# MEDIA TODAY

## MASS COMMUNICATION IN A CONVERGING WORLD

— 5TH EDITION —

# MEDIA TODAY

## MASS COMMUNICATION IN A CONVERGING WORLD

— 5TH EDITION —

JOSEPH TUROW

*University of Pennsylvania*

Routledge
Taylor & Francis Group

NEW YORK AND LONDON

**Senior Commissioning Editor:** Erica Wetter
**U.S. Textbook Development Manager:** Rebecca Pearce
**Consultant:** Heather McIntosh
**Senior Editorial Assistant:** Margo Irvin
**Assistant Editor:** Chad Hollingsworth
**Production Editor:** Alf Symons
**Project Manager:** Denise File
**Textbook Marketing Manager:** Ellie Pike
**Text Design:** Alex Lazarou
**Copy Editor:** Stephanie Ernst
**Proofreader:** Kim Hendrix
**Editorial Coordinator:** Jennifer Fandel
**Indexer:** Cynthia Swanson
**Graphics:** Keystroke
**Cover Design:** John Maloney
**Composition:** Apex CoVantage, LLC
**Companion Website Designer:** Natalya Dyer
**Illustrations:** Fakenham Prepress Solutions

Fifth edition published 2014
by Routledge
711 3rd Avenue, New York, NY 10017

and by Routledge
2 Park Square, Milton Park, Abingdon, Oxon OX14 4RN

*Routledge is an imprint of the Taylor & Francis Group, an informa business*

© 2014 Taylor & Francis

First edition published in 1999 by Houghton Mifflin Company
Fourth edition published in 2011 by Routledge

*British Library Cataloguing in Publication Data*
A catalogue record for this book is available from the British Library

*Library of Congress Cataloging-in-Publication Data*
Turow, Joseph.
  Media today : mass communication in a converging world / Joseph Turow. — [5th edition].
    pages cm
  Includes bibliographical references and index.
  1. Mass media.   I. Title.
P90.T874 2013
302.23—dc23
2013005609

ISBN 13: 978-0-415-53642-4 (hbk)
ISBN 13: 978-0-415-53643-1 (pbk)
ISBN 13: 978-0-203-11158-1 (ebk)

Printed and bound in India by Replika Press Pvt. Ltd.

About the Author

*For Oriana Avra*

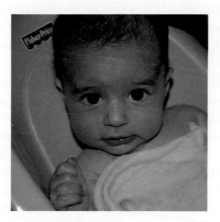

# About the Author

**J**oseph Turow is the Robert Lewis Shayon Professor of Communication at the University of Pennsylvania's Annenberg School for Communication. He has been described by the *New York Times* as "probably the reigning academic expert on media fragmentation." He holds a PhD in communication from the University of Pennsylvania, where he has taught since 1986. He has also served on the faculty at Purdue University, where he received two departmental teaching awards, and has lectured at many other universities in the United States and around the world. For 2010, he was awarded an Astor Visiting Lectureship by Oxford University. He is a fellow of the International Communication Association and was named a distinguished scholar by the National Communication Association.

Turow has authored nine books, edited five, and written more than 150 articles on mass media. His other books include *The Daily You* (Yale University Press, 2012); *Playing Doctor: Television, Storytelling, and Medical Power* (University of Michigan Press, 2010); *Niche Envy: Marketing Discrimination in the Digital Age* (MIT Press, 2006); and *The Hyperlinked Society* (coedited with Lokman Tsui, University of Michigan Press, 2008). Additionally, he is the editor of the New Media World book series out of University of Michigan Press. Turow currently serves on the editorial boards of the *Journal of Broadcasting and Electronic Media*, *Poetics*, and *New Media and Society*. He has also written about media and advertising for the popular press (e.g., the *Washington Post*, the *Los Angeles Times*, and the *Boston Globe*) and has been interviewed on National Public Radio.

# Brief Contents

# Detailed Contents

## Part I  The Nature and Business of Media
1–156

## Part II   The Media Industries
157–419

## 6   The Internet Industry ....................................168

## 7   The Book Industry ................................................191

## 8   The Newspaper Industry ...................................219

## 9  The Magazine Industry ...................246

## 10  The Recording Industry ...................**271**

# Preface

## Our Approach to Studying Media Today

Welcome to *Media Today: Mass Communication in a Converging World!* As the subtitle suggests, this fifth edition of *Media Today* uses convergence as a lens that puts the reader at the center of the profound changes in the 21st-century media world. Through the convergence lens, readers learn to think critically about the role of media today and about what these changes mean for their lives presently and in the future. The book's media systems approach helps readers to look carefully at how media are created, distributed, and exhibited in the new world that the digital revolution has created. In this way, *Media Today* goes beyond the traditional mass communication textbook's focus on consuming media, to give students an insider's perspective on how media businesses operate. How exactly does Google profit from web searches? What will the magazine look like in five years?

Joseph Turow—who has been teaching Intro to Mass Communication for well over a decade—demonstrates the many ways that media convergence and the pervasiveness of the Internet have blurred distinctions between and among various media. After looking at the essential history of each media industry, Turow examines the current forces shaping that industry and explores the impact of emerging trends. From newspapers to video games or social networking to mobile platforms, Turow's *Media Today* prepares students to live in the digital world of media, helping them to become critical, media-literate consumers of mass media and, if they go on to work in mass media industries, more alert, sensitive practitioners.

*Media Today*, Fifth Edition, is characterized by its focus on the following:

- convergence
- consumer education
- comprehensive media industry coverage
- contemporary student-friendly examples

## Convergence

Today, it is impossible to write about the workings of the newspaper, television, magazine, recording, movie, video game, advertising, and public relations industries without taking into account fundamental changes being wrought by websites, blogs, e-mail, MP3 files, and multimedia streams. Consequently, readers will find that every chapter incorporates digital media developments into the main flow of the material.

## Consumer Education

The overarching goal of the fifth edition of *Media Today* is to help students become media-literate members of society. Being media-literate involves applying critical thinking skills to the mass media. It also involves reasoning clearly about controversies that may involve the websites students use, the mobile devices they carry, the television shows they watch, the music they hear, the magazines they read, and much more. It means becoming a more aware and responsible citizen—voter, worker, adult—in our media-driven society.

After reading *Media Today*, students should be

- savvy about the influences that guide media organizations,
- up-to-date on political issues relating to the media,
- sensitive to the ethical dimensions of media activities, and
- knowledgeable about scholarship regarding media effects.

## Comprehensive Media Industry Coverage

What distinguishes mass communication from other forms of communication is the industrialized—or mass production—process that is involved in creating and circulating the material. It is this industrial process that generates the potential for reaching millions (and even billions) of diverse anonymous people at roughly the same time. *Media Today* uses this production-based approach to scrutinize the media in order to show students how the industrial nature of the process is central to the definition of mass communication.

*Media Today* also introduces the media as an interconnected system of industries—not as industries totally separate from one another. Of course, an introductory text cannot begin with a sophisticated exploration of boundary blurring. Students have to first understand the nature of the mass communication process. They must become aware that taking a mass communication perspective on the world means learning to see the interconnected system of media products that surrounds them every day in new ways.

## Contemporary Student-Friendly Examples

As much as possible, the textbook incorporates stories and events that are happening *now*. In the text, readers will find a wide variety of pop culture examples taken from across different industries—from music to TV to video games.

# How to Use This Book

Unlike other texts for the introductory course, *Media Today* takes a media systems approach out of the conviction that the best way to engage students is to reveal the forces that guide the creation, distribution, and exhibition of news, information, entertainment, education, and advertising within media systems. Once students begin to understand the ways these systems operate, they will be able to interact with the media around them in new ways.

Many features have been built into the text not only to help students learn about the inner workings of key industries in mass communication, but also to help them engage with this media, deepening their understanding of their own roles as both consumers and producers of media.

## Chapter Opening Pedagogy

### Chapter Objectives

Students are provided with the key learning objectives for the chapter at the very beginning so that they know what is ahead of them.

### Vignettes

Relevant and current stories about events or trends in the world of mass communication connect students with what they will read in the chapter and how the information applies to the world in which they live.

---

**CHAPTER OBJECTIVES**

1 Discuss what mass media convergence means and why it is important

2 Explain the differences between interpersonal communication and mass communication

3 Explain why an unorthodox definition of mass communication makes the term especially relevant in today's media environment

4 Explain the meaning and importance of culture's relationship with the mass media

5 Analyze the ways in which the mass media affect our everyday lives

6 Explain what the term "media literacy" means

7 List the key principles involved in becoming media-literate

"Whoever controls the media controls the culture."

**ALLEN GINSBERG, POET**

"Information is the oxygen of the modern age."

**RONALD REAGAN, U.S. PRESIDENT**

**The Great "Television Everywhere" Rumble**

During the year 2012, grown men and women fought in U.S. government offices over two words: "television everywhere." In one corner was Dish Network, a major satellite-television provider. On the other side was the huge entertainment company Time Warner together with Dish's major competitors, companies that own large cable systems.

The fight had been brewing since 2009, when Dish wanted to market its Slingbox service. Slingbox is a device that allows a traveler in a Seattle hotel room to watch a baseball game that is showing only locally in his hometown of Boston. Dish was offering a customized version with recording capability. The company believed the offering gave it an advantage over its satellite and cable competitors, and it wanted to use the "television everywhere" label to signal that advantage. So it asked the U.S. Patent and Trademark Office to call "television everywhere" a Dish trademark. A

---

## Quotes for Consideration

Compelling quotes from media figures draw attention to key ideas and spark discussion.

# Timelines

New timelines in all the industry chapters help students visually organize the relevant historical information that has shaped that particular industry. Students can go to the book's companion website to explore the historical events and figures in more depth using our interactive timeline feature, which links to further resources such as newspaper clippings, photos, video clips, and more.

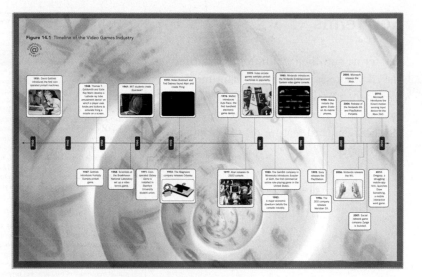

Figure 14.1 Timeline of the Video Games Industry

## MEDIA TODAY & CULTURE  BANNING OF HOLLYWOOD FILMS AROUND THE WORLD

As part of its distribution strategies, Hollywood creates movies that potentially have a global appeal. These blockbusters, as they often are called, deal with the fantasies of traveling throughout space or surviving alternate universes, such as the storylines seen in science fiction. They also show the high adventures of chases, mysteries, or quests. To tell these tales, the films rely on visual spectacles, incorporating action sequences, special effects, and brief dialogue. As a result, these films are critiqued for their lack of plot and character development.

Although these Hollywood films sometimes do gain immense profits through global distribution, not all films are received the same way in all countries. Some countries require a re-edit before the film can be shown in the country's theaters, whereas other countries ban them altogether. Reasons for both actions vary from country to country, and they often depend on cultural values, political climates, and other factors.

China, for example, issues guidelines through the State Administration of Radio Film and Television in China. One decree discourages more fantastical elements, including time travel, myths, reincarnation, and even negative thinking[1] and thus has discouraged such films as *Looper*, which involves an assassin killing targets sent back in time, and even *A Christmas Carol*. China also banned two-dimensional versions of James Cameron's *Avatar* to reduce its competition against locally produced works, even though the film went on to earn more than $182 million there.[2]

Other films are banned for their portrayals of local cultures. A more recent installment of *Rambo* was set in Myanmar (also often called Burma), and the film portrayed the Burmese soldiers as sadistic enemies.[3] Vietnam also bans films for their representations of the Vietnamese people, such as *Platoon* and *We Were Soldiers*. Nigeria banned *District 9* for its portrayal of Nigerians as gangsters who sleep with aliens and otherwise exploit them.[4]

Graphic and violent content also can be a reason for a film ban. Vietnam banned both *The Girl with the Dragon Tattoo* and *The Hunger Games*.[5] Germany banned public screenings of *Saw 3D* for its violation of a law about violent acts.[6] New Zealand banned *Hostel. Part II*.[7] Other reasons for films being banned in various countries include representations of sexuality and religion.

# Updated Media Today & Culture Boxes

New Media Today & Culture boxes provide stories about current trends in media around the world and help students appreciate the media's global impact. Discussion questions encourage students to think about how different cultural perceptions or experiences may inform the way media are experienced around the world.

# New Media Literacy Questions

Throughout the chapters, students will find media literacy questions that ask them to reflect on what it means to be a consumer of mass media and how that impacts their lives.

is known for extreme violence, which is portrayed in the show. The program came under heavy criticism after airing episodes in which extreme violence was enacted on the matriarch of the gang (Gemma): one scenario in which she was gang-raped by members of a rival gang and another in which she was severely beaten by her husband of many years.

violence by the police or military), are socially strong.

Moreover, Gerbner argues, the overall message of TV violence is that we live in a scary, mean world. He and his colleagues found support for this view through a two-pronged research design. First, they conducted a content analysis of many hours of television entertainment programming, using a careful definition of violence and noting who is violent to whom and under what conditions. Next, they conducted a telephone survey of a random sample of the U.S. adult population and asked the people questions about how violent the world is and how fearful they are. They found that heavy viewers of television are more fearful of the world than light viewers. Over time, these viewers also engage in more self-protective behavior and show more mistrust of others than do light viewers.

## THINKING ABOUT MEDIA LITERACY

When you think of the word "romance," what kind of scene comes to your mind? Do patterns of media messages "cultivate"— that is, reinforce and extend—your mental picture of romance? If so, which ones and why?

Gerbner maintains that although this phenomenon affects the individual, it also has larger social implications. The message of fear helps those who are in power because it makes heavy viewers (a substantial portion of the population) more likely to agree to support police and military forces that protect them from that scary world. Not incidentally, those police and military forces also protect those in power and help them maintain control over unruly or rebellious groups in society.

Gerbner's cultivation research and the critical approaches of political economists

# Key Terms

Key terms and their definitions have been placed where students need them most—next to their usage in the text. Students can practice their mastery of these terms by using the flash card feature on the companion website.

## EDITORIALS

Opinions regarding hard news are usually reserved for editorials. Unlike hard news and investigative reports, an **editorial** is a subgenre of news that expresses an individual's or an organization's point of view. Some editorials are written in the name of (and express the point of view of) the person who wrote the piece, whereas others are written in the name of the entire news organization—for example, the newspaper that printed the piece or the television station that aired it.

News organizations may also allow their reporters and knowledgeable people who do not work for their firm to present editorial comments. **Columnists** are individuals who are paid to write editorials on a regular basis—usually weekly, monthly, or daily. Editorials by the most famous columnists, such as Dave Barry, Peggy Noonan, and Anna Quindlen, are carried by many news outlets across the United States and even around the world. On the web, columnists may show up on journalistic websites (such as CNN.com or Slate) or on **blogs,** online sites written in the style of journal entries, often in reverse chronological order. A well-known example is the *Huffington Post* group of political opinion blogs. They include regular columns by Arianna Huffington, talk show host Tavis Smiley, and Fox program host Greta Van Susteren, as well as opinion pieces from a wide spectrum of celebrities and non-celebrities from different fields.

**editorial**
subgenre of news that concentrates on an individual's or an organization's point of view

**columnists**
individuals who are paid to write editorials on a regular basis—usually weekly, monthly, or daily

**blogs**
journalistic websites or opinion sites in which writings are in the style of journal entries, often in reverse chronological order

## SOFT NEWS

Whereas news workers generally consider hard news reporting a place for objective, accurate, and balanced reporting with little (if any) editorial commentary, they consider another news category, **soft news**, to be an area in which the reporter's opinions and biases can show through. As you may be able to tell by its name, soft news (also known as the human interest story) is the kind of story that news workers feel may not have the critical importance of hard news but nevertheless would appeal to a substantial number of people in the audience. Cooking spots, articles on the best ways to shovel snow without injuring your back, video clips highlighting local students in community plays or recitals—these are topics that news workers consider soft rather than hard news.

**soft news**
the kind of news story that news workers feel may not have the critical importance of hard news but nevertheless would appeal to a substantial number of people in the audience

## INFORMATION

One way to understand the difference between news and information—a difficult distinction to draw for some—is to say that **information** is the raw material that journalists use when they create news stories. On the most basic level, a piece of information

**information**
the raw material that journalists use when they create news stories

# New Infographics

Newly rendered art is vibrant, instructive, and provides students with a good study tool for understanding key concepts in the text.

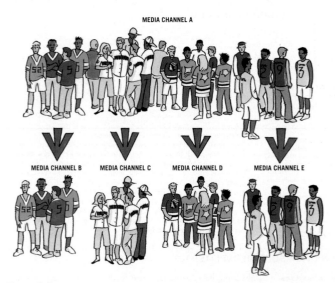

MEDIA CHANNEL A

MEDIA CHANNEL B    MEDIA CHANNEL C    MEDIA CHANNEL D    MEDIA CHANNEL E

**Figure 1.1**
The arrival of the diverse array of media channels has had a fragmenting effect on audiences—as audience members move to watch, read, or listen to a new channel, fewer people use any single channel.

# End-of-Chapter Materials

## Media Ethics Case Study

Students are given ethical issues to explore and report on based on a debate or topic that was covered earlier in the chapter.

### Case Study
### TEENS AS A CONSTRUCTED AUDIENCE

**The idea** One way to get a feel for the idea that audiences are constructed is to see how advertisers actually construct audiences. In this case study you will go through recent advertising trade magazines to see how marketing and media executives talk about an important audience—teens. You will also explore what their construction of teens means for the ways they try to reach teens and persuade them to buy products.

**The method** To conduct this study, you need to know how to use a periodical database in your school's library. The most popular databases are Factiva and LexisNexis. Knowing how to use these sorts of databases will help you learn a lot about the state of media today. Reading magazines for ad practitioners may help you get a summer—or permanent—job in a media firm.

1. Ask someone who knows how to use the database to show you how to do a full-text search of the weekly trade magazine *Advertising Age* for the past six months. Tell that person that you would like to investigate how *Advertising Age* used the term "teen" or "teenager" during that time.
2. You may find that *Advertising Age* used the term a lot during that period. Ask your professor what proportion of the articles you should read. If there are a hundred articles or more, the class might divide into groups of two or three people in each group. That way each group can share findings on different articles and summarize them.
3. For each article, note the title and date and then answer the following questions on a sheet of paper:
   a. On what topic does it mention teenagers?
   b. How does it describe teenagers? How and to what extent does it divide teens by gender, class, spending power, physical characteristics, personalities, or other categories?
   c. Does the article make comparisons between teenagers and other groups in society? If so, how?
   d. What does the article say about teenagers' value to advertisers, uses of different media, and uses of different products?
   e. What, if anything, does the article say about how media firms create media to attract teens?
   f. What, if anything, does the article say about how media firms and advertisers are creating advertisements to attract teens? With what messages and images do they think they can persuade them?
4. Once you and your group have taken notes on all the articles, make an outline of a report that discusses what you learned about how teenagers are constructed by advertisers, why, and with what consequences for commercial messages and for media.

| | | |
|---|---|---|
| collaborative activity | information | setting |
| columnists | informational ads | shelf space |
| cooperative advertising | initial public offering (IPO) | soft news |
| creative personnel | investigative reports | soft sell ads |
| demographic indicators | investment banks | stock offerings |
| demographics | journalists | subgenres |
| distribution | lifestyle categories | surveys |
| dramedy | loan | syndicate |
| editorial | mass media production firm | talent guild |
| education | media practitioners | track record |
| entertainment | objectivity | trade incentives |
| exhibition | on-staff worker | typical characters |
| focus group | patterns of action | venture capitalists |
| format | powerful distributor | vertical integration |
| formula | product placement | |

## Review Questions

End-of-chapter review questions give students the opportunity to recall topics discussed in the chapter and to test their conceptual understanding of these topics.

### Questions for Discussion and Critical Thinking

1. After reading this chapter, what reasons can you find for why media industries spend so much time trying to learn more about their audiences? What advantages does that practice offer the industries?
2. Are there any advantages for audiences in all this research?
3. What do you think of the ideas of "objectivity" in print and on camera? Do you think those principles are enough? Can you think of any news examples from either medium that seem objective by these standards?
4. How are freelancers an important part of media industries?

# New to This Edition

- **Reduced page length without reduced comprehensiveness.** Because we know student and instructor schedules are jam-packed, edits have been made to reduce the amount of detail in some areas of the text in order to allow for more space for current trends in mass communication.
- A new chapter dedicated entirely to **video games**.
- **Public relations and advertising** chapters were condensed and are now discussed as part of the chapter (chapter 4).
- Consideration of the Internet and convergence that begins in chapter 1 and flows throughout the entire book, better reflecting today's media environment.
- Enhanced discussions about and coverage of social media integrated throughout the book as it relates to all industries and the media business as a whole.

## Companion Website

A freshly updated website provides students and instructors with all the tools they will need to learn and teach their mass communication course: **http://www. routledge.com/cw/turow.**

### For Students

The student website features content-rich assets to help students expand their knowledge, study for exams, and more. Features include the following:

- *Practice quizzes for each chapter*: help students test their knowledge and prepare for exams.
- *Interactive key-term flash cards*: provide students with a fun way to review important terms and definitions.
- *Interactive timeline*: brings the timelines from the chapters to life and allows students to learn more about the important people and events that shaped the media business.
- *Chapter Recaps*: summarize the key points and themes of each chapter.
- *Media Today internship and career guide*: offers students information and job listings to help them get started in a career in media.
- *Links to further resources*: direct students to key media websites for further study and the latest news on media industries.

### For Instructors

The password-protected instructor website provides completely updated instructor support materials in the form of the following:

- *Complete, online, and downloadable instructor's manual revised for this update*: updated by Chenjerai Kumanyika of Pennsylvania State University, this manual summarizes the key learning objectives of each chapter and provides instructors with discussion starters to help build a dialogue in the classroom.
- *Correlation guide*: for instructors who were using the fourth edition of the text, this is a guide to how content has been changed or moved so that instructors can better organize their courses.
- *Extensive expanded test bank*: provides multiple-choice, true–false, and fill-in-the-blank questions as well as new short-answer questions for exams for each chapter.
- *Fully revised PowerPoint presentations*: offer lecture outlines for each chapter, along with a set of slides for every figure in the text.
- *New sample syllabi*: help instructors plan their courses using the new edition.
- *Textboxes* from previous edition of *Media Today* for instructors who would like to continue to incorporate them into their classes.
- *Links to all videos from the Interactive Timelines*, plus additional video recommendations.

# Acknowledgments

A book such as this is impossible to create alone, and so there are several people to thank. My wife Judy has with every edition been supportive with her encouragement and smart advice. At the University of Pennsylvania's Annenberg School for Communication, a number of graduate students helped with research and editorial work. Special thanks go to Nora Draper, Bo Mai, and Katherine Wong for their work on this edition. Sharon Black, the great Annenberg librarian, has always been ready to help with the best references available.

At Routledge, I am indebted to my editor Erica Wetter, whose enthusiasm and suggestions for this major revision were an important incentive. Rebecca Pearce, the development manager, has been both a vigilant taskmaster and a dedicated, creative organizer of the project. Heather McIntosh of Boston College offered smart editing advice as I wrote the chapters, in addition to authoring the "Media Today & Culture" boxes. Additional thanks go to textbook marketing manager Ellie Pike, development editor Alf Symons, copy editor Stephanie Ernst, and proofreader Kim Hendrix.

I would also like to thank all the reviewers (including those who chose to remain anonymous and are not listed here) whose suggestions during the reviewing process helped me greatly as I prepared the fifth edition:

Mimi Adams, *Louisiana Tech University*

Amy Bonebright, *Liberty University*

Carolyn Byerly, *Howard University*

David Edwards, *South Central College–Fairbault*

Tony Gault, *University of Denver*

Meredith Guthrie, *University of Pittsburgh*

Roger Heinrich, *Middle Tennessee State University*

Nina Huntemann, *Suffolk University*

Shandra R. Huntt, *Howard University*

Joonseong Lee, *California State University–San Marcos*

Chuck Lubbers, *University of South Dakota*

Nicole Maurantonio, *University of Richmond*

Heather McIntosh, *Boston College*

Connie Hicks McMahon, *Barry University*

Nora Paul, *University of Minnesota*

Whitney Pisani, *Collin County Community College*

Jack Powers, *Ithaca College*

Sharaf Rehman, *University of Texas–Brownsville*

Meghan Sanders, *Louisiana State University*

Ann Savage, *Butler University*

Tammy Trujillo, *Mount St. Antonio College*

Therese Villenueve, *Citrus College*

Scott Weiss, *Montana State University–Billings*

# To the Student

I hope that you will find *Media Today* fun to read, helpful for understanding the media-saturated world around you, and (if you're so inclined) useful for thinking about a future career in mass media. More likely than not, you've grown up with all or at least most of the media we cover in this book. Your family has probably had newspapers, books, magazines, CDs, radios, and a television set in your home from the time you were born. It's likely, too, that you have also had a computer and the Internet in your home from the time you were small. In one sense, then, you're already an "expert" at mass media: you've seen a lot of it, you know what you like, and you know what you don't like. At the same time, there's probably a lot about the content mass media present, the industries behind them, and their roles in society that you haven't considered yet.

The purpose of *Media Today* is to introduce you to these ideas, with the expectation that they will help you think about the media you think you already know in entirely new ways. To get the most out of this text, use all the bells and whistles that come with it. The chapter objectives, the marginal glossary, the timelines, the art and photo selections, and the boxed features all have been created with an eye toward making the text itself as clear and relevant as possible. The companion website **(http://www. routledge.com/cw/turow)** will also be of enormous value for learning more about book topics, studying for exams, learning about careers in mass media, quizzing yourself, and more. Get to know all these learning aids, and let us know what you think of them.

Best wishes,
*Joe Turow*

# MEDIA TODAY

# 1 Understanding Mass Media, Convergence, and the Importance of Media Literacy

## CHAPTER OBJECTIVES

1 Discuss what mass media convergence means and why it is important

2 Explain the differences between interpersonal communication and mass communication

3 Explain why an unorthodox definition of mass communication makes the term especially relevant in today's media environment

4 Explain the meaning and importance of culture's relationship with the mass media

5 Analyze the ways in which the mass media affect our everyday lives

6 Explain what the term "media literacy" means

7 List the key principles involved in becoming media-literate

> "Whoever controls the media controls the culture."

**ALLEN GINSBERG, POET**

> "Information is the oxygen of the modern age."

**RONALD REAGAN, U.S. PRESIDENT**

## The Great "Television Everywhere" Rumble

During the year 2012, grown men and women fought in U.S. government offices over two words: "television everywhere." In one corner was Dish Network, a major satellite-television provider. On the other side was the huge entertainment company Time Warner together with Dish's major competitors, companies that own large cable systems.

The fight had been brewing since 2009, when Dish wanted to market its Slingbox service. Slingbox is a device that allows a traveler in a Seattle hotel room to watch a baseball game that is showing only locally in his hometown of Boston. Dish was offering a customized version with recording capability. The company believed the offering gave it an advantage over its satellite and cable competitors, and it wanted to use the "television everywhere" label to signal that advantage. So it asked the U.S. Patent and Trademark Office to call "television everywhere" a Dish trademark. A

2

trademark is a distinctive sign or phrase that businesses connect to a product or service to tag it with a special name and personality. If the U.S. government agency gave its permission, only Dish could use the phrase "television everywhere" to market and advertise its products.

Time Warner and the cable systems cried foul. Time Warner showed the trademark office that it and its cable-industry partners had used "television everywhere" to describe its HBO Go service before Dish filed to claim the term for itself. HBO Go allows people who subscribe to Time Warner's HBO pay-cable channel to view many of the channel's programs on computers and tablets such as the iPad that connect to the internet. True enough—but why the rumble? Why did all those companies try to shoot down Dish Network's attempt to own the words "television everywhere"?

To begin understanding why large companies would spend the time and energy to face off against one another over two words, you first have to realize that the fight is actually over one word—"everywhere." Time Warner and its allies realize they are moving into a world that is like no other in history. It is a world of not just television everywhere but also newspapers everywhere, books everywhere, magazines everywhere, movies everywhere, and more. To companies involved in these media businesses, the changes are exciting and scary at the same time. Many are jockeying to shape the new world and define themselves in it. The firms fighting Dish don't want it to grab a title that symbolizes this new era.

The Dish battle represents just one small skirmish in what will certainly be a decades-long transformation of the media system in the United States. The changes will surely affect you as a citizen, as a consumer, and as a worker—especially if you choose to work in one of the media industries. It's important, then, to ask and answer some basic questions:

- Precisely what is happening that is so transformative?
- Why are those things happening?
- How will it impact me as a citizen, a consumer, and a worker?
- What can I do to help myself, my family, and my society as the changes unfold?

*Media Today* is about helping you answer these questions. Over the next several chapters we will take an excursion through industries and businesses that relate directly to our everyday lives. We will look at how the media industries got here, what they're doing, and where they seem to be going. We'll explore what is changing about them and what is not. And we'll develop a way of thinking about them that will help you analyze them long after you've read this book.

This chapter begins the journey with exploration of an everywhere-related idea that guides much of the work of executives at Dish Network and Time Warner and throughout the media system: media convergence.

## Introducing Media Convergence

Let's take the words one at a time. *Media* are platforms or vehicles that industries have developed for the purpose of creating and sending messages. Think of telephones, television, movies, music recordings, magazines, and newspapers. *Convergence* occurs when two or more things come together. *Media convergence* takes place when products typically linked to one medium show up on many media. When you can get a Red Sox baseball game broadcast in Boston to show up on your laptop computer and or your Android phone in Seattle, that is convergence. When you can transfer an Adele music album from your laptop to your iPod, iPhone, iPad, or Xbox, that is convergence.

Until recently, media convergence was not a common activity. To the contrary, people associated every medium with a particular kind of product. The telephone meant conversations via a special device between two people not located in the same place. Television meant audiovisual programs on a special set with a glass front. Movies meant audiovisual programs made for projection onto a big screen. Newspapers meant printed stories on large sheets of paper circulated daily or weekly. Music recordings were plastic discs or tape cartridges made to be played on phonographs or tape decks.

It's not as if the media were sealed off from one another. Musical recordings showed up on radio all the time. Movie plots sometimes came from books, and theatrical films did show up on television. But these activities involved negotiation by companies from different industries. (The industries that guided particular media and their products were worlds unto themselves.) Moreover, actually moving the products from one medium to another could take a lot of work. One important reason was that the technology—that is, the machinery and materials—of the media industries were very different from one another. Certainly, most members of the audience didn't have the equipment to carry out such transfers. And it was hard to imagine a print magazine such as *Cosmopolitan* sharing a screen with the ABC television program *Modern Family*.

"Wait!" you might be yelling at this page (or more likely saying to yourself). "That's still the case. When I hold *Cosmo* or *Sports Illustrated* in my hand, I can't put it into my TV set." You're right. But as the lawsuit about "television everywhere" indicates, executives in industries that have historically thought of their content as specific to particular media are now trying to get their products—the content you read, watch, and hear—in front of their intended audiences wherever they are. If you're a loyal reader of *Cosmo* or *SI* or most any major magazine, you probably know it has a website. It probably has an application ("app") for people who have an iPad or another tablet. And it likely has a way to allow access for those who want to read it on their smartphones.

But we're not talking here only of the merger of magazines and the web. Media convergence is taking place with so many media that it is quickly becoming the way media executives do their work, no matter what their industry is. If you're into college sports, you probably have heard about March Madness, the basketball tournament that pits college teams against one another toward finding a National College Athletic Association (NCAA) champion. Until just a few years ago, the only place you could see the matchups outside the stadiums was on your television set, with the CBS television network and Turner's TNT cable network showing various games. But convergence has changed everything. Take what went on during March 2012 as an example. In addition to the television presentations, the over-the-air TV network CBS, the magazine *Sports Illustrated* (owned by the same company that owns Turner), and the NCAA itself allowed free viewing of select games on their websites. For true sports fanatics there was even more. If they paid $3.99, CBS and Turner would allow them full access to all 2012 NCAA Division 1 Men's Basketball Championship games. Moreover, they could watch the games on their computers, on their mobile phones, and on tablets: truly "television everywhere."

Why is media convergence happening now? Why do companies carry it out? When do they do it? How do they do it? When are companies—and workers and industries—winners because of convergence, and when are they losers? How are individuals and society at large affected by the new developments in media today? How might they be affected in the future? Are there government policies or other organized initiatives that try to ensure the best possible outcomes for all involved with the media system?

You probably realize that these questions cannot be answered in two or three paragraphs. Answering them is a project for this book as a whole. The goal is to help you answer these questions not just right now but also in the future, as you move through your personal and professional life. To start, it's useful to step back and ask what the media we will be exploring have in common. The answer is that they are all involved in the process of mass communication. Media convergence is, in fact, a central aspect of mass communication today. This chapter will unpack what that means. We will explore and define communication, media, and culture, and we will consider how the relationships among them affect us and the world in which we live. We will also consider why the term "mass communication" remains relevant in the 21st century, contrary to what some writers say.

## Introducing Mass Communication

To understand why some writers suggest that the idea of mass communication doesn't connect to what's going on in today's world, we have to look at how the term has traditionally been used. Over the past hundred years, people who wrote about mass communication tended to relate it to the size of the audience. That made a lot of sense at one point. From the mid-19th century onward, new technologies such as high-speed newspaper presses, radio, movies, and television provided access to the huge "masses" of people. Not only were those audiences very large; they also were dispersed geographically, were quite diverse (i.e., made up of different types of people), and typically were anonymous to the companies that created the material. The essential reason that newspapers, radio, television, and other such media were considered different from other means of communication had to do with the size and composition of the audience.

This perspective on mass communication worked well until recently, when the key aspects of the traditional definition of mass communication as reaching huge, diverse groups no longer fit. The reason is that the arrival of many channels—including the growing number of radio and TV stations, the rise of video recorders, the multiplication of cable networks, and the rise of the web—led to **audience fragmentation** (see Figure 1.1). That is, as people watched or read these new channels, there were fewer

**audience fragmentation**
the process of dividing audience members into segments based on background and lifestyle in order to send them messages targeted to their specific characteristics

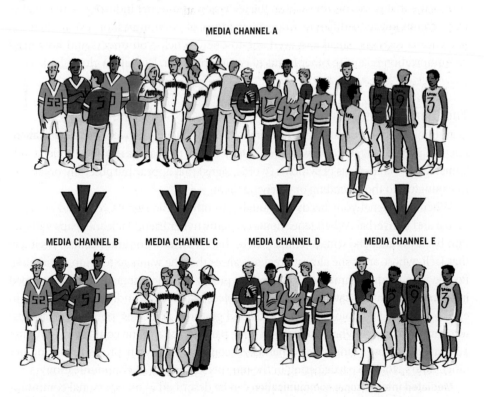

MEDIA CHANNEL A

MEDIA CHANNEL B   MEDIA CHANNEL C   MEDIA CHANNEL D   MEDIA CHANNEL E

## Figure 1.1
The arrival of the diverse array of media channels has had a fragmenting effect on audiences—as audience members move to watch, read, or listen to a new channel, fewer people use any single channel.

people using any one of them. Because these new media channels do not necessarily individually reach large numbers of people—the "masses"—some writers have suggested that we can abandon the term mass communication.

However, the view in this book is that mass communication is still a critically important part of society. As we will see, what really separates mass communication from other forms of communication is not the size of the audience—it can be large or small. Rather, what makes mass communication special is the way the content of the communication message is created.

**mass production process**
the industrial process that creates the potential for reaching millions, even billions, of diverse, anonymous people at around the same time

---

# THINKING ABOUT MEDIA LITERACY

Throughout the chapters you will see media literacy questions such as this one. These questions will ask you to engage that chapter's ideas and concepts critically, often asking you to connect them with your own experiences.

Mass communication is integral to how our society functions. Can you think of some ways that society would change if the different forms of mass communication disappeared? How might those changes be beneficial? Detrimental?

---

**industrial nature**
the aspect of industrialized—or mass production—processes involved in creating the message material that distinguishes mass communication from other forms of communication. This industrial process creates the potential for reaching billions of diverse, anonymous people simultaneously.

**communication**
refers to people interacting in ways that at least one of the parties involved understands as messages

**messages**
collections of symbols (words, signs) that appear purposely organized (meaningful) to those sending or receiving them

**interpersonal communication**
a form of communication that involves two or three individuals signaling to each other using their voices, facial and hand gestures, and other signs (even clothes) to convey meaning

**mediated interpersonal communication**
a specialized type of interpersonal communication that is assisted by a device, such as a pen or pencil, computer, or phone

**medium**
part of a technical system that helps in the transmission, distribution, or reception of messages

Mass communication is carried out by organizations working together in industries to produce and circulate a wide range of content—from entertainment to news to educational materials. It is this industrial, **mass production process** that creates the potential for reaching millions, even billions, of diverse, anonymous people at around the same time. And it is the **industrial nature** of the process—for example, the various companies that work together within the television or internet industries—that makes mass communication different from other forms of communication even when the audience is relatively small and even one-to-one. To help you understand how mass communication relates to other forms of communication, let's take a closer look.

## The Elements of Communication

Communication is a basic feature of human life. In general, the word "**communication**" refers to people interacting in ways that at least one of the parties involved understands as **messages**—collections of symbols (words, signs) that appear purposefully organized (meaningful) to those sending or receiving them.

When you signal your needs or thoughts to others, the signals you send are both verbal and nonverbal. When Jane shouts excitedly to her friend Jack and leaps with joy into his arms after she wins a tennis match, that's a form of communication. It's likely that Jack, whose arms she almost breaks, realizes that she wants to tell him something. People who study communication would typically call the interaction just described **interpersonal communication**, a form that involves two or three individuals signaling to each other using their voices, facial and hand gestures, and other signs (even clothes) to convey meaning. When you talk to your parents about your coursework, discuss a recent movie over dinner with friends, or converse with your professor during her office hours, you are participating in the interpersonal form of communication

**Mediated interpersonal communication** can be described as interpersonal communication that is assisted by a **medium**—part of a technical system that helps in the transmission, distribution, or reception of messages. The medium helps communication take place when senders and receivers are not face-to-face. The internet is an example of a medium, as are radio, CD, television, and DVD. (Note that the term "medium"

A common sight today, interpersonal communication through both direct and mediated means. Mediated interpersonal communication methods such as Skyping allow people to keep in touch in a more visual way than was ever possible in the past.

is singular; it refers to one technological vehicle for communication. The plural is media.) When you write a thank-you note to your grandmother, send an e-mail to your graduate teaching assistant, or call a friend on the phone, you are participating in the mediated form of interpersonal communication.

Although interpersonal, mediated interpersonal, and mass communication have their differences, they have a central similarity: they involve messages. Eight major elements are involved in every interaction that involves messages: the **source**, **encoding**, **transmitter**, **channel**, **receiver**, **decoding**, **feedback**, and **noise**.

Take a look at Figure 1.2. It illustrates how these eight elements appear in the process of interpersonal communication in an imaginary conversation between TV personality Jon Stewart and a student named Sally. Now take a look at Table 1.1. It lays out the ways these elements are similar or different across interpersonal communication, mediated interpersonal communication, and mass communication. The table also presents examples that highlight these similarities and differences.

The main difference between mass communication and the two forms of interpersonal communication relates to the nature of the source and the receiver. In the interpersonal modes the source and the receiver are individual people—Jon Stewart schmoozing face-to-face with Sally in the library, for example, or Jon gossiping over the phone with another student named Geraldo. In the case of mass communication, the source is an organization—for example, the Comedy Central television channel (where you can view Jon Stewart's show) or the *USA Today* newspaper. When you read a particular newspaper article or watch a particular program, you may think that sources are individual people, not organizations. After all, the name of the author is on the article, and you can see the actors who work on the show. Why, for example, shouldn't we consider Jon Stewart the "source" on Comedy Central's *The Daily Show*?

The answer is that he is only the most visible of an entire firm of people that prepared the mass media material. If Jon were in the same room as you telling you

**1** The source (Sally) encodes a message using the brain and transmits it through the airwaves (a medium) using parts of her body (vocal cords, facial muscles).

**3** The receiver (Jon) hears Sally's voice, decodes the message using his senses, and prepares to encode his answer. This process of responding is called interpersonal feedback.

SO HOW CAN I GET AN INTERNSHIP AT THE DAILY SHOW?

**2** The message travels through the air (the channel) to reach Jon (the receiver).

**5** The message once again travels through the air to reach the other person.

THEY POST INTERNSHIPS ON VIACOM'S WEB-SITE – BUT I'LL PUT IN A GOOD WORD FOR YOU!

**6** Sally (the former source) is now the receiver. She decodes his message and prepares to encode an answer. In this way, the interpersonal communication episode continues.

**4** Jon encodes his response using his brain and transmits it (the feedback) using parts of his body. When transmitting, Jon becomes a source.

**Figure 1.2**

In this model of interpersonal communication, information moves from a starting point at the source (Sally), who transmits the message over the channel, to the receiver (Jon) for decoding.

about what he just read in the newspaper, he—as an individual—would be a source. But when you watch him do his monologue on *The Daily Show*, Jon is no longer the source. That's because behind him is an organization that is creating the news satire for him to present. Sure, Jon is reading the messages, and so it may seem that he should be called "the source." But the writing team of *The Daily Show* helped him write the script, produced and edited the videos he introduces, and prepared his set for the broadcast. Moreover, the photos and clips he satirizes sometimes come from news firms, such as ABC News. So Jon is really just the most visible representative of an organizational source. And the Comedy Central organization is interacting with other organizations (ABC News, companies that provide it with supplies for

**Table 1.1** Comparing Elements Across Different Forms of Communication

| Element of communication | General meaning of the element | How do we understand that element in interpersonal communication? | How do we understand that element in mediated interpersonal communication? | How do we understand that element in mass communication? |
|---|---|---|---|---|
| Source | The originator of the message | It is an individual. | It is an individual. | It is one or more organizations. |
| Encoding | When the source organizes and prepares to send the message | It takes place in an individual's brain. | It takes place in an individual's brain. | It takes place in an organization using technology. |
| Transmitter | Performs the physical activity of sending the message | It is the person's vocal cords. | It is the person's vocal cords and technology (e.g., a phone). | It is a person's vocal cords and technology (e.g., a phone). |
| Channel | Pathway through which the transmitter sends the message | It is the air. | It is the air and technology (e.g., wires). | It is the air and technology (e.g., wires). |
| Receiver | The person or organization that gets the message | It can be one person or a few individuals in the same location. | It can be one or many individuals in one or more locations. | It is typically many people in different locations. |
| Decoding | The process by which the receiver makes sense of the message | It takes place in an individual's brain. | It take place first via technology and then in an individual's brain. | It take place first via technology and then in an individual's brain. |
| Feedback | A response to the message | It is immediate and directly to the source. | It is immediate and directly to the source. | It may be immediate or delayed and is generally indirect: other parts of the organization receive it and tell the source. |
| Noise | A sound in the communication situation that interferes with the delivery of the message | It can be environmental (e.g., noise in a park), mechanical (the person coughs so much the message gets lost), or semantic (the speaker doesn't know the language well). | It can be environmental, mechanical (e.g., park noise or static on the line), or semantic. | It can be environmental, mechanical, and semantic, sometimes caused by organizations. |

the programs, advertisers that support the program, and many more) in order to get *The Daily Show* on the air.

## Mass Communication Defined

And so we come at last to the definition of mass communication that we have been building: mass communication is the industrialized production and multiple distribution of messages through technological devices. The industrial nature of the process is central to this definition of mass communication. Figure 1.3 illustrates this point by using *The Daily Show* as an example.

As the definition suggests, mass communication is carried out by mass media industries. Think, for example, of the movie industry, in which many different companies—from production studios to film providers to catering firms—work

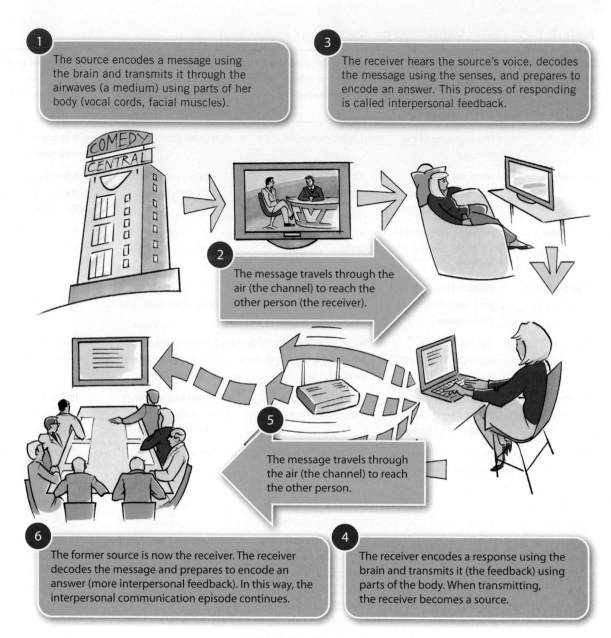

**1** The source encodes a message using the brain and transmits it through the airwaves (a medium) using parts of her body (vocal cords, facial muscles).

**3** The receiver hears the source's voice, decodes the message using the senses, and prepares to encode an answer. This process of responding is called interpersonal feedback.

**2** The message travels through the air (the channel) to reach the other person (the receiver).

**5** The message travels through the air (the channel) to reach the other person.

**6** The former source is now the receiver. The receiver decodes the message and prepares to encode an answer (more interpersonal feedback). In this way, the interpersonal communication episode continues.

**4** The receiver encodes a response using the brain and transmits it (the feedback) using parts of the body. When transmitting, the receiver becomes a source.

**Figure 1.3**

In this model of mass communication, the elements (source, message, transmission, etc.) are all marked by industrial production and multiple distribution by mass media organizations.

**mass media**
the technological vehicles through which mass communication takes place (note that the term "mass media" is plural and refers to more than one vehicle; the singular version is mass medium)

**mass media outlets**
companies that send out messages via mass media

to make and circulate movies. **Mass media** are the technological instruments—for example, newsprint, the internet, television, and radio (both traditional and satellite)—through which mass communication takes place. **Mass media outlets** are companies that send out messages via mass media—for example, *Time* magazine, foxnews.com, and the NBC television network.

Mass communication's power allows media consumers to share the materials they are reading and listening to with millions of people. This sharing is made possible, of course, because of the industrial nature of the activity and its technology of production and distribution. When complex organizations comprising many workers join to use the latest technology to produce media, those organizations have the potential to distribute the same message to huge numbers of people.

Consider the typical television broadcast of the Grammy Awards, the ceremony in which the recording industry honors its most successful talent. It is transmitted via satellite from Los Angeles to broadcast television production facilities in New York and then distributed "live" to every corner of the United States, as well as to many other parts of the world.

Or consider a typical presidential news conference. It is covered by dozens of newspaper reporters and television and radio news crews. Snippets of the event then will commonly confront Americans around the country in many different forms during that day and the next on national TV news, on internet news and blog sites, on the local news, and in morning papers and throughout the day on hourly radio news reports.

As a third and slightly different example, consider a mega-hit film such as the first of the *Twilight* movies. Millions of people around the world saw it in theaters within a few months of its release. In addition, word of the movie's popularity sped around the globe as Summit Entertainment, its distributor in the United States and many regions outside the United States as well, revved up a publicity and advertising machine. It peppered as many media outlets as possible with word of the high-octane action and head-lopping digital effects.

*Twilight*, the presidential news conference, and the Grammy Awards represent only three examples of activities that happen all the time in industrialized countries such as the United States. Linking large numbers of people to share the same materials virtually instantly has become standard practice for the broadcast television, internet, radio, cable TV, and satellite television industries. Just as significant is the sharing that takes place relatively more slowly when newspapers, magazines, books, movies, billboards, and other mass media release their messages. Because of mass media industries and their abilities to mass-produce media content, millions of people within the United States and around the world can receive the same messages within a fairly short time. Think about it—here are huge numbers of people who are physically separated from one another, have no obvious relationship with one another, and most often are unknown to one another. Yet on a daily basis they are watching the same news stories, listening to the same music, and reading the same magazine articles.

## THINKING ABOUT MEDIA LITERACY

Drawing on the examples of *Twilight*, a presidential press conference, and the Grammy Awards, can you think of any forms of mass communication from your own experiences? Do you think that a viral video of a cat talking on YouTube is an example of mass communication? Why or why not?

## Mass Media and Convergence

If you spin out the logic of our descriptions of mass communication and mass media, you can see how closely they are related to the process of convergence that we began to explore at the beginning of this chapter. Recall that we said media convergence takes place when products typically linked to one medium show up on another. We noted that when a Red Sox baseball game broadcast in Boston shows up

In analog technology, like a vinyl record, the grooves in the record are reproductions of the music that was generated by the instruments or the singer's voice. In digital technology, there is no physical reproduction of the music—instead, the music is coded into bits. Thus, the sequence of the code is what creates the sounds we hear when we listen to CDs or MP3s.

on your laptop computer in Seattle, that is convergence. Let's take apart that example a bit to show its connection to our definition of mass communication.

It's actually not a hard connection to make. The Boston broadcast is a straightforward case of mass communication: a collection of companies—the Red Sox organization, the local broadcast station, the advertisers, and more—working together to produce the game and distribute it via broadcast television technology. As for the game showing up on your computer in Seattle, remember that the Dish Network makes this possible through Slingbox. That means the satellite firm joins with the technology firm that makes the Slingbox to allow Dish subscribers to tap Slingbox's potential to send video signals across the internet. Also involved are firms that cooperate with one another in internet distribution of Slingbox signals—the one that provides the connection from the Slingbox in your home to the internet, the firms that carry the video of the game across the internet (we'll discuss how that works in chapter 7), and the firms that provide you with an internet connection in your Seattle hotel.

We have here what might be called the three Cs of mass media convergence: content, corporations, and computers. The first two Cs reflect the definition of mass communication presented earlier. *Content* refers to the "messages"—in this case, the ball game, the announcers' descriptions and interviews, and the commercials shown around all of that. *Corporations* refers to the companies that interact to create and distribute the content. It is the third C—the use of computers by corporations to create and distribute content—that brings convergence into the mass communication picture. To understand how, you need to think about the difference between computer-centered mass media such as the internet and media technologies that don't rely on computers for production and distribution of content.

A crucial difference between computer-centered mass media and other media technologies is that the former are digital rather than analog. A simple way to understand the distinction between digital and analog is to think about what distinguishes an old-fashioned vinyl record from a CD. If you look at a record, you will see grooves. When the phonograph needle moves through the grooves, it picks up vibrations that were made by the sound coming from the singer's vocal cords. When the record was made, a machine cut grooves that reproduced these vibrations into the vinyl. The record grooves, then, hold a literal physical reproduction—an **analog**—of the singer's sound that can be reproduced with the right equipment.

The CD, by contrast, does not contain a physical reproduction of the sound. During the CD's recording process, computers transform the singer's voice patterns into a string of binary digits, or bits (0s and 1s). Each sequence, or string, of 0s and 1s represents a different sound. The strings serve as a code—a symbolic representation of the sound. This **digital** code is placed on the CD in an order that conforms to the sequence of

**analog**
electronic transmission accomplished by adding signals of varying frequency of amplitude to carrier waves of a given frequency of alternating electromagnetic current. Broadcast and phone transmissions conventionally have used analog technology

**digital**
electronic technology that generates, stores, processes, and transmits data in the form of strings of 0s and 1s; each of these digits is referred to as a bit (and a string of bits that a computer can address individually as a group is a byte)

sounds made by the singer. When you turn on your CD player, a laser beam reads the code and sends it to a computer chip in the player. The computer chip is programmed to recognize the code and to understand which strings of numbers represent which sounds. At the speed of light, the chip transforms the code into electrical impulses that, when sent through an amplifier and sound system, reproduce the singer's voice.

The basic idea applies also to digital music files that reside in your computer, your digital music player, or your mobile phone. In that case, you don't even have a piece of plastic that carries the tune into the device. Rather, you download a digital file in one of a number of formats (MP3, WAV, AAC, or others), and if your device has the ability to recognize and decode the file, it transforms it into sounds that reproduce the original. If the file you are using is not copy-protected (and MP3 and WAV files are not), you can copy the music from your phone to one of your other players. Being able to move digital files (music or not) from one device to another is an example of the **convergence** of media technologies; it involves the ability of different media to interact with one another easily in parallel digital formats. As a result of convergence, different media can end up carrying out similar functions because they all accept digital information. A laptop computer, a phone, and a tablet (such as the iPad) can take on the functions of a DVD player, a CD player, and a cable television set. That means, for example, that you can start watching the *Twilight* movie trilogy on your bedroom cable TV, continue viewing it on your phone during a train ride to work, and finish it during an airplane trip via your iPad. And you can toggle listening to the newest music album by Taylor Swift on your phone, your laptop, your tablet, and your CD player (if you still use it).

The digital nature of content also means that you and others can rather easily get the technical capability to alter mass media materials for your own purposes. You can, for example, humorously overlay a *Twilight* scene with a Bruno Mars song and share it with your friends over the web or in some other way. The ability of members of the audience to easily manipulate the products of mass communication is a recent development, made possible by the rise of digital technology. Realizing this, some media companies invite their audiences to send them materials they can use for their commercials, websites, or television shows. Dove soap, for example, has run a contest that involves creating a commercial. And the news network CNN has an iReporter program that encourages people who take photos or videos of news with any devices— cameras, phones, iPads, you name it—to send these images or videos to the network, which might place them on the CNN website and show them on its cable channels.

**convergence**
the ability of different media to easily interact with each other because they all deal with information in the same digital form

## THINKING ABOUT MEDIA LITERACY

Through convergence, we now can access media industry materials online. Most of us view the materials, maybe comment on them, and maybe even share them, but some people go further and modify these materials in different ways. First, why do you think people share materials with others online? Second, why do you think people go through the trouble of modifying these materials?

Scholars have pointed to the audience's ability to become part of mass media activities as a new development in the relationship between the audience and the companies that produce and distribute media materials. Some note that audience members are increasingly becoming part of the production process. We will see a lot of this phenomenon as we move through this book.

# Mass Media, Culture, and Society

## How Do We Use the Mass Media in Our Daily Lives?

The interest people have in sharing and sometimes manipulating media materials they like speaks to the role these materials play in the most personal parts of our lives. Media industries help us connect ourselves and our friends to parts of the world beyond our private circumstances—worlds of music, politics, war, and much more.

Because they do that, mass media industries are a major force in society. To understand what this means, we have to dig deeper into how people use the media and what they get out of them.

Scholars have found that individuals adapt their use of mass media to their own particular needs. Broadly speaking, people use the media in four ways: for enjoyment, for companionship, for surveillance, and for interpretation. Let's examine these uses one at a time.

**Enjoyment** The desire for enjoyment is a basic human urge. Watching a television program, studying the Bible, finishing a newspaper crossword puzzle, networking on Facebook, or even reading an advertisement can bring this kind of gratification to many people.

News stories, daytime soap operas, sports, and prime-time sitcoms can ignite everyday talk with friends, relatives, work colleagues, and even strangers. During the mid-1990s, for example, many local television stations around the United States were advertising their morning talk programs by saying, "We give you something to talk about." This process of using media content for everyday interpersonal discussions is called using media materials as **social currency**, or coins of exchange. "Did you hear Jay Leno's monologue last night?" someone might ask around the water cooler at work. "No, I watched Letterman," one person might reply, triggering a chain of comments about late-night TV comedy that brings a number of people into the conversation.

Of course, another way people can bring mass media material into friendly conversation is by experiencing the content together. If you have attended Super Bowl parties, you have an idea of how a televised event can energize friends in ways that have little to do with what is taking place on the screen. You may even have a tablet or television-set app that allows you to text friends—or make friends—around the particular TV shows you are viewing. In this way, the media provide us with the enjoyment we seek as a basic human need.

**Companionship** Mass media bring a sense of camaraderie to people who are lonely and those who are alone. A chronically ill hospital patient or a homebound senior citizen may find companionship by viewing a favorite sports team on TV or listening to the music of days gone by on the radio. A *Grey's Anatomy* fan might feel like part of a community by reading the blogs written by the show's writers.

Sometimes, media can even draw out people who feel troubled and in need of friends. The term "**parasocial interaction**" describes the psychological connections that some people establish with celebrities they learn about through the mass media—typically feeling a sense of bonding with those celebrities. Actors' Facebook pages and Twitter posts might lead fans to feel a special knowledge of and relationship with the person. You might know someone who gets so involved with media images of rock or rap stars that they sometimes act as if they know them well. In a few publicized cases,

Watching televised sporting events, either at someone's home or out at a bar, unites large groups of audience members who may then go on to talk about the game in various ways that connect them to that larger audience—whether it's talking about the game with coworkers, Tweeting, or blogging about it. Online activities, such as Fantasy Football leagues, connect hundreds of thousands of sports fans from around the country, creating a new kind of social currency.

**social currency**
media content used as coins of exchange in everyday interpersonal discussions

**parasocial interaction**
the psychological connections that some media users establish with celebrities whom they learn about through the mass media

this feeling has gotten out of control, leading individuals to stalk and even harm the media figures who were the objects of their adulation. In 2009, for example, a man was arrested for trying to get into a vehicle with *American Idol* host Ryan Seacrest, while possessing a knife. A month later he was arrested for attempting to approach the star in his workplace. A judge therefore forbade him from coming within 100 yards of Seacrest, his home, his car, or his places of employment.

**Surveillance** **Surveillance** users of the media employ them to learn about what is happening in the world. We all do this every day, often without realizing it. Do you turn on the radio or TV each morning to find out the weather? Do you check the stock listings to find out how your investments are faring? Have you read classified ads in print or online to look for a job, concert tickets, or used furniture? Have you ever called or logged on to Fandango or Moviefone to find out where and when a film is playing? All these activities are illustrations of using the mass media for surveillance. Of course, our surveillance can be more global. Many people are interested in knowing what is going on in the world beyond their immediate neighborhood. Did the flooding upstate destroy any houses? Will Congress raise taxes? What's going on with the negotiations for peace in the Middle East?

**surveillance**
using the media to learn about what is happening in the world around us

## THINKING ABOUT MEDIA LITERACY

Think back to your media consumption habits throughout a typical day. What kinds of information might you look up? How might you access this information? Why would you take the time to learn this information? In other words, what do you do with this information once you have it?

**Interpretation** Many of us turn to the media to learn not only what is going on but also why and what, if any, actions we should take. When people try to find reasons that things are happening, they are looking for **interpretation**. We may read newspaper editorials to understand the actions of national leaders and to come to conclusions about our stand on an issue. We know that financial magazines such as *Money* and *Barron's* are written to appeal to people who want to understand how investment vehicles work and which ones to choose. And we are aware that libraries, bookstores, and some websites (e.g., http://www.howstuffworks.com) specialize in "how to" topics ranging from raising children and installing a retaining wall to dying with dignity. Some people who are genuinely confused about some topics find mass media to be the most useful sources of answers. Preteens, for example, may want to understand why women and men behave romantically toward each other but may feel too embarrassed to ask their parents. They may be quite open to different opinions—in the *Twilight* films, on Oprah, in Justin Timberlake's music, or in *CosmoGirl* magazine—about where sexual attraction comes from and what the appropriate behavior is.

But how do people actually use the explanations they get from the mass media? Researchers have found that the credibility people place on the positions that mass media take depends on the extent to which the individuals agree with the values they find in that content.[5] For example, a person who is rooted in a religiously conservative approach to the Bible would not be likely to agree with a nature book that is based on the theory of evolution; a political liberal probably would not be persuaded by the interpretations that politically conservative magazines offer about ways to end

**interpretation**
using the media to find out why things are happening—who or what is the cause—and what to do about them

poverty. Keep in mind, however, that in these examples, these people would probably not search out such media content to begin with. Unless people have a good reason to confront materials that go against their values (unless they will be engaging in a debate on the ideas, for example), most people stay away from media that do not reflect (and reinforce) their own beliefs, values, or interests. And if they do come across materials that go against their values, they tend to dismiss them as biased.

**Multiple Use of Mass Media Content**  The example of a preteen seeking interpretations of romance from four very different outlets—a movie series, a television talk show, a musical record, and a magazine—raises an important point about the four uses that people make of the mass media: the uses are not linked to any particular medium or genre. If we take television as an example, we might be tempted to suggest that enjoyment comes from certain sitcoms or adventure series, that companionship comes from soap operas, that surveillance is achieved through network and local news programs, and that interpretation can be found in Sunday morning political talk shows such as *Meet the Press*, as well as from daily talk fests such as *The View*. In fact, we may divide many kinds of content in these ways. Communication researchers point out, however, that individuals can get just about any gratification they are seeking from just about any program—or any kind of mass media materials.

You might find, for example, that you use the *NBC Nightly News* for enjoyment, surveillance, and interpretation. Enjoyment might come from the satisfaction of watching reporters' familiar faces day after day (is a little parasocial interaction working here?); surveillance might be satisfied by reports from different parts of the globe; and interpretation might flow from stray comments by the reporters and those they interview about what ought to be done to solve problems.

In thinking about the multiple uses of mass media content, consider too that the application of computer codes to mass media materials allows audience members to carry out enjoyment, companionship, surveillance, and interpretation in ways that did not exist before computer-centered mass communication. With the right tools, users can often manipulate the print, audio, or audiovisual materials to suit their needs and interests. (Think of a person whose keen interest in college sports has led him to create a website with links to the college sports sections of newspaper and TV websites.) Audience members who are connected to the producers of an audio or audiovisual program via a cable or telephone line can respond to those producers via the computer. The producers, in turn, can send out a new message that takes the response—the feedback—into consideration. This sort of manipulation and response—which is much easier in digital than in analog technology—is known as **interactivity**.

## How Do the Mass Media Influence Culture?

When we use the term "**culture**," we are broadly talking about ways of life that are passed on to members of a society through time and that keep the society together. We typically use the word "**society**" to refer to large numbers of individuals, groups, and organizations that live in the same general area and consider themselves connected to one another through the sharing of a culture.

What is shared includes learned behaviors, beliefs, and values. A culture lays out guidelines about who belongs to the society and what rules apply to them. It provides guideposts about where and what to learn, where and how to work, and how to eat and sleep. It tells us how we should act toward family members, friends, and strangers and much, much more. In other words, a culture helps us make sense of ourselves and our place in the world.

**interactivity**
the ability to track and respond to any actions triggered by the end user, in order to cultivate a rapport

**culture**
ways of life that are passed on to members of a society through time and that keep the society together

**society**
large numbers of individuals, groups, and organizations that live in the same general area and consider themselves connected to one another through the sharing of a culture

A culture provides people with ideas about the kinds of arguments concerning particular subjects that are acceptable. In American culture, people likely feel that on certain topics (e.g., vegetarianism) all sorts of positions are acceptable, whereas on other topics (e.g., cannibalism, incest) the range of acceptable views is much narrower. Moreover, American culture allows for the existence of groups with habits that many people consider odd and unusual but not threatening to the more general way of life. Such group lifestyles are called **subcultures**. The Amish of Pennsylvania who live without modern appliances at home represent such a subculture, as do Catholic monks who lead a secluded existence devoted to God.

For better or worse, it is not always easy to find direct evidence of who belongs and what the rules are by simply looking around. The mass media allow us to view clearly the ideas that people have about their broad cultural connections with others and where they stand in the larger society. When mass media encourage huge numbers of people who are dispersed and unrelated to share the same materials, they are

**subcultures**
groups with habits that many people consider odd and unusual but not threatening to the more general way of life

## MEDIA TODAY & CULTURE  THE SHIFT TO MEDIATED COMMUNICATION

Consider these two brief scenarios:

You are walking across campus, and you recognize a person you met at a student gathering last weekend coming from the other direction. Just as the two of you are about to meet, the other person pulls out a cell phone and begins sending a text message as he walks by, denying you the chance to say hello.

You are out to dinner with some of your friends. As you sit in the booth waiting for your food to arrive, you notice that no one is talking to each other. Instead, everyone is occupied with his or her cell phone. Lisa is sending a text message, Brian is checking his e-mail, Adnaan is looking up something on Google, and Preeti is looking for a video she wants to share with everyone.

According to Sherry Turkle, we have entered an era when we are "alone together." Turkle is a scholar at the Massachusetts Institute of Technology who studies how technologies are changing not only the ways in which we communicate, but also the ways in which we construct ourselves.

We are able to customize our media to our interests and needs. We can maintain connections to people we want to keep connected to, and we can access media content that we want to see and filter out what we don't want to see. And we can connect to these people and this content at almost any time we choose.

These media also allow us to construct ourselves—our self-images—in ways that we want. We can share what information we choose, and we can choose how to share it. We can edit and even remove whatever has been shared previously.

But all these connections are changing the ways in which people communicate in person. The technologies allow us to shut other people out and avoid having a real-life conversation with them. Instead of talking to the stranger sitting next to us on the bus, we are more likely to ignore that person and send a text message to someone we do know. People use earphones to send a visual signal to others that they want to be left alone. These instances occur on campus, in public, and even in business.

Although this situation makes for a neat and tidy world, we miss out on the rich complexities of human relationships and human conversations. According to Turkle, "human relationships are rich; they're messy and demanding. We have learned the habit of cleaning them up with technology." But in the process of cleaning them up, we miss out on patience and self-reflection. Turkle even suggests that Apple's digital assistant Siri will become a companion for some people in the future.

Why do you think these shifts from interpersonal to mediated interpersonal communication are occurring at such a rapid rate? Do you find yourself engaging with media instead of talking with people? What do you think needs to be done in changing this situation?

PART 1    THE NATURE AND BUSINESS OF MEDIA

focusing people's attention on what is culturally important to think about and to talk and argue with others about. In other words, mass media create people's common lived experiences, a sense of the common culture, and the varieties of subcultures acceptable to that common culture.

The mass media present ideas of the culture in three broad and related ways: they help us (1) identify and discuss the codes of acceptable behavior within our society, (2) learn what and who counts in our world and why, and (3) determine what others think of us and what people "like us" think of others. Let's look at each of the ways separately.

**Identifying and Discussing Codes of Acceptable Behavior**  A culture provides its people with notions about how to approach life's decisions, from waking to sleeping. It also gives people ideas about the arguments that are acceptable concerning all these subjects. If you think about the mass media from this standpoint, you'll realize that this is exactly what they do. Newspapers continually give us a look at how government works, as do internet sites such as *Politico* and the *Huffington Post*. TV's *CSI* series acts out behavior the police consider unacceptable and opens up issues in which the rules of police and "criminal" behavior are contested or unclear. Magazine articles provide ideas and a range of arguments about what looks attractive and how to act toward the opposite sex. We may personally disagree with many of these ideas. At the same time, we may well realize that these ideas are shared and possibly accepted broadly in society.

**Learning What and Who Counts in Our World—and Why**  Mass media tell us who is "famous"—from movie stars to scientists—and give us reasons why. They define the leaders to watch, from the U.S. president to religious ministers. News reports tell us who these people are in "real life." Fictional presentations such as books, movies, and TV dramas may tell us what they (or people like them) do and are like. Many of the presentations are angrily critical or bitingly satirical; American culture allows for this sort of argumentation. Through critical presentations or heroic ones, though, mass media presentations offer members of the society a sense of the qualities that we ought to expect in good leaders.

Felix Baumgartner, an Austrian skydiver and daredevil, was elevated to celebrity status after the media attention received by his Red Bull Statos project in which he skydived to Earth from a height of 24 miles, reaching speeds up to 834.4 mph.

Fiction often shows us what leaders ought to be like—what values count in society. Actor Denzel Washington excels at playing law enforcement officers or other social protectors who are courageous, smart, loyal, persevering, strong, and handsome; think, for example, of the movies *Déjà Vu*, *Inside Man*, and *The Story of Eli*. (Recently, though, he seems to revel in going somewhat against this type, as in *Safe House*.) Sometimes, mass media discussions of fiction and nonfiction merge in curious ways. During the election of 2000, for example, several mass media commentators noted that President Bartlett of the then-popular TV drama *West Wing* would be a better choice than any of the real candidates because of his better leadership qualities.

**Determining What Others Think of Us—and What People "Like Us" Think of Others**  Am I leadership material? Am I good-looking? Am I more or less religious than most people? Is what I like to eat what most people like to eat? Is my apartment as neat as most people's homes? How do I fit into the culture? Mass media allow us, and sometimes even encourage us, to ask questions such as these. When we read newspapers, listen to the radio, or watch TV, we can't help but compare ourselves to the portrayals these media present. Sometimes we may shrug off the comparisons with the clear conviction that we simply don't care if we are different from people who are famous or considered "in." Other times we might feel that we ought to be more in tune with what's going on; this may lead us to buy new clothes or adopt a new hairstyle. Often, we might simply take in ideas of what the world is like outside our direct reach and try to figure out how we fit in.

At the same time that the mass media get us wondering how we fit in, they may also encourage feelings of connection with people whom we have never met. Newscasters, textbooks, and even advertisements tell us that we are part of a nation that extends far beyond what we can see. We may perceive that sense of connection differently depending on our personal interests. We may feel a bond of sympathy with people in a U.S. city that the news shows ravaged by floods. We may feel linked to people thousands of miles away who a website tells us share our political opinions. We may feel camaraderie with Super Bowl viewers around the country, especially those rooting for the team we are supporting.

Similarly, we may feel disconnected from people and nations that mass media tell us have belief systems that we do not share. U.S. news and entertainment are filled with portrayals of nations, individuals, and types of individuals who, we are told, do not subscribe to key values of American culture. Labels such as "rogue nation," "Nazi," "communist," and "Islamic extremist" suggest threats to an American sense of decency. When mass media attach these labels to countries or individuals, we may well see them as enemies of our way of life, unless we have personal reasons not to believe the media portrayals.

**Criticisms of Mass Media's Influence on Culture** Some social observers have been critical of the way mass media have used their power as reflectors and creators of culture. One criticism is that mass media present unfortunate prejudices about the world by systematically using **stereotypes**, predictable depictions that reflect (and sometimes create) cultural prejudices, and **political ideologies**, beliefs about who should hold the greatest power within a culture and why. Another is that mass media detract from the quality of American culture. A third criticism, related to the first two, is that the mass media's cultural presentations encourage political and economic manipulation of their audiences.

Criticisms such as these have made people think deeply about the role that mass media play in American culture. These criticisms do have their weak points. Some might note that it is too simplistic to say that mass media detract from the quality of American culture. Different parts of the U.S. population use the mass media differently and, as a result, may confront different kinds of images. Related to this point is the idea that people bring their own personalities to the materials they read and watch. They are not simply passive recipients of messages. They actively interpret, reshape, and even reject some of the messages.

Nevertheless, the observations about stereotypes, cultural quality, and political ideology should make us think about the power of mass media over our lives. Many people—most people at one time or another—do seem to see the mass media as mirroring parts of their society and the world beyond it, especially parts they do not know firsthand. Most people do accept what the mass media tell them in news—and

**stereotypes**
predictable depictions that reflect (and sometimes create) cultural prejudices

**political ideologies**
beliefs about who should hold the greatest power within a culture

even in entertainment—about what and who counts in their world and why. Many seem to believe that the mass media's codes of acceptable behavior accurately describe large numbers of people, even if the codes don't describe their own norms. And they accept the mass media's images as starting points for understanding where they fit in society in relation to others and their connection with, or disconnection from, others. They may disagree with these images or think that they shouldn't exist. Nevertheless, the media images serve as starting points for their concerns about and arguments over reality. There will be further discussion about critical views on the effects of media in chapter 2.

## THINKING ABOUT MEDIA LITERACY

Among the criticisms of the mass media listed here, which one, in your opinion, seems the most detrimental to society? What do you think are the media's responsibilities to address these criticisms?

## Media Literacy

The aim of this book is to help you learn how to seriously examine the mass media's role in your life and in American life. The goal is not to make you cynical and distrustful of all mass media. Rather, it is to help you think in an educated manner about the forces that shape the media and your relationships with them so that you will better evaluate what you see and hear. The aim is to give you the tools you need to become media-literate.

A media-literate person is

- knowledgeable about the influences that guide media organizations,
- up-to-date on political issues relating to the media,
- sensitive to ways of seeing media content as a means of learning about culture,
- sensitive to the ethical dimensions of media activities,
- knowledgeable about scholarship regarding media effects, and
- able to enjoy media materials in a sophisticated manner.

Being media-literate can be satisfying and fun. For example, knowing movie history can make watching films fascinating because you will be able to notice historical and technical features of the films that you wouldn't have otherwise noticed. Having a comparative understanding of different forms of news can help you think more clearly about what you can expect from journalism today and how it is changing. Understanding the forces that shape the entertainment we see and hear, as well as the social controversies around stereotyping and violence in entertainment, can make your daily use of the media a jumping-off point for thinking critically about yourself in relation to images of others in society. All these and other media activities can also start important conversations between you and your friends about the directions of our culture and your place in it. That, in turn, can help you become a more aware and responsible citizen—parent, voter, worker—in our media-driven society (see Figure 1.4).

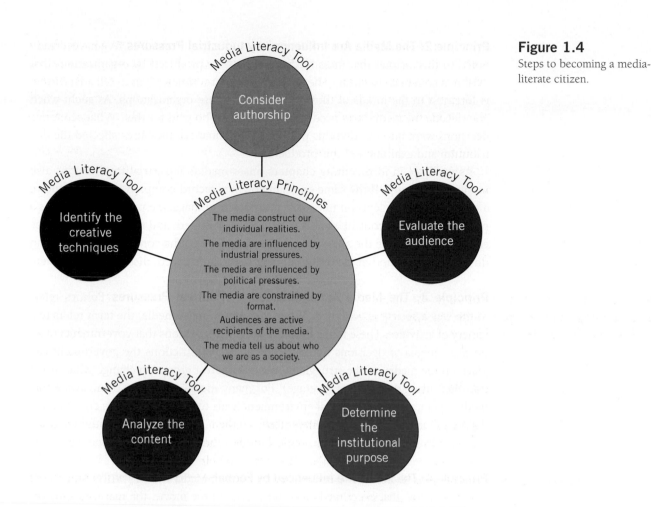

**Figure 1.4**
Steps to becoming a media-literate citizen.

## Principles of Media Literacy

When we speak about **literacy**, we mean the ability to effectively comprehend and use messages that are expressed in written or printed symbols, such as letters. When we speak about **media literacy**, however, we mean something broader. To quote the National Leadership Conference on Media Literacy, it is "the ability to access, analyze, evaluate and communicate messages in a variety of forms."

Much of what we know about the world comes from what we see and hear in the media. Beyond simply mirroring what our world looks like, the media interpret, alter, and modify our reality. To develop media literacy skills and become responsible, media-literate consumers who can critically examine the way the media work in our lives, we first need to understand some basic principles about mass media materials—principles that help us engage in and understand the media's role in our daily lives.

**Principle 1: The Media Construct Our Individual Realities** Along with our personal observations and experiences, media materials help us to create our own individual notions of reality. Much of what we see as reality comes from the media we've experienced, and it is sometimes difficult to distinguish between our personal experiences and the world of the media. When we read newspapers, watch TV, and surf the web, we need to be aware that what we are seeing and hearing is not reality—even so-called reality TV. Rather, media materials are created with specific purposes in mind. They are constructions—that is, human creations that present a kind of script about the culture. Even when media materials appear to be particularly "natural" or reflective of reality, many different business decisions and constraints have contributed to the way they are constructed.

**literacy**
the ability to effectively comprehend and use messages that are expressed in written or printed symbols, such as letters

**media literacy**
the ability to apply critical thinking skills to the mass media, thereby becoming a more aware and responsible citizen—parent, voter, worker—in our media-driven society

**Principle 2: The Media Are Influenced by Industrial Pressures** We have already noted in this chapter that mass media materials are produced by organizations that exist in a commercial setting. The need to bring in revenues, often to sell advertising, is foremost in the minds of those who manage these organizations. As such, when you decode the media, you need to ask yourself, Who paid for this? What economic decisions went into creating this product? What financial pressures affected the distribution and exhibition of this product?

As we'll see in forthcoming chapters, mass media's industrial implications also involve ownership. If the same company owns a record company, a movie studio, a cable service, a television network, and book and magazine publications, it has a powerful ability to control what is produced, distributed, and therefore seen. Large companies also have the ability to take advantage of media convergence more than do small ones—another factor influencing what is produced, distributed, and seen.

**Principle 3: The Media Are Influenced by Political Pressures** Politics refers to the way a society is governed. When it comes to mass media, the term refers to a variety of activities. These range from the specific regulations that governments place on mass media to decisions by courts about what restrictions the government can place on the media, to the struggle by various interest groups to change what media do (often using government leverage). For many media observers, being aware that media operate within a political environment leads to the idea that this environment deeply influences the media content itself. To them, this means we should be aware that the ideas in the media have political implications—that they are ideological.

**Principle 4: The Media Are influenced by Format** Media scholar Patricia Aufterheide and others note that every medium—the television, the movie, the magazine—has its own characteristics, codes, and conventions, its own ways of presenting cultural reality.

Although you probably haven't thought about it, it's a good bet that you recognize the differences between the ways these media do things. A report on a presidential press conference looks different depending on whether it was written for a newspaper or a magazine, presented on TV as news, described on a website's blog, or put together for the big screen. You probably also recognize, though, that mass media are similar in some of their approaches to presenting the world—they organize the world into a number of basic storytelling forms that we recognize as entertainment, news, information, education, and advertising. As a media-literate person, you should ask yourself, What about the format of this medium influences the content? What about the format limits the kind of content that is likely to be shown?

**Principle 5: Audiences Are Active Recipients of the Media** The process of making meaning out of media is an ongoing interaction between the reader and the materials. As individual audience members, we filter meaning through our unique experiences: our socioeconomic status, cultural background, gender, and so on. However, emphasizing the input of the individual does not take away from the broad social importance of the media. Because so many people share mass media materials, large segments of society see mass media as having cultural importance for society as a whole.

**Principle 6: The Media Tell Us about Who We Are as a Society** People may like what they see about their society, or they may complain about it. They may want people to view media images about themselves and others, or they may fear that others will be influenced negatively by certain products (e.g., stereotypes and violence). Even with an active audience, then, mass media hold crucial importance for society's visions of itself. A media-literate person searches out bias and explores the assumptions and the values in everything that is made through the production, distribution, and exhibition processes.

## Media Literacy Tools

To be a critical consumer in a mediated society, you need to equip yourself with tools that enable you to distinguish between different media forms and know how to ask basic questions. From the media literacy principles we discussed previously flow a series of five basic categories of questions that you can use to begin to take apart and explore any media message. Typically you would apply this questioning process to a specific media "text"—that is, an identifiable production or publication, or a part of one: an episode of *The Vampire Diaries*, an ad for Pepsi, an issue of *Wired* magazine, a billboard for Budweiser beer, photos and articles about a bank robbery on the home page of a news site, or the Super Bowl telecast. Sometimes a media "text" can involve multiple formats. A new animated Disney film, for example, involves not only a blockbuster movie released in thousands of theaters but also a whole campaign of advertising and merchandising—character dolls and toys, clothes, lunchboxes, and so on—as well as a website, storybooks, games, and perhaps eventually, a ride at one of the Disney theme parks. Consider, too, that with the convergence of digital media, the movie that appears in theaters also will likely appear in other media—as will the games, storybooks, and other products based on it.

Let's take a look at these skill-building categories one at a time. They all involve asking questions about the media. Don't worry if you don't feel comfortable answering them now. You'll feel much more able as you move through this book.

**Consider Authorship**  Ask yourself, Who created this message, and why are they sending it? To explore the idea of "authorship" in media literacy is to look deeper than just knowing whose name is on the cover of a book or all the jobs in the credits of a movie. Companies make media texts just as buildings and highways are put together. Lead companies make the plans and then call on a variety of firms to make the products and do the work, the building blocks are brought together, and ordinary people get paid to do various jobs. Whether we are watching the nightly news, passing a billboard on the street, or reading a political campaign flyer, the media messages we experience are created, distributed, and exhibited by various organizations in which individuals (and often teams of individuals) have written the words, captured the images, and worked the technical marvels.

Be aware, too, that in this creative process choices are made. If some words are spoken, others are edited out. If one picture is selected, dozens may have been rejected. If an ending to a story is written one way, other endings may not have been explored. However, as the audience, we don't get to see or hear the words, pictures, or endings that were rejected. We see, hear, or read only what was accepted! Rarely

Although all of these media news outlets may be covering the same story, the way in which the story is delivered or what elements of the story receive more attention than others is likely to vary since each news outlet makes different creative choices and may even be targeting different segments of the audience. Do you find yourself preferring a particular news organization over the others?

23

does anybody ever explain why certain choices were made. Rarely, too, do creators bring up alternative ways to interpret the world we see through our media channels. It is up to us to consider the constructed nature of our media realities and, when possible and important to us, to look for a variety of perspectives on the same realities.

**Evaluate the Audience** This proposition involves two broad questions. The first is, who are the intended targets of these media materials? The second is, how might different people understand these materials similarly and differently?

Thinking about the intended targets gets us back to the point that industries typically construct media materials to make money. As we will see, that often means deciding what types of people would want certain kinds of content and creating products designed to fit these interests. As straightforward as this idea sounds, we will see that it is really quite complex. Entire companies revolve around helping firms describe lucrative target audiences, evaluate their interests, and figure out how to reach them. Other firms make money evaluating whether the audiences that were targeted actually attended to the messages. "Audience research" is, in fact, a big business that is increasingly important to all media industries, from books and newspapers to the internet and video games. The more you learn about it, the more you will understand the multitude of factors that lead to the sometimes different media worlds that different people encounter. Moreover, in a world were convergence is common, media firms are likely to try to follow their target audiences with the same content across a variety of platforms. ESPN, for example, will want you to tune into its cable channel, its internet site, its tablet app, and its phone feed.

As we will see, the companies that produce, distribute, and sponsor media materials often have certain ideas in mind about what specific audiences will share as funny, sad, repulsive, scary, and exhilarating. Even though they contend that these notions are based on research, they also may be rooted in social stereotypes. Thinking about audience when you confront media materials will force you to dive into some of the most interesting questions about their creation and the roles they play in society.

**Determine the Institutional Purpose** Ask yourself, Why is this content being sent? This question flows from the previous questions about the audience. We noted that much of the world's media were developed as moneymaking enterprises and continue to operate today as commercial businesses. As we will see, with the rise of digital convergence, companies associated with products from particular industries are trying to make money from those products across various media platforms. We will see in chapters 8 and 9, for example, how newspaper and magazine publishers are redefining their output for the laptop, the tablet, and the mobile phone—while still trying to sell printed versions of their products. Chapters 8 and 9 also discuss how newspapers and magazines decide how much space they can devote to different kinds of material based on the amount and kinds of advertisements they sell. Chapter 3 sets up the more general idea that what is really being sold through commercial media is not just the advertised products to the audience, but also the audience to the advertisers!

**Analyze the Content** Ask yourself, What values, lifestyles, and points of view are represented in (or omitted from) this message? Because all media messages are constructed, choices have to be made. These choices inevitably reflect the values, attitudes, and points of view of the ones doing the constructing. The decisions about a character's age, gender, or race mixed in with the lifestyles, attitudes, and behaviors that are portrayed, the selection of a setting (urban or rural, affluent or poor), and the actions and reactions in the plot are just some of the ways that values become part of a TV show, a movie, or an ad. As we will discuss in chapter 3, even the news reflects values in the decisions made about which stories go first, how long they are, what kinds of pictures are chosen, and so on.

Our discussion of scholarly media research in chapter 2 will provide you with a variety of tools for analyzing content. There, as well as throughout this book, we address two major complaints that many people have about the widespread mass media: (1) less popular or new ideas can have a hard time getting aired, especially if they challenge long-standing assumptions or commonly accepted beliefs; and (2) unless challenged, old assumptions can create and perpetuate stereotypes, thus further limiting our understanding and appreciation of the world and the many possibilities of human life.

**Identify the Creative Techniques** Ask yourself, What creative techniques are being used to attract my attention? This question relates partly to the need to identify the ways that media materials provide clues to their institutional purpose and choices made. You should think about how a message is constructed to connect with its intended audience, including the creative components that are used in putting it together--words, still images, moving images, camera angle, music, color, movement, and many more components. Apart from the issue of targeting, understanding the creative techniques of mass media will aid your appreciation of the artistry involved. All forms of communication—whether print magazine covers, television advertisements, or horror movies—depend on a kind of "creative language." For example, use of different colors creates different feelings, camera close-ups often convey intimacy, and scary music heightens fear. As we will see, learning the history of a medium involves learning the ways that companies have organized words and images to draw and captivate audiences. Go beyond what you learn here to immerse yourself in the creative languages of media that you love—whether they are comic books, romance novels, hip-hop recordings, cowboy films, daily newspapers, video games on mobile devices, or other elements of media culture. Try to understand how the techniques involved in creating those products change when companies adapt them for other media. What you learn will undoubtedly be fascinating, and it will make your everyday interactions with those media extremely interesting.

## The Benefits of a Media-Literate Perspective

Armed with the principles of media literacy and the tools to evaluate any media message, you are on your way to developing a media-literate perspective. For those who adopt this perspective, the power held by the mass media raises a host of social issues, including the following:

- Do media conglomerates have the ability to control what we receive over a variety of media channels? If so, do they use that ability? How do their activities affect the way digital convergence is taking place?
- Are portrayals of sex and violence increasing in the new media environment, as some critics allege? Do media organizations have the power to lower the amount of sex and violence? Would they do it if they could?
- Does the segmentation of audiences by media companies lead to better advertising discounts and greater diversity of content for groups that those firms consider more attractive than for groups that those firms consider less important? If so, what consequences will that have for social tensions and the ability of parts of society to share ideas with one another?

- What (if anything) should be done about the increasing ability of mass media firms to invade people's privacy by storing information they gain when they interact with them? Should the federal government pass laws that force companies to respect people's privacy, or should we leave it up to corporate self-regulation? What do we know about the history of corporate self-regulation that would lead us to believe that it would or wouldn't work in this situation?

- Should global media companies adapt to the cultural values of the nations in which they work, even if those values infringe on free press and free speech?

Our exploration of these and related questions will take us into topics that you may not associate with the mass media business—for example, mobile telephones, toys, games, and supermarkets. It will also sometimes take us far beyond the United States because American mass media companies increasingly operate globally. They influence non-U.S. firms around the world and are influenced by them. As we will see, their activities have sparked controversies in the United States and abroad that will likely intensify as the 21st century unfolds.

# CHAPTER REVIEW

Visit the Companion Website at www.routledge.com/cw/turow for additional study tools and resources.

## Key Terms

You can find the definitions to these key terms in the marginal glossary throughout this chapter. Test your knowledge of these terms with interactive flash cards on the *Media Today* companion website.

| | | |
|---|---|---|
| analog | interpersonal communication | parasocial interaction |
| audience fragmentation | interpretation | political ideologies |
| channel | literacy | receiver |
| communication | mass media | social currency |
| convergence | mass media outlets | society |
| culture | mass production process | source |
| digital | media literacy | stereotypes |
| decoding | mediated interpersonal | subcultures |
| encoding | communication | surveillance |
| feedback | medium | transmitter |
| industrial nature | messages | |
| interactivity | noise | |

# Questions for Discussion and Critical Thinking

1. After reading about the different ways of approaching media literacy, how do you think you might apply them to your own media consumption? Do you think they might change how you "see" media? Why or why not?
2. Think about a television format with which you are familiar, such as a type of reality show, sports show, or situation comedy. What are basic features of this format? What are some other shows that also follow this format?

What does the format allow? What are some of its limitations?
3. What are some codes of acceptable behavior shown within the format you are considering?
4. Look back to the comparisons of analog and digital media. What everyday tools depend on digital technologies in order to be useful or "cool"? Could these tools function as analog technologies? Why or why not?

## Case Study
### THE MEDIA AS SOCIAL CURRENCY

**The Idea** How much do media really influence what people discuss with you? This study will help you begin to find out by tracking how often people bring up media-related topics with you over the course of a day.

**The Method** The challenge will be to get some sense of a day's media-related conversations that people initiate with you. The trick will be to keep a record of what people talk to you about from the media, but without encouraging them to do it and without making them so self-conscious that they will stop right away or refrain from doing it again during the day. Here are suggestions about how to go about it:

1. Prepare a small notebook that you can carry in your pocket or pocketbook. On each page write the following column heads, leaving space underneath each one: "Time," "Who," "Topic," "How Long?"
2. Go through your day normally. Each time a person (or group of people) brings up a topic that in some way or another relates to something that the person clearly says he or she saw or heard in the media (e.g., in the news or in an ad), or that he or she clearly thinks you saw or heard in the media, pay particular attention. Involve yourself in the conversation as you normally would. When the conversation has ended and the others involved have left (or if you can absent yourself for a bit), get out your notebook and fill in the topics on the page: What time did the media-related conversation start? Who was involved as speaker(s) and listener(s)? What did they talk about, and for how long? Remember that listeners can also be speakers and that a conversation can have far more than a single media-related topic.
3. For the purpose of this study, you should note only media-related conversations that people initiate with you. The reason is that you might go out of your way to initiate such activities, and that would make the results hard to generalize. Make sure, though, to include mediated conversations—for example, phone calls, Skype calls, text messages, and e-mail—that people use to discuss media with you or to direct you to websites or other media. Also pay attention to evidence of the effect of media convergence. A person might, for example, mention an HBO program she often watches on cable but today viewed on her iPad.
4. You might also write notes about topics of conversation that you think originated from the media when the speaker did not clearly note the connection. A person might talk about the war in Iraq, for example, but not say that he or she learned about it from the media. In fact, the story may have come from a friend who saw it on TV.
5. The next day, pull out your notebook and make a table that notes each occurrence and what you wrote about each one. Separate the clear cases from the ones that aren't explicit. Write a short (two-page) essay summarizing the findings. What might this mean about media's role in the way people interact with you? Compare your findings with the findings of others in the class, and try to figure out why they are similar or different.

# 2 Making Sense of Research on Media Effects and Media Culture

## CHAPTER OBJECTIVES

1 Identify and explain what mass media research is

2 Recognize and discuss the mainstream approaches to mass media research

3 Recognize the shift from mainstream approaches to critical approaches

4 Recognize and discuss the critical approaches to mass media research

5 Recognize and discuss the cultural studies approaches to mass media research

6 Harness your media literacy skills regarding media research and effects to understand and evaluate the media's presence and influence in your life

"There are in fact no masses; there are only ways of seeing people as masses."

**RAYMOND WILLIAMS, CULTURAL PHILOSOPHER**

Imagine a communication major, Jessica, who is a junior at a college near a large U.S. city. Jessica works on the Culture and Arts beat for the school's daily newspaper. In recent weeks she's been watching a lot of reality television. Her viewing runs a broad gamut of programs, from *Survivor* to *The Great Race* to *Top Chef*. She is, however, particularly fascinated and disgusted by series on the Bravo cable network that claim to shed light on housewives of particular areas of the United States, shows such as *The Real Housewives of Beverly Hills, The Real Housewives of Orange County*, and *The Real Housewives of Atlanta*. After tuning into several episodes, she begins to worry that viewers, especially young women her age, will get the impression that the women portrayed are typical of many American housewives. Having grown up in a loving Italian American home in New Jersey, Jessica becomes particularly concerned about *The Real Housewives of New Jersey*. While growing up, Jessica was quite aware that television and movie representations of Italians and her state portrayed gangsters and dysfunctional families; HBO's *The Sopranos* was the most famous example. Under the guise of comic realism, the show continually showcased outrageous remarks, catfights, soap-operatic family lives, and ridiculous spending of female characters, some of whom just happened to be Italian.

Having just learned about media convergence in one of her Communication classes, Jessica is also aware that Bravo is extending all the *Housewives* programs from cable TV into other media. She can view episodes on her laptop and iPad, buy an entire season on DVD, access key storylines on the Bravo website, and even follow the tweets of the "characters" on her mobile phone. In Jessica's eyes this makes the programs especially disturbing. She becomes even more concerned after reading an article by Amanda Espitia in the Chicago section of the *Huffington Post* that points out how reality programs such as the *Housewife* shows contain domestic abuse—verbal, emotional, physical, financial, and/or sexual—as a natural part of the characters' relationships. "The pervasiveness of this violence," Espitia writes, "and the fact that it is widely accepted as having a high entertainment value has served to confuse people, especially youth, about what constitutes domestic violence."

"I know lots of college students who follow these programs," Jessica says to her boyfriend Jim over lunch. "I'm sure many of them think that many of the moms I know back home are like the ones on Jersey Housewives."

"Well," Jim replies, "loads of people around here pay attention to those shows."

"But why?" Jessica presses him as she finishes her iced tea. "Why would Bravo air these sorts of portrayals?"

Jessica finds that a number of friends at the paper share her concerns about the depiction of women in the *Housewives* series and other such reality programs. Zoe, a criminology major, confides that she phoned her local cable company about the programs after reading the Espitia

piece. She wanted the cable system to allow her time to present criticism of the series before every episode to alert viewers to alternative ways of thinking about the show. The community-relations manager listened politely to her complaints, she says, but never got back to her. "The need to attract large numbers of viewers for advertisers obviously exceeds their desire to be publicly responsible," Zoe suggests. But Jessica is determined to go beyond what her friend has done. She decides to start a group to put public pressure on the cable system and Bravo to allow debate on Bravo about the *Housewives* series.

But how should she start? Jim suggests that she start with the basics: "You need to research the effects of TV and how cable TV news operates. If you go out there and start complaining publicly with no knowledge, you may come off looking foolish. And the people who run the cable system and Bravo will have had their way." Jim suggests that her first step might be to talk to her advisor. "Get his input into how this all works, what effects these sorts of images might have, and the best ways to influence the companies that put them on the air," he says.

Jessica decides to give it a try, so she shares her concerns with her advisor, communication professor David Berg. "It's an interesting topic," Professor Berg says. "In fact, it's an issue I would love to pose to the graduate students in my Media Theory class. Why don't you come to the class next week, and I'll get the students to help you brainstorm?" Jessica tells him that's a great idea, but she secretly worries that the grad students might be more inclined to think about "ivory tower" concepts and not about her concerns about the cable programs. Nevertheless, she shows up in the graduate class to find that she has hit on a hot-button topic with a substantial proportion of the grad students, who are eager to express their viewpoints and link them to scholarly research. In this chapter are the kinds of things you might hear if you were in on the discussions.

## The Nature of Mass Media Research

Research is the application of a systematic method to solve a problem or understand it better than in the past. **Mass media research** involves the use of systematic methods to understand or solve problems regarding the mass media.

The research we are concerned with in this chapter tries to answer questions that relate to society's bottom line, not to a company's bottom line. Understanding how the research developed also means understanding how the mass media developed and how people responded to them. The research we review here asks about the role

**mass media research**
the use of systematic methods to understand or solve problems regarding the mass media

mass media play in improving or degrading the relationships, values, and ideals of society and the people who make up that society.

# The Early Years of Mass Media Research in the United States

Nearly a hundred years ago, two major media issues preoccupied the thinkers of the day. The first was the media's role in helping to keep a sense of American community alive. The second was the media's role in encouraging bad behavior among children—an issue that faded rather quickly, only to reappear many years later.

## Searching for Community: Early Critical Studies Research

The early 20th century was a time of enormous social change in American society. The industrial revolution was in full swing, and factories were turning out machine-made consumer products at low cost in numbers that had never been seen before.

Many of these factories were located in cities, and they drew millions of workers who streamed out of farming communities in order to take advantage of the higher salaries and better opportunities of urban life.

Even more numerous than the workers who came to the cities from U.S. farms were the immigrants from central and eastern Europe who were teeming into American ports looking for a piece of the American dream. For many, the dream turned out to be a bit of a nightmare, at least at first. A large number of the newcomers, poor and unable to speak the English language, led a difficult, even hand-to-mouth existence that contrasted dramatically with the lives of the wealthy urban industrialists of the day and the relatively modest, yet still quite comfortable situation of most nonimmigrants.

Social observers in this period considered this a very serious situation. It wasn't just the poverty that concerned them. They also worried that this new urban, often non-English-speaking population of immigrants who knew little of American values would endanger the small-town democratic community that they believed had characterized American society before the late 19th century. Could the traditional sense of community—that shared sense of responsibility that people felt toward their neighbors and their nation—be sustained in cities where so few people knew or cared about one another? Could the torrents of immigrants be brought into the mainstream of American society so that they considered its values their own?

You may not agree that the questions these social observers asked were the correct ones. You may feel that these people were romanticizing small-town communities. Or you might argue that those who already lived in the United States did not have the right to impose their "American" values on the new immigrants. These are quite legitimate objections, but at the turn of the 20th century, many people considered U.S. society's biggest problems to be preserving a sense of small-town community and making sure immigrants "assimilated."

Mott Street in downtown New York City circa 1900—an area known as "Little Italy" because it was home to many of the Italian immigrants. During this time, newcomers to America banded together to create self-sustaining neighborhoods where inhabitants shared cultural values and the same language, making it difficult to pressure the immigrants into assimilating.

The pessimists among them concluded that there really was no hope—that urban society, especially immigrant urban society, would destroy the connectedness that they associated with small-town America. Drawing on late 19th-century European writings on the dangers of the "crowd" (or the "masses" as they were sometimes called), the prejudiced among U.S. citizens saw these urban crowds as having dangerously irrational tendencies. There was, they felt, a good reason to keep immigrants away from U.S. shores.

A group of prominent sociologists at the University of Chicago argued publicly and in their scholarly writings that it was precisely because of the mass media that the situation in "mass society" was not nearly as bleak as some thought. Professors Robert Park, John Dewey, and Charles Cooley suggested that the widespread popularity of newspapers and magazines in the early 20th century allowed for the creation of a new type of community (see Figure 2.1).

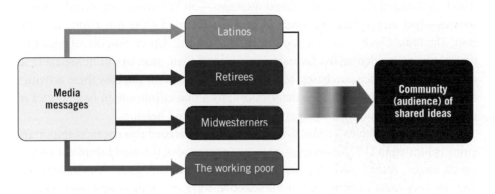

### Figure 2.1
According to the Chicago School, media have power to bring disparate individuals together by broadcasting the same notions of society to large numbers of people who might otherwise never interact, thereby creating a new type of community.

These researchers argued that the media brought together large numbers of geographically separated, diverse individuals who would otherwise be disconnected from one another and from a common notion of society and allowed them to share ideas about the society without assembling in the same geographic area. They said that if media firms acted responsibly, Americans—both newcomers and those here from birth—could learn ideas that were essential to their democracy from the media's messages. Robert Park conducted a study of the immigrant press in the United States and concluded that, far from keeping the foreigners in their own little ethnic worlds, the immigrant newspapers were helping people (over time) acclimate to American society. Immigrants, he said, were using their foreign-language media to learn how to be good citizens.

Cooley and Dewey were social philosophers. Their work tended to be conceptual rather than empirical. Park, a former newspaper reporter, was more empirically oriented. All three were the most prominent members of what became known as the Chicago School of Sociology. Many of their ideas are fresh and interesting even today. Not everyone agreed with them then (and not everyone agrees with them now). Nevertheless, they were among the first U.S. academics to show how systematically presented ideas and research about the mass media could feed into important social issues.

## Fearing Propaganda: Early Concerns about Persuasion
At about the same time that Cooley, Dewey, and Park were writing about ways the mass media could help society maintain an informed democratic public, other researchers were expressing strong concerns about unethical rulers using the power of the mass media to reach huge numbers of people for undemocratic ends.

University of Chicago political science professor Harold Lasswell saw mass media organizations as powerful weapons of persuasion because they reached enormous

**propaganda**
messages designed to change the attitudes and behavior of huge numbers of otherwise disconnected individuals on controversial social issues

**agenda setting**
the notion that the media create "the ideas in our heads" about what is going on in the world

**propaganda analysis**
the systematic examination of mass media messages that seem designed to sway the attitudes of large populations on controversial issues

Chief of Staff George C. Marshall enlisted well-known director Frank Capra (who later directed *It's a Wonderful Life*, among other films) to create a series of seven propaganda films that the government showed American soldiers during World War II to explain why it was important for them to be fighting in this war. Propaganda analysts would examine films such as these for their efficacy in convincing soldiers that the United States was right to be involved in the war in Europe.

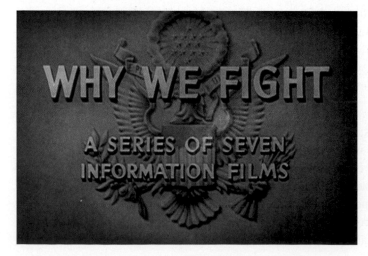

numbers of geographically dispersed people in very short periods of time. Never before in history had this been possible, Lasswell and other researchers pointed out. They feared that powerful interest groups in a society would use mass media as **propaganda**—messages designed to change the attitudes and behavior of huge numbers of otherwise disconnected individuals on controversial social issues. Under the right conditions, they feared, such propaganda would enable rulers to spread lies through the media and manipulate large numbers of people to support their views. Those in the society who opposed these rulers would be at a substantial disadvantage.

One reason that such fears abounded in the United States had to do with the successful manipulation of newspaper reports and photographs by both the Allies and the German government during World War I. The head of the U.S. propaganda effort, George Creel, wrote a popular book, *How We Advertised America* (1920), in which he boasted that expertly crafted messages—on billboards, on records, and in movies—had moved huge numbers of people to work for the war effort. In addition, *The Brass Check* (1919), a book by the social critic Upton Sinclair, alleged that major advertisers demanded favorable coverage of their products in newspapers in exchange for ad space purchases. Many liberal thinkers of the day saw these activities as fundamentally threatening to democracy, given that citizens often had no idea of the intentions behind the messages they were seeing and hearing.

Some writers, such as journalist Walter Lippmann, argued that the most important culprits hindering U.S. newspapers' objective portrayal of the world were not propaganda forces. Rather, said Lippmann, the culprits were U.S. journalists themselves. Because they were mere mortals with selective ways of seeing things, and because they worked in organizations with deadlines, restrictions on story length, and the need to grab readers' attentions, news journalists often portrayed predictably patterned (stereotyped), limited views of the world. In his book *Public Opinion* (1922), Lippmann argued that the news media are a primary source of the "pictures in our heads" about the external world of public affairs that is "out of reach, out of sight, out of mind." Lippmann's notion that the media create "the ideas in our heads" about what is going on in the world is referred to as **agenda setting**.

Other academic thinkers of the era were more likely to emphasize the propagandistic aspect of the press. Academics of the 1920s and 1930s, such as Leonard Doob, Alfred McLung Lee, Ralph Casey, and George Seldes, saw the importance of systematically exploring the forces guiding media companies and the value of analyzing media content. They felt that by letting people know how media firms operate, they could help citizens to protect themselves from the undue power of those firms. They called the activity **propaganda analysis**, a type of content analysis that systematically examines mass media messages designed to sway the attitudes of large populations on controversial issues. In their propaganda analysis studies, specially trained coders examined messages (articles, movies, radio shows) for elements that the researchers believed to be significant.

For example, analysts in the late 1930s were concerned that U.S. newspapers were negatively portraying the communist Soviet Union and potentially harming the chances for a U.S.–Soviet collaboration against Hitler's Germany. To find out what influential newspapers were doing, the researchers might have systematically examined two years of articles about the Soviet Union in major U.S. newspapers. The researchers would be trained (and tested on their ability) to note a variety of topics included in the coverage of that country, from music to crime to politics. After analyzing the findings, the researchers would be able to come to quantitative conclusions about the messages about the Soviet Union that major press outlets were presenting to large numbers of Americans.

Some writers on the history of mass communication research have suggested that propaganda analysts took a **magic bullet or hypodermic needle approach** to mass communication (see Figure 2.2). By this, they mean that the propaganda analysts believed that messages delivered through the mass media persuaded all people powerfully and directly (as if they had been hit by a bullet or injected by a needle) without the people having any control over the way they reacted. For example, critics say that propaganda analysts believed that a well-made ad, an emotionally grabbing movie, or a vivid newspaper description would be able to sway millions of people toward the media producers' goals.

magic bullet or hypodermic needle approach<br/>
the idea that messages delivered through the mass media persuade all people powerfully and directly (as if they were hit by a bullet or injected by a needle) without the people having any control over the way they react

But the terms "magic bullet" and "hypodermic needle" are too simplistic to describe the effects that propaganda analysts felt the media had on individuals. For one thing, the propaganda analysts certainly did not believe that all types of messages would be equally persuasive. (They stated, for example, that audiences would more likely accept messages that reinforced common values than messages that contradicted common values.) For another, they emphasized that propaganda is more likely to work under circumstances of media monopoly than when many competitive media voices argue over the ideas presented. They believed, too, that people could be taught to critically evaluate (and thus not be so easily influenced by) propaganda.

Nevertheless, propaganda analysts of the 1920s and 1930s tended to focus more on media producers and their output than they did on members of society. They assumed that most members of society shared similar understandings of media messages, and they didn't focus on the possibility that individual audience members might interpret messages in different ways. However, another way of seeing media influence—one that suited very different social questions—was developing.

**Figure 2.2**
The hypodermic needle or magic bullet approach has been used by researchers as a punching bag to illustrate what they believe is a simplistic view of media effects.

## Kids and Movies: Continuing Effects Research

By the mid-1920s, large numbers of parents, social workers, and public welfare organizations were worried about whether specific films might be negatively affecting youngsters. Invented just a few decades earlier, the movies had become very much a part of Americans' leisure activities by the 1920s. As children and teenagers became accustomed to moviegoing, adults fretted that the violence, sexual suggestiveness, and misrepresentations of reality in many of the films they watched might bring about a slew of problems in their lives. Among the ills suggested were bad sleep patterns, improper notions of romance, and violent conduct.

These ideas may sound very modern to have been around as early as the 1920s. You may know (and we'll note later in the book) that in recent years television programs, comic books, video games, sports programs, the internet, and songs, as well as movies, have all been accused of encouraging these same problems among U.S. youth.

These early controversies over movies marked the first time that social researchers carried out systematic research to determine whether these accusations had any basis in reality. The most important of these projects, formally known as Motion Pictures and Youth, is more commonly referred to as the Payne Fund Studies because a foundation called the Payne Fund paid for the project. The research effort was led by Professor W. W. Charters of Ohio State University and was conducted by the most prominent psychologists, sociologists, and educators of the day. The studies, published in 1933, look at the effects of particular films on sleep patterns, knowledge about foreign cultures, attitudes about violence, and delinquent behavior.

The researchers used a range of empirical techniques, including experiments, surveys, and content analysis. One especially interesting survey was qualitative: a sociologist interviewed female college students about the extent to which and ways in which movies had affected their notions of romance. A noteworthy experiment was aimed at determining whether children who had seen violent films slept more restlessly than those who had seen only nonviolent films. The children in the experiment were shown a movie featuring a lot of fighting, whereas those in the control condition saw a film with no combat at all. To determine the effects of the films on sleep, the researchers had the children sleep where they could observe them. Among other aspects of the children's sleep, the researchers measured their "restlessness" by attaching equipment to their beds that would note how often they moved and turned. They found that the children who had viewed the violent film tossed and turned more than the ones who had not.

Some popular commentators in the 1930s suggested that the results showed that individual movies could have major negative effects on all children—a kind of hypodermic needle effect. Most of the Payne Fund researchers themselves, though, went out of their way to point out that youngsters' reactions to movies were not at all uniform. Instead, these reactions very much depended on specific social and psychological differences among children. A sociologist in the group, for example, concluded that a particular film might move a youngster to want or not want to be a criminal. The specific reaction, the sociologist found, depended to a large extent on the social environment, attitudes, and interests of the child.

The psychologists in the group, for their part, pointed out that the way children reacted to films often depended on individual differences in mental or cognitive ability. So, for example, two researchers looked at children's emotional reactions to a film by hooking them up to instruments that measured their heartbeat and the amount of sweat on their skin. They found that children varied widely in emotional stimulation, and they suggested that differences in response to specific scenes were caused by varied abilities to comprehend what they saw on the screen.

## THINKING ABOUT MEDIA LITERACY

Why do you think people had such strong concerns about the impacts of media on children so early on? Can you think of some examples of how these concerns about media impacting children still exist today?

### Social Relations and the Media

At Columbia University's sociology department in the early 1940s, a new contribution to this emphasis on people's different reactions to media materials emerged. It was the idea that **social relations**—interactions among people—influence the way individuals interpret media messages. For example, when people watch movies, read newspapers, listen to the radio, or use any other medium, they often talk with other people about what they have seen or heard, and this can affect their opinions about what they have seen or heard. To understand how media content affects one person differently from another, then, we might want to know more about whom people speak to about what they've seen, read, or heard in the media.

It wasn't until the early 1940s that researchers began to think of placing social relations alongside individual social and psychological differences as a major factor in helping determine the different understandings that people draw from the media. Paul Lazarsfeld and his colleagues at Columbia were the first to make this discovery, and their research started in a large-scale survey of the voting attitudes and activities of people in Erie County, Ohio, about the 1940 presidential election.

Lazarsfeld and his colleagues interviewed four similar samples of approximately 600 people about their use of radio and newspapers in relation to the election. The researchers split the people up in this way because they were using a technique called a **panel survey**. In a panel survey, the same individuals are asked questions over a period of time. The purpose is to see whether and how the attitudes of these people change over time. In the early 1940s, panel surveys were an innovative design. Lazarsfeld wanted to find out whether asking people questions once a month during the election campaign (May to November) would lead to their answering questions differently from the way they would answer if the investigators asked them questions a few times during the period, only once during the period, or only at the end of the period. After comparing the answers given by the four samples, Lazarsfeld concluded that surveying people every month did not affect their answers. The good thing about surveying them every month, however (despite its expense), was that the researchers could track the changes in the people's opinions regarding the candidates.

When the Columbia researchers concentrated on the roles that radio and newspapers played in individuals' decisions regarding the campaign, they found that news about the race seemed to change few people's voting intentions. However, when Lazarsfeld and his colleagues turned away from the issue of direct media influence to knowledge about the election, they got a surprise. The researchers were struck by the importance of voters' influence on one another. In short, voters who participated in the survey reported that instead of being exposed to the election through news coverage, they learned what was going on through discussions with friends and acquaintances.

Building from their data in a somewhat shaky manner, Lazarsfeld and his colleagues offered the **two-step flow model** (see Figure 2.3). This model states that media influence

**social relations**
interactions among people that influence the way individuals interpret media messages

**panel survey**
asking the same individuals questions over a period of time in order to find out whether and how the attitudes of these people change over time

35

**Figure 2.3**

Model of the two-step flow model
of media influence.

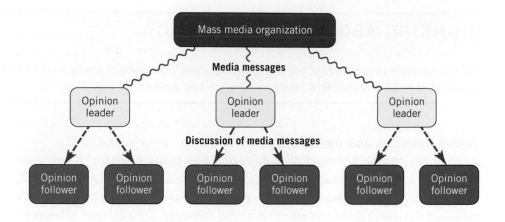

often works in two stages: (1) media content (opinion and fact) is picked up by people who use the media frequently, and (2) these people, in turn, act as opinion leaders when they discuss the media content with others. The others are therefore influenced by the media in a way that is one step removed from the actual content.

## THINKING ABOUT MEDIA LITERACY

How do social media such as Facebook and Twitter fit within the two-step flow model? Who do you think are most likely to be opinion leaders and why? Are there any limitations to applying this model to social media? Why or why not?

**active audience**
the idea that people are not simply passive recipients of media messages; they respond to content based on their personal backgrounds, interests, and interpersonal relationships

**uses and gratifications research**
research that studies how people use media products to meet their needs and interests; it asks (and answers) questions about why individuals use the mass media

As an everyday example, think of a friend whose taste in movies is similar to yours and who is much more likely than you to keep up with the latest news about films. When the movie companies put out new releases, he not only reads newspaper and magazine reviews but also checks the web and reads the trade press. At least once a week, over lunch, you and that friend talk about the new releases and discuss the possibility of seeing "the best one" that weekend. Clearly, media discussions of the new movies are influencing you through your friend. The two-step flow moves first from the various media to your friend and then to you.

Paul Lazarsfeld, his colleague Robert Merton, a graduate student named Elihu Katz, and other members of Columbia's sociology department went on to conduct several other studies on the relationship between opinion leaders, the two-step flow, and the mass media. In addition to these important works, the Columbia program also conducted research that examined the relationship between the media and their audiences—research that emphasized the idea of the active audience. By **active audience**, they meant that people are not simply passive recipients of media messages. Rather, they respond to content based on their personal backgrounds, interests, and interpersonal relationships.

The best-known aspect of this research, which came to be known as **uses and gratifications research**, studies how people use media products to meet their needs and interests. The aim of this research was  to ask (and answer) questions about why individuals use the mass media. Underlying these studies is the belief that it is just as important to know what people do with media as it is to know what media do to people. You may remember that in chapter 1 we discussed why people use the media and raised such topics as enjoyment, companionship, surveillance, and interpretation.

All these are ideas that sprang from scholarly writings about the uses and gratifications people make of and get from the mass media.

Uses and gratifications research typically employs two research methods. One method involves interviewing people about why they use specific media and what kinds of satisfactions (gratifications) they get from these media. Often such research involves a small population so that the research can be conducted in depth. The second research method involves surveys that try to predict what kinds of people use what media or what certain kinds of people do with particular media.

Consider a researcher who is interested in whether computers in nursing homes can enrich the lives of seniors. He might want to use both of these methods. One way to start such a project would be to go to nursing homes that provide internet access and interview residents about the extent to which they use the internet and what they get out of it. You might object that such a small-scale study is not clearly generalizable to other situations. You're right about that, but the researcher might sacrifice getting a representative sample of the population in return for the ability to really learn the habits and ideas of these people. He then might test what he learns in other circumstances or through large-scale surveys. In fact, the researcher might want to use the survey technique to canvass nursing homes with web access around the country. One goal might be to find out whether certain characteristics of seniors—their age, their health, or their attitudes about the future, for example—predict the kinds and extent of their web use.

## The Limits of Propaganda: Limited Effects Research

Amid all this interest in how difficult it is for media to change people's attitudes and behaviors, even propaganda research was turned on its head. Remember how powerful the propaganda analysts of the 1920s and 1930s considered the mass media to be? Well, in the 1940s, social psychologists were pointing out that even media materials specifically designed to persuade people would succeed only under limited circumstances and with only certain types of people.

The issue was by no means just a theoretical one. Propaganda became an important tool during World War II in the 1940s and during the height of the Cold War with the Soviet Union in the 1950s and 1960s. During World War II, military officials became especially interested in the ability of movies, filmstrips, and other media to teach soldiers about the reasons for the war and to increase their motivation to serve. Research on the power of these media was carried out as part of a wide investigation called "The American Soldier."

Because a soldier's duty is to do what he or she is told, a team of social psychologists under the leadership of Carl Hovland conducted careful naturalistic experiments with large numbers of people, a task that is typically difficult to accomplish. A **naturalistic experiment** is a study in which randomly selected people are manipulated in a relatively controlled environment (as in an experiment) without knowing that they are involved in an experiment. Some (who make up the experimental group) see the media message that is being evaluated, whereas others (the control group) do not. Researchers ask both groups the same questions at different points in time. The researchers take care to separate the questionnaire from the viewing so that the subjects don't suspect the relationship between the two. The before/after answers of the two groups are then compared. This approach is usually more reflective of real life than a typical experiment, in which groups of randomly chosen subjects know that they are involved in an experiment and often participate in a laboratory setting.

**naturalistic experiment**
a study in which randomly selected people are manipulated in a relatively controlled environment (as in an experiment) without knowing that they are involved in an experiment

Hovland and his colleagues used a variety of techniques with different subjects, but all were shown movies explaining America's reason for entering World War II. The 4,200 soldiers involved in the study were not told they were involved in an experiment. Instead, they were told they were being given a general opinion survey; the questionnaires they were given before seeing the film were different from those they received a week after seeing the film, to disguise the real purpose of the questionnaire. Some of the experimental groups were also given questionnaires nine weeks after seeing the movie to study the long-term effects of the film. Control groups did not see the movies, but they were given questionnaires to fill out to see if changes happened without their having viewed the movies.

Hovland's naturalistic experiments showed how difficult it is to change an individual's opinions. As an example, consider the researchers' findings when they evaluated the effects of *The Battle of Britain* (a short film that explored in vivid detail how Britain fought bravely against the Nazis, why the United States went to war to help Britain, and why it was necessary to fight to win) on men enrolled in the military. The team found that the movie had strong effects on what men learned about the battle; how much they learned depended on their educational background. When it came to convincing the men in the study that the British and French were doing all they could to win, however, the film had much less effect; few soldiers who were suspicious of the French and British before they saw the film changed their opinion.

The film was also ineffective in strengthening the overall motivation and morale of the soldiers. Specifically, one item on the questionnaire given after the experimental group saw the film asked whether the soldiers preferred military service at home or joining the fighting overseas. Only 38 percent of the control group said they wanted to fight. For the film group—supposedly fired up by the film—the comparable figure was 41 percent, not a significant difference. Even Hovland (who later went on to run the influential Program of Research on Communication and Attitude Change at Yale University) agreed that the findings did not contradict what by the 1950s was the mainstream verdict about media influence: under normal circumstances, in which all aspects of the communication environment could not be equal, the mass media's ability to change people's attitudes and behavior on controversial issues was minimal.

## Consolidating the Mainstream Approach

The seeds planted by the Columbia School, the Yale School, and to a lesser degree the Payne Fund Studies bore great fruit in the 1950s and beyond, as researchers in many universities and colleges built on their findings. We can divide these later approaches into three very broad areas of study: opinion and behavior change; what people learn from media; and why, when, and how people use the media. Let's look at these one at a time.

### Studying Opinion and Behavior Change

Many researchers have been interested in understanding why some people's opinions or behaviors are influenced by certain types of content, and those of others are not. Some of these researchers became involved in the most contentious issues involving media in the second half of the 20th century—those centering on the effects of TV violence on children and the effects of sexually explicit materials (pornography) on adults.

In general, researchers seem to agree that the ways in which most adults and children react to such materials depend greatly on family background, social setting, and personality. At the same time, they also agree that consistent viewing of violent television shows or movies may cause some children to become aggressive toward others regardless of family background. Researchers have come to similar conclusions about violent sexual materials, the kind in which men hurt women or vice versa. There is mounting evidence that in the case of some viewers, irrespective of their background or initial attitudes, heavy exposure to such materials may desensitize them to the seriousness of rape and other forms of sexual violence. For example, in one study viewers of sexual violence had less concern about the supposed victim of a violent rape than the control group viewers who hadn't seen such materials. Because most of these findings are based on lab experiments, though, there is a significant amount of debate about whether they apply to the real world.

## Studying What People Learn from Media

A large number of researchers have been interested in who learns what from mass media material and under what conditions. There are many facets to this study area, but two particularly important ones stand out. The first is whether media can encourage children's learning of educational skills. The second looks at who in society learns about current national and world affairs from the media.

**Can Media Encourage Learning Skills in Children?** *Sesame Street*, which made its TV debut in 1969, has been the subject of a great deal of research into what children learn from it. Researchers have found that the program can teach boys and girls from different income levels their letters and numbers and can be credited with improving the vocabulary of young children.

Professor Ellen Wartella, an expert on this topic, summarizes other findings on children's learning of education skills this way:

Educational programming, such as *Sesame Street*, has been heavily researched with respect to media effects and how such programming can impact the young children who watch it.

> Since the success of Sesame Street, other planned educational programs, such as *Where in the World Is Carmen Sandiego*, *Bill Nye the Science Guy*, *Square One Television*, *Reading Rainbow*, *Gullah Gullah Island*, *Blue's Clues* and *Magic School Bus*, have been found both to increase children's interest in the educational content of programs and to teach some of the planned curriculum. In addition, other children's shows, which focus less on teaching cognitive skills but more on such positive behaviors as helping others and sharing toys, can be successful. The most important evidence here comes from a study of preschool children's effective learning of such helping or pro-social behaviors from watching *Mister Rogers' Neighborhood*.

**Which Individuals Learn about National and World Affairs from the Mass Media?** Researchers who examine what people learn about national and world affairs from the mass media would probably argue that they too are looking at pro-social learning, but of a different kind. The basic belief that guides their work is that a democratic society needs informed citizens if public policies are to be guided by the greatest number of people. Some of their questions center on Walter Lippmann's agenda-setting concept that we discussed earlier in this chapter.

Agenda-setting scholars agree with the mainstream position that differences among individuals make it unlikely that the mass media can tell you or me precisely what opinions we should have about particular topics. They point out, however, that by making some events and not others into major headlines, the mass media are quite successful at getting large numbers of people to agree on what topics to think about. That in itself is important, these researchers argue, because it shows that the press has the power to spark public dialogue on major topics facing the nation.

Professors Maxwell McCombs and Donald Shaw at the University of North Carolina, Chapel Hill, demonstrated this agenda-setting effect in research for the first time in a 1970 article. They surveyed Chapel Hill voters about the most important issues in the presidential campaign. They also conducted a content analysis of the attention that major media outlets in Chapel Hill paid to issues in the presidential campaign. McCombs and Shaw showed that the rankings of the importance that voters placed on certain issues in the presidential election campaign were related not to the voters' party affiliation or personal biases but to the priorities that the media outlets in Chapel Hill presented at the time.

This one study on the influence of the media agenda on the public agenda led to more than 200 others. The agenda-setting power of the press has generally been shown to operate in both election and nonelection studies across a variety of geographic settings, time spans, news media, and public issues. Researchers have also described an effect called priming as a "close cousin of agenda-setting."

**priming**
the process by which the media affect the standard that individuals use to evaluate what they see and hear in the media

**Priming** is the process by which the media affect the standard that individuals use to evaluate what they see and hear in the media. The idea is that the more prominent a political issue is in the national media, the more that idea will prime people (that is, cue them in) that the handling of that issue should be used to evaluate how well political candidates or organizations are doing their jobs.

But the power of agenda-setting and priming is by no means the entire story. Researchers have found that mass media agenda-setting has the ability to affect people's sense of public affairs priorities and that mass media coverage primes people with respect to the criteria they use to evaluate particular issues. Nevertheless, researchers emphasize that individual backgrounds and interests weaken these effects. That is, these factors bring about a lot of variation in what issues people pick up as important, how they prioritize these issues, and whether or not they use these issues as evaluation criteria. The weakening of the effects of agenda-setting and priming occurs primarily because people's differences lead them to pay attention to different things in the media. As with the Yale studies described earlier, the strongest agenda-setting effects have been found in experimental studies, which suggests that a major condition for obtaining these effects is attention, given that in experiments subjects are essentially forced to pay attention, whereas under naturalistic conditions some people do and others don't, based on their interest in what is going on.

## THINKING ABOUT MEDIA LITERACY

Both priming and framing limit our understandings of the world around us. Drawing on media literacy, how might you analyze media messages for these frames and their limitations? What might you do to learn more about the "bigger picture"?

If it is sometimes difficult to get people to pay attention to current events via the headlines, imagine how difficult it is to get them to pay attention to less obvious aspects of our political culture. In fact, in the decades since World War II, researchers have found a wide variation in what individuals learn from the mass media. Education has consistently been a major factor that is positively associated with differences between those who pick up knowledge of public affairs and those who do not. It seems that people are more likely to remember the events and facts that media present if they have frameworks of knowledge from schooling that can help them make sense of the news events they see or hear.

In the late 1960s, Professors Phillip Tichenor, George Donahue, and Clarice Olien of the University of Minnesota came upon a sobering survey finding that relates to the difference in the amount of current events information that different people learn from the media. They found that in the development of any social or political issue, the more highly educated segments of a population know more about the issue early on and, in fact, acquire information about that issue at a faster rate than the less educated segments. That is, people who are information-rich to begin with get richer faster than people who are information-poor, and so the difference in the amount of knowledge between the two types of people will grow wider.

## MEDIA TODAY & CULTURE FACEBOOK AND SOCIAL JUDGMENTS

Media industries constantly change, and the new technologies and applications they develop and offer to audiences impact society in multiple ways. Communication research methods help explain how people are using those technologies, how those technologies are changing the ways people communicate, and even how those technologies might be impacting society.

The social networking site Facebook has become enormously popular worldwide, with over a billion registered users. Its popularity has drawn researchers to explore how people use Facebook for personal and professional reasons. These studies often focus on the site's interactive features, such as the ability to post pictures, update statuses, and like posts or pages.

Several studies are finding motivational differences in how men and women use the site. One study, titled "Contingencies of Self-Worth and Social-Networking-Site Behavior," found that self-worth often served as a motivation and explained people's online activities. Authors Michael Stefanone, Derek Lackaff, and Devan Rosen found that women who placed value on their appearance often shared more photos than those who placed their values elsewhere. The photo-sharing served as a means for seeking affirmation.

Another study from the University of Missouri also looked at pictures but focused specifically on profile pictures and the comments they drew. Authors Kevin Wise and Seoyeon Hong looked closely at how the comments offered cues for how to perceive the person, including their attractiveness and social value. They found that impressions from others carry more weight than self-projected images. They also found that images of people doing something associated with their interests or profession, such as playing sports or a musical instrument, generated a more favorable response than static headshots. They concluded that people should be careful when choosing profile pictures and when comments appear on those pictures because of the impressions other people might form from them.

Both of these studies involved asking people questions. In their conclusions, both of these studies also upheld the ideas that first impressions are important and that people will make judgments based on pictures, even with social networking.

If you were to conduct a study of Facebook, what kinds of questions might you ask about people's uses of it? How might you modify one of these two studies? What other social networking sites might be useful for studying here?

**knowledge gap**
a theory that holds that, in
the development of any social
or political issues, the more
highly educated segments of a
population know more about
the issues early on and, in fact,
acquire information about that
issue at a faster rate than the less
educated segments, and so the
difference between the two types
of people grows wider

Professors Tichenor, Donahue, and Olien concluded that this growing **knowledge gap** was dangerous for society in an age in which the ability to pick up information about the latest trends is increasingly crucial to success. Because the study found that the information-rich in society were often the well-schooled and well-off financially, a growing knowledge gap might mean that the poorer segments of society could not participate meaningfully in discussions of social issues. It also might mean that they would not know about developments that would help them prepare for—and get—better jobs.

## Studying Why, When, and How People Use the Media

Some of the most basic questions that researchers ask about mass media in society center on who uses them, how, and why. As we noted earlier, it was a group of scholars at Columbia University who created the first notable research program that went beyond basic factual descriptions of the numbers of newspaper readers and radio listeners to ask what motivated people to use certain kinds of content.

They asked, for example, "Why do people like such programming as radio soap operas and quiz shows?" This question may have gotten sneers from some of their elitist colleagues. Nevertheless, over the decades, this uses and gratifications research has received a lot of attention. The focus is on when, how, and why people use various mass media or particular genres of mass media content.

True to the spirit of the mainstream approach, uses and gratifications research has at its core a belief in the active audience, which again means that individuals are not just passive receivers of messages. Rather, they make conscious decisions about what they like, and they have different reasons for using particular media, depending on different social relationships as well as on individual social and psychological differences. Moreover, people are physically active when they use media. When it comes to TV, for example, studies have shown that people do not sit quietly, transfixed by the tube, as some cartoon stereotypes would have it. Rather, they move around, do other things, and talk to friends and family.

A huge amount of literature explores how people use a variety of media and why. Some very interesting work connects uses and gratifications research with effects research, linking how or why people use media content with the extent to which it changes their opinions, actions, or ideas about the world.

Much of this work is interesting and important in its own right. It is useful to know, for example, what percentage of poor families have been connecting to the internet compared with the percentage of middle-class and wealthy families. The findings that there are sharp differences in income between families that are online at home and those that are not has sparked discussion of a **digital divide** in the United States—a separation between those who are connected to "the future" and those who are being left behind (see Figure 2.4). That, in turn, has led to efforts by governments and corporations to place web-linked computers with instructors in libraries and community centers that are within easy reach of people who cannot afford the internet at home.

**digital divide**
the separation between those who
have access to and knowledge
about technology and those who
(perhaps be cause of their level of
education or income) do not

Activists argue that there is a lot more to do in this area. Of particular concern are economically disadvantaged children in the United States and elsewhere in the world who are falling behind in their ability to be part of the modern world. More than a few of their advocates point out that although providing them with new technology is a beginning, it is not enough. Teaching them how to use the technology in ways that will benefit them and their societies is a critical part of bridging the digital divide.

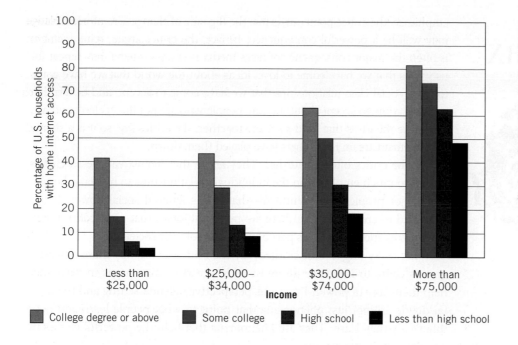

**Figure 2.4**
Now, more than ever, the gap between those people and communities who can make effective use of information technology and those who cannot is widening. Although a consensus does not exist regarding the extent of this digital divide, most researchers acknowledge that a divide exists at this point in time, as this figure shows.

## The Rise of Critical Approaches

As you can see, the **mainstream approaches**—the research models that developed out of the work of the Columbia School, the Yale School, and the Payne Fund Studies—have led to valuable work that has helped many researchers contribute to society's most important debates. At the same time, however, other researchers insist that the questions asked by mainstream approaches are not really the most important ones when it comes to understanding the role of mass media in society.

**mainstream approaches**
the research models that developed out of the work of the Columbia School, the Yale School, and the Payne Fund Studies

### Moving from Mainstream Approaches to Critical Approaches

According to critics of the mainstream approach, there are two major problems with even the best mainstream research. One problem is its stress on change rather than continuity. The other is its emphasis on the active role of the individual—the active audience member—in the media environment and not on the power of larger social forces that control that media environment.

Let's look at the first problem. In referring to a stress on change over continuity, critics of mainstream research mean that much of this research focuses on whether a change will occur as a result of specific movies, articles, or shows. Critics say that this approach ignores the possibility that the most important effects of the media have to do not with changing people but with encouraging them (or reinforcing them) to continue certain actions or perspectives on life.

Mainstream researchers might focus, for example, on whether a girl will hit her little brother after watching the violent antics of a Three Stooges film or whether a woman will learn about politics from a website or TV news program. Now, there's nothing wrong with such questions, the critics allow. But, they add, fascination with these questions of change often hides the importance of the media in encouraging the reinforcement of actions and beliefs among many in society.

Mainstream researchers emphasize that most people's opinions and behaviors don't change after they view television or listen to the radio. What the researchers don't

# KARL MARX

Karl Marx's *Das Capital* was his manifesto in which he heavily criticized capitalism as an economic model because he felt it was heavily dependent on the exploitation of the working class by business owners and the upper class, creating many cultural and societal problems for countries adopting this economic model. The interaction between capitalism and culture was of great interest to those in the Frankfurt School during the 1930s and 1940s.

**capitalism**
as defined by Karl Marx, the ownership of the means of production by a ruling class in society

emphasize, the critics point out, is that the flip side of change—reinforcement—may well be a powerful consequence. In fact, the critics argue, reinforcement is often the major consequence of mass media messages. Media may repeat for us values that we have come to love, ideas about the world that we have come to trust, social class relationships that we have come to accept, and beliefs that we have come to accept about the way people who are not like us look and act. These are the ideas that hold a society together, the critics say, so it is a shame that the mainstream researchers have played them down.

But the critics often go further. They argue that mainstream research has placed so much emphasis on the individual's relationships to media—the second major problem we identified—that it has ignored social power. It has neglected to emphasize that there are powerful forces that exert control over what media industries do as part of their control over society.

What really ought to be studied, say the critics, is the way these powerful groups come to influence the most widespread media images in ways that help them stay in power. From this perspective, agenda-setting and the digital divide are not just phenomena that point to what people learn and how differently they learn. They are phenomena that help the powerful classes in a society retain their power.

Clearly, we have here a major difference of opinion about how to look at mass media, about where their powers lie, and about which of their aspects should be studied. Many critics of the mainstream approach prefer an avenue of research that recalls the most sophisticated of the propaganda analysis. Like the propaganda analysts, contemporary critical scholars emphasize the importance of systematically exploring the forces guiding media companies. They also place great value on analyzing media content to reveal the patterns of messages that are shared broadly by the population. Like the propaganda analysts, their aim is often to expose to public light the relationships between media firms and powerful forces in society. They want to publicize their findings in order to encourage public understanding and, sometimes, to urge government regulations that would promote greater diversity among creators of media content and in the content itself.

The "critical" label describes a wide variety of projects relating to the mass media. Three prominent perspectives that guide critical researchers are the critical theory of the Frankfurt School, political economy research, and cultivation studies.

**The Deep Political Influence of the Media: The Frankfurt School's Critical Theory** The Frankfurt School is a shorthand name for a group of scholars who were associated with a place called the School for Social Research during the 1930s and 1940s. This shorthand name comes from the original location of the institute in Frankfurt, Germany. The researchers who made significant contributions to this school of thought are Theodor Adorno (philosopher, sociologist, and musicologist), Walter Benjamin (essayist and literary critic), Herbert Marcuse (philosopher), and Max Horkheimer (philosopher and sociologist). Each of these philosophers shared the basic view of capitalism set forth by the 19th-century philosopher Karl Marx. According to Marx, **capitalism** is the ownership of the means of production by a ruling class in society. Marx insisted that in societies that accept this economic approach, capitalism greatly influences all beliefs. He further insisted that capitalism and the beliefs it generates create economic and cultural problems. They exploit the working class and celebrate that exploitation in literature and many other aspects of culture. Marx believed that the direction of history was toward labor's overthrow of the capitalist class and the reign of workers in a society in which everyone would receive what he or she needs.

The Frankfurt School focused on the cultural aspect of this issue, and its members were pessimistic about it. Marxist and Jewish, they were exiled from Germany to the United States because of the rise of Nazism during the 1920s and 1930s. In New York (where they established the New School for Social Research), the members of the Frankfurt School explored the relationship between culture and capitalism in an era in which economic depression, war, and mass exterminations made it difficult to be optimistic about the liberating potential of culture. Their writings about the corrosive influence of capitalism on culture came to be known as **critical theory**. Writings by Adorno stress the power of "the culture industry" to move audience members toward ways of looking at the world. Writings by Marcuse suggest to researchers how messages about social power can be found in all aspects of media content, even if typical audience members don't recognize them. For example, **co-optation** is a well-known term that Marcuse coined to express the way capitalism takes potentially revolutionary ideas and tames them to express capitalist ideals. For an example of co-optation, consider how advertisers take expressions of youthful rebellion such as tattoos and colored hair and turn them into the next moneymaking fads. Marcuse would say that this sort of activity shows how difficult it is for oppositional movements to create symbols that keep their critical meanings.

Many media scholars today feel that the members of the Frankfurt School tended to overemphasize the ability of mass media to control individuals' beliefs. Nevertheless, over the decades, the philosophies collectively known as critical theory have influenced many writings on mass media.

**Political Economy Research** **Political economy** theorists focus specifically on the relationship between economics and the culture. They look at when and how the economic structures of society and the media system reflect the political interests of society's rich and powerful. In this vein, professor and media activist Robert McChesney examined ownership patterns of media companies in the early 2000s. He concluded in his 2004 book *The Problem of the Media* that we have reached "the age of hyper-commercialism," where media worry far more about satisfying advertisers and shareholders than about providing entertainment or news that encourages people to understand their society and become engaged in it. McChesney blames government legislators and regulators for allowing the rise of huge media conglomerates that control large portions of the revenues of particular media industries for the purposes of selling advertising time and space. One alarming consequence, he contends, is a journalistic system that focuses more on attracting the attention of audiences than on trying to build an informed society like that imagined by Jefferson and Madison. As alarming to McChesney is the notion that, because U.S. media firms are so powerful internationally, this commercially driven perspective on journalism is spreading through the world. He and political economist Edward Herman put that idea succinctly in a 1997 book called *The Global Media*:

> Such a [global] concentration of media power in organizations dependent on advertiser support and responsible primarily to shareholders is a clear and present danger to citizens' participation in public affairs, understanding of public issues, and thus to the effective workings of democracy.

Another writer from a political economy perspective, Ben Bagdikian, points out in his book *The Media Monopoly* that huge media firms are often involved in many

**critical theory**
the Frankfurt School's members' theories focusing on the corrosive influence of capitalism on culture

**co-optation**
a term coined by Marcuse to express the way in which capitalism takes potentially revolutionary ideas and tames them to express capitalist ideals

**political economy**
an area of study that focuses specifically on the relationship between the economic and the cultural and that looks at when and how the economic structures of society and the media system reflect the political interests of society's rich and powerful

businesses outside of journalism. Comcast, the main parent of NBC News, owns many cable systems, for example. Disney owns theme parks around the world as well as ABC News. News workers who are employed by these firms may be afraid to cover controversies that involve those operations; in fact, corporate bigwigs may keep them from doing so.

The problem is not just theoretical: when ABC News investigative reporter Brian Ross was putting together a report on child abuse issues in theme parks, he was ordered by executives of the Walt Disney Company, which owns ABC News, not to report on possible problems with child care in Disneyland (Figure 2.5). ABC officials denied that the corporate linkage influenced their decision to pull an investigative report on allegations involving Disney. "Disney: The Mouse Betrayed," a *20/20* segment produced by Brian Ross, alleged, among other things, that Disney World in Florida

**1** ABC's investigative reporter, Brian Ross, learns of sex offenders being hired at Disneyland—a theme park that draws large numbers of children.

**2** As Ross further investigates this story, executives at Disney become aware of his plans to run a story on Disneyland's failure to run security checks on ABC's prime-time news program 20/20.

**3** David Westin, ABC News executive, orders that Ross drop the Disneyland story, maintaining that it has nothing to do with ABC's ownership by Disney.

**Figure 2.5**
A conflict of interest can arise when conglomerates with a direct stake in businesses outside of journalism own many of the media outlets through which the public is informed, as was the case for Brian Ross's "Disney: The Mouse Betrayed" news segment.

fails to perform security checks that would prevent the hiring of sex offenders and has problems with Peeping Toms. According to an ABC spokeswoman, news president David Westin's killing of the story had nothing to do with any network reluctance to criticize its parent company. "The fact that this particular story involved Disney was not the reason it did not make air," claimed an ABC spokesperson (http://www. washingtonpost.com/wp-srv/style/tv/features/abckillsstory.htm).

The work by McChesney, Herman, and Bagdikian looks into the economic relationships within the media system and tries to figure out their consequences for issues of social power and equity. It is concerned with looking at how institutional and organizational relationships create requirements for media firms that lead the employees of those firms to create and circulate certain kinds of material and not others. These scholars might explore, for example, whether (and how) major advertisers' relationships with television networks affect programming. They would look at the extent to which advertisers' need to reach certain audiences for their products causes networks to signal to program producers that shows that aim at those types of people will get preference.

The topics that political economists choose vary greatly. Some, such as Herbert Schiller, explore global issues. An example is the study of factors that encourage the spread of Western (often U.S.) news and entertainment throughout the world. These political scientists consider such activities to be cultural colonialism. **Colonialism** means control over a dependent area or people by a powerful entity (usually a nation) by force of arms. England and France practiced colonialism in places such as India and Vietnam for many years. **Cultural colonialism** involves the exercise of control over an area or people by a dominant power, not so much through force of arms as by surrounding the weaker countries with cultural materials that reflect values and beliefs supporting the interests of that dominant power. The political economists who explore cultural colonialism argue that by celebrating values such as commercialism and immediate gratification, the cultural colonizers encourage markets for goods that reflect those values and so help their own country's business interests.

Other political economists focus on the concerns of media in individual countries. They look, for example, at the extent to which ethnic or racial minorities can exert some control over mainstream media. Their fear is that social minorities often do not get to guide their own portrayals in their nation's main media. The result is underrepresentation and stereotyping of these groups by producers who are insensitive to their concerns. These political scientists urge changes so that minority producers and actors can have input regarding their groups' depictions.

**Cultivation Studies** Cultivation researchers are also interested in depictions, but in a different way. Such studies are different from political economy studies in that they focus not on industry relationships but on the information about the world that people pick up from media portrayals. You might object that this sounds very much like what many mainstream effects researchers do. On the surface it does. Where cultivation researchers differ is in the perspective they bring to the work and how they interpret their findings. **Cultivation studies** emphasize that when media systematically portray certain populations in unfavorable ways, the ideas that mainstream audiences pick up about those people help certain groups in society retain their power over the groups they denigrate. Stereotypes, they believe, reinforce and extend ("cultivate") power relationships.

Cultivation work is most associated with Professor George Gerbner and his colleagues at the University of Pennsylvania's Annenberg School for Communication

**colonialism**
control over a dependent area or people by a powerful entity by force or arms

**cultural colonialism**
the exercise of control over an area or people by a dominant power, not so much through force of arms as by surrounding the weaker countries with cultural materials that reflect values and beliefs supporting the interests of that dominant power

**cultivation studies**
studies that emphasize that when media systematically portray certain populations in unfavorable ways, the ideas that mainstream audiences pick up about those people help certain groups in society retain their power over the groups they denigrate

The program *Sons of Anarchy* on FX network follows the story of the leader of a motorcycle gang that sells illegal guns and is known for extreme violence, which is portrayed in the show. The program came under heavy criticism after airing episodes in which extreme violence was enacted on the matriarch of the gang (Gemma): one scenario in which she was gang-raped by members of a rival gang and another in which she was severely beaten by her husband of many years.

from the 1960s through the 1980s. Gerbner began his work with the perspective that all mass media material—entertainment and news—gives people views of the world. Those views, he said, are the mass-produced output of huge corporations. These corporations have a vested interest in perpetuating their power along with the power of established economic and cultural approaches in U.S. society. Their power is seen especially in the way violence is used in television entertainment, the most widely viewed entertainment medium in the United States.

Across all channels on the tube, argues Gerbner, TV violence is a kind of ritual ballet that acts out social power. Although TV violence may sometimes encourage aggression, most of the time it cultivates lessons about strength and weakness in society. For example, Gerbner contends that the "hidden curriculum" of TV violence tells us that women and blacks, who tend to be the objects of violence, are socially weak. White males, who tend to be perpetrators of violence (including legal violence by the police or military), are socially strong.

Moreover, Gerbner argues, the overall message of TV violence is that we live in a scary, mean world. He and his colleagues found support for this view through a two-pronged research design. First, they conducted a content analysis of many hours of television entertainment programming, using a careful definition of violence and noting who is violent to whom and under what conditions. Next, they conducted a telephone survey of a random sample of the U.S. adult population and asked the people questions about how violent the world is and how fearful they are. They found that heavy viewers of television are more fearful of the world than light viewers. Over time, these viewers also engage in more self-protective behavior and show more mistrust of others than do light viewers.

## THINKING ABOUT MEDIA LITERACY

When you think of the word "romance," what kind of scene comes to your mind? Do patterns of media messages "cultivate"—that is, reinforce and extend—your mental picture of romance? If so, which ones and why?

Gerbner maintains that although this phenomenon affects the individual, it also has larger social implications. The message of fear helps those who are in power because it makes heavy viewers (a substantial portion of the population) more likely to agree to support police and military forces that protect them from that scary world. Not incidentally, those police and military forces also protect those in power and help them maintain control over unruly or rebellious groups in society.

Gerbner's cultivation research and the critical approaches of political economists and the Frankfurt School helped to add another dimension to the way U.S. scholars looked at the mass media. In the past couple of decades, a third broad avenue of inquiry has added to the mix of ideas about media power and consequences. This avenue is widely known as cultural studies.

# Cultural Studies

L et's say that you accept the importance of emphasizing the connection between mass media and social power, but you're a bit uncomfortable with what you feel is the too-simplistic perspective of the political economy and cultivation theorists. "Media power isn't as controlling as they would have it," you say. "I don't believe that everybody in society necessarily buys into the images of power that these systems project. People have minds of their own, and they often live in communities that help them resist the aims of the powerful."

If that's your perspective, you would probably find one of the many approaches within cultural studies to be up your alley. The approach taken by cultural studies was developed in Europe and had been used there for many years before it attracted a large following in the United States during the 1980s. Writings in this area often tie media studies to concepts in literature, linguistics, anthropology, and history. **Cultural studies** scholars often start with the idea that all sorts of mass media, from newspapers to movies, present their audiences with technologies and texts and that audiences find meaning in them. Major questions for these scholars center on how to think about what "making meaning" of technologies and texts means and what consequences it has for those audiences in society. As you might imagine, there are many ways to answer these questions.

## Historical Approaches to Cultural Studies

One way to answer cultural studies questions is from a historical perspective. Professor Lynn Spigel, for example, explores the expectations that men and women have had for audiovisual technologies in the home and how those expectations have tied into larger social issues. She points out, for example, a historical relationship between home TV use and social fear:

> Communications technologies have promised to bring the outside world into the home since the late 19th century. At the time of industrialization, when urban centers were linked to the first suburban towns, there were endless speculations about the joys and potential pitfalls of a new design for middle-class living which would allow people to be joined together in an electrical public space without ever going outside. Middle-class families could, in this way, enjoy social encounters while avoiding the elements of urban space—such as labor unrest or ethnic immigration—which made them feel most threatened.

## Anthropological Approaches to Cultural Studies

Another way to look at what technologies mean in the context of social class and social power is to take an anthropologist's approach and closely examine the way people use media. Cultural studies researchers tie people's uses of the media to their class, racial, or gender positions within society. Here, for example, is Professor Ellen Seiter writing in 1997 on differences between men and women in the use of television and computers in the home. Consider whether you think the particulars she emphasizes apply today.

> Television sets and computers introduce highly similar issues in terms of placement in domestic space, conflicts among family members over usage and control, value in the household budget, and we can expect these to be articulated

**cultural studies**
studies that start with the idea that all sorts of mass media, from newspapers to movies, present their audiences with technologies and texts and that audiences find meaning in them; scholars then ask questions that center on how to think about what "making meaning" of technologies and texts means and what consequences it has for those audiences in society

with gender roles in the family. Some research on gendered conflicts over computers (Giacquinta; Murdock; Haddon) reproduces themes of family-based studies about control of the television set. Already researchers have noted a strong tendency for men and boys to have more access to computers in the home. Television studies such as Ann Gray's, David Morley's and my own work suggest that women in nuclear families have difficulty watching a favorite television show (because of competition for control of the set from other family members, and because of shouldering the majority of childcare, housework and cooking). If male family members gravitate towards the computer as hobbyists, the load of chores relegated to female family members will only increase, and make it more difficult for female members to get time on the home computer. Computers require hours of trial and error experimentation, a kind of extended play demanding excess leisure time. Fully exploring the internet needs time for lengthy downloading, and patience with connections that are busy, so much so that some have dubbed the World Wide Web the World Wide Wait.

## Linguistic and Literary Approaches to Cultural Studies

You probably found the paragraphs by Ellen Seiter and Lynn Spigel quite straightforward and easy to understand. The same can't typically be said for the areas of cultural studies that apply linguistic and literary models to the meaning of media texts. They tend to use the complex phraseology of linguistics and the jargon of literary analysts to make their points. That is unfortunate because some of the scholars involved in this area often proclaim that their goal is to encourage viewers and readers to "resist" the dominant models of society that are suggested in the text.

Moreover, these discussions are actually quite interesting and important, once you cut through the language. A major topic of discussion is just where the meaning of a text lies. Is it preset in the written or audiovisual material (e.g., the book or the TV show), is it in the way a person using the material understands it, or is it in some relationship between the two? That may sound like an odd question, but it is significant because it speaks to the power of the media to guide people's understanding of the world.

**polysemous**
open to multiple meanings

At one extreme are scholars who believe that a text is open to multiple meanings (they say that it is **polysemous**) because people have the ability to subject media content to endless interpretations based on their critical understanding of the world. So, for example, Professors Elihu Katz and Tamar Liebes interviewed people in Israel and Japan to find out how they understood the popular 1980s U.S. TV series *Dallas*. They found that Japanese viewers, Israeli viewers originally from Morocco, and Israeli viewers originally from Russia had quite different interpretations of the program and its relevance to their lives. According to such findings about multiple interpretations, people in this camp have a clear idea of where they should apply their public interest energies. They would say, for example, that trying to limit the power of media conglomerates is not nearly as important as teaching people how to interpret media critically, in ways that resist any support of the dominant system.

## THINKING ABOUT MEDIA LITERACY

Think of your favorite television show. When telling a new friend who hasn't seen it about the show, what do you tell her and why? What do you think someone who dislikes the show would tell her? How about someone who could take or leave the show?

Against this notion of a program or book being open to multiple meanings is the opposite idea that the meaning is in the text itself. Scholars with this view argue that the shared culture of a society leads individuals to share the basic meaning of the text. To them, firms that create agendas in news and entertainment have enormous power that cannot be overcome simply by teaching criticism. Active work to limit the power of these conglomerates is also necessary.

Philosophically, most scholars take a position between these two extremes. They accept the notion of polysemy, but they argue that most people's interpretations of media texts are very much shaped by the actual texts themselves and by the industrial and social environments in which these texts are created. They stress that texts are likely to "constrain" meaning in directions that benefit the powerful. That is, because of the way the text is created, viewers or readers notice the "preferred" meaning, the meaning that members of the establishment would likely find most compatible with their own thinking. Certainly, audience members can disagree with this take on the world. Even if they do, however, they may get the strong idea that most other people would not disagree with the text's approaches to racial, gender, ethnic, and religious stereotypes; tales of who is strong and who is weak; or portrayals of what the universe is like, how we (as Americans and humans) fit in, and how we should act toward it. Such scholars might be likely to enthusiastically support media criticism as well as public actions to limit the power of huge media conglomerates.

## Using Media Research to Develop Media Literacy Skills

We now return to the story of Jessica. She has heard the grad students discuss everything that you've read in this chapter's pages, as they present ways of looking at the issues about local news that she has brought to them. Each student gives her a thumbnail summary of the history and nature of different aspects of mass communication research. Jessica's head is spinning from the variety of ways to look at the same media material and the hundreds of questions it is possible to ask.

You may feel the same way she does. But if you think about it a bit more, you'll see that understanding the history of mass media research provides tools with which to figure out three key ideas that a media-literate person must know. One is where you stand with respect to the effects of media on society. A second is how to make sense of the discussions and arguments about media effects. A third is how to get involved in research that can be used to explore concerns you might have about mass media.

### Where Do You Stand with Respect to Media Effects?

While reading this chapter, it's likely that you found yourself agreeing with some of the media approaches and disagreeing with others. Maybe you dismissed political economy as a lot of baloney, but you felt that uses and gratifications research and some aspects of cultural studies really make sense. That's fine; part of becoming media-literate involves taking an informed stand on why the media are important. Learning about the ways in which people have grappled with concerns about the mass media over the decades can help you sort out your concerns. You personally may be more convinced that the individual interpretations and uses of the media are what make a difference for people. You may not be convinced by those who emphasize social issues, such as political economists, cultivation researchers, and even people involved in studying agenda-setting.

It's really important, though, that you do not close your mind to the possibilities. New ideas keep coming up; your ideas about life keep changing as well. You can keep up with what media researchers are saying by reading press articles about them or maybe even by going to journals such as the *Journal of Communication*, *Critical Studies in Media Communication*, *Journalism and Mass Communication Quarterly*, or the *Journal of Broadcasting & Electronic Media*. What you have learned here and what you learn in the future may well affect how you relate to the media yourself, how you introduce your children to different media, and what you tell parents who ask your opinion on how to think about the media's consequences for their children.

## How to Make Sense of Discussions and Arguments about Media Effects

When you do read about research in the popular press or in academic journals, think back to this chapter to help you place the work in perspective and critique it. Here are some questions you should ask yourself:

**Are the questions the researcher is asking interesting and important?** Think of the issues you have learned about in this chapter. How important are the ones dealt with in the study you are considering? Do you wish the researchers had devoted their energies to other topics that you consider more relevant to your life or the life of the country?

**Into what research tradition does the study fall?** Is it a study of priming, an example of cultivation research, a study of message persuasion, or a representation of another one of the streams of work that we have discussed (see Table 2.1)?

**How good is the research design?** Whereas journal articles lay out the method used in research quite carefully, press reports of research often don't give you a lot of information about how the work was carried out. Even in the popular press, however, you can often find some of the specific questions the investigators used and some details about the method. When you think about the research design, be skeptical. Think about the type and size of the sample. If the study was an experiment, how realistic was it?

**How convincing is the analysis?** If the researcher is claiming that the media caused something to happen, are there any other explanations for the findings? Does it appear that the researcher thought about reliability? How valid does the study seem in terms of the real world? These and other questions should roll around in your head as you decide whether accept the conclusions of the researchers or others who are quoted.

**What do you wish the researchers would do next in their research?** Asking this question, involving whether or not you like the research, will encourage you to think more deeply than you otherwise might about the role of media in society. Talking with your friends about especially interesting or problematic research is another way to play out some of the meanings that the research holds for you and for others in society.

## How to Explore Your Concerns about Mass Media

What are the implications of the research for your personal life as well as for public policy? For example, a well-done study of attitudes toward the web and uses of the

**Table 2.1** Comparing Media Research Theories

| Theory/research study | Approach | Participating researchers | Aim | Example |
|---|---|---|---|---|
| Chicago School | Early philosophy and sociology of media | Dewey, Cooley, Park | Searching for community | The immigrant press |
| Propaganda analysts | Early concerns about media persuasion | Lasswell, McLung, Casey | The activities of media producers and the resulting content | Content analyses of newspapers |
| Payne Fund researchers | Early research on children and movies | Charters | Explorations of media effects via multiple methods | How violent movies affect children's sleep patterns |
| Columbia School | The media and social relations | Lazarsfeld, Katz, Merton | Research on how interpersonal relations intervene in media effects | The "two-step flow" influence of radio and newspapers during a presidential election campaign |
| American Soldier propaganda research | The limits of propaganda | Hovland | Movies, learning, and persuasion | An evaluation of the effects of *The Battle of Britain* |
| Yale Program of Research on Communication and Attitude Change | The limits of propaganda | Hovland | Research on the conditions that encourage audience persuasion | Experiments to determine whether and when fear appeals were more persuasive than appeals not using fear |
| Various | Mainstream effects research | | Studying behavior and opinion change | |
| Various | Mainstream effects research | | Research on whether television can encourage learning skills in children | Research on what youngsters learn from *Sesame Street* |
| Various | Mainstream effects research | McCombs and Shaw; Tichenor, Donahue, and Olien | Research on which individuals learn about national and world affairs from mass media | Research on agenda-setting; research on the knowledge gap |
| Various | Mainstream effects research | | Why, when, and how people use the media | Investigations of the active audience; research on the digital divide |
| Frankfurt School | Critical approaches to mass media | Adorno, Marcuse, Horkheimer | The relationship between capitalism and culture | Critical theory about the culture industry |
| Various | Critical approaches to mass media | Bagdikian, Schiller | Political economy research | Research on media monopolies |
| Annenberg School | Critical approaches to mass media | Gerbner | Cultivation studies | Research on TV violence and perceptions of a mean world |
| Various | Cultural studies | Spigel | Historical approaches | Historical relationship between home TV use and social fear |
| Various | Cultural studies | Seiter, Murdock, Haddon | Anthropological approaches | Differences between men and women in use of TV and computers |
| Various | Cultural studies | Katz and Leibes | Literary and linguistic approaches | Research on polysemous meanings |

web by people over the age of 75 might have great meaning to you if you work in a senior center and want to get seniors engaged with the internet. The study might inform members of Congress who are thinking of providing funding to connect senior centers to the Web. The study might also be relevant if you have a parent or grandparent over that age, and you have wondered whether and how to introduce e-mail and other web-related technologies to her or him.

A desire to learn the implications of research for her personal life and public policy, you'll remember, is what brought communication major and student journalist Jessica to Professor Berg's graduate seminar. She now understands that all the research perspectives that the students have presented, from mainstream effects and uses and gratifications research to cultivation research to political economy and cultural studies, can be relevant to understanding the *Real Housewives* series.

"There are so many possible important approaches to this issue that I almost feel paralyzed just worrying about which to choose," she says to the assembled group. "Where should I begin? How should I begin?"

As they continue discussing her concerns, though, Jessica realizes that she must choose the approach to mass media that best fits the concerns she personally has about the media and the specific questions that she is asking. She goes home convinced that what she has had all along is a critical studies take on the issue.

Jessica suggests to her friend, who is a sociology major with an interest in women's issues, that they get a group together to conduct a systematic content analysis of the programs with the help of one of the professors. Their goal is to find out the extent to which and ways in which women and ethnic groups—especially Italians and African Americans—come across negatively and positively in the shows. Part of the challenge for the researchers, of course, will be to figure out exactly what they mean by *negative* and *positive*. After the content research is completed, the group will interview graduate students to prepare a review of agenda-setting and cultivation literature, to make the point that the Bravo programs' systematic presentations can have a real impact on the way viewers think about marriage, relationships, and especially ethnic marriages and relationships. When all that is done—Jessica estimates it will take five months—she and her group will examine their findings. If their expectations about negative depictions are confirmed, they will present their material to the local cable systems and to Bravo, as well as to newspaper reporters and academics. Their hope is that the work will encourage people and even some advertisers to place pressure on the program creators to rethink their depictions and show housewives and their relationships in more balanced ways. "Maybe I'm quixotic," Jessica tells her group, "but I really do think it can be done."

Jessica's story is not an unusual one. Every day, all sorts of mass communication research, from all sorts of perspectives, is brought to bear on a multitude of public issues. Local, state, and federal governments draw on the results of mass communication research, and they often commission it. Of course, scholars don't always carry out research with specific public policy questions in mind. Nor, it should be emphasized, do they "cook" their results to conform to their particular political points of view. Nevertheless, as we have seen in this chapter, over the past century academics have asked questions not from the irrelevance of an ivory tower but as human beings concerned with the best ways to think about some of the most important topics of their day. As you read the rest of this book, consider that you can explore the topics and issues systematically from one or more of the perspectives sketched previously in this chapter. You might find carrying out such an inquiry fascinating and rewarding.

# CHAPTER REVIEW

 Visit the Companion Website at www.routledge.com/cw/turow for additional study tools and resources.

## Key Terms

You can find the definitions to these key terms in the marginal glossary throughout this chapter. Test your knowledge of these terms with interactive flash cards on the *Media Today* companion website.

active audience

agenda setting

capitalism

colonialism

co-optation

critical theory

cultivation studies

cultural colonialism

cultural studies

digital divide

knowledge gap

magic bullet or hypodermic needle
    approach

mainstream approaches

mass media research

naturalistic experiment

panel survey

political economy

polysemous

priming

propaganda

propaganda analysis

social relations

two-step flow
    model

uses and gratifications
    research

## Questions for Discussion and Critical Thinking

1. Why do you think early media researchers were so concerned with the effects of propaganda? Do you think today's audiences are less susceptible to propaganda's influence because media are more prevalent now? Why or why not?

2. Media representations of violence get more and more violent as the decades go on. As these violent depictions increase and grow more intense, do you think that we still should be as concerned about their effects on adult populations as observers were in the 1930s? Why or why not?

3. Think of a question you might have about the media that could be studied through one of the approaches discussed in this chapter. What question would you want to explore? What approach would you use to explore it and why? What might you hope to find?

4. In addition to media scholars, what other groups do you think might find these methods useful and why? What would they use these methods for?

# Case Study
## EVALUATING A SCHOLARLY ARTICLE

It takes some training to evaluate a scholarly article. The main thing to remember is that just because a study has been published in an academic journal doesn't mean that it is perfect. Sometimes published articles have many flaws as well as good points. Hone your scholarly reading skills in the following manner:

Read an article about an empirical study that is published in a scholarly journal such as the *Journal of Communication*, *Journal of Broadcasting and Electronic Media*, *Critical Studies in Media Communication*, or *Journalism and Mass Communication Quarterly*.

Write a summary of the main points of the article in a page or less, focusing on the major questions, the theory the authors are working with to help understand or address those questions, the method used to carry out the study, the major findings, and the authors' conclusions about what the study means.

Then evaluate what you like and don't like about the study from the standpoint of the features discussed in this chapter: the nature of the sample, the size of the sample and the way it's collected, the design of the study, the reliability of the study, the soundness of the analysis, and the validity of the study.

In general, do you think the topics or questions that the author addressed are important? Why or why not? How convinced are you that the way the authors addressed those topics sheds an important light on the topics or questions?

The point here is to alert you to what it means to be a literate consumer of mass media research. If you understand the basics of evaluating research, and you get an overview of the kinds of concerns media researchers have had over the decades, you will be able to ask the right questions and critically evaluate the answers to those questions.

# The Business of Media

3

"If anyone said we were the radio business, it wouldn't be someone from our company. We're not in the business of providing news and information. We're not in the business of providing well-researched music. We're simply in the business of selling our customers' products."

**LOWRY MAYS, CLEAR CHANNEL CEO**

## CHAPTER OBJECTIVES

1   Recognize how mass media personnel consider the audience an integral part of business concerns

2   Describe the primary genres of the materials created by various mass media industries

3   Identify and discuss the process of producing, distributing, and exhibiting materials in mass media industries

4   Explain the way media firms finance the production, distribution, and exhibition of media materials

5   Harness your media literacy skills to evaluate what media forms mean to you as a media consumer

Understanding the changing media system and the issues surrounding it can help us to be responsible citizens—parents, voters, workers—in our media-driven society. If you know how news is created, you might be able to read a paper or watch a TV news magazine with a much keener sense of what's going on. If you know how TV entertainment shows get on the air and how and why the firms that produce them are changing, you may be able to come up with strategies for influencing those changes that will benefit social groups that you care about. If you are aware of the strategies of media conglomerates and their relation to convergence, you may have a better understanding of why certain companies want to move into

certain businesses. You also may be able to decide whether the government officials you voted for are doing the right thing by allowing or not allowing them to do that.

The difficulty with getting up to speed on these topics is that understanding a mass media industry can be a bewildering experience. Let's say that community leaders in the neighborhood where you live have begun to complain about billboard advertising because of the overwhelming number of signs featuring sexual images or advertising beer. In order to help a community group petition billboard company executives to change their companies' ad policies, you decide you must learn about the billboard business. You quickly find that billboards are part of a large and growing "outdoor advertising" industry. More-over, you learn that mass media conglomerates own some of the biggest companies in the industry. These conglomerates also run several radio stations and other media outlets in your city.

You are faced with a number of crucial questions here. First, how do you get enough of a grasp on the outdoor advertising industry to learn about the factors that affect its policies for accepting ads and how those policies can be changed? Second, is the local radio business tied to some of the goals of the outdoor firms, and if so, does that make it harder or easier to influence ad policies? Third, in terms of your interest in changing outdoor advertising policies, is it relevant that the mass media conglomerates own both the outdoor firms and the radio stations? If so, how?

You want to learn as much as possible about the outdoor advertising industry to understand how its policies on beer and sex can be changed. But should you also learn about the radio industry and the conglomerates? If so, what should you learn? And where do you start? Must you conduct research on each industry separately, as if the activities in one industry cannot help you understand the activities in another? If that's the case, you may find yourself thinking that it's not worth the time and effort.

This chapter aims to assure you that becoming knowledgeable about the business of mass media is not as intimidating as it may sound. By learning a small number of general points about the mass media business, you will understand particular conglomerates and mass media industries much better than if you started from scratch every time.

## Identifying an Audience for Mass Media Content

In its 2011 Communications Industry Forecast, consulting firm Veronis Suhler Stevenson (VSS) estimated that 2010 spending on media in the United States by companies and individuals was a bit over one trillion dollars. That number will give you one sense of the large overall size of the media business. As we move through this book, we will see that the revenues of individual media industries come to tens of billions of dollars and sometimes far more. Table 3.1 gives you another sense of the media economy by presenting the revenues of the five biggest media firms. As the table notes, these five companies alone brought in almost $119 billion in 2010.

No media business can exist (or continue to take in revenues) without content that attracts consumers, or **audiences**—the people to whom mass media firms are directing their products. **Media practitioners**—the people who select or create the material that a mass media firm produces, distributes, or exhibits—are keenly aware that their content must be attractive to audiences if money is to flow their way instead of to their competitors. In fact, audiences pose enormous risks as well as great opportunities for success for

**audiences**
the people to whom a media product is directed

**media practitioners**
the people who select or create the material that a mass media firm produces, distributes, or exhibits

**Table 3.1** The Top Five Largest Media Companies by U.S. Revenue, 2010

| Rank | Media company | Headquarters | U.S. revenue ($ billions) |
|------|---------------|--------------|---------------------------|
| 1 | Comcast Corp | Philadelphia, PA | 44.5 |
| 2 | DirecTV | El Segundo, CA | 20.7 |
| 3 | Walt Disney Co. | Burbank, CA | 18.6 |
| 4 | Time Warner | New York, NY | 18.2 |
| 5 | Time Warner Cable | New York, NY | 16.8 |

Source: *Advertising Age*, http://adage.com/datacenter/datapopup.php?article_id=230087, accessed May 2, 2012. For this table, *Advertising Age* defines "media" as "information and entertainment content distribution systems in which advertising (including branded entertainment) is a key element." Customer revenues are also included, however.

media practitioners. To best manage these risks and increase their chances of success, practitioners must carefully consider the following questions:

1. How should we think about our audience? How should we define our audience?
2. Will the material we are thinking of creating, distributing, or exhibiting to attract that audience generate adequate revenues?
3. Were the people we thought would be attracted to our products in fact attracted to our products? Why or why not?

## Defining and Constructing a Target Audience

Executives who are charting the direction of media firms do not think about the members of their audience in the same way that they think about themselves. Take, for example, Kaya. She thinks of herself in a number of ways—as a hard worker who juggles her communication studies major with her 20-hour-a-week job at a local restaurant; as a daughter who visits her parents twice a week; as a moderate churchgoer (about two Sundays a month); as a girlfriend who makes time for her boyfriend, Omar; and as a loyal friend who tries to keep up with high school classmates by phone and e-mail.

Now consider how executives at a magazine that Kaya gets—call it *Style & Beauty* (*S&B*)—think of her. Of course, they are not really thinking specifically about Kaya at all. Instead, *S&B* executives focus on the characteristics that they can use to show potential advertisers the types of people they can reach through their magazine. *S&B* got some of its data from a questionnaire that Kaya filled out after she received a student discount to the periodical. Other data came from lists that the magazine bought from companies that bring together information about millions of people and sell it to media firms.

To *S&B*, Kaya is (among other things) in the 18–34 age group, a female, a student, a small-car owner, unmarried, childless, an apartment renter, an earner of $30,000 a year, the possessor of two credit cards, an avid moviegoer, not a big TV watcher, and someone who has taken at least three airplane trips in the past two years. The major reason that *S&B* collects this information it does have about Kaya is that these are some of the characteristics that major advertisers consider when they think about buying space in magazines. A car manufacturer who is thinking of advertising in the magazine doesn't care how many times a month Kaya goes to church or whether she visits her parents (though other advertisers may well consider that information useful as a predictor of buying patterns). The car manufacturer does care about her age, her gender, her income, and the kind of car she presently owns because it believes this information predicts the likelihood that she will buy its brand. Kaya's age and student status make her attractive to advertisers such as car manufacturers, even though she doesn't make a lot of money; they believe these factors indicate that she will make a lot more some day.

Because *S&B* magazine gets at least half of its revenue from advertising, its executives want to keep subscribers who are attractive to advertisers. They therefore use the information they have about Kaya and subscribers like her—and about other groups of subscribers that they have identified as being attractive to advertisers—to help them decide what kinds of materials in the magazine will keep these people as subscribers. These identified and selected population segments, then, become the desired audience for *S&B*. Once the magazine's executives have identified the target segments, they try to learn things about those segments that will lead to an increase in sales of space to advertisers. That, in turn, leads to more research to understand the groups. Figure 3.1 illustrates this process by focusing on

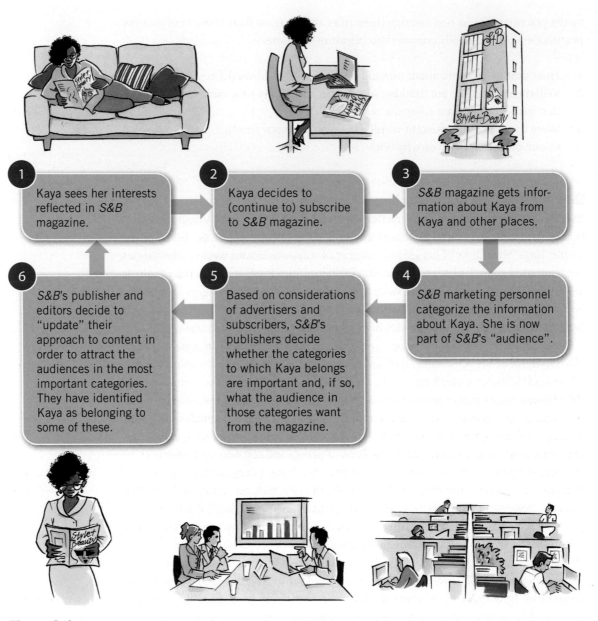

**Figure 3.1**
Kaya and the constructed audience

Kaya. The example assumes that *S&B* marketers are attracted by what they know about Kaya and want her to be part of their audience. If they didn't find Kaya and people with similar characteristics attractive as consumers, they would produce content that speaks to different interests and that might drive Kaya away, rather than encourage her to renew her subscription.

Thinking about the audience, then, means learning to think of people primarily as consumers of media materials and other products. For media professionals, thinking about people in this way requires a combination of intuition and solid knowledge of the marketplace. As the example of Kaya and *S&B* magazine suggests, when advertisers contribute all or part of a firm's revenue stream, the firm's executives have three challenges: First, they have to create content that will attract audiences. Second, recognizing the importance of convergence, they have to place the content, or content like it, on a variety of media—the printed magazine, the magazine's website, *S&B* apps for tablets and smartphones, and even brochures for fashion shows that *S&B* puts on in malls. Third, the *S&B* executives also must make sure that the content and the audience it brings in will be attractive to advertisers on one or several of these media so that money flows to *S&B* instead of to its competitors. To do this, they need to decide whether enough advertisers want to reach that audience in order to provide **adequate revenue**—enough cash to allow the enterprise to pay for itself and give the owners or bankers who put up the money the desired return on their investment.

Sometimes, in fact, media executives reverse the order of the questions. They first ask which audiences advertisers want to reach and then look for ways to attract those audiences. In recent decades, companies have been quite targeted in their audience aims: they try to appeal to particular segments of society rather than to the population as a whole. Often executives have to ask what segments should be the targets— women or men; the rich, the middle class, or the poor; Asians, Latinos, whites, or blacks; people who live in the eastern United States or those who live in the Midwest; or some combination of these and other categories?

Executives try to verify their intuitions and control their risks with research. In conducting this research, they think about the types of people who make up their audience—that is, they construct their audience—in three broad ways: through demographics, psychographics, and lifestyle categories.

**Demographics** **Demographics**—one of the simplest and most common ways to construct an audience—refers to characteristics by which people are divided into particular social categories. Media executives focus on those characteristics, or factors, that they believe are most relevant to understanding how and why people use their medium. **Demographic indicators** include such factors as age, gender, income, occupation, ethnicity, and race. Our fictional *S&B* magazine focuses on the first three when it tells potential advertisers that its readership is 90 percent female and 47 percent between 18 and 34 years old and that 37 percent make $100,000 or more per year. The management's hope is that these attractive "demos" will attract lots of upscale advertisers.

**Psychographics** Media organizations also differentiate groups by **psychographics**, or by categorizing people on the basis of their attitudes, personality types, or motivations. Let's imagine that the management of *S&B* magazine wants advertisers to understand its readership beyond the demographics of female, high-income, and at a point in their lives i.e., age) when they are likely to acquire new things. The magazine executives hire a research firm to interview a large number of subscribers and create psychological profiles of them. The researchers find that the readers can be divided into three psychographic types: comparers (25 percent of subscribers), who like to read the magazine to see how their clothes stack up against the apparel on the pages; idea hunters (60 percent of subscribers), who read it to help them with their own sense of clothes and cosmetics; and luxury lovers (15 percent), who subscribe because they like to look at the expensive clothes and accessories that appear in the magazine's articles and ads each month. The researchers also find that the three psychographic categories differ in terms of the length of time people remain subscribers. Those readers who are classified as idea hunters stay the longest time (an average of five years), and those classified as luxury lovers stay the shortest time (two years), with the comparers in the middle (three years). The magazine execu-

**adequate revenue**
enough cash to allow the enterprise to pay for itself and give the owners or bankers who put up the money the desired return on their investment

**demographics**
characteristics by which people are divided into particular social categories

**demographic indicators**
factors such as age, gender, occupation, ethnicity, race, and income

**psychographics**
a way to differentiate among people or groups by categorizing them according to their attitudes, personality types, or motivations

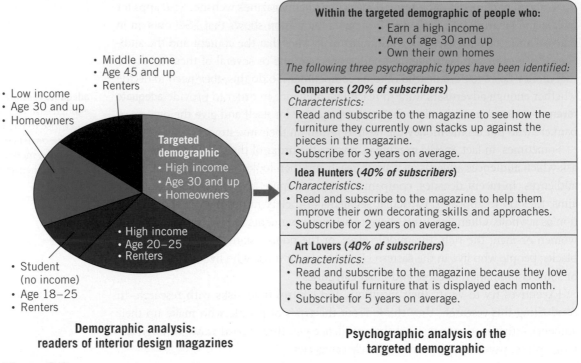

**Demographic analysis:
readers of interior design magazines**

**Psychographic analysis of the
targeted demographic**

**Figure 3.2**
Psychographic indicators can help media executives further shape their product to attract the audience members their advertisers seek.

tives can use this construction of the audience to shape their articles to appeal to the idea hunters and comparers and to find advertisers that are interested in any of the groups (see Figure 3.2).

**lifestyle categories**
activities in which potential audiences are involved that mark them as different from others in the population at large

**Lifestyle Categories**  We can also describe media audiences using **lifestyle categories**—that is, by finding activities in which potential audiences are involved that mark them as different from others in the audience or in the population at large. Suppose, for example, that *S&B* magazine conducts another research study that finds that its readers go to restaurants, own expensive cars, and travel outside the United States far more than the average for the U.S. population. In this way, the magazine's employees are categorizing readers from a lifestyle point of view.

Keep in mind that what media professionals learn about their audiences through research is relevant only if it relates to making money by attracting advertisers or by keeping them as audience members. The lifestyle characteristics that our fictional magazine found are terrific—just the sort that will attract major automobile, airline, hotel, and restaurant advertisers. The demographics and psychographics are also useful for getting sponsors as well as for thinking about the kind of content that will keep particular groups as part of the audience.

## THINKING ABOUT MEDIA LITERACY

In what lifestyle category or categories do you think you fit? How might a magazine target its content toward one of those categories? Overall, why would advertisers find that category appealing?

often steeped in the formulas' history. Writers and producers in all mass media often "borrow" plot elements, characters, and settings from previously successful stories. Their hope is that the basic elements of the formula will stay popular and that they can reshape these elements to fit what they believe are the interests of contemporary audiences.

Examples are all around us, but you have to know something about the history of a mass medium to notice them. Perhaps you've seen the remakes of classic horror movies that have appeared in movie theaters over the past few years—for example, *Friday the 13th* (2009), *The Echo* (a 2009 remake of the Philippine film *Sigaw*), *The Wolfman* (2009), and Halloween (2007). If you go back to the originals, you will see how the contemporary writers borrowed settings, characters, and

In crime dramas such as *Bones,* there is a fairly set pattern of action involving the finding of human remains and an investigation into the cause of death and identity of the victim, and the show is typically resolved with the identification and capture of the person responsible for causing the victim's death.

plot elements from the originals and then changed them to fit their idea of what audiences of the 2000s would like. Watching TV, going to the movies, reading novels, and even playing video games will take on a whole new dimension once you are aware of this borrowing.

Apart from updating genres, writers and producers are also eager to find new ways to mix entertainment subgenres to entertain their target audiences. The term **"hybrid genres"** can be used to describe mixed genres; the process of mixing genres within a culture and across cultures is called **hybridity**. Hybrid genres are all around us. Consider, for example, the music of Taylor Swift, which consciously blurs the boundary between country and teen pop music. Hybridity can also take place across cultures. Think of attempts by U.S. producers and writers to mix plots, settings, and characters of Indian Bollywood films with traditional Hollywood plots, characters, and settings. For example, *Bride and Prejudice* is a 2004 movie that inserts an Indian family into the basic plot of the Jane Austen novel *Pride and Prejudice* and follows them through Indian, U.K., and U.S. locales. The advertising tagline for the movie, which was filmed in India, the United Kingdom, and the United States, trumpeted this hybridity: "Bollywood meets Hollywood ... and it's the perfect match."

**hybrid genres**
a term used by some academic writers to describe mixed genres

**hybridity**
the process of mixing genres within a culture and across cultures

Beyond combining specific entertainment subgenres, some producers and writers try to get people's attention by blending the rules associated with drama (serious) and comedy (funny) into what some media practitioners call a **dramedy**. Dramedies have shown up fairly frequently on U.S. television in recent years. Think of *Desperate Housewives, Psych, Monk, Ugly Betty,* and *Californication*. These programs don't have laugh tracks, and they can veer from a hilariously funny scene to one that tugs strongly at viewers' heartstrings. *New York Daily News* TV critic David Hinckley zeroed in on that quality in *Monk* when commenting on the series' final episode. The closing drama brings Adrian Monk (Tony Shalhoub) back to the show's original launching point: the unsolved murder of his wife, Trudy. As Hinckley noted,

**dramedy**
a subgenre that blends the rules associated with drama (serious) and comedy (funny)

Trudy's death gave the show a bed of tragedy and Monk a terrible sadness that passing seasons did not diminish. It also left him with a nightmare of phobias, quirks and general obsessive compulsion. He was afraid of germs, of closed areas, of pretty much anything involving people. But the show's genius, and Shalhoub's, was that all this somehow honed his skills. He solved case after case even as he couldn't crack the one he most cared about.

The finale carried these features to a conclusion that combined formula-driven TV with a wonderful understanding of the program's characters. Hinckley wrote that "it's so well-written and so true to the wonderfully tragicomic tone of the whole show that you won't even mind the fact that the actual plot wrapup is pretty formulaic."

## THINKING ABOUT MEDIA LITERACY

Can you think of any of your own examples of hybrids? On what other genres does the hybrid draw? Do you think the combination is successful? Why or why not?

### News

News, like entertainment, involves the telling of stories. We often don't think of news in this way, but it is useful to pause and consider this point. When you watch *NBC Nightly News*, in one sense news anchor Brian Williams is telling you a tale with a beginning, a middle, and an end. Of course, Williams reads most of the story and shows short video clips of the accompanying action, whereas other storytelling media genres (such as the sitcom) continuously illustrate the story through acting. The tales that Brian Williams tells during his newscast, however, may not be that different from the sitcom you will be viewing just two hours later on the same network. In fact, many of the ideas for non-news television programming are generated from news. NBC's *Law & Order*, in fact, used to boast that its plots were "ripped from the headlines." The program's ads stopped saying that because of the producers' fear they might be sued for libel by the people whose news stories they adapted. Nevertheless, even casual viewers of *Law & Order* or other drama programs would notice that the program drew on news stories.

**journalists**
individuals who are trained to report nonfiction events to an audience

Reporters, directors, editors, producers, and other people who work in the news business are called **journalists**. A journalist is someone who is trained to report nonfiction events to an audience. Journalists' reporting can be in print (newspapers, magazines) or electronic media (radio, TV, the web). Historically, newspapers have been central to the circulation of news in America. But as we'll see in later chapters, big changes taking place are eroding the presence and power of newspapers in people's lives. Today's journalists are learning that they must present news in many media, including audio and video reports on the web. Convergence has become a fact even in the news divisions of the major TV networks. You can find Brian Williams reading the news on your tablet, laptop, and smartphone in addition to on your TV set.

**Subgenres of News** How would these people explain the difference between what they produce and other storytelling genres, such as entertainment? They would undoubtedly argue that there is one clear distinction: news stories are constrained by facts, whereas entertainment stories are not. The writer of the screenplay for a TV show that is "based on a true story" or "ripped from the headlines" can decide whether a character who is accused of rape is guilty or innocent. The reporter of the real-life news event, however, should never make such a judgment. Building on this basic distinction, news workers divide news broadly into four subgenres:

- Hard news
- Investigative reports
- Editorials
- Soft news

## HARD NEWS

**Hard news** is what most people probably think of as news. It is the firsthand reportage of a battle, the coverage of a congressional bill's passage, or the details of a forest fire. News workers use four guidelines when deciding what is and what isn't hard news. An event that fits only one of these guidelines will probably not be considered hard news. Additionally, the more of these guidelines that apply to an event, the more likely news workers are to cover it.

- *Timeliness*. A hard news event must have happened recently—typically within the past day or so. A murder that happened yesterday might deserve coverage. A murder that happened last year would not, unless new information about it has been released or discovered.
- *Unusualness*. Hard news events are those that most people would consider unusual. To use the classic example, "Dog Bites Man" is not news, whereas "Man Bites Dog" is.
- *Conflict*. Struggles between opposing forces—conflicts—often lie at the center of hard news stories. Often these struggles are physical; they can be wars or barroom brawls. Sometimes the conflicts involve wars of words, as between members of Congress. Other times they pit humans against nature (a fire or other natural disaster).
- *The closeness of the incident*. An event is more likely to be seen as hard news if it happens close by than if it takes place far away. Note, however, that closeness carries two meanings: it can mean geographically close (physically near to the audience), or it can mean psychologically close. An incident is psychologically close when members of the audience feel a connection to it even though it takes place far away. Because of Boston's large Irish population, for example, newspaper editors in Boston may consider certain happenings in Ireland to be hard news, whereas editors in areas of the United States with small Irish populations would not cover those events.

Once they have decided that something is hard news, news workers must decide how to present it. Journalists use the word "**objectivity**" to summarize the way in which news ought to be researched, organized, and presented. Most journalists would agree that it is impossible to present a totally objective view of an event, if that means a view that is the absolute truth with no personal viewpoints inserted. The fact is that no two people will see the same thing in exactly the same way. Most journalists would say that what they mean by an objective report is a report that presents a fair, balanced, and impartial representation of the events that took place.

Over the decades, journalists have agreed on certain characteristics that an objective story will have. These characteristics give a reporter the tools to describe an incident efficiently in ways that his or her editor (or any other editor) will consider fair and impartial. Here are four major characteristics of an objective story, particularly with regard to print news:

- It should be written in a form that journalists call an inverted pyramid (see Figure 3.4). This means that the reporter should place in the first paragraph (the lead paragraph) a concise recounting of the entire story. In the paragraphs that follow, the reporter should give increasingly specific information about the material in the lead paragraph. An objective story should be told in the third person:

**Figure 3.4**
The inverted pyramid approach to reporting the news begins with the most general statement of the story and grows increasingly more specific.

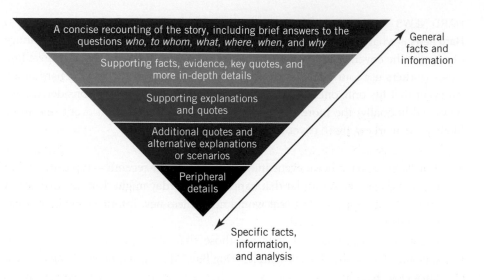

A concise recounting of the story, including brief answers to the questions *who, to whom, what, where, when,* and *why*

Supporting facts, evidence, key quotes, and more in-depth details

Supporting explanations and quotes

Additional quotes and alternative explanations or scenarios

Peripheral details

General facts and information

Specific facts, information, and analysis

that means writing as if the journalist is a novelist telling the tale but is not involved in it (i.e., the person doesn't use personal pronouns such as "I" or "me"). An objective story should report at least two sides of a conflict. If a politician is accused of corruption, the objective report must also note the politician's denial of the charges.

• An objective story uses quotes from those involved or from experts on the topic to back up statements.

These characteristics can be used in creating objective news stories for any medium. If you watch television news programs carefully, however, you may note that reporters also convey the idea of objectivity in a visual way. Here are three camera rules for an objective story:

• There should be a title on the screen telling the viewer whom the reporter is interviewing.
• The camera should film the reporter or a person being interviewed from the height of a normal person, not from the ground staring up at the person or from above the person staring down.
• The camera should give as much time to a person representing one side of the conflict as it does to a person representing the other side. Anything less would be considered biased.

**accuracy**
reporting factually correct information

In addition to being objective, hard news reports are also held to strict standards of accuracy. **Accuracy** means reporting factually correct information. Many news organizations expect their reporters to check "facts" with at least two sources before they use them in stories, and many news-oriented magazines employ fact-checkers who review stories for accuracy before they are released to the public.

## INVESTIGATIVE REPORTS

**investigative reports**
in-depth explorations of some aspects of reality

**Investigative reports** are in-depth explorations of some aspects of reality. This news subgenre shares the same standards of objectivity, accuracy, and fairness or balance with hard news. However, a major difference between hard news and investigative reports is the amount of time journalists can devote to the project. When it comes to hard news, journalists typically work on tight schedules; their time limit (deadline) for the completion of an assignment is often only a few hours after they begin it. In contrast, journalists who work on investigative reports have quite a bit more time to do their research, interview their sources, and write their script. Their deadlines can be days or weeks from the time they begin, or even longer.

Investigative reporters often seek to uncover corruption or other problems in government or business, and the tone of the report resembles that of a detective story. A few broadcast television news series, such as *60 Minutes*, *Dateline NBC*, and *20/20*, present this type of material. They spread their output across a variety of digital media, too. Propublica is a nonprofit organization that often creates investigative reports with the cooperation of other journalistic organizations based in print, broadcast, cable, or digital media.

## EDITORIALS

Opinions regarding hard news are usually reserved for editorials. Unlike hard news and investigative reports, an **editorial** is a subgenre of news that expresses an individual's or an organization's point of view. Some editorials are written in the name of (and express the point of view of) the person who wrote the piece, whereas others are written in the name of the entire news organization—for example, the newspaper that printed the piece or the television station that aired it.

News organizations may also allow their reporters and knowledgeable people who do not work for their firm to present editorial comments. **Columnists** are individuals who are paid to write editorials on a regular basis—usually weekly, monthly, or daily. Editorials by the most famous columnists, such as Dave Barry, Peggy Noonan, and Anna Quindlen, are carried by many news outlets across the United States and even around the world. On the web, columnists may show up on journalistic websites (such as CNN.com or Slate) or on **blogs,** online sites written in the style of journal entries, often in reverse chronological order. A well-known example is the *Huffington Post* group of political opinion blogs. They include regular columns by Arianna Huffington, talk show host Tavis Smiley, and Fox program host Greta Van Susteren, as well as opinion pieces from a wide spectrum of celebrities and non-celebrities from different fields.

**editorial**
subgenre of news that concentrates on an individual's or an organization's point of view

**columnists**
individuals who are paid to write editorials on a regular basis—usually weekly, monthly, or daily

**blogs**
journalistic websites or opinion sites in which writings are in the style of journal entries, often in reverse chronological order

## SOFT NEWS

Whereas news workers generally consider hard news reporting a place for objective, accurate, and balanced reporting with little (if any) editorial commentary, they consider another news category, **soft news**, to be an area in which the reporter's opinions and biases can show through. As you may be able to tell by its name, soft news (also known as the human interest story) is the kind of story that news workers feel may not have the critical importance of hard news but nevertheless would appeal to a substantial number of people in the audience. Cooking spots, articles on the best ways to shovel snow without injuring your back, video clips highlighting local students in community plays or recitals—these are topics that news workers consider soft rather than hard news.

**soft news**
the kind of news story that news workers feel may not have the critical importance of hard news but nevertheless would appeal to a substantial number of people in the audience

## INFORMATION

One way to understand the difference between news and information—a difficult distinction to draw for some—is to say that **information** is the raw material that journalists use when they create news stories. On the most basic level, a piece of information

**information**
the raw material that journalists use when they create news stories

is a fact, an item that reveals something about the world. Generally, we must bring together many pieces of information in order to draw conclusions about a person, place, thing, or incident.

All of us use pieces of information as tools in our personal and professional lives. Students gather information as part of paper-writing assignments. Accountants bring together the facts of a client's expenses and wages to fill out the client's tax return. Professors compile information to prepare (interesting, it is hoped) lectures. Similarly, journalists often stitch together facts when they create a news story.

Sometimes searching for relevant facts means speaking to individuals (as reporters might), looking at old bills (as accountants might), or reading scholarly books (as professors might). Often, however, people find the information they want in special collections of facts called databases. Journalists search motor vehicle records, collections of trial transcripts, gatherings of old newspaper articles, and city real estate files. Students, too, use databases: computerized and manual library catalogs are databases; so are dictionaries, LexisNexis, Factiva, and the *Reader's Guide to Periodical Literature*.

Information is a widely used and lucrative mass media commodity—bringing together facts and packaging them in a multitude of ways. A trip to any library's reference collection reveals an extensive array of categorized facts on an enormous number of subjects that are waiting to be used for papers, dissertations, or books or just to settle arguments.

But although a major library's collection of databases may appear quite impressive, it is merely the tip of a huge iceberg of information that mass media firms collect and offer for sale. The information industry creates and distributes much of its product for companies, not individual consumers.

**Information Gathering and Distributing** One major segment of the information industry aims to help businesses find, evaluate, and understand their current customers. For example, Trans Union Credit Information Company and Equifax hold collections of information about the income and debts of hundreds of millions of people worldwide. These firms are in the business of selling selected segments of that information to banks, insurance companies, and other organizations that are interested in the creditworthiness of particular individuals.

Information activities affect you directly when you are approved (or turned down) for a loan or a credit card. This part of the information business also provides lists of names to the marketers who send you postal mail or e-mail—or phone you (often in the middle of dinner)—with "great" offers. Catalog companies often rely on information companies to help them find new customers too.

**Information Research and Retrieval** Another major segment of the information industry focuses on providing quick retrieval of data for people whose work requires them to get facts quickly. Consider the services provided by LexisNexis, for example. The Nexis information service, owned by publishing giant Reed Elsevier of the Netherlands, enables journalists, professors, and students—in fact, researchers of all kinds—to search for and retrieve virtually any fact in more than 2.5 billion searchable documents. Lexis, a sister service, enables attorneys and paralegals to find, analyze, and validate information from countless legal documents by keywords via computer networks. For example, through Lexis's database, legal professionals can retrieve background information on public and private companies, find information about individuals, identify an organization's assets, and research judges, expert witnesses, and opposing counsel, among other things.

The subscription for services such as those offered by Reed Elsevier, News Corporation (e.g., Factiva), and other similar firms in the information business can be costly. Information industry executives tie their high prices to the expense of collecting the data, trying to ensure their accuracy, storing them and protecting them from hackers, preparing print or computer retrieval methods, and distributing the data to clients. But the high price of information is also based on the realization that certain types of information can be extremely valuable, allowing companies to make (or save) millions of dollars. Quick access to the right information helps businesses and governments go about their work efficiently.

## Education

When it comes to genres of media, **education** means content that is purposefully crafted to teach people specific ideas about the world in specific ways. Education is a large segment of the media marketplace. In fact, spending for "instructional materials" by elementary and high schools reached $8.2 billion in 2010. Spending on instructional materials for traditional private and state colleges hit $11 billion. Much of this money was spent on textbooks, the medium that most of us conjure up when we think of instructional materials for schools.

But the genre of education extends far beyond textbooks and other types of printed materials. Consider for a moment the wide variety of media that you've encountered in your long trek through school. The aforementioned spending includes not just textbooks but also workbooks, course packs, wall maps, flash cards, software, online services, and more. In addition, there is a vast amount of educational media material produced primarily for home use. When you were a child, your parents might have set you in front of the TV to view *Sesame Street* or *Reading Rainbow*. Perhaps you watched *Bill Nye the Science Guy*, or *Where in the World Is Carmen San Diego?* when you got a bit older. Maybe your parents gave you the Math Blaster, Fraction Fever, LeapFrog, or JumpStart computer programs for a birthday present. These are just a few of the products that media companies have explicitly designed to teach basic skills.

**education**
content that is purposefully crafted to teach people specific ideas about the world in specific ways

## Advertising

A traditional definition of an **advertisement** is that it is a message that explicitly aims to direct favorable attention to certain goods and services. The message may have a commercial purpose or be aimed at advancing a noncommercial cause, such as the election of a political candidate or the promotion of a fundraising event.

As we will see in chapter 4, advertising involves far more than explicit messages. People who work in the advertising industry help their clients with a range of activities from package design to coupon offers. A broad definition of advertising even includes **product placement**, which is the paid insertion of products into TV shows and movies in order to associate those products, often quietly, with certain desirable characters or activities.

**advertisement**
a message that explicitly aims to direct favorable attention to certain goods and services

**product placement**
the process by which a manufacturer pays—often tens of thousands of dollars and sometimes far more—a production company for the opportunity to have its product displayed in a movie or TV show

**Subgenres of Advertisements** No matter what the medium, advertising practitioners speak about three broad subgenres of advertisements:

- Informational ads
- Hard-sell ads
- Soft-sell ads

**informational ads**
advertisements that rely primarily on the recitation of facts about a product and the product's features to convince target consumers that it is the right product for them to purchase

**hard-sell ads**
messages that combine information about the product with intense attempts to get the consumer to purchase it as soon as possible

**soft-sell ads**
advertisements that aim mostly to create good feelings about the product or service by associating it with music, personalities, or events that the creators of that product or service feel would appeal to the target audience

## INFORMATIONAL ADVERTISEMENTS

**Informational ads** rely primarily on a recitation of facts about a product and the product's features to convince target consumers that it is the right product for them to purchase. An advertisement in *Sound & Vision* magazine that carefully details the specifications and capabilities of a set of Bose speakers would be informational in nature. Similarly, a television announcement aired during PBS's *This Old House* noting the program's support by Home Depot is another example of an informational ad.

## HARD-SELL ADVERTISEMENTS

**Hard-sell ads** are messages that combine information about the product with intense attempts to get the consumer to purchase it as soon as possible. For example, a TV commercial in which a car salesman speaks a mile a minute about the glories of his dealership, shouts about a two-day-only sale, and recites the address of the dealership four times before the spot ends is a hard-sell ad.

## SOFT-SELL ADVERTISEMENTS

**Soft-sell ads** aim mostly to create good feelings about the product or service by associating it with music, personalities, or events that the creators of that product or service feel would appeal to the target audience. Television commercials for a wide variety of products, including soft drinks, beer, and athletic footwear, are soft-sell ads. Remember the "Got Milk?" ads for milk producers, the Clydesdale horse commercials for Budweiser, or the "Mac versus PC" ads for Apple? These are classic examples of ads that aim to create a "hip" feeling about a product that will lead consumers to want to be identified with it.

It is important to note that these three types of ads—informational, hard-sell, and soft-sell—mainly differ in the amount of stress they place on facts about the product, the intensity of the sales pitch, and the emotional connection between the consumer and the product. There are, however, circumstances in which much longer ads are created, and the advertisers can then combine informational, hard-sell, and soft-sell tactics. If you watch TV shopping channels such as HSN, you might see this mix. A hostess may provide a demonstration of a gold necklace that mixes specific information about the necklace ("beautiful 14-karat gold, 30 inches long, with a sturdy lock, as you can see") and hard-sell encouragement ("these necklaces are going so fast that if you don't call us right now, we might run out of them") with soft-sell tactics that include joking around by people on the set and an attempt to build an entertaining environment for selling.

Dean Winters stars in a series of commercials for Allstate Insurance in the role of Mayhem, in which he is responsible for creating a variety of comical scenarios in which a person falls victim to an unfortunate mishap as a result of Mayhem's mischief and is stuck with poor insurance that will not cover the damages caused.

## THINKING ABOUT MEDIA LITERACY

Can you think of your own example of a hard-sell ad? How about a soft-sell ad? An informational one?

# Mixing Genres in a Convergent Media System

You have probably noticed that soft-sell advertising sometimes shows up as part of entertainment-oriented TV shows. When the Lifetime cable network paraded L'Oreal products as part of the action on *Project Runway*, that was a clear case of mixing genres. Clearly, L'Oreal executives believed that audiences would get a favorable feeling for their brand if the audiences saw their products pop up within a popular entertainment program. As we will discuss in depth in chapter 4, hybridity involving advertising and entertainment—and other content genres—is becoming increasingly common. Of course, advertising is not the only genre that mixes with other genres. Media practitioners who work in the fields of entertainment, information, and education explore the value of this sort of hybridity in order to attract and hold audiences. Media practitioners and advertisements often borrow comedic, dramatic, festival, and gaming elements to attract and hold audiences. Writers for *Sesame Street*, for example, often deliver their educational messages in segments that resemble situation comedies, game shows, and musical variety programs.

As you probably know by now, the organizations that create material based on any of the genres, or any combination of genres, have a strong incentive to follow the logic of convergence by moving their material across media boundaries so that as many people as possible in their target audience will see it. Think of the commercials that advertisers create around the Super Bowl—say the Budweiser beer ads that tell cute stories via the entertainment genre about those iconic Clydesdale horses. Many advertisers place their commercials on popular websites such as YouTube for people to view either before or after the game. Then they try to create interest in going to those sites by getting journalists or other media creators to use their commercials in *their* stories on television, in newspapers and magazines, or on the web.

## THINKING ABOUT MEDIA LITERACY

What advantages does targeting an audience with specific content have for media practitioners? Does that targeting offer any advantages to the audiences?

Knowing how to use genres and their formulas to create materials that are popular with carefully targeted audiences across multiple platforms is a highly valued skill in mass media industries. But there's a lot more to creating a work valued by audiences than just thinking it up. We have already discussed audience construction and research as important factors in content selection. All mass media organizations also must be concerned with five other primary business activities:

- Production
- Distribution
- Exhibition
- Audience research
- Finance

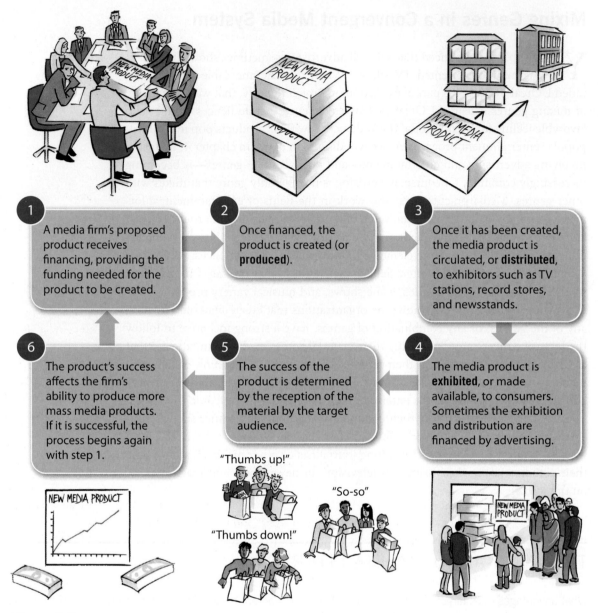

**Figure 3.5**

Organizations involved in production, distribution, and exhibition, activities central to the function of all media organizations, must first secure financing before they can proceed.

As Figure 3.5 shows, production involves creating the content. Distribution involves circulating the material to exhibitors (e.g., music stores and TV stations). The exhibitors, in turn, make the material available to consumers. Let's examine these steps, which lie at the heart of what goes on in mass media industries, one at a time.

## Production of Mass Media Content

**production**
the creation of mass media materials for distribution through one or more mass media vehicles

Production is the beginning of the chain of events that brings mass media content to audiences. **Production** for the mass media means the creation of materials for distribution through one or more mass media vehicles.

## Media Production Firms

A **mass media production firm** is a company that creates materials for distribution through one or more mass media vehicles. The Washington Post Company, which publishes the Washington Post, is a production company. So is Routledge, the publisher of this book, and its parent company, Informa. So are Time Inc. magazine company (a division of Time Warner), which creates *Time* magazine; Comcast's NBC Universal, which produces *NBC Nightly News*; and TheHuffingtonPost.com (a division of AOL).

**mass media production firm**
a company that creates materials for distribution through one or more mass media vehicles

**Who Does the Work?**  The making of all these media products requires both administrative personnel and creative personnel. **Administrative personnel** make sure the business side of the media organization is humming along. They must thoroughly understand that the media business they are in and their daily jobs—in, for example, accounting, law, marketing—have much to do with the success of the organizations for which they work. Their work does not, however, relate directly to the creation of their firm's media materials. **Creative personnel** do that. They are the individuals who get initial ideas for the material or use their artistic talent to put the material together.

**administrative personnel**
workers who oversee the business side of the media organization

In all media industries, work on the creative side of a production firm can be done in two ways, on-staff or freelance. An **on-staff worker** has secured a full-time position at a production firm. For example, most, though not all, art directors in advertising agencies are on-staff workers. They work for the same agency all the time; the projects they work on may change, but the company that issues their paycheck remains the same. **Freelancers**, on the other hand, are workers who make a living by accepting and completing assignments for a number of different companies—sometimes several at one time. Most movie actors work as freelancers, for example; when they finish one film, they look for work on another film, which may be made by a different company.

**creative personnel**
individuals who get initial ideas for the material or use their artistic talent to put the material together

**on-staff worker**
a worker who has secured a full-time position at a production firm

**freelancers**
workers who make a living by accepting and completing assignments for a number of different companies—sometimes several at one time

Although freelancing can be highly lucrative for some (we are familiar with the names of well-paid freelance creatives such as the novelist John Grisham and the film actor Tom Cruise), historically freelancing has been a difficult road for many creatives. Even when salaries are high (and they frequently are not), many freelance creatives do not work as often as they would like because of the heavy competition for desirable assignments. Historically, this competition has given tremendous power to the production companies that hire these freelance creatives. Freelancers, from actors, to book editors, ghost writers, and cinematographers, have reported that production companies have used this power to "borrow" innovative ideas discussed in job interviews, force them to work unusually long hours, and withhold their due credits when the assignment is completed.

To establish a power of their own, many freelance creatives have banded together to create talent guilds. A **talent guild** is a union formed by people who work in a particular craft; consider, for example, the Writers Guild of America, the Screen Actors Guild, and the Directors Guild of America. These guilds negotiate rules with major production firms in their industries regarding the ways in which freelance creatives will be treated and paid.

**talent guild**
a union formed by people who work in similar crafts to help negotiate rules with major production firms in their industries regarding the ways in which freelance creatives will be treated and paid

The administrative and creative personnel of mass media production firms recognize that the previous successes of individual freelance creators—their positive track records—can help reduce the risk that a project will fail. In an effort to manage their risks, movie companies typically will not allow high-budget movies to be made unless a high-profile actor (such as Matt Damon or Robert Downey Jr.) signs on.

Similarly, book publishing firms have been known to pay popular writers quite a lot for the rights to their next work. In 2006, various firms agreed to pay $7 million for books to Warren Buffett's ghostwriter, more than $8 million to former U.S. Federal Reserve head Alan Greenspan, and over $10 million to evangelist Joel Osteen. The economic downturn of the late 2000s made it harder for publishers to make these levels of upfront payments. Word in the trade was that book publishers liked reality TV hosts because of their high name recognition and built-in following but also because they tend to accept advances in the mid-five-figure to low six-figure range, far lower than other celebrities watched by millions every week. Nevertheless, in 2008 the Dutton publishing company agreed to pay "in the millions" for a novel by Anthony Zuiker, creator of TV's highly popular action series *CSI*, that leads people from the hard-copy book to online motion picture and interactive elements.

**How Does Production Take Place?** The personal vision of an actor, novelist, or scholar can sometimes make it to the screen or the page. Inserting such a personal vision into a work is called authorship. Generally, however, production in media industries is a **collaborative activity**, in which many people work together to initiate, create, and polish the end material. The collaborative nature of production holds true for every mass media product, from movies to scholarly books. Some types of production require more creative hands than others. When there are many creators, the "author" of the work may not be a person, but rather a group or company.

Compare the production of a scholarly book with that of a typical commercial movie starring a well-known actor (see Figure 3.6). In addition to the writer, a scholarly book requires an acquisitions editor, who finds the author and might help with the initial plan for the work; a few readers (usually other scholars or development editors) who suggest ways in which the writer can improve the book; a copy editor, who helps with the manuscript's style; and design personnel, who craft the look of the book and perhaps its jacket.

Now consider the film. The well-known actor is chosen by an executive producer or studio head, with the assistance of the actor's business representatives. In addition, the film will need screenwriters to write and rewrite the script; other actors to work with the star; a casting director with assistants to choose the other actors; a set designer and assistants to plan the backdrops; a director and assistants to organize the filming; a cinematographer and assistants to photograph the scenes; an editor and assistants to put the scenes together into a finished movie; and many more collaborators. Although individual authorship of the scholarly book may be fairly clear, the same cannot be said of the movie. Because so many people are involved on the creative side, it is often very difficult to argue that the final version of a Hollywood film is one person's vision.

**collaborative activity**
an activity in which many people work together to initiate, create, and polish the end material

**Figure 3.6**
Individuals involved in two types of media production. The mass media production process is almost always a collaborative process.

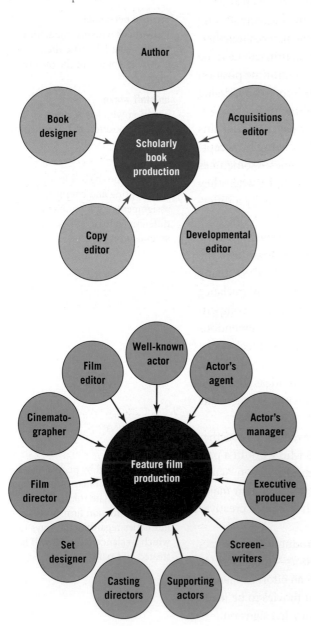

We commonly regard the results of production in terms of individual items—a particular movie, book, magazine, or TV show. Actually, though, it is possible to find many cases in which what is produced is not an individual item, but rather a stitching-together of already-existing products that, taken together, make up a whole. Take ABC television as an example. ABC creates many, but not all, of the programs that it airs. It leases some programs from other production companies, which grant the network the right to sell time between parts of the shows to advertisers. ABC then sends these shows to TV stations in cities and towns via satellite, and they in turn broadcast the shows to the public.

But if you look at ABC's work another way, you will realize that the company could be considered heavily involved in TV production even if it didn't actually produce any of its shows. That conclusion comes from seeing production not in terms of individual programs but in terms of the **schedule**, or the pattern in which the programs are arranged. ABC employs programmers who create regular schedules for different parts of the day. The goal of these schedules is to attract viewers to ABC and to keep them watching ABC's shows and commercials for a number of hours. During the early 2010s, for example, ABC fielded a successful Thursday evening schedule (including the medical series *Grey's Anatomy* and *Private Practice*) from 8:00 to 11:00 p.m. (EST). Clearly, the product that ABC programmers were creating was not an individual show but a flow of shows, put together with a particular audience-attracting goal in mind.

In mass media industries, "format" is the term commonly used to describe the rules that guide this flow. A **format** is the patterned choice and arrangement of elements that make up specific media material. The material may be a flow of programs, such as ABC's schedule, or it may be an arrangement of video, audio, or text presentations that people upload to a website, such as Facebook, YouTube, or Pinterest. Most radio stations use formats that convey their personalities by combining certain types of songs, disc jockeys' sounds, and jingles that identify the station. The concept of format applies to magazines, too. *Vogue's* creative personnel are involved not only in the production of individual articles that appear in the periodical, but also in choosing the topics of the articles to begin with and arranging the articles in a flow that is designed to convey an image and entice readers through the magazine.

**schedule**
the pattern in which the programs are arranged and presented to the audience

**format**
the rules that guide the flow of products that are put together with a particular audience-attracting goal in mind; a formula that describes a particular media product

## Distribution of Mass Media Content

Most of us tend to think of production when we think of mass media industries. After all, it is the output of this production—the newspapers we read, the cable TV shows we watch—that grabs our attention, that makes us happy or angry, interested or bored. Moreover, most public discussion about mass communication tends to center around production. The latest gossip about which actor will be in which film, the angry comments a mayor makes about the violence on local TV news, the newest CD by an up-and-coming music group—these are the kinds of topics that are most often the focus of our attention when we discuss media.

However, media executives and media-literate citizens know that production is only one step in the arduous and risky process of getting a mass media idea to an audience and that distribution is just as important as production. **Distribution** is the delivery of the produced material to the point where it will be shown to its intended audience. Although the activity takes place out of public view, distributors often have a large say in marketing the products to the target audience.

**distribution**
the delivery of the produced material to the point where it will be shown to its intended audience

Before a newspaper or magazine can be put out into a newsstand, supermarket, or deli, it has to be delivered to these locations by the company producing it.

We have already mentioned that ABC acts as a distributor when it disseminates television programming to TV stations via satellite. When Philadelphia Media Network delivers its *Philadelphia Inquirer* to city newsstands, when Twentieth Century Fox moves its movies to the Regal Cinema Theaters, and when Sony Music sends its newest releases to Apple to be sold over the iTunes website, they are all involved in distribution to exhibitors.

Note that these firms—Philadelphia Media Network, Twentieth Century Fox, and Sony Music—use their own distribution divisions rather than rely on other independent distribution firms to do the job. This background ought to underscore for you the importance of successful distribution in the world of media business. Some executives argue that although "content is king," distribution ought to share the crown. The reason is simple: without a distributor, a production firm's media product would literally go nowhere. It would stack up in the warehouse or on a computer, eventually to be destroyed. To get a feel for the power in distribution, consider that you could "publish" a book quite easily. That is, you could take any work of art you've created—some doodles, a love poem, notes to this book—and get it photocopied and bound at the nearest store, such as Kinko's. Say you splurge and print 500 copies. For a bit more money than you'd spend in the copy shop, you could put a fancy binding on the product, so that it would look like a "real" book. Even easier, you could format the document on a computer to look like a book.

Of course, now that you have a printed and/or digital book, the trick is to sell it. You might try to get the university bookstore to carry it, but chances are the store won't. Barnes & Noble Booksellers probably won't touch your book with a 10-foot pole. It's likely, in fact, that no legitimate bookstore will carry it. This is not necessarily because your writing is bad; your book might actually be a true work of art. The real reason that your chances of getting your book into a bookstore are so poor is that your book does not have a powerful book distributor behind it. Even if you manage to get Amazon to carry your book online (a special Amazon program does that for authors), without a track record to get potential readers' attention and without money for promoting the book, you have little chance of getting people to buy it among Amazon's millions of offerings. If, however, you could persuade a major publishing company to add your book to its distribution list, have its publicity force pitch your book to offline bookstores, and have you interviewed by radio and print journalists, you might have a pretty good chance to get your book sold.

Production, then, is useless without distribution. Without a powerful distributor, the material that a production firm's executives believe could be tremendously successful will have much less chance of achieving its potential. Some people believe that the internet reduces the importance of distribution because just about anyone can post—that is, distribute—just about anything online for very little cost. But putting something on a personal website or even on a backwater page of a popular exhibition site such as YouTube or MySpace does not ensure that anyone but your friends will go to it. Perhaps you will get lucky, and the clip you posted to YouTube will become a popular viral video viewed by millions. In most cases, however, the key is to have the clout to place the content in a position where many people have a good chance of seeing it. That means getting the attention of a powerful distributor.

**powerful distributor**
a firm that can ensure the media products it carries will end up in the best locations at the best exhibitors to the best audience

What makes a **powerful distributor**? Simply put, a distributor's power is measured in terms of the firm's ability to ensure that the media products it carries will end up in the best locations of the best exhibitors to the best audience. To understand what that means, we have to look at exhibition.

# Exhibition of Mass Media Content

The exhibition of mass media material is closely linked to the distribution in the sense that both are steps in bringing the content to the audience. Sometimes the same company carries out both activities. Because exhibition is quite a different business from distribution, though, it often involves different firms.

**Exhibition** is the activity of presenting mass media materials to audiences for viewing or purchase. When media executives speak about the importance of exhibition, they often mention shelf space. **Shelf space** is the amount of area or time available for presenting products to consumers. Think of bookstores with their long rows of shelves and display tables. As large as typical chain stores are today, production firms want to rent and sell more types of titles than will fit into even the biggest stores. As a result, store executives must decide which categories of products and which company's products within those categories are carried and which get more room than others.

Consequently, book distribution firms that rely on stores to present their products to consumers must compete furiously for shelf space. The distributors that wield the most power are those with products that the stores need to have because consumers demand them. These distributors have more ability to negotiate shelf space for new products than do distributors of goods that are not so important to the stores.

The same is true elsewhere in the media business. Magazine and book producers must compete for shelf space in bookstores, on newsstands, and in supermarket aisles. Moreover, some spots in stores and on newsstands are more valuable than others. The area toward the front of a bookstore is most valuable because all customers pass through it. Racks on a newsstand that are at eye level are more valuable than those at floor level because consumers are likely to look at the racks at eye level first. The exhibitors (i.e., the stores) often charge book or magazine distributors money for placing their products in such privileged positions.

For cable TV, movies, broadcast TV, radio, the web, mobile phones, and other media, the concept of shelf space has to be stretched just a bit, but it applies just the same. Executives think of the limited number of channels of a cable system as its shelves. Similarly, some broadcast television executives see the 24 hours in a day as their stations' shelves, because time limits what they can air. In cable, radio, and broadcast TV, certain time slots and channels (or stations) are more valuable than others. The same goes for high-traffic pages on websites such as Auto.com and the space mobile phone companies reserve for applications (apps) that come with a smartphone at the time of purchase.

Now imagine a particular case: feel the tension that Marisol Durán, a salesperson for a newly formed independent book distribution firm, experiences as she waits to speak to a purchasing executive at the large bookstore chain Barnes & Noble. Marisol represents small publishing firms specializing in science fiction. Because of their small size, these firms don't have the money to hire their own salespeople. She knows that Barnes & Noble's shelves hold many books, but she also knows that the number of books published each year alone would take up far more space than those shelves can hold. She has been successful in placing many of the titles she carries in bookstores that specialize in the science fiction genre. She has ambitions beyond these small stores, however. A chance to catch the eyes of science fiction readers who shop at Barnes & Noble would, she believes, surely result in a strong increase in sales.

**exhibition**
the activity of presenting mass media materials to audiences for viewing or purchase

**shelf space**
the amount of area or time available for presenting products to consumers

81

**trade incentives**
payments in cash, discounts, or publicity activities that provide a special reason for an exhibitor to highlight a product

**cooperative advertising**
(also known as co-op advertising) advertising paid for in part by media production firms or their distributors in order to help the exhibitor promote the product

**vertical integration**
an organization's control over a media product from production through distribution to exhibition

She knows, however, that she would get a better hearing at Barnes & Noble—and would place more books there—if she worked for the distribution arm of a publishing house such as Random House or Simon & Schuster, two giants of the book business. One reason is that such publishing giants can afford to advertise and promote their titles to the public better than her struggling publishers can, and such publicity can strongly affect sales.

The large publishers also may be better able than smaller ones to offer **trade incentives**—payments in cash, discounts, or publicity activities that provide a special reason for an exhibitor to highlight a product—that could influence large stores such as Barnes & Noble to carry their books. To make sure that a bookstore chain exhibits key titles at the entrances to its stores, for example, a publisher might have to offer—through its distributor—to pay the bookstore chain a sum of money for taking up that space. Bringing the author in for special book readings and book signings and helping to pay for ads in newspapers (a practice called **cooperative advertising**) might also be part of the deal.

As this hypothetical experience suggests, linking up with a powerful distributor is of great benefit to producers in every mass media industry. Not surprisingly, the major production companies either own or are otherwise strategically linked to the major distribution organizations. In these cases, it is important to keep in mind that power over production and distribution is self-reinforcing: creative personnel with strong track records are attracted to the production firm in part because it has powerful distribution. In turn, the company has powerful distribution in part because its production arm attracts creative personnel with strong track records.

In some industries, major firms consolidate their strength by owning not only the distribution organizations but the major exhibition firms as well. Television networks such as NBC, CBS, and ABC, for example, have production divisions that create fiction, sports, and news programs. They also own broadcast TV networks that distribute their programs and broadcast stations in key cities that exhibit them. This control of the entire process from production through distribution to exhibition is called **vertical integration**, and it represents yet another way in which media companies try to reduce the risk that their target audiences will even have an opportunity to choose the material that competitors create (see Figure 3.7).

**Figure 3.7**
The CBS television network—which owns production divisions, distribution channels, and exhibition venues—is a successful example of vertical integration.

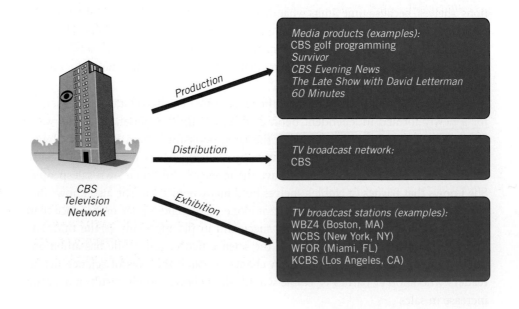

# Financing Mass Media Content

As you can probably guess, the production, distribution, and exhibition of mass media materials requires a lot of money. Starting a publishing company, even a very small one, costs hundreds of thousands of dollars. Creating a one-hour program for a major broadcast or cable television network costs more than a million dollars. Starting a new magazine can cost even more. Want to buy a radio station? Despite the recent slowdown of growth in radio advertising, stations still go for tens of millions of dollars.

The cash coming into a mass media firm can be divided into two categories:

- Money to fund new production
- Money to pay for already-completed products

We'll explore each in detail.

## Funding New Production

Executives in mass media enterprises may need to raise funds to expand into new areas, or they may want to build up areas in which they are already operating. A movie exhibition chain may want to expand by building new theaters in Europe. A publishing firm might want to start a new unit to create oversized coffee table books. A company might want to buy an AM radio station. In such cases, executives may not want or be able to use the company's current revenues to cover the costs of the new venture.

A company generally has two ways to get money in anticipation of production: it can take out loans, or it can encourage investments in the company.

**Taking Out Loans**  A **loan** is money borrowed from an organization, usually a bank, for a certain price (a percentage of the loan called an interest rate). To get a loan, executives must persuade the lending organization that their plans will realistically bring in the cash they expect so that the firm will be able to repay the amount of the loan (its principal) plus the interest in a timely way. The lender will also want to be sure that it has a claim on some of the current value (assets) of the firm—for example, the real estate of an exhibition chain or the current holdings of a radio station owner—in case the firm does not pay back the loan.

**Investment banks** are companies that arrange to lend millions, even tens and hundreds of millions, of dollars to companies and that also arrange stock offerings. Some investment banks specialize in particular industries, and the executives of these investment banks feel that they understand quite well the risks involved. Large investment banks hire experts in particular industries to guide the banks' lending activities in their areas of expertise. These investment bankers assess the firms that want loans and put together the terms of agreement. When very large amounts of money are involved, the investment banker will organize a **syndicate**, a group of banks that agree to share the risks and rewards of the lending deal. Because it takes on more responsibility, the lead bank (the bank that organizes the syndicate) makes more money on the deal than the others.

**loan**
money borrowed from an organization, usually a bank, for a certain price (a percentage of the loan called an interest rate)

**investment banks**
companies that arrange to lend millions, even tens and hundreds of millions, of dollars to companies and that also arrange stock offerings

**syndicate**
a group of banks that agree to share the risks and rewards of the lending deal, organized by investment banks when very large amounts of money are required

**stock offerings**
selling units of ownership in the company, or shares of stock, to organizations and individuals

**venture capitalists**
individuals or companies that invest in startup or nonpublic firms in the hope that the firms' value will increase over time

**initial public offering (IPO)**
the offering for sale to the general public of a predetermined number of shares of company stock that were previously owned by a limited number of individuals and the listing of the company's shares on the stock exchange

On May 12, 2012, Facebook made big news by going public and holding its IPO. Founder Mark Zuckerberg had long resisted taking the company public but finally had to make the leap once the number of shareholders (smaller private investors, mostly from tech-related companies) reached more than 500.

**Encouraging Investments** Whereas bankers worry that firms will not be able to pay back the money they have borrowed, executives of those firms worry about how much money the loans are costing them. That is, paying the interest on the loans requires cash that the company could use for other purposes. Consequently, executives may prefer to raise money through **stock offerings**. A share of stock is a unit of ownership in a company. All corporations, whether they are owned by only a few people or by millions of people, issue stock. When a company engages in a stock offering, it sells these units of ownership to organizations and individuals.

For example, let's say that DigitalFeast, a media organization that creates specialized restaurant and recipe sites for the web and mobile devices, wants to expand. One of its computer engineers has just devised software that executives believe will revolutionize the industry and make the firm a leader.

The three founders of the company still own all the stock; because there is no public market for the stock, the value of each founder's holdings equals the assets of the firm divided by three. The founders (who also run the firm) are concerned that taking out loans in addition to the loans they already have would make the interest payments too high for the firm to afford, given that they don't expect the new device to be profitable for at least a year. They decide to open up ownership of the company to people other than themselves.

Working with the company's accountants and with outside specialists, the company's founders determine the value of the company. That amount includes the worth of its equipment and also its goodwill—that is, the value of its reputation among its clients and potential clients in the online world. The founders decide that the company should issue six million shares; each of the founders will keep one million of those shares, and DigitalFeast will offer the other three million at $2 each. Consequently, if the company is able to sell all of the nonpartners' shares, it will receive $6 million, which will be enough to expand the venture.

In view of its small size, DigitalFeast will probably sell its stock to **venture capitalists**. Venture capitalists are individuals or companies that invest in startup or nonpublic firms in the hope that the firms' value will increase over time. These people and firms are in the business of assuming the high risks of investing in such firms in the hope of receiving high rewards. In the case of DigitalFeast, they are assuming that the company's earnings will increase because its new device will bring in more business. That increase in earnings will make the company more valuable, and so each share will be worth more than the amount the venture capitalists paid for it. If the company were then sold, the venture capitalists would get substantially more money than they invested.

There are other ways in which DigitalFeast can raise more money. Assume, for example, that after the sale of stock to the venture capitalists, DigitalFeast's board of directors (which now includes some of the venture capitalists) decides on an **initial public offering (IPO)** of the company's stock. The board needs to convince an investment banker that the company's future is so great that investment companies and individual investors would buy five million new shares of the company's stock at $10 a share. The investment bank agrees to manage (or underwrite) the offering for a fee. Because five million new shares will be created, the shares that already exist will represent a smaller percentage of the ownership than they did before the IPO. Still, the market value of the early stockholders' shares will go from $2 to $10 a share. DigitalFeast, meanwhile, has $50 million more to chew on.

## Funding When Production Is Already Complete

A primary indicator of the health of any company is its **profits**—the amount of money brought in by the completed products (the revenues) minus expenses. Even if a company is run efficiently and its expenses are low, it still needs to bring in ever-increasing amounts of revenue in order to increase its profits and satisfy its investors and lenders. In mass media firms, there are several ways to bring in revenues.

**Direct Sales** The purchaser pays the production firm or a separate distributor or exhibitor for the item and can use it in any way she or he sees fit—keep it forever, throw it away, give it to someone else, or even resell it. In college textbook publishing, for example, most of the money comes from sales to consumers (the students).

**License Fees** A person or organization pays the production firm or a separate distributor or exhibitor for the use of a product, but the producer has ultimate control over the way it is used. For example, a toy company may pay Warner Bros. for the right to use the image of Bugs Bunny on toy banks for five years. Similarly, if you have Microsoft Word on your computer, what you have actually bought is a license to use it. (Remember the notice telling you that if you use the software, you are accepting the "license agreement"? One consequence is that, according to the agreement, you are prohibited from reselling the software to someone else.)

**Rentals** The production firm or a separate distributor or exhibitor charges for the right to employ (read, view, or hear) a mass media product for a certain period of time and then gets the product back. For example, with movie rentals, the store typically buys the video from the production firm and tries to make a profit by renting it to you and many others.

**Usage Fee** The amount the producer or the separate distributor or exhibitor charges for a mass media product is based on the number of times the product is employed. For example, an internet database of articles may charge you for the number of articles or "page views" you print.

**Subscriptions** The producer or the separate distributor or exhibitor charges for regularly providing a media product or service. (Think of a magazine subscription, a subscription to a cable system, and a subscription to a company that provides you with internet service.)

**Advertising** A company buys space or time on a mass medium (a page in a magazine, 30 seconds on a radio station) in which it is allowed to display a persuasive message (an advertisement) for a product or service. We will have a good deal to say about the workings of the advertising industry in chapter 4. What is important to remember here is that the advertising industry is the dominant support system for the mass media. If advertising did not exist, the amount you pay for magazines, newspapers, internet content, and cable television, not to mention broadcast television and radio, would skyrocket. Reliable estimates suggest, for example, that because of advertising, people on average pay half of what they would otherwise pay for magazines and substantially less than half for newspapers.

**profits**
the amount of money brought in by the completed products (the revenues) minus expenses

The mention of magazines and newspapers brings up another important point about the sources of cash in mass media industries. Particularly in an era of convergence, companies work hard to bring in money from what economists call multiple revenue streams. Magazine and newspaper firms, for example, sell ads for their print editions as well as their web and tablet versions. They also ask consumers to pay for the print versions, and many magazines and newspapers charge for tablet access as well. Movie companies, we will see, have even longer revenue streams. They bring in money for their titles from theaters, DVDs, on-demand cable and satellite services, hotels, and other places. Local TV broadcasters, by contrast, overwhelmingly have long lived off only a single revenue stream, advertiser support; viewers do not have to pay them. This revenue stream happens to be quite an outpouring: in 2010, local TV stations took in $21.4 billion from advertisers. But as competition tightens in the television industry, as costs go up, and as advertisers have the option of placing ads in other media if the local stations raise their advertising rates, the single revenue stream does not look as lucrative as it once did. That is why the stations are demanding that cable systems pay them for carrying their signals to their customers (what is called a **retransmission fee**). The stations are also trying to make money via advertising on their websites.

By now, the complexity of trying to navigate the mass media environment should be quite clear. But wait—there's more! Not only do media practitioners have to worry about production, distribution, exhibition, and finance; they also have to concern themselves with **government regulation**. Government regulation involves a wide variety of activities and laws through which elected and appointed officials at local, state, and federal levels exercise influence over media firms. The different forms of regulation are so important to what media firms can and cannot do when it comes to production, distribution, exhibition, advertising, and finance that we devote an entire chapter—chapter 5—to them.

## Media Literacy and the Business of Mass Media

At this point, you may be asking yourself two questions: How does knowing about the business of media help me to be a more aware consumer of mass media materials? And what difference might being an aware consumer make in my life? The questions speak, of course, to the important topic of media literacy, which we introduced in chapter 1.

Think back to the billboard scenario that began this chapter. Remember that the premise was that community leaders in the neighborhood where you live had begun to complain about billboard advertising featuring beer and sex, and you wanted to help these community leaders influence billboard executives to change their ad policies. At the beginning of this chapter, you could mostly just list what you didn't know. Now (after reading the chapter), you ought to know enough to help your community deal with billboard (or "outdoor") firms.

- To begin with, you know that billboard companies are the exhibition point of a chain that often also involves companies that create the ad ideas and other firms that actually make the posters and distribute them to the billboard owners. Your community group will try to persuade the exhibitors to change their policies, but if they refuse, you now know that there may well be two other levels of firms

**retransmission fee**
amount a cable system or satellite firm pays to a broadcaster for the right to pick the broadcaster's signal off the air and send it to cable or satellite subscribers.

**government regulation**
a wide variety of activities and laws through which elected and appointed officials at local, state, and federal levels exercise influence over media firms

to which you can bring your demands. You might put pressure on the ad agencies that thought up the ads or on the companies that manufactured them and delivered them to the billboard firm. The ad agencies may be more sensitive to organized pressure and anger than the billboard company.

- You now bring to your talk with company executives a basic understanding of the advertising genre that will give you credibility with them and help you make your arguments. You know, for example, that sex and violence are often used in soft-sell advertising. The issue here is twofold: whether the practice is ethical when it is used for selling beer and whether it is ethical in areas where there are children who might consider the ads attractive and hip and so consider the combination (sex and beer) attractive and hip.

- Our discussion of the way media firms think about audiences and of the importance of segmentation and targeting to today's media should sensitize you to the issues that outdoor firms consider when they put up their billboards and that advertisers think about when they decide to place their ads on the billboards. By examining the locations of the most objectionable billboards, you might be able to show the billboard firms that you know that their supposed targets—adults—are not their only targets. You might, for example, find several of the objectionable billboards within a few blocks of high schools. That can get you into an interesting discussion about the ethics of targeting that audience and lead to leverage that you can apply to the firms.

Even if there is still much to learn about this billboard issue as well as other aspects of media, the hope is that you have already begun to watch TV, read the newspaper, and use the web with a new awareness of what is going on. Have you begun to dissect the formats of your favorite TV shows or magazines? When you open up "junk" mail or get an ad on the web or phone, have you tried to figure out what target audiences you fit into and where the firms got your name? When you've gone into a bookstore, have you thought of the relationships among exhibition, distribution, and production? Have you watched and read the news with an eye to the subgenres that journalists use and, if it is hard news, the way they present the sense of an "objective" approach to the world through their use of the verbal and visual conventions we discussed?

If not, you ought to try; it will open up new ways to view reality and the forces that create it.

# CHAPTER REVIEW

 Visit the Companion Website at www.routledge.com/cw/turow for additional study tools and resources.

## Key Terms

You can find the definitions to these key terms in the marginal glossary throughout this chapter. Test your knowledge of these terms with interactive flash cards on the *Media Today* companion website.

accuracy
adequate revenue
administrative personnel
advertisement
analysis of existing data
audiences
blogs
collaborative activity
columnists
cooperative advertising
creative personnel
demographic indicators
demographics
distribution
dramedy
editorial
education
entertainment
exhibition
focus group
format
formula

freelancers
genres
government regulation
hard news
hard-sell ads
hybrid genres
hybridity
information
informational ads
initial public offering (IPO)
investigative reports
investment banks
journalists
lifestyle categories
loan
mass media production firm
media practitioners
objectivity
on-staff worker
patterns of action
powerful distributor
product placement

production
profits
psychographics
research and development
   (R&D)
retransmission fee
schedule
setting
shelf space
soft news
soft-sell ads
stock offerings
subgenres
surveys
syndicate
talent guild
track record
trade incentives
typical characters
venture capitalists
vertical integration

## Questions for Discussion and Critical Thinking

1. After reading this chapter, what reasons can you find for why media industries spend so much time trying to learn more about their audiences? What advantages does that practice offer the industries?

2. Are there any advantages for audiences in all this research?

3. What do you think of the ideas of "objectivity" in print and on camera? Do you think those principles are enough? Can you think of any news examples from either medium that seem objective by these standards?

4. How are freelancers an important part of media industries?

# Case Study
## TEENS AS A CONSTRUCTED AUDIENCE

**The Idea** One way to get a feel for the idea that audiences are constructed is to see how advertisers actually construct audiences. In this case study you will go through recent advertising trade magazines to see how marketing and media executives talk about an important audience—teens. You will also explore what their construction of teens means for the ways they try to reach teens and persuade them to buy products.

**The Method** To conduct this study, you need to know how to use a periodical database in your school's library. The most popular databases are Factiva and LexisNexis. Knowing how to use these sorts of databases will help you learn a lot about the state of media today. Reading magazines for ad practitioners may help you get a summer—or permanent—job in a media firm.

1. Ask someone who knows how to use the database to show you how to do a full-text search of the weekly trade magazine *Advertising Age* for the past six months. Tell that person that you would like to investigate how *Advertising Age* used the term "teen" or "teenager" during that time.
2. You may find that *Advertising Age* used the term a lot during that period. Ask your professor what proportion of the articles you should read. If there are a hundred articles or more, the class might divide into groups of two or three people in each group. That way each group can share findings on different articles and summarize them.
3. For each article, note the title and date and then answer the following questions on a sheet of paper:
   a. On what topic does it mention teenagers?
   b. How does it describe teenagers? How and to what extent does it divide teens by gender, class, spending power, physical characteristics, personalities, or other categories?
   c. Does the article make comparisons between teenagers and other groups in society? If so, how?
   d. What does the article say about teenagers' value to advertisers, uses of different media, and uses of different products?
   e. What, if anything, does the article say about how media firms create media to attract teens?
   f. What, if anything, does the article say about how media firms and advertisers are creating advertisements to attract teens? With what messages and images do they think they can persuade them?
4. Once you and your group have taken notes on all the articles, make an outline of a report that discusses what you learned about how teenagers are constructed by advertisers, why, and with what consequences for commercial messages and for media.

# 4 Financing and Shaping the Media

## Advertising, Public Relations, and Marketing Communications

## CHAPTER OBJECTIVES

1 Describe the roles that advertising, public relations, and marketing communications play in the media system

2 Describe the kinds of firms involved in these activities and what they do

3 Analyze the process of producing and creating ads and public relations material

4 Explain how advertising, public relations, and marketing communications relate to convergence and what that means for the media system

5 Discuss debates between critics and defenders of these businesses regarding topics such as commercialism, hidden persuasion, and targeting communication

"The trouble with us in America isn't that the poetry of life has turned to prose, but that it has turned to advertising copy."

**LOUIS KRONENBERGER, AUTHOR AND CRITIC**

You buy a book from a local bookstore. You go to the movies and pay at the box office (even though your date offers to do it). You download a song from iTunes, and it gets charged to your account. You forget to write a check to the cable company two months in a row—you thought your roommate was supposed to do it—but you get the notice in time not to have the service shut off. We all pay to use certain kinds of media content. A major consulting firm estimates that Americans shelled out $218 billion on "media content and services" during 2010.

"Content" means specific materials such as music and books. "Services" refers to the companies and devices we use to get the content. That may include the mobile phone you buy or rent, the cable company you deal with, or the Roku box you use to stream Netflix from the internet to your television set. But here's a point you might initially find odd: even though we put in a lot of money for media, companies supply a lot more money than that to pay for media we use. That same consulting firm figures that during 2010 firms spent about $370 billion to support media content and services we receive. How can that be? Well, if you think about it, you'll realize that much of the content that you receive is supported by advertising. You listen to the radio, and it doesn't cost you. You may pay a cable bill, but you could receive CBS television over the air (or online) for free. If you subscribe to a magazine, the fee is likely only half the magazine firm's cost of producing the issues you receive. In all these cases, companies pay for the content so that they can send messages (ads) to you to persuade you to purchase particular products and services.

It turns out, though, that the $370 billion includes more than advertising. Advertising is the company support of media that we can see. Under the hood of the converging media world, though, are activities that also support media firms but in a more hidden and indirect way than advertising. They fall under the label "public relations." Consider a local television news reporter who is trying to think up a story for the weekend broadcast. A representative of the largest museum in the area suggests a story about the Van Gogh exhibit that has just started there. The representative provides the reporter with great video regarding the paintings and the artist. Can you see

how that kind of activity is an important indirect media support? It gives the reporter a useful idea and supplies material that could have been expensive for the television station to create by itself. The museum, in turn, receives the ability to call attention to its new presentation on a major television outlet. Multiply such TV news spots by similar activities thousands and thousands of times a day across virtually every media firm, big and small. That's a lot of media support. You can see, then, that public relations (PR) and advertising are crucial support systems for the media. This chapter explores how they work, including how advertising and PR often combine in new forms under the umbrella of marketing communications. We will see that the advertising and PR industries help media platforms pay the bills while performing other important activities for companies they represent. In doing so, advertising and PR exert major influence on media content. We will see how social observers debate whether the widespread influence of advertising and public relations practitioners has had problematic consequences for the view of life the media present. Let's start with an overview of the advertising industry.

## The Advertising Industry

**A**dvertising is the activity of explicitly paying for media space or time in order to direct favorable attention to certain goods or services. Three points about this definition deserve emphasis. First, advertisers pay for the space or time that they receive. Second, advertising clearly states its presence. When you see an ad, you know what it is for, and you often know quite easily who is sponsoring it. Third, advertising involves persuasion—the ability or power to induce an individual or group of individuals to undertake a course of action or embrace a point of view by means of argument, reasoning, or emotional plea.

Advertising is a large and widespread operation, and as we suggested previously, the amount of money advertisers shell out is impressive. Table 4.1 provides details about what advertisers spend on particular media. According to the consultancy firm Veronis Suhler Stevenson, in 2010 advertisers in the United States spent around $61 billion in support of television programming and about $15.5 billion to fund radio broadcasting. In addition, the ad industry spent $30.3 billion on advertisements in newspapers (including their online and mobile versions), compared with the $9.8 billion that consumers shelled out to buy the papers. Advertisers funded consumer magazines (including their online and mobile versions) to the tune of about $11 billion, and consumers dropped a smaller $8.8 billion into the periodicals' coffers. When it came to supporting internet and mobile platforms that are unattached to traditional media brands—industry people call them pure-play digital platforms, from websites to mobile apps to tablets—advertisers put out about $22 billion to support them. The total amount is huge. As Table 4.1 indicates, Veronis Suhler Stevenson

**advertising**
the activity of explicitly paying for media space or time in order to direct favorable attention to certain goods or services

**Table 4.1** Advertising Spending by Media Industry, 2010 versus 2005*

| Industry | US$ billions | |
|---|---|---|
| | 2010 | 2005 |
| Broadcast television | 45.2 | 42.3 |
| Subscription television | 30.0 | 21.4 |
| Newspapers | 30.3 | 55.1 |
| Pure-play internet** | 19.7 | 8.8 |
| Broadcast and satellite radio | 15.6 | 20.1 |
| Consumer directories/yellow pages | 11.5 | 15.4 |
| Consumer magazines | 11.7 | 13.1 |
| Business-to-business media | 9.2 | 9.1 |
| Pure-play mobile | 1.2 | 0.12 |
| Out-of-home*** | 7.8 | 6.6 |
| Other entertainment-based advertising**** | 1.2 | 0.33 |
| Total | 183.5 | 177.7 |

*Numbers for traditional media industries include online advertising activities within these industries.

**Includes digital revenues for firms (e.g., Salon) with no traditional media counterpart.

***Includes billboards, kiosks, mall boards, transit ads, and other outdoor vehicles.

****Includes cinema advertising, in-game video game advertising, and advertising on film, music, video game, and consumer book websites. Does not include advergaming or product placement in video games; these are considered marketing services, not advertising.

estimated that in 2010 about $183.51 billion was spent in the United States on all types of advertising. As you can see, that is actually almost $6 billion less than the media industry spent in 2005.

You will also notice that the decisions by advertisers regarding what media to fund have changed as well. Newspapers have lost out, whereas the internet has won many advertising dollars. In future chapters, we explore reasons for these changes. But you can imagine that when advertisers start removing their money from particular media industries in large amounts, that can ignite great anxiety among people in those industries. The plummeting advertising in newspapers, for example, has led to much speculation about the future of that business. By contrast, the huge increases in pure-play internet advertising (think of Google and Facebook as examples) have caused enormous positive excitement among entrepreneurs that the advertising industry will support their digital plans.

## An Overview of the Modern Advertising Industry

The number of companies involved in advertising is also huge. Just about every business advertises somewhere. Sometimes the executives of the business write the ads themselves and then place them in newspapers and magazines. Other times—and this is particularly true of larger firms—the executives turn to companies that specialize in the creation of ads and their placement in media that accept payment for exhibiting those ads. These companies are called **advertising agencies**. The companies that hire them and pay for their work are called advertisers. In the ad industry, when

**advertising agencies**
companies that specialize in the creation of ads for placement in media that accept payment for exhibiting those ads

an agency takes on an advertiser's business, it is said to take on an account.

The biggest advertising agencies are owned by large companies known as **agency holding companies**. These are umbrella firms that own two or more ad agencies, plus research firms, public relations consultancies, or other organizations that contribute to the business of selling products, services, or ideas. Such holding companies offer clients a range of services beyond advertising, including public relations. They own more than one agency under their conglomerate umbrella to be able to serve firms that compete with one another. Traditionally, companies would not think of giving business to an agency that has such **client conflicts** for fear that confidential information might be shared among employees and get to competitors. If a totally different agency network is involved, though, most advertisers don't mind—even if both agencies are controlled by one firm. They accept the claim that those parts of the two businesses are kept quite separate. As Table 4.2 shows, the top eight holding companies (which are by far the biggest) have substantial business outside the United States. In fact, in 2006 only one, Interpublic, made more than half of its revenue in the United States.

Whether or not they are owned by a holding company, the largest agencies tend to be located in the largest cities, especially New York, Chicago, and Los Angeles. But big cities are by no means the only sites for ad agencies. There are about 3,000 advertising agencies in the United States, and they are scattered throughout the country. Ad agencies range from one-site operations with just a few people to organizations with several offices and thousands of employees. The kinds of things ad agencies do also vary. We can describe them along four dimensions:

- Business-to-business agencies versus consumer agencies
- General agencies versus specialty agencies
- Traditional agencies versus direct-marketing agencies
- Agency networks versus stand-alone firms

Many people have found it interesting to watch the series *Mad Men*, which follows an advertising agency during the 1960s.

**agency holding companies**
firms that own full-service advertising agencies, specialty agencies, direct-marketing firms, research companies, and even public relations agencies

**client conflicts**
situations that occur when agencies serve companies that compete with one another

**Table 4.2** The "Big Eight" Marketing Agency Holding Companies, 2011

| Holding company | Headquarters | Worldwide revenues ($) | U.S. revenue ($) | U.S. percentage of total revenue |
| --- | --- | --- | --- | --- |
| WPP Group | Dublin | 16.10 billion | 5.05 billion | 31 |
| Omnicom Group | New York | 13.87 billion | 7.10 billion | 51 |
| Publicis Group | Paris | 8.01 billion | 2.95 billion | 37 |
| Interpublic Group | New York | 7.02 billion | 3.78 billion | 54 |
| Dentsu | Tokyo | 4.10 billion | 316 million | 3 |
| Havas | Suresnes, France | 2.30 billion | 724 million | 31 |
| Hakuhodo DY Holdings | Tokyo | 1.90 billion | 0 | 0 |
| Aegis Groupy | London | 1.82 billion | 198 million | 10 |

Source: *Advertising Age*, http://adage.com/5388/datacenter/datapopup.php?article_id=234318, accessed May 2, 2012.

**business-to-business agencies**
advertising agencies that carry out work for companies that are interested in persuading personnel in other companies to buy from them instead of from their competitors

**consumer agencies**
advertising agencies that carry out work for advertisers that want to persuade people in their nonwork roles to buy products

**general ad agency**
an advertising agency that invites business from all types of advertisers

**specialty ad agency**
an advertising agency that tackles only certain types of clients (and accounts)

**internet agency**
an advertising company that promotes its expertise in understanding the technology for reaching people online, for creating the ads and websites that will lead to customer responses, and for measuring those responses

**direct-to-consumer (DTC)**
a type of advertising used most effectively by the pharmaceutical industry, which presents a prescription drug as a medial solution and encourages viewers to ask their physician to order the medicine if appropriate

**traditional ad agency**
an advertising agency that creates and distributes persuasive messages with the aim of creating a favorable impression of the product in the minds of target consumers that will lead them to buy it in stores

**direct-marketing agencies**
agencies that focus on consumer mailings, telephone marketing contacts, TV commercials, and other appeals to target audiences so as to elicit purchases right then and there

**agency networks**
advertising agencies with branch offices in a number of different cities worldwide

**Business-to-Business Agencies versus Consumer Agencies.** **Business-to-business agencies** work for companies that are interested in persuading personnel in other companies to buy from them instead of from their competitors. For example, a zipper manufacturer might want to inform a pants manufacturer about its great new development in the fly business. **Consumer agencies**, by contrast, work for advertisers that want to persuade people in their nonwork roles to buy products. An agency that touts a client's cereal to children and their parents is one example. Individual agencies typically do not do both.

**General Agencies versus Specialty Agencies.** A **general ad agency** invites business from all types of advertisers, whereas a **specialty ad agency** tackles only certain types of clients. One type of specialty agency that works in both the consumer and business-to-business areas is the **internet agency**. This is a company that promotes its expertise in understanding the technology for reaching people online, for creating the ads and websites that will lead to customer responses, and for measuring those responses. A different type of specialty agency deals with health care advertising. A big source of clients is the pharmaceutical industry because firms in this industry are constantly competing to persuade physicians that their prescription products are best. In recent years, pharmaceutical firms' desire to get consumers to nudge their doctors to order new prescription drugs for them has led to a specialty called **direct-to-consumer (DTC)** pharmaceutical advertising, and ad firms focusing on that business have developed. Advertising to ethnic and racial groups is also a big specialty in the consumer area. You can find agencies that claim to have particular knowledge of how to persuade African Americans, others that tout their abilities to move Latinos to buy, others that go after Irish Americans, and still others that specialize in Asian or Russian immigrants—and the list can go on.

**Traditional Agencies versus Direct-Marketing Agencies.** A **traditional ad agency** creates and distributes persuasive messages with the aim of creating a favorable impression of the product in the minds of target consumers that will lead them to buy it in stores. **Direct-marketing agencies** have a different mandate. Their job is not just to create a favorable image that will eventually result in purchases; they also have to shape consumer mailings, telephone marketing contacts, TV commercials, and other appeals to target audiences so as to elicit purchases right then and there. Traditional advertising practitioners generally consider direct-marketing approaches more gruff, fast-talking, and even obnoxious than the traditional rhetorical tools. For their part, direct-marketing people believe that they are the only ones who really show that advertising can sell things, given that the results are immediate: either people buy the product, or they don't.

**Agency Networks versus Stand-Alone Firms.** The biggest advertising agencies tend to be traditional, consumer-oriented companies (see Table 4.3). They often have offices in a number of cities in the United States as well as in foreign countries; the trade press calls firms such as these **agency networks**. These types of agencies are different from firms that have only one location. The agency networks typically work for large national advertisers such as Procter & Gamble (P&G), Philip Morris, General Motors, Sears, Ford, and McDonald's. Because national advertisers tend to sell many products, they will often appoint a number of ad agencies to work for them, each working on a different product or a different set of products.

Specialty racial and ethnic firms sometimes enter the mix. For example, in addition to relying on Saatchi and Saatchi for general advertising of Pampers, P&G called

**Table 4.3** Top 10 Agency Networks, Ranked by 2012 Worldwide Network Revenue

| Rank | Agency (Parent) | Headquarters | Worldwide revenue ($ millions) |
| --- | --- | --- | --- |
| 1 | Dentsu (Dentsu) | Tokyo | 3,409 |
| 2 | Young & Rubicam Brands (WPP) | New York | 3,280 |
| 3 | McCann World Group (Interpublic) | New York | 2,920 |
| 4 | DBB World Communications Group (Omnicom) | New York | 2,223 |
| 5 | Ogilvy & Mather (WPP) | New York | 2,343 |
| 6 | BBDO Worldwide (Omnicom) | New York | 2,323 |
| 7 | TWBA Worldwide (Omnicom) | New York | 1,700 |
| 8 | Publicis Worldwide (Publicis) | Paris | 1,400 |
| 9 | DraftFCB (Interpublic Group of COS) | New York | 1,400 |
| 10 | Euro RSCG Worldwide (Havas) | New York | 1,328 |

Note: A portion of revenues of some of these firms come from divisions that carry out public relations and other activities not under the traditional definition of advertising.

Source: *Advertising Age*, http://gaia.adage.com/images/random/datacenter/2012/agencynetworks2012.pdf, accessed May 2, 2012).

on Burrell Communications Group in Chicago for its advertising to African American consumers. It used Conill in Miami to pitch Pampers to Hispanics.

Popular books, movies, magazine articles, and television shows encourage most people to think of a large and powerful "full-service" ad agency such as JWT or Young and Rubicam when they think about the advertising industry. In today's complex marketing world, though, even large agencies such as JWT work with other organizations in the industry to carry out the three basic functions of ad work: **creative persuasion**, **market research**, and **media planning and buying**. We can explain how these three functions are carried out by exploring how they fit into the three basic activities of media industries: production, distribution, and exhibition.

## Production in the Advertising Industry

It is through their work with their clients that the biggest advertising agencies channel hundreds of millions, even billions, of dollars into various media—a major source of support for American media industries. But the advertising industry does not really spend its money to support media. It spends money to persuade people to buy products, services, or ideas. How does it go about doing that?

The production of persuasive advertising messages goes on with the approval and often the direct involvement of executives from the client/advertiser. To ensure that clients continually understand what the agency is doing for their products, agency heads appoint an **account executive** for every account. The job of the account executive is to move information between the advertiser and the agency as well as to make sure that all production, distribution, and exhibition activities take place as planned.

Production activities involve the individuals whose work relates directly to the creation of their firm's media materials; people in the ad industry call such individuals **creatives** or **creative personnel**. They include copywriters (who write the words for the ads), art directors (who guide the creation of artwork), print production personnel

**creative persuasion**
the set of imaginative activities involved in producing and creating advertisements

**market research**
research whose end goal is gathering information that will help an organization sell more products or services

**media planning and buying**
a function of advertising involving purchasing media space and/or time on strategically selected outlets that are deemed best-suited to carry a client's ad message

**account executive**
a person who moves information between the advertiser and the agency and also makes sure that all production, distribution, and exhibition activities take place as planned

**creatives** or **creative personnel**
people whose work relates directly to the creation of their firm's media materials

**Figure 4.1**

Structure of a typical advertising agency

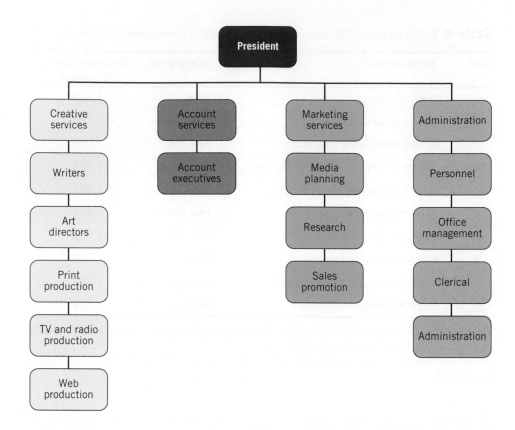

(who supervise the final production of magazine and newspaper ads), and TV–radio production personnel (who supervise the final production of TV and radio commercials) (see Figure 4.1).

But the work of the creatives does not take place in a vacuum. Copywriters and art directors generally do not concoct a print ad or TV commercial out of just any ideas that come to them. On the contrary, they work hard to determine which ideas will lead target consumers to purchase the product. Typically, a client does not expect that an ad will be directed toward the entire population. For example, a cosmetics company would generally expect its lipstick ads to be directed to women (not men). However, for reasons having to do with the nature of the lipstick or the company's marketing strategy, company executives may want to advertise a particular lipstick to a few specific groups of women—say, women from 18 to 34 years or executive women from 18 to 34 years. Dividing society into different categories of consumers is an activity called **market segmentation**. Agency creatives must understand the segments they are aiming at before they produce their ads. In fact, both when ad agency executives are competing for new business and when they are working on products for current clients, they place a high priority on learning a lot about both the product they are seeking to represent and the audience they are trying to reach. What are the product's strengths? What do consumers think about it? What kinds of people buy it? Who are the best potential customers? Why do they—or don't they—buy the product?

**market segmentation**
dividing society into different categories of consumers

## THINKING ABOUT MEDIA LITERACY

Think about an advertisement directed to an audience that you don't belong to. What market segment is it trying to reach and how? Why do you think it is trying to reach that market and not others?

Answering these questions often requires drawing on the market research function of the ad agency. Such research might involve compiling the results of previous investigations on the product or its competitors. It might involve commissioning original surveys or experiments with potential customers to check the persuasiveness of a new ad or the success of one that already has been introduced to the marketplace. It might involve joining other firms in ongoing "syndicated" studies that inquire about social trends, general product use, media habits, or other characteristics of the American population.

Through these and other approaches, researchers construct detailed portraits of the intended audience and its position within the society at large. Then creatives mix those portraits with their own sensibilities and apply the results to their work. Armed with these imaginings, a creative team can concoct a **sales pitch**—a message that portrays the world of the intended audience, a problem in that world, and actions that show how the product can solve that problem.

The next step is to illustrate the sales pitch in stories and settings that the creatives believe the target audience will accept. Often an agency develops different campaigns for distinct audiences. Editing and casting decisions take into consideration research findings about how different audiences look at the product and the world. This approach enables agencies to create an image of the product that matches what they believe will lead various audiences to feel good about the product and to purchase it.

**sales pitch**
a presentation to a client, portraying the world of the client's intended audience and actions, to show how the client's product is valuable in that world

## MEDIA TODAY & CULTURE ASIAN AMERICAN STEREOTYPES AND AD CAMPAIGNS

According to the Pew Research Center, Asian Americans now represent the fastest-growing ethnic group in the United States.[1] This population boasts the highest income and best education rates, ahead of African Americans, Hispanics, and whites.[2] As such, advertisers have found them a desirable market to try to reach. However, the advertising still relies on stereotypical representations of Asian Americans.

One stereotype used in representing Asian Americans is the model minority. The model minority possesses a strong work ethic, attains higher educational degrees, and understands business environments well.

Another stereotype associates Asian Americans with technology. They are shown as experts on technology's uses and developments. For example, an ad for Verizon shows a salesperson offering a smartphone with gaming, geopositioning, video and still cameras, e-reader, and several hundred thousand apps to a customer carrying around separate devices for all those functions on a belt. The customer is white, and the salesperson is Asian American.[3]

In another example, Metro PCS developed a series of commercials with characters Ranjit and Chad, two cell phone tech-support types who tout the benefits of Metro PCS's plans. Ranjit and Chad are of Indian descent, playing on the stereotyping that many call-center support employees are from India but also drawing on the intelligence associated with technology and its operation. Debates emerged around whether these commercials were racist.[4] Some critics predicted that the campaign would fail, but sales increased more than 20 percent during the quarter the ads debuted.[5]

At first glance, these stereotypes appear to be positive ones, and in these commercials they are used for humor, not harm. But to cast all Asian Americans in this light overlooks the vast diversity of experiences and backgrounds among this group. It creates an unrealistic picture that some members of the group find themselves being pushed to conform to or being teased about. And the stereotype is being used to sell a product in the end.

Advertising holds an enormous influence in culture, yet it relies on stereotypes of Asian Americans and other groups to sell products. Why do you think the advertising industry relies on these stereotypes instead of trying to change them? What do you think the industry could do differently? Do you think the changes might be effective? Why or why not?

**branding**
creating a specific image of a product that makes it stand out in the marketplace

Creating a specific image of a product that makes it stand out in the marketplace is called **branding** it. Ad practitioners consider the creation and nurturing of these product images—these brands—to be among their most important activities. The reason is their belief that people will pay more for a well-regarded brand than for a product they do not know or about which they have a bad feeling. Think about it: Which would you rather buy from your supermarket for a party—Pepsi or Coke (whichever you prefer) or something called Pop-Soda Cola? Even if your supermarket guarantees the quality of Pop-Soda Cola and says it tastes "like the big guys," and even if it's a dollar less expensive, you might feel funny serving it to your guests. Chances are you would choose Pepsi or Coke. These are brands you trust; perhaps, after years of seeing commercials, you may even think that these products *belong* at parties.

## Distribution in the Advertising Industry

Creating a series of ads and spending money to test them would be totally useless if the ad agency had no idea how and where to distribute them. Decisions on how to distribute ads have been affected by improvements in technology. Because of cooperation between ad agencies and media firms, now ad practitioners can actually send finished print and television ads directly to media outlets by satellite. In some cases, print ads can be sent in digital form directly to the computers of the magazines or newspapers in which they will appear. From that standpoint, distribution of ads is constantly getting easier.

Because media fragmentation has dramatically increased the number of ad vehicles, however, deciding where to place advertisements is not getting easier; instead, it is becoming more and more challenging. Making these decisions is the work of an agency's **media planners**. To get an idea of the challenges they face, think of where you would place TV commercials for GEICO Insurance if that firm wanted to reach young adults. Where, too, would you place web ads that aim to convey the same message about the company to young adults?

**media planners**
agency personnel who make decisions about where to place advertisements

The answer is that media planners track computerized data about the number and kinds of people that various media outlets (specific magazines, radio stations, or TV networks) reach. Much of this information about individual media outlets is collected in syndicated studies by audience research firms such as Nielsen (for television and cable) and comScore and Nielsen NetRatings (for the internet); the Traffic Audit Bureau and Nielsen Outdoor (for billboard advertising); Arbitron and RADAR (for local and network radio); the Audit Bureau of Circulation (for newspapers and magazines); and Simmons and MRI (for magazines). Sometimes the planners pay attention to custom research findings presented to them by individual media firms that want to impress them with further details. The custom research may add to the demographic data that syndicated research provides; for example, it might explore the religious affiliations or occupations of an audience. The research might present **psychographic data**, information that links demographic categories to the personality characteristics of an audience—for instance, whether they are "materialistic" or "confident" or people who want to lead rather than follow.

**psychographic data**
information that links demographic categories to personality characteristics of an audience

The research might also provide details about the lifestyles of the audience that could impress potential advertisers: how many vacations they took last year, what cars they drive, whether they play golf regularly. *Seventeen* magazine executives, for example, might commission research about how many of their teen readers have begun to use cosmetics or go to the movies each week or own cars. They then would present these data to potential cosmetic, movie, and car advertisers in the hope of convincing them to include *Seventeen* in their **media plan**—that is, in the list of media outlets in which they advertise their products.

Outdoor and in-store media are of increasing importance for some marketers, and an insurance company such as GEICO may be one such marketer. Outdoor media encompass a great variety of stationary billboards and signs as well as moving media such as buses and trains. The term "**in-store media**" refers to a raft of print and audiovisual ads that people see when they walk into retail spaces. In a growing number of supermarkets, a company called MediaCart sells ads on grocery carriages. Supermarkets show videos and ads at checkout too. In stores such as Wal-Mart and Best Buy, PRN Corporation (owned by Thomson) sells ad space on checkout screens. Captivate Network, a company owned by the Gannett newspaper firm, sets up screens in office building elevators that run ads along with entertainment, weather, or news. Accent-Health, a company owned by Discovery Holdings, has TV screens with CNN clips and targeted ads in more than 10,000 doctors' offices across the country. And supermarket firms fill their stores with the audio announcements of sales, shelf signs, floor mats with ads, and video screens showing ads at checkout. The locations for ads seem to be boundless. To hype its shows during 2007, CBS even had a company stamp 35 million supermarket eggs with its trademark "eye" logo, as well as the names and logos of the programs in its fall television lineup.

In evaluating a media outlet, media planners examine syndicated and custom demographic, psychographic, and lifestyle research to decide whether the audience segment they are aiming at can be found at that outlet. If it can, the planners then ask the following questions:

- What is the outlet's reach with respect to (ad planners use the term "against") the target audience? That is, what percentage of the entire target audience (say, teenage girls) will the outlet reach?
- Considering the costs of running an ad there, how efficient is the outlet in reaching that audience compared with other outlets?

In studying *Seventeen* for a makeup client, ad planners may find that it sells 22 million copies, the overwhelming percentage of which are sold to teenage girls. Moreover, *Seventeen* provides lifestyle research that contends that many of these readers are trying makeup for the first time. Just as important, the planners learn that although the cost of buying space for a four-color, full-page ad in *Seventeen* is similar to the cost of buying such an ad in women's magazines with larger circulations, the **cost per thousand (CPM)** of teenage girls is quite a bit lower. That is because of the selectivity of the magazine: magazines such as *Glamour* reach lots of teenage girls, but an advertiser would not be able to target an edition directly to them, and so much of the ad money would be wasted. Because *Seventeen* reaches virtually only teenage girls, the CPM of the target audience is lower.

This factor makes *Seventeen* an efficient buy compared with women's magazines, but how does *Seventeen* compare with *Teen Vogue*, for example, or with MTV? Ad planners have to study their own research, their syndicated research, and the research presented to them by the magazine and cable companies to make a decision. They might decide to see whether one or another of the teen magazines would give them a discount for the bulk of the makeup ad money. Or they might discuss the pros and cons of splitting their ad purchases equally among major teen periodicals and teen-oriented cable networks.

**media plan**
the list of media outlets in which companies advertise their products

**in-store media**
the print and audiovisual ads that people see when they walk into retail spaces

**cost per thousand (CPM)**
the basic measurement of advertising efficiency in all media; it is used by advertisers to evaluate how much space they will buy in a given medium and what price they will pay

Considerations such as these constantly occupy media planners. Perhaps by now you're beginning to get a strong sense of how powerful the decisions they make are to the success or failure of particular media companies. The executives of newspaper firms, magazine companies, websites, television stations, and even TV networks worry constantly whether they are reaching the types of people advertisers want to reach. If market research shows they are not reaching the right targets, the firms may well change their content to try to attract the ones advertisers want to reach. During the late 2000s, for example, a few radio stations in Philadelphia learned, based on a new audience-measurement device, that they were not reaching nearly enough of the kinds of listeners advertisers wanted. A few stations drastically changed the music they played—and the DJs who introduced the music—as a result.

## Exhibition in the Advertising Industry

**ad campaign**
the entire set of advertisements using a particular theme to promote a certain product for a certain period of time

The goal of the production and distribution of an ad is to exhibit it across a variety of media to a target audience. Once the media plan for an **ad campaign**—the entire set of advertisements using a particular theme to promote a certain product for a certain period of time—has been created, it is up to the advertisers' media buyers to carry it out. The buyers often work for separate media-buying companies. (Although Martin Agency creates and produces GEICO's ads, it works with Horizon Media to plan ad-placement strategy; Horizon does the actual buying.) Every mass media firm publishes its rates for space or time. It also makes a pitch for different target audiences that advertisers crave. For example, MTV's online division has organized its sales staff to sell to advertisers "against" three psychographic groups: kids and family, men and gaming enthusiasts, and youth music. The division's digital sales director noted in 2006 that the company was reaching over 30 million unique visitors per month and so could deliver the large numbers—the "online scale"—that advertisers want.[1]

For media buyers representing large advertisers, however, these charges are just the starting point. They dangle the large amounts of cash that they control as they attempt to negotiate discounts from the basic rates. Media firms, for their part, know that buyers like to follow audiences across different platforms. So, for example, Fox's *House* in 2009 created a webpage for fans to express their regrets about a character who had inexplicably committed suicide on one of the season's episodes.

Eventually, with the right technology, the goal is to help advertisers track individuals across many media, so as to reach them when they are most ready to receive ads. One hint of the way that might happen relates to mobile phone companies' ability to track their customers' locations. If the customers agree, the companies can send them

During the 2012 Olympic Games, Procter & Gamble launched a massive and memorable ad campaign titled "Thanks, Mom" in which they focused on the important role "Mom" plays in helping young athletes achieve their dreams of participating in the Olympics. In addition to the series of commercials on television, there were online and social media campaigns linked to this ad campaign.

Thank you, Mom by P&G
506,755 likes · 26,084 talking about this

reports and e-mail blasts aimed at shareholders as well as news firms that reach the general public or a their particular industry. Their internal relations counterparts also may use media to communicate to their large number of employees. They may do so through websites, e-mail summaries of company developments, or (in really big companies) even video news programs about the company for employees in offices around the globe.

Just as the work of PR departments in companies often involves fueling media content of one sort or another, so public relations agencies often aim to "subsidize" media firms with content that benefits their clients. The U.S. Census Bureau found more than 7,000 public relations firms in the United States in 2006. Companies large and small hire such "outside" PR companies for various projects, ranging from special lobbying that may or may not involve the media to getting or controlling media exposure. Public relations companies often charge fees based on the number of hours that their employees work for a client. Sometimes clients make "retainer" deals with an agency, under which the company agrees to carry out a PR program at an agreed-upon rate per month.

Not all public relations companies do the same things. Large firms such as Fleishman-Hillard help their clients with virtually any area of communication, including teaching their top executives how to speak on TV and in front of large groups. Many smaller public relations firms, however, specialize in a particular part of their industry's work. Examples of medium-size independent agencies that specialize include Healthstar, a health care agency; Cerrell Associates, a public affairs and environmental agency; and Integrated Corporate Relations, a company that helps firms speak to stock analysts, institutional investors, financial media, and other corporate audiences.

The biggest public relations firms are widely considered to be Fleishman-Hillard, Weber Shandwick, Hill & Knowlton Strategies, Burson-Marsteller, Incepta, Edelman Worldwide, BSMG Worldwide, Ogilvy PR, Porter Novelli, and Ketchum. All of these companies with the exception of Edelman and Incepta are owned by one of the agency holding companies known as **the Big Four** Omnicom, WPP, Interpublic, and Publicis (see Table 4.4). As we noted earlier, agency holding companies are firms that own large ad agency networks, public relations firms, and a multitude of branding, market research, and marketing communications firms.

**the Big Four**
the largest agency holding companies, including Omnicom, WPP, Interpublic, and Publicis

**Table 4.4** Major PR Firms Owned by Large Agency Holding Companies

| WPP | Omnicom Group | Interpublic | Publicis |
| --- | --- | --- | --- |
| Burson-Marsteller | Fleishman-Hillard | Weber Shandwick | Publicis Consultants Public Relations |
| Hill & Knowlton | Ketchum | Golin Harris | Schwartz Communications |
| Cohn and Wolfe | Porter Novelli | Rogers & Cowan | Hanmer MSL (India) |
| Ogilvy PR | Brodeur Worldwide | PMK/HBH | Genedigi (China) |
| Carl Byoir | Clark and Weinstock | Carmichael Lynch Spong | |
| GCI Health | Cone | | |
| Dewey Square Group | | | |

Sources: Holding company websites.

Global reach is key to the activities of the biggest firms. Hill & Knowlton Strategies, part of the WPP holding company, reports on its website that it has 83 offices in 46 countries throughout the world. "Our firm has been in the wisdom business for more than 80 years," says its CEO on the firm's website,

> and our world-class teams of trusted advisors and creative experts have a wealth of experience in strengthening brands, reputations and bottom lines. Our teams collaborate across time zones, languages and cultures to engage in public conversations that help clients make solid decisions and craft compelling messages.[3]

## THINKING ABOUT MEDIA LITERACY

Why do you think globalization plays such an important role in both advertising and public relations? Can you think of any public relations examples that became global news or issues? What did the company do to get media attention, and how did the company respond to it?

Especially prominent public relations activities fall into these areas:

- Corporate communications
- Financial communications
- Health care
- Public affairs
- Crisis management

The biggest firms tackle many of these categories, though not always all of them. Moreover, some companies may combine one or another category in organizing their expertise and personnel. Table 4.5 defines each of these activities and gives an example of the ways a public relations agency may influence hard news and soft news in carrying it out for a client. (For a discussion of these news forms, see chapter 2.) The examples suggest the broad range of clients these agencies serve and the wide range of topics we see and hear in various media that result from such public relations activities.

How does this work of placing topics and products into the media get accomplished? As we did with advertising, we can answer by approaching the activities through the lenses of production, distribution, and exhibition.

### Production in the Public Relations Industry

We've already noted that the term "media relations" covers all dealings with members of media organizations who might tell a story about a client. Much of that work involves hard news or soft news. In some of these dealings, journalists take the initiative—for example, when reporters want to know what is going on during a company crisis. Other dealings with the media take place at the initiative of PR practitioners who want to spread the word about their clients' activities. Your university probably uses a PR staff to spread good news about research that is being carried out and about the success of its sports teams. The goal is to make both alumni and current students so proud of the institution that they will want to donate money.

**Table 4.5** Examples of Ways Public Relations Agencies May Influence Media Content through Prominent Public Relations Activities

| Activity | Definition | Type of client and aim | Influence on hard news | Influence on soft news |
|---|---|---|---|---|
| Corporate communications | The creation and presentation of a company's overall image to its employees and to the public at large | An automobile manufacturer wants to spread the notion that it is a technologically advanced yet socially responsible company. | The firm sponsors a coast-to-coast solar-car race named after the company on college campuses and makes sure all the local TV and radio stations in the areas of the cars cross cover the race. | The company convinces the star of an action TV series to work with the team from his college alma mater. The company donates a car to a charity the actor chooses. |
| Financial communications | Helping a client's interactions with lenders, shareholders, and stock market regulators proceed smoothly | A pharmaceutical firm wants its shareholders to trust that the firm's management is doing excellent work guiding new drugs with great profit potential to market. | The company's public relations firm offers a popular newsmagazine an exclusive look at the firm's state-of-the art drug-innovation facilities. The company places the newsmagazine's article and mails copies to shareholders. | |
| Health care | Helping hospitals, health maintenance organizations, pharmaceutical firms, and provider organizations such as the American Medical Association and the American Nursing Association in relation to government regulations, international sales, tensions with organizations that purchase their goods and services, and confused, angry, and even frightened members of the public | A major medical center wants to encourage people bordering on high obesity to visit the medical center's new weight-loss clinics in different cities across the United States. | On the day the clinic chain opens, the director manages to land a *Today Show* interview in which she champions the mix of exercise and drugs that the clinic offers for severely obese people. | On the day the drug is released, the firm manages to schedule an interview on HLN and *The Tonight Show* with a well-known actress who lost 50 pounds using a new drug the clinic has been testing in clinical trials. |
| Public affairs | Helps companies that depend on government contracts that worry about lawmakers imposing regulations that will have negative effects on the firms | A large internet advertising firm is concerned that the public is angry at the firm for gathering information about its audiences without their explicit opt-in permission. The worry is that large numbers of people might encourage Congress to push for opt-in laws. | The company's public relations firm makes the advertising firm's persuasive CEO available to editorial boards of major newspapers to lay out his belief that the audiences are happy with an opt-out approach that allows them to stop the gathering of information if they like. | The company's PR firm persuades that charismatic CEO to play the saxophone at the South by Southwest Festival in Austin, TX, with the hope that his musicianship—and he—will get wide favorable press coverage. That, the PR firm believes, might move people to be favorable toward the firm. |
| Crisis management | The range of activities that help a company respond to its business partners, the general public, or the government in the event of an unforeseen disaster affecting its image or products | A petroleum company responsible for a huge oil spill in the Gulf of Mexico wants the public and the government to believe it is doing the cleanup correctly and with the residents of the area in mind. | The firm's CEO makes the rounds of the major TV news networks with news of the company's huge donation to the towns affected by the oil spill as well as its rollout of new technologies that will make such oil spills "nearly impossible." | A popular singer whose parents live in one of the towns getting the donation agrees to appear on celebrity news programs and *Nightline* with baby birds who recently hatched in the area where the oil company paid for the cleanup. |

PR practitioners often spread news by building good relationships with relevant journalists and editors. That way, the public relations staff will have the best chance at getting its organization's desired point of view across in a media story. Getting a desired viewpoint across usually means more than just answering incoming calls and sending out information. Most media relations work is proactive. So in addition to providing interested parties with relevant facts and information for their stories, PR staff members have to go the extra mile by doing much of the journalists' job for them—for example, thinking up, selling, and sometimes even writing sample stories.

Of course, journalists have the final word on which stories they'll choose to write or rewrite and finally run, and they are often suspicious of their PR contacts. In addition, journalists have a large number of choices among PR-initiated stories, given that so many companies are involved in media relations activities. These two circumstances create a lot of pressure on the PR practitioner.

**press release**
a short essay that is written in the form of an objective news story

The most basic product of a public relations firm's attempt to influence the media is the **press release**—a short essay that is written in the form of an objective news story. Because the goal is to get a reporter or editor to write about a particular aspect of the client's activities, a successful press release finds a hook in the client's tale that the reporter can use. PR practitioners know that reporters will dismiss as propaganda stories that simply tout the views of the firm's executives or present the firm's accomplishments. The trick is to write a story with an angle that the journalist will see as interesting to her or his audience and that also can include other firms and other points of view. A press release that is too obviously self-serving will rarely get picked up.

Because of the importance of knowing what attracts journalists to particular stories, PR firms and PR departments of organizations often hire former journalists as their press contacts. Hill & Knowlton's LinkedIn page proudly notes,

> We have a reputation for handling complex media situations in positive circumstances as well as in times of crisis. Our media relations professionals—including former journalists, press secretaries and communications officers—have delivered results throughout the world.
>
> Using solid research and analysis, messaging, journalistic skills and close media relationships, we can deliver real business impact.[4]

As these lines suggest, writing press releases is just part of a PR firm's media duties. The company must also hire practitioners who can field questions from members of the press who come to them for stories. PR practitioners are also increasingly involved in reaching out to entertainment companies to coordinate the production of audiovisual materials that present the points of view of their companies to various constituencies. A mobile phone company, for example, might send a video to high schools to describe for students the new technologies it is using to keep rates down while providing the best service. A university might prepare a home page on the internet that gives prospective students tours of the campus. Also important is the role of digital vehicles that encourage target audiences to interact with companies and feel friendly toward them. PR firms help clients set up Facebook pages or Twitter feeds that inform about discounts, answer questions, quash rumors, and exude a likable personality.

Smart companies shift their marketing focus to reflect changing media consumption habits. Others play digital catch-up in order to remain relevant and competitive. Either way, companies need to know how to harness the power of social media by building community around an issue or a brand, driving engagement, and building strong relationships with all audiences—and all this in a way that is open, honest, and genuine.

Companies involved in consumer public relations often decide to reach people in a less-than-open way—by turning out their own TV "news" stories. For example, a computer chip manufacturer might create a short video for use on local news programs that shows how cutting-edge computer chips allow typical home users to perform an enormous number of tasks faster and make these tasks more fun. The trick to getting such a spot on the air is to make it seem like a soft news story created by the TV station. PR practitioners know that they should mention their client, the chip manufacturer, only in passing and show its logo only a couple of times. Subtlety is important. Overtly pushing the company and its products would be the kiss of death for a spot; a news show would never use it.

## Distribution in the Public Relations Industry

Once materials for the media part of a public relations campaign have been prepared, the PR firm must distribute them to the proper publicity outlets. A **publicity outlet** is a media vehicle (e.g., a particular magazine, a specific TV interview program, or a particular radio talk show) that has in the past been open to input from public relations practitioners. "Proper" in this case has two meanings: it refers to both outlets that reach the kinds of people the firm is targeting and outlets that are appropriate for the particular ideas, products, or services that the firm is trying to push.

Public relations practitioners keep lists of the publicity outlets in different areas that are appropriate for different types of products and for reaching different groups of people. When they are working on a particular campaign, they use these lists to determine which outlets to concentrate on and whom to contact. Sometimes only a press release will be sent. At other times, PR practitioners will be so familiar with the individuals involved that they will phone them directly. In fact, having good connections among media people, especially the press corps, is a crucial asset in the PR business.

Advanced distribution technologies also have become crucial to the PR industry during the past few years. PR practitioners use e-mail and (less often) fax machines to send press releases. They pay firms to track the discussions—the buzz—about their clients in chat rooms and on blogs, Facebook, Twitter, and elsewhere, and they respond by paying people to go online and insert comments that reflect the positive spin that fits the aim of the PR campaign. (They're supposed to say they represent the firm, but they don't always do that.) PR practitioners use satellite linkups to set up interviews with TV reporters from around the country and the world for their clients. They also use satellites to send video press releases to appropriate publicity outlets. These are packages of photographs, video clips, and interviews from which a reporter can choose to create a story. A video press release for a new adventure film, for example, might contain short clips from the movie, a background piece on the special effects used to make the movie, and separate as well as combined interviews with the male and female stars. Each piece would be designed to be used as a feature story on a local television newscast. The interviews would be shot in a way that allows news people in local stations to create the impression that the discussion was created exclusively for their broadcasts.

**publicity outlet**
a media vehicle (e.g., a particular magazine, a specific TV interview program, or a particular radio talk show) that has in the past been open to input from public relations practitioners

## Exhibition in the Public Relations Industry

"But," you may ask, "why do TV and print journalists use this material? Don't journalists pride themselves on their objectivity and independence?" Good question. The answer lies in the costs of news reporting in the print and electronic worlds. Costs here relate both to monetary expense and to the amount of time involved. Reporting stories totally from scratch can cost a lot of money. It can also cost reporters an enormous amount of time, time that they often do not have because of deadlines.

Imagine how many reporters the *Washington Post* would have to assign to the Departments of State and Agriculture, the Treasury, and the other cabinet-level divisions of the U.S. government if there were no systematic way to find out about meetings, speeches, reports, and other materials emanating from each. The paper could not afford to ferret out all that information, but it doesn't have to do so because each department's public relations division provides the newspaper with its basic schedule. Moreover, in key parts of the government, such as the State Department, public relations representatives summarize key issues for reporters and answer their questions.

In addition to allowing news organizations to allocate fewer journalists to government agencies, these press briefings help journalists budget their time efficiently. The briefings enable journalists to gather the basic information needed to write their daily stories. They can then spend the rest of their time following up issues raised by the briefings; each journalist hopes that his or her stories will stand out from those of other journalists who were also at the meetings.

As you can see, PR practitioners help the media get their work done. Communication professor Oscar Gandy calls this sort of help to media organizations and their personnel "**information subsidies**." The term means that PR people's help with information is akin to advancing money and time. Faced with a beautifully done clip that is part of a video press release, a TV station's news director may genuinely believe that some of the material in that clip is interesting enough to warrant a story. She or he also knows that the low cost of putting that spot on the air will offset the extra expenses of a locally produced story.

The danger of information subsidies from a client's standpoint is that they may not be used. News organizations receive many more offerings from PR firms than they have room for, and journalists can often be quite selective. The most successful—and most expensive—public relations practitioners work hard to establish strong relationships with members of the press to help grease the path to coverage. In the mid-1990s, the *New York Times* reported that Sard Verbinnen, the head of the PR agency with that name, would get pieces in the news by currying favor with journalists: giving an "exclusive" about a deal or an interview with a chief executive to one newspaper and then offering a behind-the-scenes look at a transaction to a reporter of another paper that did not get the original exclusive. By doing that, he would be able to call on both sources to help him with coverage when he needed it.

For Verbinnen or anyone else, though, coverage doesn't always work out the way the PR practitioner wants it to. Good journalists do their own independent investigations of material suggested by a press release or some other PR initiative. Consequently, what begins as an attempt to present a favorable image of a firm or a person may backfire if the reporter finds material that contradicts the original report.

**information subsidies**
the time and money that PR people provide media practitioners that helps the latter get their work done

# The Rise of Marketing Communications

As we have seen, public relations is potentially very useful but also unpredictable when it comes to getting a company, person, or product specific and favorable mass media coverage aimed at a particular audience. In contrast, advertising can provide quite predictable media coverage (because the advertiser pays for time or space), but it can be quite a bit more expensive than public relations work and may not be as persuasive as PR stories that appear as news.

During the past several years, the awareness that advertising and PR can complement each other has led executives to attempt to coordinate the two types of activities to get the best of both worlds. Some have dubbed this approach **integrated marketing communications (IMC)**, or often simply **marketing communications**. The goal is to blend (integrate) historically different ways to communicate to an organization's various audiences and markets. Under the best of circumstances, integration means creating a campaign that sends different yet consistent messages around particular themes to present and potential consumers of a firm's products as well as to its employees, to the companies that sell to it and buy from it, and to government regulators.

In addition to traditional advertising and public relations, IMC often brings three related activities into its mix: branded entertainment, direct marketing, and relationship marketing. Let's take a look at each.

## Branded Entertainment

**Branded entertainment** involves associating a company or product with media activities in ways that are not as obviously intrusive as advertisements. The word "branded" refers to linking the firm or product's name (and personality) with an activity that the target audience enjoys. The three most common forms of branded entertainment are event marketing, event sponsorship, and product placement.

**Event Marketing** Event marketing involves creating compelling circumstances that command attention in ways that are relevant to the product or firm. These activities typically take place at sports and entertainment venues, by way of mobile trailers or road shows that publicize products, and on college campuses, in malls, and in bars. Some of the activities are termed "grassroots." That is, companies pay nonprofessionals (say, moms who like their products) to set up parties or other meetings that promote the items. These are activities that bring the products in front of people in unusual ways. Other activities are called "guerrilla" events. An example is when a company planted blinking electronic devices around Boston in a publicity stunt for a Cartoon Network show. Figure 4.2 presents the proportions of different forms of event marketing in 2009.

**integrated marketing communications (IMC)** or **marketing communications**
a type of PR, the goal of which is to blend (integrate) historically different ways to communicate to an organization's various audiences and markets

**branded entertainment**
the act of linking the firm or product's name (and personality) with an activity that the target audience enjoys

**event marketing**
creating compelling circumstances that command attention in ways that are relevant to the product or firm. These activities typically take place at sports and entertainment venues, by way of mobile trailers or road shows that publicize products, and on college campuses, in malls, and in bars.

### Figure 4.2
Shares of spending on consumer event marketing, 2009

Note: "Others" includes mall, nightlife, and guerilla marketing.

Source: Veronis Suhler Stevenson, *Communications Forecast 2009–2013* (New York: VSS, 2009), part 3, p. 17.

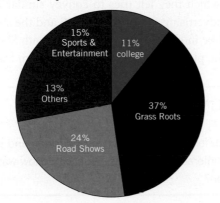

15% Sports & Entertainment
11% college
13% Others
37% Grass Roots
24% Road Shows

Note the placement of company logos throughout the hockey arena of the L.A. Kings indicating their sponsorship of the arena and/or the team.

**event sponsorship**
situation in which companies pay money to be associated with particular activities that their target audiences enjoy or value. Examples include sports, concerts, and charities

**barter**
process by which products used in movies and TV shows are provided by the manufacturer to the producers for free in exchange for the publicity

**product integration**
the act of building plot lines or discussions for talk shows and reality TV around specific brands

Spring break presents huge opportunities for event marketing. If you've gone to Florida or Texas for spring break, you may have seen companies such as Hawaiian Tropics set up bikini pageants. Often, these activities get more elaborate. In 2009, for example, the college network mtvU, aired on more than 750 college campuses around the country, sponsored events that framed spring break in Panama City, Florida. Performers included Lil Wayne, the All American Rejects, Flo Rida, Asher Roth, and Jim Jones. The network also sponsored a $20,000 rock-paper-scissors tournament along with other games and giveaways. MtvU's goal was clearly twofold: first, to get viewers who hadn't traveled to Panama City to watch the events on the cable network and second, to publicize the channel to the Panama City revelers so that they would watch the network when they got back to school and tell others about it.

**Event Sponsorship**  In event marketing, the product is the focus of the activity. By contrast, **event sponsorship** occurs when companies pay money to be associated with particular activities that their target audiences enjoy or value. It happens a lot with sports, concerts, and charities. Sport has long been the largest entertainment-sponsorship category, with NASCAR and the NFL being particular draws for companies. A notable concert sponsorship in 2008 was by the Clorox Company. To promote its KC Masterpiece sauces and Kingsford Charcoal, Clorox paid to support the U.S. stops of singer Keith Urban's tour.

**Product Placement**  Product placement takes place when a firm manages to insert its brand in a positive way into fiction or nonfiction content. Think of AT&T, Ford, and Coca-Cola on the TV series *American Idol* or the appearances of particular car models in movies, TV shows, and video games that you've seen. Traditionally, products used in movies and TV shows were provided by the manufacturer to the producers for free in exchange for the publicity. That is called **barter**, and it still represents the largest percentage of product placement. But in recent years, paid product placement has been increasing, though observers say it still takes place less often than barter. Some marketers have paid producers of so-called reality shows and talk shows to build plot lines or discussions around their brands. The activity is called **product integration**, and it is increasing, particularly online. In 2012, for example, Chrysler's Ram trucks bought a season-long sponsorship of *Longmire*, a drama series on the A&E cable network. Because the show centers on a sheriff whom an A&E executive called "hard-working, tough dependable, and gutsy," network advertising salespeople pitched the sponsorship to Ram, which they felt tries to convey similar qualities. But the deal quickly went beyond advertising sponsorship. A&E and the show's producers agreed that the vehicle would be integrated into the content, with Sheriff Longmore driving it and with points in the plot that would "convey core Ram features."[5]

## THINKING ABOUT MEDIA LITERACY

The next time you watch a television show or a movie, watch for and note the different name-brand products you see. Were the products just visible in the scene, or did the characters interact with them in some way? How was that interaction used? As humor? As character development? Some other motivation?

## Direct Marketing

**Direct marketing** uses media vehicles created by the marketer (phone messages, e-mail, postal mailings) to send persuasive messages asking that the consumers who receive them respond to the marketer. Think of any of the late-night TV commercials you've watched that urge you to phone them via an 800 number or a web ad that asks you to click to buy a product or service. Nowadays, most direct marketing involves **databases**. These are lists of customers and potential customers that can be used to determine what those people might purchase in the future. The marketer contacts the people on these lists with advertising or PR messages. The practice of using these computerized lists is called **database marketing**.

Although the use of lists in marketing dates back to at least the 1800s, the past few decades have seen a huge growth in the use of computers to store information about people and their habits. This growth in marketers' ability to cross-link and retrieve huge amounts of information about people took place at the same time that the introduction of toll-free numbers, more efficient mailing techniques, and fast delivery firms made shopping from home easier than ever in the decades before the internet. These changes led to a huge increase in targeted persuasion through direct marketing.

## Relationship Marketing

**Relationship marketing** involves a determination by the firm to maintain long-term contact with its customers. This can be done by regular mailings of custom magazines, brochures, letters, or e-mails or through frequent user programs that encourage repeat purchases and keep the person connected to the firm.

# Advertising, Public Relations, and Convergence

By this point in the chapter you should be getting a pretty good feel for the idea that advertising, public relations, and marketing communications together exert a substantial impact on the media. Although public relations activities tend to relate to hard and soft news, the same firms that carry out PR also often have divisions that work the entertainment beat for their clients. The *Longmire* series that linked Ram trucks with an A&E cable show provides a good example of the way advertising and marketing communications work together. One can imagine, in fact, how the public relations practitioners could parlay the Ram-*Longmire* linkup into a spot on a celebrity TV show such as *Entertainment Tonight*. The show's producers might well want to interview the show's star, and he might casually insert references to the truck into the conversation. Or perhaps the *ET* people might like the idea of directly describing the ways in which some of Longmire's plots are crafted with the Ram in mind.

With the word "convergence" in this section's heading in mind, you might realize multiple media are often involved as a result of the work that advertising agencies, public relations agencies, and marketing communications specialists perform for their clients. When a PR practitioner puts out a press release, he or she does it with the hope that the story will be picked up by many media outlets. Often the practitioner prepares an audiovisual version along with a print version so that television stations can use the story. And of course the material will show up on the company's websites and on its Facebook and Google+ pages—and people might be drawn to it through Twitter posts and ads on Facebook and Twitter aimed at the kinds of people who would be interested in that aspect of the client's activities. Carried out

**direct marketing**
marketing that uses media vehicles created by the marketer (phone messages, e-mail, postal mailings) to send persuasive messages asking that the consumers who receive them respond to the marketer

**databases**
lists of customers and potential customers that can be used to determine what those people might purchase in the future

**database marketing**
practice of constructing computerized lists of customers and potential customers that can be used to determine what those people might purchase in the future. The marketer then contacts the people on these lists with advertising or PR messages.

**relationship marketing**
a firm's process of maintaining long-term contact with its customers

Actor Adrian Grenier (*Entourage*), Sungevity founder Danny Kennedy, and SHFT's Peter Glatzer attend SHFT Pop-Up Gallery and Shop. Grenier and Glatzer cofounded SHFT and partnered with the auto manufacturer Ford in order to create a greater awareness of the need and possibilities for environmental sustainability.

with skill, stories that benefit the client can nowadays take advantage of media convergence so as to reach substantial percentages of the target audiences at least once—and often more than that.

When marketing communications is added to the advertising and PR mix, the convergence canvas on which companies can work to reach their audience is especially wide. Consider the Ford Motor Company's goal in 2012 to position itself and its cars as a thought leader in sustainability by encouraging consumers to take a more eco-friendly approach to their lives. Some of the marketing initiatives connected to this effort included a nationwide electric vehicle education program in partnership with Green Festival, where the automaker awarded $5,000 grants to green initiatives in major U.S. cities. Ford also donated an electric charging station to more than 25 communities at locations voted on by local residents. All these activities—especially the donations—likely received press coverage in the communities they impacted. To make the case for sustainability more broadly via the media, Ford partnered with a company called SHFT.com, which was founded by Adrian Grenier, an actor who had starred on the HBO series *Entourage*, and Peter Glatzer, a Hollywood producer. SHFT.com created "The Big SHFT: 10 Innovators Changing Our World." The website featured short films profiling 10 innovators who work to affect ecologically sound activities in food, fashion, urbanization, technology, design, and other key areas of life. Ford and SHFT arranged for the programs to run on several platforms, "notably AOL and its Huffington Post property, as well as SHFT.com, Ford's own media properties, and U.S. Virgin Airlines' in-flight entertainment." Ford's hope: that through 2012 Americans would catch a whiff of its campaign in one or another medium and take seriously the idea that the auto[6] company (and its products) are at the vanguard.

## Media Literacy Issues Related to Advertising and PR

You might imagine that Ford's marketing executives along with the advertising, public relations, and marketing communications agencies that work for Ford are happy that today's converging media scene gives them the ability to spread ideas about Ford. More generally, if this chapter has done its job, you might now be impressed by the power of advertisers' sponsorship decisions to support certain media firms and doom others. And you might be impressed by the ability of advertising, PR, and marketing communications practitioners to spread content to target audiences across a multitude of media outlets.

But what about people who are members of the larger society? What should citizens who want to live in a democratic, peaceful, thriving world think about the relationship between these businesses and media? This is an important question, if only because advertising, public relations, and integrated marketing communications—what might be called the persuasion industries—are all around us. Many scholars suggest that we really ought to think deeply about them. A few writers even contend that the future of world civilization depends on redefining society's relationship to these media support systems. That may sound like an extravagant claim about industries that sell cars and candy bars. But is it really that far-fetched? See what you think as we review three issues that center on these industries, the mass media, and society: advertising and commercialism, truth and hidden influence, and the social impact of targeting. As we will see, all three issues are quite interrelated.

## Advertising and Commercialism

"**Commercialism**," a term often associated with advertising and its impact on American life, refers to a situation in which the buying and selling of goods and services is a highly promoted value. Many people say that the United States is a nation in which commercialism runs rampant. Everywhere we turn, we see a sales pitch.

Defenders of commercialism insist that Americans never would have achieved the high standard of living that many now have—or acquired the products that they take for granted—were it not for the industrial competition that commercialism has encouraged. Detractors of commercialism question this notion of progress. They insist that many difficulties come along with making commercialism a central tenet of American society. The most common problem, they say, is leading people to purchase things that they don't really need.

From the time Americans are very young, the critics say, they are presented with a daily barrage of ads. These ads are important not primarily because they aim to sell individual products or services; sometimes they succeed at that, and sometimes they don't. Rather, the importance of the advertising barrage is that it is part of what some observers call a **hidden curriculum**—a body of knowledge that people unconsciously absorb when consuming ads. Advertising critics argue that what advertising teaches—and what Americans accept as a basic lesson from the ad "course" they receive—is that society is merely a huge marketplace and that buying products and defining oneself through them is an essential aspect of life.

Supporters of advertising say that even if this hidden curriculum exists in as powerful a manner as its critics suggest, it is not harmful. People need to feel good about themselves, and advertising provides a vehicle—products—for doing that. Critics respond, however, that commercialism has dire side effects. They especially highlight the exploitation of children and the destruction of the global environment.

**The Exploitation of Children** Media critics contend that advertising to children is ethically unacceptable. They point out that children aged 2 through 12 years are often treated just like any other consumers. Ad people know that children influence their parents' spending and, as they get older, also have their own purchasing power from gifts and allowances. The critics cite scholarly research showing that the youngest children (those under four or five years) often don't have the skills to be critical of advertisers' claims—and often can't tell an advertisement from other types of content. As for the older kids, the critics contend that by getting children hyped for toys, foods, and other products that their parents must approve, the advertisers may be encouraging family arguments. In fact, marketers and media firms that invite children into a separate channel to advertise to them are quietly setting themselves up in opposition to the children's parents—a situation that, the critics argue, is morally highly questionable.

**Destruction of the Global Environment** Some critics argue that when so many people are taught that the continual purchase of new products is the key to the good life, their resulting activities place an enormous burden on the earth's resources. The

**commercialism**
a situation in which the buying and selling of goods and services is a highly promoted value

**hidden curriculum**
a body of knowledge that people unconsciously absorb when consuming ads

energy used to create the products they buy, the energy (and pollution) created by the use of the products, the garbage problems that are created when people throw away things that they could still use but that aren't fashionable—all these activities make the earth a more and more difficult place to inhabit. Supporters of advertisers counter that these problems are not really so bad, that people are living better now than ever before in history. The critics reply that the ecological disasters caused by commercialism are just beginning. As the billions of people in developing countries such as China buy into the commercialist philosophy of countries such as the United States, the pressure on the earth's environment will mount to unacceptable levels. Advertising critics such as Sut Jhally have argued that this predicament will literally lead to the end of the earth's ability to sustain human beings.

## Truth and Hidden Influence in Public Relations

Advertising is the industry that most scholars mention when discussing commercialism. Our examples of public relations—Ford's ecology campaign was one—demonstrate that a lot of what public relations practitioners do promotes commercialism as well. Scholars tend to focus on PR when they raise the issue of truth and hidden influence. They argue that when a company deliberately hides the sponsor or power behind a media message (as PR practitioners typically do), the action very much represents a problem of truth. Leading an audience to get the wrong impression of a story by encouraging it to believe that the story had one author rather than another—for instance, a TV station rather than the pharmaceutical firm that supplied the video and gave the station the idea for the story—is very close to promoting a lie.

Critics of advertising, PR, and marketing communications—which, again, together might be called the persuasion industries—argue that their practitioners can never really be truthful because their business is to portray people, products, and organizations purposefully in ways that do not reveal problems. Advertising, PR, and IMC practitioners respond that there is nothing wrong with emphasizing the positive aspects of something, as long as what is emphasized is not demonstrably wrong. Their critics reply that it is possible to create an ad or public relations campaign that deceives even when the text in the ad is legally truthful. Think about all the ads you see in which men are attracted to women—or women are attracted to men—who use certain products. Technically, these ads are truthful because they never contend that using these products will automatically make you alluring. Still, the critics argue, there is a fundamental deception in photographs that imply over and over that material goods will make you sexually attractive.

A pioneering professor of public relations, Scott Cutlip, worried about the industry's problem with the truth. He admonished,

> Reality says … that the public relations [practitioner] should be seen as the advocate … not as a dedicated purveyor of truth to serve the public interest. Many [practitioners] serve as advocates of institutions and causes in the same way that lawyers serve clients, to put the best possible face on the facts they can, regardless of merit or truth.

He added that because of this, "as many PR practitioners shade the truth and deal in obfuscation as they purvey accurate, useful information to the public via the news media."[7]

Executives in the persuasion industries usually shrug off such complaints. They argue that not being able to suggest that a product will bring psychological benefits or that a company has a warm personality would seriously hamper their ability to create successful advertising and public relations campaigns. When it comes to ethics, they focus instead on circumstances that can hurt them legally or economically. Can the government hold them legally liable for deception in an ad or PR campaign? Are competitors making incorrect statements about their products that are likely to hurt sales? Will unscrupulous practices by competitors lessen the credibility of their industry and prompt government investigations?

To make the rules clear and to deter government regulators from intruding on their business, industry leaders have turned to self-regulation. That means they have created professional associations that develop norms for the industry and write them into codes of good practice. The American Association of Advertising Agencies and the American Advertising Federation, for example, both circulate similar standards that their members promise to follow. Among their many prohibitions are misleading price claims and misleading rumors about competitors. In a similar vein, the Direct Marketing Association compiles lists of "deceptive and misleading practices" that its members should avoid. The Public Relations Society of America also has a code of "professional standards" that includes such topics as safeguarding "the confidences of present and former clients," not engaging "in any practice which tends to corrupt the integrity of channels of communication or the processes of government," and "not intentionally" communicating "false and misleading information."[8]

Some critics contend that public relations and advertising firms violate these rules every day. Moreover, no society can force a nonmember to even pay lip service to its rules. Attempts to enforce complaints by one member against another do exist. If, for example, one advertiser believes that another advertiser is harming its products by broadcasting misleading or inaccurate commercials, the advertiser can complain to the National Advertising Division (NAD) of the Council of Better Business Bureaus. The NAD will investigate. If it finds the advertiser's work misleading, the charge is reviewed by the National Advertising Review Board, which consists of industry practitioners. That industry body will act as a referee and make a report on its conclusion available to the public. It will also suggest how the commercial might be changed. For the sake of self-regulation, advertisers typically agree to follow these suggestions.

Although critics of advertising point out that industry disputes over accuracy are only the tip of the iceberg of problems with the truthfulness of information, they acknowledge that at least an ad is out in the open for its audience to see. A person who sees an advertisement almost always knows that it is an ad and so can be sensitive to claims and images that may be exaggerated or are unsupportable. Public relations, in contrast, is by its very nature an activity that hides its creators from public view. That, say its critics, makes it almost impossible to examine its products for accuracy as one might examine an ad. In fact, as we noted previously, this is one of the persuasive advantages over advertising that PR practitioners cite. People naturally suspect an ad, they say, whereas in the case of PR, they don't even know it is taking place.

The negative social effects of public relations' hidden nature can be considerable. As we have seen, many media activities today are influenced by the information subsidies that various types of public relations agencies supply. These subsidies can be as seemingly harmless as products placed by companies in entertainment or as clearly outrageous as fake atrocity stories orchestrated to sway the news media, the public, and Congress to support a war. In all cases, though, public relations practitioners are manipulating mass media content to their clients' commercial and political benefit without letting the public know about it.

People who don't consider the impact of public relations on news and entertainment may believe what they see because they trust the news or entertainment organization that they think is the source. They may act against their best interests because they don't realize that the real source of the story is quite different from the one that they believe instigated and interpreted the story. At the same time, people who are aware of the power of PR over the mass media typically will still not be able to figure out whether a PR organization is behind a particular story or how or why. The result of this inability to know may be a cynical view that everything in the media is tainted by PR and therefore is not what it seems. In either case, the hidden nature of public relations may have an unfortunate, even corrosive effect on the way people understand those parts of society that are outside their immediate reach.

## Targeting by Advertising and Public Relations Firms

The past two decades have seen tremendous growth in the ways advertisers and public relations practitioners create, combine, and use lists to reach target audiences. Americans have told pollsters in growing numbers that they worry that too much information about their lives and personal preferences is being exchanged without their knowledge. It also seems clear to direct marketers that people believe that they are receiving too much junk mail and too many telemarketing calls. Moreover, both pollsters and academics predict that the growth of online services will increase worries about privacy as more ways of collecting personal information are created.

Another possible consequence of targeting that deserves mention involves marketing and media firms surrounding people with content that speaks so much to their own particular interests that those people learn little—and care little—about parts of society that do not relate directly to those interests.

Critics, including this book's author, point out that the ultimate aim of 21st-century marketing is to reach consumers with specific messages about how products and services tie in to their personal lifestyles. Target-minded media help advertisers and public relations practitioners do this by building what we might call "primary media communities." These are not real-life communities where people live. Rather, they are ideas of connection with certain types of people that are formed when viewers or readers feel that a magazine, radio station, or other medium harmonizes with their personal beliefs and helps them to understand their position in the larger world.

Some media are going a step beyond trying to attract certain types of people. They make an active effort to exclude people who do not fit the desired profile. This makes the community more "pure" and thereby more efficient for advertisers. Media executives accomplish this objective simply by purposefully placing material in their medium that they know will turn off certain types of people while not turning off others (and while maybe even attracting others). The message of target radio stations, cable networks, and magazines is often that "this is not for everyone."

*Jackass*, a coarsely funny reality program, filled this role for MTV during the early 2000s when the network was working to position itself as a young adult-oriented channel. *Dexter* and *Nurse Jackie*, Showtime series about, respectively, a likable serial murderer and a drug-addicted, adulterous, yet likable nurse did the same for that network in 2009. These programs had so much "attitude" that they sparked controversy among people who were clearly far removed from their "in" crowds. Executives involved with scheduling the shows hoped that the controversies surrounding them would crystallize the channels' images and guarantee that the channels would be sampled by the people they wanted to attract. The executives acknowledged that they also expected these "signature shows" to turn off viewers whom they didn't want in their audience.

An even more effective form of targeting goes beyond chasing undesirables away. It simply excludes them in the first place. **Tailoring** is the capacity to aim media content and ads at particular individuals. With just a little effort (habit, actually), people can listen to radio stations, read magazines, watch cable programs, surf the Web, and participate in loyalty programs that parade their self-images and clusters of concerns. With seemingly no effort at all, they receive offers from marketers that complement their lifestyles. And with just a bit of cash, they can pay for technologies that further tailor information to their interests—through highly personalized news delivery, for example.

Customized media are still pretty expensive, so PR and advertising practitioners mostly reserve them for upscale audiences. The high cost of introducing interactive television that can customize programming for large populations has caused the process to take longer than some media firms would like. But the competition to develop interactive technologies has not faded. The momentum toward creating targeted spaces for increasingly narrow niches of consumers is both national and global.

All signs point to a 21st century in which media firms can efficiently attract all sorts of marketers by offering three things. One is **selectability**— the ability to reach an individual with entertainment, news, information, and advertising based on knowledge of the individual's background, interests, and habits. The second is **accountability to advertisers**—the ability to trace an individual's response to a particular ad. The third is **interactivity**—the ability to cultivate a rapport with, as well as the loyalty of, individual consumers.

Some companies, to be sure, want to get their brands out to the broad population as quickly as possible and will continue to find mass market media useful. They will support the presence of billboards, supermarket signs, and the few TV broadcasts that still draw mass audiences, such as the Super Bowl, the World Series, and the Miss America Pageant. This kind of programming helps create immediate national awareness for a new car model, athletic shoe, or computer.

But even this material will be targeted in the future. For example, Warner Bros. Television might try to reach as many people as possible to offset the high production costs of a TV movie about nuclear disaster that involves major battle scenes with impressive computer-generated special effects. Yet it might achieve this by public relations activities aimed at targeting people's personal TV navigators with tailored plot synopses— one for people who are interested in science and a different one for people who like the lead actor. At present, it is cheaper to customize news and information programs than to customize top-of-the-line entertainment. For instance, NBC might tailor its election coverage to viewers with different interests. Consumers who care about foreign affairs, agricultural topics, or environmental issues might be able to choose the network feed that features detailed coverage of election results in their special-interest area.

Over and over, some media critics predict, different versions of news will present different social distinctions to different people. And even when the content is the same (as in the nuclear disaster movie), producers will aim different PR and ad campaigns to different types of people or different media communities, thus encouraging

*Nurse Jackie*, a Showtime original series based around a drug-addicted and troubled nurse, is targeting an audience that is more accepting of, relates to, or is interested in this type of character—specifically 25- to 54-year-olds.

**tailoring**
the capacity to aim media content and ads at particular individuals.

**selectability**
ability to reach an individual with entertainment, news, information, and advertising based on knowledge of the individual's background, interests, and habits

**accountability to advertisers**
the ability to trace an individual's response to a particular ad

**interactivity**
the ability to cultivate a rapport with, as well as the loyalty of, individual consumers

the perception that the viewing experience in America is an enormously splintered one. The net result will be to push separation over collectivity.

These critics argue that it will take time, possibly decades, for the full effects of the emerging media world to take shape. Even when the new media environment does crystallize, consumers will still seek media that are not specifically aimed at them. Increasingly, though, the easiest path will be to go with the customized flow of media and marketing paraphernalia. For you and me—individual readers and viewers—this segmentation and targeting portends terrific things. If we can afford to pay, or if we're important to PR or advertising sponsors who will pick up the tab, we will be able to receive all the news, information, and entertainment we like. Who would not welcome media and sponsors that offer to surround us with exactly what we want when we want it?

A critical view of the situation would argue that although this may benefit us as individuals, it could potentially have a harmful effect on society. Customized media driven by target-oriented advertising and PR allow—even encourage—individuals to live in their own personally constructed worlds, separate from people and issues that they don't care about and don't want to be bothered with. This kind of segmentation of the population diminishes the chance that individuals who identify with certain groups will even have an opportunity to learn about others. In a society in which immigration is increasing ethnic variation and tensions, the goal should not be to use the media to connect people. Rather, the media should encourage people to do the hard work necessary to become aware of other cultures' interests, to enjoy various backgrounds collectively, and to seek out media interactions to celebrate, argue, and learn with a wide spectrum of groups in the society.

The problem, say media critics, is that the advertising and public relations industries are working with media firms to go in the opposite direction. Their goal is to ease people into media environments that comfortably mirror their own interests so that they can be persuaded more easily. Media practitioners see nothing wrong with this approach. Media analyst Sut Jhally is among those who disagree. He argues that the tendency of the persuasion industries to play to people's self-interests rather than the larger society's interests is quite predictable. "The market," he says, "appeals to the worst in us … and discourages what is best in us." As you move through the media world, it's useful to keep both perspectives in mind.[9]

# CHAPTER REVIEW

 Visit the Companion Website at www.routledge.com/cw/turow for additional study tools and resources.

## Key Terms

You can find the definitions to these key terms in the marginal glossary throughout this chapter. Test your knowledge of these terms with interactive flash cards on the *Media Today* companion website.

| | | |
|---|---|---|
| account executive | creative persuasion | market research |
| accountability to advertisers | creatives or creative personnel | market segmentation |
| ad campaign | database marketing | media plan |
| advertising | databases | media planners |
| advertising agencies | direct-to-consumer (DTC) | media planning and buying |
| agency holding companies | direct-marketing agencies | media relations |
| agency networks | event marketing | press release |
| barter | event sponsorship | product integration |
| the Big Four | general ad agency | psychographic data |
| branded entertainment | hidden curriculum | publicity |
| branding | in-store media | publicity outlet |
| business-to-business agencies | information subsidies | relationship marketing |
| click-through ad | integrated marketing communications | sales pitch |
| client conflicts | (IMC) or marketing communications | selectability |
| commercialism | interactivity | specialty ad agency |
| consumer agencies | internet agency | tailoring |
| cost per thousand (CPM | location-based advertising | traditional ad agency |

## Questions for Discussion and Critical Thinking

1. Some critics claim that advertising to children is unethical. What might be some reasons that support their claim? Are there any counterarguments that advertisers might make?

2. What do you think of the idea that advertising has a "hidden curriculum"? In general what do you think advertising is trying to teach us? Do you think the curriculum is really that hidden?

3. As you will see throughout this book, the internet has made significant impacts on all media industries and their audiences. What impacts do you see the internet having on advertising and publication relations activities?

4. If you were in charge of placing GEICO ads online, where would you put them and why? What specific sites might you use? How would you balance social media against regular websites?

## Case Study
### EXPLORING MARKETING COMMUNICATIONS

**The Idea** As this chapter notes, traditional forms of public relations and advertising are two of the several approaches that marketers are using to reach target audiences. As we saw, "marketing communications" is the broad term that media and marketing personnel give to approaches that represent a wide gamut, from product placement to event sponsorship and from buzz marketing to viral marketing. This case study will give you the opportunity to examine forms of marketing communications and their relation to mass media.

**The Method** A convenient way to investigate marketing communications is to visit the website of the Big Four agency holding companies: Omnicom, WPP, Interpublic, and Publicis. Go to the website of one of these firms and explore the companies that they own that do not fall under the labels of advertising or public relations. These companies are sometimes listed as "marketing services" firms. The websites typically describe these firms and give examples of their work.

Choose two of these subsidiaries that seem to deal with a form of outreach to consumers. An example might be a company that is involved in helping marketers develop "brand" images of products. Another might be interested in using the internet to track consumers' discussions of products and decide how to react to those discussions. Still another might be involved in deciding how to use mobile media to reach customers.

For each of the two marketing communications firms, describe (1) the work the company carries out, (2) why the company says it is important, (3) in what mass media the company's activities (or the result of the company's activities) take place, and (4) in what areas of the world the firm operates. Then consider an example of each firm's activities from the website or from another periodical. In view of what you've learned about each firm, comment on how you think firms that carry out the two forms of marketing communications represented by these examples are influencing the media materials that audiences receive.

## Government Regulation, Self-Regulation, and Ethics

"What progress we are making. In the Middle Ages they would have burned me. Now they are content with burning my books."

**SIGMUND FREUD (1856–1939), JEWISH AUSTRIAN PSYCHIATRIST, 1933**

## CHAPTER OBJECTIVES

1 Explain the reasons for and the theories underlying media regulation

2 Identify and describe the different types of media regulation

3 Analyze the struggles between citizens and regulatory agencies in the search for information

4 Discuss the ways in which media organizations self-regulate

5 Identify and evaluate ethical dilemmas facing media practitioners today

6 Harness your media literacy skills to comprehend how media regulation affects you as a consumer

If you fired up your web browser and traveled to Google. com on June 18, 2011, you would have found the colorful Google letters blacked out. If you clicked on the word, you would have been directed to a page explaining that the company was protesting two bills passing through committees of the U.S. Congress, one in the House of Representatives and one in the Senate. The two bills might end up as law, Google told its visitors, and protest was necessary to prevent their passage.

The legislation—the Stop Online Piracy Act (a House bill commonly called SOPA) and the Protect IP Act in the Senate (called PIPA)—aimed to help U.S. attorneys general and copyright holders to crack down on websites that display or link to copyrighted intellectual property (i.e., materials such as books, songs, and videos owned by particular individuals or companies) without the permission of their owners. If websites did display or link to these materials, they could be placed on a list of websites that would be blocked by internet service providers. The owners of the copyrighted material could also ask the court to force online advertising companies to stop doing business with the website that was allegedly linking without permission. The copyright owners could also force payment processors such as PayPal and MasterCard to stop allowing financial transactions on the allegedly infringing site. They could even stop search engines from listing such sites.

"What's wrong with such a law?" you might say. "If I worked for a company that owns movies or songs, and someone was making money off of them without my firm's permission, I would want to find a way to stop them from doing it." That's certainly what representatives of the movie, music, television, and book industries believed when they encouraged members of Congress to write the bills. They noted that internet criminals outside the United States were pirating American works, allowing people access to them and making money from them without permission. They hoped that SOPA and PIPA—combined into one law after going through the two halves of Congress—would give the U.S. government the ability to stop criminals from benefiting from the pirated works by stopping links to them, consumer payments to them, and advertising cash to them.

Google and other companies that make money from the internet saw the issue quite differently from the companies that create and own the content. They argued that they firmly oppose piracy. Nevertheless, they said, allowing the U.S. government to force internet providers, including search engines, to block links to foreign websites accused of piracy would cause confusion and amount to government censorship. Even after the bills' sponsors offered to take out that provision, the opponents insisted that the other parts—the right to stop advertising and payment systems and get search engines to stop listing the sites—were unacceptable. That's why Google and some of the web's most popular destinations—for example, Wikipedia, MoveOn.org, Craigslist, Boing Boing, and Firefox—blacked out all or part of their sites for the day. They urged their startled visitors to contact their elected representatives in protest of PIPA and SOPA.

Members of Congress were flooded with angry messages from constituents endorsing the internet industry's view. A few lawmakers removed their support for the bills, and neither bill made it to a vote. Some observers saw the situation as reflecting the new clout of the internet technology industry with U.S. lawmakers. Historically, the interests of Hollywood and print publishing had their ears. Ethan Zuckerman, director of the Center for Civic Media at the Massachusetts Institute of Technology and a supporter of the internet side, wasn't willing to declare victory. "It's a long boxing match," he told *USA Today*. He said grassroots organizers and tech companies "did an excellent job making the point clear. But I'm not ready to declare [the legislation] dead. It's wounded."[1]

## Why Do Media Firms Care About What Government Does?

The "boxing match" that Ethan Zuckerman noted takes place all the time between media industries as well as among individual media companies. They clash over government regulations they worry will hurt or help them. When we talk about the regulation of mass media, we mean the laws and guidelines that influence the way media companies produce, distribute, or exhibit materials for audiences. Government regulation of mass media covers a wide range of territory. It can mean regulation by federal, state, county, or city government.

"Wait!" you may hear yourself saying to this page. "I remember from high school history classes that the U.S. Constitution says we should have freedom of the press. That means that there should be no government restrictions on the work of content creators. How, then, can you say that government regulation has such an effect on media firms?" This is a good and important question. A short answer is that the value of a free press has turned out to be less straightforward than it may seem. Sometimes the constitutional value of free press conflicts with another constitutional value. For example, the Constitution guarantees an author's ownership of a creative work for a period of time. If you have created a video or poem, does your ownership of the work mean that you have the right to stop a website from publishing it without your permission? Or does the website have a free-press right to do so? Sometimes freedom of the press conflicts with an important social value. If a television program is spreading ugly, untrue, and potentially hurtful rumors about you, do you have the right to halt them even though they have freedom of the press? At other times, conflicting parties argue that freedom of the press is on their side. Say your firm runs an internet news site and makes money through advertising on the site. Should a company that provides households in Chicago with internet service be allowed to stop people from reaching your firm's website unless the firm pays the internet service provider money?

These are just three kinds of situations where courts or elected officials (or both) have had to make decisions about how to interpret freedom of the press for one party when it may interfere with the press freedom, or other freedoms, of another party. Attorneys who specialize in media law—perhaps you might be interested in becoming one—spend their entire professional lives trying to understand how to argue for clients in situations where the free-press rights of one group clash with the free-press rights or other social rights of other groups. Large media companies and organizations representing media industries also hire lobbyists to argue that laws they favor are best for society as well as for their industry and don't contradict the Constitution. We saw some of that with the fight over SOPA and PIPA.

The aim of this chapter is to give you a broad sense of the way three key arguments—over how to define freedom of the press, what a good media system means, and how much government should guide it—have shaped media laws in the United States. As we've already suggested, the story must start with the U.S. Constitution, which is the basis for the authority of the country's government and courts. The legal foundation for government's regulation of the press is the First Amendment to the Constitution, which is one of a group of 10 amendments collectively known as the Bill of Rights. Let's look at what it says and what it means.

## The First Amendment

The First Amendment to the Constitution reads,

> Congress shall make no law respecting an establishment of religion, or prohibiting the free exercise thereof; or abridging the freedom of speech, or of the press; or the right of the people peaceably to assemble, and to petition the Government for a redress of grievances.

The First Amendment's statement that "Congress shall make no law . . . abridging the freedom of speech, or of the press" seems to rule out any type of government interference in journalistic organizations ("the press") and even in media that present content other than news. The country's founders were determined that, in the new nation, no one would need the government's permission to communicate ideas to a wide public.

As we have noted, the reality of lawmaking has been quite different, however. Over the decades, the federal government has been involved in regulating media firms, which raises continuing debate about the precise meaning of the First Amendment. The U.S. Supreme Court has repeatedly sorted out fights between government agencies that seek to curtail mass media content and companies interested in protecting and extending it. Consider these questions:

**What Does the First Amendment Mean by "No Law," and Where Does It Apply?**
Since the time the First Amendment was passed, lawmakers and lawyers have understood that its phrase "make no law" means that the federal branches of government cannot

make laws abridging press freedoms. But here's a question: does the First Amendment apply to the states as well? The issue is an important one. Imagine you are the publisher of a newspaper that prints controversial views about politicians throughout the United States. You would like to be sure that the Constitution protects your work, no matter which politicians object to it. If the legislature of the state in which you work has the right to stop you from publishing your views, your newspaper would likely go out of business.

In 1925, this question was resolved by the Supreme Court in the case of *Gitlow v. New York*. Socialist agitator Benjamin Gitlow published a circular called the *Left Wing Manifesto*, calling for an uprising to overthrow the government. This upset local authorities, and Gitlow was convicted of "criminal anarchy," a wrongdoing in New York State. Gitlow then appealed his case to the U.S. Supreme Court. His lawyers argued that the Constitution (and therefore the First Amendment) should override any state law that contradicts it. The U.S. Supreme Court agreed with Gitlow and his lawyers, ruling that the First Amendment's phrase "Congress shall make no law" should be interpreted as "government and its agencies shall make no law," regardless of the location or level of government.

## MEDIA TODAY & CULTURE FACEBOOK AND THE DILEMMA OF GOVERNMENT CONTROL IN CHINA

In pursuit of business, should an American media company accept perspectives of other countries that do not conform to American values of free speech and press? Facebook is one firm confronting this tough question.

Facebook is the largest social networking site in the world, with more than one billion registered users from the United States and around the world. In order for Facebook to continue adding users, the company must reach global audiences. In that regard, China appears crucial for Facebook's growth. But since 2009, Facebook has been blocked in China, though there seems to be unsanctioned use of the service.[1] The reason: social media face tough scrutiny and quick cut-offs at the hands of the Chinese government when certain topics—such as Chinese suppression of Tibetan culture, the Tiananmen protests of 2001, and pornography—are discussed. Facebook has so far refused to allow this type of government interference.

Several websites operating within China offer alternatives to the sites blocked by the firewall. With over 400 million users, SinaWeibo[2] offers a combination of Facebook and Twitter functionalities on its microblogging site. Another site is Pengyou.com, with "pengyou" meaning "friends" in Chinese. It offers functions such as sharing, apps, and games. Other social networking sites include Renren, Kaixin001, Tencent, and 51.com.[3] Although there is a lot of political discussion on these sites, they too face scrutiny and restrictions from the Chinese government if users mention taboo topics. To discourage people from crossing the line, the government requires real names for registration as well as identification. The sites also engage in self-censorship, blacklisting certain words or names, removing potentially offensive content, and blocking users if necessary.

So if Facebook entered the Chinese market, it would face competition from other social networking companies, none of which dominates the market. Furthermore, Facebook would face regulations and restrictions from the Chinese government. Yet with a population of about 1.3 billion, China would present a huge economic prize if Facebook could gain a good foothold there. In its filing for public company status, Facebook asserted that it is continuing to consider entering the Chinese market. The company has cited several challenges to doing so, however, including political instability, regulation challenges, currency exchange rate fluctuations, and foreign law compliance.[4]

In view of these considerations, do you think Facebook should continue to pursue business in China? How might the company have to change in order to adapt to the Chinese government's restrictions? Or would it be better off pursuing other markets instead?

**What Does the First Amendment Mean by "the Press"?** When the founders wrote that "Congress shall make no law . . . abridging the freedom of speech, or of the press," how did they define the term "press"? The founders could not have possibly imagined the complex world of media messages and channels in which we currently live. So which segments of the media are included under the First Amendment's definition of the press?

If only newspaper companies fell under the protection of the First Amendment, then book publishers, magazine firms, television stations, movie companies, websites, and advertising firms would be subject to government interference. This, in turn, might place a chill on the creation of entertainment and fiction, given that companies might fear getting in trouble with federal and state governments. But more than 150 years after the writing of the Constitution, the Supreme Court agreed with the notion that entertainment and nonprint media make up "the press" along with print news media. It may seem difficult to understand today, but as late as 1919, the Court ruled that films were not a protected form of expression because they were entertainment, not the kind of serious information that would make up "the press."

In 1952 the Supreme Court overturned this view. This decision was part of a trend that began around the middle of the 20th century. The Court's justices adopted an increasingly broad view of "the press" that included factually truthful advertising and many forms of entertainment in film, television, and radio as well as print media. The justices also agreed that when media firms circulate incorrect facts about individuals or organizations that are created by mistake or even sloppiness (though not by a clear desire to harm those described), the errors are protected under the First Amendment. That protection, the Court emphasized in 1967, applies to errors in entertainment as well as in news. In explaining, Justice William Brennan quoted a previous Court ruling that both forms of content "must be protected if the freedoms of expression are to have the 'breathing space' that they 'need . . . to survive.'"[2]

**What Does the First Amendment Mean by "Abridging"?** The term "abridge" means "to cut short" or "to curtail." In fact, the Supreme Court has often approved government restrictions on speech or the press that place limits on the time, place, and manner of an expression. Such restrictions are legal as long as those limits

- are applicable to everyone,
- are without political bias,
- serve a significant governmental interest, and
- leave ample alternative ways for the communication to take place.

The issue of restriction has come up a lot in the area of outdoor advertising. Over the decades, communities upset about both the clutter that billboards bring and the content of some of them—sexual images and unwholesome products—have tried to create laws regulating them. Based on the preceding points, courts have ruled that any laws restricting outdoor advertising have to apply to all businesses and cannot reflect any prejudice toward any particular lawful business. Following this logic, federal courts have ruled that liquor ads cannot be singled out for a ban on highways on the presumption that teen drivers would be influenced by them. The reasoning is that free speech should be protected as long as there are other ways to warn teenagers about the dangers of drinking and driving.

Anti-cigarette activists argue that outdoor cigarette advertising ought to be an exception to this approach. At this point, cigarette companies have stopped using large billboards as part of a "voluntary" agreement with the federal government to limit commercial messages for the product that, although it harms people, can still be bought legally.

# More Allowable Government Control over Media Content

**prior restraint**
government restriction of speech before it is made

**obscene**
offensive to accepted standards of decency or modesty

So far we have seen that the U.S. Supreme Court has tackled questions about whether and how much the First Amendment applies to entertainment, news, and advertising. We have also seen that the Court has laid out broad rules that the government must follow if it wants to abridge certain kinds of speech. As it turns out, the Supreme Court has gone even further than those broad rules of abridgment. It has ruled over the decades that the government has a right to abridge media "speech" more on certain topics and in certain situation than others.

We can divide these types of governmental media regulation into three categories:

- Regulation of content before it is distributed
- Regulation of content after it has been distributed
- Economic regulation

Let's look at each of these three types separately.

## Regulating Content before Distribution

When the government restricts speech before it is made or distributed, it is engaging in **prior restraint**. Since the 1930s, the U.S. Supreme Court has consistently ruled that the practice of regulating or restricting speech before it is made violates both the spirit and the letter of the First Amendment. At the same time, however, the Court has held that in some rare and specific circumstances, prior restraint is in the interest of the public good. Table 5.1 sketches four types of content situations that the Court says may in some circumstances warrant restriction in advance: education, national security, clear and present danger to public safety, and commercial speech. Three other such areas are obscenity, military operations, and copyright. Let's take a look at these in some detail.

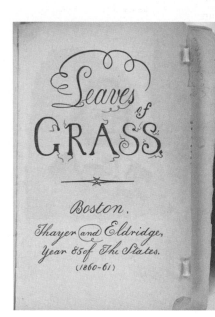

Walt Whitman's *Leaves of Grass* was written in the morally and socially conservative Victorian era. This work celebrating love, sensuality, and sexuality was met with great opposition—including a call from a Boston district attorney to the publisher of the work to remove certain poems from the collection and to stop distribution of the work. The book was banned by many of the larger, more popular book distributors. Nevertheless, the first printing sold out quickly, and Whitman went on to find a new publisher that wouldn't cave into such demands.

**Obscenity** When was the last time you saw something you considered truly **obscene**? Well, if you did see obscene material, you should know that the Supreme Court has ruled that such matter is not protected by the First Amendment. The government can exercise prior restraint and not allow the material to be distributed. This sounds like a major power of the government that it could exercise every day, even against some HBO pay-cable programs (such as *Real Sex*) that you, your friends, or your parents may not consider obscene. But over the decades the Supreme Court has set the bar for determining obscenity so high that, in practice, this sort of prior restraint rarely takes place today.

The term "obscene" means offensive to accepted standards of decency or modesty. One difficulty in determining whether something is obscene, of course, is that different people may have different standards of acceptability. Books such as D. H. Lawrence's *Lady Chatterley's Lover* and Walt Whitman's *Leaves of Grass* may not be acceptable to some in society but may be considered genuine works of art by others. (Did your high school assign J. D. Salinger's *Catcher in the Rye*? Some school systems classify it as obscene, whereas others assign it as a classic.) Of course, the same holds with respect to images on television and websites.

**Table 5.1** Additional Examples of Types of Content for which the Supreme Court Allows Prior Restraint

| Content category | Definition | Example | Note |
| --- | --- | --- | --- |
| Education | The right of primary and secondary school administrators to dictate school-newspaper policy and refuse to allow articles to appear | A school principal's objection to publishing a story about a pregnant student | The Supreme Court held that when the school newspaper is part of the school's educational mission, it is not entitled to First Amendment protections "even though the government could not censor similar speech outside the school." |
| National security | Information that if revealed would pose a clear and present danger to the ability of the United States to defend itself against enemies | Information on government plans during wartime | Supreme Court has emphasized this prior restraint should be used rarely: "Paramount among the responsibilities of a free press is the duty to prevent any part of the government from deceiving the people and sending them off to distant lands to die." |
| Clear and present danger to public safety | A situation in which media content itself poses a threat to the physical welfare of citizens | A Ku Klux Klan video that urges members to commit physical violence against African Americans at a particular date, place, and time | Supreme Court has emphasized this prior restraint should be used rarely: when the danger is close in time, likely, and lawless in approach. |
| Commercial speech | Messages designed to sell products or services | A soup company's television commercial that uses marbles at the bottom of a soup bowl to make it look as if it contains big pieces of meat and vegetables | Many public advocacy groups argue that the government should exercise prior restraint on commercials and product placements of high-calorie foods and drinks in TV programs with large audiences of children. |

## THINKING ABOUT MEDIA LITERACY

Did you read any books or plays in high school that raised controversy because of their topic or writing? If not, why do you think no readings generated controversy? If yes, how did teachers, other students, and parents address the controversy? Looking back, do you agree with what they said? Why or why not?

Further complicating these disagreements about obscenity is the dilemma that the public's collective standards of what is obscene and what is not obscene change and shift almost constantly. Communities that deemed a book or film obscene in the 1970s might not agree with that assessment today. In 1957, the U.S. Supreme Court ruled that explicit depictions of sex need not be obscene. It noted that "sex, a great and mysterious motive force in human life, has indisputably been a subject of absorbing interest to mankind through the ages; it is one of the vital problems of human interest and public concern." So when is explicit sex obscene, to the Court? "Obscene material," it wrote, "is material which deals with sex in a manner appealing to prurient interests."[3]

All right, does that make it clear when something is obscene? Well, not really. You see, the Court made a number of additional specifications about the definition of obscenity that make giving something that label quite difficult. For example, the work has to portray in a *clearly offensive manner*—in pictures or writing—certain sexual conduct specifically described as unallowable by state law. The Court also said that the media product—such as a television episode or entire film—must be considered in its entirety, not just an excerpt. So, for example, the company circulating the material in question might argue that a particular sex scene may indeed be quite explicit but that it is necessary to explain the character's personality as it evolves through the movie. And if that doesn't make labeling something as obscene difficult enough, the Court added that the standard of "appealing to prurient interests" must be community-based. It stipulates that an *average person*, applying current standards of the community, would have to find that the work as an entirety reflects an obsessive interest in sex. Finally, it states that a *reasonable person* has to agree that the work lacks serious literary, artistic, scientific, or political usefulness.

These criteria make it quite difficult for the government to make the case for prior restraint on the basis of obscenity, even if content is pornographic—that is, sexually explicit. There are, it is important to note, other ways to control certain kinds of sexual content, even if they do not meet these tests of obscenity. Materials can still be restricted under import regulations, postal regulations, zoning ordinances, and other laws. For example, child abuse laws have been used to bar materials that feature nude children.

**Military Operations** The regulation and control of news during times of war has taken place since the Civil War. At times, media personnel have been required to submit their scripts and stories for governmental review before distribution.

During World War I, Congress passed the Espionage Act (1917) and the Sedition Act (1918), which together formalized wartime censorship of the press by preventing "disloyal" publications from being mailed via the U.S. Postal Service. During World War II, the Espionage Act was again put into effect—allowing the government to control broadcasting from 1941 until 1945. During this time, the Office of Censorship had the power to censor international communication at its "absolute discretion." With a staff of more than 10,000 censors, the office routinely examined mail, cables, newspapers, magazines, films, and radio broadcasts. Its operations constituted the most extensive government censorship of the media in U.S. history and one of the most vivid examples of the use of executive emergency powers.

In cases in which the United States is involved in a military operation but has not officially declared war, the government may seek to control access to information, rather than officially censoring that content. When U.S. troops were sent to the Caribbean island of Grenada in 1983, the Pentagon took control of all transportation to and from the island and refused to transport reporters to the island to cover the conflict. Journalists protested this military news "blackout." In 1989, when U.S. troops were sent to Panama, the Pentagon instituted a system of **pool reporters**—selected members of the media who get access to a news event and share facts, stories, images, and firsthand knowledge of that event with others. Journalists were skeptical about the system, and as it turned out, their skepticism was well-founded. Reporters in the press pool were held in a briefing room at a military post and were given briefings that consisted of little more than history lessons on the relationship between the United States and Panama. As a consequence, journalists soured on the idea of a specially chosen pool of reporters, and the practice faded.

**pool reporters**
selected members of the media who are present at a news event and share facts, stories, images, and firsthand knowledge of that event with others

## THINKING ABOUT MEDIA LITERACY

In general, reporters are supposed to maintain a professional and personal distance from the people they write about. Embedded reporters, or embeds, travel with the troops during wartime, facing the same dangers as the troops do. Embeds face the identical risks of attack and even injury, and as a result some embeds develop strong ties to the troops they travel with. How might this situation influence a reporter when he or she is covering a story about a botched invasion or a soldier accidentally killed by friendly fire? Why might the reporter be reluctant to write stories that might portray troops in a negative light?

In the Iraq War that began in 2004, as well as in the parallel, continuing Afghanistan conflict, the military allowed **embeds**—reporters who received permission to travel with a military unit across the battlefield. The Defense Department required all embeds to agree not to break military information embargos, not to report on ongoing missions without clearance, and not to reveal deployment levels below large numbers such as troop corps and carrier battle groups. Nevertheless, some news outlets such as CNN and the United Kingdom's ITN did reveal certain information about the fighting that the military would have liked to keep secret, and they were periodically threatened with losing the right to have embeds. Despite the restrictions, many of the embeds in Iraq were able to report the battlefield in great detail; one book calls the initial U.S. invasion of Iraq "the most covered war in history."[4] According to one reporter who studied the embed approach, journalists who were embedded in Iraq "experienced a freedom to do their jobs that journalists had not had since the Vietnam War."[5]

Critics pointed out that a disadvantage of the embed approach was the tendency for such journalists to be highly sympathetic to the troops with whom they lived and on whom they depended for survival. These critics argued that self-censorship was sometimes the result. To address these criticisms, the military allowed other journalists to work as unilaterals—to travel through the war zone by themselves.

**Copyright** When we speak about **copyright**, we mean the legal protection of a creator's right to a work. According to the U.S. Constitution, the purpose of copyright is "to promote the progress of science and the useful arts." The framers of the Constitution believed that only if people could profit from their work would they want to create materials that could ultimately benefit the nation as a whole. At the same time, the framers wanted lawmakers to strike a balance between the rights of authors to gain personally from their work and the right of the society to draw on the information.

The hesitancy of government agencies to stop the press from circulating content does not apply to copyright violations, for two reasons. The first is that authors ought to be able to control how their work—their intellectual property—is used. The second is that authors should be paid fairly for the use of their work.

The **Copyright Act of 1976** lays out the basic rules as they exist in the United States today. The law, as later modified (in 1978 and again in 1998), recognizes the rights of an individual creator (in any medium) from the time he or she has created a work and protects a creative work for the lifetime of its author plus 70 years.

As an example, let us say that Hector, an English student, writes a poem. From the moment Hector finishes the poem, he holds an automatic copyright on the poem for his lifetime plus 70 years. He may, if he decides, send the poem to the U.S. Copyright

**embeds**
reporters who receive permission from the military to travel with a military unit across the battlefield

**copyright**
the legal protection of a creator's right to a work

**Copyright Act of 1976**
a law that recognizes the rights of an individual creator (in any medium) from the time he or she has created a work and that protects a creative work for the lifetime of that author plus 70 years

Office to register it for a small fee. Even if he does not do this, however, he is protected as long as he can prove that he wrote the poem before anyone else did. In order to prove when a work was created, some people mail a copy of the work to themselves and do not open it. The cancellation by the post office serves as proof of the date the material was sent. Let's say that Hector does this with his poem.

Hector is proud of his poem, and he also sends it to his friend Paloma, a former classmate in a summer poetry workshop. Now let's say that Paloma is envious of Hector's poem. She submits the poem to an online literary journal as her own, and the journal accepts it, pays her a small honorarium, and publishes it under her name, not Hector's. At this point, Paloma has violated U.S. copyright law, and she can be prosecuted if Hector pursues the case, since she falsely passed herself off as the poem's true author.

But even if Paloma had not lied about the poem's authorship—let's say she submitted it to the journal under Hector's name to surprise him—Paloma (and the journal) probably would not be allowed to publish the poem, or even parts of it. Apart from not asking Hector's permission to publish the poem, Paloma has also violated the second proposition of copyright law—that authors must be paid fairly for the use of their works. Hector might in the future want to earn money from publishing the entire poem or parts of it. Sometimes, even a line of a poem or a song may be considered crucial to the work's value. As you can see, Paloma and the editors of the literary journal would have to think hard before they printed all or part of Hector's poem without getting his permission.

The copyright rules for musical compositions are similar to those for poems. If a magazine or website wants to publish selected words or music from a tune by Paul McCartney, it needs the permission of his publisher. Copying parts of copyrighted musical material from someone else who has paid for it is also illegal. For decades, although businesses paid attention to this law, individuals ignored it. Friends would often lend albums to their friends so that they could copy them onto tapes or CDs. If recording industry executives minded, they generally didn't make noise about it. One reason might be that the taped copies were not as good in sound quality as the originals. As we will see when we discuss the recording industry in chapter 10, their perspective has changed drastically. With the advent of perfect digital copies and the ability to share them over the internet, recording industry officials started hauling into court people who shared copyrighted music without the publisher's permission. We will review the pros and cons of this activity in chapter 10, but here it is relevant to note what those officials have not emphasized: even copying part of a song without permission can make one a copyright violator. The same is true regarding movies, which, as we will see in chapter 12, have also become a target for illegal uploading and sharing.

## FAIR USE

Although Congress has generally supported the right of copyright holders over the desire of individuals to copy their material, one exception involves writers, documentary producers, artists, or academics who want to quote from copyrighted material in order to carry out critical analyses. A poet, artist, novelist, or movie studio might charge an exorbitant rate for use of their works, and this might make it impossible for a scholar to share critical responses to it. To get around these problems, the law provides exceptions via **fair use regulations**. Generally, these regulations indicate that under certain conditions, a person or company may use small portions of a copyrighted

**fair use regulations**
provisions under which a person or company may use small portions of copyrighted work without asking permission

work without asking permission. Nonprofit, educational purposes have more leeway than for-profit ventures.

Another important consideration in fair use decisions is the commercial damage that copying may cause to the copyright material. The less potential damage, the greater chance it will be considered fair use. A third criterion in favor of fair use is the transformative use of the copyrighted material. A use is considered **transformative** when it presents the work in a way that adds interpretations to it so that some people might see it in a new light. So, for example, an online magazine essay on World War II movies that links to short snippets of such flicks to show how views of the war have changed over time would likely be considered fair use. By these criteria, when scholarly critiques of popular culture quote from copyrighted materials to make their points, this is almost surely fair use.

**transformative**
when use of copyrighted material presents the work in a way that adds interpretation to it so that some people might see it in a new light

---

## THINKING ABOUT MEDIA LITERACY

Within your current class that is using this textbook and in other media classes, you most likely will see a variety of clips, or short segments, from films and television shows. Keeping in mind the basic tenets of fair use, how does this exception benefit students and teachers in these classes? What challenges might teachers face if fair use did not allow them to use these materials? Can you see how the concept of fair use can be important to you as a student as well as to your teachers?

---

Despite fair use regulations, college copy shops must contact publishers and get permission when they want to use entire articles in "course packs" for classes. You may not know it, but photocopying a work for your own pleasure is normally not fair use. One curious exception to fair use guidelines relates to the videotape recorder. The Supreme Court ruled in 1984 that viewers may record copyrighted TV shows for their personal, noncommercial use. A majority of the justices reasoned that taping was legal because people used the tapes for *time shifting*—that is, taping for later viewing what they would have watched anyway.

Today, time shifting is a way of life for many people who record TV shows and movies on digital video recorders (DVRs). Although the practice is legal, it has brought interesting headaches to media companies and their advertisers, given that people view the programs they copy but not the commercials that support them. Even greater headaches have come with the rise of digital technologies that make it simple for people to copy all sorts of copyrighted materials (including music and movies) in circumstances that do not fall within the fair use rules. Some copyright owners call these behaviors "piracy" and demand that audiences stop doing it. The activities raise important legal and ethical issues that we will explore in chapters to come.

### PARODIES

A **parody** is a work that imitates another work for laughs in a way that comments on the original work. A number of major court cases have ruled that when artists add new perspectives to copyrighted material, in the process critiquing it and encouraging people to see it in different ways, that is fully legal. Supreme Court Justice David Souter even suggested that parodies have stronger rights than other kinds of fair use material in that the creator of a parody "may quite legitimately aim at destroying [the original] commercially as well as artistically."[6] The problem with parodies from

**parody**
a work that imitates another work for laughs in a way that comments on the original work

Defining a work as a parody can be legally risky. Many observers saw the "Blue Harvest" episode of "Family Guy" as a parody of "Star Wars," but the program's producers still sought the copyright holder's permission to make sure there would be no lawsuit.

**defamation**
a highly disreputable or false statement about a living person or an organization that causes injury to the reputation that a substantial group of people hold for that person or entity

**slander**
spoken communication that is considered harmful to a person's reputation

**libel**
written communication that is considered harmful to a person's reputation

a legal standpoint, though, is that the line between fair use and copyright violation is sometimes hard to figure out.

For one thing, not all comically altered versions of songs are fair use. Weird Al is a performer who has based his professional career on writing and recording parodies of popular songs. Pieces such as "My Bologna" (a take on the Knack's "My Sharona"), "I Love Rocky Road," "Another One Rides the Bus," "Eat It," "Like a Surgeon," "I Think I'm a Clone Now," and "Smells Like Nirvana" have given him long-term popularity with a huge number of fans around the globe. Yet Weird Al is actually pretty conservative regarding his parodic creations. His lawyers may have pointed out to him that although his lyrics are funny, they don't really criticize the originals; nor does his musical take on the originals vary much from them. Perhaps as a result, Weird Al notes that he always seeks permission from the artists and writers of the songs before he puts his spin on them. "The parodies are all in good fun and good taste," he says, "and most of the artists normally take it that way. I prefer to have them on my team and I like to sleep well at night."[8]

## Regulating Content after Distribution

There are some types of content where courts have stated that authorities must wait until after distribution to press charges of illegal activity. The two biggies in this area are defamation and invasion of privacy.

**Defamation**  An act of **defamation** is a highly disreputable or false statement about a living person or an organization that causes injury to the reputation that a substantial group of people hold for that person or entity. One hopes that will never happen to you, but can you imagine if it did? Let's say someone you know (and who doesn't like you) is a columnist for the local newspaper website. In the course of arguing that several people who lost their jobs during the recession deserved it, he describes a person that everyone in your community recognizes as you. He asserts that when you left a job two years ago, it wasn't because of the bad financial situation of the company (as you claimed) but because you stole money from one of the employees. The "real fact" about your job loss circulates, people bring it up in conversation, and as you decide to look for a new job, you worry it is inhibiting local employers from seriously considering you. What recourse do you have against the person and the newspaper that published that horrible stuff?

If, in a panic, you read up on the subject of defamation, you will find there are two forms: slander and libel. Traditionally, **slander** has been seen as spoken communication considered harmful to a person's reputation. **Libel** has traditionally been seen as written communication that is considered harmful to a person's reputation. In the 19th century the courts treated slander and libel differently. They considered written defamation the more serious offense. The reasoning was that libel lasted longer, was more widely circulated, and seemed to be more planned than slander (a spoken comment might be made in a flash of anger). The distinction between spoken and written defamation fell apart in the 20th century, with the rise of sound media. Now even spoken communication is circulated broadly and can be planned ahead of time (as, for example, through use of a script). As

**Table 5.2** Libel Per Se

Listed below are some "red flag" words and expressions that courts have generally considered libelous per se:

| | | |
|---|---|---|
| ignoramus | rascal | amoral |
| bankrupt | slacker | unprofessional |
| thief | sneaky | incompetent |
| cheat | unethical | illegitimate |
| traitor | unprincipled | hypocritical |
| drunk | corrupt | cheating |
| blockhead | | |

experts in media law have noted, it's no longer useful to distinguish between oral and written forms of communication. Table 5.2 contains "red flag" words and expressions that courts have generally considered **libel per se**—that is, libel on their face. But some words, expressions, and statements that seem, on their face, to be innocent and not injurious may be considered libel in their actual contexts; they are called **libel per quod**. For example, saying that Bradley is married to Marisol doesn't sound libelous, but if you know that Bradley is married to Nadia, being married to Marisol would make him a bigamist. And that statement is libelous.

It is also important to recognize that there are two categories of libel plaintiffs: public figures and private persons. A **public figure** may be an elected or appointed official (a politician) or someone who has stepped (willingly or unwillingly) into a public spotlight (e.g., movie stars and TV stars, famous athletes, or other persons who draw attention to themselves). A **private person** may be well known in the community, but he or she has no authority or responsibility for the conduct of governmental affairs and has not thrust himself or herself into the middle of an important public spotlight. The distinction between private and public individuals is important because it is much more difficult for a public figure to win the kind of libel claim we have fictitiously noted for you.

**libel per se**
written communication that is considered obvious libel

**libel per quod**
words, expressions, and statements that, at face value, seem to be innocent and not injurious but that may be considered libelous in their actual context

**public figure**
a person who is an elected or appointed official (a politician) or someone who has stepped (willingly or unwillingly) into a public role

**private person**
an individual who may be well known in the community, but who has no authority or responsibility for the conduct of government affairs and has not thrust himself or herself into the middle of an important public role

## THINKING ABOUT MEDIA LITERACY

Public figures include politicians, famous actors, athletes, and even those people trying to hang on to their 15 minutes of fame after the reality shows end. These people frequently draw both positive and negative media attention. Yet public figures face difficulties when suing for defamation. What challenges do you think they face? Why are their challenges so different from those of a private individual? Do you think this situation is fair? Why or why not?

The difficulty for public figures claiming libel was made particularly clear in a 1964 Supreme Court decision regarding the case of *New York Times v. Sullivan*. The case profoundly altered libel law and set legal precedent that is still in effect today. On March 29, 1960, a full-page advertisement titled "Heed Their Rising Voices" was placed in the *New York Times* by the Committee to Defend Martin Luther King Jr. and the Struggle for Freedom in the South. The ad criticized police and public officials in several cities for tactics used to disrupt the civil rights movement and sought contributions toward bail for the Rev. Martin Luther King Jr. and other movement leaders. The accusations made in the advertisement were true for the most part, but the copy contained several rather minor factual errors. L. B. Sullivan, police commissioner in Montgomery, Alabama, sued the *New York Times* for libel, claiming that the ad had defamed him indirectly. He won $500,000 for damages in the state courts of Alabama, but the U.S. Supreme Court overturned the damage award, reasoning that Alabama's libel laws violated the *New York Times'* First Amendment rights.

In issuing its opinion, the Supreme Court said that the U.S. Constitution protected false and defamatory statements made about *public officials* if the false statements were not published with actual malice. The Court defined **actual malice** as reckless disregard for truth or knowledge of falsity. Note that actual malice considers a defendant's attitude toward truth, not the defendant's attitude toward the plaintiff. This differs from **simple malice**, which means hatred or ill will toward another person.

Because actual malice is difficult to prove, this ruling makes it difficult for a public official to win a libel suit. Additionally, the Supreme Court has broadened the actual malice protection to include public figures as well as public officials. The Court's reasoning is simple: the actual malice test sets a high bar, but it does so to protect the First Amendment rights of the media. At the same time, it allows media outlets to pursue legitimate news stories without the constant fear of being sued by the subjects of news stories. In the end, concern for the First Amendment takes precedence over libel laws as they relate to media.

Supreme Court decisions have also made it hard for a person who is neither a public figure nor a public official to sue a media firm for libel. The Court has ruled that the First Amendment requires proof of **simple negligence**—lack of reasonable care—even when private persons sue the mass media for libel. So in our hypothetical situation, for you to win a libel suit against the columnist and the newspaper (which can pay you more money for your lost employment opportunities than can the columnist), you would have to prove that neither the columnist nor the paper's editors tried to check the column's "facts" with your employer and that the columnist didn't camouflage your identity well in the piece.

**Invasion of Privacy** Now that you have a feel for what it means to be defamed, how about getting a feel for the law you would turn to if a media firm invaded your privacy? Here's one way that could happen: Suppose a TV station is creating a news report about the growing use of heroin by middle-class residents of your city. To illustrate the idea that "average" citizens are increasingly involved in the problem, the producer films footage of people walking down the streets of the city; you happen to be one of them. Turning on the local news one evening, you see a report that shows you quite clearly walking down the street just as the narrator notes that average residents are becoming hooked on heroin. You are angry at the TV station. What rights do you have?

Before answering directly, let's step back a bit to look at the larger topic. **Privacy**—the right to be protected from unwanted intrusions or disclosures—is a broad area of the law when it comes to media industries. Almost every state recognizes some right of privacy, either by statute or under common law. Most state laws attempt to strike a balance between the individual's right to privacy and the public interest in freedom of the press. However, these rights often clash.

---

**actual malice**
reckless disregard for truth or knowledge of falsity

**simple malice**
hatred or ill will toward another person

**simple negligence**
lack of reasonable care

**privacy**
the right to be protected from unwanted intrusions or disclosures

The law regarding privacy is aimed at protecting what the law has come to call a person's "reasonable expectations of privacy." Only a person can claim a right of privacy; corporations, organizations, and other entities cannot. In view of what we previously said about public figures when it comes to defamation, you'd be right to expect that public figures have a limited claim to a right of privacy. Past and present government officials, political candidates, entertainers, and sports figures are generally considered to be public figures. According to the law, they have voluntarily exposed themselves to scrutiny and have waived their right of privacy, at least regarding media coverage of matters that might have an impact on their ability to perform their public duties.

Although private individuals can usually claim the right to be protected from unwarranted intrusions or disclosures, that right is not absolute. For example, if a person who is normally not considered a public figure is thrust into the spotlight because of her participation in a newsworthy event—say, a state lottery—her claims to a right of privacy may be limited. Table 5.3 presents brief definitions and examples of four areas of privacy that particularly affect how news organizations can go about

**Table 5.3** Invasion-of-Privacy Activities Media Firms Sometimes Carry Out When Creating Content

| Activity | Definition | Example | Note |
|---|---|---|---|
| False light | Publishing material that falsely suggests an individual is involved in an illegal or unethical situation | To illustrate the idea that "average" citizens are increasingly involved in using heroin, a TV news producer tapes footage of people walking down the streets of the city. You happen to be one of them when the narrator states that average citizens are hooked on heroin. | Courts do not particularly favor false light cases because very often they conflict with freedom of speech. A plaintiff is required to prove "by clear and convincing evidence" that the defendant knew of the statement's falsity or acted in reckless disregard of its truth or falsity. In this case, the producer could argue viewers would understand the crowd scene was used to make a broad point and not to focus on any individual in it. |
| Appropriation | The unauthorized use of a person's name or likeness in an advertisement, poster, public relations promotion, or other commercial context | A magazine publishes photographs of living cancer survivors without their permission. | Judges have allowed the use of such images without permission for newsworthy purposes—that is, for stories tied to a timely event. But when the story stops being "news," the photo's subject can claim appropriation. |
| Intrusion | When a person or organization intentionally invades a person's solitude, private area, or affairs | A reporter records a phone conversation with a subject in a state where permission is required to record. | The intrusion can be physical (e.g., sneaking into a person's office) or nonphysical (e.g., putting an electronic listening device outside the office but in a position to hear what is going on inside). |
| Public disclosure | Truthful information concerning the private life of a person that a media source reveals and that both would be highly offensive to a reasonable person and is not of legitimate public concern | A newspaper reveals private, sensational facts about a person's sexual activity and economic status. | First Amendment considerations have tended to grant media businesses the right to reveal information about individuals. How the information was obtained and its newsworthiness often determine liability in cases of public disclosure. If a journalistic organization obtains information unlawfully—whether or not the information is truthful—the organization may be held liable for invasion of privacy under the rules of public disclosure. |

**false light**
invading a person's privacy by implying something untrue about him or her

**appropriation**
an invasion of privacy that takes place via the unauthorized use of a person's name or likeness in an advertisement, poster, public relations promotion, or other commercial context

**intrusion**
an invasion of privacy that takes place when a person or organization intentionally invades a person's solitude, private space, or affairs

**public disclosure**
an invasion of privacy that occurs when truthful information concerning the private life of a person (that would be highly offensive to a reasonable person and is not of legitimate public concern) is revealed by a media source

doing their work: **false light**, **appropriation**, **intrusion**, and **public disclosure**. If you've been following the logic of the legal thinking until now, you will not be surprised that courts have made it difficult to win suits against journalists in these four areas. Just as concerns for the First Amendment have given mass media firms a great deal of latitude when it comes to libel, First Amendment considerations have tended to grant media businesses the right to reveal information about individuals in one way or another. In short, you'd have a tough time winning a suit against the producer of that TV program about heroin use.

## DATABASES AND PRIVACY CONCERNS

Separate from these four areas is another world of media activities that some call an invasion of privacy but others simply call business. It involves media firms' collection of many types of data about individuals for marketing purposes. This area of data-privacy regulation is still emerging. It's a great example of how government decisions and indecisions about what media firms should be able to do can have major effects on the way media industries take shape. We'll be discussing different aspects of this boxing match in forthcoming chapters. Here let's sketch out the major sides of the controversy.

On one side are media firms and marketers who want to take advantage of new digital technologies to reach specific audiences with their media products and advertising—and make money doing it. To do that, they have developed techniques to learn loads of information about the individuals who visit them or might visit them, either by name or anonymously. One popular way is by silently tracking what you do on your computer, on your tablet, or on your phone. For example, when you visit a website via a web browser on these devices, the site may place a hidden text file called a cookie in the browser. Every time you visit the site, the cookie identifies you, probably by an identification number, unless you gave the site your name. This action allows the company to record your movements through the site. Over time, the company that created the cookie develops a profile of your interests that it can bring together with other profiles to offer to advertisers. There is an active trade in cookies with particular characteristics, and technologies to target individuals with specific backgrounds—from age to income to lifestyles and much more—are developing quickly. Web publishers can now offer to advertisers the ability to reach certain types of people—say, women searching for baby carriages—in real time, as they are entering their sites.

Chapter 6 covers digital advertising targeting and how it works in more depth. The point of bringing it up here is that whereas media and marketing practitioners laud its possibilities as the major future business model for the media system, organizations critical of these uses of databases want the government to limit them strictly, pointing to many possibilities for harm. Take health data: a company might use a person's online comments about diabetes or clicks on a diabetes site, for example, as a consideration against giving the person a job (because of the possible medical costs). A college may track tagged photos of applicants to decide whether their behavior in the photos befits the standards of the school. Finance companies may use data that evaluate how well your Facebook friends pay back their loans to decide whether or not to give you a loan and how much to charge. More broadly, a marketer may use online data it buys about you to decide whether and how to advertise toward you and whether to give you discounts (and if so, how much).

Organizations that represent marketers typically don't respond to these criticisms directly, but they do argue that there is already sufficient protection for the public.

They note that a law called Gramm-Leach-Bliley prevents banks and credit card companies from selling certain kinds of sensitive data about Americans. Similarly, a law called the Health Insurance Portability and Accountability Act (HIPAA) stops health providers from sharing your personal medical information with marketers. The Children's Online Privacy Protection Act (COPPA) requires online publishers and advertisers to get parents' permission if they want to collect information from children younger than 13 years of age. The critics respond that there are plenty of ways to find out health, financial, and family information without breaking these laws. What you look at when you are on a medical website isn't protected by HIPAA, for example. Critics want clearer and stronger limitations on what information organizations and individuals can track and store about people without their explicit permission. This is a long-term, major media boxing match, with a diverse assortment of media companies and advocacy groups making various pleadings to various government entities at the state and federal levels.

## Economic Regulation

Media firms and advocacy organizations regularly keep an eye on government actions that define and limit media activities, such as defamation and privacy invasion. They know that laws and court decisions will affect how companies can make money and what audiences read, see, and hear. But regulations regarding content make up only one part of the influence government has over media industries. **Economic regulations** make up another important government leverage. These are rules the government sets about how firms are allowed to compete with one another—in essence, about what constitutes "fair play" when it comes to doing business in the media space. Economic regulation of media organizations greatly affects the ways in which those organizations finance, produce, distribute, and exhibit their products. Two types of media economic regulation are most common: antitrust laws and direct regulation by government agencies.

**Antitrust Laws** One way to expand the marketplace of ideas without directly making rules about content is to limit excessive market control by mass media corporations. Excessive market control is behavior by one company or a few companies that makes it nearly impossible for new companies to enter the marketplace and compete. For example, a production company might gain this kind of power by buying up competitors and making sure that exhibitors do not deal with any new competitors. Distributors and exhibitors might do the same thing: a few bookstore chains might swallow up their retail competition to the point that all publishers must deal primarily with them. When it comes to mass media, excessive control over the market might directly affect consumers or advertisers, or both.

Control of the market by one firm is called a **monopoly**. Control by a select few firms is called an **oligopoly**. Great concern over train and steel monopolies and oligopolies in the late 1800s led U.S. legislators to begin to take special actions with respect to these activities, in order to maintain competition. These laws came to be known broadly as **antitrust policies**, and in the following decades they were carried out in three ways:

- Through the passage of laws
- Through enforcement of the laws by the U.S. Department of Justice and by state attorneys general

**economic regulations**
rules set by the government about how firms are allowed to compete with one another

**monopoly**
control of the market by a single firm

**oligopoly**
control of the market by a select few firms

**antitrust policies**
policies put in place to maintain competition in the U.S. economy, carried out through the passing of laws, through enforcement of the laws by the U.S. Department of Justice and state attorneys general, and through federal court decisions that determine how far the government ought to go in encouraging competition and forcing companies to break themselves into a number of smaller companies

**Federal Trade Commission (FTC)**
a federal agency whose mission is to ensure that the nation's markets function competitively; its coverage can include any mass media—print or electronic—as long as the issue involved is related to the smooth functioning of the marketplace and consumer protection in that sphere

**Federal Communications Commission (FCC)**
a federal agency specifically mandated by Congress to govern interstate and international communication by television, radio, wire, satellite, and cable

**Figure 5.1**

Comparison of the roles of the FCC and FTC in the regulation of media.

• Through federal court decisions that determine how far the government ought to go in encouraging competition and forcing companies to break themselves up into a number of smaller companies

Over the years, regulators and the courts have ruled that certain activities by firms involved in mass communication represent excessive market control. Typically, these activities have involved the use of vertical integration by a few firms to control an industry. We will note the most important of these cases when we deal with particular industries in the chapters to come.

**Direct Regulation by Government Agencies**   The **Federal Trade Commission (FTC)** and the **Federal Communications Commission (FCC)** are the two most important federal agencies involved in regulating the mass media (see Figure 5.1).

The first thing to remember when comparing the two agencies is that the FTC's coverage can include any of the mass media—print or electronic—as long as the issue involved

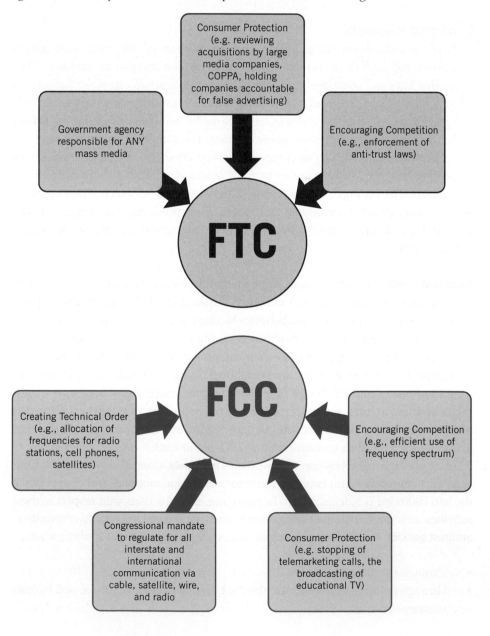

is related to the smooth functioning of the marketplace and consumer protection in that sphere. By contrast, the FCC is specifically mandated by Congress to govern interstate and international communications by television, radio, wire, satellite, and cable.

The FTC describes its overall mission as carrying out three responsibilities that very much relate to media today: creating technical order, encouraging competition, and consumer protection. These three responsibilities can also be said to apply to the FCC in its domain. Let's briefly take a look at them.

## CREATING TECHNICAL ORDER

Many of the FCC's most important activities are aimed at simply creating technical order in an electronic environment that could become chaotic without some kind of regulation. It is through the FCC that radio stations get licenses that allow them to broadcast on specific wavelengths (the numbers we associate with the stations—e.g., 105.1 FM). The FCC is also in charge of allocating the frequency spectrum among various other technologies, including satellites and cellular phones. Although some of these technical activities have nothing to do with mass media, many of them do. Most major news organizations use satellites and cell phones for their work. Many consumers pay to get TV programming via satellite. Increasingly, too, consumers are getting news, information, and advertisements through their mobile phones. FCC decisions about how to allocate spectrum space help define which and how many companies can afford to get into this business in different parts of the country. That, in turn, affects the number of companies consumers have to choose from and how much they will have to pay.

## ENCOURAGING COMPETITION

Encouraging competition, to the FCC, means promoting efficient use of the frequency spectrum. To the commission, that means eliminating regulations that discourage innovation and "allocating frequencies in a manner to facilitate entry into the market of new competitors," as well as "the introduction of new applications and technologies" for the frequencies it oversees.[8] Examples would be allowing satellite radio services, enacting regulations that allow mobile wireless firms to use new faster technologies, and allowing the auction of spectrum space with the idea that companies bidding the most for it will use it in innovative ways. As you might imagine, there are those who believe the FCC has not nearly encouraged the efficient use of the spectrum as it claims. One strain of criticism insists that the commission has not allowed the development of many low-power radio stations that could reach only a small number of square miles but that would, in the process, serve many local communities. The commission's reasoning has been that the frequencies of such stations might interfere with existing stations or disrupt communications between pilots and the control tower at local airports. Critics say the real reason is that the larger radio stations don't want to compete with smaller ones for audiences and that they have persuaded the FCC to their side—using interference as an excuse.

At the Federal Trade Commission, in the meantime, encouraging competition means enforcing federal antitrust laws. Again, these are laws designed to prevent one or a few companies from controlling such a large percentage of an industry that they can dictate high prices and so harm the consumer. As with the FCC, FTC decisions in this area generate controversy.

Consider the FTC's decision to review the announcement by Google in 2009 that it would like to purchase the firm AdMob for $750 million. AdMob tracks people's mobile phones and serves ads to them based on their location and data about their web use.

The FTC contacted Google for more information about the deal, possibly out of concern that it might deter future competition in the mobile space. Reinforcing this perspective was a joint letter sent to the commission by two advocacy groups, Consumer Watchdog and the Center for Digital Democracy. They argued that Google was buying its way to dominance in the mobile advertising industry by diminishing the competition "to the detriment of consumers." According to a press release by the organizations, the letter asserted, "The mobile sector is the next frontier of the digital revolution. Without vigorous competition and strong privacy guarantees this vital and growing segment of the online economy will be stifled." The two groups added that the deal raised substantial privacy concerns because both companies involved in the deal gather tremendous amounts of data about consumers.[9] As it turned out, the groups were disappointed. The FTC approved the AdMob deal, considering it not anticompetitive. As you can see, the "boxing match" we discussed early in the chapter goes on continuously.

## CONSUMER PROTECTION

Both the FCC and the FTC pay attention to consumer protection as it relates to mass media. Of course, consumer protection can mean many things, so this area can be especially controversial. At the FCC, consumer protection has meant stopping marketers from using unsolicited prerecorded telemarketing calls ("robocalls"), making sure broadcasters and cable systems do not allow commercials that are louder than the programs around them, making rules about wireless 911 emergency phone lines, and promoting hearing aid compatibility for wireless telephones.

More controversially, the FCC has tried to make sure broadcasters use their spectrum "in the public interest"—in ways that are not always aimed at making the most money. You might be surprised that the commission has this sort of influence. It is the case that the basic principles of freedom of speech and of the press apply in electronic media just as they do in print media. Yet from the early days of broadcasting, Congress viewed it as different from print because the available wavelengths for radio and TV signals were limited (or scarce). According to Congress, this wavelength scarcity justified the creation of an agency such as the Federal Communications Commission to oversee the distribution of frequencies and to ensure competition of ideas over the airwaves.

Congress's notion of wavelength scarcity applies to broadcasting only—not to cable or satellite television. This limitation has sometimes put Congress and the FCC in the strange position of announcing content regulations for broadcasters that do not apply to hundreds of cable and satellite channels. For example, in 1996 the FCC announced that each week broadcast TV stations must air three hours of educational television programs aimed at children aged 16 and under that serve their "intellectual, cognitive, social, and emotional needs." Broadcasters complain that it is unfair that they alone, not cable or satellite networks, are required to spend the time and money on such programming. They also say that the requirement is outdated in an era of specialized children's channels such as Nickelodeon and the Disney Channel. Supporters of the rule argue that broadcasters should have greater obligations than other media firms because broadcasters are using valuable public airwaves that reach virtually everyone. The rule's supporters also claim that broadcasters do not always air programs that match the spirit of the FCC rule. In the case of Univision, the country's largest Spanish-language broadcaster, the commission agreed. In 2007 it forced Univision to pay a record $24 million fine for airing telenovelas (soap operas) that simply included children in plots during the time it claimed it was fulfilling the children's educational requirement from 2004 to 2006.[10]

The Federal Trade Commission's consumer protection work covers a wide territory, from combating deceptive advertising to protecting children's privacy on the web. As we have noted, the FTC was placed in charge of implementing and administering the Children's Online Privacy Protection Act, or COPPA. To implement the act, the FTC had to create rules that specified exactly what websites were covered by the act, exactly what rules should apply to them, and when the rules would go into effect. To administer the act, the FTC had to create a system for monitoring websites on a regular basis to make sure that they were adhering to COPPA.

The FTC also sues firms that it contends have engaged in false advertising that has harmed consumers. For example, it brought charges against the Skechers footwear company, saying that it deceived consumers with weight-loss and toning claims related to Shape-ups shoes and other toning products. At issue were ads (many starring the celebrity Kim Kardashian) urging consumers, "Shape up while you walk" and "Get in shape without setting foot in a gym." In 2012 the commission announced that Skechers had agreed to pay $40 million to settle the charges, though it didn't admit wrongdoing. Skechers' settlement with the FTC was part of a broader agreement with attorneys general from nearly all 50 states; consumers who bought the sneakers could request compensation.[11]

---

## THINKING ABOUT MEDIA LITERACY

Advertising often uses "creative" claims to get our attention about various products. Some of these claims might seem reasonable, whereas others, such as the Skechers ad, seem far-fetched. Can you think of any advertisements that raise some questionable or reaching claims about what their products can do or what benefits their products offer? Do you think the FTC's decision about Skechers' advertising has led or will lead people to think less of its footwear? What about if the FTC pursued actions against the ads you thought of? Why or why not?

---

## Media Self-Regulation

As you might imagine, advertising executives do not welcome actions of this sort from the government. Media executives in general don't welcome government interference. Even competitors within a media industry are not always happy when the FTC or FCC—or any government agency—responds to a problem by forcing other firms to act in certain ways. They worry that once the government gets involved in one company's activities, regulators may begin to exert unwanted influence on what other companies do too. Executives therefore often believe that it is best to create self-regulation regimes. **Self-regulation regimes** are sets of codes and agreements among companies in an industry to ensure that employees carry out their work in what industry officials agree is an ethical manner.

It's important to recognize that pressures toward self-regulation don't always originate from the government. Some of the pressures come from other places outside the industry. Some even come from within the media industry itself. Three major external sources of influence are members of the public, public advocacy organizations, and advertisers. Two sources from within the industry are professional groups and concerned leaders. Let's briefly look at these.

**self-regulation regimes**
codes and agreements among companies in an industry to ensure that employees carry out their work in what industry officials agree is an ethical manner

## External Pressures on Media to Self-Regulate

**Pressure from Members of the Public**   When individuals are disturbed about media content, they may contact the production, distribution, or exhibition firms involved to express their displeasure and demand alterations in the content. Pick any topic—from racism to religion, from politicians to businesspeople—and you will probably find that some sector of society is concerned about the portrayal of that topic in the mass media. People who see the mass media as a series of windows on the world often want to see the people, behaviors, and values that they hold dear portrayed fairly in the media products they use.

As we noted in chapter 2, media executives understand that they must think of their audiences as consumers who buy their products or whom they sell to advertisers. The complaining individual might be successful in getting the content changed or even removed if he or she convinces the media executives that they might otherwise lose a substantial portion of their target market. But an individual's concern will garner little attention if it is clear that the person does not belong in the target audience. The editors from *Cosmopolitan* magazine, which aims at 20-something single women, for example, are not likely to follow the advice of an elderly-sounding woman from rural Kansas who phones to protest what she feels are demeaning portrayals of women on covers of the magazine that she sees in the supermarket. Yet the magazine staff might well act favorably if a *Cosmo* subscriber writes with a suggestion for a new column that would attract more of the upscale single women they want as readers.

**advocacy organizations** or **pressure groups**
collections of people who work to change the nature of certain kinds of mass media materials

**Pressure from Advocacy Organizations**   Individuals who are particularly outraged about certain media portrayals may try to find others who share their concerns. They might join or start **advocacy organizations** or **pressure groups**, which work to change the nature of certain kinds of mass media materials.

Some advocacy organizations are specific to media. For example, the Center for Media Education concentrates on children and television, the Committee for Accuracy in Middle East Reporting in America (CAMERA) is devoted to promoting its view of accurate coverage of Israel in the media, and the Center for the Study of Commercialism criticizes advertising and marketing. Other advocacy organizations pay attention to media as part of more general concerns. For example, People for the American Way supports politically liberal approaches to social problems, GLAAD (formerly the Gay & Lesbian Alliance Against Defamation) advocates for fair representations of lesbian, gay, bisexual, and transgender people in the media, and the conservative American Family Association monitors all aspects of society for attacks on its preferred image of the family.

Representatives of these organizations may try to meet with the heads of media firms, start letter-writing campaigns, or attempt to embarrass media firms by attracting press coverage about an issue. If their target is an advertiser-supported medium, they may threaten to boycott the products of sponsors. They also may appeal to government officials for help.

**Pressure from Advertisers**   Advertisers are a powerful force in pressuring the media to make changes in their content. Many advertisers like to buy space or time for their commercial messages within media content that reflects well on their products. Companies such as Hallmark and Procter & Gamble, which spend enormous amounts of money on advertising, sometimes have the clout to persuade media firms to tone down certain kinds of portrayals that don't fit their brand image.

Consider, for example, efforts by marketers to generate more "family-friendly" programming to sponsor during prime time on television networks. In 1998, such advertising giants as Johnson & Johnson, AT&T, Bristol-Myers Squibb, Coca-Cola, Ford Motor Company, General Motors, Gillette, IBM, Kellogg's, McDonald's, Procter & Gamble, and Unilever United States became concerned that the increased level of sex and violence on TV was angering many of their customers. These elements of TV programming were also making it difficult for them to reach both parents and children at the same time.

In response, the marketers created the Family Friendly Programming Forum. It seeks to stimulate the production of shows meant to appeal to broader, multigenerational audiences and suitable to run between 8:00 and 10:00 p.m. (Eastern and Pacific times). "We want to sit and watch TV with our families and not be embarrassed," explained Steve Johnston, vice president for advertising and brand management at Nationwide Mutual Enterprises in Columbus, Ohio.[12]

NBC's quickly-cancelled series *Animal Practice* followed the story of a successful veterinarian who is painfully socially inept. Situational comedies such as this, which generally lack many (if any) references to violence or sex, are considered suitable family-friendly programs.

## THINKING ABOUT MEDIA LITERACY

How would you define "family-friendly" programming? What are some shows that fit with your definition? What are some shows that challenge it? Why do you think family-friendly shows might be popular with audiences?

Critics of this coalition fear that it wants to create programs that romanticize a kind of fictional nuclear family. The advertisers insist, however, that it is possible to be both contemporary and family-friendly. "We have to be realistic; families may not be gathered around one TV anymore, and they're not your traditional families," said Susan Frank, executive vice president and general manager of the Odyssey Network in Studio City, California, a cable channel owned by Hallmark Cards that focuses on family-oriented programming. "But there are times you can bring family members together with content that's thought-provoking, done in a good, quality way," she added. "You have to be relevant to the way people live today."[13]

By 2009, the Family Friendly Programming Forum had come directly under the wing of the Association of National Advertisers (ANA) and changed its name to the ANA Alliance for Family Entertainment. The name change indicated a broadened mission to reflect the changing media environment, "to ensuring there are programming choices on broadcast/cable networks, internet, mobile devices and gaming platforms, wherever consumers look for family entertainment." To emphasize that it was building on past successes, the alliance noted on its website that it had "played a significant role in bringing 20 primetime programs to air, including hits *The Gilmore Girls, Chuck, Everybody Hates Chris,* and *Friday Night Lights*."[14] Although this project has itself created controversy, it does show how powerful advertisers can respond to concerns they perceive in their target audience and act to influence media.

## Internal Pressures on Media to Self-Regulate

To maintain their credibility with the public at large (and their target audiences in particular) and to avoid pressures from government and other outside entities interfering with their firms' activities, media executives set up self-regulation policies and codes. This internal self-regulation can take a number of forms, including editorial standards and ombudspersons at the level of individual organizations and professional codes of ethics, journalism reviews, and content ratings at the industry level.

**editorial standards**
written statements of policy and conduct established by media organizations as a form of self-regulation

**policy books**
guidelines for fairness, accuracy, and appropriateness of station content and the like, adopted by media organizations in the interest of self-regulation

**operating policies**
policies, most often used by print media organizations, that spell out guidelines for everyday operations, such as conflicts of interest, acceptable advertising content, boundaries of deceptive information-gathering practices, payment to sources for news stories, and so on

**editorial policies**
policies, most often used by print media organizations, that identify company positions on specific issues, such as which presidential candidate the paper supports and whether the paper is in support of certain governmental policies

**ombudsperson**
an individual who is hired by a media organization to deal with readers, viewers, or listeners who have a complaint to report or an issue to discuss

**code of ethics**
a formal list of guidelines and standards designed to establish standards of professionalism within an industry

**journalism reviews**
publications that report on and analyze examples of ethical and unethical journalism

**Editorial Standards**   Most media organizations have established **editorial standards**—written statements of policy and conduct. In the case of the network television industry, these policies are maintained and enforced by a department known as Standards and Practices, which makes difficult decisions regarding the acceptability of language in scripts, themes in plotlines, and images used in visual portrayals. At the local television station level, policy and conduct are most often guided by **policy books**, which help to lay down guidelines for fairness, accuracy, and appropriateness of station content, among other things.

Newspapers and magazines are most often guided by two kinds of editorial standards. The first kind of standards, **operating policies**, spell out guidelines for everyday operations, such as conflicts of interest, acceptable advertising content, boundaries of deceptive information-gathering practices, and payment to sources for news stories, among other things. The second kind, **editorial policies**, identify company positions on specific issues, such as which presidential candidate the paper supports and whether the paper is in support of certain governmental policies.

**Ombudspersons**   An **ombudsperson** is hired by a media organization to deal with readers, viewers, or listeners who have a complaint to report or an issue to discuss. Although an ombudsperson is employed directly by a media organization, his or her role is to act as an impartial intermediary between the organization and the public.

**Professional Codes of Ethics**   One of the oldest approaches to self-regulation is the professional **code of ethics**. This is a formal list of guidelines and standards that tell the members of the profession—in this case, media practitioners—what they should and should not do. These codes are designed to establish internal standards of professionalism and are often administered by societies or associations that represent an industry's interests to the outside world.

Examples of such organizations are the Society of Professional Journalists, the American Society of Newspaper Editors, the Radio-Television News Directors Association, the American Advertising Federation, and the Public Relations Society of America. Each has an established code of ethics, and you can find these codes online.

**Journalism Reviews**   **Journalism reviews**—publications that report on and analyze examples of ethical and unethical journalism—are yet another internal force that helps the media self-regulate. These reviews include publications such as *Quill*, *Columbia Journalism Review*, and *American Journalism Review*. Take a look at the print copies of these journals or their counterparts on the web. What you'll see are vehicles that explore the realities of the news business and stand up for the values of journalism and for the rights of journalists around the world.

**Content Ratings and Advisories** Another way in which media organizations regulate themselves is through the adoption of ratings systems. Most prominent are those of the film, television, and video game industries. The Motion Picture Association of America (MPAA) created the first of these three voluntary ratings systems in 1968; it was revised in 1990. Film ratings are determined by a full-time Ratings Board, located in Los Angeles, California. The board is made up of 8 to 13 people who are not specially qualified in any way, other than the fact that they all have "parenthood experience." When a film is submitted to the Ratings Board, each member estimates what most parents would consider to be an appropriate rating for the film. The criteria the board considers are theme, violence, language, nudity, sensuality, and drug abuse, among other elements. After a group discussion, the board votes on the film's rating, which is decided by a majority vote.

The Ratings Board process sounds quite rational, but movie executives and members of the public have complained that the decisions to rate films PG, R, or NC-17 are often quite subjective and based on the particular, sometimes eccentric judgments of the committee members. A film about the movie ratings process, *This Film Is Not Yet Rated* (2006), emphasizes these limitations to a process the movie industry likes to portray as rational, systematic, and predictable. This movie's release seems not to have deterred the industry from using the ratings as its primary form of self-regulation. The success of the approach has led other industries to copy it.

The video game and television industries are cases in point. They model their ratings after the MPAA approach. Games' ratings are set by the Entertainment Software Rating Board (ESRB), an organization of industry leaders created in the early 1990s as a result of threatened federal intervention because of public outcry over violence and sex in certain video games. Like the movie ratings, the ESRB ratings are determined by a specially chosen panel of "regular" people. Table 5.4 and Table 5.5 present the ratings categories for movies and video games along with their meaning.

**Table 5.4** The Entertainment Software Ratings Board Ratings Categories

- EC: *Early childhood.* May be suitable for children aged 3 and older. Contains no material that parents would find inappropriate

- E: *Everyone.* May be suitable for persons aged 6 and older. These titles will appeal to people of many ages and tastes. They may contain minimal cartoon, fantasy, or mild violence and/or infrequent use of mild language. This rating was formerly known as Kids to Adult (K–A).

- E10+: *Everyone ten and older.* May be suitable for ages 10 and older. Titles in this category may contain more cartoon, fantasy, or mild violence, mild language, and/or minimal suggestive themes.

- T: *Teen.* May be suitable for ages 13 and older. Titles in this category may contain violence, suggestive themes, crude humor, minimal blood, simulated gambling, and/or infrequent use of strong language.

- M: *Mature.* May be suitable for persons aged 17 and older. Titles in this category may contain intense violence, blood and gore, sexual content, and/or strong language.

- AO: Adults only. Should be played only by persons 18 years or older. Titles in this category may include prolonged scenes of intense violence and/or graphic sexual content and nudity.

**Table 5.5** The Motion Picture Association of America Ratings Categories

- G: *General audience—all ages admitted.* This is a film that contains nothing in theme, language, nudity and sex, violence, and so on that would be offensive to parents whose younger children view the film.

- PG: *Parental guidance suggested—some material may not be suitable for children.* This is a film that needs to be examined or inquired into by parents before they let their children attend.

- PG-13: *Parents strongly cautioned—some material may be inappropriate for children under 13.* This is a film that goes beyond the boundaries of the PG rating in theme, violence, nudity, sensuality, language, or other content but that does not quite fit within the restricted R category.

- R: *Restricted—anyone under 17 requires accompanying parent or adult guardian.* This is a film that definitely contains some adult material, possibly including hard language, tough violence, nudity within sensual scenes, drug abuse, or a combination of these and other elements.

- NC-17: *No one under 17 admitted.* This is a film that most parents will consider patently too adult for their youngsters under 17. No children will be admitted.

**Table 5.6** The National Association of Broadcasters Ratings Categories

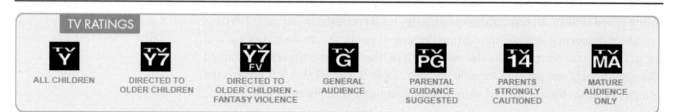

- TV-Y: *All children.* This program is designed to be appropriate for all children, including children aged 2 to 6.

- TV-Y7: *Directed to older children.* This program is designed for children aged 7 and above.

- TV-G: *General audience.* Most parents would find this program suitable for all ages. It contains little or no violence, no strong language, and little or no sexual dialogue or situations.

- TV-PG: *Parental guidance suggested.* This program contains material that parents may find unsuitable for younger children. The theme itself may call for parental guidance, and/or the program may contain one or more of the following: moderate violence (V), some sexual situations (S), infrequent coarse language (L), or some suggestive dialogue (D).

- TV-14: *Parents strongly cautioned.* This program contains some material that many parents would find unsuitable for children under 14 years of age. This program contains one or more of the following: intense violence (V), intense sexual situations (S), strong coarse language (L), or intensely suggestive dialogue (D).

- TV-MA: *Mature audience only.* This program is specifically designed to be viewed by adults and therefore may be unsuitable for children under 17. This program contains one or more of the following: graphic violence (V), explicit sexual activity (S), or crude indecent language (L).

You undoubtedly have seen some of the letters during the course of your leisure activities. You also may be familiar with the categories the television industry uses to help parents sort through the huge volume of material available through their cable or satellite feeds. Also modeled after the movie ratings, these guidelines consist of six categories (see Table 5.6). Rather than using "regular" people, the networks and producers of each show determine the show's parental guidelines. A monitoring board formed by the National Association of Broadcasters works to achieve accuracy and consistency in applying the parental guidelines by examining programs with inappropriate guidelines and reviewing programs that have been publicly criticized.

## THINKING ABOUT MEDIA LITERACY

Ratings on films, television shows, and video games often draw controversy because audiences disagree with the ratings boards' decisions. Have you ever seen a film or purchased a video game that has a rating you disagree with? What rating did it have, and why did you disagree with it? What rating would you have given it instead?

These ratings do seem to have done what their industries wanted them to do: stop lawmakers from threatening companies with some sort of punishment if they didn't calm large sectors of the public about their products. Still, the ratings are controversial in some circles. Some people believe they are merely a fig leaf to cover the huge amount of objectionable material these industries produce and promote. Others take a very different view. They point out that mainstream exhibitors such as movie theaters, stores, and websites hesitate to carry products with ratings that are for adults only. These critics believe that the difficulty of getting "objectionable" materials in front of the public means that works with controversial yet important themes and images will not be made—or, if made, will not get the attention they deserve.

They point to the documentary film *Bully* (2011) as an example. The producers created it with the goal of getting schoolchildren to see the terrible nature of bullying and its consequences for young people. After being exposed to the coarse language of the bullies in the movie, though, the ratings board gave it an NC-17 rating, and so major movie theater chains refused to show it. It was only when the film's distributor, the Weinstein Company, launched a public relations blitz pointing out the folly of this decision that executives of the largest chains changed their minds and scheduled *Bully* in their theaters.

The initial ratings of the documentary *Bully* (NC-17 and R) would have made it much more difficult for the intended audience of the film (adolescents 17 years old and younger) to see the film since they would have to be attended by an adult guardian. Katy Butler, a 17-year-old student from Michigan, launched a campaign to have the Motion Picture Association of America lower the rating so that teens would be able to see the movie without a guardian. She managed to secure a petition with more than 200,000 signatures.

**ethics**
a system of principles about what is right that guides a person's actions

## The Role of Ethics

**E**thics is a system of notions about right and wrong that guides a person's actions. Let's look a bit more carefully at the topic of ethics and the way it relates to business requirements.

### Making Ethical Decisions

Every day you find yourself in situations in which ethical decisions need to be made, whether those situations involve the mass media or not. How do you make these decisions? What sort of moral reasoning process should you follow—not only as a media consumer but also and more importantly as a good citizen?

Bob Steele, a senior faculty member at the Poynter Institute, outlines a model that media literates and professionals alike can use to evaluate and examine their decisions and to make good ethical decisions. Steele is concerned specifically with journalism, but the ethical thinking process that he suggests can work for all sorts of media practitioners and consumers. Steele says to ask yourself these 10 questions:[15]

1. What do I know? What do I need to know?
2. What are my ethical concerns?
3. What is my journalistic (or informational, entertainment, advertising, or educational) purpose?
4. What organizational policies and professional guidelines should I consider?
5. How can I include other people, with different perspectives and diverse ideas, in the decision-making process?
6. Who are the stakeholders—those affected by my decision? What are their motivations? Which are legitimate?
7. What if the roles were reversed? How would I feel if I were in the shoes of one of the stakeholders?
8. What are the possible consequences of my actions in the short term and in the long term?
9. What are my alternatives to maximize my truth-telling responsibility and minimize harm?
10. Can I clearly and fully justify my thinking and my decision to my colleagues, to the stakeholders, and to the public?

## Ethical Duties to Various Constituencies

When combined with larger philosophies of ethics, Bob Steele's questions can help media practitioners think about their day-to-day responsibilities and prepare for events that raise grave ethical dilemmas. Ethical dilemmas often come about because we are torn over an issue, pulled in a number of directions. The perspective that media ethics scholars Clifford Christians, Mark Fackler, and Kim Rotzoll contribute to this topic can help bring a sharper focus to the issues Steele raises when it comes to knotty ethical situations. In order to reach a responsible decision, these scholars write, an individual must clarify which parties will be influenced by a decision and which ones the person feels particularly obligated to support.[16]

Imagine, for example, that you are a movie theater executive who must make the decision of whether to carry *Bully* with an NC-17 rating. How would you use Steele's previously listed questions to think through your decision? Where would you stand before and after the Weinstein PR blitz—and why? What considerations would guide your decisions? Christians and his colleagues stress that as you make this decision—or carry out the production, distribution, or exhibition of any media product—you should realize you have obligations to five parties, or constituencies. These five parties are you, the audience, the employer, the profession, and society. To these five, we will add one more: the people to whom we've made promises, such as publics and (in the case of journalists) sources.

- *Duty to self.* As a media practitioner, you clearly feel a duty to make sure your actions do not harm you. In fact, a key goal of your work is to make yourself look good—to shine in your job—and to act in ways that allow you to feel ethically correct.
- *Duty to audience.* As a media practitioner, you also have a duty to make sure that what you do takes the nature and expectations of the audience into consideration.
- *Duty to the employer.* The company that pays your salary is also an important consideration. At the very least, a practitioner owes the firm good work—a product that meets the expectations that caused the person to be hired in the first place.

- *Duty to the profession.* Most practitioners feel an allegiance to their profession. Movie scriptwriters feel an obligation to keep up the reputation and pay of the people who ply that craft. Similarly, reporters feel a responsibility to help other journalists who are in trouble and to make sure that their profession is taken seriously by editors and publishers.

- *Duty to promise holders.* If you made promises to people during the course of covering a news story, putting a movie together, or making an ad, you may (and should) feel an obligation to those people when you move forward with your work. If a source requested anonymity, you can't divulge the source's name even if your editor thinks the article would be better if it were there. If you promised a young TV talk show host the first interview about your new film, you are obligated to give that show the first interview, even though Jay Leno wants you first.

- *Duty to society.* Many practitioners also feel an obligation to society at large. You live in a real world, with neighbors, children, stores, churches, and governments. If you produce recordings, edit movies, write sitcoms, or illustrate children's books, you may feel that what you produce should have a positive social impact. At least, you may say, what you produce should not have a negative social impact.

## Forming Ethical Standards for the Mass Media

If you think about these ethical systems, about Bob Steele's 10 questions, and about the constituencies that Clifford Christians and his colleagues discuss, you will see that ethical standards for the mass media often involve at least three levels:

- The personal level
- The professional level
- The societal level

Most media practitioners find that they cannot exist on one level only. How their standards develop at each level has to do with their values and ideals. From these two sources come their principles—the basis for their ethical actions at every level.

**Values** reflect our presuppositions about social life and human nature. They cover a broad range of possibilities, such as aesthetic values (how harmonious or pleasing something is), professional values (innovation and promptness), logical values (consistency and competency), sociocultural values (thrift and hard work), and moral values (honesty and nonviolence).

**Ideals** are notions of excellence or goals that are thought to bring about greater harmony to ourselves and to others. For example, American culture respects ideals such as tolerance, compassion, loyalty, forgiveness, peace, justice, fairness, and respect for persons. In addition to these human ideals, there are institutional or organizational ideals, such as profit, efficiency, productivity, quality, and stability.

**Principles** are those guidelines we derive from values and ideals and are precursors to codified rules. They are usually stated in positive (prescriptive) or negative (proscriptive) terms. Consider, for example, the motto "never corrupt the integrity of media channels"—a principle derived from the professional value of truth-telling in public relations—or the statement "always maximize profit," a principle derived from belief in the efficacy of the free enterprise system. The ideals, values, and principles of media practitioners, organizations, and industries will differ according to the differing goals and loyalties of each.

**values**
those things that reflect our presuppositions about social life and human nature

**ideals**
notions of excellence or goals that are thought to bring about greater harmony to ourselves and to others

**principles**
those guidelines we derive from values and ideals that are precursors to codified rules

# Media Literacy, Regulation, and Ethics

The high risks involved in today's highly competitive media environment often make decisions that may seem straightforward—such as allowing the exhibition of *Bully*—complex. The high risks also create pressure on individuals to conform to organizational activities that, although legal, might be considered unethical. An individual's duty to the media organization may conflict with his or her duty to society; an individual's personal values may conflict with the organization's values.

For example, consider the use of graphic violence in TV dramas, in local TV news programs, in ads, and in music recordings. Many of the distributors and exhibitors of the material—and even its creators—may personally abhor some elements of what they are doing. In their business lives, though, they may feel they have to use those elements. Why? Because they "work"—that is, they seem to sell the product to the right audience in a manner that supports the organization and brings paychecks to its members. A well-paid writer of TV movies once yelled at me for asking him questions that implied respect for his craft. "I write junk!" he shouted. He added that he knew he used violence and sex as props to advance his plots and that he wrote according to the most blatant pop-cultural formulas. He said, "I do it because I have a family to support and a big mortgage to pay off for this house in Brentwood! I do it, but I know it's junk. Don't forget that!"

Whereas this writer may condemn his own scripts as contributing to the violent and mediocre nature of popular culture, the producers of the programs that were based on these scripts might argue that they were handsome creations that explore issues of good and evil in ways that are accessible to large audiences.

There also may be ambiguity regarding how to apply ethical principles. Ethical criteria may seem straightforward, but they are not always so. Take the principle of not misleading people—a notion that most people would agree is a basic ethical principle. Consider a famous case from the 1970s in light of this principle: The Campbell Soup Company's ad agency put marbles in the bottom of a bowl of soup in an ad to emphasize the soup's chunkiness by making it look as if it contained many big pieces of meat and vegetables. Responding to complaints from competitors, the Federal Trade Commission forced the company to withdraw the ad. But one can ask, was that really misleading? Campbell's argued that the company was trying to emphasize a genuine feature of its soup that the camera couldn't easily reflect without the marbles. The Federal Trade Commission disagreed, but that doesn't mean that Campbell's employees felt that they were acting unethically—do you believe they were?

Sometimes, though, executives do acknowledge that business competition leads them to act unethically. One way to guard themselves and their competitors from improper behavior is by encouraging rules that prohibit it. From one point of view, then, media laws and regulations can be seen as a way to formally enforce agreed-upon norms of behavior. The First Amendment is a proposition that reflects ethical values regarding the government's relation to media, information, and the public. Similarly, antitrust laws, laws against deceptive advertising, and self-regulatory ratings voice norms about how media firms and media practitioners ought to behave.

## Media Regulations and the Savvy Citizen

Thinking about the rules that guide the media is crucial for a media-literate consumer. You can undoubtedly think of many examples of anger directed at the media. Activists who believe in a woman's right to choose abortion might be deeply offended by the portrayals of teen pregnancies in a TV movie shown by one of the networks. They might feel that doing nothing about these portrayals invites further support of the antiabortion position by the producers when they work on other shows. They also might believe that the portrayals will reinforce in the audience unfortunate images of and actions toward teen abortions in society. So they might mobilize to prevent the network from showing the film again and to force the network to air a film or series that is more sympathetic toward teenagers who choose abortions.

However, at the same time that the pro-choice activists are voicing their complaints, groups that find any portrayal of abortion to be reprehensible might make totally opposite demands of the network. They might argue that such portrayals encourage children and others to think that abortion is acceptable in society and that this erodes family values—the very values that define American society. Consequently, they might demand that the network never portray any abortions.

Three points about these opposing groups and their demands deserve attention here. One point is the similarity in their approach: although they are far apart ideologically, their concern about the media comes not so much from a worry about how the members of their immediate groups will react to the movie as from concern about how members of society who are less informed on the subject—especially children—will relate to the material. This type of concern is common among media activists. Arguments with media firms are often based on fear about the media's effects on other segments of society.

A second point is that the two groups are divided on the question of what is ethically correct for the media to do in this case. One side has notions of ethically proper images that involve certain positive portrayals of abortion. The other side considers any depiction of abortion as playing a legitimate part in mainstream society to be unethical.

Finally, it should be clear that this is an ethical conflict that cannot be resolved by government regulation. As we have seen, the First Amendment protects the creators of media materials, including most forms of entertainment, from government interference. The First Amendment would apply in the abortion fight. In other circumstances, however, other laws might take precedence, and a concerned citizen would need to understand when it is appropriate to ask the government to intervene. We have seen, for example, that in the case of libel of a nonpublic figure in a TV entertainment program, the person who was insulted likely would be allowed to have her or his day in court.

Knowing the laws that relate to particular media in particular circumstances is critical to understanding the rights and responsibilities that apply to you, media firms, and government when it comes to materials you like or don't like. In many cases, you will find that no governmental law will help you to force certain media organizations to act in what you believe is an ethical manner. You will also find out that there are few easily agreed-upon media ethics in a nation as complex and varied as the United States. Of course, people who care about media ethics should not give up trying to persuade media organizations to alter their notions of proper behavior. However, persuading media organizations to do things involves much more than simply insisting on the ethical value of one person's or one group's suggestions; as we have seen, there may be others who insist on the ethical value of totally opposite actions. So it is also necessary to understand the following: controversial proposals likely will not be accepted by media organizations as a result of social debate unless the party making the proposal is able to exercise economic and political power.

# CHAPTER REVIEW

 Visit the Companion Website at www.routledge.com/cw/turow for additional study tools and resources.

## Key Terms

You can find the definitions to these key terms in the marginal glossary throughout this chapter. Test your knowledge of these terms with interactive flash cards on the *Media Today* companion website.

| | | |
|---|---|---|
| actual malice | false light | parody |
| advocacy organizations or pressure groups | Federal Communications Commission (FCC) | policy books |
| | | pool reporters |
| antitrust policies | Federal Trade Commission (FTC) | principles |
| appropriation | ideals | prior restraint |
| code of ethics | intrusion | privacy |
| copyright | journalism reviews | private person |
| Copyright Act of 1976 | libel | public disclosure |
| defamation | libel per quod | public figure |
| economic regulations | libel per se | self-regulation regimes |
| editorial policies | monopoly | simple malice |
| editorial standards | obscene | simple negligence |
| embeds | oligopoly | slander |
| ethics | ombudsperson | transformative |
| fair use regulations | operating policies | values |

## Questions for Discussion and Critical Thinking

1. The opening of this chapter discussed SOPA and PIPA from the points of view of copyright holders and internet industries. If either or both of these bills had passed, how do you think they would have affected consumers? Would consumers have benefited from this legislation? Why or why not?

2. One of the rules for determining obscenity states that the entire work must be deemed obscene and not just one sequence, scene, or image. Can you think of shorter parts of media texts you are familiar with that might be deemed obscene? How might it be difficult to label the entire television show or film obscene?

3. The documentary *This Film Is Not Yet Rated* shows how the MPAA movie ratings are inconsistent from one film to another. For example, drug use might earn an R rating, but extreme violence might earn a PG-13 rating. Do you think the movie industry and other industries with internal

review boards should standardize their criteria and make them public? Or do you think they need not do this? Why or why not?

4. We all grow up with different ideas of what is right and what is wrong, but we may not stop and think about these ideas as systems of ethics. If you were to get a job working as a reporter for your hometown newspaper, what ideas of right and wrong might you bring to the job?

5. The Children's Online Privacy Protection Act (COPPA) requires websites to get parents' permission if they want to get identifiable personal information (e.g., full name, e-mail address, phone number) from children under the age of 13. When the bill was first introduced to Congress, many privacy advocates wanted to raise the age to 17 or under, or at least older than 13. Do you think that the age limit should have been raised to older than 13? Why or why not? Why do you think that the age was not raised?

# Case Study
## JOURNALISTS AND ETHICAL DILEMMAS

**The Idea** Reading about the ethical dilemmas that media practitioners experience is not the same thing as experiencing them firsthand. You might be able to understand these dilemmas and the ways media practitioners and their organizations deal with them better by talking directly to them about it.

**The Method** Interview a local journalist about an ethical dilemma that he or she confronted during his or her career. Come prepared with questions, and take notes during the interview, or ask the journalist for permission to record it. To get the journalist to be most honest, you may have to promise that when you write your essay about the interview, you will not reveal his or her name.

Ask what the dilemma was. With whom did the journalist share the dilemma inside and outside of his or her media organization? How did the journalist resolve the dilemma? Why? How did it affect the story that the journalist wanted to tell?

In writing an essay about the interview, ask yourself if the resolution the journalist found for the dilemma fits with one or more of the ethics models described in this chapter. Also consider whether you would have resolved the dilemma in the same way or in a different way.

# The Media Industries

## The Forces Driving Convergence in Media Industries

The first part of this book covered the big picture of today's media industries. It looked at the components of those industries. It analyzed how they relate to the ideas of "mass communication," "mass media," and the interrelationship of media with culture. It described the interactive nature of digital media and how companies today often encourage members of the audience to act as consumers and producers of digital media. It surveyed ways that researchers have studied the impacts of media on society and individuals. It outlined ways to look at content genres across the media industries. It explored the advertising and public relations structures that fund the media, and it laid out U.S. laws that guide them.

The second part of this book shifts gears. Now that you have a bird's-eye view of the system and the parts that make it work, we will focus on key media industries within that system. Those industries create the content (and the culture) that we associate with media today. Think about what your world would be like without books, newspapers, magazines, recorded music, radio, movies, television, and video games. Think, too, what it would be like without the internet, which we often take for granted when we use it to bring the content of books, newspapers, video games, and more to us in digital forms. Decisions about the creation, distribution, and exhibition of these different media materials take place in particular industries. The people who work in them typically see the industries as separate, with distinct histories within the larger media system described in the first section of the book. So, for example, to understand who chooses the books we see in stores and online and why, we have to explore the book industry. To trace the considerations that lead to the films shown in local movie theaters, we need to take a look at the movie industry. That's the kind of thinking we will be doing in the next several chapters.

An aim of this part of the book is to stress the importance of convergence in media industries and to sketch the considerations that cause convergence to happen even while the media practitioners see themselves as working within particular industries. You probably recall from chapter 1 that media convergence is the presentation across several media of content traditionally associated with one medium, such as when you can watch a film on a movie screen, a television set, a laptop, and a cell phone. You may remember that in chapter 1 we described three elements—corporations, content, and computers—that need to be brought together if convergence as a mass communication process is to occur. That is, convergence in the mass media requires corporations serving content via networked computers to their audiences. Today, the corporation-content-computer relationship is commonplace, and media convergence is skyrocketing. Take a look at any computer-related device—your laptop, tablet, smartphone, or video game console, for example—and you'll undoubtedly find the capability to download movies, music, magazine articles, books, and much more content that you could also find on other devices.

But why does convergence take place? Why do people in the book and newspaper industries see a need to move the content they produce to e-readers? Why do movie companies move their films from theaters to hotels, airplanes, and DVDs? One answer—to make money—may seem obvious. But that begs another question. What developments are taking place in industries that make it possible to make money through the movement of materials across traditional media boundaries?

It turns out that convergence is being propelled by five developments that stand at the heart of today's media industries:

- The spread of digital media
- The importance of distribution windows
- Audience fragmentation and segmentation
- Globalization
- Conglomeration

Understanding these developments is critical to understanding the changes taking place in all media industries today. They all have different histories. The importance of distribution windows, audience fragmentation and segmentation, globalization, and conglomeration came into being even before the spread of digital media. Digital media, however, have encouraged and extended these processes. In turn, the processes, as well as the further spread of digital media, have encouraged convergence. These developments will show up in the following chapters on particular media industries. There we will discuss not only why it is *possible* to move materials across media boundaries but also why it is often *necessary*. Here we will sketch the five developments briefly as a foundation for the following chapters—so that you will understand them and their importance when you encounter them later.

## The Spread of Digital Media

**digital media**
devices with computer processors that allow access to textual, audio, and/or visual material

We start with the spread of digital media because today these media stand at the core of so many convergent activities. **Digital media** are devices with computer processors that allow access to textual, audio, and/or visual material. As we've noted, among the most popular digital media are MP3 music players, tablets, and smartphones, as well as laptop or desktop computers. One key aspect of the spread of these and other digital media is their link to the internet. If content is placed on the web, it then becomes rather easy to use that content on many different devices.

An important reason for the acceleration of convergence, then, is the technical ability to carry it out as a result of the spread of the internet among the U.S. population. The internet accelerates the spread of convergence. In 2012, about

76 million U.S. households had internet access. That number represented about 67 percent of all U.S. households and 95 percent of computer-owning households. At this point, you might be marveling at how digitization has created enormous opportunities for companies. But digitization also has created major challenges for firms involved in the production, distribution, and exhibition of media materials. One challenge is that all these new devices bring potential for lots more competition among publishers. To executives in the 21st century, a publisher is a person or organization that produces, markets, and distributes content. For example, on the web both the *New York Times* newspaper and the CBS television network are publishers. The more important point, though, is that on the web those two large media firms compete with untold numbers of other news and entertainment producer-distributors. Because of the low costs of making digital documents and distributing them on the web, almost anyone can be a publisher today.

Digital media *are* now commonplace, among both the old and especially the younger generations. Tablets, iPods, and portable video game consoles make it possible to engage with digital media in the home and outside the home thanks to 3G and 4G technology and the growing abundance of wireless hotpots.

The competition among producers and distributors of media material also extends to exhibitors. Recall from chapter 1 that exhibitors present distributed materials to targeted audiences for them to choose. Before the digital media era, for many types of media materials, competition among exhibitors within a particular area was fairly limited. As an example, a neighborhood might have just one or two video stores, one newspaper home-delivery firm, a few newspaper and magazine stands and pay boxes, a couple of bookstores, and a cable system that competes with two TV satellite operators. With the rise of the web, all that has changed. Now the video stores (if they still exist) compete directly with digital streaming-movie sites such as Netflix and Amazon. The bookstore (if it remains in business) must compete with Amazon and Barnes & Noble online. The newspaper vendors must worry that people who live in the area will access local, national, and even international newspapers on the web. And the cable and satellite operators, apart from competing with one another, must face sites such as Netflix, Hulu, Hulu Plus, Amazon Prime, and YouTube that offer many of the same programs.

## The Importance of Distribution Windows

The mention of Netflix, Hulu, and YouTube brings up the importance of distribution **windows**. The term "windows" refers to the various exhibition points distributors use to generate revenues for a product—for example, a movie theater, a newspaper, or a cable network. The concept of windows predates the rise of digital media. Companies have long used the idea of windows in the analog (non-digital) media world to bring in revenues from different places for the same materials. This approach is not too different from the British TV firm ITV's way of selling its hit series *Downton Abbey* in the United States during 2011 and 2012. It sold the first window—the Public Broadcasting Service (PBS)—the rights to show every new season's program episode by episode. After every season of the series ended, ITV yanked repeat episodes off PBS and made money from the season's episodes through other windows: physical stores (with the episodes packaged as a DVD set), online stores (as a DVD set), and rental locations such as video stores and digital streaming sites.

**windows**

the various exhibition points distributors use to generate revenues for a product—for example, a movie theater, a newspaper, or a cable network

As the *Downton Abbey* example indicates, media producers try to increase revenues by moving their content across a number of windows. Different media industries have tended to approach this activity in different ways. In the television and film businesses, where production costs are quite high, the challenge of covering costs has forced production organizations to design their output with an eye toward moving it across mass media boundaries.

When companies make theatrical films, their windows are quite a bit more varied than that of TV producers. Blockbuster movies such as *Men in Black 3* likely move through a gauntlet of platforms, including movie theaters, store-bought DVDs, video stores, Redbox video machines, streaming sites such as Netflix, hotel pay-per-view channels, video-on-demand cable and satellite channels, airline flights, premium subscription cable/satellite networks such as HBO and Showtime, non-premium cable/satellite networks such as USA Network, and (rarely nowadays) finally, broadcast networks and local stations (see Figure P.1).

In the digital world, distributors' desire to have as many windows as possible for their products has encouraged the growth in convergence—that is, the movement of the same content across different digital media.

Why do distributors want more and more windows? As you might suspect, the answer has to do with money. Of course, the use of all these windows to cover costs and make a good profit assumes that people will want to view the movies and TV shows across the various windows. When we get to the chapters on print media—books, newspapers, and magazines—we will see that making money from windows, especially digital windows, is not at all a sure thing. The rush is to use the convergence of media by exhibiting through as many digital windows as possible or be left out of the new world.

### Figure P.1

An example of distribution windows for a movie. Contracts between the distributor and the exhibitors determine the order of windows and time between them.

# Audience Fragmentation and Segmentation

The previous section explored the challenges and opportunities of using convergence to exploit new windows with the aim of increasing a media firm's revenues and extending the value of its brands. At the same time, media producers, distributors, and exhibitors must also confront another major development: the growth of audience fragmentation and segmentation. As with windows, audience fragmentation and segmentation preceded the rise of digital media. And as with windows, the process influences more than media convergence. So we will now describe audience fragmentation and segmentation and examine their role in media today and, especially, in the growth of convergence.

Audience segmentation is a direct result of channel fragmentation. As we discussed in chapter 1, the term "**channel fragmentation**" refers to the great increase in the number of mass media outlets that has taken place during the past two decades. This fragmentation started well before the web. It was particularly startling in the case of television. In 1975, a family in Philadelphia could receive television signals only over the air, which meant they had access to seven channels. During the 1980s, cable television companies began to spread across the city, and during the 1990s satellite TV firms came in. Today, most households subscribe to a cable or satellite service and receive well over 100 channels. This is the pattern throughout the United States.

Although channel fragmentation preceded the internet, the internet rise accelerated the trend. To understand how the web has multiplied TV fragmentation substantially, consider the number of places you can find short and long video clips online. The same holds true with any medium that has digital competition. Local newspapers now must share space with journalistic services that are thousands of miles away. Traditional magazine firms confront competition with a multitude of web outlets that cover the same subjects. The steep rise of digital media clearly encourages the movement of material that might have been locally available only in print or video to find homes in many digital spaces.

As with channel fragmentation, audience erosion by no means started with the internet. The most important erosion of magazine and newspaper audiences began as a result of the introduction of television in the late 1940s. Erosion of AM radio audiences began with the introduction of FM radio in the 1960s. Since the 1980s, media and advertising practitioners have noted that the audiences for all media are eroding at an increasing pace. Much of that erosion is due to the dramatic splintering of audiences for broadcast television. From the late 1940s until the early 1980s, fully 90 percent of all those watching television were tuned in to ABC, CBS, or NBC, according to the Nielsen audience ratings company. By the mid-2000s, though, the three networks' "share" had slid to about 51 percent—that's a 39 percent drop. According to Nielsen, the missing population could be found at the relatively new Fox network (which had about 13 percent of the audience); at the smaller, newer broadcast networks (e.g., CW and Univision); at cable networks; and playing DVDs and video games.

The spread of digital media—and the nearly limitless number of websites and apps a person can access through many media—makes audience fragmentation a bigger issue now than ever. Instead of trying to attract everybody, today's media executives respond to the situation by focusing on a specific audience. They are trying to define

**channel fragmentation**
the great increase in the number of mass media outlets that has taken place during the past two decades

and hold an audience niche—to earn the loyalty of specific portions of the population while other companies in the fragmenting media world try to attract other groups. As media executives think about their desired audiences more and more carefully, they engage in what is known as audience segmentation.

**audience segmentation**
producers and distributors try to reach different types of people with content tailored specifically for them

The term "**audience segmentation**" refers to the practice by which producers and distributors try to reach different types of people with messages tailored specifically for them (see Figure P.2). No individual media materials can attract all of the approximately 314 million individuals in the United States. Instead, these materials reach segments, or parts, of society. These segments vary greatly in terms of the number of people involved and the time it takes for most of them to receive the material. *Grey's Anatomy* is an example of a television program that reaches tens of millions of viewers virtually instantaneously. Conversely, the unexpected death of pop icon Michael Jackson in 2009 showed how huge audiences can build over a period of time—although many heard the "breaking news" on television, many more learned about it in news programs, newspapers, and web reports.

**targeting**
when a mass media organization sets its sights on having as its audience one or more of the social segments it has identified in the population

Increasingly, though, the pursuit of relatively small audiences by firms involved in the production, distribution, and exhibition of messages is purposeful and profitable. **Targeting** occurs when a mass media organization sets its sights on having as its audience one or more of the social segments it has identified in the population. Consider, for example, a magazine company that, for decades, has put out a periodical aimed at women in general. Women, of course, constitute an audience segment—quite a large one (women make up a bit more than half of the U.S. population). Greater audience segmentation on the part of the publisher might involve deciding to create two websites: one goes after specific types of women aged 18–35 who are mothers, and the other is set up to attract women aged 40–54 whose children have left home. One form of targeting would involve advertising to women who fit that profile in the hope that they will visit the website and keep coming back. An additional approach would be to publish articles on topics clearly aimed at one group or another so that those articles show up high on organic search-engine results when people of that group search for the topic. That would lead women to the magazine, and maybe they would return.

## Figure P.2

An example of audience segmentation from LoudDoor. It categorizes members of a company's "ideal customers" based on the companies the customer chose to become a fan of on Facebook. (Courtesy of LoudDoor, www.louddoor.com)

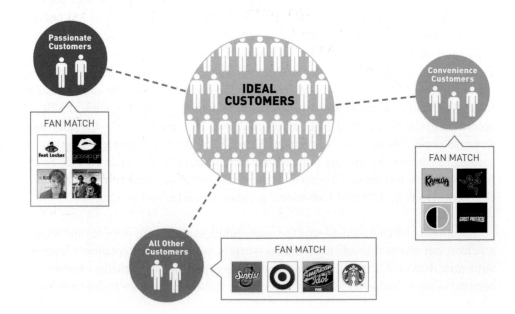

Why would a media company want to reduce its audience by segmenting and targeting in a particular way? The answer is that decisions to segment and target are based on business considerations. Why and how executives engage in segmentation and targeting differs according to whether or not their media outlet is supported primarily by advertising funds. Recall from chapter 2 that some media companies rely mostly on advertising for their revenues. Other companies get support from a balanced combination of advertising and subscriptions. Still others get most of their support from individual purchases or subscriptions. If a marketer sees that particular segments are well off economically or are more likely than other segments to purchase its products, the marketer will target more lucrative segments and pay less attention to the others.

## Globalization

In the face of media fragmentation, audience erosion, and the need to move materials to more digital windows in order to increase revenues, U.S. production and distribution executives are looking to the global marketplace as a way to solve their revenue problems. Digital media allow for that to happen more quickly and efficiently. That fueling of **globalization**, like the other developments we've discussed so far, fuels convergence.

It's not as if U.S. mass media firms have been ignoring the rest of the world until now. On the contrary, the movie, recording, radio, television, book, and magazine industries have all to some extent been distributing their products internationally for a long time. However, during the first three-quarters of the 20th century, "going global" meant taking materials that had already generated profits in the United States and adding to those profits by selling them elsewhere.

**globalization**
the movement of media content around the world

Today, a new mindset about the world outside the United States' borders is at work. Its logic is as follows: Media fragmentation and audience erosion make it difficult for mass media distributors to reach the huge audiences they would like in the United States. When producers use audience segmentation to attract advertisers or cultivate consumer loyalty, they inevitably lower the number of American consumers who will view those products. Global consumers are a way to make the audience larger. In this way, media executives view countries around the world as part of the initial marketplace for these mass media materials. Moreover, the internet provides the opportunity for U.S.-based media firms to reach people globally. It allows these firms to take advantage of convergence by presenting these audiences with news, movies, digital books, music, games, and more.

A member of the Hamar tribe of southern Ethiopia searching online. Even though the members of this tribe live a primarily pastoral existence, they are connected via the internet and digital technology. They are therefore potential targets for advertising and other media messages.

For media critics, there are two questions about this global approach that particularly stand out. First, these critics ask, "Who's to say that there are audience segments outside the United States that have tastes similar to those of Americans?" Second, they ask, "Don't those parts of the world that have strong and growing consumer economies—Europe, Asia, and Central and South America—have their own mass media firms that create materials aimed at their own consumers?" As we will see in the chapters to come, companies in different media industries answer these questions differently. Recording companies, for example, have decided that they can't, in fact, take it for granted that people throughout the world share American tastes. Tastes in music are often vastly different within each country, let alone worldwide. But the costs of producing a CD or selling digital copies through iTunes or another web music store are so relatively low that it is often quite profitable to pursue audience segments within a country. Consequently, even the biggest firms have split themselves into different subsidiaries that concentrate on different parts of the world and funnel the profits back to the home office. The U.S. movie industry, by contrast, derives a lot of its revenues from sending the same movies around the world. At the same time, the major U.S. film producers have been getting more involved than ever in international coproductions. A **coproduction** is a deal between two firms for the funding of media material. So, for example, Warner Bros. may collaborate with Village Roadshow Pictures of Australia in financing a movie. The two companies would split the costs and perhaps the distribution duties. They would also split the profits.

**coproduction**
a deal between two firms for the funding of media material

Looking at global possibilities, then, mass media executives see both opportunities and risks, particularly because convergence potentially provides the space for companies to reach across the world for audiences, advertisers, and the meeting of the two. Moreover, as convergence allows for increased global media competition, the companies involved may push for even more convergence—that is, for the movement of more content across a larger number of digital technologies. But although competition across a wide waterfront of media, analog and digital, may sound great to consumers, many executives get nervous that their firms will lose out if too many products fight for audience attention. Other—typically large—companies can do more because their ownership of content and exhibition windows around the world and in the United States allows them to reach huge audiences (and advertisers) internationally on both digital and non-digital media. These companies represent the rise (and power) of conglomeration.

## Conglomeration

**conglomeration**
the activities involved in becoming and acting like a company's becoming a mass media conglomerate

**mass media conglomerate**
a company that holds several mass media firms in different media industries under its corporate umbrella

In the media world, **conglomeration** refers to the activities involved in becoming and acting like a a mass media conglomerate. A **mass media conglomerate** is a company that holds several mass media firms in different media industries under its corporate umbrella. Mass media conglomerates are not new. What is relatively new is the approach that their corporate leaders are taking.

Until the 1980s, the executives who ran media conglomerates typically did not require the different parts of their firm to work with one another. To them, the value of owning magazines, TV stations, music labels, and the like lay in the ability of each business to generate profits separately for the parent firm. Things began to change in the 1980s for a number of reasons. One reason was simply that top media executives and financiers got caught up in the greedy merger-and-acquisition mania that swept through corporate America during that decade. An even more intense period of combinations took place during the mid-1990s, with multibillion-dollar linkages between such companies as Time and Warner and then between AOL and Time and Warner; Twentieth Century Fox and News Corporation; Sony and Columbia; Disney and ABC; and CBS and Viacom.

To justify the high costs of these mergers, the chief executives of these companies describe the media world evolving in a way that requires them to have holdings in several mass media industries if their companies are to remain major players in the 21st century. They believe the danger for a media firm otherwise is that its competitors will prevent it from accessing the distribution and exhibition outlets that it needs if it is to carry out its revenue-generating mission. True, they can make agreements with other firms that allow them to use outlets owned by those other firms on the condition that those firms also can use *their* outlets. But ultimately, they believe, a company's destiny in the new media world will be determined by its ability to own, alone or with others, the distribution and exhibition outlets that it needs in order to reach its audiences. Perhaps 10 or 15 companies from around the world will achieve this power. Executives of large firms want their companies to be among them.

Recall that we have used the term "vertical integration" to describe an organization's control of a media product from the production of content through its distribution and exhibition. Vertical integration is now in the TV industry and, to a certain extent, in the theatrical motion picture industry. In circumstances in which vertical integration hasn't been legalized (as was the case in the movie and broadcast TV industries until recently), companies have tried to grab control of two of the three stages—production and/or distribution and/or exhibition—to keep their industry clout.

What the leaders of media conglomerates urge today is horizontal integration in addition to as much vertical integration as possible. **Horizontal integration** (see Figure P.3) has two aspects. First, it involves the ownership of production facilities, distribution channels, and/or exhibition outlets in different, even potentially competing companies across a number of media industries. Second, it involves bringing those parts together (integrating them) so that each can profit from the expertise of the others. A term that is similar to horizontal integration and that became a buzzword among media executives is "synergy." **Synergy** describes a situation in which the whole is greater than the sum of its parts. It is synergy at work when Time Warner's DC Comics provides the characters for Time Warner's Warner Bros. movies, which in turn provide the inspiration for *Batman* clothing, and when all of these elements get publicity through the following:

- Time Warner's CW broadcast network (which it owns with CBS)
- Time Warner's TNT, TBS, and CNN cable networks

**horizontal integration**
the ownership of production facilities, distribution channels, and/or exhibition outlets in a number of media industries and the integration of those elements so that each can profit from the expertise of the others

**synergy**
a situation in which the whole is greater than the sum of its parts; the ability of mass media organizations to channel content into a wide variety of mass media on a global scale through control over production, distribution, and exhibition in as many of those media as possible

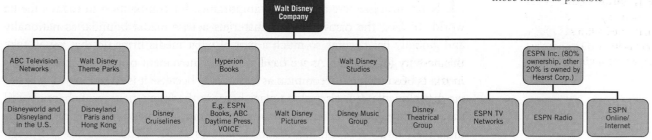

## Figure P.3
The Walt Disney Company's various divisions allow for much horizontal integration. Can you see how and think of some examples?

- All of Time Warner's websites and mobile apps
- The expressed enthusiasm by the target audience on *Batman* Facebook fan pages
- *Batman* feeds on Twitter
- The encouragement of more media attention to *Batman* as a result of real-time monitoring of these activities by DC Comics and its PR agency

The goal of synergy underscores that at the turn of the century, executives of mass media conglomerates were defining market power in a sweeping way. They saw it as the ability to channel products into a wide variety of mass media on a global scale through control over production, distribution, and exhibition in as many of those media as possible. They considered the best content for these cross-media activities to be genres that were likely to cross national borders, reach audiences that are attractive to advertisers, and not raise the political hackles of certain governments. These executives believed that children's programs, sports, variety shows, action adventures, direct marketing, headline news, and certain kinds of music were the genres that traveled best globally across media.

As you can see from some of the examples (and you undoubtedly have been thinking of some of your own), convergence is a major aspect of these synergistic activities. As we noted earlier, all media companies have as a goal crossing digital media in order to be accessible to their target audiences whenever and wherever they want their content. Because of their wealth and multimedia capabilities, media conglomerates pursue this goal as well, but with the kind of money that links tens and even hundreds of millions of people with techniques of audience segmentation, windows, and globalization across a panoply of media.

Media companies need help from other firms in order to compete globally across media boundaries. To get that help, they can join up with larger firms or turn to one or more of the thousands of smaller firms eager to extend their niches in the global media environment. Called **joint ventures**, these alliances involve companies agreeing to work together or to share investments. The television network Animal Planet, for example, is a joint venture between Discovery Communications and the BBC in all parts of the world except the United Kingdom and Italy, where Discovery controls it.

## Moving Forward

The bottom line is that companies are moving forward with convergence quickly because they are aware of its importance for competition in today's media world. In fact, the distribution of materials across media boundaries nationally and globally has become so much a part of what media firms do that we all take this activity for granted. As we have seen, the movement of much content across media is becoming more common at least partly because it is technologically easier via digital media. It is also taking place because the fragmentation of channels and the segmentation of audiences encourage attempts to make target audiences cumulatively larger through distribution windows across media industries, through globalization of distribution, and through the kind of conglomeration that gives companies a lot of clout in analog and digital distribution of the content within their countries and around the world.

**joint ventures**
alliances formed between a large media firm and one or more of the thousands of smaller firms that are eager to extend their niches in the global media environment; the companies either work together or share investments

These activities will show up in the forthcoming chapters on individual media industries. As we'll see, the five drivers of media convergence have provoked concern both from within the media system and from critics outside it. Perhaps some anxious thoughts about the possible impact of globalization or conglomeration crossed your mind as you read the previous pages. We may well discuss your worries in future chapters, or we may bring up other issues relating to convergence. The exploration of particular media industries today is a fascinating, many-sided activity. Let's get started.

## Key Terms

| | | |
|---|---|---|
| audience segmentation | digital media | mass media conglomerate |
| channel fragmentation | globalization | synergy |
| conglomeration | horizontal integration | targeting |
| coproduction | joint ventures | windows |

# 6 The Internet Industry

## CHAPTER OBJECTIVES

1  Discuss the history of the internet and the devices that link to it

2  Understand the internet as a technology

3  Describe be the internet industry, its relationship to convergence, and its impact on media organizations and their consumers

4  Analyze concerns that observers hold about internet privacy issues

"The internet, like the steam engine, is a technological breakthrough that changed the world."

**PETER SINGER, PROFESSOR OF BIOETHICS AT PRINCETON UNIVERSITY**

How often do you watch TV on an actual television set? You may be like the increasing number of people who, surveys indicate, view "television" programs on their desktop computers, their laptops, their tablets, and even their phones. The research firm Ypulse found in 2012 that 71 percent of people born between 1983 and 1994 say they have recently watched TV by streaming it to their desktop computer, their laptop computer, or a mobile device such as a tablet (e.g., an iPad, Kindle, Galaxy, or Surface) or phone—compared to 66 percent who say they have recently watched TV on a regular TV set.[1] Do you fit this description? Perhaps you also use social media—Facebook, Twitter, Yahoo! Chat, chatabouteverything, live.twit.tv—to chat with others about the shows you're viewing online or on the traditional box. Or you may also find yourself using your phone or tablet to find out the score of a game while you watch a drama series on your laptop. Ad agency researchers have found that distraction from TV

screens by smartphones and tablets may be fairly severe.[2] But the number of social media devices associated with television keeps going up.

The internet stands at the center of this convergence of technologies around television content. The internet is also central to so many other aspects of media convergence—for example, watching movies on your "smart TV," reading books on your e-reader, browsing magazines and newspapers on your tablet, listening to music on your phone or MP3 player, playing a video game with faraway strangers, and seeing ads on all of them. As you can imagine, and as we'll see in the following chapters, the people who work in industries that produce, distribute, and exhibit materials for these media are quite aware of the importance of the internet for their livelihoods. Much of their work takes place with the internet in mind.

The internet is so important to media today that to understand books, newspapers, magazines, recorded music, radio, the movies, television, and video games (the subjects of the forthcoming chapters), it's crucial that we first understand the internet. Our goal here is to answer three basic questions: Exactly what is the internet? Where did it come from? How does it work? We will see that an entire industry has built up around the internet. The internet industry is involved in producing, distributing, and exhibiting its own content as well as connecting with other media industries that want to distribute and exhibit their own content via the "net."

## Rise of the Internet

The **internet** is a global system of interconnected private, public, academic, business, and government computer networks that use a standard set of commands to link billions of users worldwide. ARPANet, as it was first known, was conceived by the Advanced Research Projects Agency (ARPA) of the Department of Defense in 1969. The aim was to create a network that would allow a research computer at one university or military installation to "talk to" research computers at other universities or military installations even if part of the system were destroyed by war or disaster. The system of data transfer was fundamentally different from the way telephone conversations made their way from one person to another. In a standard landline phone conversation, the entire flow of voice "data"—the electrical impulses representing what each person says—is continuous. Every phone call, therefore, continuously takes up a wire connection until the people hang up, even if there is silence on the line for seconds or minutes.

The unique aspect of the new system was that it allowed for a transmission line to carry more than one data "conversation" at a time. It did that by breaking down messages into segments called **packets** and sending the packets through parts of the network that had the fewest other packets moving through them at a particular moment. The packets contained digital instructions that allowed them to be reassembled properly at the same time at the destination. Because packets could be

**the internet**
a global system of interconnected private, public, academic, business, and government computer networks that use a standard set of commands to link billions of users worldwide

**packets**
segments of messages that contain digital instructions that allow them to reassemble properly at the same time at the destination

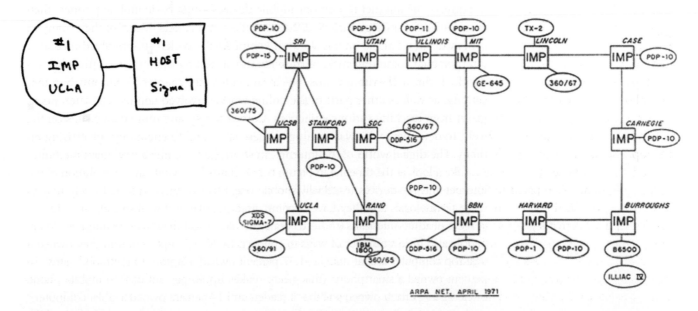

The left drawing, from 1969, notes the first two nodes of the ARPANET, created that year. The right diagram, created just 3 years later, shows that 14 nodes of ARPANET were in operation by 1971. (Source: Computer History Museum, http://www.computerhistory.org.)

routed or rerouted in more than one direction in the process of looking for the most efficient paths of a network, ARPANet could continue to function even if parts of it were destroyed in the event of a military attack or other disaster.

But some computer scientists had even more ambitious ideas. They didn't want the internet to be simply a vehicle for transferring messages or documents between individuals. Instead, they wanted to create a way for large groups of people to access and work on the same files. They also wanted to be able to direct people to those documents through **hyperlinks**, or specially coded words or pictures that, when clicked, connect the user to a particular file, even to a specific relevant part of a document. Researchers at the Center for European Nuclear Research (CERN) in Geneva, Switzerland, made this linking possible in 1989. Tim Berners-Lee and Sam Walker from the United Kingdom and Robert Cailliau from Belgium created **HyperText Markup Language (HTML)**, a computer language system that allowed people to access a system of interlinked documents through the internet. HTML is used to define the structure, content, and layout of a page by using what are called tags. The CERN researchers built this system to work via the internet, and they called it the World Wide Web. A key aspect of this web was that users could go to the materials by typing in a specific World Wide Web address or by clicking on a link in a document that contained the address, which would automatically connect them to that place.

Internet messages at the time had to be transmitted in text form. Sending graphical images was possible, but the images had to be decoded by the receiver before viewing. That situation changed in 1993, when computer scientists at the University of Illinois created the web browser, a graphical way to access the World Wide Web. They called it Mosaic. With its successor browsers—for example, Apple's Safari, Microsoft Internet Explorer, Google Chrome, or Mozilla Firefox—a computer user today can easily view complex drawings or photographs.

By the mid-1990s, the internet had moved far beyond its original military and academic purposes to become a vast societal communication system. Scientists figured out ways to attach devices such as desktop and laptop computers to the internet with both indoor wired and wireless connections. They also figured out ways to connect the internet to outdoor mobile devices—first basic mobile phones, then more powerful smartphones, and then e-readers and tablets. Much of the activity in cyberspace (i.e., in the online world of computer networks) still involved mediated interpersonal communication or individuals interacting one-on-one with other individuals through written words, voice, and video (see chapter 1). But much of that activity, as well as other parts of the online world, involved commercial attempts to profit from reaching various audiences. Companies sprang up to create sites on the web, to determine who was coming to these sites, and to encourage advertising on them. The digital world of the internet, in short, had become a new mass medium.

Take a look at the timeline in Figure 6.1. It charts key points in the evolution of the internet and the devices (especially mobile ones) that connect to it. Relatively new as these technologies are, they have become quite popular and widespread. In 2012, 85 percent of adult Americans (those 18 years and older) said they "use the internet." Many people also have a number of ways to connect. In 2011, 55 percent said they owned a desktop computer at that time, and 57 percent owned a laptop. In the mobile area, 46 percent owned a smartphone (this group makes up 60 percent of U.S. mobile phone owners), 19 percent owned an e-book reader, and 19 percent owned a tablet computer.[3]

As Table 6.1 shows, internet use is more common among younger people than adults over 65 years old and among those with higher education and higher incomes. Somewhat

**hyperlinks**
highlighted words or pictures on the internet that, when clicked, will connect the user to a particular file, even to a specific relevant part of a document

**HyperText Markup Language (HTML)**
a computer language system that allowed people to access a system of interlinked documents through the internet. HTML is used to define the structure, content, and layout of a page by using what are called tags.

**Table 6.1** Demographics of Internet Users
*Below is the % of each group of American adults who use the internet, according to our August 2012 survey. For instance, 85% of women use the internet.*

|  | % who use the internet |
| --- | :---: |
| **All adults** | 85 |
| Men | 85 |
| Women | 85 |
| **Race/ethnicity** | |
| White, Non-Hispanic | 86 |
| Black, Non-Hispanic | 86 |
| Hispanic (English- and Spanish-speaking) | 80 |
| **Age** | |
| 18–29 | 96 |
| 30–49 | 93 |
| 50–64 | 85 |
| 65+ | 58 |
| **Household income** | |
| Less than $30,000/yr | 75 |
| $30,000–$49,999 | 90 |
| $50,000–$74,999 | 93 |
| $75,000+ | 99 |
| **Educational attainment** | |
| No high school diploma | 61 |
| High school grad | 80 |
| Some College | 94 |
| College + | 97 |

Sources: The Pew Research Center's Internet & American Life Project's Tracking Survey conducted July 16–August 7, 2012. N=2,253 adults ages 18 and older, including 900 interviews conducted by cell phone. Interviews were conducted in both English and Spanish.

smaller proportions of Hispanics (in comparison to white or black non-Hispanics) say they use the internet, yet the numbers are still way over 50 percent. And teenagers, particularly, are connected: 96 percent of Americans aged 12 to 17 reported using the internet.

These findings come from the Pew Internet and American Life Project, which continually surveys the U.S. population regarding its internet use, knowledge, and habits.[4] Table 6.2 reflects the answers that representative national samples of adults gave Pew regarding uses that they make of the internet. Other Pew research shows that there are generational differences in some activities—use of social networking sites, for example, goes down with age. But there are other areas—such as using e-mail and getting news—for which large percentages of almost every age group find the internet valuable. Clearly, young adults find social, informational, and commercial uses for the web—social networking, searching, viewing videos, and buying products—that show that the internet is a central aspect of their world.

# Figure 6.1 Timeline: History of the Internet

**1931**: Emanuel Goldberg and Robert Luther in Germany receive a U.S. patent for a "Statistical Machine" that uses photoelectric cells and pattern recognition to search for specific words on microfilm documents.

**1945**: Scientist Vannevar Bush publishes an article "As We May Think" in The Atlantic magazine predicting the invention of technology that would allow ideas in different parts of text to link to one another.

**1961**: Len Kleinrock, professor of Computer Science at UCLA, writes the first paper on "packet switching."

**1958**: President Eisenhower requests funds to create the United States Defense Advanced Research Project Agency (ARPA).

**1966**: ARPANet project begins in Cambridge Massachusetts; Larry Roberts is in charge.

**1972**: Ray Tomlinson creates the first email program, along with the @ sign to signify "at."

1930s — 1940s — 1950s — 1960s — 1970s

**1947**: University of Pennsylvania engineers create ENIAC, the Electronic Numerical Integrator and Computer.

**1965**: Larry Roberts at MIT sets up an experiment in which two computers communicate to each other using packet-switching technology.

**1969**: ARPANET connects computers at four U.S. universities.

**1973**: ARPANET establishes connections to two universities in the UK and Norway.

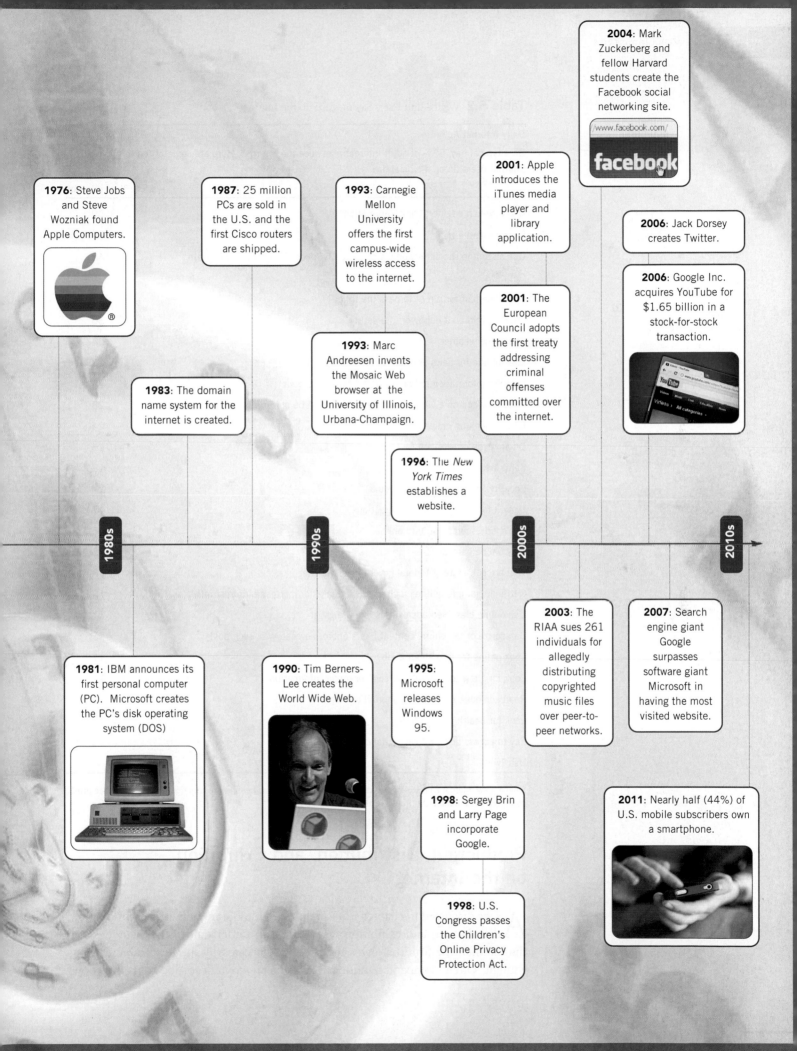

**2004**: Mark Zuckerberg and fellow Harvard students create the Facebook social networking site.

www.facebook.com/
facebook

**1976**: Steve Jobs and Steve Wozniak found Apple Computers.

**1987**: 25 million PCs are sold in the U.S. and the first Cisco routers are shipped.

**1993**: Carnegie Mellon University offers the first campus-wide wireless access to the internet.

**2001**: Apple introduces the iTunes media player and library application.

**2006**: Jack Dorsey creates Twitter.

**2006**: Google Inc. acquires YouTube for $1.65 billion in a stock-for-stock transaction.

**1993**: Marc Andreesen invents the Mosaic Web browser at the University of Illinois, Urbana-Champaign.

**2001**: The European Council adopts the first treaty addressing criminal offenses committed over the internet.

**1983**: The domain name system for the internet is created.

**1996**: The *New York Times* establishes a website.

**1980s**　　**1990s**　　**2000s**　　**2010s**

**2003**: The RIAA sues 261 individuals for allegedly distributing copyrighted music files over peer-to-peer networks.

**2007**: Search engine giant Google surpasses software giant Microsoft in having the most visited website.

**1981**: IBM announces its first personal computer (PC). Microsoft creates the PC's disk operating system (DOS)

**1990**: Tim Berners-Lee creates the World Wide Web.

**1995**: Microsoft releases Windows 95.

**1998**: Sergey Brin and Larry Page incorporate Google.

**2011**: Nearly half (44%) of U.S. mobile subscribers own a smartphone.

**1998**: U.S. Congress passes the Children's Online Privacy Protection Act.

**Table 6.2** What Adult Users Say they Do on the Internet

**Daily Internet Activities**

On a typical day, 82% of adult internet users use the internet. Here are some of the things that internet users do on a typical day.

| | % of internet |
|---|---|
| Use a search engine to find information | 59 |
| Send or read e-mail | 59 |
| Use an online social networking site like MySpace, Facebook or LinkedIn | 48 |
| Get news | 45 |
| Go online just for fun or to pass the time | 44 |
| Look for info on a hobby or interest | 35 |
| Check the weather | 34 |
| Look online for news or information about politics | 28 |
| Look for information online about a service or product | 28 |
| Watch a video on a video-sharing site like YouTube or Vimeo | 28 |
| Do any banking online | 24 |
| Do any type of research for your job | 23 |
| Send instant messages | 18 |
| Look for information on Wikipedia | 17 |
| Search for a map or driving directions | 17 |
| Get sports scores and info online | 15 |
| Play online games | 13 |
| Visit a local, state or federal government website | 13 |
| Get financial info online, such as stock quotes or mortgage interest rate | 12 |
| Use online classified ads or sites like Craigslist | 11 |
| Categorize or tag online content like a photo, news story or blog post | 11 |
| Look online for info about a job | 11 |
| Look for "how-to," "do-it-yourself" or repair information | 11 |
| Read someone else's online journal or blog | 10 |
| Look for health/medical info | 10 |
| Pay to access or download digital content online | 10 |
| Use Twitter | 8 |

Source: Pew Internet and Society Program, based on a compilation of survey results from 2008-2012. See http://pewinternet.org/Trend-Data-(Adults)/Online-Activities-Daily.aspx

# Production, Distribution, and Exhibition on the Internet

As we discussed in chapter 1, it is helpful to think of the activities of production, distribution, and exhibition when trying to understand media activities. On the internet, the firm that owns the site is not necessarily the firm that creates its content. Often, companies and individuals create content for locations they don't control. An example is a video production firm paid to create a travel video for Frommers.com. Very different would be an individual who makes a travel video during a recent trip to Spain and posts it on YouTube and Facebook. Creative products made by individuals who visit sites are often called **user-generated content (UGC)**. The *Huffington Post* is an example of a popular current events website that uses a lot of UGC to fill its space and attract users. Although it does that, the parent firm TheHuffingtonPost.com still plays an important role in production: it formats the material and finds relevant photos, for example.

Apart from this shared production role, TheHuffingtonPost.com also acts as a distributor by placing and marketing *The Huffington Post* online. Websites in general fulfill this role as distributors. NYTimes.com, for example, is a major distributor of the material produced by the *New York Times* newspaper. This is also the case with Amazon.com, which produces and distributes its retail website online. Google produces and distributes its search engine to people who tell their browser to go to it. And Facebook produces and distributes its software that allows people to create mini-sites within its site that their friends can access in various ways.

**user-generated content (UGC)**
creative products, such as videos and music, generated by people who visit websites such as Facebook, YouTube, and Instagram

## THINKING ABOUT MEDIA LITERACY

Many websites generate traffic and gain popularity through user-generated content. YouTube, for example, features videos created and uploaded by people for sharing with their friends and others. Surrounding each video is an abundance of advertising, and much of the revenues go back to YouTube itself. Do you think that some of this advertising revenue should go back to the content creators? Why or why not?

But who is the exhibitor in this situation? Recall from chapter 1 that an exhibitor is a company that provides the public with access to the material it accepts from a distributor. From one standpoint, we can say that the sites themselves exhibit the materials to their visitors, much as customers visit physical stores that show their products. Another, perhaps better view is that the internet exhibitor is the **internet service provider (ISP)**, the firm that provides the technology through which the person can access the internet. There's a fair chance that much of college students' contact with the online world is through their school. In that case, the school typically picks up the tab for your e-mail and your connections to the college's online resources (such as the library catalog), as well as to the internet. Outside colleges, the firms that carry out this role tend to be cable companies such as Time Warner or Comcast, phone companies such as Verizon or Sprint, packagers of internet services such as Earthlink, and mobile phone companies such as AT&T and T-Mobile.

**internet service provider (ISP)**
a company that sells access to the internet

Most ISPs today provide their customers with the ability to connect via **Wi-Fi**. Wi-Fi is a radio technology (called IEEE 802.11) that engineers designed in the late 1990s to provide secure, reliable, fast wireless connectivity. Many consumer devices use Wi-Fi—personal computers can network to each other and connect to the internet, mobile computers can connect to the internet from any Wi-Fi hotspot, and digital cameras can transfer images wirelessly. There are four types of Wi-Fi—a, b, g, and n—and each provides faster connection to the web router (see Figure 6.2). Because Wi-Fi frequencies don't travel more than a few hundred yards, it takes many Wi-Fi transmitters to cover an area such as a college campus.

**Wi-Fi**
a radio technology (called IEEE 802.11) that engineers designed in the late 1990s to provide secure, reliable, fast wireless connectivity

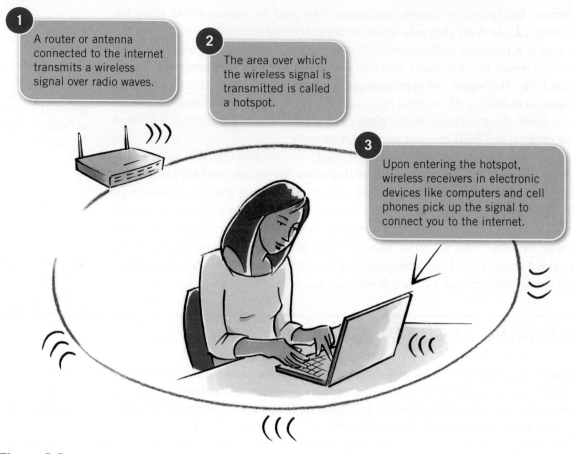

**Figure 6.2**

How Wi-Fi works. Wi-Fi technology allows an internet connection to be broadcast and received using radio waves. Technology in computers, video game consoles, smartphones, MP3 players, tablets, and other wireless-enabled devices can pick up the signals to connect to the internet when they are within range of a wireless network. The area in which one can connect to a wireless network is known as a hotspot.

Some internet service providers have rules about how much downloading from the internet you can do before you have to pay them more money. Someone who regularly streams movies to a cell phone, for example, may be charged a substantial extra charge. A cable company may not charge more, but it may "throttle" the data speeds, or slow down the service. ISP executives explain that they do this because people who download or stream movies and other products that take up a lot of electronic space—bandwidth—often clog the ISP's system and make it difficult for other customers to have their packets delivered efficiently.

## The Net Neutrality Controversy

It is important to note, though, that so far no ISPs have stopped their customers from going to a site they type into the URL box. That is why the notion of the ISP as exhibitor may not seem as important to the producer and distributor as does a cable provider or a newsstand, where the owners decide what material to accept and what to reject for presentation to the public. Some companies do restrict their workers' ability to use the firms' computers to visit sites that the companies feel will waste workers' time (e.g., game sites and Facebook) or embarrass other employees (e.g., pornography sites).

Imagine, though, if the internet service provider for your home computer decided that it would allow only certain websites to reach its clients but not others. The ISP might do this in order to get websites to pay to "exhibit" the sites in people's homes. Or the ISP may tell certain websites that it might slow them down (thus encouraging users to go to other sites) unless they pay fees to get the fastest speeds.

As a consumer, you may think this is a terrible idea because it might make it difficult or impossible to reach certain sites. But some ISP executives argue that they should have the right to charge some sites for "exhibition" because the sites use up enormous amounts of bandwidth (by providing videos, for example) that they have to provide to their customers and for which they do not get compensated. Website executives and consumer advocates respond that the ISPs do get money back by charging their customers for access. Moreover, they argue that the internet has become so important to society that to restrict or diminish the use of it could have unfortunate consequences for what people know and what they can share with one another.

This argument is called the **net neutrality controversy**. The term refers to the desire by websites and advocates to make sure that ISPs do not charge sites for transmission. At this point, no ISPs seem to do that, but the Federal Trade Commission (FTC) accused Comcast of violating the concept of net neutrality by slowing down the availability of certain sites that use lots of bandwidth. Comcast executives said they were doing it to make sure that the majority of their customers didn't suffer a general slowdown because of the few using those sites. A court later ruled that the FTC was wrong to censure Comcast. Nevertheless, the company said it would not regulate its web traffic by picking on specific sites—even as it repeated that the FTC had no right to proclaim net neutrality and enforce it. That right, Comcast and the court said, must come from Congress.

**net neutrality controversy**
the desire by websites and advocates to make sure that ISPs do not charge sites for transmission

## THINKING ABOUT MEDIA LITERACY

After reading through this discussion on net neutrality, where do you stand on the issue? Do you think that internet service providers have a valid point in their arguments? Why or why not?

## Social Media Sites and Search Engines

Let's leave the topic of exhibition and return to our discussion of producers and distributors of content on the web. You'll recall we mentioned NYTimes.com, TheHuffingtonPost.com, Amazon, Google, and Facebook. These five firms reflect three different kinds of content businesses that exist online. The *New York Times* is an example of a firm from another industry that, seeing the need for digital convergence, has brought its business online. TheHuffingtonPost.com and Amazon represent firms that started on the web but that are carrying out activities that resemble offline firms. (The *Huffington Post* acts somewhat like an offline newspaper, whereas Amazon acts somewhat like a big offline retail catalog. We will discuss these newspaper and catalog forms and their relation to the Internet in forthcoming chapters.) As a search engine and a social media site, respectively, Google and Facebook are examples of businesses that don't exist outside the internet environment, even though other media industries (such as newspapers and retail advertising) make great use of them.

**social media site (social networking site or SNS)**
an online location where people can interact with others around information, entertainment, and news of their own choosing and, often, making

**search engine**
websites that allow users to find sites relevant to topics of interest to them

**web crawlers (web spiders)**
programs used by search engines that search the internet to retrieve and catalog the content of websites

**algorithm**
a complex set of mathematically based rules that search engines use to come up with sites that relate to your search terms

**natural or organic search results**
websites that come up based on a search engine's algorithm without any influence from advertisers

A **social media site** (sometimes called a social networking site) is an online location where people can interact with others around information, entertainment, and news of their own choosing and, often, making. Facebook, Google+, Twitter, and LinkedIn are popular social media locations that offer people quite different approaches to interacting. Twitter requires users to communicate via messages of no more than 140 characters, though they can add links, photos, or videos. LinkedIn invites people to connect around business networks. Facebook and Google+ see themselves as ways in which friends can stay connected with each other on a continuing basis. All four social media locations also offer companies ways to maintain an important presence. If you've been to a fan page on Facebook or followed a company on Twitter, you know how popular those places can be.

Whereas people go to social media to find people and companies on those sites, they go to search engines to find people, products, services, and ideas—just about anything—on the internet. *Merriam-Webster's Collegiate Dictionary* defines a **search engine** as "computer software used to search data (as text or a database) for specified information." The search engine developed out of the need of people using the web to find sites relevant to topics of interest to them. You undoubtedly have gone to Google, Bing, Yahoo!, or another search program to find out about a person, location, or fact. Search engines work by using **web crawlers** (also known as **web spiders**), programs that automatically browse the World Wide Web to create copies of all the visited pages. The search engine software then catalog or "index" the downloaded pages so that a person searching for a word in them will find it quickly. Depending on the search engine, the spiders index more or less of the web, but they never catalog the entire web. Not only would it take too much time (and the crawlers have to keep doing their jobs over and over again to update their findings), but there are also some parts of the web that they cannot enter because they are protected by passwords.

When you type in search terms, you activate a complex set of mathematically based rules, called an **algorithm**, that comes up with sites that relate to your search terms. Algorithms are the "secret sauce" of search engines. It is quite well known, though, that Google's approach to search involves a particular definition of popularity: the number of websites that are linked to a site that uses the search term. The search engine will also take into consideration what Google knows about you based on previous searches, your location, and information you gave Google if you signed into the site. So, for example, if you type "pizza" into a Google search box, the top links that appear will probably be for pizza stores near your house. After those, you might get a Wikipedia article about the history of pizza.

The main list of sites that you get in response to typing "pizza" in the Google search box is called Google's **natural or organic search results**. That means that the sites come up based on Google's algorithm without any influence from a pizza restaurant or any other advertiser. Yahoo! and other major search engines work this way too because they want to maintain their credibility in the eyes of their users. The way these search companies survive is by sending advertising to their users. If natural results were intermingled with ads, users might have a tough time knowing whether a link was placed higher because it was really relevant or because a company paid for its placement there.

Although it may seem that search engines and social media sites are quite different from one another, during the past few years companies in both areas have begun

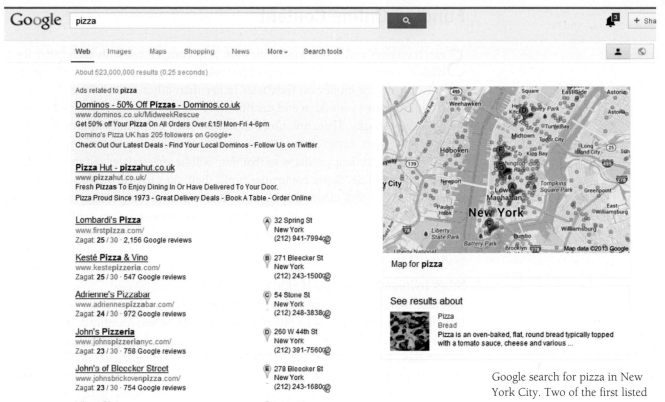

Google search for pizza in New York City. Two of the first listed results are advertisements and links to Pizza Hut and then Dominos, followed by the Wikipedia entry for pizza. It isn't until the fourth search result that local pizza results are returned. Google and the Google logo are registered trademarks of Google Inc., used with permission.

to realize that they may well end up in similar businesses. The reason for this is the emergence of what they call **social search**, a search carried out to find what people in a person's social circle say about an item. Let's say you are deciding whether to go to a new *Batman* movie called (for this example) *Batman's Cape*. You could go to Google or Bing and type in the movie's name along with the word "review" to find out what critics have said about the film. Or you could go to Facebook and type *"Batman's Cape"* into the search box, and out would come comments that your Facebook friends have made about the film. These comments might be more relevant to you than anonymous Google reviews. In fact, the utility of this sort of search has led Google to integrate its social network, Google+, into members' search findings when they are signed into the network. Bing has gotten into the act, too, by integrating Facebook comments from people's friends into their search results.

**social search**
a search that is carried out to find what people in a person's social circle say about an item

## THINKING ABOUT MEDIA LITERACY

Google is one of the most popular search engines, if not *the* most popular, in the world. Why do you think Google is so popular? What does it offer that other search engines do not? Do you use Google? If so, through what devices do you access it? If you use another search engine, which one and why? What does it offer that Google does not?

# Funding Online Content

Search engines and social media sites are very competitive with each other for a basic reason: they survive through advertising revenues, and they must convince advertisers to place money on their sites rather than other sites. In fact, very many sites support their production and distribution of content by attracting audiences to advertising messages. There are, however, others ways companies approach making money on the web. Some companies see their sites as helping to build good images for themselves and their products so that they will be able to later sell their products online and/or offline. Some companies build their sites to sell products directly to people who visit. Still others display content aimed at making money by attracting audiences through subscriptions. Sometimes, firms approach sites with more than one of these goals. Let's take a look at each.

### Sites Involved in Image-Making

The idea behind using a site for image-making activities is typically to encourage fans of a product or service to purchase the product or service offline. Kraft Foods' Jell-O website, for example, is a site that provides recipes based on various forms of the product. The site also allows people to watch Jell-O commercials and learn about Jell-O products. The site further urges people to use various forms of the product with other Kraft products (e.g., Cool Whip). Across the web, Jell-O also hosts a fan page on Facebook. None of these activities directly makes any money for Kraft. Instead, they cultivate a friendly, healthful, family-oriented image for Kraft Foods that they hope will yield purchases in supermarkets and other physical stores.

### Sites Selling Products or Services

If you have ever bought anything online (and a large majority of internet-enabled individuals have), you are familiar with websites that sell products or services. This selling method has much in common with an old-fashioned catalog, except that online you sometimes have an opportunity to see a video of the products in operation. Amazon.com is a major company that sells only online; at this writing it has no physical (or brick-and-mortar) stores. Although Amazon, Amazon-owned Zappos, and iTunes are internet-only retailers that do extremely well, it should come as no surprise that the most popular brick-and-mortar stores are among the most popular online stores. For example, Walmart, JCPenney, and Home Depot draw millions to their websites. People in the industry refer to firms with both an online and an offline sales presence as **click-and-mortar companies**.

**click-and-mortar companies**
firms with both an online and an offline sales presence

### Content Sites Selling Subscriptions

Netflix is a site that charges a subscription fee for access to movies and TV shows. Subscription fees also work for specialized business magazines and databases because companies may be willing to pay for their employees to access important information related to their industries. For example, the legal database Lexis charges for entry to and use of its site. Along these lines, the trade magazine *Advertising Age* requires a subscription to get into parts of its site with especially desirable information about the advertising industry.

Generally, though, the idea of a publisher charging people subscriptions to see the content of a site hasn't worked very well on the web. It seems that people who are spending hundreds, even thousands, of dollars for hardware and monthly payments to receive the internet have come, over the decades, to expect that media content will be free or very low-cost. Moreover, the competition among websites means that people can find adequate (or even the same) news, information, and entertainment for free rather than for a fee. Publishers of music and audiovisual entertainment have learned, to their dismay, that if they charge more than a little (or even anything!) for their products, online people will go to pirate sites to get the material.

Nevertheless, as sites such as LinkedIn, Netflix, Rhapsody, and Hulu can attest, companies do try to find ways to make subscriptions work. The *Wall Street Journal*, the *Financial Times*, and the *New York Times* newspapers also have created subscription models for their websites. Netflix and the *Journal* charge a flat subscription fee, perhaps after a trial period. The approach LinkedIn, Rhapsody, Hulu, the *Financial Times*, the *New York Times*, and others use involves multilevel (or *tiered*) content offerings: The site will allow users to have some materials without charge, perhaps at the price of receiving advertisements. If the users want other materials, or if they want to get the materials without ads, they will have to pay.

Unfortunately for many online publishers, though, charging for content seems to draw significant numbers of paying customers only on prominent sites. Over the past decade, many newspapers and magazines that have tried subscription models have abandoned this approach for all but archives of their periodicals. Instead, they have turned to advertising as the way to support their online ventures.

## Selling Advertisements

As with so much of the media we have explored in previous chapters and as we will see in forthcoming chapters, a huge part of the web is supported by advertising. Advertising of all types brought in $39.5 billion to websites in 2011, a growth rate of 23.3 percent from the previous year at a time when most traditional media were growing slowly or losing money.[5]

The pitch that websites make to advertisers is that they attract the best potential customers for their products. Because the online world is so diverse, they argue, advertisers can find sites that reach people with very specific interests. They also provide advertisers with technology that, they claim, can actually ensure that certain ads will be seen by some people on their sites and that other ads will be seen by different people.

Web marketers argue that this ability to target individuals makes online advertising more "customizable" than any other mass medium in history. One way to customize an advertising message is by **keyword advertising**, one approach used by search engines. Say you type the words "cat food" into a search box. Not only will the search engine find websites about cat food, but it will also show you ads for companies interested in reaching people who search for cat food. Related to keyword advertising is **contextual advertising**, in which software determines what a person is reading and sends the person ads for products that advertisers consider related to the topic. Say you are reading an article about cat food that the search engine found for you. There may be advertisers who want to reach people who read articles about cats and even about cat food, and so the website you are on will send you that sort of ad.

**keyword advertising**
when software determines what a person is reading and sends the person ads for products that advertisers consider related to the topic

**contextual advertising**
when software uses the words in the search box to send the person ads for products that advertisers consider related to the topic

**profiling**
creating a description of someone based on collected data

Because tailoring messages in this way requires information about particular members of the audience, website owners engage in online data gathering to find out as much as they can about the individuals who visit their domains. Creating a description of someone based on collected data is called **profiling**. One straightforward method a firm can use to get data for profiling is to ask people to register to get access to a site. When you sign up for Facebook, for example, the company asks you to fill out your name, gender, age, and e-mail address. As you continue the sign-up process, the company asks for your high school, college, and employer's name. That information may not be reliable because you could make up everything except your e-mail address (the Facebook computer tries to check that the e-mail address is correct). A second profiling method that sites use (and which yields different sorts of data) is to ask people what topics they want to learn about through the site. The *New York Times*, for example, allows you to choose news and entertainment categories as guides to the material it sends you.

**cookie**
information that a website puts on your computer's hard drive so that it can remember something about you at a later time; more technically, it is information for future use that is stored by the server on the client side of a client/server communication

A third method of profiling yields still other kinds of data: the computer tracks your choices as you move through a particular website or across websites. These choices are stored on your computer in a tiny hidden text file called a **cookie**. Note that the cookie doesn't know your name or address, or even your e-mail address, unless you told its owner or the company went through special means to get it. But each time you visit the site, the cookie identifies you by a number and allows the company to record your mouse clicks, or **clickstream**, through the site. Over time, the company that created the cookie develops a profile of your interests that it can bring together with other profiles to offer to advertisers. The company can track your behavior within its site, and many advertising networks track your behavior with their cookies across sites. The process of following your behavior and then sending you material tailored to what was learned about you is called **behavioral targeting**.

**clickstream**
computer jargon used to describe user movement through websites

**behavioral targeting**
the process of following people's behavior and then sending them material tailored to what was learned about them

## THINKING ABOUT MEDIA LITERACY

Behavioral targeting allows websites and advertisers to send content to you based on your past online activities. Although the preceding paragraphs suggest the advantages to the advertisers, can you think of any advantages this targeting offers to web users? What might be some disadvantages?

**data mining**
the process of gathering and storing information about many individuals—often millions—to be used in audience profiling and interactive marketing

The process of gathering and storing information about many individuals—often millions—to be used in audience profiling and interactive marketing is called **data mining**. In addition to the three forms of online data gathering just mentioned, data miners try to find offline information about individuals—for example, drivers' license records, mortgage information, and credit ratings—that they can link by computer to other data in the website's collection. Companies also have a means to match cookies from different sources that relate to the same person. Because of the wide interest in data gathering on the web, an entire data-mining industry has grown up around these activities. Its goal is to help web companies sort through the many pieces of information they have on the individuals who come to their sites so that the producers of the sites can profitably use mass customization in editorial and advertising content. Figure 6.3 illustrates this data-mining process in action.

Such data mining helps websites get advertisers. And even sites that don't rely on ads want to know about the people who visit. They believe that very specific audience data can help them better customize their content and more persuasively encourage people to buy their products or services. Then there are other types of firms that

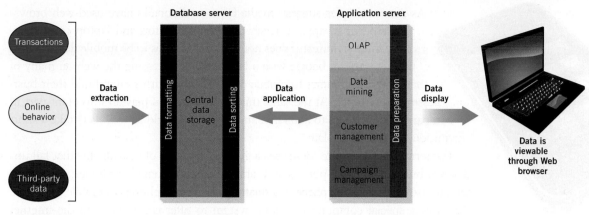

**Figure 6.3**

The data-mining process in action. This figure illustrates how information on individuals is "extracted" from various sources and analyzed. The database server stores the information for the application server, which takes the information and sorts it to make profiles (a process called data mining), to create lists of types of profiles (data management), and to create web ad campaigns and other online targeting activities. OLAP stands for "online analytical processing," an activity that analyzes new and old data about an individual in real time.

collect information about people who travel the web so that they can use the information to make money from advertisers and publishers. One such type of company is an **ad network**—or a collection of many websites that a company knits together in order to sell ads on them. The ad-serving company then shares its revenues with the sites on which it places the ads. Another way advertisers can get in front of target audiences on the web is by using **ad exchanges**. These are electronic auctions in which various publishers and ad networks offer advertisers the ability to reach specific types of people (e.g., women aged 18–24 or men who are considering the purchase of a BMW), often at exactly the moment those people are entering certain sites.

**ad network**
a collection of many websites that a company knits together in order to sell ads on them

**ad exchanges**
electronic auctions in which various publishers and ad networks offer advertisers the ability to reach specific types of people, often at exactly the moment those people are entering certain sites

## "Web-Centered" and "App-Centered" Businesses

People are so used to going on the web (i.e., accessing information through browsers such as Google Chrome, Internet Explorer, Firefox, and Safari) that they typically believe that the web *is* the internet. As we have seen, though, the web is a system of linked data that works *through* the internet. There are other types of internet activities—such as certain types of e-mail (e.g., accessed through Outlook) and audio messaging—that use the internet but not the web. For companies involved in producing, distributing, and exhibiting materials ("media content") for audiences, the most important distinction is between web-centered and app-centered businesses. A web-centered business involves reaching out to target audiences through web browsers. For example, the web-centered business of the *New York Times* can be found at its website address, NYTimes.com. An app-centered business involves reaching people not through the web but through **applications** or "**apps**." An app is software that uses the internet, but not the web system, to bring material to audiences. A person must download the app to get the material. If you have a smartphone or a tablet, you probably can download an app for the *New York Times* that will present its materials to you in ways that may be different from the ways they look on the website.

**applications ("apps")**
software that uses the internet, but not the web system, to bring material to audiences

Apps on smartphones have gone far beyond the basic calendar, music, and e-mail functionality. More and more apps are being released every day, ranging from no-cost to more than $1,200 as technology allows for more sophisticated capabilities from the palm of your hand. They include surveillance technology and specialized apps for medical professionals and scientists, such as DDS GP for dentists and Agro (for agronomists, which costs $999.99).

**feature phone**
a mobile telephone that carries extras unrelated to calling ("features" such as texting, calendars, cameras, and media players) but does not have the sophisticated web-browsing, app-importing operating system of a smartphone

**smartphone**
a mobile telephone that uses a special computer operating system to offer connections to the internet through a web browser as well as through special applications (apps) that are compatible with that operating system

**mobile application (mobile app)**
computer software designed to help the user of a mobile device perform specific tasks

As these examples suggest, media firms traditionally have used web browsers rather than apps to reach people on desktop and laptop computers. (The internet industry does not consider laptops to be mobile devices even though you can boogie with a laptop while accessing the web on many of them.) When it comes to mobile devices, media firms often build their businesses around apps. At the same time, web browsers play an important part in companies' approaches to audiences in the mobile world as well. Let's take a short definitional detour to explain.

The term "mobile device" describes a growing number of instruments that fall under two broad categories: phones and tablets. When it comes to phones, Americans tend to use either a **feature phone** or a **smartphone**. A smartphone is a mobile telephone that uses a special computer operating system to offer connections to the internet through a web browser as well as through special applications (apps) that are compatible with that operating system. The most common smartphone operating systems are Google's Android and Apple's iOS, though Nokia, Microsoft, and Blackberry offer competition in the area. Feature phones do not have these complex operating systems, and although they often carry a variety of extras unrelated to calling ("features" such as texting, calendars, cameras, and media players), many to do not have web browsers, and most do not allow the importation and use of apps.

A **mobile application** (or **mobile app**) is computer software designed to help the user of a mobile device perform specific tasks. Apps are available through app stores, which are typically operated by the owner of the mobile operating system of the smartphone or tablet. Think of the Apple App Store, Google Play, Windows Phone Store, and BlackBerry App World. Some apps are free, whereas others cost money. After you pay, your app is downloaded from the platform to your device—for example, your Android phone or iPad.

Because of their ability to connect to the web and download apps, smartphones are more expensive to buy than feature phones, and they are often more expensive to keep. Feature phone owners often pay extra for text messaging, but smartphone owners often pay a lot more because connecting to the web and apps requires payment for monthly data plans as well as for the ability to make voice calls. Apps often cost money too, and people download many of those. In 2012, 19 percent of Android phone owners and 26 percent of iPhone owners reported more than 20 apps on their phone.[6]

In late 2012, according to the Pew Research Center, 44 percent of Americans had a smartphone. Of those, 46 percent carried one with an Android OS, and 38 percent carried the iPhone operating system. During the same period, one in four Americans owned a tablet.[7] A tablet is a computer that is larger than a mobile phone but smaller and lighter than a laptop and is operated primarily by touching the screen. In 2012, 52 percent of tablet owners owned an Apple iPad, 48 percent owned a tablet based on the Android operating system (e.g., the Samsung Galaxy), and 21 percent owned a Kindle Fire tablet. These numbers add to 121 percent because a substantial number of these owners owned both an e-book reader and a tablet not specifically designed for reading.[8]

## THINKING ABOUT MEDIA LITERACY

Do you use or have you used a tablet? If so, which one and why? Why do you think tablets have gained such an immense following within just a few short years of their initial introduction?

As the costs of smartphones and tablets decrease, the proportion of Americans who use this technology is likely to grow larger and larger. Many technology experts predict that some of the most important developments in media during the next decade will center on mobile devices. Businesses are certainly paying a lot of attention. During the past several years, two major developments have marked the spread of mobile devices. One is that some publishers are making sure that the sites they present to mobile owners are different from those that show up on desktop and laptop computers. The other is the creation of apps designed specifically for the devices.

Not all publishers show mobile users a different view of the web. If you went to the *New York Times* site via a laptop browser in 2012, for example, you would see the same home page that popped up when you went online via your phone's browser. Some companies, however, do change the look and functionality of their websites to make them easy to load on a phone and tablet, where the speed of the device's computer processor and the size of the screen (especially in the case of phones) might not work well with the graphics-intensive websites that they have created for desktops and laptops. For example, if you went to Facebook on the iPhone's Safari browser that year, Facebook directed you to m.Facebook.com, to a page that aimed to optimize its look on mobile.

Another, increasingly common reason for customizing a website for mobile involves making sure the content you receive relates directly to what the publisher believes are your needs on a device that often moves with you and can make phone calls. Google's search engine takes this approach. Type the word "pizza" into the Google search engine on a laptop during 2012, and you were likely to find a list of local restaurants serving the food, with a map and their addresses and phone numbers. The mobile version showed a map as well but also had buttons for phone calling, specific directions, and the website. If you typed in "Italy" in a new search afterward, the mobile Google returned a Wikipedia entry on the country and then names of pizza restaurants with the word "Italy" in their name, though not necessarily in the right location. The laptop version of Google, by contrast, referenced sites on travel to Italy, with no pizza-restaurant links in sight.

Apps provide another popular approach to getting specific information in the mobile realm. Going on the web via a mobile device is still a more common activity than using mobile apps, but Apple noted in late 2012 that from the start of the Apple App Store in July 2008 visitors have downloaded 35 billion apps to their various Apple mobile technologies—the iPhone, iPod touch, and iPad.[9] These apps run the gamut from electronic book (e-book) readers to games, banking instruments, meditation timers, running programs, and much more. Many of the publishers of these apps also have websites with similar material, but many do not. Why do publishers choose to distribute their content via apps in addition to, or instead of, the web? For some app developers, an app provided a way to get around the slowness of loading websites on mobile browsers in the early 2010s. Apps have built-in features that load immediately, and they update information through an Internet channel that does not use a web browser. For example, after you pay for and download a book-reading app from your mobile device's store, you may be able to use the book-reading app regardless of whether you are connected to your cellular network or to a Wi-Fi network. But your app would need to connect to the internet to purchase a new book or make changes in the book reader.

From everything we have discussed, you can see that, in the mobile industry, publishers are often also both content creators (when they do create the content they carry) and distributors of the content to the point of its public exhibition. As in the online industry, exhibition is carried out in the mobile web and app space by the internet service provider. But other digital players may also take on the role of exhibitors. When a website or app sells items to visitors (as Amazon's mobile website and the Apple App store do), it is acting as an exhibitor as well as a distributor.

Firms that follow Americans' use of mobile devices are also aware that people use tablets and smartphones in the home while they are watching television. Table 6.2 lists the popularity of certain activities based on a Pew Internet & American Life survey. Checking e-mail is the most popular. Note, too, that 38 percent of tablet owners say they have looked up information related to the TV program they were watching, and 44 percent visited a social networking site during the program. Seeing the relationship between mobile devices and TV-set viewing, many cable systems offer apps that turn a phone or tablet into a remote control. Then there is the social aspect of viewing. As we will discuss in chapter 13, IntoNow, MyTVBuddy, and Tapcast are among the applications that help people interact with others—friends or perfect strangers—around programs they are watching.

## THINKING ABOUT MEDIA LITERACY

Think for a moment about your media consumption habits and the devices you use to access those media. Do you often find yourself engaging with multiple media through multiple devices at once? If so, which ones and how? Why do you think you engage in these practices?

In view of the increasing popularity of mobile apps and the mobile web in so many circumstances, it should not be surprising that advertising is increasingly part of the mobile industry. Newspapers and magazines, which for generations have made revenues only in print, are connecting to readers on the mobile web and via apps and trying to find sponsors to help them pay for it. Although ads have not historically been a common feature of the book industry, Amazon decided to buck that tradition by inviting ads on its e-reader for those who want to pay less for the device. Other digital-only publishers such as Google, Yahoo!, Facebook, Twitter, and AOL are trying to turn rapidly expanding mobile usage into an important source of advertising money.

Advertising companies are using the same kinds of activities on the mobile web that they use in the online space—behavioral targeting via cookies through publishers, ad networks, and exchanges. Apps don't accept cookies, though, so publishers and ad networks have had to use other techniques, such as linking the user to an identification number of the device, to track and target people. For advertisers and their agencies, the holy grail of advertising is to be able to track an individual across all sorts of digital devices, from laptops to tablets, TV sets, retail checkout machines, and more.

# Media Ethics: Confronting Internet Privacy

As we will see in forthcoming chapters, executives from various media industries see these targeting capabilities as extremely helpful for bringing in advertising money in their highly competitive business environments. Critics, however, worry that the 21st-century media world might also cause trouble by trampling on people's privacy. They point out that the phenomenal growth of digital media, as well as the convergence that has come along with it, has made so much of what we do every day a two-way experience. It is interactive. In one direction we bring news, information, advertising, e-mail, retail forms, bank information, Tweets, Facebook and Foursquare updates, and more into our devices. In the other direction, we respond by clicking on links, writing blogs, transferring money, filling out retail forms, creating Tweets, creating Facebook and FourSquare updates, and more. All these activities describe our lives, the critics point out, and they contain information—about who we are, what we do, our likes and dislikes—that we might not want others to know.

As more and more people use online social networking sites, such as Facebook, advertisers are increasingly interested in finding ways to reach out to potential customers and to learn more about their web browsing and online behavior that might help them better reach those people. In addition, because many people aren't necessarily thinking about their privacy when they are interacting with these media, they often reveal information about their appearance (e.g., posting photos) and their location and other information that might be abused by criminals, such as identity thieves.

That, say concerned individuals and organizations, is a major problem we have to think through as a society. They argue that we are moving into a new era when it comes to information. It is an era, they say, in which governments will be able to find out far more about citizens than the citizens want them to know. And it is an era in which companies will be able to find out far more about their customers than those customers realize or want them to know. In the new age of digital convergence, critics say, more and more devices are two way and so people must be aware of companies' secret use of their data.

The first stirrings of concern began in the 1970s, when companies began to use computers to combine enormous amounts of information from public and private records about virtually everyone in the nation and sell this information to marketers. Among the largest of these companies are Experian, Equifax, Acxiom, and Choicepoint. Many marketers use these firms' universal databases (called that because they hold information on almost everyone) to find people whose profiles make them potential customers.

But privacy really took off as a media issue with the rise of marketing on the World Wide Web in the mid-1990s. Recall our discussion of interactive marketing and cookie technology earlier in this chapter. Interactive media firms see the ability to track clickstreams as a great way to find out what users want and how best to serve them. It is important to point out that placing a cookie in a person's computer does not allow a marketer to learn the name, postal address, or any other so-called **personally identifiable information (PII)** about the person who owns the computer. Many online marketers contend that this anonymity makes following people online and creating cookie profiles about them perfectly acceptable. Critics of this viewpoint, though, point out that many ad networks and websites can easily determine PII by relating a cookie to the name or e-mail address used when the person has registered on a site. When no registration information is available, a marketer can encourage a person with a cookie to sign up for a sweepstakes. The personal information provided then can get linked to the cookie data. Critics add that even when marketers and websites don't have personally identifiable information, they still surround individuals with ads and other content

**personally identifiable information (PII)**
the name, postal address, or any other information that allows tracking down the specific person who owns a device

that are tailored to their understanding of what that individual is like. Based on profiles they have created without people's knowledge or permission, they are creating views of the world for people and giving certain people discounts that they don't give others.

Rarely will media executives argue publicly that people should have no right to stop firms from collecting information about them. Under government pressures, many often concede that members of the public should have the right to know that material about them is being collected. Media executives emphasize, however, that in today's competitive media world, being able to show advertisers that a medium can deliver specific, desirable types of people is crucial for media companies' survival. Supporters of data collection also use the argument that this invasion of privacy has its positive side. They argue that the more marketers know about people, the more they will be able to send individuals materials that these individuals will find relevant to their lives. The result, they say, is that people will be unlikely to complain that they receive junk mail. Nowadays, most web marketers say that they understand people's desire to keep certain information private. They also insist, however, that many individuals are willing to give up information about themselves if, in return, they get something that they consider valuable. Many privacy advocates agree that people should have the right to decide whether they want to give up private information as part of a transaction. They disagree with the web marketers on the way in which consumers should be informed about the data that will be collected about them—which often occurs without their knowledge.

Privacy advocates want members of the public to have to opt in when it comes to giving out information. That is, marketers should not be permitted to collect information about a person unless that person explicitly indicates that it is all right for them to do so (say, by checking a box online). Marketers contend that getting **opt-in** permission is too difficult because people either are too lazy to give it or are concerned about their privacy when the question is put to them in that manner. The marketers prefer an **opt-out approach**. That means that they will be permitted to collect personal information from consumers as long as they inform people of what they are doing and give them the opportunity to check a "no" box or otherwise refuse to allow it.

Note that these privacy issues are not related only to the web. What people do on mobile devices is already of interest to many advertisers; some government agencies might want to see these data as well. The same is the case with what and how people play video games. In fact, as home-based television viewing becomes a two-way activity (we'll discuss this in the TV industry chapter), getting data about what individuals do with the medium will also interest marketers and, possibly, certain branches of government. As these types of surveillance continue to take place, various advocacy groups will argue against them and ask for legal safeguards against the misuse and abuse of people's data. Clearly, the fight over U.S. consumer privacy in the digital age will continue.

## Determining Your Point of View as a Critical Consumer of Media

As you consider the preceding paragraphs, you may end up deciding that what is happening with people's data is fine. Or you might decide that important changes should be made. You may also feel strongly (pro or con) regarding the windows, globalization, and conglomeration activities we described in the introduction to Part 2. More and more, these activities are taking hold in all media industries, and they are beginning to affect all our lives profoundly. Think about where you stand on these issues when you read about individual industries in the rest of the book. Remember that today every mass media industry is part of the big, cross-media picture.

**opt-in approach**
the view that marketers should not be permitted to collect information about a person unless the person explicitly indicates that it is all right for them to do so

**opt-out approach**
the view that marketers should be permitted to collect personal information from consumers as long as they inform people of what they are doing and give them the opportunity to refuse

## MEDIA TODAY & CULTURE SOCIAL MEDIA AND THE KOREAN MUSIC INDUSTRY

The South Korean popular music industry has expanded globally over the last decade or so, riding into North America on what has been called the second "Korean Wave." The nine-member band Girls' Generation appeared on *The Late Show with David Letterman* and *Live! with Kelly* in 2012, performing their song "The Boys" in English. Solo artist Psy appeared on shows such as *Ellen* and NBC's *Today* show, performing his hit "Gangnam Style" on the latter. Despite what might seem like sudden successes, Korean pop music artists actually go through a rigorous process before becoming stars. Building awareness about these artists took a long time, particularly within foreign markets. Korean popular music, also called K-pop, has history of popularity in countries such as Japan, Malaysia, and Thailand. Building awareness of new artists required partnering with local countries' companies and even releasing albums recorded for those countries. It was a timely and costly process.

Social media changed this situation. With sites such as YouTube, Twitter, and Facebook, the Korean music industry could reach the audiences in foreign countries and cultivate fans without local industry partnerships. It also could engage in these activities cheaply and the process takes less time to develop audiences for its artists. Before the process took around 5 years, but social media cut that time in half (or even less).

Psy's video for "Gangnam Style" originally was uploaded in July 2012. By December 2012, the video had broken viewing records previously held U.S. artist Justin Bieber, exceeding one billion. Prior to this video, Psy had released six albums in Korea, but the viral video quickly brought him to global attention. All around the world, people began creating their own fan videos and imitating the dance moves. The success of the video led Psy to sign a global management deal with Island Records, though YG Entertainment still manages his career in Korea.

In addition to promotional purposes, the Korean artists use social media to connect with their fans in a more personable and friendly way than U.S. stars. According to Kenneth Cho, vice president of marketing of Seoul-based Chiel, "Korean stars are usually good at using social media to communicate with their fans. They speak about their personal lives (their family, their pets, etc.) and even post their 'no-makeup' photos." He continues, "Using these social/digital media, K-pop stars become . . . very approachable, someone who's very close to me."

# CHAPTER REVIEW

Visit the Companion Website at www.routledge.com/cw/turow for additional study tools and resources.

## Key Terms

You can find the definitions to these key terms in the marginal glossary throughout this chapter. Test your knowledge of these terms with interactive flash cards on the *Media Today* companion website.

ad exchanges
ad network
algorithm
applications ("apps")
behavioral targeting
click-and-mortar companies
clickstream
contextual advertising
cookie
data mining
feature phone

hyperlinks
HyperText Markup Language (HTML)
the internet
internet service provider (ISP)
keyword advertising
mobile application (mobile app)
natural or organic search results
net neutrality controversy
opt-in approach
opt-out approach
packets

personally identifiable information (PII)
profiling
search engine
smartphone
social media site (social networking site or SNS)
social search
user-generated content (UGC)
web crawlers (web spiders)
wireless fidelity (Wi-Fi)

# Questions for Discussion and Critical Thinking

1. The "packet-switching" technology of the internet does have advantages over standard telephone technology. Sometimes, though, when audio or video technology is sent via packets, the results can be distorted. (You might hear it sometimes when you use Skype.) Use the internet to explore this problem and how companies use a technique called "buffering" to solve it.

2. Some journalists worry that user-generated content can hurt their livelihoods. Why do you think they would have this concern? Do you think the concern is justified? Do you think the audience for the content should be concerned about journalists' worries?

3. Under net neutrality, internet service providers would make no effort to restrict or promote your access to websites. Instead, they would deliver all sites to you equally without restriction. But what about websites that pose threats to certain populations, such as ones that promote human trafficking or celebrate child pornography? Under net neutrality, ISPs would offer equal access to them. Do you think ISPs should restrict the public's access to these types of sites? If so, why? If not, should other measures be taken against those sites? If so, what?

4. Websites use cookies and other techniques to "personalize" your experience with them. In some cases, that personalization might mean offering you a lower price on a product, while offering someone else a higher price. Or it might mean offering one person a 20 percent discount while offering you a 10 percent discount. What advantages does this system offer to the advertisers? What advantages and disadvantages does this offer customers? Overall, does this system seem fair? Why or why not?

5. Many marketing executives contend that teenagers and young adults don't worry much about the privacy of their data. The marketers say that as long as these individuals receive content and offers relevant to them, they don't mind advertisers mining data about them. Do you think the executives' claims are valid? Why or why not?

## Case Study
### THE USE OF MOBILE DEVICES FOR PRICE COMPARISONS

**The Idea** To get a sense of the ways that people use mobile devices to check prices and products while they are shopping—and the extent to which store prices are competitive.

**The Method** Pick a major chain store with a lot of traffic—for example, Best Buy, Bed Bath & Beyond, or Macy's. Spend an hour in an area of the store and note how many people appear to be using their mobile devices to check prices or evaluate products. When you see someone doing it, politely ask them if they are checking prices, evaluating a product, or both. Find out how they carried out their comparison—via what website or app? Ask them their conclusion—did they find out good things about the product? Did the store have a lower or higher price than available elsewhere?

Write a report of what you learned and compare your findings with other members of the class. Based on your research and their research, what conclusions can you draw about the extent to which—and ways in which—people use mobile devices for price comparisons? Also, what conclusions can you draw about the extent to which those stores have competitive prices?

# The Book Industry

"If I rely on just the bookstore sales, I won't make a living. Putting [my book] online does not put my livelihood at risk; you make a living finding new ways to do business."

**CORY DOCTOROW, SCIENCE FICTION WRITER AND BLOGGER**

## CHAPTER OBJECTIVES

1 Understand today's books in terms of the development of books over the centuries

2 Differentiate among the different types of books within the book publishing industry

3 Explain the roles of production, distribution, and exhibition as they pertain to the book publishing industry

4 Realize and evaluate the effects of new digital technologies on the book publishing industry

5 Analyze ethical pitfalls present in the book publishing industry

If you were a book publishing executive, what would you do when faced with the following situation? You realize that, more and more, people are buying electronic versions of books to read on e-readers—that is, on tablets such as the Kindle, the Nook, the iPad, and the Sony Reader, through which people download the electronic copies, which get charged to an online account. Your company used to make most of its money by selling its mystery and horror titles to the small independent bookstores that populated the American landscape for over a century as well as to the handful of large bookstore chains (e.g., Borders, Barnes & Noble, Books-A-Million) that seemed to be fixtures of so many strip malls around the nation. Now many of those outlets are closing, and

you learn that the readers of your books are purchasing hard copies online, and many others are buying the electronic versions. The rise of the electronic book would be terrific—a new platform for selling mystery and horror—except for one major problem: Amazon, the 800-pound gorilla of the electronic space, is selling your books (and the books of many other publishers) for a loss at $9.99, in comparison with the $13 or more that you would like to charge. The problem with that, you worry, is that other online bookstores will hesitate to carry your books, fearing they cannot compete with Amazon on price—or they will force you, the publisher, to lower your price to them. "What kind of book world is being created?" you may ask yourself. "Apart from Amazon keeping our prices low and stifling competition, consumers may grow accustomed to inexpensive e-books and limit publishers' ability to sell more expensive titles."

A tough situation, isn't it? So what would you do if Apple representatives contacted you and laid out a plan under which Apple would sell your books and those of other publishers through its online store for the prices the publishers would set, and Apple would take a 30 percent cut of that. Apple also would require that publishers using its store not let other electronic retailers (including Amazon) sell the same book at a lower price. The idea would be that if enough publishers agreed to that plan, they could then go to Amazon and require it to follow Apple's lead.

Sound like a good idea? Would you join other publishers in this venture? Well, the U.S. Justice Department claims several did and broke the law. As the *Wall Street Journal* reported it, "The Justice Department believes that Apple and the publishers acted in concert to raise prices across the industry, and is prepared to sue them for violating federal antitrust laws."[1] Although a few publishers that the government accused of that collusion admitted wrongdoing, others held back, arguing they had done nothing illegal. During 2013 a court declared Apple guilty, but Apple insisted it had not colluded with any publisher and would appeal. Moreover, whereas some in the book publishing industry applauded Justice for stopping a blatant attempt to keep book prices high, others took the opposite position. They argued that Amazon's activities would have a long-term dismal effect on book publishing, making it difficult for many book companies to stay in the business of taking risks on authors and their works. As of late 2012 this case was still percolating; perhaps by the time you read this, it will have reached a conclusion. The point to make here, though, is that the circumstances surrounding this case highlight the tumultuous changes taking place in one of the oldest mass media industries.

The book you are reading now is a product of one area of the transforming book industry: the college textbook segment. *Media Today* is available via the Kindle. Moreover, if you think of the "extra" materials that come with the print version of the book—the website and the terms you can download to your mobile device, for example— you will realize that in this area, too, book publishers in the converging media environment are going beyond the printed page in various ways. Their biggest long-term concerns involve figuring out how to compete in a digital environment, in which paper is only one way to deliver the information in books.

For one of the oldest communication media—books are older than newspapers—and for an industry that has typically been pretty set in its ways, that is a tall order. It's by no means an impossible one, though, as we will see. If you were involved in the task, probably the first thing you would have to do is ask two basic questions: What *are* the essential features of a book that have drawn readers over the centuries? And what are the essential elements of today's book industry that would encourage or discourage bold new movements into the digital age?

## The History of the Book

We should begin by making one point clear: despite the startling growth of e-book readers during the past several years, people still read paper books in far greater numbers than electronic ones. According to the Association of American Publishers, electronic books represented only 6 percent of the book industry's revenues in 2010—meaning that 94 percent of the revenues came from paper books. So why are publishers so worried about Amazon's pricing of electronic books? And why are they so worried about the future of their industry?

The answer is that the growth of e-books has been so fast that many in the industry feel it indicates that a great transformation is upon them. Consider that although the percentage of e-books in 2010 was rather small at 6 percent, only two years earlier it was far smaller—less than 1 percent. Moreover, the rise in e-book revenues between 2009 and 2010 was astonishing: 1,040 percent. And if we look at the area where e-books are most popular—adult fiction—we find that they now make up 14 percent of that part of the industry's revenues.[2] Book publishing executives look at these revenues and see a world in transition that might create problems for their companies if they don't respond in appropriate ways.

They are certainly not the first people in history who had to confront changing technologies when it came to the book. This history of the book is, at its heart, a story of humans trying to use technology to record and circulate ideas. Although the book as we know it can be traced back only about 500 years, the idea of the book is much older. Scholars consider the papyrus roll in Egypt around 3,000 BCE to be an early ancestor of the modern book. Papyrus was made from a reed-like plant in the Nile Valley, and it resembled paper. Scribes laid out sheets of papyrus, copied a text on one side of the sheets, and then rolled up the finished manuscript. The Greeks adopted the papyrus roll from the Egyptians and stored their rolls in great libraries. In fact, the Greeks considered the book so important that they began to use it, rather than memorizing poems and speeches (called the oral tradition), as the main way to make ideas "public"—or available to large numbers of people. Greek writers of the era refer to a market in books and to prices paid for them. Large libraries maintained scriptoria where many books were copied by hand.

These manuscripts in the scriptoria don't sound at all like the books we know, do they? Take a look at the book timeline (Figure 7.1), and you'll realize just how long it took for the idea of a book as we know it to emerge. Study the timeline carefully, and you'll probably notice three important themes:

1.  *The modern book did not arrive in a flash as a result of one inventor's grand change.*

Instead, pieces of what we know as the printed book developed slowly and came together at certain important stages. For example, Johannes Gutenberg's invention of the printing press in 1440 was certainly a milestone because it allowed far more copies of a particular book to be created than was possible when copies were written by hand. But Gutenberg's amazing step forward drew on innovations made centuries earlier. He didn't wake up one morning and say, "Hey, I think I'll develop a printing press."

Rather, as the timeline makes clear, people in China had already developed the ink that Gutenberg needed for his technology, and traders had brought the recipe to Europe. Similarly, Asians had also pioneered the process of carving on wooden blocks, inking them, and "printing" what was on the blocks onto a variety of materials. Gutenberg knew of these developments. He also knew that although the communication of meaning in China took place through pictures, European languages such as Latin conveyed meaning through individual letters of an alphabet. Gutenberg's genius, then, was in deciding the "blocks" needed to be letters. Doing that, he created movable type. The machine that he invented to hold the type, allow it to be inked, and then allow the inked type to be pressed on the paper became what we know as the printing press. Even the printing press wasn't a totally original invention. He borrowed the design from a wine press.

Other parts of the book timeline also reflect this idea that the technology evolved rather than appeared suddenly. It is a theme we will see in the history of other media industries.

2.  *The book as a medium of communication developed as a result of social and legal responses to the technology during different periods.*

It is impossible to separate the decisions of those who wrote, created, and sold books from the beliefs of their time, the reading ability of the population, and the government actions of the historical period. It is no accident that one of the first titles

# Figure 7.1 Timeline of the Book Industry

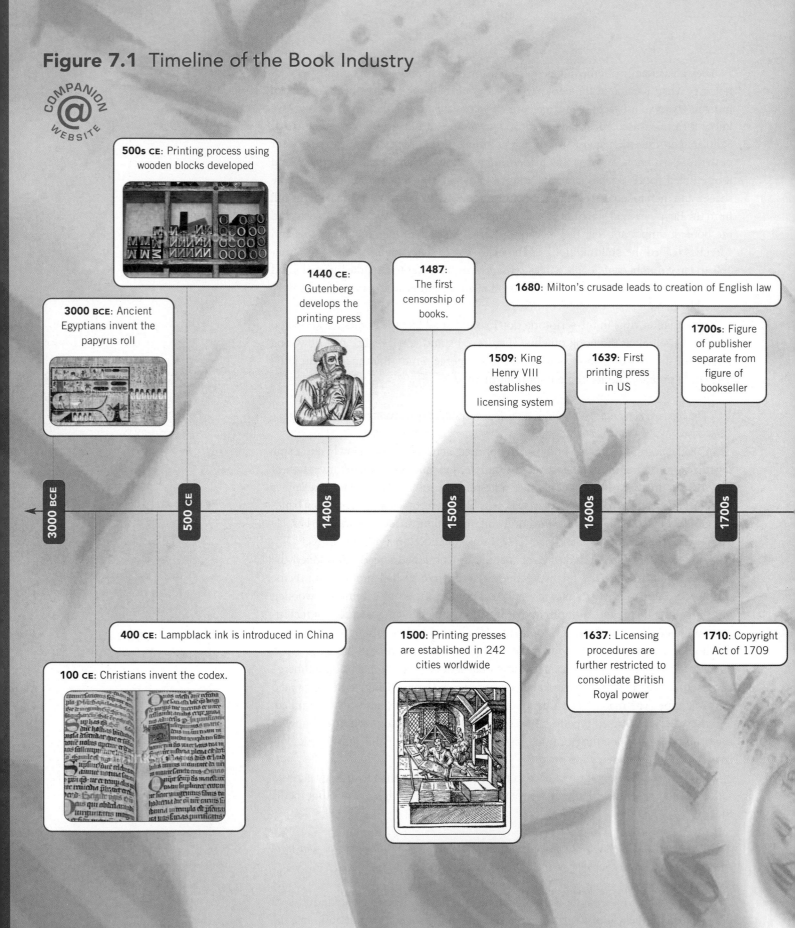

**500s CE**: Printing process using wooden blocks developed

**3000 BCE**: Ancient Egyptians invent the papyrus roll

**1440 CE**: Gutenberg develops the printing press

**1487**: The first censorship of books.

**1680**: Milton's crusade leads to creation of English law

**1509**: King Henry VIII establishes licensing system

**1639**: First printing press in US

**1700s**: Figure of publisher separate from figure of bookseller

**400 CE**: Lampblack ink is introduced in China

**100 CE**: Christians invent the codex.

**1500**: Printing presses are established in 242 cities worldwide

**1637**: Licensing procedures are further restricted to consolidate British Royal power

**1710**: Copyright Act of 1709

3000 BCE | 500 CE | 1400s | 1500s | 1600s | 1700s

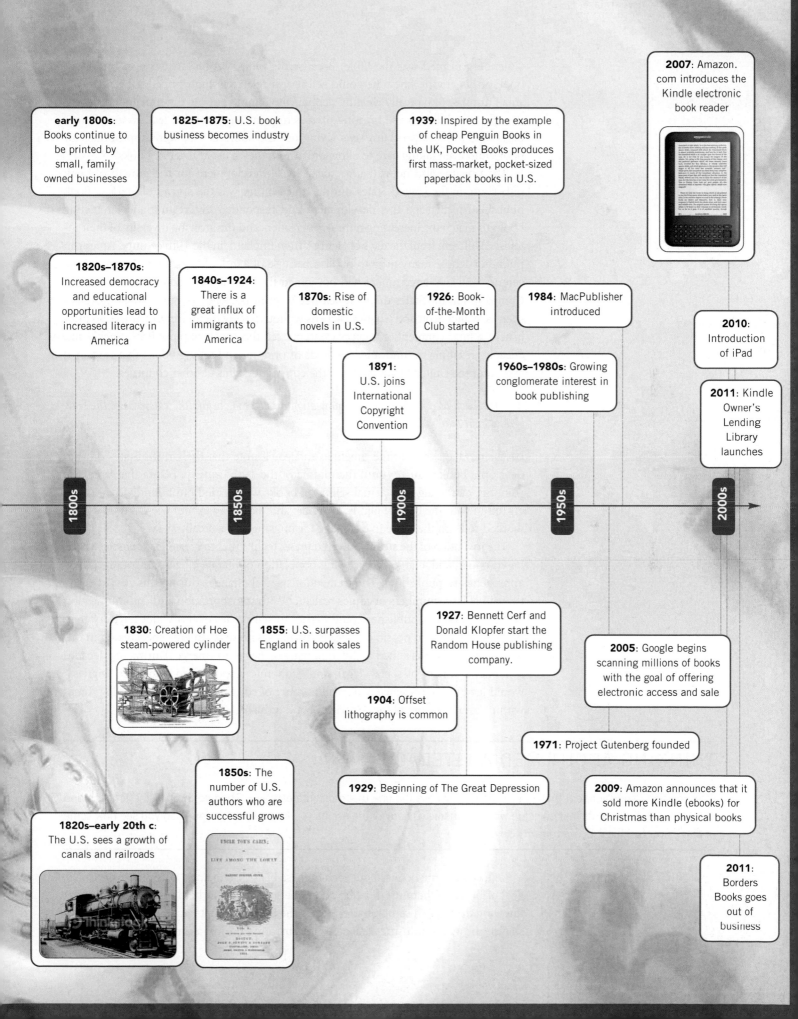

**early 1800s**: Books continue to be printed by small, family owned businesses

**1825–1875**: U.S. book business becomes industry

**1939**: Inspired by the example of cheap Penguin Books in the UK, Pocket Books produces first mass-market, pocket-sized paperback books in U.S.

**2007**: Amazon.com introduces the Kindle electronic book reader

**1820s–1870s**: Increased democracy and educational opportunities lead to increased literacy in America

**1840s–1924**: There is a great influx of immigrants to America

**1870s**: Rise of domestic novels in U.S.

**1926**: Book-of-the-Month Club started

**1984**: MacPublisher introduced

**2010**: Introduction of iPad

**1891**: U.S. joins International Copyright Convention

**1960s–1980s**: Growing conglomerate interest in book publishing

**2011**: Kindle Owner's Lending Library launches

**1800s**    **1850s**    **1900s**    **1950s**    **2000s**

**1830**: Creation of Hoe steam-powered cylinder

**1855**: U.S. surpasses England in book sales

**1927**: Bennett Cerf and Donald Klopfer start the Random House publishing company.

**2005**: Google begins scanning millions of books with the goal of offering electronic access and sale

**1904**: Offset lithography is common

**1971**: Project Gutenberg founded

**1850s**: The number of U.S. authors who are successful grows

**1929**: Beginning of The Great Depression

**2009**: Amazon announces that it sold more Kindle (ebooks) for Christmas than physical books

**1820s–early 20th c**: The U.S. sees a growth of canals and railroads

UNCLE TOM'S CABIN;
LIFE AMONG THE LOWLY

**2011**: Borders Books goes out of business

Gutenberg printed was the Bible. Because the Bible was by far the most important book of his era, he knew he could sell it at a relatively high price to the relatively small number of typically wealthy people who could read. As the timeline indicates, though, the ability to use printing presses to print any book led leaders in different parts of Europe to proclaim laws laying out the subjects that were appropriate for books and even taking care to allow only those they trusted to print books.

The timeline also notes that a crucial social development for the growth of book publishing in the United States during 19th century was the spread of literacy. Book publishers recognized this development and responded by creating and circulating books to match the increasing numbers of readers and the growing diversity of their interests. Different from the days of Henry VIII in England, in the 19th century, American publishers chose many titles to publish because of a *lack* of laws: until the end of the century, the U.S. government had not joined the international copyright convention. Companies in the States therefore felt free to print books by popular British novelists such as Walter Scott and Charles Dickens without paying them. Among American publishers, a huge competition took place to put out the novels of those Brits quickly and cheaply, resulting in innovative methods of printing and selling books that remained even after the United States accepted the copyright claims of other countries.

3.  *The book as a medium of communication existed long before the existence of the book industry.*

Again, take a look at the timeline, and you'll note that the United States did not develop a book industry until the middle of the 19th century. Before that time, the printing, marketing, and actual selling of books was carried out by individual printers, often with the help of family members and maybe an apprentice—a trainee who worked to learn the trade in exchange for housing and a small salary.

The invention of the steam-powered press, techniques to create inexpensive wood-based paper, and a large and growing population of literate citizens encouraged new approaches to publishing. The tremendous social changes during this period made the sale of large numbers of copies realistic. With transportation and communication becoming easier, a publisher could expect to sell copies over a wider territory than previously had been possible. Large companies with departments specializing in different types of books aimed at different markets began to emerge. During the decades to come, a variety of social, legal, and economic responses to publisher "bigness" would lead to the presence of a small number of conglomerates as the leading forces within several sectors of the American book industry.

## THINKING ABOUT MEDIA LITERACY

After reading carefully about these three themes, choose the one that most interests you. Then go through the timeline and see if you can find events that coincide with that theme. Do any of the events you found surprise you? Can you see how some of these events impact books today? If so, how?

One could write books about each of these historical themes, and people have. The goal of bringing them up in a text about media today is to help you understand that knowing the past is useful for interpreting the present. What happened in the past has shaped the media industries that currently surround us. Just as important, the industry processes that the themes describe apply to the present as well as to years ago. We have already noted in this chapter's introduction that contemporary books are evolving in new digital forms (theme 1). In the following pages we will explore that topic further. We will also see that the book business is responding to new social and legal developments (theme 2) and that the book industry is transforming even as we study it (theme 3). Being familiar with historical versions of these themes may well help you better understand—and even predict—how they will work in the 21st century. So let's get to it.

## The Book Industry Today

Book publishing is a big and generally healthy business with sales totaling $27.94 billion in 2010, according to the BookStats research organization. The people who work in the industry make a variety of distinctions among types of books. The most general distinction is between professional and educational books on the one hand and consumer books on the other. **Audiobooks**, however, are a type that can include professional and educational as well as consumer books. Let's get a bird's-eye view of each category.

### Educational and Professional Books

Educational and professional books focus on training. Most professional and educational books are marked by their use of **pedagogy** (or particular teaching approaches), which includes features such as learning objectives, chapter recaps, questions for discussion, and the like. Although a good deal of what professional and educational publishers turn out look like traditional books, the publishers are the first to acknowledge that a growing proportion of the publications flowing from their firms aren't books in the traditional sense. An example is what educators call "digital basal materials"—these are basic teaching tools for children in early grades, but they are electronic rather than on paper. Industry observers also point to math workbooks, corporate training manuals, college course packs, online versions of textbooks, and text-related videos. Because some of the materials are not standard books (or even books at all, as we understand the term), some writers on the topic have come to refer to this area broadly as "educational and training media," suggesting that a new converging industry is developing with books as a part of it. Other experts still consider the area to be part of book publishing because the nonbook products are often closely connected to traditional books in the learning environment. People who work in the industry recognize three types of educational and training books: **K–12 books and materials**; **higher-education books and materials**; and **professional books**.

### Consumer Books

Unlike the publishers of professional and educational books, publishers of **consumer books** are aiming their products at the general public. They target readers

**audiobook**
a recording in which someone reads a printed book or a version of it

**pedagogy**
the use of features such as learning objectives, chapter recaps, and questions for discussion; this is characteristic of educational books

**K–12 books and materials**
books and materials created for students in kindergarten through the 12th grade

**higher-education books and materials**
books and materials that focus on teaching students in college and post-college learning

**professional books**
books that help people who are working keep up-to-date in their areas as well as rise to the next level of knowledge

**consumer books**
books that are aimed at the general public

Textbooks for undergraduates and graduate students often contain pedagogical elements, such as review questions, chapter summaries, and marginal glossaries, and link to further resources available online via a website that has been created to complement the text.

in their private lives, outside their roles as students and highly trained workers. Informal teaching is certainly a significant part of consumer publishing in areas as varied as religion (the Bible), science (*A Brief History of Time*), history (*Guns, Germs and Steel*), cooking (*Rachel Ray Express Lane Meals*), and ethics (*The Book of Virtues*). Noneducational genres are also a major part of consumer book publishing; these include everything from romance novels to joke books to travel books. Publishing personnel use these subject classifications and many more when they create titles.

When it comes to defining the major categories of the consumer book publishing business, though, publishers identify them quite differently. Using terms originated by the Association of American Publishers (AAP), people involved in publishing talk about the following categories:

- Trade
- Mass market paperback
- Religious
- Book club
- Mail-order
- Scholarly
- Subscription reference

Rather than describing the subject matter of books, all the AAP categories (with the exception of religion) refer to the way in which books are distributed or produced. Figure 7.2 shows the amount of money consumers spent for each of these categories in 2010. Let's explore each of these categories one at a time.

**trade books**
general-interest titles, including both fiction and nonfiction books, that are typically sold to consumers through retail bookstores (both traditional and web-based) and to libraries

**Trade Books** **Trade books**—general-interest titles, including both fiction and nonfiction books—are typically sold to consumers through retail bookstores (both traditional and web-based) and to libraries.

**Figure 7.2**
Consumer spending on trade books (2010)

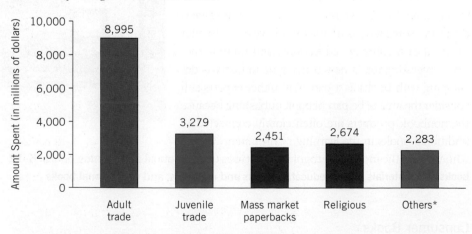

Source: *Communications Industry Forecast, 2011–15* (New York: Veronis Suhler Stevenson, 2011), chapter 14, p. 9.

* = book clubs, mail-order, university presses, self-publishing

Publishing personnel further distinguish between adult and juvenile trade books. In 2010, they shipped about 449.2 million of the former and 394.6 million of the latter to retailers. Employees also distinguish between trade books that are hard-bound (165.4 million copies of juvenile units and 196.8 million copies of adult units shipped in 2010) and those that are paperbound, called **trade paperbacks** (a combined total of 481.6 million shipped).[3]

**Mass Market Paperbacks** Pocket-size paperback books smaller than trade paperbacks are called **mass market paperbacks**. They are designed to be sold primarily in so-called **mass market outlets**—newsstands, drugstores, discount stores, and supermarkets. Many types of books come in this format, but romance novels and science fiction tales are among the most common. Publishers shipped 319.4 million mass market paperbacks in 2010.

**Religious Books  Religious books** are essentially trade books that contain specifically religious content. They are sold in general bookstores as well as in special religious bookshops. The success of this category seems to vary with the level of interest in the topic. In the early 2000s, the sales figures hovered above $3 billion. The late 2000s saw the numbers dip; in 2010 U.S. consumers spent $2.83 billion on religious books and bought 204 million copies. That figure includes sales of the Bible, the best-selling book of all time. It also includes Rick Warren's *The Purpose-Driven Life*, which its publisher Zondervan (owned by News Corp's HarperCollins) contends is the best-selling nonfiction book in history (apart from the Bible), with more than 30 million copies sold worldwide.[4]

**Scholarly Books**  This area covers titles published by scholarly societies, commercial publishers, and university presses for those involved in primary research in academic, corporate, or government settings. Many such books are published by university presses; these presses are typically not-for-profit divisions of universities, colleges, museums, or research institutions, and they publish mostly scholarly materials—that is, books that are read by professors and graduate students. These are not the best of times for university presses. Their main outlets, libraries, are seeing their book-buying budgets shrink because of the rising costs of electronic databases and journals. The situation has forced many university presses to reduce output.

**Book Clubs and Mail-Order**  This industry category is used for books distributed through **book clubs**, whose members can select books from the club's catalog and purchase them through the mail or via the club's website, often at a discounted price. There are general-interest clubs, such as Book of the Month Club, and special interest clubs that aim at people with specific passions—cooking, the outdoors, history, the military, and many other topics. When you join a club, you get a certain number of books for a small amount of money, and then the company sends you a catalog every month with new choices that you can purchase.

In a nation with so many bookstores and the internet to help people find and access books, though, the allure of book clubs is not huge. The total sales of this publishing segment in 2010 amounted to around $1 billion, a small fraction of consumer trade book sales.

An even smaller business nowadays is **mail-order books**. You've undoubtedly seen TV ads or received promotional mailings for books on home repair, the Civil War, or gardening. You call an 800 number and give the operator your credit card number, and within several days the book shows up on your doorstep. Both book clubs and

---

**trade paperbacks**
standard-size books that have flexible covers

**mass market paperbacks**
smaller, pocket-size paperback books

**mass market outlets**
venues where mass market paperbacks are generally sold, including newsstands, drugstores, discount stores, and supermarkets

**religious books**
trade books that contain specifically religious content

**scholarly books**
titles published by scholarly societies, commercial publishers, and university presses for those involved in primary research in academic, corporate, or government settings

**book clubs**
organizations through which individuals who have joined can select books from the club's catalog and purchase them through the mail or via the club's website, often at a discounted price

**mail-order books**
books that are advertised on TV or in promotional mailings that can be ordered directly from the publisher and are shipped to the consumer's home

mail-order businesses ship titles directly to the consumer. The principal difference between the two is that the mail-order publisher actually underwrites new titles—creates new, original books—whereas the book club sells existing titles. Although mail-order sales made up 10.5 percent of the U.S. consumer book industry in 1982, the number had dropped to less than 1 percent by 2008. Of course, people still buy many books through the mail—for example, after ordering online from Amazon—but this bookselling business does not fit the definition of mail-order.

**subscription reference books**
titles such as "great books" series, dictionaries, atlases, and sets of encyclopedias that are marketed by their publishers to consumers on a door-to-door or direct-mail basis

**Subscription Reference Books** The term "**subscription reference books**" refers to dictionaries, atlases, and sets of encyclopedias that are marketed by their publishers to consumers on a door-to-door or direct-mail basis. It is a separate category from mail-order because the distribution typically involves one large package deal—several volumes at a time—with a deferred payment schedule.

## THINKING ABOUT MEDIA LITERACY

Today, you can find many free dictionaries and encyclopedias online. Many of these sites are supported by advertising, but they allow free searching for key terms and ideas. What do you think are some advantages to online access to dictionaries and encyclopedias? Can you think of any disadvantages? If so, what are they? Can you think of any advantages that the print versions offer over the online ones?

Consumers receive the encyclopedia set right away, but they pay for the material by subscription, over a number of months. Perhaps your parents bought the *World Book Encyclopedia* or *Encyclopedia Britannica* in this way; millions of people have done so. During the past two decades, this category has been affected negatively by the rise of internet references; the *Britannica* and *World Book* are themselves available online. Their sales make up a tiny 0.1 percent (that's one-tenth of 1 percent) of book industry sales.

## Variety and Specialization in Book Publishing

No matter how obscure a subject is, there is probably a book about it. In fact, there may even be a publisher specializing in the topic. Many publishers have imprints that focus on particular types of books. An imprint is a name or brand that the publisher places on the bottom of a book's spine as well as on the main title page. It signifies a publishing firm or one its divisions. Random House is an imprint of the large Random House, Inc. publishing company. But Random House also has many other imprints that deal with particular topics or aim at particular audiences. Fodor's, for example, is Random House's travel imprint. ESPN is its sports imprint. One World is an imprint devoted to "African-American, Asian, Latin, and Native American interest." Schocken puts out Jewish-themed books.

With imprints in mind, take a virtual stroll through your nearest university library's catalog, through Amazon's online bookstore, or through the "subject" section of *Books in Print*, a reference volume that you can find in print or online in any library or bookstore. Even though you've been dealing with books all your life, a close examination of the breadth of titles is likely to surprise you. Are you interested in maritime issues? *Literary Marketplace*, a standard reference volume on book publishing, lists 61 imprints in the United States that deal with the subject. Among the other specialties noted, 52 firms mention Hindu religion, 57 note real estate, 37 list wine and spirits, and 22 claim veterinary science. Many of the publishers involved are quite small. *Literary Marketplace* devotes more than 10 pages to listing "small presses," which it considers to be firms that publish fewer than three books per year.

### Financing Book Publishing

These examples only begin to suggest the immensity of the book publishing business in the United States. More than 75,000 publishing houses issued more than 275,000 new titles and editions in 2008.

Part of the reason for this huge number is that publishing a basic book really doesn't cost that much, although some titles (such as this textbook) can be very expensive to put together. For a few thousand dollars, a person can put out a handsome product to sell in fairly large numbers. The low entry costs allow zealous entrepreneurs or people who are committed to disseminating certain ideas to get in on the activity. Moreover, new printing technologies allow publishers to make a profit turning out copies of books in small numbers or even "on demand"—that is, only when someone pays for the book. (In the past, the nature of printing efficiencies meant that a publisher had to go through the expense of producing and storing lots of copies of a title so that the copies could be priced competitively.)

Sometimes small publishing ventures can yield bonanzas in terms of readership and revenue. A great recent example is the erotic (and controversial) *Fifty Shades* series of three titles: *Fifty Shades of Grey*, *Fifty Shades Darker*, and *Fifty Shades Freed*. Written by a British woman named E. L. James, the book began as a contribution to a fan fiction site centering on the *Twilight* book and movie series. Believing her writing had potential as a stand-alone book, James refashioned and extended her story and published it through Writers' Coffee Shop, a small publisher in Australia that released it as an e-book and a print-on-demand paperback. Because the publisher had a small marketing budget, it relied on blogs about books for early publicity. Then it seems word-of-mouth recommendations, Facebook sharing, and rave reviews on blogs aimed at women pushed the title to enormous popularity. It has more than 16,000 reader reviews on the social networking site Goodreads, and it sold out in many bookstores. The series has sold over 31 million copies worldwide and set the record as the fastest-selling paperback series of all time, beating the Harry Potter titles.[5]

*Fifty Shades of Grey* was practically an overnight success, selling more than 31 million copies worldwide, and its success resulted in the contracting of two more related novels (*Fifty Shades Darker* and *Fifty Shades Freed*) and a series of informational books for couples looking to liven up the romance in their lives.

Such success for small publishers is highly unusual. Although many small publishers are founded every year, a handful of companies still dominate the most lucrative areas of the book publishing business. For example, three titles—Merriam-Webster, Random House, and American Heritage—regularly dominate the field of English-language dictionaries, with a combined 90 percent or greater share. The same publishing company may put out books under many different imprints. It turns out that under their own imprints and the imprints of subsidiaries, only six publishers accounted for

88.7 percent of hardcover and 88.9 percent of paperback consumer trade books on the U.S. best-seller lists in 2012: Random House, Simon & Schuster, Penguin USA, Hachette Book Group USA, HarperCollins, and Macmillan. These firms are themselves owned by major media conglomerates. Here is a brief snapshot of who owns each firm along with its well-known imprints:

- **Random House**: Random House is the largest English-language trade publisher in the world and is a full subsidiary of the German conglomerate Bertelsmann. The Random House American Division is divided into several publishing groups, including the Random House Publishing Group, the Knopf Doubleday Publishing Group, and the Crown Publishing Group. Each group has its own set of unique and specialized imprints.
- **Simon & Schuster**: Owned by the CBS Corporation, Simon & Schuster publishes through imprints that include Pocket, Free Press, and Scribner.
- **Penguin Group**: Owned by the British conglomerate Pearson PLC, Penguin is the second-largest trade publisher in the world. Penguin is still known largely for its classic paperbacks. Well-known imprints are Penguin, NAL, and Ace Books, the oldest continually operating science fiction publisher in the United States.
- **Hachette Book Group, USA**: Formerly the book publishing firm owned by the Time Warner conglomerate, Hachette Book Group (HBG) now belongs to Hachette Livre, the second-largest publisher in the world. Hachette Livre is itself a wholly owned subsidiary of the French conglomerate Lagardere Group. Little Brown and Company, one of HBG's subsidiaries, has a number of important imprints, including Little Brown and Back Bay Books. Among other HBG imprints are FaithWords, 5-Spot, and Grand Central Publishing.
- **HarperCollins**: Owned by Rupert Murdoch's News Corp, HarperCollins owns imprints that publish books in different parts of the world. Among the well-known imprints are William Morrow, Zondervan, HarperTeen, and Walden Pond Press.
- **Macmillan**: Owned by the German firm Holtzbrinck, Macmillan is a collection of trade and scholarly publishers. Among the well-known publishers in its trade stable are St. Martin's Press (which itself has five imprints), Henry Holt, and Farrar Straus & Giroux.

The power of these firms raises a logical question: if producing a book is often relatively inexpensive, how is it that only a few companies dominate parts of the industry? The answer is that some parts of book publishing can be extremely expensive, and the greatest expenses are typically related to aspects other than the physical creation of the book.

The overwhelming majority of publishers do not own the basic machinery of bookmaking—a printing press and a machine that places bindings on finished pages. Typically, publishers contract out these services to firms that specialize in these activities. Publishers also contract out **composition** services, the work involved in inserting into a manuscript the codes and conventions that tell the page-making program or the printing press how the material should look on the page.

Color photographs and special layouts can be expensive. To sell the book at a reasonable price, the publisher has to sell many thousands of copies simply to make back the manufacturing costs. Still, the ability to contract out such services at reasonable costs is what makes the mere entry into book publishing so easy.

At its heart, though, book publishing is not really about writing or editing or printing. It is about finding, preparing, marketing, distributing, and exhibiting titles in ways that will get particular audiences to notice them and buy them. This process takes place

**composition**
the work involved in inserting into a manuscript the codes and conventions that tell the page-making program or the printing press how the material should look on the page

in different ways in different sectors of the industry. Much more money is required in some sectors than in others to compete at the top level. As a result, in these sectors, the wealthiest companies can take the lead and keep it. To give you a sense of what book publishing means, we'll focus on comparing adult hardcover trade publishing and university press publishing from the standpoint of production, distribution, and exhibition.

## Production in the Book Publishing Industry

As we've noted, the production of books involves finding them and preparing them for the marketplace. The same basic activities take place at every kind of book publisher.

### Production in Trade Publishing

An **acquisitions editor** recruits and signs new authors and titles for the company's list of books. In major firms, because of the cost of running the company, acquisitions editors must find and produce a certain number of new titles that have a certain sales potential. The titles can come as completed manuscripts or as proposals for manuscripts. A contract is drawn up that promises payments to the author. Sometimes the payments are in the form of a flat fee for producing the work. Often the payments are in the form of **royalties**—shares of the sales income, usually based on the number of copies sold. After the acquisitions editor receives a completed manuscript, permission to go ahead with publication must typically be granted by an executive committee (sometimes called a publication board) of the firm. Once the go-ahead is received, the manuscript goes to a developmental editor. That person reads and edits the work carefully to make sure that it is clear and internally consistent. After the author addresses the developmental editor's suggestions, the manuscript is transmitted from the developmental editor to a production editor in the production department. The production editor then arranges all of the technical aspects of the book—from copyediting to design to pagination—until the book is in final page-proof form (see Figure 7.3).

This process sounds straightforward, but it can be quite complex. Probably the hardest step is the first, and it belongs to the acquisitions editor—identifying the "right" manuscript. You might not think that finding manuscripts would be a big deal; we all know people who are eager to get their ideas into print. Yet acquisitions editors have to deal with two major considerations when they sift through proposals. First, they have to find topics that match the personality of their imprint, and second, they have to find authors who can write about those topics and whose books can make profits for the firm. Getting the topic and the author together is the really hard part, the editors will tell you. Not surprisingly, acquisitions editors have developed strategies to overcome this challenge and reduce their risk of failure. These strategies require the editor to be familiar with the sales goals of the firm, with the intended audience, and with the way in which books are marketed to that audience.

Adult hardcover trade acquisitions editors rarely read unsolicited manuscripts or proposals for manuscripts unless these are brought to them by known literary agents. A **literary agent** is a person who, on behalf of a client, markets the client's manuscripts to editors, publishers, and other buyers, based on knowledge of the target market and the specific content of the manuscript. Agents understand the personalities of different imprints, and they make their pitches to the ones best suited to particular authors. This system saves editors enormous amounts of work, although some authors undoubtedly fall through the cracks because of it. If an agent succeeds in placing a

**acquisitions editor**
a person who recruits and signs new authors and titles for the company's list of books

**royalties**
shares of a book's sales income that are paid to an author, usually based on the number of copies sold

**literary agent**
a person who, on behalf of a client, markets the client's manuscripts to editors, publishers, and other buyers, based on knowledge of the target market and the specific content of the manuscript

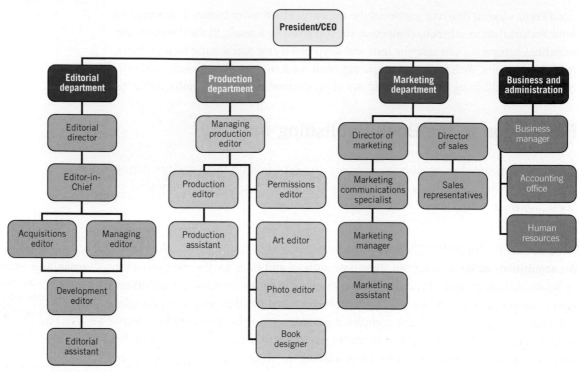

**Figure 7.3**

The organizational structure of a typical book publishing house.

work, the agent receives a commission, typically 10 percent of all income related to the book that is received by the author.

Trade presses usually sell their titles through bookstores. Consumers find out about them by browsing through the shelves, reading reviews in newspapers and magazines, or noting discussions with the author in print or on TV.

In hardcover trade publishing, achieving success with a book means selling at least 50,000 copies. Achieving **best-seller** status means selling more than 75,000 hardcover copies or 100,000 paperback copies. And beyond the best seller looms the realm of the blockbuster, which is a book that sells well over 100,000 hardcover copies—constituting an immense success. Major trade presses spend enormous amounts of money on marketing and publicity departments that have the expertise and resources to take books that have the potential to be best sellers or **blockbusters** and help them sell the requisite number of copies. The acquisitions editor's job is to find books with that potential.

## Production at a University Press

Publishing at a university press is very different from adult hardcover trade publishing in this respect. In university press publishing, a "hit" realistically means selling several thousand copies. A title reaches hit status if it commands respect from professors, who then tell their students and university libraries to buy it.

Scholarly and trade publishers take different approaches to recruiting and acquiring authors whose books may or may not be hits. To reduce the risk that academics will not like their books, editors at scholarly presses try to get manuscripts by well-known professors from well-known universities. Because acquiring books only from these professors would not yield enough titles for their lists, the editors go after the next best thing: young professors on their way up the academic ladder. To find them, the editors turn to consultants: well-known academics that have a reputation for being able to spot innovative new work in their field that their colleagues are likely to appreciate. Sometimes these academics get paid for their services. In addition to the help of consultants, many academic editors will read unsolicited manuscripts sent to them by professors from around the country in the hope of finding something good.

In contrast to the way trade books are sold, university presses usually publicize their books at academic conferences and by mail. Academic associations rent space at their conventions to booksellers. Salespeople set out titles that they think the professors and graduate students who are attending the convention might like and then discuss the books with interested passersby. In addition, the marketing departments of these publishing companies send brochures specifically to academics who specialize in a book's topic; the brochures contain descriptions of the author and the topic along with blurbs by other professors who like the work.

## Book Production in the Electronic Age

During the past few years, the biggest book publishers have been active in creating books for the electronic market—placing titles for sale online at the same or a lower price than hard-copy versions. Some observers have wondered what the rush is about. In 2007, Daniel O'Brien, a book analyst for Forrester Research, called electronic books a solution in search of a problem. "Our research with consumers indicates very little interest in reading on a screen," he told the *New York Times*. "Maybe someday, but not in a five-year time frame. Books are pretty elegant." But Jack Romanos, president of Simon & Schuster, one of the first traditional publishers to begin selling electronic books, argued that "the logic of electronic books is pretty hard to refute—we see it as an incremental increase in sales as a new form of books for adults and especially for the next generation of readers."

It turns out that Romano was far more correct. With the release of various Kindles by Amazon, Nooks by Barnes & Noble, the iPad, Sony Reader, and other portable devices, on e-books has soared. In 2010, in fact, one analyst suggested that sales of hardbound fiction and mass market paperback fiction had dropped because people were purchasing the books on e-readers. In fact, e-books were accounting for as much as 50 percent of new best-seller sales.[6]

As we will see when we discuss exhibition in book publishing, the technological revolution in bookselling is having huge consequences for book publishers of all sorts—especially textbooks. The result is that in the early years of the 21st century, major book publishers believe they must get involved with digital books. It may well be that electronic book publishing is, to quote the editor in chief of *Publishers Weekly*, "the next major thing after Gutenberg." Still, don't hold your breath waiting for the disappearance of the book. Even the just-quoted editor was adamant that books won't go away. What seems certain is that book industry executives will respond to competitive pressures from electronic—and other—currents around them.

Portable reading devices, which can be as simple as a standard ePub reader or as sophisticated as a tablet, are typically web-enabled. That makes it possible for owners to sample books, purchase them, or borrow them electronically from libraries.

## MEDIA TODAY & CULTURE LIBRARIES AND THE CHALLENGES OF LENDING E-BOOKS

Tablets such as iPads and e-readers such as the Kindle and Nook have changed the way people experience reading books. E-readers allow almost instant access to millions of e-books, and online booksellers such as Amazon and Barnes & Noble offer them in a range of prices.

But what about borrowing an e-book from your local library? Many readers use their local libraries to check out physical books, but what happens when they want to check out digital ones?

Digital book lending has been a challenge for libraries and for the book industry. Libraries have been trying to build their digital collections in order to address the growing popularity of digital borrowing among its patrons. The New York Public Library, for example, offers more than 88,000 e-book titles,[1] and the library has seen a sharp increase in digital borrowing.[2] Using a service called Overdrive, a software company that manages digital lending for libraries, the New York Public Library makes materials available for lending on a wide variety of consumer devices.[3] Patrons must install software on their devices in order to access the materials, but that small inconvenience overshadows the conveniences of browsing books, choosing titles to check out, and finding them automatically returned, all without leaving home.[4] The biggest inconvenience, it seems, is the wait.[5]

But the conveniences of digital lending from libraries makes the book publishing industry nervous about preserving their profits, and the publishers have implemented systems to restrict their content or limit its uses in different ways. Some publishers, such as Simon & Schuster, Macmillan, and Hachette, find the digital lending model unsustainable for business and refuse to make e-books available to libraries.[6] Other publishers refuse to make newer titles available.

Another recent restriction is through limiting the number of times patrons can check out books before libraries must renew the licenses for these books. HarperCollins, the first publisher to make this move, restricts the digital lending of its more popular titles to 26 times, at which point libraries must purchase another license.[7] The second license costs less than the initial license.[8] These limitations concern libraries facing increased patron demands and smaller budgets.

Smaller publishers fail to share the concerns of the larger publishers. Instead, more than 1,000 of them make their digital books available to libraries.[9]

Do you think the larger publishers are right in withholding their digital titles from lending through public libraries? Do HarperCollins' license restrictions seem fair to you? Or are these publishers missing out on opportunities for reaching audiences that might buy their other books? What do you think might be a more workable compromise?

### Reducing the Risks of Failure during the Production Process

These sorts of concerns come up all the time as authors, agents, and editors struggle to make books and, in turn, see those books make money. Book publishers use a number of strategies to reduce the risk of failure, including the following:

- Conducting prepublication research
- Making use of authors with positive track records
- Offering authors advances on royalties

Let's look at each of these strategies individually.

**prepublication research**
research conducted in order to gauge a title's chances of success with its likely audience

**Conducting Prepublication Research** You might wonder whether companies involved in publishing university press and trade books conduct **prepublication research** to gauge a title's chances of success with their likely audiences. In fact, they do, but they do it in a rather informal way. Editors may meet with people who are representative of their audience and ask them questions about the book being developed. In scholarly publishing, editors often pay a few professors to read the manuscript and comment on its prospects for success. Going a lot further in research, such as testing each title with large numbers of likely consumers to gauge their reactions, might raise the expense of publishing the book so much that to make a profit, it would have to be priced at an unrealistically high level. About the only systematic research that publishing executives carry out regularly is seeing how previous books on a topic sold. That information gives them an indication of whether going ahead with the book is worth the company's money.

**Making Use of Track Records**  Of course, some authors have already proven their worth: they have **track records**, or histories of successes, in the book marketplace. Editors naturally like to sign these authors because doing so lowers the risk of failure. The authors' names are so well known in their area of publishing that their new titles almost sell themselves.

In academic publishing, prestige tends to be the best tool for successfully snagging an author with a substantial track record. Typically, the acquisitions editor who wants to snag such authors must work for one of the most prestigious scholarly presses—Harvard, Yale, Cambridge, Oxford, MIT, Chicago, and a few others. So the most prestigious presses continue to collect the most prestigious academic authors and thus to dominate the scholarly sector.

In adult trade publishing, almost anything goes with regard to authors with positive track records or authors who for other reasons are expected to have high sales. The authors who garner large advances and are successful in sales are often those with some specific characteristics:

- Previously hugely successful (e.g., John Grisham, Stephen King, Patricia Cornwell)
- Controversial (e.g., former U.S. senator and presidential candidate Hillary Clinton, former Alaskan governor and presidential candidate Sarah Palin)
- Well known outside of book publishing (e.g., Madonna, Hilary Duff)

**Offering Advances on Royalties**  Offering authors an **advance on royalties**—a payment of money before the book is published that the publisher anticipates the author will earn through royalties on the book—to sign a contract is not as common in academic publishing as in trade publishing. One possible reason is that academic titles do not sell that many copies. Another is that the firms can lure academic writers without advances, as they are called. Trade book authors note that even when book advances sound substantial, they get eaten up by the cost of conducting research and simply living while writing full-time. Take a reported six-figure advance, the president of the Authors Guild told the *New York Times* in 2009:

> That may mean $100,000, minus 15 percent agent's commission and self-employment tax, and if we're comparing it to a salary let us recall (a) that it does not include any fringes like a desk, let alone health insurance, and (b) that the book might take two years to write and three years to get published. . . . So a six-figure advance, while in my experience gratefully received, is not necessarily enough, in itself, for most adults to live on.[7]

The amount of money that trade publishers offer in order to lure star authors—or people they suspect will be stars—can be impressive. In 2009, the Scribner publishing company (owned by Simon & Schuster, which is in turn owned by CBS Corporation) paid $5 million for Audrey Niffenegger's second novel, *Her Fearful Symmetry*. She had previously penned *The Time Traveler's Wife*, which had become a hit. More spectacularly, in 2006 Simon & Schuster offered Houston televangelist Joel Osteen

**track records**
the previous successes or failures of a product, person, or organization

**advance on royalties**
a payment of money before the book is published that is based on what the publisher anticipates the author will earn from royalties on the book

$10 million for the right to publish his 2007 book, *Become a Better You*. The reason? His book *Your Best Life Now: 7 Steps to Living at Your Potential*, published by small publisher FaithWords, had sold millions of copies since its release in 2004. Probably at least as important was that its audience bought audiobooks, calendars, and other spinoffs that seemed to suggest the pastor's writing career had legs. He also has television and radio gigs that continually keep him in the eye of the people who might buy his books.

Those who are involved with such deals clearly believe that they are worth the cost. In addition to considering whether the book will sell enough in hardcover to justify the advance, the publishing firm considers the title's future attraction to paperback and foreign publishers—in return for the advance, the hardback publisher typically gets the opportunity to sell the paperback and foreign rights to other publishers. In the case of an attractive title, the hardback publisher might make back a substantial portion of the advance through the sale of these rights. As the advance to Osteen suggests, the largest advances typically go to authors whose involvement in other media can help them sell copies. A title based on a popular movie or one that is written by a popular sports figure will similarly have the instant recognition among certain audiences that will help it move off the shelves.

Of course, not all titles succeed, no matter what strategies the publishers might have taken to reduce the risk of failure. *Publishers Weekly* (PW) lists standard reasons that books with hopes for great sales end in disappointment: "one too many sequels, a book where a magazine article would do, a celebrity whose day has come and gone." When a string of similar books sells strongly at the outset but ends with disappointing sales, acquisitions editors generalize about the kinds of titles in which people have temporarily or permanently lost interest. It also works the other way. When one or two books on a topic take off, editors begin to think a trend is at work, and they look for books that relate to the same or similar topics. The large number of sudoku puzzle books that have poured into stores in recent years is one example. Another example, perhaps stranger and more tentative, is a seeming mini-trend of books that try to promote atheism. *Publishers Weekly* pointed out in 2007 that at the same time that religious books were selling well, three titles against religion had also been garnering large numbers of readers: Christopher Hitchens's *God Is Not Great: How Religion Poisons Everything* (published by Twelve), Richard Dawkins's *The God Delusion* (Houghton Mifflin), and Sam Harris's *Letter to a Christian Nation* (Knopf). A *PW* reporter noted that "these brainy, skeptical takes on God and religion have quickly ascended to the top of national bestseller lists" and in interviewing editors found that they saw the topic as a reaction to fundamentalism among substantial segments of U.S. society. To the editors, that meant room for more and a chance for substantial sales. As a Houghton Mifflin editor said, "If another great book came along tomorrow that I felt really advanced the issue, I'd snap it up."

## Distribution in the Book Industry

Ideas that are not well conceived or well executed and trends that have passed their peak can explain the failure of titles in every sector of book publishing, from juvenile hardback to mail-order. At the same time, though, acquisitions editors and other executives in all areas of the industry realize that distribution can play an important part in making or breaking a title.

## The Role of Wholesalers in the Distribution Process

The biggest trade publishers—Random House, Simon & Schuster, HarperCollins—distribute books themselves to the largest bookstore chains (Barnes & Noble and Books-A-Million) and a few others, such as the huge online bookseller Amazon. Otherwise, these publishers and others rely on three huge wholesalers—Baker & Taylor, Ingram, and Brodart—to distribute their books to bookstores and libraries. These wholesalers stock enormous numbers of titles from a great number of publishers in massive warehouses. This system allows librarians and book dealers to obtain a variety of books more quickly than if they had to order from individual presses.

The process works this way: A wholesaler purchases copies of a book from a publisher at a discount and then resells them to a retailer (the exhibitor) at a somewhat higher price. Both the wholesaler and the publisher share the risks in their relationship. When a wholesaler purchases a certain number of copies of a title, it is committing itself to devoting valuable warehouse space to that title and to fulfilling orders for the book. The publisher, though, is not off the hook when the wholesaler receives the title. In the book industry, copies of the book that don't sell can ordinarily be returned to the publisher for credit toward other titles (see Figure 7.4). As a result of

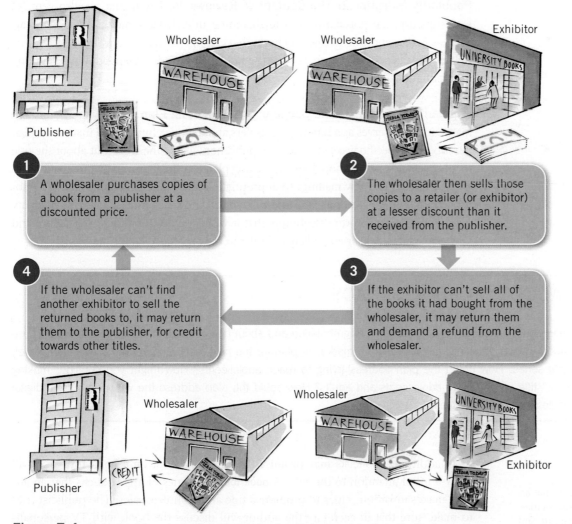

**Figure 7.4** The role of the wholesaler. The wholesaler plays a crucial role in the book publishing process.

**print run**
the number of copies of a book
that are printed

this returns policy, publishing executives must be realistic regarding the **print run**, or the number of copies printed.

## Assessing a Title's Popularity

Throughout the distribution process, wholesalers keep a careful eye on indicators that help them to gauge how popular a book will be. Doing that allows them to decide how many copies should take up valuable space in their warehouses.

**Popularity Indicator 1: The Size of the Print Run** The size of the print run signals to wholesalers how popular a publisher expects a book to be. That indication helps wholesalers decide how many copies of the title to stock. Looking at the publishing imprint also helps. Wholesalers associate certain imprints with certain levels of marketing power as well as with certain types of books. Imprints, therefore, telegraph expected sales. A distributor is more likely to stock up on a title with the Random House imprint than to take a large quantity of a title from Pantheon or Schocken, even though Random House owns those imprints.

**Popularity Indicator 2: The Content of Reviews** Review media are also vehicles for estimating the popularity of a forthcoming title. Review media are periodicals such as *Kirkus* and *Choice* that receive early versions of books from their publishers. Review magazine staff members read the books and predict their popularity among different audiences.

**Popularity Indicator 3: The Scope of the Marketing Plan** Finally, the publisher's marketing plan serves as a hint to wholesalers about a title's future. The marketing plan describes the specific ways in which the publisher will get the word out about the title to its target audience. Although the marketing plan of a small university press will probably be limited to a few mailings to appropriate libraries and academics, a trade publisher with high expectations for a title will typically do much more. The firm's publicity department might inform distributors that it will advertise the title in magazines and newspapers that deliver an audience similar to the one expected for the book.

## THINKING ABOUT MEDIA LITERACY

In chapter 6, you read about convergence and audience fragmentation and about how the industries must respond to those challenges. Think about how a publisher might develop a marketing plan for the next teen vampire and/or werewolf novel, similar to the *Twilight* series. How could the plan address trying to reach adolescents? How might you consider making the book a "crossover" title of interest to adolescents and adults? How could the plan address the various forms of digital technologies, alongside analog technologies?

**book tour**
a series of appearances that an
author makes in various cities
in order to promote a title and
stimulate sales

In addition, publicists may promise to send the author on a book tour that will draw a lot of attention to the title. A **book tour** is a series of appearances that an author makes in various cities to promote a title and stimulate sales. The publicist tries to make sure that in each city the author will discuss the book with TV personalities, radio talk show hosts, and newspaper columnists. In addition, publicists might arrange for the author to appear in bookstores to talk about the book and sign copies for customers. The belief in book publishing is that a vigorous and well-put-together book tour can spike the sales of a title substantially.

## Exhibition in the Book Publishing Industry

The concern that trade publishers and distributors feel about printing and circulating the appropriate number of copies is shared by the companies that sell the books to the public. When it comes to book exhibitors, you probably think of bookstores. Of course, there are many different kinds of bookstores. There are the nationwide chains, such as Barnes & Noble and Books-A-Million. University bookstores are often quite big and sometimes part of a chain (e.g., Follett or a spinoff of Barnes & Noble). They distinguish themselves by carrying textbooks and academic books that general bookstores typically would not stock. Then there are the "independents"—companies that are based in a particular area and have at most a few locations, though often only one. A large independent is Powell's Books, based in Portland, Oregon. Powell's stocks a huge number and variety of new and used books. Other independents, such as the Seattle Mystery Bookshop, are small and specialize in particular storytelling or nonfiction genres.

An important sign of exhibition in the 21st century is that all the types of exhibition establishments can be found online as well as offline. This online presence, along with the growth of electronic publishing, is changing exhibition in the book industry just as it is changing production and distribution. To illustrate, let's look at exhibition of consumer books and textbooks.

Book tours are one way publishers promote the sale of titles. Tours often include the opportunity for attendees to ask the author questions about the book they wrote. *Fifty Shades of Grey* employed such marketing techniques as having author E. L. James interviewed by sexologist Dr. Logan Levkoff at a Barnes & Noble in New York City.

### Exhibition of Consumer Books

Think about where you went the last time you bought a hardback title for yourself or a friend. Did you purchase it from a physical bookstore with real doors and shelves (sometimes called **brick-and-mortar stores**) or from an online bookseller? If you bought it from a bookstore, do you remember if it was a chain bookstore or an independent bookseller? Traditionally, the independent bookstore was the place where Americans went to buy hardback trade books. In the mid-1990s, bookstore chains overtook them, and many independents are now struggling to survive.

The brick-and-mortar bookstore chains, meanwhile, are themselves struggling to compete with a type of company that hardly existed in the 1990s: the online-only bookseller, especially Amazon. By 2008, Amazon topped all outlets, accounting for 14 percent of book sales, ahead of Barnes & Noble, which held a 12.5 percent share of the market. In fact, the internet overall accounted for 23 percent of units sold, just beating out the major physical sides of the bookstore chains, which had a 22 percent market share. (When physical independent and religion bookstores are added to the chains, brick-and-mortar bookstores did beat the web, accounting for 30 percent of book purchases that year.) A report released in 2009 underscored the importance of the internet to the book industry beyond even exhibition. It noted that the internet is not only selling more books than ever; it is also playing an increasing role in making consumers aware of books. One out of five book buyers

**brick-and-mortar stores**
stores that have a physical presence in the offline world

said they became aware of a book through an online promotion or ad rather than through the many offline opportunities they might have had to learn about titles.

One particular difficulty for brick-and-mortar book exhibitors is that they often cannot compete on price with online retailers, especially Amazon. Amazon often charges far less for popular titles than brick-and-mortar bookstores. Moreover, customers who pay an annual membership fee or buy a certain dollar-value of books get free shipping. Plus, as we saw in the beginning of this chapter, Amazon often charges far less for the electronic edition of titles it suspects will be popular than for the hardcover versions of those books.

These activities deter many readers from purchasing books from their local bookstores. Instead, the brick-and-mortar stores—in the book industry and other industries—have noticed people using their places for window shopping. They look at the window or amble down the aisles and take note of interesting books. Then they buy them online.

As you can imagine, such activities do not encourage a healthy bottom line for traditional retailers. The bankruptcy of the large bookstore chain Borders is one indication of the precarious health of brick-and-mortar retailers. Borders had not developed a robust-enough online footprint to compete with Amazon in that retail space. Barnes & Noble, by contrast, has managed to keep its foot in the brick-and-mortar world while also developing a major presence with the online sale of physical books and e-books. In fact, online bookselling has outstripped physical bookstore-chain outlets as the dominant way people buy consumer books.[8] With its online presence, Powell's calls itself the "largest independent used and new bookstore in the world." Powell's online book emporium highlights new and used books, and the company contends it is doing quite well, even though it doesn't always compete with Amazon and Barnes & Noble on price.

This major disruption and transformation of the publishing industry as a result of technological and social changes should remind you of the processes described in themes 2 and 3, presented earlier. The switch has not affected all parts of publishing as greatly or in the same way. Recall, for example, that we noted that more than 50 percent of adult trade fiction best sellers are purchased in electronic form. It turns out that is not true regarding juvenile titles. Juvenile trade publishers and exhibitors have learned that parents still want to buy picture books that their daughters and sons can hold, perhaps to give them the sense of the feel of a traditional book, perhaps because the color of most e-books still doesn't match that of a beautiful traditional picture book. Teenagers also seem to read paperbacks more than they read books on tablets.[9] That may be a matter of the tablet's price.

## Exhibition in Textbook Publishing

Textbooks represent another type of book that is clearly having some success in digital form. To understand why textbooks are different from consumer books, you have to consider who buys them and how they are bought. K–12 texts and college texts are quite different in terms of exhibition. The "exhibition" area for K–12 texts is not primarily the schools; it is special evaluation boards that inspect various titles to determine their appropriateness for children in their area. In many states, this evaluation takes place at the state level. California and Texas are the largest states with centralized selection, and board decisions can influence whether a textbook publisher has a chance of selling thousands upon thousands of copies. As you might imagine, textbook company executives pay a lot of attention to the likes and dislikes of members of the selection boards in these states. The executives often instruct their authors to make sure they write in ways that will appeal to the selection boards of California and Texas.

## THINKING ABOUT MEDIA LITERACY

How do nonfiction consumer books differ from college texts? Think about a textbook in a history class and a nonfiction book about a historical event that has been reinterpreted. What would you expect the history textbook to include about the event? What features might the book have? What would you expect the nonfiction book to have about the event? How would its features differ from the textbook and why?

This activity, in turn, has bred resentment among teachers and parents in states that buy fewer books. They have expressed anger that the attitudes of a few people should have so much influence over what American children learn. You may not have known it when you were in grades K through 12, but K–12 textbooks are controversial commodities.

At the college level, instructors choose the titles they want to use and require students to buy them (sound familiar?). Presumably, if the students don't like a text, their feedback will encourage their teacher to look for a replacement. College textbook publishers regularly send professors free copies of new textbooks in the hope they will like what they see better than whatever they are currently using and will order the new book for their classes. Acquisitions editors must be alert for new trends in teaching that would suggest new text ideas, even while they encourage authors of current books to update their titles with new editions.

New editions of texts have two purposes. Most obviously, a new edition includes facts or ideas that have come to light or have been incorporated into the course as it is usually taught since the earlier edition went to press. (The changes in media that take place between this book's updates are often quite dramatic.) But there is also a strong marketing motive for new editions. Textbook publishers know that many students sell their texts after they use them and that the books then go on sale in the used-book market. The result is that publishing revenues from an edition plummet after the first year because students purchase used copies. The production of a new edition every three years or so is an attempt to derail this process, since students cannot get the updated version from used-book vendors. Revised versions of popular titles keep textbook publishers in business.

College students often complain about the high price of textbooks. During the last several years, a number of advocacy groups and politicians have taken up their cause, asserting that they are indeed paying too much and that publishers are encouraging professors to order too many extra materials—workbooks and online materials, for example—with the texts. Publishers reply that although their prices are high, the used-book market means that many students pay far less than the original price and that the extra (or "bundled") materials are useful to instructors and students. Nevertheless, during the past several years a number of states have taken action. In 2006, Connecticut passed a law requiring publishers to disclose textbook prices to college

More and more classrooms throughout the country are providing students with tablets and digital media through which they can interact with their textbooks and other educational materials.

faculty, presumably so that the faculty would consider costs in their decisions. In 2005, Virginia passed a law discouraging faculty from asking students to buy new editions that are minimally different from older ones that can be bought on the used-book market.

Enter the digital revolution. A number of school districts around the United States have experimented with giving their students Apple iPads loaded with their textbooks instead of giving hard copies of the books. This way the districts can get updates of the books more cheaply every year; the kids can use the tablets for their work at school and at home; and the children's backs aren't strained terribly by the weight of heavy textbooks that they must lug home every day.

## Convergence and Conglomeration in the Book Industry

The emergence of electronic copies of paper book titles along with the soaring popularity of reader technologies such as the Amazon Kindle, the Apple iPad, the Barnes & Noble Nook, and the Microsoft Surface point to the active presence of convergence in the book industry. These activities also reflect the blurring of media boundaries, of course. We have noted other types of boundary blurring as well, especially when it comes to trade books. Publishers promote trade book titles across a variety of media, from television shows to magazines and newspapers to the web.

The footprints of media conglomerates show up here, too. You might have noticed when reading the chapter the mention that one of the largest book publishers, Simon & Schuster, is owned by CBS Corporation. You might not be surprised, then, that synergy is sometimes at work here: Simon & Schuster is the primary publisher for books related to various program franchises owned by parent CBS, such as *Mission: Impossible*, *Star Trek*, and *CSI*. Consider some joint ventures that reflect common ownership: The National Amusements movie theater chain controls both CBS and Viacom, so National Amusements makes sure that many Viacom products stay in the corporate family. For example, Simon & Schuster has published books that tie into Viacom's Nickelodeon and Nick Jr. cable programs.

As chapters 1 and 6 noted, convergence that is often tied to corporate synergies or joint ventures goes to the heart of how publishers believe they must operate in today's media world. Mass media executives today increasingly believe that to reach their target audiences, they must pursue these audiences across media boundaries. We should therefore expect not only more multimedia promotion of books but also more books that are *presold*. A **presold title** is one that publishers expect will sell well to specific audiences because it ties into material that is already popular with those audiences across other media. For example, a book by Oprah Winfrey or highlighted on her cable channel is presold to fans of her channel and magazine.

Many book lovers are nervous about this fixation on presold books and books that can be easily publicized across media boundaries. They worry that the books with the highest profile in bookstores and in the media are those that are reflections of popular characters or plotlines from other media—television, radio, magazines, the movies, or the web. Our age is one in which the most powerful media conglomerates own the

**presold title**
a book that publishers expect will sell well to specific audiences because it ties into material that is already popular with those audiences across other media

largest book companies. These cross-media relationships are not likely to change. In fact, for reasons we suggested in chapter 6, cross-media activities may accelerate in the name of synergy. As a media-literate person, you might want to ask the following questions as you move through the book world:

- To what extent are the books that are getting most of the media attention today generated as a result of an author's or a character's popularity in another medium?
- Are we seeing an increase in cooperative activities between movie companies and book publishers owned by the same conglomerate? That is, are movie companies mostly using the publishers to sell books that publicize the movies, and are book companies trying to come up with titles that can become films?

An optimist would answer, "Surely not." She or he would point out that many publishers publish trade books that have no connection to TV or movies and have no interest in making a TV show or movie of these books. A pessimist would concede this point but would emphasize that increasingly the titles that get the most publicity both in and out of the bookstore are those that fit the cross-media, conglomerate profile. As this chapter has shown, the history of the book is a long and complex one. Books have changed through the ages, with the currents of culture and interests of those who have the power to produce them. This long view is useful to take when you think about the future of the book.

## Ethical Issues in Book Production

The process of finding and developing ideas and authors for books is filled with ethical pitfalls for authors, agents, and publishers. One of the biggest issues is that of stealing ideas. **Plagiarism**—using parts of another person's work without citing or otherwise crediting the original author—unfortunately seems to be much more common than many in publishing would like to believe. Sometimes such an act is clearly illegal, as when an author lifts sentences or paragraphs from copyrighted material. Plagiarism is not illegal when the author uses material that has not been protected by copyright; however, it remains a serious breach of ethics.

**plagiarism**
using parts of another person's work without citing or otherwise crediting the original author

**Ethical Issues for Authors** Literary scholars and critics have concluded that many writers have been guilty of plagiarism, although the issue rarely makes the front pages. You might remember the case of Harvard student Kaavya Viswanathan. In 2006, the Little Brown publishing company released her first novel, *How Opal Mehta Got Kissed, Got Wild, and Got a Life*. Soon afterward, her publisher asked bookstores to remove the book from their shelves, having confirmed accusations that she had used paragraphs from two other novels without citing them. One of the most prominent authors to be accused of plagiarism in recent years was Alex Haley, the author of *Roots*, the best-selling book that became one of the most-viewed television miniseries of all time. In 1978, Harold Courlander sued Haley for extensively lifting material for *Roots* from his book *The African*. That book itself had done quite well when it appeared in 1967: it sold 300,000 copies and was translated into several languages.

Haley eventually agreed to settle. Courlander received $650,000 just before the judge was to issue a ruling. Yet until Haley's death, he continued to claim that the numerous similarities between the books were unintentional and minor, even though a lot of evidence introduced in court indicated that he had used *The African* substantially in writing *Roots*. Courlander himself felt that the basic issue of copying never really made it onto the public agenda. He later noted that although he had felt vindicated at the time of the court settlement, public interest in the incident quickly disappeared. Haley, he added, "was a very persuasive public speaker" who dismissed questions about the settlement. "Nobody really raised the issue of literary ethics, and he continued to receive honorary degrees—it didn't slow him up. This troubled me."

An ethical issue swirling around nonfiction authors involves making up facts. In recent years a number of American writers—in newspapers and magazines as well as books—have betrayed their readers in this way. An example is Jonah Lehrer, who as a 32-year-old rising star at the *New Yorker* magazine, admitted that he had concocted a quote by the songwriter Bob Dylan for his book *Imagine*. According to an expert on Dylan's life and music, who accused Lehrer of making up the quote when he didn't recognize it from any of his research on Dylan, Lehrer also used quotes from Dylan in ways that did not at all reflect the contexts in which they had been said. Houghton Mifflin Harcourt, the publisher of *Imagine*, took the drastic and expensive step of withdrawing the book from publication. That included recalling all printed copies of the book from exhibitors and distributors. Nevertheless, *Imagine* had already sold more than 200,000 copies in hardcover and e-book.[10]

**Ethical Issues for Editors and Literary Agents** Editors and literary agents, as well as authors, also confront major ethical issues. Let's say you're an editor, and you get a manuscript chapter out of the blue from an unknown author. She proposes a nonfiction book about how mothers who travel frequently on business balance home and work. You don't know the writer, and you don't intend to use her. You do, however, like the topic, and you can think of at least two authors who have written for you who would do a great job with such a book. What do you do? Should you go ahead with using the idea? Is it ethical to take one person's ideas for a book and pay someone else to write it?

---

## THINKING ABOUT MEDIA LITERACY

What do you think? Is it ethical for you to take an idea from a stranger who wrote to you and give it to an author who you know will do a terrific job? Knowing it is legal (because no one can copyright ideas), should you do it to help yourself and another writer even if you're troubled that you took the idea from the aspiring author?

---

Or let's say you are a literary agent just starting out on your own. You already represent a few authors, but you need to bring in more money. You know that among literary agents the rule is that you charge a percentage of an author's earnings, but you do not demand a fee for simply representing an author. The reason is that agents who accept fees have been known to represent authors simply to get their money, not because the agents really think the authors will succeed in finding a publisher. You also know, however, that there are many aspiring writers out there who would love to have your input, even for a fee. You tell yourself you can be honest with them. Should you do it?

As we have seen, this concern is only one of the many issues people in the book publishing industry must contend with every day. It's a challenging business facing a challenging present and future. If you care about ideas and stories, the shape of the book industry in the 21st century should certainly be on your radar.

# CHAPTER REVIEW

 Visit the Companion Website at www.routledge.com/cw/turow for additional study tools and resources.

## Key Terms

You can find the definitions to these key terms in the marginal glossary throughout this chapter. Test your knowledge of these terms with interactive flash cards on the *Media Today* companion website.

| | | |
|---|---|---|
| acquisitions editor | higher-education books | presold title |
| advance on royalties | and materials | print run |
| audiobook | K–12 books and materials | professional books |
| best seller | literary agent | religious books |
| blockbuster | mail-order books | royalties |
| book clubs | mass market outlets | scholarly books |
| book tour | mass market paperbacks | subscription reference books |
| brick-and-mortar stores | pedagogy | track records |
| composition | plagiarism | trade books |
| consumer books | prepublication research | trade paperbacks |

## Questions for Discussion and Critical Thinking

1. What are the threats to variety and diversity in the book industry? Do you think people who worry about such threats exaggerate the problem? Why or why not?

2. What segments of the book industry will gain, and which ones will lose, if a large number of people start using digital book readers? (Hint: Consider the suppliers of paper.)

3. What ethical issues relating to book publishing concern you the most? Why?

4. In what ways is the book publishing industry contributing to the digital media environment?

5. If you worked in book publishing, what career would you choose? Why?

## Case Study
### INDEPENDENT VERSUS CHAIN BOOKSTORES

**The Idea** The number of independent bookstores has diminished over the past few decades as big chains and online bookselling have made it difficult for them to compete. Many independents have folded, and others have adapted so that they can compete successfully. How are independents faring in your community?

**The Method** Using electronic databases such as Nexis and Factiva, find statistics and discussions about the national trends regarding independent bookstores. What is happening and why? Is the death of independents accelerating, decelerating, or remaining the same? Why?

   Then identify independent bookstores in your community. If they don't exist now, when did they cease business, and what took their place? If they do exist, what do they seem to be doing to compete with the chains in your area? Interview the owners or managers of the bookstores to get their perspectives. Write a report of your findings in which you lay out what you have found and suggest whether or not you believe the balance of independents and chains in your community is a good one.

# The Newspaper Industry 8

> "Half of the American people have never read a newspaper. Half never voted for President. One hopes it is the same half."

**GORE VIDAL**

## CHAPTER OBJECTIVES

1 Describe key developments in U.S. newspaper history

2 Explain the production, distribution, and exhibition processes of various types of newspapers

3 Recognize and discuss the challenges faced by the newspaper industry today and some approaches to dealing with them

4 Describe the ways that newspapers have begun to reach out to audiences through digital technologies, on the internet and elsewhere

5 Apply your media literacy skills and ethical compass to evaluate activities of the newspaper industry and their impact on your everyday life

Ryan Frank (pictured above), the publisher of the *Oregon Daily Emerald*, the nonprofit student news organization at the University of Oregon, had hope in mind when he read the 2012 "State of the News Media" report from the respected Project for Excellence in Journalism. A former reporter for the *Oregonian* newspaper, Frank scanned the key findings in search of solutions to the dire financial difficulties of the U.S. newspaper industry—"the industry," he wrote, "that has been my daily passion since I fell in love with journalism at my high school newspaper." On a blog aimed at media-business strategists, he wrote that the Pew report left him with a mixture of optimism and alarm. The optimism came from Pew's finding that "news and information are increasingly important in people's lives, and newspapers remain the primary source for civic affairs reporting." The alarm came from so much else Pew noted about the newspaper industry. Here are three examples:

- Declines in print newspaper advertising revenue are taking place far faster than the growth of digital revenue— by a ratio of 10 to 1.

- Newspapers are the only one of seven media industries to report a substantial drop in audience between 2010 and 2011. Newspapers also reported the largest decline in revenue.
- More and more executives predict that daily newspapers will not offer daily home delivery by 2017.

In the face of such dismal markers—and the layoffs of many newspaper reporters—some particularly pessimistic observers foresee the end of physical newspapers and the growth of entirely new forms of journalism quite separate from today's newspaper industry. Frank urged newspaper executives not to despair for their industry's future. Instead, he says, they need to know that local newspapers still have their credibility to readers and their readers' interest in local news and politics, which they can use to compete with

digital giants such as Google, Facebook, and Yahoo!. The key, he noted, is to "build our readership and revenue in the digital world while still preserving the revenue that the print editions generate."

Most newspaper industry executives would agree with this goal—but they would also point out how hard it is to achieve. The aim of this chapter is to provide a snapshot of the newspaper industry at this scary point in its history and to address the following questions: What historical influences shaped the newspaper business as we know it? How do print and online newspapers work today—and why are online versions bringing in so much less revenue than their print counterparts? What are newspaper firms trying to do to keep print going and to make their digital versions profitable? And if these attempts fail, are there socially useful alternatives to the traditional newspaper industry?

## The Development of the Newspaper

**newspapers**
printed products created on a regular (weekly or daily) basis and released in multiple copies

**N**ewspapers are printed products created on a regular (weekly or daily) basis and released in multiple copies. By this definition, newspapers did not exist before Johannes Gutenberg invented the printing press in the middle 1400s (see chapter 7). And although Gutenberg's printing press made it possible for newspapers to be produced, having the technical means to do so did not immediately result in an explosion of newspaper publishing (see the timeline, Figure 8.1).

In England, regular newspapers weren't even produced during most of the 1600s. England's ruling monarchs feared newspapers and greatly restricted their production. These rulers felt that if newspapers were to report on happenings in the land, they might provoke political discussions that could lead to revolution. Newspapers published in Europe tended to mix political news with business news. Merchants were the main audience because they needed to know what was going on politically and economically throughout Europe and in the "New World" that was being colonized by European nations. In the late 1600s, England's ruling monarchs were forced to yield power to a feisty Parliament, and the nation began to flex its naval and trading muscles—and newspapers become a regular feature in the country.

Recall the three themes about media history that we introduced when we discussed books in chapter 7. You may be able to see elements of that first theme here, in connection with newspapers:

1. *The modern newspaper did not arrive in a flash as a result of one inventor's grand change.*

Look online for a photo of *The Daily Courant*, the first regularly published English-language newspaper, from the 1600s. It doesn't much look like the newspapers you know, does it? It took hundreds of years for the printed newspaper as we recognize it to come into being. You'll probably agree that the photo beside it of a *New York World* front page from the early 1900s appears closer to a contemporary

daily paper. Explore the newspaper timeline, and you'll follow the chain of technological innovations that affected the nature of the newspaper across the centuries.
Critical changes in the paper's look came about with the development of methods for
creating headlines across the page, ways to reproduce photographs, ways to include
color pictures and photos, and far more. Critical changes in the ability to reach more
people came as a result of the steam-powered press, the rotary press, and computerized printing technologies. Then there are the technologies that helped bring the
information—the news—to newspapers from outside their offices, including the telegraph, the telephone, the computer, and more.

But the newspaper we know is not just a product of technology. It's the result of
people pushing the technology in certain directions in order to make money telling
stories to others in the society. It's a point that leads to theme 2.

2. *The newspaper as a medium of communication developed as a result of social and legal
responses to the technology during different periods.*

If you read through the timeline with this theme in mind, a number of fascinating incidents will pop out and connect. From Peter Zenger to American colonists'
anger over the British "tax" on knowledge to the Constitution's First Amendment,
we witness the rise of a belief in an **adversarial press**—a press that has the ability to
argue with the government. On a different front, we see how the rise of literacy, the
example of union papers of the 1820s, and the success of British papers aimed at the
"common man" combined with fast printing-press technology and cheap paper to
encourage the growth of a new kind of newspaper—the penny press—beginning in
the 1830s. It was the penny press that really marked the start of newspapers in the
United States aimed at virtually anyone. With that came new definitions of news, wire
services to help report it from around the world, and new ways to use technologies
such as the telegraph, the camera, and the telephone to report news.

Along with these developments came the development of a newspaper industry.
And here's where theme 3 becomes relevant.

**adversarial press**
a press that has the ability to
argue with the government

3. *The newspaper as a medium of communication existed long before the existence of the
book industry.*

As the timeline indicates, it wasn't until the 19th century that American society
witnessed the development of a newspaper *industry*—that is, a set of organizations that
interact regularly to produce, distribute, and exhibit that journalistic product. Before
the penny press, the entire process of writing the articles, printing the paper, and even
delivering it to readers was typically carried out by a publisher, his family, and perhaps
an assistant. Sometimes the post office helped with the delivery. But with the success
of the penny press came the growth of a news organization, with reporters covering
particular topics, editors checking their work before publication, and business departments devoted to increasing circulation and bringing in advertising.

Follow the timeline into the late 19th century, and you'll see how big-city newspapers became big business as their circulations swelled and advertisers paid handsomely to reach their readers. The timeline shows how the newspaper industry
expanded in circulation despite various challenges of the Depression of the 1930s
and competition from television. A long-term decline in daily newspaper readership
that began in the 1950s sped up in the 2000s, as younger consumers migrated to

# Figure 8.1 Timeline of the Newspaper Industry

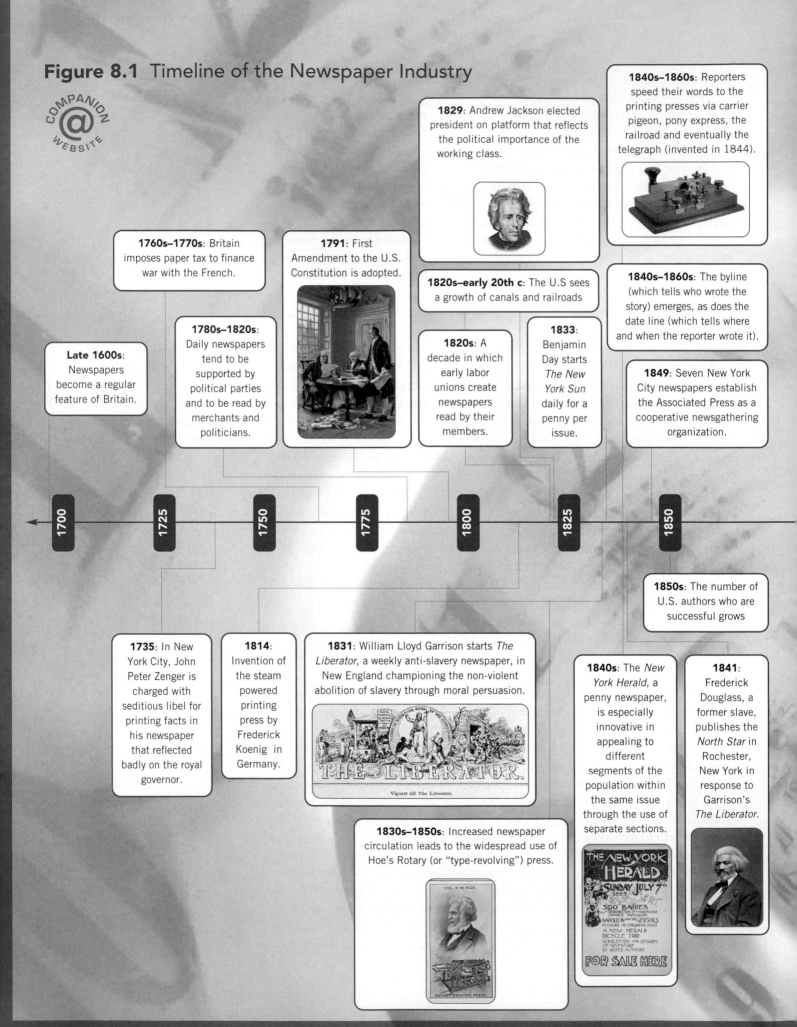

**1829**: Andrew Jackson elected president on platform that reflects the political importance of the working class.

**1840s–1860s**: Reporters speed their words to the printing presses via carrier pigeon, pony express, the railroad and eventually the telegraph (invented in 1844).

**1760s–1770s**: Britain imposes paper tax to finance war with the French.

**1791**: First Amendment to the U.S. Constitution is adopted.

**1820s–early 20th c**: The U.S sees a growth of canals and railroads

**1840s–1860s**: The byline (which tells who wrote the story) emerges, as does the date line (which tells where and when the reporter wrote it).

**1780s–1820s**: Daily newspapers tend to be supported by political parties and to be read by merchants and politicians.

**Late 1600s**: Newspapers become a regular feature of Britain.

**1820s**: A decade in which early labor unions create newspapers read by their members.

**1833**: Benjamin Day starts *The New York Sun* daily for a penny per issue.

**1849**: Seven New York City newspapers establish the Associated Press as a cooperative newsgathering organization.

**1700**  **1725**  **1750**  **1775**  **1800**  **1825**  **1850**

**1735**: In New York City, John Peter Zenger is charged with seditious libel for printing facts in his newspaper that reflected badly on the royal governor.

**1814**: Invention of the steam powered printing press by Frederick Koenig in Germany.

**1831**: William Lloyd Garrison starts *The Liberator*, a weekly anti-slavery newspaper, in New England championing the non-violent abolition of slavery through moral persuasion.

**1850s**: The number of U.S. authors who are successful grows

**1840s**: The *New York Herald*, a penny newspaper, is especially innovative in appealing to different segments of the population within the same issue through the use of separate sections.

**1841**: Frederick Douglass, a former slave, publishes the *North Star* in Rochester, New York in response to Garrison's *The Liberator*.

**1830s–1850s**: Increased newspaper circulation leads to the widespread use of Hoe's Rotary (or "type-revolving") press.

**1890s**: Full – color presses, first used in Paris, are adapted in the United States and used especially for Sunday comics.

**Late 2000s**: A global recession along with huge debts on the part of certain newspaper chains lead to major decreases in total newspaper revenues during 2008 and 2009.

**1870s–1900**: The number of English – language general – circulation dailies increases from 489 in 1872 to 1,967 in 1900.

**1880s–1910**: A new business philosophy in newspapers develops: using advertising instead of circulation revenues for their profits.

**1890s**: The term "yellow journalism" is used for a newspaper characterized by irresponsible, fickle, and sensational news-gathering and exhibition.

**1930s**: In the midst of the Depression, powerful newspaper chains – that is, companies that own a number of papers around the nation – become established.

**1990s – present**: The migration of younger consumers to Web – based news sources such as blog and news collection (or *aggregation*) sites such as Google News speed up newspaper circulation declines.

1875    1900    1925    1950    1975    2000

**1860s**: During the Civil War, reporters on both sides fear the telegraph wires will be cut, leading them to quickly summarize their facts in a style that will become known as the "inverted pyramid."

**1898**: Sensationalistic coverage of the Spanish-American War.

**1930s**: The Great Depression and the rise of radio adversely impact the newspaper industry.

**1920s**: Rise of the tabloids: the most popular of this sort of newspaper was the *New York Daily News*, which dubbed itself "New York's picture newspaper."

**1950s**: By the late 1950s, most US homes (86%) have at least one television set.

**2008**: Four newspaper companies file for bankruptcy protection under Chapter 11 of the US bankruptcy code.

**2008**: The *Seattle Post-Intelligencer* moves to an online-only format to save money.

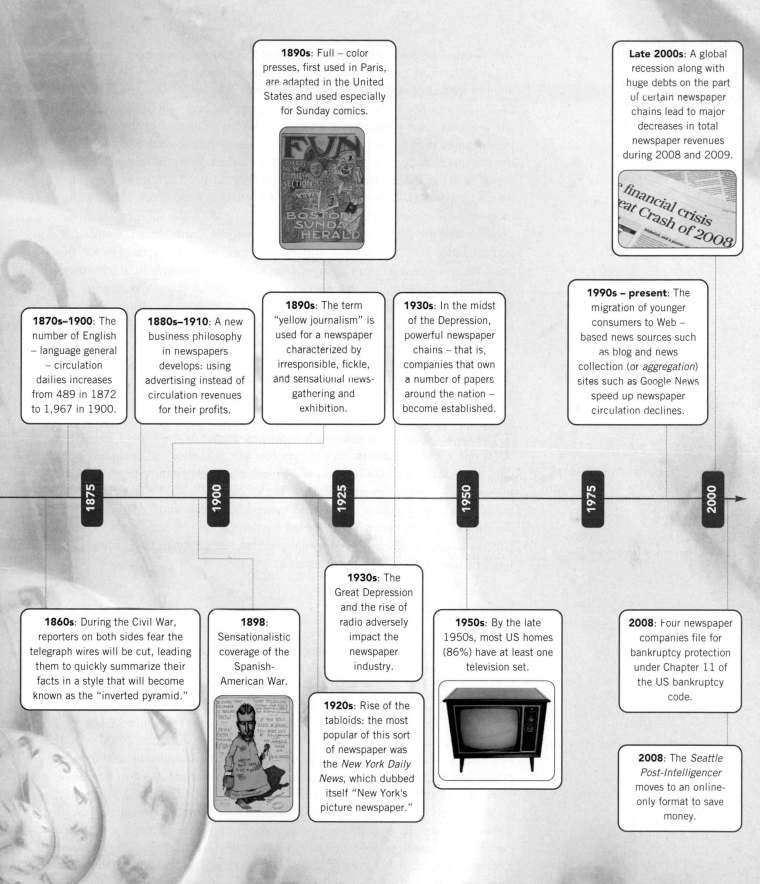

web-based news sources such as blogs and news collection (or aggregation) sites such as Google News or Yahoo! News. Many advertisers followed those people to the web, and newspapers consequently lost advertising money as well.

And so we arrive at the present—to a newspaper industry with a long and generally profitable history undergoing a major transition. Influenced by the rise of digital technologies and convergence, the current developments will likely transform the newspaper industry for the 21st century as profoundly as the late 19th-century events noted in the timeline shaped great mass-circulation, advertising-dependent dailies for the 20th century. The changes are affecting some types of newspapers more immediately and dramatically than others. To grasp the ways in which convergence and the digital world are affecting newspapers' production, distribution, and exhibition activities, it is first important to understand the types of papers that exist, the companies that run them, and the support they receive from advertisers. This will also make it clear that the newspaper industry today is quite varied, and it is important to get a sense of that variety before making generalizations about the future of "the newspaper."

## An Overview of the Contemporary Newspaper Industry

**dailies**

newspapers that are published on newsprint every day, sometimes with the exception of Sunday

**weeklies**

newspapers that are published on newsprint once or twice a week

Perhaps the broadest way to think about newspapers in the United States is to divide them into **dailies** (newspapers that are published on newsprint every day, sometimes with the exception of Sunday) and **weeklies** (newspapers that are published on newsprint once or twice a week). According to the newspaper trade magazine *Editor & Publisher,* in 2009 there were 1,397 dailies and 7,319 weeklies. Of the dailies, morning papers outnumbered evening papers 869 to 528. Of the newspapers mentioned, 919 had Sunday editions. That was a substantial rise from 1970, when there were only 586 Sunday editions.

### Daily Newspapers

The circulation of printed daily newspapers has moved downward over the past quarter-century, even though the nation's adult population has grown by more than a third. In 2010, it hovered at about 42.5 million. That was a 7.2 percent drop from 2009 and almost 12 million fewer print readers than in 2005.[1] The three dailies distributed across the country—the *Wall Street Journal,* the *New York Times,* and *USA Today*—have seen differing fortunes. Since 2001, the *Journal* has climbed substantially in average daily (Monday–Friday) print circulation, from around 560,000 in 2001 to 1.5 million in 2010; the *Times* has fallen, from around 1.1 million in 2001 to about 800,000 in 2011; and *USA Today* has dropped even more sharply, with 2.1 million print copies circulating daily in 2001 and 1.7 million in 2011.

Newspapers aimed at particular localities also have often seen circulation drops, sometimes quite big ones. In San Francisco, for example, the *Chronicle* lost 17 percent of its circulation in 2005; circulation kept going down toward the decade's end. Observers pointed out that enthusiasm for the web was widespread earlier in San Francisco than in many parts of the country, and they saw the declines there as a leading indicator. It underscored for newspaper-industry watchers that the poor state of the economy is not the only, or even the primary, factor threatening the business of many newspapers in the early 2010s. It is, rather, the availability of so many other news sources, particularly digital ones. The *Economist* magazine even suggested in 2009 that San Francisco could become the first major American city without a daily newspaper. Reflecting on how much physical newspapers had become devalued by certain groups, the magazine quoted the city's major as saying, "People under 30 won't even notice."

## THINKING ABOUT MEDIA LITERACY

What do you think about the quote from the mayor saying that people under 30 wouldn't notice a missing daily printed newspaper? Do you agree with the mayor's assessment, or do you disagree? Do you think you would notice the paper missing from your hometown? Why or why not?

**Daily Newspaper Chains** It's important to note that, with only a few exceptions, daily newspapers tend not to have competition from other printed dailies. (The major exceptions are free papers known as *Metro* in Boston, New York, and Philadelphia; similar products in other cities tend not to be competition because they are owned by the city's own daily newspaper firm.) Moreover, most of the dailies in the United States are controlled by a few large firms. In 2000, for example, newspaper chains (or groups) controlled about 1,083 dailies; only about 400 were independent. More recent data are not available, but observations of mergers and acquisitions in the industry suggest that the number of independent dailies certainly has not grown. The logic of chain ownership has traditionally been quite strong. A daily newspaper that was the only one in its area could pretty well dictate prices to local advertisers—car dealers, department stores, movie theaters—that wanted to reach high percentages of the population on a regular basis. Historically, daily newspapers' margins of profit were quite high, far higher than most other industries.

In recent years, newspaper executives and their investors have begun to worry that this logic no longer holds. Losses in readership and increased competition for local advertising by websites, the free newspapers in some cities, and other local media have led investors to downgrade the monetary value of some of the biggest newspaper companies. In 2008 and 2009, a national mortgage crisis that left many people without homes, a weak job market, and reduced consumer spending drove many of the large newspaper firms into a tailspin, as advertising plummeted and circulation went down. A number of newspaper chains that had borrowed lots of money now found it hard to pay their debts. With online competition growing every day, analysts began to wonder whether the newspaper industry could rebound.

The result was that many newspaper companies were struggling to stay afloat, and publicly traded newspaper companies experienced sharp drops—as much as 90 percent—in their stock value. Both these companies and privately held firms laid off reporters and closed bureaus in state and national capitals. The Tribune Company, parent to the *Chicago Tribune* and *Los Angeles Times*, among other papers, declared bankruptcy and struggled through the 2010s to right itself. The Hearst Corporation stopped publishing a print edition of the *Seattle Post-Intelligencer*. It kept a web version alive but still cut 80 percent of the newsroom staff. The E. W. Scripps Company fully closed Denver's *Rocky Mountain News* in 2009. McClatchy Company, parent company of the *Miami Herald* and *Kansas City Star*, among many other papers, cut its work force by 4,000, or one-third of its previous full-time workers. In 2008 alone, the newspaper industry dropped about 325,000 jobs overall, including 5,900 positions of reporters and editors. Although the layoffs between 2007 and 2010 were particularly large, the situation for print journalists was still difficult in 2010. The American Society of News Editors employment census of 2011 counted a loss of 1,000 full-time newsroom jobs.[2]

Weekly "alternative" papers, such as the *Village Voice* in New York City, focus on local news and events. The *Voice* is released in print for free each Tuesday and is also available online.

**alternative weekly**
a paper written for a young, urban audience with an eye on political and cultural commentary

**shoppers**
free, nondaily newspapers, typically aimed at people in particular neighborhoods who might shop at local merchants and designed primarily to deliver coupons and advertisements, though they may also carry some news or feature content

## Weekly Newspapers

Weekly newspapers have been somewhat less buffeted by the enormous challenges that daily newspapers have been experiencing. In 2009, about 20 million people paid for a weekly paper, and about 24 million got them free, a total circulation of about 44 million. Many weeklies have succeeded in carving out topic or audience areas that (so far) daily newspapers have not been able to cover easily. Four coverage topics stand out. Three are geographic—coverage of neighborhoods within cities, of suburbs, and of rural areas. The fourth area of coverage focuses on certain types of people—particular ethnic, racial, occupational, or interest communities. Often those communities cannot support a daily paper, and so a weekly takes hold. A hot type of city paper has been the **alternative weekly**. This is a paper written for a young, urban audience with an eye on political and cultural commentary; the *Chicago Reader* is an example. **Shoppers** are another popular form of weekly newspaper that bears noting. These papers are typically aimed at people in particular neighborhoods who might shop at local merchants and are designed primarily to deliver coupons and advertisements, but they may also carry some news or feature content.

## The Variety of Newspapers

As the newspaper categories suggest, the variety that exists among daily and weekly papers is fascinating. When was the last time you read the *Arctic Sentry*, a weekly North Pole paper that claims a circulation of about 4,000? Are you a lawyer in Philadelphia? If so, you might know that the five-times-a-week *Legal Intelligencer* in Philadelphia counts 5,000 subscribers. If you're a resident of New Orleans, perhaps you will be interested in the *Gambit Weekly* of New Orleans, a self-described locally owned "alternative weekly" that distributes 50,000 copies to 400 locations throughout the area. Did you say you're a college student? You're probably aware that virtually every campus has a newspaper, and most such papers are free to students and supported by advertising. The largest college paper is the University of Minnesota's *Minnesota Daily*, which actually is a daily during the normal school season and a weekly during the summer. And it's a printed daily Monday through Thursday during the normal school season, with an online-only version appearing on Fridays.

The African American press includes about 200 newspapers. With the exception of a few papers such as the *Philadelphia Tribune*, which is published four days a week, almost all appear weekly. Among foreign-language newspapers, Spanish newspapers are the most common. Latino papers range from the seven-days-a-week *El Diario* of New York City (circulation 50,000) to the weekly *Conejos County Citizen* of La Jara, Colorado, to the twice-monthly *El Veterano* published in Vineland, New Jersey. Spanish, though, is only the tip of the iceberg of foreign-language newspapers in the United States. Daily or nondaily newspapers target speakers of Mandarin, Vietnamese, Russian, Yiddish, and Ukrainian, among many other languages.

---

## MEDIA TODAY & CULTURE THE RISE OF HISPANIC NEWSPAPERS

According to the U.S. Census Office, the Hispanic population in the United States increased by 15.2 million from 2000 to 2010. That represents a growth rate of 43 percent, outpacing the 10 percent growth rate for the total population. This growing population has not gone unnoticed by marketers and media.[1] NBCUniversal, owned by Comcast, has a particular interest in Hispanic Americans because it owns Telemundo, the Spanish-language television network. iVillage, an NBCUniversal site that targets women aged 18–49, recently partnered with Telemundo to create Mujer de Hoy,[2] a site that attempts to reach digitally connected Latinas.[3]

Newspapers compete to target this growing audience. Some newspapers, such as *La Raza* in Chicago and *El Nuevo Herald* in Miami, publish their online editions only in Spanish. Other newspapers, such as *Reflejos* in suburban Chicago or *El Aguila del Hudson Valley* in New York, print stories on paper in both English and Spanish. The *Reflejos* website is bilingual, whereas *El Aguila* is only in Spanish. Newspaper companies that have traditionally been English-only are responding to this market as well. *El Nuevo Herald* in Miami, for example, is part of the large McClatchy chain.[4]

Despite these efforts, Hispanic newspapers and websites face multiple challenges. A key one is the diversity of the audience and the audience's experiences. Some readers are long-term residents of the United States, whereas others are new immigrants. Readers may have their roots in Cuba, Mexico, Central or South America, or sometimes Spain. These differences contribute to diverse experiences.

What advantages might a niche publication offer a mainstream newspaper publisher? Do you think a local Spanish-language paper and its website can compete with Telemundo's *Mujer de Hoy*? Why or why not?

---

## Financing the Newspaper Business

No matter what their size, topic, or language, newspapers need to make money. They can generate revenues in two ways: from advertising or from circulation. Advertising is by far the dominant source of money. Historically, printed daily newspapers have received about 75 to 80 percent of their revenues—and weekly newspapers about 90 percent of their revenues—in this way. Individual papers may have higher or lower percentages, depending on the ad environment. Larger newspapers and weeklies that charge for their copies receive a higher share of their revenues from circulation than do smaller papers and free weeklies.

### Advertising

You've undoubtedly seen a lot of advertisements in physical newspapers. Advertising can show up in newspapers next to the actual stories (the most common way) or as inserts, often called **freestanding inserts (FSIs)**. These are preprinted sheets that advertise particular products, services, or retailers. When advertisers buy space in newspapers, a major way they evaluate the purchase is by looking at the **cost per thousand readers** (often abbreviated **CPM**, for **cost per mil**, "mil" being Greek for thousand). This is the basic measurement of advertising efficiency in all media; it is used by advertisers to evaluate how much space they will buy in a given newspaper or other medium and what price they will pay. If a full-page ad in a particular newspaper that reaches a hundred thousand people costs $10,000, the CPM is $10. Because advertisers often compare media in terms of CPM, even firms that have the only daily newspapers in their cities worry about coming up with ad prices that can compete with radio and TV or even local ads inserted into national magazines.

**freestanding inserts (FSIs)**
preprinted sheets that advertise particular products, services, or retailers

**cost per thousand readers** or **cost per mil (CPM)**
the basic measurement of advertising efficiency in all media; it is used by advertisers to evaluate how much space they will buy in a given newspaper or other medium and what price they will pay

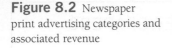

**Figure 8.2** Newspaper print advertising categories and associated revenue

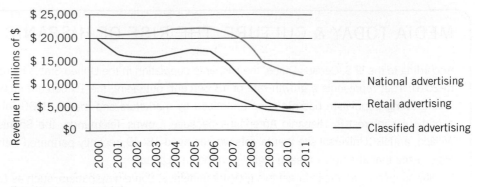

Note: Numbers are rounded.

Source: Newspaper Association of America, March 2012

In 2008, daily and weekly newspapers together brought in about $34 billion in advertising, about $4 billion of which came from digital advertising. That sounds like a lot of money, and it is. But consider that in 2005 the amount was $53.1 billion, and it decreased every year afterward. To understand what's going on, you need to know that the term "advertising" as it applies to newspapers really refers to three different areas: retail advertising from companies with local outlets, classified ads, and national ads. Let's focus on print advertising in the daily papers, where the difficulty stands out most starkly. Figure 8.2 can help you compare these forms of advertising in relation to one another and over time.

**Retail Advertising** Local retail advertising is carried out by establishments located in the same geographic area as the newspaper in which the ad is placed. Think of ads from computer electronics stores, department stores, hospitals, car dealerships, restaurants, realtors, and movie theaters. Some of these advertisers may be parts of national chains, but the purpose of the ads is to persuade people to shop in the local outlets. Retail advertising is the most important of the three main areas of newspaper advertising. In 2011 it made up about 57 percent of the total advertising revenues for print daily papers. The problem for the newspaper industry is that although the amount of money brought in from retail businesses that year was $11.9 billion, just six years earlier it was $22.2 billion—more than the entire amount of advertising revenues the industry earned in 2011.

## THINKING ABOUT MEDIA LITERACY

Although Craigslist has taken over many of the functions of classified advertising, what might be some advantages to placing a classified ad in your local newspaper? Does the local newspaper offer any advantages? If so, what? What about in smaller or larger communities?

**classified ad**
short announcement for a product or service that is typically grouped with announcements for other products or services of the same kind

**Classified Advertising** The second most lucrative type of newspaper advertisement is the classified ad. A **classified ad** is a short announcement for a product or service that is typically grouped with announcements for other products or services of the same kind. Newspapers typically sell classified ad space by the line to people who want to offer everything from houses to beds to bikes. In recent years, the amount of money daily print newspapers have generated through classified ads has plummeted—from about $17 billion and 37 percent of daily newspaper advertising in 2003 to $5 billion and 24 percent in 2011. The drop has a lot to do with the rise of online real estate, auto, and general classified sites, especially free (or very cheap) ones such as Craigslist. They provide users with continually updated information, interactivity, and immediate responsiveness that papers cannot possibly match.

**National Advertising** **National ads** are advertisements placed by large national and multinational firms that do business in a newspaper's geographic area. Airline and cruise line ads are often national purchases. Political advertisements and movie ads also often fit the "national" tag. The distinction between retail and national ads may not always be clear. Sometimes what appear to be retail ads are actually national ads. The reason is that national marketers often provide co-op advertising money to retailers that carry their products. In co-op advertising, manufacturers or distributors of products provide money to exhibitors in order to help the exhibitor with the cost of promoting a particular product. A soup manufacturer, for example, might provide a local supermarket chain with an allowance to purchase ads that highlight the manufacturer's soups. The money may be used to buy time on local radio and TV, as well as ads in local newspapers.

> **national ads**
> advertisements placed by large national and multinational firms that do business in a newspaper's geographic area

Since at least 2003, national advertising has represented between 17 and 19 percent of daily newspaper advertising. As with retail and classified advertising, though, the actual amounts represented by those numbers declined sharply in the late 2000s. In 2003 national ads revenue amounted to $7.8 billion, and in 2005 it amounted to $7.9 billion, but in 2008 it dropped to $6 billion, and in 2011 it was $3.8 billion.

## Circulation

If you were a newspaper executive, you would probably find the retail, classified, and national advertising trends in the industry depressing and scary. But there's more: as if the problem of advertising were not enough, circulation presents another major revenue challenge for newspapers. We have already noted that a downturn in readership of printed copies has caused alarm among newspaper executives. Although newspaper income from circulation is far less than that from advertising, it is still critical because advertisers typically buy space in newspapers because of circulation numbers. Two particular circulation issues concern many daily newspaper executives. One is whether young people will stop reading printed papers because they are so heavily involved in electronic media. The other is whether young people or anyone else will pay for digital newspapers in amounts that will allow newspapers to survive as the printed version decreases in importance and the amount of advertising they receive online is not enough to support staffs of professional journalists.

Executives see the question about young people as critical. They believe that newspaper publishers' inability to attract new young readers is a major factor in the circulation declines. Consider the Newspaper Association of America's finding that whereas in 1988 57 percent of those aged 18–24 reported being a daily newspaper reader, only 26 percent said that in 2009. Similarly, whereas in 1989 67 percent of those aged 35–54 said they read daily newspapers, the proportion dropped to 43 percent in 2009. Frankly, though, even a higher percentage of Americans 55 years and older

Online news sites such as Google News have become increasingly popular. Newspaper industry observers believe that the availability of such sites is hurting print newspaper sales.

admit to not reading the paper daily nowadays compared to the late 1980s, though the percentage who say they do so is higher than the percentage for younger Americans: 68 percent of those 55 and older in 1989 and 51 percent in 2009. One analysis of these declining numbers concluded that "the decline in overall readership can be attributed to the migration of readers to other media offering around-the-clock news coverage, including cable news networks and internet news sources" such as search engines, blogs, social networking sites such as Facebook, and Twitter. The analyst didn't mention that people may well go to their own local newspaper's website. That would be good for the newspaper, if it could make money from their visit through subscriptions and advertising.

In fact, many newspaper websites attract large numbers of readers, and newspaper executives want to spread the message that when advertisers consider circulation, they should include online subscribers as well. They note, for example, that a study by the web rating firm comScore found that around 112 million individuals were visiting U.S. newspaper websites during fall 2011.[3] In fact, beginning in 2011, the organization that tracks readership for the industry, the Audit Bureau of Circulation, began to include paying online subscribers in the total circulation. But it is important to note that the advertising money that newspapers collect from activities online, though growing, represents a small percentage of the ad revenues they bring in. Recall that daily newspaper companies made about $4 billion from online advertisers in 2008. That sounds like a lot until you recognize it's only 12 percent of the $34 billion worth of ads in their printed pages. You might think that there is really no problem here—as advertisers move their ads to the internet, the $40 billion that they have been investing in the newspaper's printed page will simply move over to its electronic one.

But it doesn't work that way. Advertisers have been leaving newspapers to put money on the web, but they often have been doing it in places other than those newspapers. Often they desert the papers because the other places are cheaper or because they can reach younger people than the ones who read the papers' sites. As for the advertisers who do come to the newspapers' sites, they insist on paying far less per thousand readers than they would pay in the print addition. They can do that because the competition for ads online among websites is so fierce that it has driven down prices drastically. The upshot is that even when newspapers attract more people online than they do offline, the amount of money they make advertising to them is far lower. One seasoned analyst of the industry put the dilemma this way: "In 2011, according to Newspaper Association of America statistics, online advertising was up $207 million industry-wide compared to 2010. Print advertising, though, was down $2.1 billion. So the print losses were greater than the digital gains by 10 to 1."[4]

If you've been putting yourself in the place of a newspaper executive, you realize that you cannot simply give up on print, despite the consistently lower number of readers and advertising figures. Print simply brings in too high a percentage of the company revenue to dismiss it. You also then undoubtedly understand the dual dilemma facing the business: (1) to keep drawing advertising and circulation profits from the declining print product while (2) building digital products that are on track to replace print as the future of the business. As we will see, most still have not figured out how to solve either problem, though new ideas keep coming. Print strategies involve trying to create products that are both attractive to readers and profitable. Digital strategies involve trying to rethink the presentation and delivery of news as well as who should pay for it. Both strategies affect the agenda of the news that newspaper firms are offering their audiences. Let's look at them through our familiar categories of production, distribution, and exhibition.

## Production in the Newspaper Industry

In discussing the production of newspapers, we will focus on two general areas. One involves the creation of the content that goes into the papers, and the other involves the actual technical process of putting together a newspaper.

### Creating Newspaper Content

The way a newspaper's content is created differs between dailies and weeklies and between newspapers with large circulations and those with small ones. We can, however, generalize about the basic approach to creating content (see Figure 8.3). The newspaper's publisher is in charge of the entire company's operation, which includes financial issues (getting advertising, increasing circulation), production issues, and editorial issues. "Editorial" in this case has two meanings. In a narrow sense, it means the creation of opinion pieces by the firm's editorial writers. More broadly, it means all non-advertising matter in the paper.

The publisher sets an **advertising–editorial ratio**, which determines the balance between the amount of space available for advertisements and the amount of space available for editorial matter in one issue of a newspaper. A typical daily newspaper carries 60 percent advertising and 40 percent editorial content. Weeklies have a higher percentage of advertising; some are virtually all advertising. For any particular issue of the paper, the number of pages left over and available for editorial matter (based on the number of pages needed for advertisements) is called the **news hole**. The executive in charge of all the operations required to fill the news hole is called the **editor**. He or she is aided by a **managing editor**, who coordinates the work of the sections (or departments) of the paper if there are any.

**advertising–editorial ratio**
set by the publisher, this ratio determines the balance between the amount of space available for advertisements and the amount of space available for editorial matter in one issue of a newspaper

**news hole**
the number of pages left over and available for editorial matter (based on the number of pages needed for advertisements)

**editor**
the executive in charge of all the operations required to fill the news hole

**managing editor**
individual who coordinates the work of the sections (or departments) within the newspaper

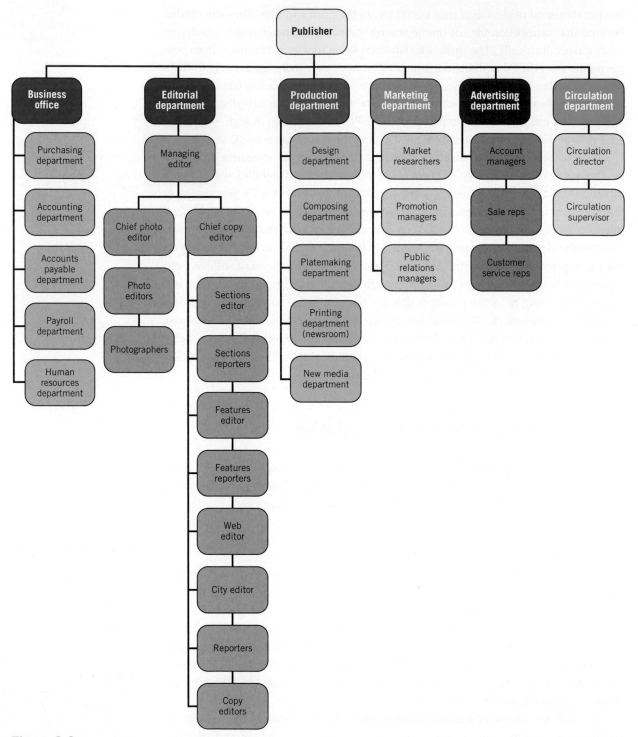

**Figure 8.3**

The organizational structure of a typical newspaper

**general assignment reporters**
newspaper reporters who cover
a variety of topics within their
department

In a daily urban newspaper, typical departments might be sports, lifestyles, entertainment/leisure, business, TV, city news, a "neighborhoods" section, and real estate. Each department has one or more reporters assigned to it, and the editor may tell them what topics to cover and when and where. Reporters who cover a variety of topics within their department are called **general assignment reporters**.

If the newspaper's editor and publisher consider a department especially important, they may give the editor the money and personnel to assign reporters to particular places or topics—for example, city hall and crime in the city news department, college athletics in the sports department, or movie reviewing in the entertainment/leisure department. Such specific long-term assignments are called **beats**.

However, a fair amount of a paper's editorial matter will not be written by members of the newspaper's staff. Sometimes an editor may hire individuals who accept creative assignments from a number of different newspapers to write such pieces as music or book reviews; these people are called **freelancers**. If the paper is owned by a group—Gannett or Knight-Ridder, for example—that group may have its own news service that provides stories created by other papers in the chain. A substantial number of stories also will come from **wire services** such as the Associated Press and Reuters. These services, for a fee, supply via high-speed telephone, cable, and/or internet connections a continual stream of hard news and feature stories about international, national, and even state topics for which the newspaper may have no reporters. Special wire editors and others continually check the stream of stories that "come over the wires" for likely material.

**Syndicates** also provide important materials for newspapers. A syndicate is a company that sells soft news, editorial matter, cartoons, and photographs to newspapers for use. There are hundreds of syndicates that supply a variety of content for different departments and different audiences, including the following:

- The Washington Post Writers Group, the syndication arm of the *Washington Post*, circulates the work of columnists such as Ellen Goodman, George Will, and David Broder.
- The Copley News Service sells editorial cartoons.
- The Universal Press Syndicate offers a wide range of choices, from "Dear Abby" and Jeane Dixon's "Your Horoscope" to Marshall Leob's "Your Money" column to the *Doonesbury* comic strip

As you might imagine, syndicates supply some of the most popular parts of a paper.

For every issue, editors from all departments draw on all these sources to make up the paper. Under the watchful eye of editors, reporters on beats and those assigned to particular stories carry out their assignments. When it comes to the print version, everyone knows the paper's **deadline**—the time when the final version of their work has to be in. The news staff enters the stories into computers, which are linked to the managing editor and copy editors, as well as to others on the paper. **Copy editors** read the stories the reporters write and edit them for length, accuracy, style, and grammar. Headlines are written, and photographs and design work to accompany the stories are selected. Computer-ready syndicated material is chosen and added to the mix. The newspaper is ready to be printed.

Until around 2005, that was it: the work cycle of a newspaper centered on the time at which one or more editions had to be printed. When newspaper organizations began putting their material online, they still followed this approach. To a large extent what readers saw on the web was a reproduction of the printed product. Updates rarely happened, and editors were hesitant to put a story online that would reveal happenings that would override or contradict the printed product. That reluctance changed rather quickly, as newspaper executives realized that they were now competing with local and national television sites, including all-news channels, that were

**beat**
a specific, long-term assignment that covers a single topic area

**freelancers**
workers who make a living by accepting and completing creative assignments from a number of different newspapers—sometimes several at one time

**wire services**
organizations that, for a fee, supply newspapers with a continual stream of hard news and feature stories about international, national, and even state topics via high-speed telephone, cable, and/or internet connections

**syndicates**
companies that sell soft news, editorial matter, cartoons, and photographs to newspapers for use

**deadline**
the time when the final version of reporters' work has to be in

**copy editors**
the individuals who edit stories written by reporters; they edit for length, accuracy, style, and grammar and write headlines to accompany the stories

**24/7**
around-the-clock news
organizations that constantly
update stories and present new
ones

**blog**
a sort of diary or journal that may
describe the events surrounding
the coverage and that invites
reader responses

All the major newspapers in
the country (and around the
world) have an online version
of their paper, allowing readers
(or "users") to engage more
interactively with the content of
the site and even the reporters.

**users**
the audience of newspaper
websites

**pagination**
the process by which newspaper
pages are composed and
displayed as completed pages,
with pictures and graphics, on
screen

constantly updating stories and presenting new ones. Newspaper executives decided they had to do that as well, and so many newspaper websites have become round-the-clock—or **24/7**—operations. Today, stories are just as likely to premiere online as in the printed edition.

Moreover, the difference between the online and offline reporting staff is blurring. For certain topics not covered in the printed version—say, technology or certain local neighborhoods—the newspaper might hire special staff for the website. In general, though, the expectation today is that reporters will create for both the print and online products. That often means that they have to learn new skills that go beyond straightforward reportage. Creating for the online "paper" sometimes means preparing a photographic or videographic version of the written material. In many cases, it also means writing a web log, or **blog**, which is a sort of diary or journal that may describe the events surrounding the coverage and that invites reader responses.

As you might imagine, this is a lot of work, and reporters have complained that the need to produce ever more materials for analog and digital forms does more than make them tired. The piling on of new reportorial tasks, they say, makes them focus so much on getting out the product in different ways that they have little time to conduct time-consuming legwork and thinking that will help them get below the surface of stories. Publishers and editors, though perhaps sympathetic, state that an expectation of intense cross-media activity is the direction in which the news world is moving.

If you've been to a newspaper website, you have probably noticed that the contents do not stop with the staff's takes on the day's news. Increasingly, newspaper websites aim to encourage their audiences—oddly called **users** on the web—to engage with the site in numerous ways. On many sites, for example, you can e-mail a reporter whose story you have read; join a "community" of readers to discuss particular news topics; register approval of a story by "liking" or "sharing" it; respond to a story in the comment section that accompanies it; create a blog around any topic you like; search the week's news by using key words of your choosing; browse an archive of newspaper issues that may go back decades and beyond; watch video reviews, product demonstrations, or news stories from the paper's staff or one of the wire services; click on an article so that the computer will read it to you; and (of course and importantly for the sites) click on ads.

## The Technology of Publishing the Paper

Despite this seeming cornucopia of material in the digital version of the daily or weekly newspaper, many people still do read the printed version or both. Creating a website for them to read on a 24/7 schedule is a challenging and expensive activity. It requires information technology professionals who tie the journalists into a world involving the creation of sites with many layers and the storage of huge amounts of material. Interestingly, much of the printed product starts out digital too. Computers and related digital technologies are the mainstays of contemporary newspapers. Reporters now can go anywhere with portable computers and send stories to the home department in a form that can be immediately read and printed. Digital cameras, which translate the visual world directly into computer code, allow images to be instantly entered into the computers.

Key to the activity is a process called **pagination**—the ability to compose and display completed pages, with pictures and graphics, on screen. In large daily and weekly newspapers, the technology enables the editors to transmit these images to the plates of the company's printing presses.

Smaller papers use similar, though much less expensive, approaches. With personal computers, editors can use desktop publishing software to create the paper's layout. They can then take the results to a local printing shop, where the material can be printed relatively inexpensively. The costs of the operation are low enough that classified notices and ads from local merchants can support these small papers. The result has been the rise of free weekly papers that focus on sports, shows, politics, or neighborhood events in sections of large urban areas. Typically, the staff is quite small, and the advertising–editorial ratio is quite high. Nevertheless, some observers see these smaller local newspapers as providing a wider range of information to their audiences than the dailies provided when they had monopolies.

## Distribution in the Newspaper Industry

**N**ewspaper distribution means bringing the finished issue to the point of exhibition. For a newspaper, that might be a person's house, a newsstand, a supermarket, or a vending machine—or a computer or mobile device. Populating a news website on a 24/7 schedule—that is, distributing material to it—is at least as challenging as creating the material. The company's information technology professionals must coordinate the serving of textual, graphical, and video stories to users who use their computers or mobile devices (tablets or smartphones) to access the newspaper's website or the newspaper's special apps for the iPhone, Android, and Windows systems. They must distribute links to their paper's digital stories to people who request e-mail or Twitter updates. They must ensure the serving of ads to those users (often with the help of separate ad-serving companies). And they must run software that learns about users (in part to help sell ads) by getting them to register and by tracking their activities on the sites.

Distributing physical newspapers is enormously challenging as well. Newspaper firms, especially dailies, typically distribute their own products. The task is carried out by the circulation department's personnel, under the authority of the business manager and publisher.

**newspaper distribution**
bringing the finished issue to the point of exhibition

### Determining Where to Market the Newspaper

The most basic question the circulation department must confront has to do with the geographic area in which it will market the paper. Many considerations go into making the decision. Among them are these factors:

- The location of consumers that major advertisers would like to reach
- The location of present and future printing plants
- The competition of other papers
- The loyalty to the paper, if any, that people in different areas seem to have

Any or all of these considerations can change, of course. New major advertisers may be found, new printing plants can be built in certain places and not others, and marketing can try to encourage loyalty to the paper and beat the competition. The newspaper's businesspeople, however, must examine the costs and benefits of every decision. The solutions they arrive at must necessarily vary with the newspaper's circumstances.

Executives at the *New York Times*, for example, have decided that their audience is an upper-income, educated class of readers that reaches far beyond the borders of New York City. As a result, they distribute a digital version of the paper by satellite to printing plants throughout the United States every day. The *Times* contracts with local companies to print and distribute the paper in those areas.

Most daily newspapers do not have such lofty circulation goals, but their executives do have to decide on the limits of their marketing territory. In deciding on those limits, they may lose out on some ads from chain stores that have branches in the outlying areas that they have excluded. On the other hand, the paper won't incur the substantial costs of marketing and delivering papers beyond its primary territory.

**Alternative Distribution and Marketing Tactics**  In recent years, some newspaper groups have been having their cake and eating it too when it comes to winning chain store ads and not incurring the high costs of "fringe" circulation. Their tactic has been to buy dailies that serve adjacent communities. The groups then offer advertisers, particularly national and regional retailers, a single buy for the larger geographic area. The newspaper groups also save substantial amounts of money by combining their existing production facilities and staff. At the same time, each individual paper keeps its traditional coverage area and the loyalty of the readers in that area.

One example of a group using this tactic is Media General Newspapers, a group that owns, among other media holdings, three daily papers along U.S. Highway 29, an important business and residential corridor from Danville, Virginia, to the outskirts of Washington, DC. A shopper company that takes this approach is Newport Media, which owns weekly "pennysavers" across New York City, Long Island, and New Jersey. The latter firm boasts that it can offer advertisers "near 100% saturation advertising."

## Exhibition in the Newspaper Industry

Exhibition of print newspapers hasn't changed all that much in recent years, despite the exploding trend of online papers. For people who prefer to purchase individual copies of a newspaper, they are still sold on newsstands and in vending machines.

An online newspaper has a distribution site; see the *Washington Post*'s website, www.washingtonpost.com, for an example. Like other online news outlets, it is distributed through exhibitors—typically cable and telephone companies—to computers, smartphones, and other devices wherever users can and want to access it. In the physical world, the exhibition point of a newspaper is more specific and depends on its type. Free weeklies are often placed in special boxes in stores or on streets, with placards inviting people to take a copy. Weeklies and dailies that cost money can, of course, also be found in stores and in coin-operated boxes on streets as well as on newsstands.

However, circulation executives for paid weeklies and dailies prefer the exhibition point for their papers to be their readers' homes or places of work, as opposed to a newsstand. The reason is that delivery to a home or office implies a subscription to the paper, a paid-in-advance commitment to receive the product. Such commitments help the paper's businesspeople sell advertising in the paper by enabling them to guarantee that advertisers can reach a fixed number of consumers in particular locations.

money U.S. newspapers received through print and online advertising sources between 2000 and 2011. It shows that the strong increase in online ads has not stopped the decline in advertising revenue.

As you know, online advertising doesn't bring in nearly enough money to support a traditional news organization, and news executives worry that in the future, digital sites might have to carry the costs of most of the news-gathering activities. During the past few years they therefore have tried to find ways to charge people for using their sites. This barrier is called a **paywall**. Most online newspapers don't erect a complete paywall for fear of driving away audiences and advertisers. Instead, they allow people access to parts of their sites or to a certain number of articles per month for free, and they require payment from individuals who want to go beyond those limitations. The goal is to keep the number of visitors high while also developing a good flow of online subscription money. Often access to the newspapers' tablet apps comes with the online payments.

The most prominent U.S. newspapers to successfully adopt limited paywalls are the *Wall Street Journal* and the *New York Times*. Gannett is one of the newspaper chains instituting these forced payments in local newspapers around the country. It's important to stress, though, that limited paywalls by no means solve newspapers' struggle to make ends meet in the digital world. The payments do not make up enough for the low price of online newspaper ads for most newspapers to survive online only without drastically cutting their news-gathering staff. Newspaper publishers hope this problem will be solved in the years to come, as they try (in the words of one analyst) to "find the optimal balance between free, free with a paywall, and all-paid circulation, and advertising pricing models."[5]

**paywall**
a barrier that prevents people from accessing digital material without first paying money

## The Future of Newspapers versus the Future of Journalism

That ability to make money is at the heart of the concerns that knowledgeable observers have about the newspaper's future. Some of them believe that the print version is doomed to disappear and that the digital versions of most will not be able to make enough advertising money to support the staff that is required to put out an acceptable product. One controversial writer, the media consultant Henry Blodget, wrote bluntly on his blog in 2007 that "newspapers are screwed." More sober, but still pessimistic, was the 2007 assessment by the famously savvy investor Warren Buffett. Buffett, who owns a portion of the *Washington Post* and has a long connection with the newspaper business, wrote that "fundamentals are definitely eroding in the newspaper industry, and the skid will almost certainly continue." He went on to state that

> the economic potential of a newspaper internet site—given the many alternative sources of information and entertainment that are free and only a click away, is at best a small fraction of that existing in the past for a print newspaper facing no competition.

Buffet and Blodget made their pronouncements before the economic downturn. The recession that began in 2008 underscored the dilemma, as physical newspaper advertising went south and as the growth of online newspaper advertising slowed considerably.

Now and in the foreseeable future, then, what you will see when you look at the newspaper industry and its products is a search for business models that will ensure the industry's viability. Many newspapers would like members of the public to believe that the health of journalism—and of democratic ideals—rests with the survival of the newspaper organizations we know today. Cheerleaders for this venture argue that without it American society will suffer greatly. Where, they ask, will the great investigative reports come from? Where will the great editorials about local issues appear? Certainly, they argue, neither bloggers nor volunteer reporters can play the role that newspapers have taken on for 200 years in keeping people in touch with their society, communities, and democracy.

Such arguments involving the future of democracy might well induce enough guilt to make some Americans shell out money to support their digital big-city newspapers, however begrudgingly. That is a proposition you should examine critically—because there is another perspective. As we learned in chapter 2, the profession of journalism is not tied to the newspaper. There may be ways to encourage professional journalism that do not come from traditional newspaper companies. Some newspaper companies may still turn out to have the most persuasive solutions for keeping you and me abreast of what we need to know of the world. If so, we should pay for them. As for those that cannot survive, we should see their predicaments as an encouragement to rethink as a society what professional journalism means, why we should care about it, and how it should be supported.

## THINKING ABOUT MEDIA LITERACY

The rapid growth and popularity of digital media have encouraged debates surrounding the demise of print newspapers. What are some of the arguments that suggest their demise? What are some of the arguments for their continuing? Where do you stand on this argument? Will print newspapers continue, or will they all transition to digital eventually?

## Ethics and New Models of Journalism

Some newspaper workers reading the preceding paragraph may have a response about competition they face, competition that they say is unethical and destructive not only to the newspaper industry but to the journalism profession as a whole. Their argument is that a significant reason for newspapers' difficulties earning sufficient revenues in digital media relates to two unscrupulous activities that non-newspaper websites carry out. One activity involves those entities' use of newspapers' work without paying them. The other involves the creation of "content farms" that edge out newspapers' work and pay journalists low wages.

The first activity—use of newspapers' work without paying them—has been of special concern to executives at major newspapers. They have noticed that many sites simply fill their pages with descriptions of what the newspapers have written that morning, with links to those papers. The sites' argument is that they are just advising readers of what is available in those papers and that the readers will then click to go to those sites. But newspaper executives argue that only a small percentage of readers actually click on the links; mainly, the sites are receiving the benefit of the enormous resources that went into creating the material. Simply linking is totally legal, but newspaper publishers such as Rupert Murdoch have fulminated against sites such as *Google News* and the *Huffington Post* that create headlines, photos, and sometimes even longer summaries around the links. Sites should pay for that privilege, the newspaper leaders argue. In fact, during 2011 a number of major papers started a consortium that searches the web for sites that use the member papers' stories in this way. The consortium warns them that they are treading on shaky legal ground and urges them to pay a syndication fee to use the members' work. In this way, the newspapers hope to bring in a robust new revenue stream.

The second activity—content farms—involves another way of destroying newspapers' playing field, say executives. A content farm is an unfavorable way of describing a company that turns out thousands of pieces of "news" a day with the aim of catching peoples' interest on search engines. Among the largest are Demand Media and Associated Content (which is owned by Yahoo!). They work this way: Computers in those firms keep constant track of the words people are using when they search on Google and Bing. When they note topics that are "trending"—that is, that seem to be increasingly popular—they put out the word that articles and videos need to be quickly written about those topics. The articles and the headings for the articles are written to show up high on the "organic" search results—those lists of links that show up in the center of the page after you hit the search button. Their high position means that people who search for the topics are likely to click on those links—which then gives the content farm an opportunity to serve them ads and put a cookie in their browser. (See chapter 2 for an explanation of how this works.)

These activities get newspaper journalists really angry. Many argue that these activities are rampant, and they accuse the *Huffington Post* (owned by AOL) and About.com of acting like content farms. They argue that rushing articles onto the web based on trending search topics inevitably leads to superficial writing. They note that many of the articles merely stitch together facts and ideas the writers find by searching on the web. There is little, if any, original research. In the meantime, good journalistic pieces on the topics that lie in newspapers' digital archives—articles that the content-farm writers may have used to write their pieces—show up down the list because they haven't been written or positioned in the crafty ways the content farms use. That hurts the newspaper's ability to attract advertisers, the papers' employees argue. Moreover, they continue, the content farms are pushing further down the salaries of journalists because although some of the people who prepare the content-farm works are full-time employees, many are freelancers who get paid a small amount for every piece they prepare. Sadly, among these freelancers are recent journalism graduates who can't find newspaper jobs and former newspaper reporters laid off in the bad economy.

The journalistic outcry against content farms led Google in 2011 to announce it was adjusting its search algorithm to give priority to stories and videos that use new information about a topic and appear more substantial. Google would not say exactly what that means, but its new approach does seem to have devalued the most obvious content-farm stories. This basic approach to news writing continues, though, and newspapers argue that it unethically exploits their legacy articles and that readers' believe that a link that is high on search results is the better link than one below it. The companies that carry out these activities argue that they are performing a service and making money legally. Newspaper executives, they say, are simply complaining when they must learn to adjust to this competition that will not go away.

## THINKING ABOUT MEDIA LITERACY

Newspaper content, which is the product of a journalist's efforts to get information, has faced this kind of borrowing before. When radio first started, broadcasters would read newspaper stories over the air as part of their news segments. Now, news aggregator sites such as Google and Yahoo! bring together stories from other newspapers under their banners. Or sites offer summaries of news stories and link back to the source. What do you think of this practice? Does it hurt journalism as much as some critics might think, or does it help promote the original sources? What other concerns do newspapers have with this practice? How do audiences benefit? How might they lose out?

# CHAPTER REVIEW

 Visit the Companion Website at www.routledge.com/cw/turow for additional study tools and resources.

## Key Terms

You can find the definitions to these key terms in the marginal glossary throughout this chapter. Test your knowledge of these terms with interactive flash cards on the *Media Today* companion website.

| | | |
|---|---|---|
| 24/7 | deadline | newspaper distribution |
| adversarial press | direct mail firms | newspapers |
| advertising–editorial ratio | editor | pagination |
| alternative weekly | freelancers | paywall |
| beat | freestanding inserts (FSI) | podcasts |
| blog | general assignment | RSS feed |
| classified ad | reporters | shoppers |
| co-op advertising | managing editor | syndicates |
| copy editors | marriage mail outfits | total market coverage (TMC) |
| cost per thousand readers or cost | mobile feed | users |
| per mil (CPM) | national ads | weeklies |
| dailies | news hole | wire services |

## Questions for Discussion and Critical Thinking

1. What relevance does the history of newspapers have to our understanding of the current situation of the newspaper?
2. From what you have read and seen around you, how pessimistic or optimistic are you about the newspaper's future. Why?
3. If you or some friends do not read a newspaper or visit a newspaper site, what would it take to encourage you (or them) to do that? Are the steps the industry is taking persuasive?
4. Do you agree with those who argue that localism—even hyper-localism—is the way for newspapers to remain relevant and profitable in an age of so many information sources? Why or why not?

## Case Study
### ANALYZING A NEWSPAPER'S ATTEMPT TO ENGAGE ITS AUDIENCE

**The Idea** As this chapter notes, many newspaper websites today are attempting to attract audiences by creating a variety of ways to receive the sites' content as well as encouraging them to interact around, and even contribute to, the websites' content. Examples are blogs, conversation areas, RSS feeds, and mobile capabilities. The purpose of this assignment is to encourage you to explore the techniques that your local paper is using and to carry out a hands-on examination of them.

**The Method** Examine your local newspaper's website for ways that it is trying to interact with audiences and to encourage audiences to interact with each other around its content. Spend a week using these tools yourself. Then write a report of about four pages about your experience. In your paper, answer the following questions: To what extent did this effort allow you to get closer to news you want? To what extent did it extend your understanding of various sorts of news? Did the blogs or chat areas make you want to come back to the site more than you would if you hadn't connected with them? In general, how successful were these techniques in creating bonds between you and the newspaper?

# 9 The Magazine Industry

## CHAPTER OBJECTIVES

1 Connect the importance of understanding magazine history to understanding magazines today

2 Describe the physical and digital production, distribution, and exhibition of different types of magazines

3 Explain the view that magazines are brands that need to follow their readers across a variety of converging platforms

4 Analyze ethical issues regarding the influence advertising on magazine content

> "Most women's magazines simply try to mold women into bigger and better consumers."
>
> **GLORIA STEINEM, WRITER**

"How YouTube Could Kill Off Women's Magazines": that title for Nicole Martinelli's article was probably meant to be controversial. But writing in June 2012 on IJNet.org, a international website for journalists, Martinelli seemed to be quite serious in arguing the point. Her evidence was Hello Style, a new channel on YouTube. The powerful Hearst magazine company created Hello Style in response to Google's 2011 announcement that it wanted to make part of its YouTube video site a place for professionally produced content. Google executives recognized that major advertisers feel more comfortable placing their ads near content created by well-known firms, so they proposed to help pay for "branded channels" created by well-known individuals and firms from the fields of TV, film, music, news, and sports. Enticed by YouTube's offer of $10 million, Hearst was one of the magazine powerhouses

that stepped up to the plate. It created Hello Style by tapping the resources of its *Cosmopolitan*, *Harper's Bazaar*, *Marie Claire*, and *Seventeen* magazines as well as the company's RealBeauty.com website.

Martinelli was impressed by Hello Style's collection of videos with posted comments and links to Pinterest, Facebook, and other social media sites. She concluded that in the digital age, electronic magazines would trump paper ones. She observed, "The initial line-up is a banquet of fresh content, offered five days a week, including 'Sexy vs. Skanky,' 'Big Girl in a Skinny World' and 'Visible Panty Lines.'" These "go down so easy," she said, that "it makes the paper editions of these magazines seem obsolete." There is a place for paper periodicals, she allowed—but only barely. "You might thumb through Cosmo at the hairdresser's or a doctor's office, but if you want to try the manicure style du jour you'd be better served watching the quick tutorial on Hello Style," she wrote. Martinelli might have added that if you bring your iPad or Nexus tablet with your favorite magazine apps to the doctor's office (with any luck your doctor will have Wi-Fi if you don't have a cellular connection), you might not even have to look at paper there. Her conclusion: a large portion of the work of tomorrow's magazine journalists will involve creating videos, answering reader comments online, and pushing out news on social media, if Hearst's Hello Style YouTube channel is any indication.

As we will see in this chapter, magazine industry executives don't really disagree that much of their business will be based in digital technology. They do, however, worry about how to navigate these changes while maintaining and building the revenues of their companies and the industry as a whole. The level of angst showed up poignantly in 2007 when Ann Moore, the top executive at Time Inc., the largest U.S. magazine publisher, talked to the industry trade association about the anxiety her job had brought her. With her staff, she had been immersed in trying to remake her magazine division of Time Warner into a powerful force that could attract large and desirable audiences and advertisers in print, on the Web, and in other areas of the digital environment. "Steering an organization through change is hard," she said, knowing that many of the magazine publishing executives in her audience were feeling the same pressures. "You know," she advised, "everybody stay calm. This is a great business we're in."

The year 2007 was a long time ago when it comes to changes in the magazine industry. Yet the nervousness mixed with optimism that Moore revealed then still characterizes people in the industry today. Two questions loom large: What form will the digital magazines ultimately take? And will the digital magazines really "kill" the paper ones, or will paper and digital titles with the same names actually serve different purposes?

In this chapter we will explore how the industry is trying to shape answers to these questions. Doing that means examining the very meaning of the word "magazine" and its relevance to our age of convergence. As you probably expect by this point in the book, we'll start our exploration with a bit of history to understand the forces that shaped what we know today as the magazine and the magazine industry.

## The Development of Magazines

The word "magazine" is French; it means storehouse. When you think of it, that is, at core, what defines magazines. They are collections of materials (stories, ads, poems, and other items) that their editors believe will interest their audience. If you look at the photos of historical magazines that accompany the timeline (Figure 9.1), you'll note how different early magazines were from the ones of today. You'll also notice that slowly, over the centuries and decades, the magazines began to look like the ones we read today. Study the timeline, and the ways that happened will come into focus. So will magazine versions of the themes we have seen in the book and newspaper chapters.

1. *The modern magazine did not arrive in a flash as a result of one inventor's grand change.*

As we said, the pictures begin to tell that story, and the timeline's details help fill it in. Follow the chain of technological innovations that influenced the look of the magazines. As with the newspaper, magazines through the early 19th century were produced in a decidedly nonindustrial manner, by a hand-powered press. Although the type was often impressive, it was tight and rarely relieved by drawings or designs. The 19th century saw critical developments in the magazine's look, with respect to both the covers and the internal layouts. There was more white space, and there were more illustrations and different fonts—in fact, this meant

## Figure 9.1 Timeline of the Magazine Industry

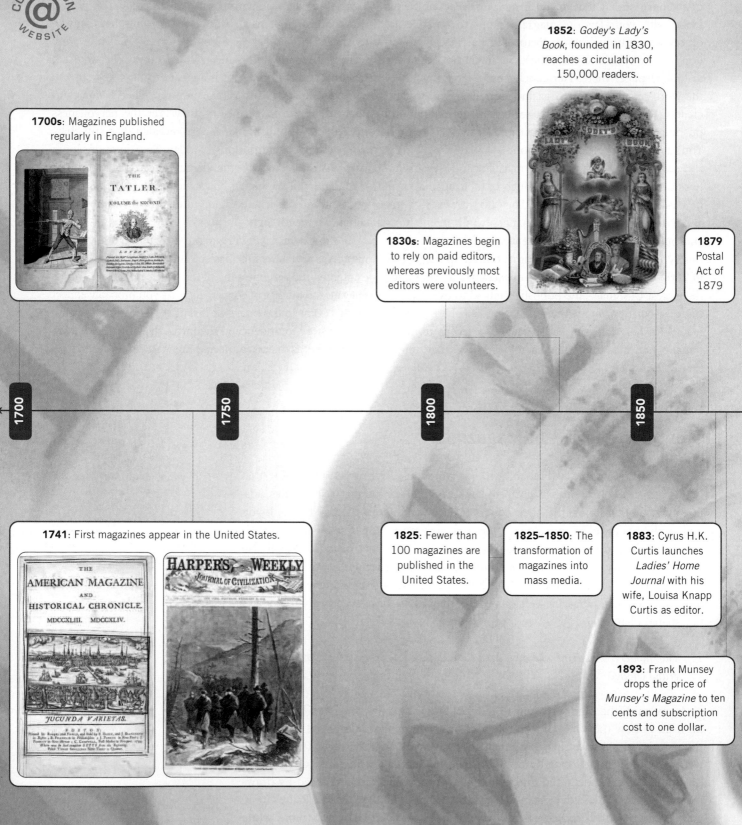

**1700s**: Magazines published regularly in England.

**1852**: *Godey's Lady's Book*, founded in 1830, reaches a circulation of 150,000 readers.

**1830s**: Magazines begin to rely on paid editors, whereas previously most editors were volunteers.

**1879** Postal Act of 1879

**1700**  **1750**  **1800**  **1850**

**1741**: First magazines appear in the United States.

**1825**: Fewer than 100 magazines are published in the United States.

**1825–1850**: The transformation of magazines into mass media.

**1883**: Cyrus H.K. Curtis launches *Ladies' Home Journal* with his wife, Louisa Knapp Curtis as editor.

**1893**: Frank Munsey drops the price of *Munsey's Magazine* to ten cents and subscription cost to one dollar.

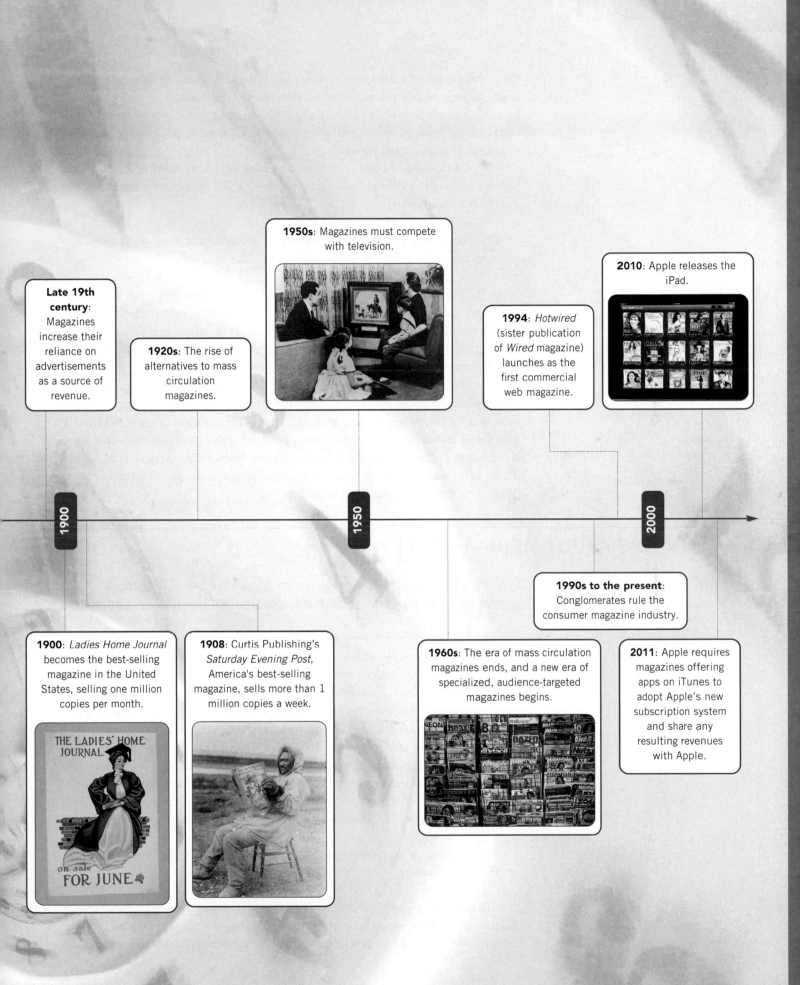

**1950s**: Magazines must compete with television.

**2010**: Apple releases the iPad.

**Late 19th century**: Magazines increase their reliance on advertisements as a source of revenue.

**1920s**: The rise of alternatives to mass circulation magazines.

**1994**: *Hotwired* (sister publication of *Wired* magazine) launches as the first commercial web magazine.

1900

1950

2000

**1990s to the present**: Conglomerates rule the consumer magazine industry.

**1900**: *Ladies Home Journal* becomes the best-selling magazine in the United States, selling one million copies per month.

**1908**: Curtis Publishing's *Saturday Evening Post*, America's best-selling magazine, sells more than 1 million copies a week.

**1960s**: The era of mass circulation magazines ends, and a new era of specialized, audience-targeted magazines begins.

**2011**: Apple requires magazines offering apps on iTunes to adopt Apple's new subscription system and share any resulting revenues with Apple.

the development of a discipline of magazine designers. These design changes also affected the look and placement of advertisements. Ads existed virtually from the beginning of magazines, but they did not take up a lot of space and tended to be placed at the back of issues. The 20th century saw more ads than ever, and they appeared throughout the issues.

Why did this flood of design changes and advertisements happen? It wasn't just because of the good ideas of individual publishers and printing-press inventors. The answer ties into theme 2.

2.  *The magazine as a medium of communication developed as a result of social and legal responses to the technology during different periods.*

As the timeline indicates, in 1825 fewer than 100 magazines were being published in the United States. The number changed drastically over the next 50 years. The spread of literacy, the spread of railroads across the nation, and postal laws that substantially lowered the cost of mailing magazines encouraged entrepreneurs to try their hands at the business. In addition, the great expansion of American business after the Civil War's end in 1865 had a major positive impact. As more and more factories sprang up across the United States, the large number of items being produced increased the competition among manufacturers of similar goods. One result was the creation of **brands**—products with distinctive names and identities that make them stand out from their competitors. But to make money on a particular brand of soap or any other mass-produced item, a manufacturer had to make sure that hordes of people recognized the brand and bought it.

**brand**
a name and image associated with a particular product

---

## THINKING ABOUT MEDIA LITERACY

Think of one of your favorite products and the advertising for it. How does the company sell that brand? What characteristics are associated with it? How do you recognize the products as belonging to that particular brand? How does the product differ from other similar products?

---

In earlier decades, readers' subscriptions covered a large percentage of the publishers' costs. However, magazine owner Frank Munsey showed how advertising could pay most of the costs of producing the magazine. His low subscription prices for *Munsey's* magazine attracted a large number of readers, which in turn attracted advertisers who wanted to reach those readers. Munsey charged the advertisers for reaching his audience, and he proved quite successful. It wasn't long before Munsey's approach caught on industry-wide. For the first time, magazine publishers aimed to attract hundreds of thousands, even millions, of customers in order to deliver them to advertisers. And so we transition to theme 3.

3.  *The magazine as a medium of communication existed long before the existence of the magazines industry.*

As the timeline shows, it was the explosive growth of magazines after the Civil War and into the 20th century that marked the beginning of a magazine industry in the United States. Large firms developed with staffs of editors, illustrators, and writers as well as marketing and circulation specialists. The magazine publishers established important relationships with major advertising clients and their advertising agencies. The industry had its major ups and downs. Notably, the shift of advertisers to television marked the beginning of the end of America's mass-circulation magazines, despite their large readerships.

It took the magazine industry a few years to adjust to the drop in advertising brought about by television, but by the early 1970s, executives had developed a new approach to their business. Although some magazines already were tailored to particular ethnic, religious, occupational, and hobby groups, new magazines tried to go beyond those categories and tap into the newer, narrower interests and lifestyles of the relatively affluent in U.S. society—target audiences that advertisers especially wanted. This potential for great profits drew giant firms that soon dominated the magazine industry by the early part of the 21st century. Time Warner's Time Inc. magazine company is the advertising and circulation leader. Other leading consumer magazine groups are Hearst Magazines, Advance Publications, and the Meredith Publishing Company.

But if the 1990s were a time of strong revenues and confidence, the 2000s and beyond are, as noted earlier, a time of worry and sober concern about the future. Let's look at the current profile of the industry.

## An Overview of the Modern Magazine Industry

American newsstands regularly display more than 2,000 magazine titles. Many others can be seen in the periodicals section of large university or city libraries. Magazines differ widely in both circulation and topic. As a mind-boggling example, consider that the 20,000 magazines that a major magazine association refers to include *AARP: The Magazine* (circulation 24.6 million), *Inc.* (circulation 711,000), *American Woodworker* (circulation 191,000), and *Gun Dog* (circulation 41,000)—all on the same association list! We can note two important traits these products share. One is that they are collections of essays or reports—articles—that their publishers gather together. The second is that their companies release them on a regular (or periodic) schedule—in these cases on a monthly basis.

A few years ago, we might have added a third shared trait: the articles are printed on paper stapled to a cover. Although the four magazines just listed as examples certainly exist in paper, they and a great majority of magazines today can be found on other media as well. Want to see *Gun Dog* magazine in a digital form? Just go to http://www.gundogmag.com/. Convergence is certainly alive and growing in the magazine industry, as we will see. Because of convergence, though, people who work in the magazine industry often have a hard time describing what a magazine is today.

### Five Major Types of Magazines

Recognizing the importance of convergence, the Magazine Publishers Association changed its name to the Association of Magazine Media. The new title recognizes that even though members' magazines started on paper, magazines now exist in many digital forms. Nowhere on the association's site, though, is there a definition

There is a magazine for just about every topic that comes to mind. Even though magazines broadly fit into one of the five topics discussed, they fit into many subcategories. Some are devoted to very specific topics, such as vegetarian cooking.

**business-to-business (b-to-b) magazine** or **trade magazine**
a magazine that focuses on topics related to a particular occupation, profession, or industry

of "magazine." The association's members seem content to accept that everyone knows a magazine when they see it. Yet within the industry, general agreement exists that if a periodical fits into one of the following five general-topic categories, it is to be considered a magazine:

- Business or trade magazines
- Consumer magazines
- Literary reviews and academic journals
- Newsletters
- Comic books

Let's see what each of these categories includes.

## Business-to-Business Magazines/Trade Magazines

A **business-to-business (b-to-b) magazine**, also called a **trade magazine**, focuses on topics related to a particular occupation, profession, or industry. Published by a private firm or by a business association, it is written to reach people who are involved with that occupation, profession, or industry.

Standard Rate and Data Service (SRDS), a firm that collects information about magazine audiences and ad rates and sells it to advertisers and ad agencies, devotes an entire reference directory to business magazines. The directory divides business specializations into more than 200 categories. Examples are advertising and marketing; automotive; banking; building; ceramics; computers; engineering and construction; health care; and hotels, motels, clubs, and resorts.

In addition to reaching their readers via paper, trade magazines now almost always have quite elaborate websites. These often carry daily updates or other articles that the print edition does not contain. The sites may also have areas that present data or special research papers that require visitors to pay a special fee (beyond the magazine subscription) to gain entry. In fact, some entrepreneurs within particular industries have reversed the traditional model: instead of focusing on paper magazines and using the website as secondary, they concentrate their resources on the web and other digital versions. Often they allow some free access and charge for deeper use of the sites. They may or may not also support a paper version.

MediaPost, a trade publisher for marketing and media practitioners, uses this model. Go to MediaPost.com, and you can subscribe to its monthly print magazines, *OMMA* magazine and *MEDIA* magazine. You can also read the magazines' articles for free online, and you can read a huge number of other articles that stay digital. The digital and the printed versions are all supported by advertising. The company also makes money by mounting well-attended conferences for digital media and digital marketing practitioners. MediaPost charges hefty entry fees for the conferences and also gets support from firms that want to advertise to the attendees.

## Consumer Magazines

Consumer magazines are aimed at people in their private, nonbusiness lives. They are sold by subscription and on newsstands and magazine racks in stores. They almost always have websites, and many have apps for the iPad and other tablets. They

**Table 9.1** Top 15 Magazines by Paid Circulation During the Last Six Months of 2011

| Rank | Magazine | Paid circulation | % change from last six months of 2010 |
|------|----------|------------------|----------------------------------------|
| 1 | AARP the Magazine | 22,407,421 | −5.6 |
| 2 | Better Homes and Gardens | 7,617,844 | −0.8 |
| 3 | Game Informer | 7,514,460 | +48.1 |
| 4 | Reader's Digest | 5,560,046 | +0.5 |
| 5 | National Geographic | 4,480,788 | −0.3 |
| 6 | Good Housekeeping | 4,341,426 | −1.7 |
| 7 | Woman's Day | 3,886,853 | −0.2 |
| 8 | Family Circle | 3,569,811 | +0.8 |
| 9 | People | 3,298,390 | −0.9 |
| 10 | Time | 3,298,390 | −0.5 |
| 11 | Ladies' Home Journal | 3,232,354 | −15.8 |
| 12 | Taste of Home | 3,230,514 | −0.7 |
| 13 | Sports Illustrated | 3,178,760 | +0.1 |
| 14 | Cosmopolitan | 3,040,013 | +4.6 |
| 15 | Prevention | 2,874,117 | −0.9 |

Source: *Advertising Age* Data Center. http://adadge.com/datacenter, accessed July 18, 2012.

are called **consumer magazines** because their readers buy and consume products and services that are sold through retail outlets and that may be advertised in those magazines. Think of a magazine that you or your friends read for fun—for example, *InStyle, Men's Health, Time, People, Essence, Cosmopolitan, Vanity Fair, Wired*, or *Maxim*. It's likely to be considered a consumer magazine. Table 9.1 lists the top 10 in terms of their print circulation in 2011. Note that most of even these high-flying magazines lost readers. The major exception was *Game Informer Magazine*, which was tapping into the surge of interest in video games.

## Literary Reviews and Academic Journals

This category includes hundreds of publications with small circulation figures—in the thousands compared to consumer magazines' tens of thousands and far more. **Literary reviews** (periodicals about literature and related topics) and **academic journals** (periodicals about scholarly topics, with articles typically edited and written by professors and/or other university-affiliated researchers) are generally nonprofit; funded by scholarly associations, universities, or foundations; and sold by subscription to individuals and libraries through the mail. Examples are the *Journal of Communication* (a scholarly journal from the International Communication Association), *The Gettysburg Review* (a literary review of short fiction, poetry, essays, and art), *Foreign Affairs* (a journal of opinion from the Council on Foreign Relations), and *Harvard Lampoon* (the oldest humor magazine in America).

Many literary reviews and academic journals have websites where visitors can learn about the publication, subscribe to it, and perhaps download a digital version of an article for a fee. If the academic journals are owned by major publishers such as Elsevier, Oxford, Routledge, and Sage, they are also likely to be included in electronic journal collections that the publishers sell to libraries. So, for example, if you go into

**consumer magazines**
magazines aimed at the general public

**literary reviews**
periodicals about literature and related topics

**academic journals**
periodicals about scholarly topics, with articles typically edited and written by professors and/or other university-affiliated researchers

your college's electronic library and search for *Journal of Communication*, you may well find decades of its issues accessible via your computer.

## Newsletters

**newsletter**
a small-circulation periodical, typically four to eight pages long, that is composed and printed in a simple style

A **newsletter** is a small-circulation periodical that is composed in a simple style. It typically runs four to eight pages when printed. The rather plain look of a newsletter often matches not only its need to suppress costs (because of its usually small circulation) but also its editorial purpose: to convey needed information in a straightforward way.

When we hear the term "newsletter," many of us may think of the information bulletin of a church or school. We are less likely to know about the large number of newsletters used in business. They often center on specific areas of an industry, and they are published frequently—usually weekly or biweekly. They address decision-makers and provide statistical trends and news about a targeted area of business. Executives pay a lot of money for those newsletters, from a few hundred to a few thousand dollars per subscription.

Today, most newsletters are circulated via the web, e-mail, or both. It's quicker than postal mail and saves lots of money on postage. Subscribers can easily print out electronic newsletters to read, if they wish. Earlier we discussed MediaPost as a trade magazine publisher. If you go to Mediapost.com, you will see that the company also describes itself as "an integrated publishing and content company whose mission is to provide a complete array of resources for media, marketing and advertising professionals." Among those resources is a "portfolio of daily and weekly email newsletters." There are over 50 of them, and they provide news in the categories of online media (e.g., *Online Media Daily*), traditional media (*MediaDailyNews*), and marketing (*Marketing Daily*). You might find one or more of the newsletters useful. There is no subscription fee; they are supported by advertising and by MediaPost's various conferences.

## Comic Books

**comic book**
a periodical that tells a story through pictures as well as words

A **comic book** is a periodical that tells a story through pictures as well as words. Comic books were developed in the 1930s, as publishers of cheap ("pulp") magazines that presented detective, romance, action, and supernatural science stories tried to take advantage of the popularity of newspaper comic strips to boost sagging sales. They put their material into comic-strip form and sold it in a complete story unit as a comic book.

Today, comic books run a wide gamut. Archie Comics publishes traditional titles, aiming at girls and boys aged 6 to 11 years—*Archie*, *Betty and Veronica*, *Sabrina the Teenage Witch*, and the like. Valiant publishes hero-centered titles such as *Bloodshot*, *H-O*, and *Archer & Armstrong*. IDW Publishing targets teens and young adults with heroic adventure and science fiction tales such as *The Transformers*, *30 Days of Night*, and *Angel*. A **graphic novel** often refers to an illustrated story that aims to be longer and more developed than a comic book. The two forms do slide into one another, though. IDW, for example, lists *30 Days of Night* versions under both its comic book and graphic novel categories.

**graphic novel**
an illustrated story that aims to be longer and more developed than a comic book

For decades, comic book characters have flown across media, including toys, T-shirts, lunch boxes, TV shows, video games, movies, and more. Movies seem to be the holy grail of adventure-oriented comic book companies. Success in that realm has been enjoyed by the two largest comic-book firms in terms of overall circulation,

Marvel Comics Group and DC Comics. Time Warner owns DC Comics, which is one reason flicks about *Batman* and *Superman* appear under the Warner Bros. movie banner. Marvel Comics is a subsidiary of Marvel Entertainment, which the Walt Disney Company bought in 2010. Spider-Man and *The Avengers* are Marvel characters that have become the hubs of hit movies. Although this sort of jackpot is the acknowledged aim of Valiant, a company executive told the *New York Times* in 2012 that despite his firm's desire to pursue movie deals, the character and action have to work first as an illustrated story. "Readers are very discerning, and they are not looking for a movie pitch in comic book form," he said.[1]

## Financing Magazine Publishing

In recent years, the advertising market has been tough for magazines. In the consumer magazine area, print advertising revenues declined 23 percent from 2007 to 2010—from $14.1 billion to $10.9 billion. In the business-to-business sector, print ad revenues went down 28 percent, from $8.8 billion to $6.3 billion. Analysts blamed some of the drop on the severe recession that began in 2008. Some marketing experts pointed out, though, that during the recession advertisers were learning how to use lower-cost digital media such as the web and mobile apps to reach audiences they had reached with magazines. Consequently, they argued, many advertisers would not bring back their previous high magazine budgets even when the economy got a lot better. As Ann Moore's comments in this chapter's introduction indicate, these considerations led magazine executives to try hard to adapt their products to the digital era.

As you might imagine, some magazines make a lot more money than others. The Magazine Publishers Association estimated that the top 50 advertisers in magazine spending brought in 39 percent of all magazine ad revenue in 2011.[2] Table 9.2 lists the magazine industry's major patrons: the advertisers who spend the most money on magazine advertisements.

Beyond money from advertising, magazines bring in money from readers. Unfortunately for industry executives, 2007–2010 saw circulation losses in single-digit percentages each year on the part of trade and consumer magazines. Not only did that

**Table 9.2**  Top 10 Magazine Advertisers by Total Ad Dollars Spent

| Rank | Company | Total ad dollars spent, 2010 (in millions) |
| --- | --- | --- |
| 1 | Procter & Gamble | 1,096.9 |
| 2 | L'Oreal | 556,1 |
| 3 | General Motors | 409.6 |
| 4 | Kraft Foods | 347.3 |
| 5 | Pfizer | 333.3 |
| 6 | Johnson & Johnson | 293.4 |
| 7 | Nestle | 285.3 |
| 8 | Time Warner | 260.4 |
| 9 | Merck & Co. | 233.1 |
| 10 | Unilever | 227.8 |

Source: *Advertising Age* Data Center. http://adadge.com/datacenter, accessed July 18, 2012.

loss reduce the amount of money brought in from single copies and subscriptions; it also meant advertisers were able to reach fewer people through magazines. Single-copy purchases particularly took a hit on the consumer side. When it comes to consumer magazines, buying single copies can be quite a bit more expensive than subscribing. A single copy of *InStyle*, for example, cost $4.99 in 2012, whereas an entire two-year subscription (26 issues) could be had for $26. When it comes to trade magazines, prices swing from high to zero. The show-business weekly *Variety* charged more than $200 for a year's subscription in 2012. At the same time, nearly two-thirds of trade magazine readers receive trade periodicals that are free.

## Controlled Circulation Magazines

Why the free trade magazines? Advertisers are so interested in paying to reach people who work in certain industries that trade publishers can support the production and distribution of these magazines at no cost to readers. This type of magazine is called a **controlled circulation magazine**. Consider, for example, *Medical Economics,* a magazine for doctors about the business of medicine. Its circulation is "controlled" in the sense that the publisher—rather than the reader—decides who gets it. *Medical Economics* creates a list of doctors whom advertisers would likely consider useful targets and mails issues to those people only. Postal rules require publishers to ask readers annually if they want to continue receiving the material.

One type of consumer magazine that often has controlled circulation is the **custom magazine**. It is typically created for a company with the goal of reaching out to the company's customers or other people (such as government officials) it wants to impress. *American Way*, given out on American Airlines flights, is one example of a custom magazine. Kraft Foods sends *Food & Family* free to 12 million homes, according to Totem Communications, which produces it for Kraft. Totem's work for Kraft is a good example of how "custom" is being transformed by the convergence of digital and paper. Several years ago, a custom magazine would have stood on its own. Now, in the words of Totem's website, it is part of a "custom media program reaching over 12 million consumers [in the United States and Canada] via an integrated magazine, video, e-newsletter and digital-content solution." Totem has also been expanding the digital components of the magazine into countries beyond the United States and Canada.[3]

## Paid Circulation Magazines

The overwhelming majority of consumer periodicals are **paid circulation magazines**—in which readers of a magazine purchase either a subscription or a single copy. Competition for advertising among consumer magazines is intense—as such, a magazine can't raise its ad rates enough to cover its production and distribution costs. As a result, consumer magazines must rely on a dual revenue stream—from both advertisers and readers.

Advertisers who are considering buying space in business or consumer magazines carry out research on the magazine's readers before they put down their money. The most basic information is **circulation**—the number of units of the magazine sold or distributed free to individuals in one publishing cycle. Publishers can hire a company such as the Audit Bureau of Circulation (ABC) or the Business Publications Audit of Circulation (BPA) to inspect ("audit") their shipments on a regular basis and certify that the number of copies they claim to circulate is, in fact, the number they

**controlled circulation magazine**
a magazine whose production and mailing is supported not by charging readers, but (typically) through advertising revenues; the publisher, rather than the reader, decides who gets the magazine

**custom magazine**
a controlled circulation magazine that is typically created for a company with the goal of reaching out to a specific audience that the company wants to impress

**paid circulation magazines**
a magazine that supports its production and mailing by charging readers money, either for a subscription or for a single copy

**circulation**
the number of units of the magazine sold or distributed free to individuals in one publishing cycle

the audience's ability to acquire products. We've already seen how *Men's Health* and *Seventeen* emphasize their readers' ability to spend. Similarly, seeking to position itself as the place for car ads, *AutoWeek* draws on information from MRI to boast to potential advertisers that its readers are influential: "72% of *AutoWeek* subscribers gave purchasing advice on specific brands of vehicles in the past 12 months."

**Drawing a Loyal Audience**  In today's competitive media environment, it is not enough for a magazine to have a distinctly attractive audience on its rolls. Any number of magazines (or other media) may make similarly alluring claims. A magazine's business executives therefore must convince advertisers that the magazine is edited so effectively that the people who receive it read it consistently and thoroughly—presumably so thoroughly that they pay attention to the ads. *AutoWeek*, for example, asserts that its subscribers "spend an average of 83 minutes reading each issue; 93% of them read 4 out of 4 issues." *Parade* magazine states that it "engages readers at home on their favorite day of the week, Sunday. For more than three generations, Americans have turned to PARADE to be inspired, informed, entertained and empowered."

## THINKING ABOUT MEDIA LITERACY

Most consumer magazines court specific audiences, but they also want to ensure that those audiences keep coming back. What do you think these magazines need to do in order to attract and retain busy audiences today? What incentives might they offer? What practices might turn audiences away?

**Creating a Conducive Environment**  As the *AutoWeek* and *Parade* statements suggest, publishers understand that from an advertiser's standpoint a magazine is above all a platform for persuasive messages. That is, advertisers want to convince audiences that certain products and services are worth buying. Advertisers particularly like magazines with articles and photos that create a conducive environment for their products or services.

It is no accident that in *Ladies' Home Journal*, *Redbook*, *Woman's Day*, and other women's service magazines, you're likely to find ads for foods in the recipe section. In fact, publishers and editors often develop new magazine sections to attract advertisers that would find these sections appealing. In the digital realm, magazines offer applications (apps) for mobile phones that bring particular aspects of the magazine features to the fan. *Style* magazine offers an app that shows mobile videos from fashion shows. Advertisers that want to be associated with such activities can sponsor the apps or advertise within them.

**Setting an Efficient Price**  Publishers know that they must present advertisers with a competitively low cost per thousand (or cost per mil, CPM) readers if they want to get or keep business. Of course, a CPM is truly low only if the consumers that the magazine reaches are the consumers that the advertiser is targeting.

Say, for example, that you represent an advertiser that wants to use *Time* to reach upper-class executives who are interested in world affairs. If you advertise in the general edition of *Time* magazine, you might get a relatively low CPM (say $15) when all the readers are taken into account. When you consider only upper-class executives who read the magazine, however, your CPM actually may be much higher because you are paying to reach so many people that you do not want. It is more efficient to use one of the special *Time* editions that target highly paid executives. In fact, *Time's* printing technology is set up so that your ad can target people based on their executive status and their geography—executives living in the northeastern United States, for example. The CPM may be higher than the CPM for *Time*'s general audience, but you will get the specific audience you want.

Cost per thousand is still an important consideration for magazines in the digital environment. Although media kits typically reveal the advertising rates for the physical magazine, they rarely do so for the digital platforms, even though they often provide information about the people who interact with the website, mobile apps, and other incarnations of the periodical. What the media kits do detail are the acceptable formats of ads on the magazine's digital properties, from the sizes in pixels of various banner ads to the kinds of animation that may be linked to them and the approach advertisers need to take to audio in the ads. (In a *Men's Health* ad, for example, sound must be initiated by the individual visiting the site.) Many online magazines offer video "articles," and they sometimes sell ads before, during, and/or after the presentations; these "in-video ads" are called pre-rolls, mid-rolls, and post-rolls, respectively. Commercials in videos are generally more expensive than banner ads because more advertisers want them, and fewer sites offer them than offer the banners. Consequently, video ads will typically have higher costs per thousand.

## Producing the Magazine as a Branded Event

An increasingly important way that a major magazine company tries to keep advertisers and get new ones is to position every title not just as paper-bound reading material but as a personality—a brand—with which readers want to engage in many areas of their lives. In doing this, magazines have become central actors in the movement of materials across media boundaries that we discussed in chapter 2. We've already seen that a major way in which they interact with their audience is through digital media. Another is by expanding into other media and staging events. In both, the magazines invite strong advertising participation. Let's look at examples.

*Forbes*, a business-oriented consumer magazine, describes its convergent approach to media as "Many Access Points. One Powerful Brand." It boasts what it refers to as "the Forbes brand," which stands for "the unshakable belief in the power of free enterprise" and an ability to deliver "information in ways that suit our audience's needs—at any given time of day, week or year—through our portfolio of Forbes brand properties." Those properties include

- the main magazine;
- several international editions;
- a separate *Forbes Asia* magazine;
- a magazine mailed to over 300,000 female readers of *Forbes*;
- a travel website aimed at upper-level executives;
- Forbes Events in which "Forbes editors and other business and lifestyle experts" offer "business leaders and affluent consumers . . . insights and information critical to their success";[5]
- *Forbes on Fox*, a weekly 30-minute program on the Fox News channel;
- Forbes Properties—art galleries in New York and a number of estates that create environments in which advertisers can "foster relationships with current and potential prospects in unique and memorable settings";[6] and
- the international edition of *Forbes* online.

In January 2013 Forbes launched its 26th international edition, *Forbes Afrique*, thereby increasing the global reach of the Forbes magazines. Forbes also has digital versions of its U.S.-based magazines and *Forbes Asia*.

One analyst on the consumer side of the business commented in 2011 that "faced with dwindling circulation and competitive pressures, magazine publishers are restructuring their business models to integrate digital platforms more prominently." The same could be said regarding trade magazines. Many of the trade publishers also have begun to place increased emphasis on setting up trade fairs and conferences as well as digital trade sites to make money.

Magazine events are by no means confined to this elite level. Look at any magazine's media kit, and you'll see how executives try to help their advertisers reach their readers beyond the page and website. For example, *Seventeen* offers its advertisers the ability to associate themselves with mall events that it stages across the country. Or consider the Martha Stewart Collection of upscale merchandise at Macy's. This venture is in addition to the image of pleasing domesticity that celebrity Martha Stewart projects not just in her magazines but also through satellite radio and television. As the SiriusXM satellite radio website declares, "Martha Stewart and her team of lifestyle experts will teach, advise, and inspire you." And all of this extends to social media such as Twitter and Facebook.

## Distribution in the Magazine Industry

**M**agazine distribution refers to the channel through which the magazine reaches its exhibition point, the place where the reader sees it (see Figure 9.3). We've already seen that magazines are now available in digital form as well as in print. The distribution activities among these forms are quite different, but executives see both realms as part of the larger goal of encouraging target audiences to see magazines as brands relevant to their lives that they want to access wherever they go.

When it comes to print materials, trade magazines are typically sent to subscribers through the mail. Comic book companies distribute their products by themselves or through wholesalers to special stores that stock them. Distribution for consumer magazines takes place in two ways. First, consumer magazines are distributed through the mail to readers who have a **subscription**—a long-term order for a magazine that is paid for in advance, for a predetermined period of time or number of issues. Second, independent distribution companies deliver consumer magazines to retail outlets where **single-copy sales**, or the sale of copies one issue at a time, take place (see Figure 9.4). Each of these avenues has its benefits and obstacles. From the standpoint of a small publisher, the mail is a useful distribution channel because the U.S. Postal Service (USPS) must accept all comers; therefore, a magazine from a major firm will not have precedence over a magazine from a minor firm. But small publishers are also angered that the USPS has raised rates for magazines that send out relatively few copies, but not for magazines that send out large numbers of copies that are bundled by ZIP codes. This "bulk-rate" approach privileges big mailers over small ones and makes it difficult for magazine publishers with small circulations to stay profitable.

**magazine distribution**
the channel through which a magazine reaches its exhibition point

**subscription**
a long-term order for a magazine that is paid for in advance, for a predetermined period of time or number of issues

**single-copy sales**
the number of copies of a magazine sold not by subscription, but one issue at a time

## THINKING ABOUT MEDIA LITERACY

What advantages do you think single-copy sales offer consumers over subscriptions? What advantages do subscriptions offer? How might a digital subscription prove more beneficial to consumers than a subscription to a print edition?

**Figure 9.3**

Magazine distribution. Although for print products, distribution methods (subscription or single-copy sales) have remained the same over time, digital distribution has revolutionized the magazine industry and accounts for an increasingly large amount of revenue for magazine publishers.

To create, build, and maintain circulation, small magazine firms may have to rely on rented lists to contact new potential readers. They also may turn to a direct-mail subscription firm such as Publishers Clearinghouse that advertises many magazines to consumers. However, subscription firms charge the magazines about 90 percent of the price the subscriber pays, meaning the magazine benefits from the new reader only as a target for its advertisers. Some magazines may nevertheless find these firms helpful in enlarging their circulation in order to attract sponsors. Although large magazine companies sometimes take the sweepstakes route, they can do a lot on their own to increase circulation. With their own expensively produced databases of potential readers, they can mail highly targeted ads that entice desirable readers to subscribe; that way, they get to keep the subscription money for themselves. Large magazine firms are also able to put a lot of money and effort into one of the most difficult aspects of their business—getting readers to renew their subscriptions—a process that can take several mailings and a lot of money.

Although creating, building, and maintaining a magazine's circulation by mail is difficult, doing it through magazine distributors is even harder. These national distribution firms reach a few hundred regional wholesalers, who in turn service well over 100,000 local retailers—typically supermarkets, drugstores, convenience stores, and newsstands. In retail, the field is complex and highly competitive, with the largest magazine racks carrying only about 200 titles. For this and other reasons, only a small number of magazines (notably *Woman's World*, *First For Women*, and *US Weekly*) use single-copy sales as their main strategy. At the same time, single-copy sales can bring in more per-copy revenues than subscriptions, which are often sold at substantial discounts off the cover price. Display on the newsstand and in the supermarket is an important way to introduce the magazine to new readers, who might use cards inside the periodical to become subscribers.

The distributor, the wholesaler, and the retailer are able to make money because they pay a discount off the cover price when they purchase the magazine. The total discount that a publisher typically gives up is about 50 percent. That is, if an issue's cover price is $4, the distributor, wholesaler, and retailer together make $2 on each issue. But as in the book publishing industry, the publisher typically takes responsibility for unsold copies. If a wholesaler gets too many copies and returns proof of the unsold ones, the publisher refunds the money to the national distributor (which credits the wholesaler and retailer) and absorbs the loss.

When it comes to websites and other digital activities, distribution means sending content through internet service providers, which act as exhibitors. To the dismay of many magazine publishers, major phone manufacturers or operating-system creators—Apple, Google, and Microsoft—have also gotten into the distribution space. They create "app" marketplaces on their devices and require that all applications that phone users don't access through the phone's web browser be routed through their marketplace. In doing so, they act as wholesale distributors between the publisher and the exhibitor. If you've ever downloaded a song or video from iTunes to a handheld device, you have participated in an app marketplace. One reason device manufacturers create these digital distribution warehouses is to make sure that the apps that go on their phones work properly. Another purpose is to collect fees from firms that want the manufacturers to sell the magazines through the marketplace. The large magazine firm Time Inc. refused to sell magazine-app subscriptions through Apple's iTunes marketplace because it didn't want to share these revenues and because Apple was keeping information about the subscribers to itself. After several months of argument with magazine executives, Apple's leadership agreed to inform magazine firms about the people who were signing up for their magazines via iTunes, and Time Inc. agreed to sell subscriptions via the service. Though the parties denied it, some observers believed Apple was giving Time Inc. a better revenue-sharing deal than its competitors because of its status as the largest U.S. magazine publisher. For their part, Time Inc. executives explained the reversal by saying they didn't want to miss out on what had clearly become an important way to gain readership.

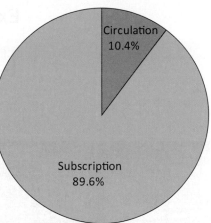

**Figure 9.4**

Today single copies make up 10.4 percent of circulation; subscriptions make up 89.6 percent. Source: http://www.magazine.org/insights-resources/research-publications/trends-data/magazine-industry facts-data/2012-new-single.

## Exhibition in the Magazine Industry

If you access the internet via a browser, you probably take your ability to download content for granted. That is the result of the pressure for net neutrality that federal regulators have placed on internet service providers (ISPs); see chapter 6. In the case of magazine apps for the mobile environment, net neutrality considerations don't exist. Nevertheless, ISPs haven't interfered with the magazine-app marketplace.

It's easy to see how a magazine can get lost in a display if the distributor is not able to pay a good slotting fee for its product.

The main limitation they place is on gigabytes. If you stream or download many movies, you may reach a service cap that prevents you from accessing your magazine via apps or a browser unless you pay extra.

Although publishers don't have to deal much with exhibitors online, the situation is quite different in the print realm. The challenge is to make sure that the wholesaler is placing the title in the retail outlets where it will sell best and in places in those outlets where it will best be seen. Walk over to a magazine stand or a supermarket checkout area, and you will see more than a few magazines vying for your attention. In view of the large number of magazines that wholesalers have to stock, they may not pay much attention to new magazines from small companies unless the magazines are heavily advertised. In fact, it may be difficult for small companies to get retailers to accept their periodicals, and when they do get picked up, they may not get prominent positions on the rack.

The largest magazine firms have an additional advantage at the newsstand. Companies such as Time Inc., Condé Nast, and Hearst own their own national distribution firms. They therefore have more influence with wholesalers concerning where and how their magazines should be placed with retailers. The large companies also have the cash to pay retailers **slotting fees**, or payments that ensure that their products will be placed prominently at the front of magazine racks or at the checkout counters of supermarkets. Smaller firms can't afford this kind of advantage.

**slotting fees**
payments that ensure that companies' products will be placed prominently at the front of magazine racks or at the checkout counters of supermarkets

Despite the attention that publishers, particularly big ones, pay to single-copy exhibition, sales are not moving in a direction that consumer magazine publishers like. From 2000 to 2008, the share of single-copy circulation declined from 15.9 percent of all consumer magazine copies distributed to 11.8 percent of the copies distributed.[10] That is a particular problem for magazines that rely on single copies to recruit new subscriptions. They have to find new ways to get potential readers to see the value of a long-term relationship with their magazines.

## Media Ethics and the Magazine Industry

Now that we have a good grasp on how the magazine business works, let's step back as citizens and explore one of the key ethical complaints that social critics have lodged against the industry. This key ethical complaint has to do with a central feature of magazines: advertising. As you know, a great deal of what we have said about the U.S. magazine business throughout this chapter comes down to attempts to attract advertisers. This fact of industry life raises another concern of media critics: the influence of advertisers on magazine content.

As the executives of consumer and business magazines feel increasing competition from other media and other periodicals, the possibility of routine advertiser influence on editorial matter looms large. Some publishers and editors may not consider this a problem. After all, they will point out, advertisers have always had a profound influence on the magazine industry because they underwrite most of the production costs. As a result, the very basic decisions about target readers—whom to attract and whom to ignore—are typically made with commercial sponsors in mind. Similarly, as we have noted, decisions about what types of sections to place in a new periodical or to add to a mature one are made with an eye toward potential advertisers. Recipe columns draw food ads. Travel columns draw travel ads. The list goes on.

Magazine publishers and editors have consistently recognized that this kind of sponsor influence is the unavoidable price of doing business in a commercial world. One long-standing principle of magazine editing, however, is that ads must be clearly separated and differentiated from other content, such as through use of a different layout and a different font. U.S. postal regulations require that ads that don't clearly look different from editorial matter be labeled "Advertisement."

Situations in which advertisers are mentioned or shown as part of the editorial content of the magazine are more difficult. Some companies, such as Time Inc., have had explicit policies that keep the business and advertising activities of its magazines away from the editorial activities. They call this separation the "church–state divide," with editorial being the church and business being the state. The partition is supposed to ensure that editors do not worry about offending advertisers, since they do not deal at all with people from the ad department. Nevertheless, for obvious reasons, most magazine editors do not go out of their way to antagonize regular sponsors, and this can sometimes lead to ethical problems. Should, for example, a women's magazine run articles about the dangers of smoking if its major advertisers are cigarette firms?

Research on the relationship between smoking ads and the lack of articles about smoking in women's magazines suggests that cigarettes have quietly "bought" protection from bad publicity by paying for ad space. Publishers counter that because cigarettes are legal, they have a right to carry these ads. Besides, publishers say, cigarette companies often purchase expensive space, such as the back cover, that is difficult to sell on a regular basis.

Publishers and their editors often face other difficult decisions relating to advertisers. For example, say you are running a controlled circulation magazine, and a potentially large advertiser agrees to purchase space on condition that the advertiser's activities will be regularly mentioned in the editorial matter of the periodical. What do you do? If your magazine needs (or covets) the money, would you say to yourself that the advertiser would probably be mentioned in the magazine anyway, so it's fine to agree? The American Business Press code of ethics states that such activities are prohibited. Trading ads for editorial coverage certainly occurs in the business press, but because this practice is rarely admitted, no one really knows how often it takes place.

## THINKING ABOUT MEDIA LITERACY

Many magazines today are publishing stories with medical and health advice. How do you think these stories might be affected by advertiser influence? How do the advertisers benefit from these stories? Do the readers benefit from them?

What about consumer magazines? How vulnerable are they to mixing advertising and editorial matter and to making themselves merely the instruments of the highest bidders? Magazine specialists J. William Click and Russell Baird years ago quoted a former editor of *Good Housekeeping* as contending that although "to set out deliberately to antagonize advertisers would be senseless . . . when there was reason to investigate and expose, there was no hesitation." Click and Baird also note that "editorial integrity is much easier to maintain if the [magazine] is in solid financial condition and does not desperately need to woo advertisers."[7] The problem is that as magazines compete for narrower audiences than ever before and as publishers worry about losing advertisers to a bad economy and other media, they worry more about their financial stability.

An article about breaking into the magazine industry quoted the advertising production manager of *Entrepreneur* as encouraging editorial people to cooperate with the advertising staff. Speaking to aspiring publishers, he said,

> You'll want to work hard to develop a strong relationship between your advertising and editorial production departments. One of the reasons we're so successful is that we've always worked well with our editorial team to develop the give and take that's necessary to make both sides of the business happy and successful.

Many people in the magazine industry would cringe at these sorts of relationships. But with even the largest magazines struggling, signs are emerging that the lines between the business and editorial departments are beginning to blur in some magazines, that the publishers of some magazines are actively encouraging "partnerships" with advertisers they feel reflect their audiences' lifestyles. The practice of seeing magazines as brands that set up events and internet sites sometimes encourages dimmed lines between the editorial department and advertisers. An example is when a fashion magazine mounts a show of the latest dresses, and the bulk of the clothes going down the runway are made by the companies sponsoring the event.

This blurring of the lines between editorial and advertising is a topic magazine executives don't like to discuss. Every now and then, though, the realities of advertiser power come through in talks at industry conferences and in trade magazine interviews. A few years ago, for example, a marketing executive for Hachette magazines, which then owned *Car and Driver* (now Hearst does), was quite clear about his desire not to alienate advertisers in videos about cars on the magazine's website. He said that although the published written review would still pull no punches, the online magazine would likely eliminate the negative aspects of the review from the video to make sponsors (likely the car company) comfortable. "If the editorial staff has said that the vehicle is overweight, we'll never say it's light," he said. Instead, "we'll focus on other aspects of the vehicle on behalf of the consumer."

This type of concern with making sure potential advertisers are not worried about editorial matter seems common. Some magazine firms are going even further, particularly in their digital versions. Not only are they trying not to offend advertisers; they are trying to attract marketers by offering to present marketers' products in ways that link them to the magazine's brand and even make them appear part of the magazine's editorial matter. The media kit of *Men's Health* suggests this possibility in a way that requires only a bit of reading between the lines. MensHealth.com, it says,

> offers a variety of custom advertising opportunities that link to highly engaging editorial platforms. We have the resources and the experience to integrate your message seamlessly within our content in ways that will align your brand with our audience of active, affluent guys in every area of their digital life.[8]

The extent of widespread editorial sensitivity to marketers and collaboration with them is one of the most basic issues that we can question about the changing magazine industry. In the interest of media ethics and literacy, it will be useful to follow this trend through industry trade magazines such as *Advertising Age* and *Folio*. In the long run, the integrity of the U.S. media system is at stake in the outcome.

The magazine industry is an enormously varied business that runs the gamut from widely read consumer periodicals to narrowly read newsletters. There are huge differences in types of readership and sources of financial support. Perhaps the one major similarity among magazine practitioners is that all are being buffeted by the changes taking place in the broad media environment. New electronic media present both challenges and opportunities. Though always intense, competition for readers is becoming more intense. In decades past, such challenges have led to profound changes in several parts of the industry. There are signs that advertisers have a growing influence on content in some areas of consumer magazines. It will be interesting to see how the magazine industry adapts to the 21st-century media world and how that affects what we get from magazines and how we get it.

# CHAPTER REVIEW

Visit the Companion Website at www.routledge.com/cw/turow for additional study tools and resources.

## Key Terms

You can find the definitions to these key terms in the marginal glossary throughout this chapter. Test your knowledge of these terms with interactive flash cards on the *Media Today* companion website.

academic journals
brand
business-to-business (b-to-b)
   magazine or trade magazine
circulation
comic book
consumer magazines

controlled circulation magazine
custom magazine
graphic novel
literary reviews
magazine distribution
magazine publisher
media kits

newsletter
paid circulation magazines
segments
single-copy sales
slotting fees
subscription
upscale readers

# Questions for Discussion and Critical Thinking

1. Consider your own use of print and online magazines. Based on your experiences, what advantages does the online edition present over the print edition? How do you think these advantages pose a threat to the print edition? Do you think this relationship might change in the future?

2. You are the editor of a women's magazine, which is having a hard time selling ads. Cigarette companies are offering to buy full-page sponsorships. Should you accept the ads? Should you run articles about the dangers of smoking if you know your major sponsors might leave? What would you do? Why?

3. Magazines increasingly need to be specialized, with a clear sense of the audience they want to reach, the topics they want to cover, and the personality (i.e., attitude and viewpoints) they want to present if they are to remain competitive in their industry. Why do you think magazines need to make so much effort in order to distinguish themselves from other publications out there? Could a magazine aimed at a more general audience even have a chance? Why or why not?

4. Several magazines described throughout this chapter have positioned themselves as brands in particular ways. Considering today's converged media environment, what advantages does this branding offer when magazines bring content to other media such as the internet, television, and radio?

5. Why do you think the conflict between "church" and "state" is more pronounced in major magazine companies today than in the past? Do you think the blurring of these lines poses a problem? Why or why not?

## Case Study
### EXPLORING MAGAZINE MEDIA KITS ONLINE

**The Idea** Many magazines post their media kits online for prospective advertisers to consider. The kits can provide interesting insight into the different ways that magazines try to position themselves among the competition and promote their ability to reach certain audience segments.

**The Method** Choose two magazines that you believe aim at similar audiences—for example, two women's magazines or two consumer automotive magazines. In Google, type the name of the magazine in quotation marks and the words "media kit" in quotation marks. For example, type "car and driver" and "media kit."

Explore each media kit along the following lines: the magazine's description of its goals or mission; the way it talks about its editorial material; the ways it describes its circulation; the ways it talks about its audience and audience segments; the various ad formats and offers for reaching its audience and audience segments; and the media activities in which it engages beyond the magazine pages. Then write a five-page report that explains the similarities and differences among the ways the magazines argue for their place and advantage within their industry.

# The Recording Industry 10

"For so long, the recording industry had control. But now that monopoly has ended, they don't know what to do."

**RICK RUBIN, MUSIC EXECUTIVE**

"Piracy is an insidious act performed in an almost offhanded way by people who would never consider stealing anything else."

**GLEN BALLARD, SONGWRITER AND MUSIC PRODUCER**

## CHAPTER OBJECTIVES

1   Sketch the history of the recording industry

2   Describe the enormous changes taking place in the industry as a result of digital technologies and convergence

3   Explain how a recording is developed, from the time an artist creates a song to the time the recording ends up in your collection

4   Explain the ways in which artists and recording companies make money

5   Decide where you stand on the major ethical issues facing the recording industry today

Can you imagine being sued for sharing songs and other kinds of music? That was the fear of many college students during the first decade of this century. The Recording Industry Association of America (RIAA)—the organization that represents major record companies—was on a tear beginning in 2003 to file charges against individuals who it claimed were circulating music illegally, without compensation to the record firms or artists whose music was being distributed. Many college students—and even a 12-year-old girl—were caught in the RIAA's dragnet. It's not clear how many people the RIAA sued. Some observers say more than 35,000, whereas the RIAA itself says the number is closer to 18,000. Evidence suggests that out-of-court settlements ran between $3,000 and $5,000.[1] People who refused to pay what was demanded, though, received even greater shocks. In 2009, for example, a jury ordered a Boston University graduate student to pay $675,000 for downloading and sharing 30 songs illegally.[2]

The RIAA's actions seemed to result from a near-panic about the future health of its industry. With the rise of digital convergence and the spread of the internet came sites such as Napster, Kazaa, Grokster, and Morpheus, which allowed people to upload music files from their computers and share the songs with anyone who visited the "file sharing" sites. One upshot was that only 37 percent of music acquired by U.S. consumers in 2009 was paid for, according to research firm NPD.[3] The RIAA itself claims that from 2004 through 2009, "approximately 30 billion songs were illegally downloaded on file-sharing networks." While all this was happening, U.S. music sales were plummeting—from $14.6 billion in 1999 to $7.0 billion in 2011.[4] Record executives were sure piracy had taken the place of legal sales.

The outcry against the RIAA's suits, though, was so high that in 2008 it announced it would cease new suits and work through internet service providers to stop service to people who carry out illegal downloading. Critics of the organization argued in the early 2000s that one reason so much illegal file sharing was taking place was that there were no inexpensive legal alternatives for consumers to get downloads of the music they wanted. That began to change during the second half of the decade. As we will see in the following pages, after a few not-very-successful attempts to sell digital music directly to consumers, the major record companies allowed Apple and its software distribution arm iTunes to sell downloads legally and inexpensively on a large scale. That, along with the rise of other services we will discuss in this chapter, helped to generate important revenues for the beleaguered recording industry.

For the people RIAA sued, this episode in U.S. music history was quite a painful one. More broadly, people in the recording industry were feeling pain as well, as they tried to adapt to a world where audiences and competitors were using new technologies to disrupt stable corporate relationships and moneymaking approaches. These disruptions are still taking place, and a "new" recording industry is still taking shape. The aim of this chapter is to investigate where the industry is now and where it seems to be going. As you might imagine, we will be aided in the exploration by our good old categories of production, distribution, and exhibition. And we will start by providing historical perspective (via the three themes and timeline) of how the industry got to where it is.

## The Rise of Records

As late as 1880 or 1890, people growing up in a middle-class U.S. household had no recorded music in their homes in the sense that we understand it today. That's not to say that homes didn't have music. For one thing, family members often played musical instruments. Pianos were especially popular in middle-class homes. Many family members learned to play, and there was a vigorous and growing industry that published sheet music and sold it in music stores around the country.

## THINKING ABOUT MEDIA LITERACY

Since the early 1900s, the number of people learning and playing instruments has declined significantly, and with that decline has come the decline in sheet music sales. Looking at the timeline, why do you think the role of music in U.S. culture has shifted from one of production to consumption? What points on the timeline offer the strongest evidence for these shifts?

How did people know which of the latest sheet-music compositions to buy? Sometimes, the salesperson at the store would play the piece so that the customer could hear it. Other times, people heard the songs they wanted to buy at concerts of musicians and singers. If audience members at these concerts liked a particular piece, they might purchase a copy from the sheet-music proprietor. As the timeline notes, two particularly important touring sources for popular new songs were the minstrel show and the vaudeville show. The first was popular around the mid-19th century, whereas the second enjoyed its run from the late 19th century through the 1920s.

People who couldn't play sheet music could enjoy other forms of music in their homes, even before the advent of records. Wind-up music boxes were a popular way of providing in-home music. Inside these music boxes were metal rolls with specially arranged pegs on them. As the rolls turned, the pegs struck steel combs. When the combs were struck, they played notes, and so the music box played a song. By around 1890, people were buying much larger music boxes that used interchangeable disks to hit the metal bars, so that one music box could play many songs.

Another popular "music machine" was the player piano, which used a perforated roll of paper and an air-powered mechanism to get the keys to hit the strings. Some player pianos reproduced not only the notes recorded on the paper roll, but also other characteristics of the original performance, such as the pressure applied to individual keys and the loudness of notes. Note that none of these devices reproduced the actual sounds of a live performance. Enter the record player, or phonograph. Well, it wasn't nearly that simple, as you probably expect if you remember the first theme in connection with the book, newspaper, and magazine industries. Here it is in relation to records:

1. *Sound (or audio) recordings did not arrive in a flash as a result of one inventor's grand change.*

Explore the timeline (Figure 10.1), and you'll see that although Thomas Edison recorded "Mary Had a Little Lamb" in 1877, it took years for what he initially described as a "toy, which has no commercial value," to become a technology that could accurately record sound in a commercially profitable manner. Notice the role of Emile Berliner, who introduced the flat disk, which could be produced more efficiently than cylinders. Berliner's gramophone had drawbacks that took a while to fix, and it wasn't until around the 1920s that the flat disk became the standard for audio recordings.

Explore the timeline some more, and you will note that the quality of sound and reproduction in audio recordings continued changing for the better throughout the 20th century. A key development was the invention of electric amplification in the 1920s. Before its introduction, record producers needed loud instruments and voices to pick up and preserve the sound in the record. Electric amplification allowed records to capture the soft, subtle sounds of voices and instruments that had previously been too soft to pick up. The timeline shows how increasing the amount of audio material on a record as well as its quality became an important goal for recording engineers.

Why did engineers have this goal? The answer may seem obvious: "it's good to make things better." Actually, the reason is more complex than that, which leads us to the second theme:

2. *Audio recording as a medium of communication developed as a result of social, legal responses to the technology during different periods.*

Go down the timeline, and you'll see how the developments in audio recordings often resulted from competition among record manufacturers as well as among the firms that made the machines to play them. They believed that their audiences

**Figure 10.1** Timeline of the Recording Industry

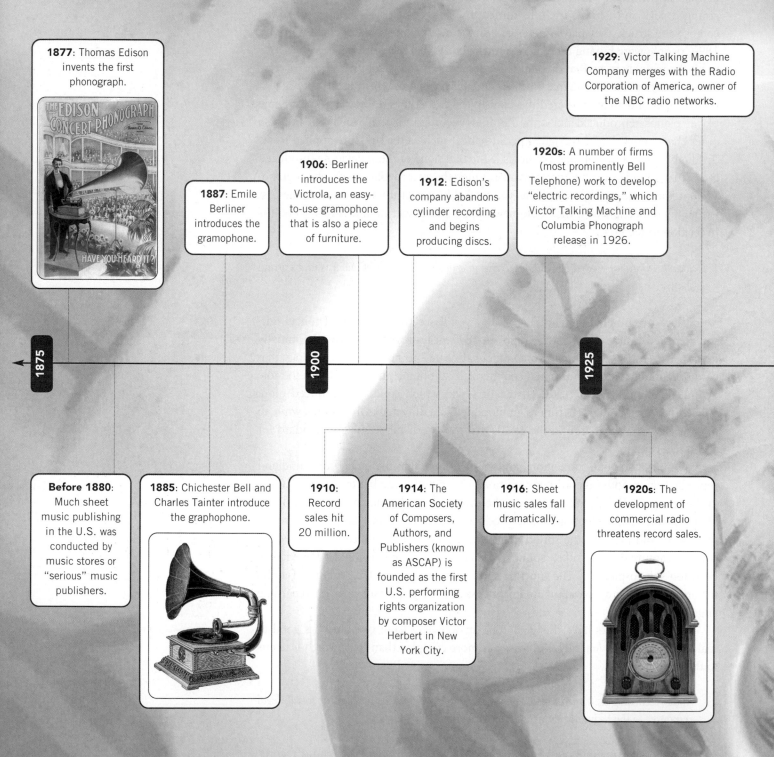

**1877**: Thomas Edison invents the first phonograph.

**1887**: Emile Berliner introduces the gramophone.

**1906**: Berliner introduces the Victrola, an easy-to-use gramophone that is also a piece of furniture.

**1912**: Edison's company abandons cylinder recording and begins producing discs.

**1920s**: A number of firms (most prominently Bell Telephone) work to develop "electric recordings," which Victor Talking Machine and Columbia Phonograph release in 1926.

**1929**: Victor Talking Machine Company merges with the Radio Corporation of America, owner of the NBC radio networks.

1875

1900

1925

**Before 1880**: Much sheet music publishing in the U.S. was conducted by music stores or "serious" music publishers.

**1885**: Chichester Bell and Charles Tainter introduce the graphophone.

**1910**: Record sales hit 20 million.

**1914**: The American Society of Composers, Authors, and Publishers (known as ASCAP) is founded as the first U.S. performing rights organization by composer Victor Herbert in New York City.

**1916**: Sheet music sales fall dramatically.

**1920s**: The development of commercial radio threatens record sales.

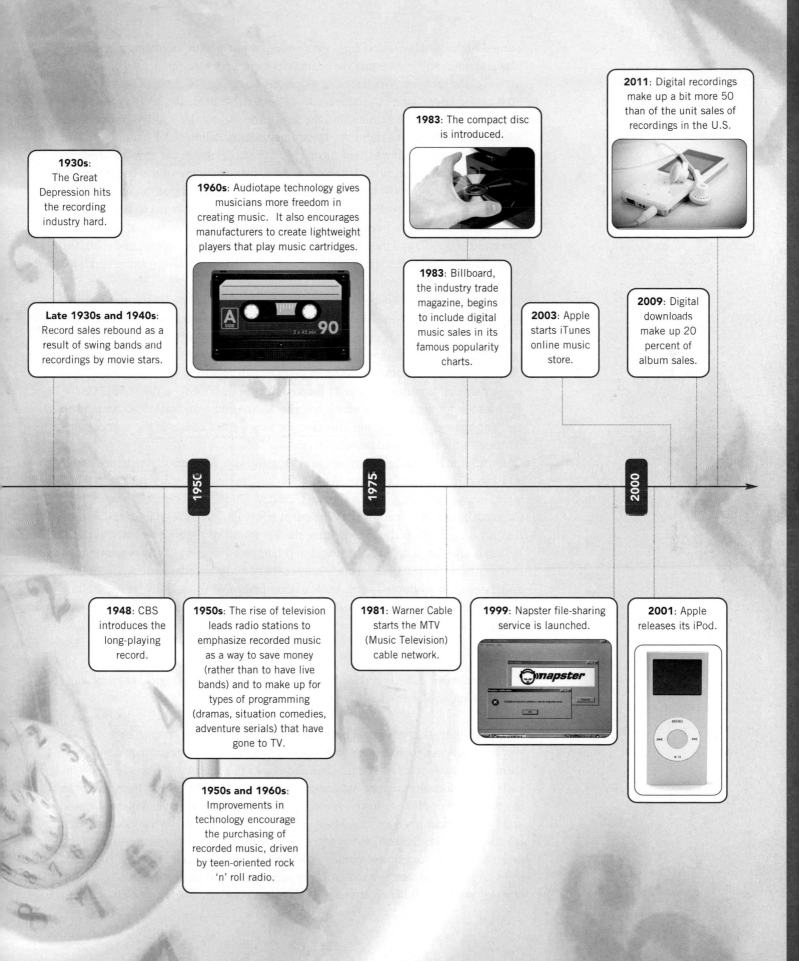

**1930s:** The Great Depression hits the recording industry hard.

**1960s:** Audiotape technology gives musicians more freedom in creating music. It also encourages manufacturers to create lightweight players that play music cartridges.

**1983:** The compact disc is introduced.

**2011:** Digital recordings make up a bit more 50 than of the unit sales of recordings in the U.S.

**Late 1930s and 1940s:** Record sales rebound as a result of swing bands and recordings by movie stars.

**1983:** Billboard, the industry trade magazine, begins to include digital music sales in its famous popularity charts.

**2003:** Apple starts iTunes online music store.

**2009:** Digital downloads make up 20 percent of album sales.

**1950**

**1975**

**2000**

**1948:** CBS introduces the long-playing record.

**1950s:** The rise of television leads radio stations to emphasize recorded music as a way to save money (rather than to have live bands) and to make up for types of programming (dramas, situation comedies, adventure serials) that have gone to TV.

**1981:** Warner Cable starts the MTV (Music Television) cable network.

**1999:** Napster file-sharing service is launched.

**2001:** Apple releases its iPod.

**1950s and 1960s:** Improvements in technology encourage the purchasing of recorded music, driven by teen-oriented rock 'n' roll radio.

wanted higher-quality sound from their products along with increasing amounts of play and durability. Sometimes the companies came up with a variety of technologies to "solve" the problem. When it came to length of recording, Columbia Records came up with the large, "long-playing record"—a platter that turned at 33 1/3 revolutions per minute (RPM), and RCA around the same time put out the 45 RPM record. Both found their places in the industry. The former became "albums" of symphonies and multiple songs, for example, and the latter became popular in the form of "singles," with one song on each side. At the same time, manufacturers of the equipment to play the music continually tried to outdo one another in claiming advantages for their devices. New formats such as the audio cassette player-recorder led to the ability to listen to recorded music in cars and on the run for up to about an hour at a time. The invention of the CD and the digital music player extended this mobility and (with the digital player) miniaturized it. The digital technologies also allowed playing music for hours at a time, far exceeding previous technologies.

It bears noting that courts have disallowed some forms of audio transfer because they violate copyright—see the timeline's items about Napster and Limewire. Also note that despite the impeccable quality of digital reproduction, sound engineers sometimes sacrificed audio quality to storability and accessibility. They did so to make their products downloadable to people with relatively slow broadband and relatively small amounts of memory for song files in their devices. An example is the MP3 format for digital audio, which compresses the audio material to accommodate efficient internet downloading. This efficient use of space comes at the cost of some richness in the reproduced music.

By now it should be pretty obvious that the developments noted previously and listed in the timeline were not the work of individuals working alone. They were the work of companies within an industry. Unlike the book, newspaper, and magazine industries we have examined in previous chapters, the audio recording industry developed not long after the invention of the first records. Edison, Berliner, and the people they worked and competed with built the beginnings of that industry. Several of the names you see on recordings today—RCA, Columbia, and Decca, for example—hark back to companies of those early years. Follow the corporate activities noted previously—the competition between RCA and CBS over a longer-playing record, for example—and you can see this new formulation of theme 3.

3.  *The recording industry developed and changed as a result of struggles to control audio recordings and their relation to audiences.*

The timeline takes you through decades of attempts by record companies to develop ways to reach out to audiences with both technologies and content that would lead them to purchase records. The timeline also shows that music publishers (e.g., Chappell) and performance rights organization (e.g., ASCAP and BMI) have been critical to the development of the industry. A music publisher ensures that the writers of music and lyrics get paid when artists use their compositions on records, on media (e.g., radio, television, and the internet), and in concerts. In return the publisher receives part of the artists' royalties—sometimes as much as 50 percent. A performance rights organization signs up artists who want to make sure they receive the royalties they deserve from radio stations, movies, or other outlets that use their compositions. These organizations keep part of the royalties as well; the rest go through the publisher to the composers and songwriters.

The timeline also shows that the recording industry and the radio industry have become intertwined. Recording artists have provided the sound of many radio shows, and radio has helped sell their records. Companies big and small have targeted various audiences by social categories (e.g., "race music"), supposed location ("country" or "hillbilly" music), age (teen music), and music genre (classical, jazz). A few firms emerged that controlled much of the industry's product.

If you follow the timeline to the near-present, you will realize that winning the struggle to control doesn't always mean success. Despite the power of many recording industry companies such as Fisher, RCA, and Sony to create technologies that define how people hear and buy audio recordings, that clout is by no means absolute. Sometimes executives have struggled to control developments they had not intended and could not control. Consider the creation by home-technology firms of products that could copy the record companies' products. The ability to transfer music from records to home tape recorders marked the beginning of the challenge to the record companies' control over their material. It's true that record-to-tape and tape-to-tape transfers could not make perfect reproductions because features of the analog sound (see chapter 1) inevitably did not copy impeccably. With the invention of the digital compact disc (the CD) and the personal computer, though, it became quite possible to make perfect digital copies (see chapter 1).

In the contemporary environment of convergence that we have discussed throughout this book, the digitization of music has meant not only that audiences can hear the same sound performances on many different devices but also that recording firms can promote their products by having them, or parts of them, hyped on many different devices. Yet from an industry standpoint there has been a major downside to these remarkable convergent technologies: the technologies have led to wholesale copying as audience members have found ways to share files across media without paying for them. Such activities led to the industry furor about piracy that we discussed at the start of this chapter.

So what is this industry like now? What new activities are emerging to take into account the digital challenges facing the recording companies and their artists in relation to production, distribution, and exhibition? Let's take a look.

## An Overview of the Modern Recording Industry

A broad look at the recording industry in the United States makes three things about the industry very clear:

1.  Its ownership is international.
2.  Its production is dispersed.
3.  Its distribution is concentrated.

Let's look at each of these areas individually.

### International Ownership
To get an idea of the international nature of the recording business, consider that only one of the three largest recording companies—Universal Music Group, Sony Music

Entertainment, and Warner Music Group—is based in the United States. Universal is owned by Vivendi, a French conglomerate. Sony Music is owned by the Sony Corporation of Japan. Warner is owned by a New York–based conglomerate called Access Industries, which has chemical and hotel as well as media holdings. The country of origin of each of these firms, however, does not typically dictate the kind of music it tries to circulate in the United States.

"Think globally; act locally" is a phrase that is very apt for executives in the recording industry. Fifteen or 20 years ago, their perspective was quite different. At that time the major firms (often called "the majors") concentrated on taking American and British hits and making them into worldwide mega-hits. Now, although many top American and, to a lesser extent, British artists still sell well globally, the real action and money seem to be in finding top local and regional talent.

Before we leave the topic of international ownership, it's important to note that until quite recently there was a fourth major, the EMI Group, based in the United Kingdom; EMI was a major global company, but it fell into hard times, with $4 billion in debt. Citigroup bought it and in 2011 announced it would sell its record division to Vivendi (owner of Universal Music Group, or UMG) and its publishing assets to a group of firms led by Sony. Critics of the transaction pointed out that EMI's addition to UMG would mean that UMG would control too high a percentage of music sales, particularly in Europe. As of late 2012, UMG was negotiating with European regulators about which of its assets it could sell that would allow it to buy EMI's record company. Nevertheless, when we report data in this chapter about the majors, EMI will typically be included.

## Dispersed Production

With or without EMI, the recording industry is dispersed at the production end. In this context, fragmentation means that there are thousands of companies turning out recordings they would like to sell. These recording firms are called independents because they are not owned by the major companies mentioned previously, which are also the major distributors in the industry. Although the United States has always had many small firms producing recordings, the number of independents has soared in the past decade. In fact, independent record distributors as a group have become the third largest distributor of recorded music in the United States, after Sony.

One reason for the rise of independent firms is that newly affordable, powerful personal digital recording technology has enabled small companies to produce high-quality sound. The availability of this technology has led to a flood of independent recordings. Many small production firms circulate their products to stores or sell them directly on the web or at concerts instead of hooking up with the major distributors. Some independents are actually quite large operations. Epitaph Records is a standout example. Guitarist Brett Gurewitz of the band Bad Religion started the company in the 1980s to sell his group's records. Over time, Gurewitz turned Epitaph into a broader business. He signed several other groups, mostly creators of punk and pop punk, to his label and helped them find ways to distribute their work. One of the label's big successes was with the band The Offspring. Epitaph released the group's 1994 album *Smash*, which had sold more than 16 million copies by 2009. That made it one of the best-selling independent label albums of all time.[5]

## Concentration of Distribution

Such huge successes by independents are highly unusual. The major recording companies are the distributors of choice because of the immense power they bring to the marketplace. Because they represent many popular artists, they have access to radio stations, cable systems, stores, and popular websites for promoting acts that small distributors might not have. Being large organizations, they are able to spend a lot of money to push artists their executives believe have promise. Figure 10.2 shows that in the United States during 2011, the four majors (including EMI) captured 88 percent of the sales of all physical albums, 84 percent of digital albums, and 85.2 percent of digital single music tracks (i.e., individual songs). Independent distributors made up the rest.

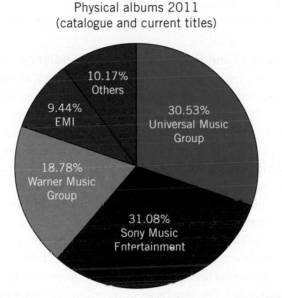

Physical albums 2011
(catalogue and current titles)

10.17% Others
9.44% EMI
30.53% Universal Music Group
18.78% Warner Music Group
31.08% Sony Music Entertainment

**Figure 10.2**

The percentages of physical albums, digital albums, and digital tracks sold by each major and "others" (the "independents")

Source: "The Nielsen Company & Billboard's 2011 Music Industry Report," Business Wire, January 05, 2012, via Lexis Nexis.

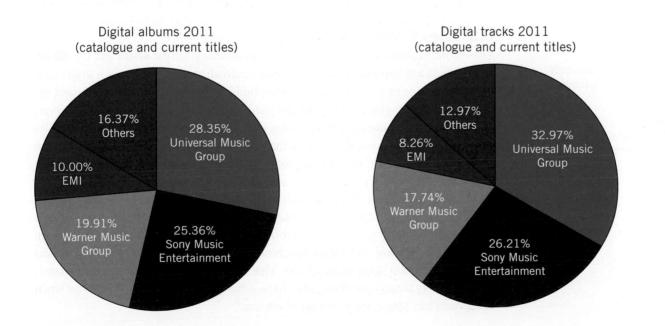

Digital albums 2011
(catalogue and current titles)

16.37% Others
10.00% EMI
19.91% Warner Music Group
28.35% Universal Music Group
25.36% Sony Music Entertainment

Digital tracks 2011
(catalogue and current titles)

12.97% Others
8.26% EMI
17.74% Warner Music Group
32.97% Universal Music Group
26.21% Sony Music Entertainment

The chart indicates that the distribution power of the majors is indeed strong. Go to the part of each company's website that describes the company (the "Overview" or even just the home page's description), and you'll see pride in this clout. The companies insist that their size and their strong international presence give them a stature and credibility that make them the distributors of choice. It's no wonder that when some performers who are signed to independent labels begin to make it big, they move to one of the majors. The Offspring, for example, moved to Sony Music two years after its *Smash* hit with Epitaph.

## THINKING ABOUT MEDIA LITERACY

What advantages do you think the music industry has in concentrating distribution as much as it has? Are there any disadvantages? How might an independent artist lose out in this situation?

### Features of the Recording Industry Audience

Who buys the output of the recording industry? Although many factors, including gender, income, geographic location, ethnicity, race, and cultural interests, undoubtedly explain why people listen to certain types of music, probably the most important category in the industry's understanding of the actual purchasing of music is age. When it comes to age in the United States, the recording industry concentrates much marketing on young people because traditionally they have bought more recordings than people in other age groups. The NDP research company regularly conducts a representative survey of people in the U.S. population aged 13 and older. The firm found that people aged 13–25 accounted for 24 percent of the spending on recordings in the United States in 2011, which is substantially more than their percentage in the population, around 15 percent. People aged 35 to 49 years and older accounted for 31 percent of the spending—also a lot more than their presence in the population at 20 percent.[6] The purchases of recordings by older people, by contrast, tended to be smaller than their percentages in the population.

### U.S. Sales: Singles versus Albums

**single**
a product that contains only one or two individual musical recordings

**album**
a collection of a dozen or more individual songs

The recording industry releases its product in two lengths: the **single** and the **album**. An album is a collection of a dozen or more individual songs, whereas a single contains only one or two songs. Singles are the building blocks of radio formats, and the airplay of these singles is often how the public first learns about an artist. However, artists and labels make their money from album sales, and the recording companies often do not price physical singles so that they are worthwhile purchases relative to the albums. As a result, in 2011 sales of physical singles (typically in CD form) were negligible compared with sales of albums; they constituted only less than 1 percent of sales. By contrast, on iTunes and other sites, digital singles are often far less expensive than albums—$1.29, 89 cents, or even 69 cents compared with several dollars. In that space, buyers go after their favorite songs. According to Nielsen SoundScan, which tracks physical and digital purchases of recordings, in 2011 U.S. consumers bought 1.27 billion single digital tracks. That's a very impressive number, but recording executives worry that their firms have a harder time maintaining profits when consumers buy single songs instead of albums.[7]

The good news for them is that digital album sales have been picking up. During 2011, Americans bought about 330 million albums—228 million physical albums and 103.1 million digital ones. That means that digital albums accounted for 31 percent of—nearly one of every three—album purchases in 2011. To see how time has changed, consider that in 2006 digital albums made up only 5.5 percent of albums sold. More important, sales of digital recordings grew by 9.2 percent in 2011 compared to 2010, offsetting the decrease in physical recording sales of 7.7 percent. The upshot was that the industry shipped slightly more recording products in 2011 than the year before. Such a year-on-year increase hadn't happened since 2004.[8] Optimists hoped their industry's fortunes were changing for the better.

## Changing Media Platforms

In addition to pointing to sales growth, 2011 was also important as the first year that the percentage of digital recordings sold was higher—even though just a teeny bit higher—than the percentage of physical sales: 50.3 percent to 49.7 percent. As you undoubtedly know, whether the recording is a single or an album, commercially sold music can be placed on a number of media. Today's physical media include compact discs (CDs), CD singles, music videos, and vinyl records. Among the physical media, about 95 percent of the units that recording companies ship are compact discs. CDs are, in fact, durable and have excellent sound quality. Increasingly, however, the convenience and low cost of digital platforms have made them the preferred choice.

The term "**digital platforms**" refers to the several ways people can purchase digital music. All typically involve a form of **downloading**, which means that the company sends the song as a digital file to the buyer's computer, tablet, or smartphone. RIAA figures show that during 2011, 91 percent of the downloads were to computers, and 7 percent were to mobile devices. The rest involved downloading songs from store kiosks and purchasing subscription services such as Rhapsody. Many sites use the popular MP3 option for downloads. Apple's iTunes site uses the AAC format, which experts say presents better sound quality at the same downloading and signal processing speeds.

Although people paying to own songs is the most common way recording companies sell music via digital platforms, the companies do have two other major opportunities: streaming and ringtones. **Ringtones** are bits of songs (or even new musical compositions) that people download to their mobile phones and that play when someone calls them. Their popularity has been declining, according to the RIAA. **Streaming**, by contrast, is on the rise. It takes place when a website sends an audio file to a computer or other device so that it can be heard while it is coming into the device and then disappears. Some sites such as Rhapsody and Spotify sell subscriptions for streaming. For example, you pay $75 a year and can stream as many songs as you want, and you can download them to your smartphone. However, you cannot share them or exchange them among devices. (The sites do give you the opportunity to buy the song or an album, though.) Sites such as Pandora, Shoutcast, and IHeart-Radio also give users the opportunity to listen to pre-chosen music streams based on certain genres—for example, jazz or classical—for free if they listen to commercials. Because it is much like a radio station, the activity has come to be known as **internet radio** or **online radio**.

**digital platform**
vehicle for receiving digital information; a computer, mobile phone, and iPad are three digital platforms for downloading music

**downloading**
transfer of data or programs from a server or host computer to one's one computer or digital device

**ringtones**
bits of songs (or even new musical compositions) that people download to their mobile phones so that they play when someone calls them

**streaming**
process in which an audio file is delivered to a computer-like device from a website so that it can be heard while it is coming into the device but cannot be saved or stored

**internet radio or online radio**
pre-chosen music streams based around certain genres—for example, jazz or classical—provided free to listeners and paid for by commercial advertisements, much like a radio station

**Table 10.1** Albums Sold by Genre (in Thousands)

| Genre | 2011 | 2010 | % change |
| --- | --- | --- | --- |
| Alternative | 55,032 | 53,727 | 2.4 |
| Christian/gospel | 23,734 | 24,226 | –2.0 |
| Classical | 9,566 | 8,957 | 6.8 |
| Country | 42,923 | 43,718 | –1.8 |
| Jazz | 11,077 | 8,780 | 26.2 |
| Latin | 11,814 | 12,350 | –4.3 |
| Metal | 32,206 | 32,554 | –1.1 |
| New Age | 1,929 | 1,660 | 16.2 |
| R&B | 55,435 | 57,871 | –4.2 |
| Rap | 28,251 | 27,328 | 3.4 |
| Rock | 105,685 | 103,709 | 1.9 |
| Soundtrack | 13,232 | 16,412 | –19.4 |
| Electronic | 10,049 | 8,735 | 15.0 |

Source: The Nielsen Company & Billboard's 2011 Music Industry Report," Business Wire, January 5, 2012, http://www.businesswire.com/news/home/20120105005547/en/Nielsen-Company-Billboard%E2%80%99s-2011-Music-Industry-Report, Accessed December 11, 2012.

### Diverse Music Genres

The recording industry releases music in many genres targeted to different slices of the music-buying public. According to Nielsen SoundScan, in 2012 rock music remained the most popular genre of physical product; it accounted for one of every three recordings sold in the United States. As Table 10.1 shows, R&B held the second spot, with country not far behind. You may (or may not) be surprised that classical music made up only 1.9 percent of the recordings, and "religious" music (which includes gospel, inspirational, and spiritual recordings) made up a higher 6.5 percent.

So we know what kinds of musical recordings have moved more quickly than others. But how do those products get to their audiences in the first place? What happens between the time someone gets an idea for a song and the moment the recording of that song is sold? To answer this basic but difficult question, we turn to issues of production, distribution, and exhibition.

## Production and the Recording Industry

Chances are you know someone who is in a band. Maybe the band plays at local college bars, and the members practice when they are not working at day jobs to pay the bills. Perhaps the band's members have even recorded a demonstration (or "demo") song at a local studio and given you a copy. They are working hard while they wait for their big break: a contract with a record company, which they know will bring them fortune and fame in Hollywood. Will they still take your phone calls when they become big stars?

Across the country, many aspiring recording artists are waiting for their big break. Most of these artists never record a professional album and eventually move on to other, more lucrative lines of work. The age-old advice to struggling artists—"Don't quit your day job"—is especially true in the record business.

## MEDIA TODAY & CULTURE WOMEN TAKE THEIR PLACE IN HIP-HOP

Hip-hop is one of the most popular music genres not only in the United States but also in the world. The world of hip-hop music is male-dominated, and the lyrics and the music videos often refer to or show misogynistic representations of women.

For example, the music video for Nelly's *Tip Drill* represents an extreme in these kinds of representations. The women are merely sex objects. Throughout the video, women clad in bikinis or less writhe about for the men. The camera focuses on their breasts and behinds as they dance. At one point in the video, Nelly throws cash at a woman's crotch area, and later he draws a credit card down a woman's behind.

Women hip-hop artists claim their place within hip-hop on their terms, however. In her article about women in hip-hop videos, Rana A. Emerson notes how "Black women are quite firmly the subjects of these narratives and are able to clearly and unequivocally express their points of view."[1] These women push past the one-dimensional representations, such as through asserting their own sexuality, flaunting their independence, and collaborating with other black female hip-hop artists.

In asserting their own sexuality, these women adopt the subject position by turning the tables and turning men into sex objects. For example, Lil' Kim responds to a verse within the song "Magic Stick," wherein rapper 50 Cent asserts his sexuality. She fires back with her own assertions, claiming, "I got the magic box." In their video for "Shoop," Salt-N-Pepa rap as they objectify the muscled men appearing with them.

Along with this assertion of sexuality, these women flaunt their independence, showing that they need no men in order to live and live well. Many represent themselves as strong black women, such as in the work of Lauren Hill or Erykah Badu. The lyrics to Destiny's Child's "Independent Woman," for example, mention all the things they are capable of buying, including their own clothes, jewelry, car, and house, while asserting, "I depend on me."

Further, these women establish their own spaces for themselves and their sisters. They frequently do this through collaborating with other women on their songs and in their videos. The remix "Not Tonight," for example, brings together Angie Martinez, Lil' Kim, Left Eye, Da Brat, and Missy Elliott. The women perform the song together, and some take turns with a solo part before rejoining the group. "Sock It 2 Me" brings together Missy Elliott, Lil' Kim, and Da Brat. In the video Elliott and Kim attempt to escape capture, and just as they are about to be caught, Da Brat arrives to save them. This sort of collaboration also pairs newer artists with more established ones, such as when Keyshia Cole worked with Missy Elliott and Lil' Kim on "Let It Go."

### Artists Looking for Labels, Labels Looking for Artists

Realistically, artists know that they are much more likely to start their recording careers with small independent firms willing to take a chance on them. Still, many struggling bands dream about being "discovered" by a label of one of the major record production and distribution companies. A **label** is a division of a recording firm that releases a certain type of music and reflects a certain personality. It is very much like an imprint in the book industry. For example, among Universal's many labels are Island Def Jam (for rap and hip-hop), Verve (for jazz and blues), MCA Nashville (for country), and Mercury Records (for classical).

The point person in a recording company for signing new artists is the label's **A&R** person. A&R stands for **artist and repertoire**, a term that dates back to the time when record executives saw themselves as shaping artists by choosing the collection of songs (the repertoire) that an artist played or sang. Today, the function of the A&R person is to screen new acts for a firm and determine whether or not to sign those acts. Like baseball scouts looking for the next Cy Young Award winner, A&R people are constantly searching for new acts for their label (see Figure 10.3).

**label**
a division of a recording firm that releases a certain type of music and reflects a certain personality

**A&R (artist and repertoire)**
recording firm executives who screen new acts for a firm and determine whether or not to sign those acts

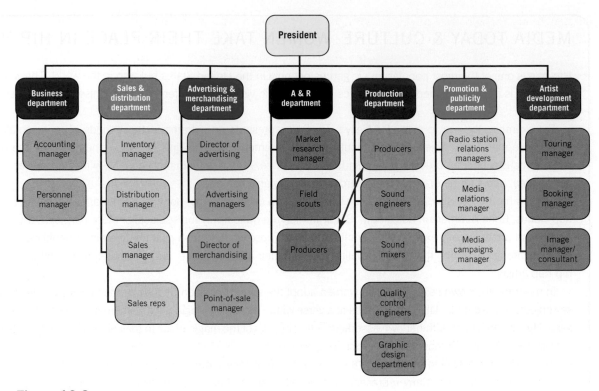

**Figure 10.3**
Organization of a typical recording company

Suppose your friends, after years of paying their dues in nightclubs throughout the state, are approached by the A&R person for Universal's Interscope record label (which distributes work by Lady Gaga, 50 Cent, and Eminem, among many others). Somehow, the record company executive learned about the band—perhaps through hearing a demo record or attending a performance at a local bar—and wants to sign it to a record deal. At this point, certain relationships come into play. Negotiating the terms and conditions of these relationships is very important. Many struggling artists, unfamiliar with the business side of the artistic process and desperate to make it in the recording industry, have entered into bad, one-sided agreements. Billy Joel, 'N Sync, Janet Jackson, and Tupac Shakur are only a few of the well-known musical acts who have fallen into this trap.

Many artists on their way up realize the necessity of hiring a competent manager to coordinate the development their career; to help arrange business opportunities for them; and to handle the receipt, disbursement, and accounting of their revenues. In return for these services, the manager earns a percentage—typically 10 to 25 percent—of all the revenue the artist earns. Of course, artists try to hire a manager who will further their career, preferably one who knows the intricacies of the music business and most of the important people in the business. Despite artists' understandable wish for a manager who will act exclusively on their behalf, good managers often handle several artists at once.

Other business relationships for the band quickly follow. Most acts hire an attorney and an accountant to assist their manager in handling their often complex business affairs. Artists may also join a union such as the American Federation of Musicians (AFM) or the American Federation of Television and Radio Artists (AFTRA), which provide access to television and motion picture work, represent the artists' interests with various media industries, and offer benefits such as group health insurance. Joining a royalty-collecting association, such as the American Society of Composers, Authors and Publishers (ASCAP) or Broadcast Music, Inc. (BMI), is also important. But of all these contractual relationships, the most important one is the one the artist develops with a record label. Simply put, the music industry today revolves around the issuance of recorded music and the joint effort of the artist and the company to sell as many records as possible.

## Finding Music to Record

Artists, of course, need music to perform. Many popular artists today perform music that they have written themselves. Yet at some point in their careers, virtually all artists record music that someone else wrote. There are several ways for an artist or group to find music. Music publishing companies maintain catalogs of songs, and many record stores still sell printed copies of music, usually intended to be played on a guitar or piano. When an artist uses any song in these libraries commercially, songwriters and their publishing companies expect to be paid a share of the money the production firm receives; this payment is called a **royalty**.

## Royalties

There are important legal steps that songwriters must take, such as filing their songs with the U.S. copyright authorities, in order to ensure that they make money from a song they have written even if they do not sing it themselves. But it is difficult for the owner of a song to keep track of where and how the song is performed. For example, songwriters are entitled to compensation whenever a radio station plays their songs, a band performs their work at a nightclub, or a record company releases their songs.

The industry distinguishes between two types of royalties for the creators of music and the words to the music: performance royalties and mechanical royalties. **Performance royalties** are paid to composers, their publishers, and their record labels when their material is used (live or recorded) in front of audiences via stage acts, jukeboxes, radio, television, or online radio. If performers or organizations want to use the music, they must obtain a "performing rights license" from music societies. Agencies such as ASCAP and BMI exist to make sure that publishers and songwriters are compensated for the use of their work. These agencies take over the daunting task of verifying compliance with the law on behalf of the rights holder. ASCAP is the largest of the performing rights organizations and represents more than 370,000 songwriters, composers, and publishers. Though the airing of one covered song on a radio station may result in a royalty payment to ASCAP or its agents of only a fraction of a penny, these small amounts add up. According to its annual report, in 2009 ASCAP received more than $846.3 million on behalf of its member songwriters and publishers. ASCAP uses formulas derived from surveys that rank the popularity of each songwriter's songs during the year to determine each member's share of the revenue after expenses and distributes that share to each member.

**Mechanical royalties** are collected as a result of the sale of physical media (e.g., CDs) and the sale or download of digital recordings, including albums, individual tracks, and ringtones. In the United States any artist has a right to record a musical work as long as the creators have already given permission to someone to make a public recording of that work. If you write the melody for a song and your friend writes the lyrics, you have the right to tell the singer Taylor Swift she cannot perform it or make a record of it. But if you have already allowed Katy Perry to release a track of the song, you have to allow Taylor to do it—though Taylor must have a mechanical license. (You can still refuse to allow Taylor to perform it onstage.) Both Taylor Swift and Katy Perry must pay you according to a royalty rate set by the U.S. government.

**royalty**
the share of money paid to a songwriter or music composer out of the money that the production firm receives from the sale or exhibition of a work

**performance royalties**
paid to composers, their publishers, and their record labels when their material is used (live or recorded) in front of audiences via stage acts, jukeboxes, radio, television, or online radio

**mechanical royalties**
collected as a result of the sale of physical media (e.g., CDs) and the sale or download of digital recordings, including albums, individual tracks, and ringtones

The Harry Fox Agency is the dominant U.S. organization that issues mechanical licenses and collects and disperses mechanical royalties. The licenses are valid only for physical or digital sound recordings distributed to the public for private use (i.e., not for use in stage shows or on radio) in the United States. If you go to HarryFox.com to learn more about mechanical royalties, you will find that the subject can get quite complex. The same is true regarding performance royalties; check out ASCAP.com, for example. A large part of this domain is the province of entertainment attorneys. Their job (for a fee) is to help composers and lyricists, as well as performing artists and record labels, navigate the terrain legally and profitably.

### Producing a Record

The firm that has signed a contract to record an artist's album will often line up a producer to oversee the recording of the album and its final sound. The producer, like the artist, is generally compensated on a royalty basis. A typical royalty percentage for a good producer is 2 to 4 percent of the total retail sales of the album.

The producer is responsible for obtaining copyright clearances, lining up session musicians if needed, staying on budget, and delivering a high-quality master tape to the record company. An important first task for a producer is to line up a good place to record. Studios with good equipment and good engineers can be found all over the world, and producers carefully select a studio where the artist will be comfortable and productive. It may come as no surprise to you that many major albums are produced in quiet, out-of-the-way places where the artists are unlikely to be disturbed.

A producer also works to keep the project on budget. Each extra day in the studio can cost thousands of dollars. Record companies can financially penalize the recording artist for cost overruns by taking the money out of the artist's royalties. After the recording sessions have been completed, the producer and artist finish mixing the songs on the album. They pay special attention to making the songs fit the specific technical requirements of the label, such as the length of each song, and also to identifying any potential singles on the album.

Taylor Swift's *Red* album was one of the top-selling albums of 2012. It sold 1.2 million copies in its first week. Swift is the only woman to have two albums achieve that kind of success. Yet much of her $57 million dollar wealth (making her the second-richest female musician in 2012—under Britney Spears) came from her tour, perfume line, and Cover Girl advertising contract.

### Self-Producing Music for Sale

For the many struggling singers and musicians who don't have a contract with a recording firm, there is another route. Because of the difficulty of getting noticed even by independent companies, some artists decide to produce their own CDs and then sell them at performances and maybe even in some stores. They also may place tracks of their music online for people to hear and perhaps even purchase. The good news is that recording studio rates have been halved in the past few years. Some artists don't even bother with studios. It is possible to make a perfectly acceptable recording in someone's basement, and people often do. Moreover, because of intense competition in the CD manufacturing business and the movement toward digital downloads, the cost of making CDs has plummeted too.

### Compensating Artists

After artists have worked on a recording, they typically want to get paid. Artists are compensated for their performance on recorded music in one of two ways. If they help to make an album but are not central to it, they are paid an hourly fee. In accordance with the rules of their union, these studio musicians or singers are remunerated with at least the industry scale. Many studio musicians and singers are quite comfortable with their predictable payments. Artists who are in great demand as backup talent for albums receive far more than scale and can make a very good living.

The central artists on the recording, in contrast, are generally not paid by the hour. They receive royalties for their work. Many artists believe that they can hit the jackpot if their recordings sell well and so prefer royalties over flat fees. A typical recording industry contract gives an artist or group 10 to 15 percent of the retail price of an album. Yet the road from laying down music tracks to making money from them can be quite rocky. Specifics about how many singles or albums a musician must sell to break even are hard to come and may vary greatly by the individual artist and his or her recording contract. Two points seem clear, though: making money is not easy, and the flow of money varies depending on the music format.

These two points are underscored in a spreadsheet that one knowledgeable observer of the industry created in 2010 to illustrate music artists' earnings.[9] The analyst looked at the format, the average retail price, how much a record label receives of the sale, and how much the musician receives of the revenue after expenses. One conclusion is that a self-pressed CD will yield the most money: a solo musician needs to sell only 143 copies of an album a month (at $9.99 per album) to make a "minimum wage" of $1,160 per month ($13,920 per year). But if the physical CD is released by a recording label, the calculations suggest that the artist must sell 3,871 copies a month to reach minimum wage. If the label sells the digital album via iTunes at $9.99, the monthly sales need to be 1,229. But if the label sells a single on iTunes rather than an album and the price is 99 cents, the musician must sell 12,399 a month to earn minimum wage.

Note that all these sales yield just the minimum wage for one musician! Members of a band would get even less. The numbers suggest how difficult it is to make a good living recording music. Independent labels generally have even more restrictive artistic contracts than the majors do. Contracts with independent labels are for a longer period than those with the majors, and they provide lower royalty rates than those of the majors, require the artists to share the copyright on songs with the labels, and may even demand a share of the artists' merchandising monies. Independent-label executives claim that such contract stipulations are necessary because a label incurs large financial risks when it subsidizes a new artist. Recording companies can spend hundreds of thousands of dollars breaking a new artist in, and many new artists, despite the best efforts of both sides, never contribute to the overall profitability of the record company. In addition, the executives argue, independent firms have to pay a percentage of their income to the firms that distribute their product.

The hope of making it truly big is always there for the artists, however. If they become superstars, their power relationship with the record label equalizes. For artists with proven market demand, their agents and lawyers can negotiate generous deals. At the height of his popularity, Michael Jackson reportedly received a royalty rate of 20 percent from one of Sony Music's labels.

## Distribution in the Recording Industry

And who says you need a CD at the start? Many musicians load their work onto sites such as MySpace and YouTube with the hope they'll get noticed. MySpace is, of course, a distribution venue, but you don't have to pay anything to get on it.

You can sell your music from it, and although the site may take a cut of the sale, the amount is far less than a label takes. If a group called the Morning Light can produce its music in a basement and release its songs on MySpace, Facebook, or YouTube just a click away from Justin Timberlake, why would any group choose to sign with a recording firm, whether an independent or a major?

## THINKING ABOUT MEDIA LITERACY

Some artists choose to make their music available for free downloading through sites such as Jamendo.com and even MySpace. Why do you think artists might choose to go this route? Further, some of these artists allow people to remix their songs through Creative Commons licenses. Do you think their act of offering this music has any impact on changes in music development? Why or why not?

Ingrid Michaelson has had great success with a small management company rather than a major record label.

It's a good question, particularly if you pay attention to stories such as Ingrid Michaelson's. Her experience makes the online model of distribution seem extremely attractive. An aspiring singer/songwriter/pianist and part-time teacher of theater to kids, Michaelson was 24 when in 2005 she set up a page on MySpace with the aim of networking with musicians and potential fans. Within a year, her soft vocals and romantic piano had attracted a management company that specializes in finding little-known acts for TV shows, advertisers, movie companies, and video games. The firm placed three of her songs on ABC's popular *Grey's Anatomy*, and the exposure sent one of her songs, "The Way I Am," to number 13 on the iTunes pop music chart. She had to pay 15 to 20 percent of her music royalties to the management company, but not having a label allowed her to keep most of what was left. The *Wall Street Journal* pointed out,

Because Ms. Michaelson doesn't have a record-label contract, she stands to make substantially more from online sales of her music. For each 99-cent sale on iTunes, Ms. Michaelson grosses 63 cents, compared with perhaps 10 or 15 cents that typical major-label artists receive via their label.

By mid-2007, she had sold about 60,000 copies of her songs on iTunes and other digital stores. She used some of that money to press (and sell) her own CDs, arrange distribution for them, make T-shirts for concerts, and hire a marketing company to produce promotional podcasts.

As of late 2012, with MySpace giving way to other online avenues for popularity, Michaelson was still distributing her albums without a label, mostly online. Go to her website, and if you click on one of her albums or singles, it will give you the choice of purchasing it from iTunes (digitally), Amazon (digitally or as a physical CD), or Barnes & Noble (as a physical CD) or going to a website run by the Coalition of Independent Music Stores, where you can purchase the physical album from a store near you. But these links represent merely the tip of a complex business, and Michaelson is by no means building it herself. She arranges her tours as well as her sale of fan-oriented clothes and doodads with the help of a management and licensing company, a booking agent, and a publicist. And like all contemporary music artists, she and her image-makers are cultivating her personality and fans carefully via Facebook, Twitter, Tumblr, and YouTube.

What, then, does a label bring to an artist's career? The short answer is sustained cross-media exposure. Getting the ears of powerful concert promoters, radio program executives, and cable gatekeepers who select music for large, though targeted audiences is a task that requires a strong organization with much experience. Don't ignore that even Michaelson didn't get her TV exposure on her own; a management company led the way. Record labels insist that they have the ability to push her further. The manager for several bands, including Death Cab for Cutie, adds that an unsigned artist risks losing momentum. "There's a lot more components to an artist's career than being featured prominently on a show, just as there's more to it than having one hit on the radio," he stated. Someone agreeing would point out that because Michaelson had no record label or distributor, her first two CDs, *Slow the Rain* and *Girls and Boys*, which she put out herself in 2004 and 2006, respectively, weren't carried by many traditional music stores, even in 2007 when she was becoming quite well known.

As in other mass media industries, having good distribution avenues does not ensure that a recording will be a hit. Without the strong ability to place recordings where people will hear them and want to buy them, the chances that a recording will be a hit diminish considerably. And having a hit with a major label builds on itself. Go to YouTube's home page for music to see the popularity of artists with major labels at work. Although you will certainly note performers distributed by independent labels—Boyce Avenue is an example—you are much more likely to find performers who have one of the majors behind them, such as Justin Bieber, Rihanna, Chris Brown, Nicki Minaj, and Katy Perry.

Distribution does not simply mean being able to send recordings to an exhibition location—for example, a local Walmart or iTunes. The real distribution power of the "Big Three" and the other major producer-distributors lies in their ability to generate buzz among an artist's potential fans that will induce brick-and-mortar and digital retailers to carry his or her records and display them properly. The task is an imposing one. The statistics must be frightening to anyone who is hoping to hit it big without the Big Three, which together have controlled over 80 percent of U.S. music sales and around 75 percent of global music sales. Powerful distributors have the benefit of big promotional teams, liaisons with radio stations, and money for cooperative advertising. Let's take a look.

## The Importance of Convergence in Promotion

More than anything else, distributors contribute marketing expertise to building a recording artist's career. Much of that involves promotion, and much of *that* takes advantage of convergence and even encourages it. Let's first define **promotion**. Promotion involves using a variety of media to lead target audiences to learn about, or hear, a recording, in order to encourage them to purchase it. It also may include cooperative advertising, which means that the recording firm provides a retailer with a portion of the money the retailer needs in order to buy space in local newspapers or time on local radio and TV stations. All this may sound easy, but in the competitive media environment it is extremely difficult. Recording firms have particular difficulty motivating people to buy the albums of new groups because people need to hear music before they buy it. Attractive cover art is nice, but it is hard to visually "window shop" for a new album. You really have to hear the music first.

The recording industry is therefore dependent on other media to inform audiences about new products. A fair amount of promotion is non-digital. Physical stores that sell recordings also allow you to sample albums, but often the choices are limited to the ones that recording firms have paid the stores to promote. Moreover, despite the incorporation of listening posts into music stores, research has shown over the decades

**promotion**
the process of scheduling publicity appearances for a recording artist, with the goal of generating excitement about the artist and thereby sales of his or her album

that customers credit radio airplay for getting them interested in buying particular music. With the rise of Facebook and other social media, that powerful role of radio may be diminishing somewhat. People share favorite artists and tracks with friends, and fan sites sometimes give people tastes of music they might like before it gets radio airplay.

Leading audiences to the artists' sites and getting buzz going often involves taking advantage of the convergent ability of digital media and their relationships with non-digital media. Promotional work takes advantage of analog media companies' common practice of also having digital outlets. Record promoters often arrange print publicity for a recording artist—for example, an interview or album review in *Spin* music magazine or charity work that will make news. Related digital promotion may include work with online versions of the magazines or their music blogs. The paper magazine *Spin*, for example, has an active website as well as apps for smartphones and tablets. Similarly, radio stations have websites and apps that not only stream the broadcast fare but also often pay special attention to artists who would interest the stations' audiences. Record promoters can encourage the convergence of these media in ways that help the media firms (they get to play new music or interview the musicians) and publicize the product.

As you might imagine, creative record promoters put a lot of effort into media convergence in the interest of their artists' output. Think of the many labels owned by the majors as well as the many independents and their labels—and then think of the many artists the labels represent—and you can see how music promotion is a real engine of cross-media convergence. The work may include uploading videos and audio files to YouTube and Facebook fan sites while generating excitement on local radio about an artist's concert tour that will come through the station's area. In return for the on-air promotion of a group and its rock concert, for example, a radio station might receive free tickets to give away, exclusive radio interview rights when the artist hits town, and the on-air mention of the YouTube and Facebook pages to increase fan excitement.

**The Recording Industry and the Radio Industry**  Despite the web's rise, radio is still very important for the music industry. Recording-industry promotion executives focus particularly on radio program directors because they are the ones who choose the particular pieces from albums (the cuts) that get airplay on the station. The relationship between the two groups is quite symbiotic; that is, each lives off the other. Both are in the business of targeting a large but fairly narrow audience by age, gender, ethnicity, or race with a particular genre of music. A hit recording keeps listeners tuned in to a radio station and helps the station in its battle to win ratings, and airplay on the radio station converts listeners to buyers, fulfilling the goals of the record company and its artists.

Broadcasting in an auto showroom, Phil Lind (l) and Dody Goodman (r) with detectives guarding Lind after he exposed disc jockey "payola" on his show.

Still, the needs of recording company promoters sometimes conflict with those of the programmers. Many radio stations are conservative about adding new music. Program directors give preference to existing artists because those artists have a track record of success and because listeners are familiar with their sound. New artists are very much an uncertainty, and gambling on new material from unknowns might hurt the station's ratings. Music promoters also face the problem of competition. In any given week, a station may add only one new song to its playlist, whereas the various record labels may have a dozen new songs that they believe fit the station's format.

Faced with the daunting task of deciding which of the many new songs that come out each week to add to their playlists, radio station programmers supplement their own impressions of the quality of music with outside data. Several firms, such as Broadcast Data Services, now electronically monitor radio stations across the country, verify the identity of every song played on those stations, and report these data to subscribers. Nielsen SoundScan automatically records the sales of music at participating retail stores and online. Each week the SoundScan findings are used to compile lists of record sales across the country. Based on such data, various trade publications compile weekly lists of the top-selling or most-played songs.

Radio programming executives often look at these lists to help them make decisions about airplay. Station program directors also monitor their own station's request line to see whether typical listeners want to hear more of a new song. Some conduct phone surveys of listeners in which they play bits of songs and ask whether they would want to hear them on the station.

Knowing that radio stations use various pieces of data to make decisions on airplay, record executives have to work hard to get the airplay in certain markets and on particular stations that will convince program directors on the largest stations to insert a song into a playlist rotation. There are many ethical ways of doing that, but the enormous pressure to succeed in radio has also led to unethical tactics. There are reports, for example, that record company representatives have organized campaigns to flood stations with requests for a particular song. An even more unsavory activity aimed at placing songs on radio stations is **payola**—the payment of money by a promotion executive to a station program director to ensure that the program director includes certain music on the playlist. In the late 1950s, the federal government made payola illegal. In view of the millions of dollars at stake in the recording industry, though, you shouldn't be surprised that prosecutions for this kind of improper influence continue. Stories consistently circulate that newer versions of payola, in the form of drugs or other noncash favors, are given to radio executives or consultants in return for adding new songs to their stations' playlists.

Although they do not constitute a significant portion of album sales, vinyl records are making a comeback, and many bands are opting to release their albums on vinyl in addition to digital platforms.

**payola**
an activity in which promotion personnel pay money to radio personnel to ensure that the latter will devote airtime to artists that the former's recording companies represent

### Video, Television, and Movie Promotions

Until now, we have discussed the convergence of media around recordings' audio sounds. But you are probably quite aware that promotion of music doesn't stop with sound alone. During the past three decades, music videos have played an important role in driving rock, pop, and rap sales. Recording companies often help artists produce these videos because of the proven ability of a sizzling video to lead consumers to stores. We have already noted that people in search of music can find much of it on YouTube and other websites; often the material is in the form of music videos. Much of this material can also be accessed on mobile devices such as tablets and smartphones—further examples of convergence.

Universal Music and Sony wanted to ensure that artists they represent are present in music videos throughout the digital universe, so they joined with the Abu Dhabi music company to create a music video player called VEVO. You can access VEVO through its website, apps for phones and tablets, and apps for the Xbox video game machine, among other devices. Universal Music's website adds that "VEVO powers music videos on artist pages across Facebook, as well as syndicates to dozen of online sites. Additionally, through a special partnership with YouTube, VEVO is accessible in over 200 countries, expanding the platform's reach around the globe."

The ability to get music this way may make theatrical films and cable-television videos seem like positively old-fashioned ways of promoting music. Nevertheless, they remain an important vehicle for introducing specific audiences to particular types of music. Movies often hype new and old songs. Examples are "Orinoco Flow (Sail Away)" by Enya in *The Girl With the Dragon Tattoo* (2011), "Hip to Be Square" by Huey Lewis and the News in *American Psycho* (2000), and "The Times They Are A-Changin'" by Bob Dylan in *Watchmen* (2009). Then there are the music video presentations on cable television. Think of Black Entertainment Television (BET) and some of MTV's various youth-oriented channels.

As Ingrid Michaelson's experience shows, television series have also become important venues for new music, particularly by new performers. For TV producers who want to reach young adults, introducing indie artists is less expensive than paying huge amounts for stars, and it may signal to the audience that the program is in tune with the newest sounds. Advertising agencies are beginning to imitate TV series' use of new songs in this way for commercials. Although these sorts of programs and commercials may not be a place for major labels to introduce big releases from hit acts, the venues may be good for relative newbies. Moreover, the indie acts that make it to TV series are getting the kind of promotion that may well make the major labels take a look at them and decide that the publicity makes them ready to move to higher levels of popularity.

## Concert Tours

Presenting live concerts across the country is a time-honored way to promote an album. In fact, in a digital world where songs are often given away free as promotions, the way artists (and, increasingly, their labels) make money is through concert tours; the songs act as vehicles to publicize the tours. Performing is second nature for most groups; after all, many groups start out by playing local gigs in their hometown. A good manager tries to book a new group as the opening act in a tour by an established superstar, thus quickly introducing the new group to the established superstar's large audience. One often overlooked fact is that although tours have the potential to generate lots of money, the expenses also are often quite high. Experienced help has to be hired, and trucks and buses must be rented. Schedules have to be reasonable so as not to wear out the artists. Millions of dollars can be lost if a major artist comes down with pneumonia and has to cancel performances. One technique for reducing the financial uncertainty of a major tour is to find a national sponsor, such as a beverage company.

At each stop along the tour, the artist seeks to build support for his or her records. The artist may visit local radio stations in an attempt to influence their decisions on airplay and help generate a large crowd at the arena. T-shirts, sweatshirts, and other memorabilia are given away free by promoters and sold at the concerts; so are albums. The total take from concert paraphernalia can be surprisingly high. Recording artists often make a substantial percentage of their income from such sales.

A promotion company may help make some of the arrangements and also share in the risks and potential rewards of putting on a concert. The largest such firm is Live Nation, which mounts or publicizes over 22,000 events a year.[10] Live Nation owns or operates large and small event locations in the United States and abroad. The challenge for artists working with it or another promoter is to make sure the arena chosen is the right size and configuration for the nature of the act. The promoter carefully prices concert tickets so that the venue will be 60 percent full at the very least. After all, it costs virtually the same amount to perform for a small audience as to perform for a large audience, but empty seats generate no revenue.

In recent years, Universal Music, Sony Music, and Warner Music have dived into concert merchandising in a bid to find new revenue avenues as sales of recorded music have declined. The majors recognize that increasing proportions of many artists' incomes are coming from concerts rather than purchased records, and the distributors want to be involved. UMG says on its website that Bravado, its merchandising company, "sells artist- and music-branded products via multiple sales point [sic] such as fashion retail, live performances, and the internet."[11] And Warner notes its growing involvement in "merchandising, touring, fan clubs, VIP ticketing, sponsorships and brand endorsements, among other music-related businesses." WMG offers these services to its artists as well as artists not otherwise signed to WMG. Its website adds,

> A growing number of our artists are signing "expanded rights" agreements or "360° deals," as they are sometimes known. Under these deals, we provide services to artists outside the recorded music business and participate economically in an artist's activities outside the recorded music business. 360° deals create more of a partnership with our artists which allows us to work together more closely to create and sustain artistic and commercial success. At the end of Q2 2009, about one-half of WMG's active global recorded music roster was signed to 360° deals[12]

## THINKING ABOUT MEDIA LITERACY

After spending money on tickets and parking, why would fans also purchase artist merchandise? What advantages does the offer of this merchandise have for the fans? How about the industries?

## Exhibition in the Recording Industry

After all the work of making the record and all the work of distributing it is completed, recordings are laid out for members of the public to choose. As we've already suggested, recordings make it into the hands of the public through two major paths, digital and physical. As you probably have gathered from the chapter so far (and may have noticed in your everyday life), the landscapes of both paths have been changing dramatically over the past few years. Let's investigate a bit.

### Digital Downloads

It's useful to start with the digital exhibition mode because we've already described it during the discussion of various vehicles for recorded music. Although internet service providers play the critical role of distributor in the sense of allowing the public to access online stores, online merchants that provide digital downloads can also be considered exhibitors in that they offer the distributors' materials to the public.

Recall from our earlier discussion that according to Nielsen SoundScan in 2011 the number of digital units of recordings (albums and singles) inched a bit above

50 percent of all unit sales. Because the revenues derived from those sales amounted to $7 billion that year, you might think that digital units accounted for just over half of the amount. Actually, the number came to a bit less than half, at $3.4 billion. That's because even when there are large sales of singles in the digital realm, the units sold are less expensive than the albums sold in the physical domain. The digital purchase of albums is growing, though. In 2011, 31 percent of all albums were purchased as downloads in online stores.[13]

Apple's iTunes online store is the largest venue for the purchase of digital recordings; the research firm NDP calculates that it accounts for about 70 percent of all single and album downloads—and, in fact, around 16 percent of all music purchases. Other popular places to purchase digital recordings online are Amazon MP3 and eMusic. Most of the downloads are to desktop or laptop computers; from there the recordings may be transferred to other devices. Nevertheless, a substantial number of purchases—short ringtones (sales of which have been declining in recent years) as well as longer singles and even albums—are made directly from mobile devices. In 2011 mobile sales of music came to $277.4 million. A relatively small amount of digital recording revenues—$3.3 million—comes from customers digitally downloading songs from kiosks in physical stores or other locations.

Although most of the recording industry's revenues come through downloads, a growing amount of revenues come through subscription services. As noted earlier, subscription services such as Rhapsody and Spotify charge a fixed amount for allowing you to stream music of your choice to one or more devices. You can listen, but you don't own the material, and you cannot move it from one device to another. These services typically provide listeners with the opportunity to purchase the singles or albums—another source of industry revenues. Offering songs for sale is also part of the business of many online-radio operations. The difference between subscription services and online radio is that the subscription firms allow you to choose individual albums or tracks to hear, whereas the online radio firms allow you limited selection of individual tracks and instead stream music to you based on your choice of genre or what they learn about your interests. Both types of services pay digital-performance royalties.

## THINKING ABOUT MEDIA LITERACY

Streaming services allow audiences convenient access to an enormous amount of music for a low monthly cost. Once subscribers stop paying for the service, however, they lose access to all the content. How does this arrangement differ from when most music was made available on media such as CDs? In what ways does this arrangement primarily benefit the recording industry?

### Physical Sales

Many people still buy physical recordings. As Figure 10.2 showed earlier, in 2011 they accounted for $3.4 billion in sales. (Of course, that was a substantial drop from 2007, when sales were $8 billion.) For decades, the record store on the street or in the mall was probably the best-known place to buy music. There were hundreds of music stores across the country. Prominent chains were Sam Goody and Tower Records. But both chains went out of business, and the other stores that still exist are struggling. Change came rapidly, for as recently as 1998, record stores accounted for

50.8 percent of the sales of recordings in the United States. By 2008, the percentage of sales linked to record stores had slid to 30 percent, and now NDP places it far lower than that. It seems that the decline can be blamed on two types of stores: physical mass-merchant stores and online stores.

A physical mass-merchant store is a retail outlet that sells many different products in huge numbers and at relatively low prices; examples include Walmart, Target, and Kmart. During 2011, 31 percent of all album purchases occurred at mass merchant outlets. Even bigger than any of these, though, is the online retailer Amazon. An online retailer is a store where you can digitally order physical recordings to be shipped to you. That usually means CDs, though old-fashioned vinyl recordings have been enjoying a bit of resurgence. Although many online retail locations sell physical recordings, Amazon.com is the most popular place. In fact, the site accounts for about 20 percent of all recorded music sales.

Record distributors fully understand the value that the biggest digital and physical distributors provide them, and they often work with them to increase sales. In fact, the biggest retailers often sell CDs through exclusive deals with big record distributors that give the sellers a reason to hype the albums and the artists. For example, in 2008 Sony Music arranged to release AC/DC's album *Black Ice* through Walmart only for a certain number of weeks. The album sold more than two million copies, making it the fifth-ranked album of that year.

## Ethical Issues in the Recording Industry

With all the changes roiling the recording industry, you would think that the last thing record executives need is a public controversy that strikes directly at the core of their activities. It turns out that they have not one such controversy to worry about, but two. One has to do with the lyrics in certain genres of popular music, especially rap. The other has to do with ways to handle piracy. Both issues raise serious ethical and social questions that have no easy answers.

### Parental Concerns about Lyrics

A large number of music consumers are also parents. In this role, many have been less concerned about the ethics of music downloads than about the lyrics of the songs their kids get off the web and buy from stores. This is not a new concern. For decades, recording companies, artists, and stores have been pelted with complaints from parents and teachers around the country that their children are purchasing music with lyrics unsuitable for the children's—and maybe some parents'—ears.

Many of their concerns came to a head during the 1980s when Tipper Gore, the wife of then–U.S. senator Al Gore, joined with other wives of influential Washington politicians and businessmen to form the Parents Music Resource Center (PMRC). The PMRC had a number of goals. It aimed to lobby the music industry to place warnings about lyrics on album covers. It wanted explicit album covers kept under the counter. It demanded a records ratings system similar to that used for films and a ratings system for concerts. The group also suggested that companies reassess the contracts of those performers who engage in violence and explicit sexual behavior onstage, and it proposed a media watch by citizens and record companies that would pressure broadcasters not to air songs that the group considered problematic.

C. Delores Tucker's fight to "clean up" rap music resulted in Time Warner getting rid of Interscope Records.

The anger succeeded in leading major recording companies to put parental advisory labels on albums that warned parents about objectionable lyrics. The nation's leading retailer, Walmart, has in fact refused to stock albums with controversial lyrics. As a result, some recording firms have resorted to distributing two versions of an album: one with safer, censored lyrics and the original one that the musician intended to distribute.

The rise of gangsta rap in the late 1980s raised more concerns about violent or sexually explicit lyrics in censored and uncensored albums. Others objected to the depiction of women in many rap songs as well as in other musical genres. In the mid-1990s, civil rights activist C. Delores Tucker launched a highly visible campaign to clean up rap music. She focused on Time Warner, whose subsidiary Interscope was home to hard-core rappers Snoop Dogg and Tupac Shakur. In 1995, Tucker and her allies succeeded in forcing Time Warner to get rid of Interscope. But Time Warner simply sold Interscope to Polygram (now Universal Music Group), and the label continued to turn out songs that Tucker and others reviled through immensely popular artists such as 50 Cent and Eminem. A dozen years later, the battle reached another crescendo, with Al Sharpton and other public figures objecting particularly to racial epithets (particularly the n-word) and sexual profanities (the omnipresent b-word) in the music.

Some people have lauded these calls for reining in rappers and other songwriters who use what they consider immoral lyrics. They have argued that popular music speaks to an enormous number of impressionable young people and teaches them about romance and love and relationships. Bleeping out a word here and there on the radio or a censored album doesn't erase many of the objectionable words and ideas in the songs, they have argued.

Many of rap's defenders have responded that outsiders should not impose their values on an important field of artistic endeavor. Rappers, they have said, reflect views that many African Americans have about their surroundings; such hard-edged views need to be heard and understood, they argue. During the past few years, though, even rap's defenders have acknowledged that sometimes the lyric writers aim for the obscene, the violent, and the derogatory simply to stand out. In 2006, the filmmaker Byron Hurt released *Beyond Beats and Rhymes*, a documentary critical of rap that, in the words of a *Time* magazine writer, was notable "not just for its hard critique but for the fact that most of the people doing the criticizing were not dowdy church ladies but members of the hip-hop generation who deplore rap's recent fixation on the sensational." Many rap artists disagreed strongly, and the arguments continued.

## Industry Concerns about Piracy

Of course, many of the songs that some people find so objectionable can be downloaded from the web. Some parents worry that their children have access to this material too easily, and so a small industry of advice-givers and software creators has arisen to help people control the access that their young people have to certain music. Record executives, for their part, have been embroiled in broader struggles with a variety of groups about access to their company's music—struggles that center on issues of piracy.

**Piracy** **Piracy** is the unauthorized duplication of copyrighted music. Two special types of concern are **counterfeiting** and **bootlegging**. Counterfeiting also involves

**piracy**
the unauthorized duplication of copyrighted material for profit

**counterfeiting**
the unauthorized duplication of copyrighted music and packaging for profit, with the goal of making the copy appear authentic

**bootlegging**
the unauthorized recording of a music performance and the subsequent distribution of that recording

unauthorized duplication, but it is more serious because the copy is packaged to look like an authentic copy so that it can be sold as authentic. Bootlegging is the unauthorized recording of a musical performance and the subsequent distribution of that performance. For example, if you go to a concert that prohibits recording devices, secretly record the program, and then sell your recording to your friends, you are bootlegging.

The counterfeiting of CDs and the bootlegging of concerts take place on a huge scale around the world. Most experts consider China the center of counterfeiting, but the sale of illegally created CDs takes place everywhere. In the United States, many people seem to have no problem buying what they know are counterfeited products, including music CDs. A 2007 Gallup poll of Los Angeles residents found that one in four residents bought pirated goods.

Although the counterfeiting of physical albums and the creation of bootlegged concert CDs remain a big problem, it is the illegal downloading of music around the world that has record executives particularly challenged. When a person grabs a song off the web without the permission of the recording firm or copyright holder, it is against the law. But it's not hard to do. Individuals continually make songs available online in a compressed file format called MP3. These files can be circulated quickly to anyone who wants them via special **peer-to-peer** (or **P2P**) downloading sites such as BitTorrent and Pirate Bay. P2P software relies on the cooperation of many computers to exchange files over the internet. Aside from being fast, P2P software makes it difficult for copyright owners to blame a website or company for the downloading. The MP3 recordings can be played on computers or on players, including iPods, that can be taken anywhere.

Digital lockers are another vehicle for piracy. A **digital locker** is an internet service that allows paying and registered users to store music, videos, games, and other files. The users can also allow others access to those files, and that's where the copyright violation takes place. The number of people using these lockers for legal or illegal purposes—about 3 percent of the internet audience, according to NDP—is quite a bit smaller than the number using peer-to-peer.[14] Moreover, observers believe that the lockers may be a bigger factor in piracy of movies than piracy of audio recordings because movies take substantially longer to download using peer-to-peer networks. Nevertheless, in early 2012 the U.S. Justice Department shut down a digital locker called Megaupload, accusing it of criminal copyright violations. People who had stored legitimate material in Megaupload's lockers were incensed. An RIAA executive was pleased with the action. "The realistic objective is not to eliminate piracy but to make it as inconvenient as possible," he said. "Some of the users you peel off."[15]

The music industry's concern relates not just to the United States. Paying for online music is rare in some countries. In 2007, almost 100 percent of music downloaded from the web in Asia was illegal, according to Leong May See, Asia director for the International Federation of the Phonographic Industry, an industry group that includes Sony Music, Universal Music, and Warner Music. In the United States illegal downloading is also rampant, but it seems to be slowing. The RIAA stated on its website in 2009 that "since 2004, the percentage of Internet-connected households that have downloading music from P2P is essentially flat." Executives and government officials who worry about this situation point out that much of the U.S. economy is based on intellectual property. When people in the United States and the rest of the world take songs without paying for them, that

**peer-to-peer (P2P) computing**
a process in which people share the resources of their computer with computers owned by other people

**digital locker**
an Internet service that allows paying and registered users to store music, videos, games, and other files

takes billions of dollars away from the economy and subtracts jobs that would otherwise exist. Exactly how much money and how many jobs this costs the U.S. economy is a matter of argument. Some people who argue that numbers relating to piracy may be inflated point out that a lot of songs may be downloaded without fee by people who otherwise would not have bought that music.

Still, most people agree that the recording industry is losing lots of money on all sorts of piracy. The industry, which has stopped suing individuals for sharing files, is moving against this problem on a number of other fronts. One is by mounting other lawsuits and encouraging the government to mount them. We have already seen the industry's encouragement of Justice Department actions against Megaupload. In 2010 the RIAA itself successfully sued Limewire, the world's most-installed P2P application, in New York district court, shutting it down. Another avenue of attack involves trying to educate young people about the ethics of piracy. A third involves getting internet service providers to threaten to remove internet service from people the RIAA determines have been downloading or sharing recordings illegally.

David Card, a New York–based senior analyst with Forrester Research, once said bluntly, "The thing is, nothing can stop piracy." His larger point was that although the recording industry must be cautious about how it circulates its music, the best approach may be to give people what they consider the best music for the best price in the easiest way possible. Some people in the industry worry that this may not be enough. It's hard to compete with "free," they say, and too many people will download songs and other materials for free if they have the chance and know they won't get caught. The industry cannot afford to give away music, they say.

Putting aside for a moment the illegality of downloading music without permission, it is useful to think about many of the points we've discussed in this chapter from the standpoint of several parties involved. We already know the position of the RIAA and the established record companies about giving away music. They want to control when it happens, and they want to stop most of it. They say that their businesses are at stake. Let's look at other constituencies—struggling artists, artists with label contracts, and consumers.

Struggling recording artists and those who are still trying to find a label and make a name for themselves might well have a different viewpoint from established ones about some of these issues. For one thing, these players and singers are likely to resent the power that just a few large firms have over the music and the musicians heard in the United States and much of the rest of the world. They realize that although music may be fragmented at the production end, it is highly concentrated at the distribution end, and it is likely to remain that way. Unlike the established artists, they may see the big recording companies not as allies but as enemies who are keeping them out of the distribution pipeline. To many aspiring artists, control of the music industry by Warner, Sony, and Universal is preventing them from achieving the success they deserve. And they may be gleeful at the prospect of the web weakening these companies' power.

Moreover, artists who are just starting out may not be upset by the trading of their music on the web. In fact, they may welcome it. Aspiring musicians can place their material on websites much more easily than they could place it on radio. For basement bands and garage bands, the web has become a great vehicle for getting their sound out and hoping that people will hear it. Some artists on their way up—

even those with label contracts—see the web in the same way. They realize that the structure of their contracts with the recording companies mean that making lots of money through their albums is a long shot. They make most of their living through the concerts they give, and they may see the pirating of their albums as great publicity that will translate into the kind of popularity that will lead people to pay to hear them at concerts. So in effect they may be grateful that fans care enough about their music to steal it.

Many consumers care little about the problems that the recording companies and their stars have with piracy. In fact, millions of people act as if sharing copyrighted music with millions of other people on the web is not a legal or ethical issue. The fact that a federal court has ruled that sharing music in this way is legally wrong hasn't stopped music lovers—especially teens and young adults—from scouring the web for MP3 cuts of their favorite new and old works. In 2009, research firm Big-Champagne calculated that U.S. fans illegally swiped one billion songs a month off the web.

Is it just selfishness that leads to these wholesale copyright violations? Some commentators argue that consumers are ignoring the interests of the recording industry because for a long time the industry—and especially a handful of firms that are intent on controlling music across as many media as possible—has ignored their interests. The top record companies, they say, have continually taken advantage of the switch to new recording forms (such as tapes, minidisks, and CDs) to charge consumers far more than necessary for singles and albums. Moreover, they say, many consumers feel that albums are often rip-offs, in that to buy two or three of a group's songs, they must purchase an album that also includes eight or nine other songs that are not terribly good. Consumers therefore have developed no loyalty to or concern for the firms and have no qualms about picking the songs that they really want off the web without paying for them. The industry, they say, ought to try to understand what consumers want and respond to their interests. Industry officials reply that this has begun to happen. They point to consumers' ability to buy many songs for 69 cents on iTunes and elsewhere. Moreover, there are so many sites—from YouTube to Revver to internet radio streams—where advertising supports listening to music for free.

In the end, of course, it is up to you to decide where you stand in relation to these issues. Arguments about piracy and about the morality of certain songs underscore the fact that recordings play a huge role in people's lives. Our trip through the recording industry in this chapter sketched the ways in which this industry produces, distributes, and exhibits products in the United States. That is changing in momentous ways. New technologies promise new opportunities, as well as challenges to traditional distribution, exhibition, and promotion routes. It will be interesting to see how the recording industry responds and how that response affects not only the recordings we can buy but also how we can buy them in years to come.

# CHAPTER REVIEW

Visit the Companion Website at www.routledge.com/cw/turow for additional study tools and resources.

## Key Terms

You can find the definitions to these key terms in the marginal glossary throughout this chapter. Test your knowledge of these terms with interactive flash cards on the *Media Today* companion website.

| | | |
|---|---|---|
| album | internet radio or online radio | piracy |
| A&R (artist and repertoire) | label | promotion |
| bootlegging | mechanical royalties | ringtones |
| counterfeiting | payola | royalty |
| digital locker | peer-to-peer (P2P) computing | single |
| digital platform | performance royalties | streaming |
| downloading | | |

## Questions for Discussion and Critical Thinking

1. Do you think that the recording industry is making too big a deal of illegal downloading, or do you think the industry is within its rights to sue people as it did? Why or why not? What might be some alternatives the industry could offer to help prevent this illegal downloading?

2. Earlier in the chapter, we mentioned that sales of vinyl records have seen a slight increase recently. Why do you think people would be returning to buying records? Who do you think the buyers might be and why?

3. If you were a member of an aspiring rock band, what are some ways in which you might generate publicity for your band? Would you want to work with a label? Why or why not?

4. Walmart is one of the largest retailers for music in the country, and often its decisions impact entire industries. Do you think Walmart is right in refusing to stock albums with lyrics it considers potentially offensive to some of its customers? Why or why not?

## Case Study
### THE "BIG THREE" WEBSITES THROUGH THE EYES OF FANS AND MUSICIANS

**The Idea** The websites of Universal Music Group, Sony Music Group, and Warner Music Group speak to at least two audiences. One consists of music fans who want to find out about their favorite groups and perhaps the labels that carry them. The other is made up of musicians who might be hoping to sign with one of the many labels owned by UMG, SMG, and WMG. This raises a basic question: who are the websites aimed at, fans, musicians, or both?

**The Method** Think about what a fan would want to know from a major recording group's website versus what a musician would want to know. Carefully explore one of the websites. While doing so, ask yourself whether the topics you are reading or viewing seem calculated to appeal to a fan or a musician. What presentations of the company's activities and capabilities would impress you as a fan? What presentations of the company's activities would impress you as a musician? Whom do you think the site would best satisfy, the fan or the musician—or neither?

Write a report of what you have learned and compare your impressions with those of others in the class who looked at the same or different websites.

# The Radio Industry 11

## CHAPTER OBJECTIVES

1 Sketch the history of the radio industry

2 Explain the relationship between advertising and programming

3 Detail the role of market research in the radio industry

4 Examine critically the issues surrounding the consolidation of radio station ownership

5 Discuss ways in which new digital technologies are challenging traditional radio

"There goes the last DJ/Who plays what he wants to play/And says what he wants to say/ Hey, hey, hey."

**TOM PETTY, SONGWRITER, "THE LAST DJ"**

In this age of media convergence, what is radio? Consider this quote from a magazine writer: "When my daughter, who is 17, wants to hear a song, she doesn't turn to radio. Nor does she go to Spotify or Pandora. YouTube is her on-demand streaming service."

For the moment, set aside whether you like the daughter's choice; we'll deal with that later in the chapter. Instead, think about what the writer (her mother) doesn't count as radio: Spotify, Pandora, and YouTube. Do you agree that these shouldn't be called radio?

Technically, she is correct. As we will see, radio in American society has historically meant audio signals transmitted ("broadcast") over the air by organizations ("stations") licensed for that activity by the Federal Communications Commission and publicly accessible via devices called radio receivers. By that definition, satellite-delivered music can be considered part of the radio industry. But neither Spotify nor Pandora, which are unlicensed by the FCC and offer music to listeners over the internet, would be considered radio. Similarly, YouTube, which is Internet-based and often includes video as well as audio, would not fit the classic definition of radio, either.

But the traditional definition begins to fall apart when you realize that Spotify, Pandora, YouTube, and similar companies compete with traditional radio-industry actors for advertisers and audiences. Thinking of internet audio and broadcast radio as part of one industry also makes sense when you realize that broadcast radio companies regularly reach out to listeners via the web and other digital platforms such as mobile phones and tablets. Recognizing this, some analysts include radio companies' digital activities as part of the radio industry. Yet many of these analysts exclude Spotify, Pandora, and other similar services because, they say, these are internet audio companies unrelated to traditional radio firms.

From the perspective that guides this book, this exclusion is a mistake. As we know, all media industries today are struggling with convergence. Radio is no exception, and it makes little sense to exclude threats to the traditional radio business when, at heart, they are extending the radio model into new technologies. Before the 1990s, radio meant over-the-air audio signals picked up by a special receiver. But in the age of convergence, the defining feature of the industry is the streaming audio it presents to audiences via various technologies. **Streaming audio** is the flow of sounds (usually music) to listeners in such a way that the sounds are meant to disappear after they are heard. This approach is quite different from the business of the recording industry (chapter 10), where the goal is to get people to pay to keep individual songs or specific collections of songs. Seen from this perspective, the various old and new platforms for radio—traditional broadcast, the web, the smartphone, the tablet—are merely competitive ways to deliver the same audio streams.

But you may ask, "Doesn't calling all streaming audio 'radio' give the word a meaning that is quite different from its original meaning?" The answer is yes, but in doing this, we—and many who work in the industry—are not treating the radio industry differently from the other media industries we have described. As we have seen, digital "books," "newspapers," "magazines," and "records" are quite different from their pre-digital versions, but they still carry the tags of the original media platforms.

This is certainly not the first time people's understanding of the radio business has shifted. "Radio" as we understand it today is quite different from how people understood it 100 years ago, 60 years ago, and even 30 years ago. To learn how we got from there to Pandora and consider what those developments mean for the future radio industry, let's turn to our timeline and three key historical themes.

**streaming audio**
the flow of sounds (usually music) to listeners in such a way that the sounds are meant to disappear after they are heard

## The Rise of Radio

The word "radio" seems to have been coined by a French physicist, Edouard Branly, in 1897. He was interested in helping developers of the new "wireless" technology detect the sounds they were radiating into the air.[1] Linking a form of the verb "to radiate" with a word to indicate flow, he concocted the word "radioconductor." The "radio" part of that term stuck in both the French and English languages. Over time, wireless activity became known in the United States as radio broadcasting. To Americans, the word "broadcasting" evoked an image of radiation, but one different from Branly's—broadcasting was originally an agricultural term referring to the scattering of seeds on a field.

The technology of radio broadcasting in the late 19th century could transmit only click-like sounds. To appreciate why this was still important, consider it in relation to the development of the telegraph. After Samuel Morse developed the telegraph in 1842, scientists began to look to send messages over the air using electric waves or frequencies. In 1895, Italian Guglielmo Marconi succeeded in sending messages wirelessly over long distances using the code of dots and dashes that Morse had developed. Because the Italian government showed no interest in Marconi's find, he took it to England, where people quickly saw its value to the far-flung British Empire. The Marconi Company was formed to equip the commercial and military ships of England, the United States, and other countries with wireless telegraphy for communicating with one another and with shore points around the world.

Clearly, what the Marconi Company was doing has little to do with the radio industry as we know it today. This point brings us to our first historical theme:

1. *Radio, as we know it, did not arrive in a flash as a result of one inventor's grand change.*

Take a look at the timeline (Figure 11.1), and you'll see the way inventions and their uses progressed to the point where radio as a technology involved the public transmission of voices and music that people could receive in their homes on receivers they bought. Even when radio first "talked," it was not for the general public but for the business of shipping and for use by the Navy. So on Christmas Eve in 1906, when the inventor Reginald Fessenden first broadcast music and speech, his radio "audience" was composed of the wireless operators on ships in various parts of the Atlantic Ocean. In another way, too, Fessenden's broadcast was not characteristic of modern radio: his audience could hear the broadcast only through earphones. It was not until a year later that Lee de Forest's Audion vacuum tube made it possible for people to listen to the radio in groups through speakers.

De Forest envisioned stations sending out continuous music, news, and other material. But as you can see in the timeline, in the United States it took more than two decades to develop the kind of radio programming de Forest imagined. This early approach to radio was quite different from the one we know today. It was more like broadcast network television in airing a diversity of genres: light talk shows in the morning, soap operas during the late morning and afternoon, children's programs after school, news after dinner, and then musical variety shows, dramas, and situation comedies in the evening.

How did we get from this model to the contemporary idea of what radio means? Follow the timeline, and you'll see that the rise of television during the 1950s, along with the rise of FM in the 1960s, forced radio companies to change their approaches to their business. Instead of full-service programming aimed at everyone in an area, stations began to target particular types of people by age (e.g., teenagers) and by interests (e.g., country music, news). As the introduction noted and the timeline illustrates, the rise of companies using converging digital technologies to compete with radio has forced executives to think yet again about what their stations should do and how they should reach out to their audiences.

This story of the transformation of radio over the decades is very much tied to our second historical theme.

2.   *Radio as a medium of communication developed as a result of social, legal, and organizational responses to the technology during different periods.*

We've already noted that it took a while for the radio system to develop programming aimed at the general public and that competition with television then forced radio firms to develop more targeted approaches to their stations' programming. We've also indicated that those approaches are now undergoing change because of competition stemming from digital convergence. If you follow these developments across the timeline with the second historical theme in mind, you will see how the technology and the content of the radio system were shaped—and continue to be shaped—by social and legal debates about what radio should be and who should control it.

You will see, for example, that when the United States entered World War I in 1917, the U.S. Navy took control of domestic radio and developed it in ways that would most benefit the military. After the war, the Navy sought congressional permission to retain control over radio for reasons of national security. Its argument was that if enemies of the United States got control of radio stations, they could disseminate propaganda that could be damaging to the interests of the country.

However, American tradition dictates that mass media should not be under government control. Allowing the U.S. Navy to dictate radio's use would mean that a

# Figure 11.1 Timeline of the Radio Industry

**1922**: AT&T allows the Queensboro Realty Company to pay $3,000 for five "talks" on AT&T's New York City radio station.

**1896**: Marconi patents the first radio transmitter.

**1907**: U.S. inventor Lee de Forest creates Audion vacuum tube.

**1917**: During World War I, the U.S. Navy takes control of domestic radio for military purposes.

**1920s-1930s**: News slowly develops into an important part of radio.

**1926**: The earliest radio networks, the National Broadcasting Company (NBC) and United Independent Broadcasters, are founded.

**1875** — **1900** — **1925**

**1895**: Italian Guglielmo Marconi succeeds in sending wireless messages over long distance using Morse code.

**1906**: Reginald Fessenden manages to broadcast speech and music with Marconi's device.

**1912**: Congress passes Radio Act of 1912.

**1919**: Congress decrees that broadcasting is to be a privately sponsored enterprise.

**1920s-1930s**: Entertainment genres develop in radio.

**1927**: The Radio Act of 1927 creates the Federal Radio Commission (FRC) to issue radio licenses and bring order to nation's radio airwaves.

**1919**: AT&T, Westinghouse, GE, and United Fruit Company form the Radio Corporation of America.

**1920**: Westinghouse Corporation founds KDKA radio station in Pittsburgh with the purpose of providing programming over the air so people will buy Westinghouse radio sets.

**1927**: United Independent Broadcasters is reorganized into Columbia Broadcasting System (CBS).

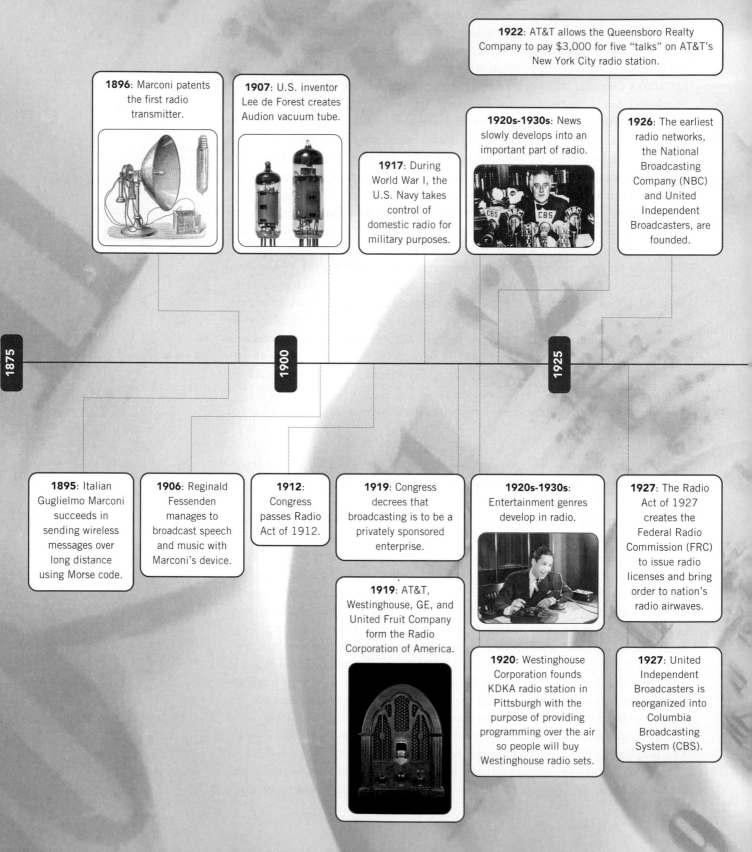

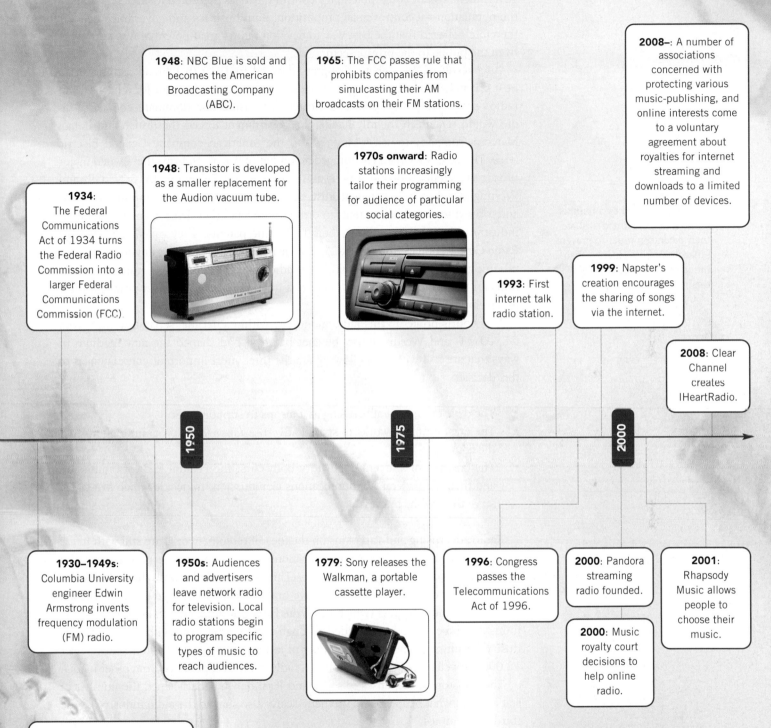

**1934:** The Federal Communications Act of 1934 turns the Federal Radio Commission into a larger Federal Communications Commission (FCC).

**1948:** NBC Blue is sold and becomes the American Broadcasting Company (ABC).

**1948:** Transistor is developed as a smaller replacement for the Audion vacuum tube.

**1965:** The FCC passes rule that prohibits companies from simulcasting their AM broadcasts on their FM stations.

**1970s onward:** Radio stations increasingly tailor their programming for audience of particular social categories.

**2008–:** A number of associations concerned with protecting various music-publishing, and online interests come to a voluntary agreement about royalties for internet streaming and downloads to a limited number of devices.

**1993:** First internet talk radio station.

**1999:** Napster's creation encourages the sharing of songs via the internet.

**2008:** Clear Channel creates IHeartRadio.

1950

1975

2000

**1930–1949s:** Columbia University engineer Edwin Armstrong invents frequency modulation (FM) radio.

**1950s:** Audiences and advertisers leave network radio for television. Local radio stations begin to program specific types of music to reach audiences.

**1979:** Sony releases the Walkman, a portable cassette player.

**1996:** Congress passes the Telecommunications Act of 1996.

**2000:** Pandora streaming radio founded.

**2001:** Rhapsody Music allows people to choose their music.

**2000:** Music royalty court decisions to help online radio.

**Late 1940s:** NBC, CBS, and ABC begin to shift the profits of their radio networks into building television networks.

government agency could potentially control the ideas presented to large segments of the population—a controversial proposition. Both business and government leaders therefore believed that the best way to develop radio's great potential was to move it from the public to the private sector.

As a result of this debate, Congress decreed in 1919 that broadcasting was to be a privately sponsored enterprise, open to any citizen who paid for a license. But radio's split from government had a catch. To ensure that dominant control of radio would remain in friendly hands, the government forced the British and Italian Marconi Company to sell its interests to the American company General Electric (GE). The U.S. Navy then encouraged a number of American firms that owned major broadcast patents (notably American Telephone and Telegraph [AT&T], GE, and Westinghouse) to form a **patent trust**, or a company owned by a number of firms and formed to share their patents in order to prevent other firms from entering their industry unless the trust allows them to use the patents. They called this trust the Radio Corporation of America (RCA) and gave it the power to force anyone interested in setting up a radio station to pay for a radio patent. RCA, in turn, imposed conditions for the use of the airwaves. The trust quickly became the most powerful force in developing the airwaves.

U.S. courts broke up this radio monopoly within a decade, separating RCA from GE, AT&T, and Westinghouse, but not before it had shaped the new medium in ways that are still with us. Following are the three most important consequences of this decision:

- The development of advertising as a means to support radio
- The creation of networks to spread advertiser-sponsored programming around the country
- The creation of a federal regulatory body (first the Federal Radio Commission and then the Federal Communications Commission) to decide which firms best serve the "public interest"

Radio advertising and variations on the idea of radio networks are still with us, as we will see. So is the Federal Communications Commission, but its power over radio has decreased over the past few decades. This is primarily because the industry has convinced the commission, the executive branch of the federal government (which oversees it), and Congress (which can write laws that determine its powers) that the industry's direction is best decided through competition from within the radio industry (resulting from the large number of radio stations in the United States—over 12,000) as well as from competition that radio stations experience from other media.

These historical responses to social and legal debates that shaped the number of stations and what people heard on them clearly also shaped the radio industry, as the third theme notes:

3. *The radio industry developed and changed as a result of struggles to control audio channels and their relations to audiences.*

The radio industry has changed enormously from its beginnings with RCA. Follow the timeline, and you'll note the rise of the Mutual Broadcasting Network, the CBS Radio Network, and later the several station "groups" (including CBS) that now dominate the radio landscape. These developments and others involved attempts by

**patent trust**
a company owned by a number of firms that is formed to share their patents in order to prevent other firms from entering their industry unless the trust allows them to use the patents

companies to take advantage of perceived opportunities. Sometimes companies have tried to block developments they do not believe are in their interests. This happened with FM radio, which stands for **frequency modulation**—an invention of Columbia University engineer Edwin Armstrong during the 1930s. From the start, leading radio executives realized that the static-free sound of FM was far superior to the sound produced by the **amplitude modulation**, or AM, technology upon which existing radio transmitters and sets were based. But for technical reasons, the FM technology could not simply be used to improve AM radio. FM would have to either replace AM or coexist with it. Broadcasters worried that their huge investment in AM would be threatened if they developed FM as a substitute. They also worried that the development of a whole new set of FM stations would reduce their profits by dividing both audiences and advertising money. For these reasons, radio executives tried hard to influence the FCC to derail the development of FM radio.

Old radio showing the AM and FM frequency bands in megahertz and kilohertz.

**frequency modulation (FM)**
a means of radio broadcasting, utilizing the band between 88 and 108 megahertz; FM signals are marked by high levels of clarity but rarely travel more than 80 miles from the site of their transmission

**amplitude modulation (AM)**
a means of radio broadcasting, utilizing the band between 540 and 1,700 megahertz; AM signals are prone to frequent static interference, but their high-powered signals allow them to travel great distances, especially at night

FM radio did emerge, though years later than its supporters wanted. By the 1960s, the FCC was not handing out new AM licenses, and the amount of money needed to buy an existing AM station soared. In the face of these developments, new business interests saw opportunities in FM radio and pressured the FCC to encourage the growth of FM by passing a nonduplication rule. The FCC passed this rule in 1965, stating that an owner of both an AM and an FM station could not play the same material on both stations more than 50 percent of the time. The rule had the effect supporters of FM wanted. FM stations, looking for things to play and not having many commercials, developed music-based formats that played long cuts or even entire albums—an approach that AM stations resisted. Many listeners migrated to FM; they liked the music and the static-free sound. In 1972, FM had 28 percent of the radio audience in the top 40 radio markets, with AM taking 72 percent. By 1990, these figures were reversed.

The FM example shows how powerful forces within the radio industry could use their leverage to delay a technology they believed would transform their industry in a way they didn't want. During the 1990s, radio broadcasters applied pressure to Congress to allow changes in the industry that they *did* want. Before that time, the FCC did not allow broadcasters to own more than one FM and one AM station in a given area. However, the industry convinced legislators who crafted the Telecommunications Act of 1996 to do away with such restrictions. The new law allowed broadcast companies to snatch up several AM and FM properties in the same market. This sparked the creation of large radio conglomerates, most notably Clear Channel Communications, which controlled large proportions of radio advertising in markets across the country.

The rise of radio conglomerates has sparked the criticism that much of terrestrial radio is repetitive, boring, and clogged with commercials. This criticism is being voiced at a time when digital media—such as satellite radio, internet-linked computers, iPods, MP3 players, mobile phones, and related technologies—are opening up new ways for people to get audio programming that radio has long provided. Once again, radio executives stand between an old and new world. They have a lot invested in traditional broadcast radio, but their audience numbers are declining. So they are trying to understand how to adapt to and compete with the new technologies. Let's take a look at the established and emerging worlds of radio. We start with today's terrestrial radio world and then examine digital competition to the radio industry and the industry's response to it.

# An Overview of the Terrestrial Radio Industry

It's certainly a world with a lot of stations. At the end of June 2012 there were 15,906 FCC-licensed radio stations in the United States.[2] Despite increased competition from digital media for advertising and audiences, the number of stations has grown—in 2008, this count was 13,977. At the same time, the ownership of the stations in and around big cities has become concentrated. As we have seen, the federal government has greatly relaxed its limitations on the number of stations one party can own. The Telecommunications Act of 1996 allowed the owners of station groups to hold up to eight stations in large markets and up to five stations in smaller markets—with no limit on the total number they can have across multiple markets. As a result, most large-market stations are now part of station groups owned by companies such as Clear Channel, Cumulus, Citadel, and CBS.

Consider Philadelphia, Pennsylvania, as an example. There are 53 stations that reach the city with strong signals. Of these, CBS owns five, Clear Channel owns six, the Beasley Broadcast Group owns four (including one in nearby Wilmington, Delaware), and Greater Media owns five. That means that four firms own 20 (38 percent) of the stations that target the city.[3] Moreover, these stations are among the most popular, so the four firms likely gather more than 38 percent of the listeners and more than 38 percent of the advertising.

## Where and When People Listen to the Radio

Arbitron, a company that makes money supplying radio ratings to the industry and its advertisers, notes in a 2011 report that radio "continues to hold a universally popular presence in the daily lives of all Americans, reaching over 93% of all persons 12+ each week."[4] Since the 1950s, radio's strength in the face of competition from other media has had to do with its portability—people have been able to use radio outside the home, where they have historically had less access to the medium's audiovisual competition. According to Arbitron, listening at home has been on a long-term decline. Whereas 53 percent of all radio listening (as measured in quarter hours) took place at home in 1986, that percentage had dropped to 39 percent by 2012. Listening to terrestrial radio has become a predominantly "away-from-home" (in cars, at work, on the beach, in the park) activity.

What Arbitron means by "listening" is tuning in at least once for five minutes during a quarter hour during a week. A somewhat tougher gauge of attention to radio is the *number* of quarter hours during a week in which a listener has spent five minutes or more with a radio station. Arbitron acknowledges that the time spent listening (TSL) has gone down. For average listeners aged 12 and older, TSL fell 30 minutes per week between 2011 and 2012.[5] Moreover, the number of Americans aged 12 and older tuning into terrestrial radio on average during a quarter hour has been declining steadily since 2003, as Table 11.1 indicates. The decline has been taking place for both in-home and out-of-home listening, as other technologies that carry music—most prominently the internet, the iPod, the mobile phone, and other digital music players—take terrestrial radio's place. As we will see, this drop in audience numbers has hurt the ability of radio stations to draw advertising revenues.

## AM versus FM Technology

You already know that terrestrial radio stations broadcast using one of two technologies, AM or FM. The two technologies operate on different ranges of frequencies

**Table 11.1** Radio Listeners (Aged 12+ Years) in the Average Quarter Hour (in Millions)

|  | 2003 | 2004 | 2005 | 2006 | 2007 | 2008 | 2009 | 2010 |
|---|---|---|---|---|---|---|---|---|
| All radio stations | 27.8 | 27.6 | 27.6 | 27.2 | 27.1 | 25.8 | 23.40 | 22.15 |
| At home | 11.4 | 11.4 | 11.0 | 10.9 | 10.8 | 10.1 | 9.26 | 8.59 |
| Out of home | 16.4 | 16.2 | 16.4 | 16.3 | 16.3 | 15.7 | 14.17 | 13.60 |
| AM stations | 5.5 | 5.2 | 5.1 | 4.9 | 4.8 | 4.5 | 3.83 | 3.34 |
| FM stations | 22.4 | 22.3 | 22.4 | 22.3 | 22.4 | 21.3 | 18.64 | 18.07 |

Source: *Communications Industry Forecast, 2011–15* (New York: Veronis Suhler Stevenson, 2012), 18–19.

(called bands) and utilize two different means of broadcasting their signal (see Figure 11.2). There are about 4,754 AM stations and 10,852 FM stations in the United States. Since the 1970s, listeners clearly have preferred FM because its sound is clearer than AM, with less static. In 1981, AM stations attracted 41 percent of the listeners per average quarter hour; in 2011, they managed to grab only 15.6 percent of listeners in an average quarter hour.[6]

## Commercial Radio Stations versus Noncommercial Radio Stations

In addition to distinguishing radio stations according to their positions in the AM or FM bands, we can also characterize them by the way they get the money they need to stay in business. In terms of funding, there are two types of radio stations:

- Commercial stations
- Noncommercial stations

The vast majority of stations in the United States—about 14,000—are **commercial stations**. As the name implies, these stations support themselves financially by selling time on their airwaves to advertisers. **Noncommercial stations** do not receive financial support from advertisers in the traditional sense of airing commercials. Most noncommercial stations are located at the very left of the FM band (between 88 and 92 MHz) because these frequencies have been reserved by the government exclusively for noncommercial use. If your college or university owns a station, it may very well broadcast here. Because the FCC does not permit these stations to sell products directly, the stations support themselves through donations from listeners, private foundations, and corporations—the latter in return for mentioning the firm or its products in announcements at the beginning and end of their programs. These announcements, called **billboards**, often sound suspiciously like the commercials these stations aren't allowed by law to run. National Public Radio is a network that uses billboards.

## Radio Market Size

Radio stations can be grouped according to the size of the market they serve (see Table 11.2). Listeners in small cities such as Laramie, Wyoming, or Kenai, Alaska, may have only a handful of stations available to them. Despite the availability of

**commercial stations**
radio stations that support themselves financially by selling time on their airwaves to advertisers

**noncommercial stations**
radio stations that do not receive financial support from advertisers

**billboards**
the mention of a sponsor's name or products at the start or end of an aired program, acknowledged in return for money

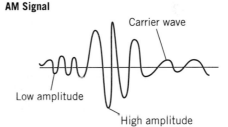

AM Signal

Carrier wave

Low amplitude

High amplitude

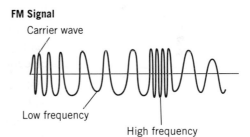

FM Signal

Carrier wave

Low frequency

High frequency

**Figure 11.2**
Both AM and FM radio stations transmit a carrier wave that is changed or "modulated" to carry audio signals such as music or voice. With AM (amplitude modulation) radio, the amplitude or strength of the carrier wave's vibration fluctuates with the sound. With FM (frequency modulation) radio, the strength of the carrier wave remains constant, and instead it is the frequency or number of vibrations within the wave that changes based on the sound.

**Table 11.2** Top 15 Radio Markets by Population, Fall 2012

| Rank | Market location | Fall 2012 population* |
|------|-----------------|----------------------|
| 1 | New York | 15,867,400 |
| 2 | Los Angeles | 11,044,200 |
| 3 | Chicago | 7,878,800 |
| 4 | San Francisco | 6,264,600 |
| 5 | Dallas–Fort Worth | 5,431,900 |
| 6 | Houston–Galveston | 5,431,900 |
| 7 | Washington, DC | 4,635,000 |
| 8 | Philadelphia | 4,517,800 |
| 9 | Atlanta | 4,385,000 |
| 10 | Boston | 4,082,100 |
| 11 | Detroit | 3,760,200 |
| 12 | Miami–Fort Lauderdale–Hollywood | 3,760,200 |
| 13 | Seattle–Tacoma | 3,538,100 |
| 14 | Phoenix | 3,255,500 |
| 15 | Puerto Rico | 3,152,100 |

*Metropolitan area, 12 year olds and older.
Source: Arbitron Radio Market Ratings, Fall 2012, http://www.arbitron.com/home/mm001050.asp, accessed December 12, 2012.

frequencies, many rural towns cannot attract the advertising or noncommercial support to field even a single radio station. Contrast this situation with that of major markets such as New York City and Los Angeles, where more than 60 stations compete for residents' ears. Despite the large number of stations fighting for listeners, a frequency in a large city can be worth hundreds of millions of dollars.

How can so many stations survive in a major urban environment? The answer lies in the second major reason that radio has so far been able to compete in the new media world: segmentation, specifically format segmentation and audience segmentation. To understand what these activities mean and how they guide the radio industry, let's turn to the categories of production, distribution, and exhibition.

## Production in the Radio Industry

Research suggests that despite the large number of signals they may be able to receive, people tend to be loyal to no more than two or three radio stations. Think about the stations that you listen to at different times during the day. Most likely you listen to a station that plays music. Perhaps you listen to a "talk station," where listeners can phone in and speak their mind, or to an all-news station or an all-sports station.

Let's focus on the music station for the moment. What does that station create or "produce"? Unless the station is broadcasting a special concert, it almost certainly does not produce the music. Today, virtually all radio stations rely on recordings for their musical repertoire. Those recordings were created elsewhere; typically, they are CDs or digital files made by recording companies.

## THINKING ABOUT MEDIA LITERACY

Consider your own radio listening habits. What stations do you listen to most frequently? What kind(s) of programming does each one offer? What motivates you to listen to each one? Does it surprise you that most people listen only to two or three stations regularly? Why or why not?

### Radio Formats

If you think about it, you'll realize that what music-oriented radio stations produce is an overall sound: a flow of songs punctuated by the comments of the DJs, the commercials, the station identification, the news, the weather, and sports. Radio industry practitioners call this flow of on-air sounds a **format**, or the "personality" of the radio station. As such, it attracts certain kinds of listeners and not others. In the highly competitive media environment, radio practitioners have found that the way to prosper is not to be all things to all people. In both commercial and noncommercial radio, profits come from breaking the audience into different groups (segments) and then attracting a lucrative segment. For commercial broadcasters, a lucrative segment is one that many advertisers want to reach. For noncommercial broadcasters, a lucrative segment is a population group that has the money to help support the station or that corporate donors want to impress.

The fragmentation of the radio industry spurred the creation of many different radio formats, as radio executives struggled for ways to reduce their risk of failure amid enormous competition. They hoped that the formats they created would help them hone in on audiences that would be large and desirable enough for local and national advertisers (or donors) to support. As Table 11.3 shows, the format with the largest number of stations is currently country music. It is carried on more than 1,700 stations. According to Arbitron, it also garners the highest share of audience listening per average quarter hour (AQH) during key parts of the day (i.e., segments of the day): the 6:00 a.m.–10:00 a.m., 10:00 a.m.–3:00 p.m., and 3:00 p.m.–7:00 p.m. time slots. Overall, it lassoed 13.7 percent of the radio audience in the fall of 2010, whereas "news/talk/information" was second in station numbers and audience share, with 12.1 percent per AQH. "Adult contemporary," "contemporary hit radio," "Spanish," and "urban" formats had lower shares of the national audience.[7]

**Determining a Station's Format** A music radio station's format is governed by four factors:

- Music style
- Music time period
- Music activity level
- Music sophistication

**Music style** refers strictly to the type of music a radio station plays, regardless of how the music is packaged for airplay. **Music time period** refers to the time of the

**format**
the personality of a station, designed to attract a particular audience segment

**music style**
the aspect of a radio station's format that refers to the type of music the station plays

**music time period**
the aspect of a radio station's format that refers to the release date of the music that the station plays (e.g., "contemporary," "oldies")

**Table 11.3** Radio Stations in the United States, November 2012

| Format category | Total counts | Commercial | Noncommercial | Total AM | Total FM |
|---|---|---|---|---|---|
| Adult contemporary (AC) | 609 | 599 | 10 | 76 | 530 |
| Adult standards | 252 | 237 | 15 | 203 | 45 |
| Alternative rock | 377 | 103 | 274 | 9 | 351 |
| Black gospel | 228 | 206 | 22 | 171 | 55 |
| Classic hits | 670 | 659 | 11 | 88 | 578 |
| Classic rock | 487 | 472 | 15 | 8 | 478 |
| Classical | 214 | 18 | 196 | 4 | 208 |
| Contemporary Christian | 1,044 | 164 | 880 | 42 | 962 |
| Country | 2,049 | 2,028 | 21 | 508 | 1,536 |
| Easy listening | 30 | 20 | 10 | 5 | 22 |
| Ethnic | 162 | 135 | 27 | 108 | 50 |
| Gospel | 29 | 25 | 4 | 21 | 7 |
| Hot AC | 438 | 425 | 13 | 6 | 431 |
| Jazz | 112 | 33 | 79 | 13 | 93 |
| Modern AC | 14 | 13 | 1 | 0 | 13 |
| Modern rock | 141 | 90 | 51 | 5 | 134 |
| News/talk | 2,261 | 1,513 | 748 | 1,315 | 910 |
| Oldies | 625 | 587 | 38 | 309 | 301 |
| Preteen | 35 | 35 | 0 | 33 | 2 |
| R&B | 160 | 132 | 28 | 10 | 139 |
| R&B adult/oldies | 54 | 50 | 4 | 22 | 28 |
| Religion (teaching, variety) | 1,613 | 342 | 1,271 | 377 | 897 |
| Rhythmic AC | 19 | 19 | 0 | 0 | 19 |
| Rock | 312 | 299 | 13 | 1 | 309 |
| Soft adult contemporary | 151 | 148 | 3 | 19 | 132 |
| Southern gospel | 283 | 170 | 113 | 135 | 138 |
| Spanish | 1,009 | 827 | 182 | 488 | 483 |
| Sports | 702 | 701 | 1 | 550 | 151 |
| Top 40 | 608 | 573 | 35 | 7 | 598 |
| Urban AC | 159 | 156 | 3 | 39 | 119 |
| Variety | 759 | 46 | 713 | 51 | 464 |
| Format not available | 20 | 18 | 2 | 7 | 12 |
| Stations off the air | 381 | 245 | 136 | 120 | 232 |
| Construction permits | 913 | 349 | 564 | 81 | 828 |

Source: Inside Radio and M Street Corp, http://ftp.media.radcity.net/ZMST/insideradio/TOTALFormats.html, accessed December 12, 2012.

music's release. "Current" music generally refers to music released within the last year, "contemporary" music generally refers to music released within the past 10 to 15 years, "oldies" generally refers to music released between the mid-1950s and the mid-1970s, and "nostalgia" generally refers to music released prior to the mid-1950s.

**Music activity level** is a measure of the music's dynamic impact, ranging from soft and mellow to loud and hard-driving. The names of some music styles include built-in descriptions of the music's activity level, such as "hard rock" or "smooth jazz." **Music sophistication** is a reflection of the simplicity or complexity of the musical structure and lyrical content of the music played. This factor often determines the composition of a station's audience, and it is also reflected in the presentation of the station's on-air staff.

**music activity level**
the aspect of a radio station's format that refers to the played music's dynamic impact (e.g., "soft rock," "smooth jazz")

**music sophistication**
the aspect of a radio station's format that refers to the simplicity or complexity of the musical structure and lyrical content of the music played

## THINKING ABOUT MEDIA LITERACY

Think of your favorite radio station. What music style does it use? What music time period does it draw from? How would you describe its music activity level? How would you describe its music sophistication? Overall, how do you think those features work in targeting you as an audience member?

**Types of Formats** Table 11.4 presents a guide to radio formats, giving the format's target demographic and a brief description of the people in the format's target audience. This list of formats, although long, is not exhaustive. By some counts there are more than 40 different formats, including "Hawaiian" and "farm," with every format having variations. Moreover, new formats are created each year.

**Table 11.4** A Guide to Radio Station Formats in the United States

| Format | Format name | Description | Demographics |
|---|---|---|---|
| AC | Adult contemporary | An adult-oriented pop/rock station with no hard rock, often with a greater emphasis on non-current music and softer hits from the 1980s and 1990s | Women aged 25 to 54 |
| AH | Hot AC, adult contemporary hits | A more up-tempo, contemporary hits format, with no hard rock and no rap | Adults aged 25 to 34 |
| AP | Adult alternative | Eclectic rock, often with wide variations in musical style | Adults aged 25 to 44 |
| AR | Album rock | Mainstream rock 'n' roll, which can include guitar-oriented "heavy metal" | Men aged 25 to 44 |
| AS | Adult standards | Standards and older, non-rock popular music from the 1940s to the 1980s, which can include softer current popular music | Adults aged 35+ |
| BG | Black gospel | Current gospel songs and sermons geared toward African Americans | Adults aged 35+ |
| CH | Contemporary hits, Top 40 | Current popular music, often encompassing a variety of rock styles, with CH-RB indicating dance contemporary hits, CH-AR indicating rock-based contemporary hits, and CH-NR indicating new rock or modern rock–based contemporary hits | Teens & adults aged 20 to 24 |
| CR | Classic rock | Rock-oriented oldies, often mixed with album cuts from the 1960s, 1970s, and 1980s | Men aged 25 to 44 |

*(Continued)*

**Table 11.4** A Guide to Radio Station Formats in the United States (*Continued*)

| Format | Format name | Description | Demographics |
| --- | --- | --- | --- |
| CW | Country | Country music, including contemporary and traditional styles; CW-OL is country oldies | Adults aged 25+ |
| CZ | Classic hits | A rock-based oldies format, focusing on the 1970s | Adults aged 25 to 44 |
| EZ | Easy listening | Primarily instrumental cover versions of popular songs, with more up-tempo varieties of this format including soft rock originals, which may be mixed with "smooth jazz" or adult standards | Adults aged 35+ |
| ET | Ethnic | Programs geared to various ethnicities, primarily in languages other than English | Variety of ages |
| FA | Fine arts–classical | Fine arts "classical" music often includes opera, theater, and/or culture-oriented news and talk | Adults aged 35+ |
| JZ | Jazz | Mostly instrumental, often mixed with soft AC, which includes both traditional jazz and "smooth jazz" or "new AC" | Adults aged 25+ |
| MA | Modern AC | An adult-oriented softer modern rock format with less heavy, guitar-oriented music than the younger new rock | Mostly women aged 25 to 44 |
| MT | Financial talk | All financial or "money-talk" | Adults aged 35+ |
| NR | New rock, modern rock | Current rock, mainstream "alternative," and heavier guitar-oriented hits | Teens & adults aged 20 to 35 |
| NX | News | All news, either local or network in origin, with stations also having this description if a significant block of time is devoted to news | Adults aged 35+ |
| OL | Oldies | Popular music, usually rock-oriented, with 80% or more non-current music, with CW-OL indicating country oldies and RB-OL indicating R&B oldies | Adults aged 25 to 55 |
| PT | Preteen | Music, drama, or readings intended primarily for a preteen audience | Children aged 12 & under |
| RB | R&B, urban | Covers a wide range of musical styles geared toward African Americans, which can also be called "urban contemporary" or "hip-hop" | Teens & adults aged 20 to 24 |
| RC | Religious contemporary | Modern and rock-based religious music | All ages |
| RG | Religious gospel | Traditional religious music | Adults aged 25+ |
| RL | Religion | Local or syndicated religious programming, often spoken-word, sometimes mixed with music | Adults aged 25+ |
| SA | Soft adult contemporary | A cross between adult contemporary and easy listening, primarily non-current, soft rock originals | Mostly women aged 25+ |
| SB | Soft urban contemporary | Soft R&B, sometimes mixed with smooth jazz, often heavy in oldies | Adults aged 35+ |
| SG | Southern gospel | Country-flavored gospel music, also includes the "Christian country" or "positive country" format | Adults aged 25+ |
| SS | Spanish | Spanish-language programming, often paired with another type of programming, with equivalents of English formats including: SS-EZ (easily listening); SS-CH (contemporary hits); SS-AC ("modern" music); SS-NX-TK (news-talk); SS-RA (ranchero music); SS-TP (salsa, tropical); SS-TJ (tejano); SS-MX (regional Mexican); or SS-VA (variety) | All ages |

(*Continued*)

**Table 11.4** (*Continued*)

| Format | Format name | Description | Demographics |
|--------|-------------|-------------|--------------|
| SX | Sports | Listed only if all or a substantial block of a broadcast day is devoted to play-by-play, sports news, interviews, or telephone-talk | Men aged 25+ |
| TK | Talk | Talk, either local or network in origin, which can be telephone-talk, interviews, information, or a mix | Adults aged 25+ |
| VA | Variety | Incorporating four or more distinct formats, either block-programmed or airing simultaneously | All ages |

Source: News Generation, Inc., http://www.newsgeneration.com/radio_resources/formats.htm, accessed December 12, 2012.

**Selecting the Right Format** Because the format is the basis for attracting a target audience, radio station executives spend a lot of time developing it—often hiring **format consultants** to analyze the competition and choose a format that will attract the most lucrative audience niche possible. Most of the formats are based on music, but the bottom-line issue is a station's ability to gather a distinct audience for sponsors, not the aesthetics or diversity of its sound. People in the industry often use the term **narrowcasting** to describe the activity of going after specific slices of the radio audience that are especially attractive to advertisers. One well-known radio consultant explained that a radio station's need for distinct listeners was the reason behind narrowcasting: "As the [audience] pie gets thinner and thinner [because of the large number of competing stations], it's not so much whether you have ten thousand listeners at any given time . . . [but] what's the difference between [stations] A, B, C, and D."

**format consultants**
individuals hired by a radio station to analyze the competition and select a format that will attract the most lucrative audience niche possible

**narrowcasting**
going after specific slices of the radio audience that are especially attractive to advertisers

## Determining Listening Patterns

**Listening patterns** describe people's habits of radio use. Radio industry executives suggest that the following five propositions about listening patterns help them effectively segment audiences:

**listening patterns**
the habits that describe people's use of radio

- Individuals tend to listen to only three radio stations at any particular period in their lives, with the most "preferred" of those stations taking up 65–70 percent of their listening time.
- In the United States, there tends to be a large and widening divide between the music preferences of black, white, and Hispanic people.
- Men and women often have separate musical interests.
- People who are 10 years apart in age tend to belong to different "music generations" with different tastes.
- Music preferences can be useful tools for identifying people with distinct styles of living and buying.

Format consultants argue, for example, that they can construct formats that will divide the African American audience by age and lifestyle. Several cities have urban/adult contemporary stations that combine the features of both adult contemporary and urban contemporary stations. They try to reach an older African American audience by playing both current songs and the "soft" tunes that were popular in these listeners' youths. In a similar vein, the news/talk format can be further divided into distinct subformats such as all news, sports talk, motivational talk, and political talk.

Consultants point out that it is the combination of a radio station's cues—the kind of music or talk, the presence of announcers and their speech patterns, the presence or absence of jingles and other identifiers (called interstitials in the business)—that keep listeners of particular genders, ages, races, and ethnicities coming back.

## Working with Formats

Once station management chooses a target audience and a format for a local station with the help of consultants, the station's personnel are typically responsible for working with the format—producing it and making it attractive to the target audience on a daily basis (see Figure 11.3).

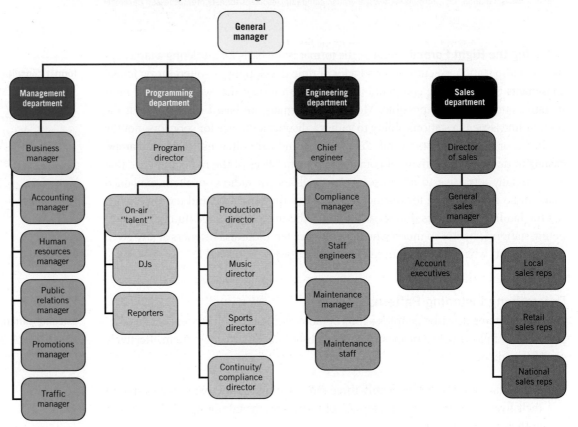

**Figure 11.3**
Organizational structure of a typical radio station

The general manager is in charge of the entire station operation. He or she represents the owners of the station and is responsible for its activities. The station's sound is controlled by the chief engineer, the news director, and the program director. The chief engineer makes sure that the station's sound goes over the air reliably and, with the help of the compliance manager, that the station's equipment complies with the technical rules of the Federal Communications Commission. The news director supervises news that is read over the air, perhaps assisted by reporters. In preparation for delivering the news over the air, these workers scan the news wires for relevant stories and conduct brief interviews with local officials in order to supplement their stories.

The program director works to ensure that the station's programming is consistent with the format and popular with the target audience and controls the station's on-air functions. Almost everything a listener hears over the air is the responsibility of the program director. The on-air personalities, or DJs, work for the program director. The program director is often assisted by a music director and a promotions manager. In many cases, these individuals also handle a shift on the air.

The average on-air personality (also known as **on-air talent**) works a four- or five-hour shift. Although this may sound like cushy work, it isn't. Running a format requires being able to handle many different, time-sensitive tasks simultaneously. During his or her hours on the air, a DJ may play up to 75 records and an equal number of commercials. In addition, the personality will answer select listener phone calls, manage on-air contests or promotions, and update the weather forecast or sports scores. Keeping all these format elements in order while sounding upbeat on the air requires a fair amount of technical skill. Using computers, station employees carefully ensure that when a song ends a new one smoothly begins. Otherwise, the station will transmit **dead air**—that is, nothing. Silence is a big taboo in radio because the mandate is to keep the target audience interested. Figuring out how to fill time attractively is a big challenge for a DJ. After their shift in the on-air studio, many disc jockeys move to a production studio, where they create items like commercials or comedy bits for later airing.

Wendy Williams, most popular for her role as a celebrity gossip "shock jockette," had a radio show on WBLS, a popular hip-hop station in New York City. Other well-known personalities, such as Steve Harvey, also had programs. Williams left broadcast radio in 2009 to host her own television talk show, *The Wendy Williams Show*.

## Producing the Playlist

Let's assume you have been named the program director of a new Top 40 station. What do you play to attract your target audience of young people in their teens and twenties? Your DJs need a playlist to guide them. The **playlist** is the roster of songs the DJs can put on the air (see Figure 11.4). The first step in creating a playlist is to find the appropriate songs that reflect the format. Most stations designate 600–700 songs that quickly signal their station's personality to listeners and that they play in rotation. In addition, stations that play contemporary music regularly highlight new songs by adding 50–100 songs to the rotation list each week. Sometimes an artist is so well known that his or her songs will be added automatically, or a new song just sounds so good that it is immediately added to the playlist. But more often than not, adding a song requires careful thought. Program directors tend to believe listeners are fickle and will tune out of a station if it plays a song they don't want to hear. When in doubt, programmers use research.

**on-air talent**
term referring to radio workers whose voices and personalities are broadcast over the radio's airwaves

**dead air**
the silence on the airwaves that is produced when a radio station fails to transmit sound

**playlist**
the roster or lineup of songs that a radio station can play on the air during a given period of time

## Conducting Research to Compile the Playlist

Research can take many forms. Stations test the general music rotation by inviting a sample of known listeners to a physical or online location and carrying out a **burn music test**. This test involves playing many of the playlist's songs for the people—or asking the surveyed people to go to a website and click on the songs—to determine which ones still draw interest and which have lost their popularity (or "burned out"). When it comes to adding new songs, executives may look at what successful stations in other cities are playing. Executives may check trade periodicals such as *Billboard*. They may go on the internet to see what people are talking about and downloading, and they may even subscribe to services offered by companies that audit what songs people are downloading illegally. They also may survey listeners in person or online from time to time and ask them about their preferences. In these surveys, the station may ask a listener to rate certain songs. Only songs that test well with the audience will receive substantial airplay.

Research can also shape the overall direction of a station. Stations or a research firm they hire may conduct **focus groups**, gathering and interviewing groups of area

**burn music test**
surveying people to determine which songs still draw interest and which have lost their popularity (or "burned out")

**focus groups**
assemblages of 8 to 10 carefully chosen people who are asked to discuss their habits and opinions about one or more topics

**Figure 11.4**

A sample playlist. This excerpted playlist from KISS 102.7—Los Angeles, California's number one hit radio station—represents some of the songs that KISS can play for a certain period of time. This playlist is from August 3, 2010.

| KISS FM playlist for March 8, 2010 | | |
|---|---|---|
| Rank | Title | Artist |
| 1 | Nothin on You | B.o.B. |
| 2 | Tik Tok | Kesha |
| 3 | Carry Out | Timbaland Feat. Justin Timberlake |
| 4 | Rude Boy | Rihanna |
| 5 | Tie Me Down | New Boyz/Ray J |
| 6 | Telephone | Lady Gaga/Beyonce |
| 7 | Solo | Iyaz |
| 8 | Imma Bee | Black Eyed Peas |
| 9 | Bad Romance | Lady Gaga |
| 10 | In My Head | Jason Derulo |
| 11 | Today Was a Fairytale | Taylor Swift |
| 12 | What Do You Want from Me | Adam Lambert |
| 13 | Bedrock | Young Money/Lloyd |
| 14 | Sexy Chick | David Guetta/Akon |
| 15 | We Are the World 2010 | Various |
| 16 | According to You | Orianthi |
| 17 | Young Forever | Jay-z/Mr. Hudson |
| 18 | Blah Blah Blah | Kesha/3 Oh! 3 |
| 19 | Lalala | Lmfao |
| 20 | Empire State of Mind | Jay-z/Alicia Keys |

residents (usually 8 to 10 per group) who fit the profile of the station's target audience. The individuals may be asked for their thoughts on various local radio stations and what they like and dislike about a certain station personality. These sessions are designed to capture the spontaneous reactions of the participants. Radio industry executives believe that focus group research gives them a feel for what their target audience really thinks about the station.

## Maintaining the Format and Retaining the Target Audience

No matter what their format, programmers work hard to please the largest possible segment of the station's target audience. To hold the interest of those who fall within the target audience but rarely listen to a particular station—that is, **fringe listeners**—the programmer wants to play only the most appropriate songs. Otherwise, when these fringe listeners tune in, they will quickly tune out again because the station is playing something they do not know or like. But the **core audience**—listeners who spend a lot of time listening to a radio station—quickly tire of hearing the same songs over and over again. A programmer must therefore carefully balance the desires of the station's fringe listeners and those of its core audience.

**fringe listeners**
listeners who fall within the target audience but rarely listen to a particular station

**core audience**
listeners who spend a lot of time listening to a radio station

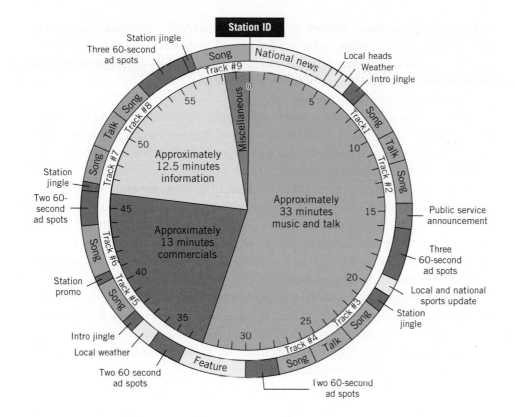

**Figure 11.5**

A sample format clock. Radio programmers and disc jockeys use a format clock like this one to arrange what will be played in one hour's time on their station—from local and national advertisements to news and songs to station jingles and promotions, all to keep the listener tuned in.

To strike this balance, most radio stations create an hourly **format clock** (also called a **format wheel**). This circular chart divides one hour of the station's format into different, timed program elements (see Figure 11.5). The clock helps the programmer to maintain stability while making sure that key service elements show up at specific times. For example, a radio station may schedule news at the top of the hour, followed by a hit song. By FCC requirements, and to help listeners remember which station they are hearing, the clock instructs DJs to broadcast the station's call letters and frequency often. Stations also may use jingles to improve their listeners' retention of the station's identity. Perhaps most important from the station owner's viewpoint, the clock dictates when on-air personalities play those vital commercials.

The clock also provides the framework for the scheduling and placement of music. Many stations use complex music-scheduling software to make sure that individual songs are properly spaced and balanced. The clock guarantees that the most popular records are repeated more often, whereas less popular records air less frequently.

The programming approach may vary somewhat during different times of the day. In radio, **drive time**—or the period when people are driving to and from work during early weekday mornings and late afternoons—is when radio stations expect to capture their largest audience. Given the large audience, advertising rates are also at their highest during these time slots. The morning shift is especially important for the station, and finding the right person or team to handle a station's early morning shift is often a great challenge. It is a strong belief within the radio business that a good morning personality will keep listeners tuned in to the station for the rest of the day. Funny morning personalities can therefore command large salaries.

Because so much listenership (and advertising money) rides on drive time, program directors cannot afford much risk in terms of what is aired. During times when

**format clock (format wheel)**
a circular chart that divides one hour of a radio station's format into different timed program elements

**drive time**
early weekday mornings and late afternoons—when people are driving to and from work—when radio stations expect to capture their largest audience

there are fewer listeners—like late at night or on weekends—program directors can be more adventurous, using these hours of lower listenership to introduce new music. Through its request line, a station can hear from members of its audience about whether they like a new song or not. This feedback might affect whether the program director will slot it during drive time.

Companies that own several stations with similar formats—for example, country music or adult contemporary—often take a group approach to programming. They conduct music tests with people from across the country, and they apply their results to all the stations. Moreover, these large radio firms—for example, Clear Channel and Cumulus—often hire on-air talent to present the music for all or some of their stations from a central location. The same DJ presents the same music to listeners in several cities while giving the impression that the program is local. In fact, a local service may cut into the program feed at precise moments to provide the traffic or weather. The aim, of course, is to save as much money as possible on local programming executives and on-air personalities.

It is interesting to note that most on-air personalities have little input into what music they play. Program directors and their general managers believe that the stakes are too high and the risk too great to allow a single DJ to decide what music to play based on his or her mood. In contemporary radio, a carefully crafted format must be consistent throughout the broadcast day.

## Distribution in the Radio Industry

In large cities more so than in small and rural ones, the sound that a station broadcasts every day may be mostly locally produced and so locally distributed. When a station group programs the DJs or talk show hosts centrally, production and distribution obviously originate from afar. But even when much of a station's live programming originates locally, there may be interest in broadcasting live programming from elsewhere—for example, concerts by famous rock acts or programs with famous talk show hosts—in order to attract the right kind of listeners to the station. Yet paying to create these programs is often far beyond the means of an individual radio station. As such, most stations depend on outside suppliers to supplement their local programming.

### The Role of Networks, Syndicators, and Format Networks

Traditionally, outside suppliers have fallen into two categories: networks and syndicators. A **network** provides a regular schedule of programming materials to its affiliate radio stations for broadcast. A **syndicator** typically makes a licensing deal for one show (or one series of shows) at a time. In recent years these distinctions have been disappearing. As an example, the *Rush Limbaugh Show* is a popular talk program distributed by Premiere Radio Networks (a subsidiary of Clear Channel). Stations may carry only a few Premiere talk programs (e.g., Sean Hannity, Rev. Jesse Jackson, *The Bob & Tom Show*) or many of its 22 programs offered during different times of the week.

The ultimate in network programming is the growing phenomenon of round-the-clock **format networks**. DialGlobal is a firm that calls itself "radio's leading provider of satellite-delivered music formats." Its website tell radio station owners that DialGlobal's

---

**network**
a company that distributes programs simultaneously to radio stations that agree to carry a substantial amount of its material on an ongoing basis; typically, a network provides a regular schedule of programming material to its affiliate stations for broadcast

**syndicator**
a company that licenses programming to radio stations on a market-by-market basis

**format networks**
programming firms that provide subscribing radio stations with all the programming they need to fill their airwaves 24 hours a day, seven days a week; often the station needs only to insert local commercial spots into the programming

"expert music programmers create a targeted format for your market."[8] The firm provides a subscribing station with all the programming it needs, and the station can insert local commercials, news, and weather when needed. A station affiliated with one of these networks no longer needs to have a fully staffed programming department, which means saving perhaps hundreds of thousands of dollars annually. These stations can still hire a person to deliver local news and weather so as to give listeners a sense that they are linked to the community.

These different forms of program suppliers typically circulate their material to stations via satellite. Sometimes the supplier charges the station. For example, Premiere often demands money from stations for carrying the highly popular *Rush Limbaugh Show*. Generally, though, stations don't pay to receive syndicated programming. Instead, programs are put on the air through **barter**. This means that the syndicator provides the show and keeps a number of minutes for the sale of commercials to advertisers. Such a company therefore makes most of its money by selling time on its programs to advertisers that want to reach the listeners of certain types of radio stations around the United States. They also may give the local station some of the advertising time available during the programming. In Philadelphia, for example, the station that airs Salem Radio Network's *The Dennis Prager Show* makes money during the first six minutes of the hour by running its own commercials during the news. During the 54 minutes of *The Dennis Prager Show*, there are 16 minutes of commercials. The Salem Radio Network makes money running commercials across its networks during 5 of those minutes. The remaining 11 minutes make up commercial time that the station can sell to local or national advertisers.

Even noncommercial stations use networks. The largest of these networks, National Public Radio (NPR), distributes cultural and informational programming to its member stations across the country. It is probably best known for its news programs such as *All Things Considered* and *Talk of the Nation*. Another large noncommercial network is American Public Media (APM), which distributes such well-known programs as *Marketplace*, *On Being*, and *Prairie Home Companion*. Because noncommercial networks are prohibited from soliciting advertisements, these networks help defray their costs by getting foundations or companies to support a program in return for being mentioned on the air, as well as by charging a fee to their affiliated stations. Foundations and companies are attracted by the chance to parade their names in front of the typically well-educated, prosperous, and influential audiences that NPR and APM deliver.

**barter**
practice in which a syndicator provides the radio program and keeps a number of minutes for the sale of commercials to advertisers

## Exhibition in the Radio Industry

From the standpoint of the radio station's owner, the purpose of producing a format and/or buying one from a distributor (a network) is to make money at the exhibition point—the moment at which the format is actually broadcast from the station.

### Advertising's Role in Radio Exhibition

For the general manager and the program director, the success or failure of their product depends on whether the station's sales team can sell enough advertising to bring the station adequate profits. Three kinds of advertising come into radio stations:

- National spot advertising
- Network advertising
- Local advertising

**national spot advertising**
form of advertising in which airtime is purchased from a local radio station by national advertisers or their representatives

**network advertising**
form of radio advertising in which national advertisers or their representatives purchase airtime not from local radio stations but from the network that serves the radio station

**local advertising**
advertising money that comes from companies within listening range of the radio station

In **national spot advertising**, airtime is purchased from a local station by major national advertisers or their representatives, such as Nabisco, Paramount Pictures, and Maybelline. The word "spot" distinguishes this kind of sponsorship from **network advertising**, in which sponsors (perhaps also Nabisco, Paramount, and Maybelline) purchase airtime not from the station but from a network that serves the station. National advertisers use spots to target certain cities with particular ads. Buying network ads is often more efficient when the aim is to reach a particular radio audience across the country.

Although spot and network advertising are important to the radio industry, local advertising is especially critical. Of the $17.6 billion of advertising funneled into radio in 2010, **local advertising** accounted for about 81 percent of the total. A radio station's local market represents advertising dollars that the station can collect from businesses in the area. To gain this revenue, the station's sales manager and staff must convince local businesses and organizations to advertise on the station.

The sales manager works with the traffic manager to coordinate the placement of commercials. The traffic manager ensures that advertisements are scheduled and broadcast correctly. For example, it is considered bad practice to schedule commercials from directly competing companies, say Pepsi and Coca-Cola, right after each other.

## Learning Who Listens

Advertisers need to be convinced that they will benefit from paying for time on a radio station. The most basic question they ask is, how many people are listening? Answering that question with certainty is nearly impossible. Newspaper and magazine companies can actually count the individual copies of the paper or magazine sold to people. For electronic media, however, the product being delivered is by definition untouchable; it is sent out free over the air. As a result, the people who choose to listen to the product must be counted. Because it is nearly impossible to ask all the people in a community what radio station they listened to this morning, radio stations pay research firms to ask this question of a sample of the population designed to represent the entire community.

## Conducting Market Research to Determine Ratings

The largest firm that conducts radio audience measurement is Arbitron. The area in which Arbitron surveys people about a station is called the station's market. Des Moines, Iowa; Los Angeles, California; and Madison, Wisconsin are radio markets of different sizes. On a regular basis, Arbitron selects a sample of listeners in each radio market to participate in its survey. Arbitron then repeatedly tries to contact its selected sample. For example, say Arbitron reaches you at your home and asks you to participate. Given your interest in the mass media, you agree. The Arbitron representative asks you to fill out a diary listing all your radio listening for a week and then to return the diary online. The company pays you a token fee—usually a dollar or two—for your participation.

The diary contains space for a week's worth of responses, and you fill it out every time you listen to the radio. You promptly submit it through the company's website at the end of the week. The firm now has an accurate survey, right? Not so fast. This technique of audience measurement has some drawbacks. First, the research firm may have had difficulty getting a random sample of everyone in the area to participate. For example, people such as college students or seasonal workers move frequently or are hard to find, so they are often underrepresented in the survey sample. In addition, evidence suggests that people with busy lifestyles are less likely to participate than those who have more time on their hands. Therefore, the assumption that the sample is representative of the community is often invalid.

In addition, many of the people who do make it into the survey drop out or fail to fill out the diary completely. Though Arbitron designs the diary to be taken with the participant throughout the day, many participants do not do so. So at the end of a day or week, these participants must try to remember their station choices and recreate their listening activity before they write it down in the diary. Even listeners who try to participate conscientiously may accidentally record incorrect information. If you are like many people, you sometimes jump between stations while you are in your car. Would you be able to record which ones you heard?

Recognizing these problems, Arbitron has rolled out a device called a **portable people meter (PPM)** for tracking radio listening both at home and on the street. At this point, the company is using it in 48 large markets—for example, New York, Philadelphia, Houston, and Cleveland—though it says it hopes to eventually replace the diary in all U.S. markets. The PPM is a mobile phone–sized device that consumers wear throughout the day. It works by detecting identification codes that can be embedded in the audio portion of any transmission. The PPM can determine what consumers listen to on the radio; what they watch on broadcast, cable, and satellite TV; what media they stream on the internet; and what they hear in stores and entertainment venues. This approach also has flaws. For example, the PPM may pick up radio stations' codes as the person carrying it is walking through a store, even if the person is not listening to their transmissions.

Although no one believes Arbitron data are fully accurate, most local stations and advertisers use the diary-based Arbitron rating results because they are the best data available. When ratings are reported to subscribing stations, employees await the news with trepidation. Ratings are to station employees what report cards are to students: rows of raw numbers that summarize many months of effort. One **rating point** equals 1 percent of the population in a market. Because typically there are dozens of stations broadcasting in major markets, the ratings for individual stations are often quite small. Stations are considered successful if they manage to garner even four or five rating points. Yet the raw number is often not the only thing of interest to a radio advertiser. The extent to which the advertiser's target audience—in demographic and lifestyle terms—is cost-efficiently being reached is often more important. For example, a concert promoter may want to know which station in town attracts the greatest share of the young adult audience so that she can effectively buy advertising to attract a rock band's core audience.

Arbitron results give radio executives and advertisers information on such basic categories as listener gender, race, and age. These characteristics form the basis for discussions between a radio station's sales force and potential advertisers about the appropriateness of the station's target audience compared with those of other stations. To gather evidence about other audience characteristics that might also attract advertisers, many radio stations subscribe to Scarborough Research surveys. Scarborough conducts telephone surveys of a market's population and asks people questions about various aspects of their lives—from purchasing habits to hobbies to radio listening preferences. Radio stations' sales forces often link these data with Arbitron data. They

**portable people meter (PPM)**
Arbitron's electronic device for tracking radio listening both at home and on the street

**rating point**
one rating point equals 1 percent of the population in a market

Justin Bieber at JingleBall
sponsored by Aeropostale. This
promotional contest, which
targeted the parents of teenagers,
included the chance for free
tickets, and one selected winner
would also get a meet and greet
with Justin Bieber after the concert.

**radio promotion**
a radio contest or event in which
prizes are given out

then use the findings to try to convince certain local advertisers that their station can deliver the most appropriate audience. This doesn't always work, however, because Scarborough studies and others like them have their own drawbacks.

Sometimes advertisers purchase time on a radio station primarily because they believe that the format is suitable for their product or message and because the sales staff has arranged to tie them to a **radio promotion** (a contest or event in which prizes are given out) that will both highlight the advertiser and result in concrete responses from listeners to the advertiser. Almost everyone knows of a radio station that has given away cash prizes, trips, or concert tickets. The prizes are geared toward the demographic and lifestyle categories of the listening population that the station's management wants to attract.

A station whose ratings are up will often try to raise its advertising rates to reflect its increased popularity. Some station employees may directly benefit from the ratings report because their salaries are tied to ratings. But the celebration cannot last too long because a new ratings report card is always being prepared. Most large radio markets, such as Chicago, are surveyed year-round by Arbitron.

## When Stations Fare Poorly in the Ratings

When stations have fared poorly in the ratings, managers may institute immediate changes. Sometimes managers blame internal factors such as a poor choice of recorded music. They also may blame factors outside the station's control. For example, many music-intensive stations have poorer ratings during severe winters because listeners flock to competing news/talk stations for updates on school closings and icy roadways. In that case, a program director of a Top 40 station, for example, will recognize that the ratings fluctuation was due to unusual circumstances and may decide to make no changes in the hope that listeners will return to their normal habits with the approach of milder spring weather.

Often, however, poor ratings lead to personnel changes. A careful analysis of Arbitron data may indicate that a particular time slot is not performing as well as the program director and station manager expected. In this case, the on-air personality during that period is likely to be replaced. When a station has a history of poor ratings and revenue performance, station owners might decide to try a new station format in an effort to grab a larger target audience and more advertisers. Overnight, a station that is known for playing classical music may start playing country tunes. With these wholesale makeovers, it is not unusual for all employees associated with the station's old format to lose their jobs.

Although management may consider it deadly to stick with an unprofitable format, instituting a new format on a radio station also has risks. Listeners of the old format are likely to feel abandoned and angry, and it may be tough to get the new target audience to find the station. Attempts to attract new listeners through publicity stunts and advertisements on billboards, on TV, and in newspapers can be quite expensive. And if the new format doesn't work, management may be in a worse situation than it was before the change. Nevertheless, the formats of certain stations do change fairly frequently; their managers believe that the benefits of responding to the shifting interests of audiences and advertisers outweigh the costs and risks of change.

# Radio and the New Digital World

Radio executives today find themselves in a world fraught with far more problems than those posed by new format trends. The most obvious change is that after decades of revenue growth, the financial strength of the terrestrial radio industry has plummeted. In 2011, advertisers spent about $17.4 billion on terrestrial radio. That may sound like a lot, but it was far less than the $20.1 billion they spent in 2006. Nevertheless, it represented a 1 percent increase from 2010 and was the second year of growth after several years of major losses.[9] Radio industry leaders attribute some of the revenue losses to the major economic downturn and predict that ad money will return as the economy improves. But radio executives recognize that the drop in revenues also reflects a realization by advertisers that the time audiences—especially young audiences—spend with radio is decreasing. Recall from Table 11.1 that the number of listeners of an average quarter hour of FM radio stations declined from 22.4 million in 2005 to 21.3 million in 2008.

The main reason for this decline is that many people have taken advantage of digital convergence to shift toward digital sources of music. They download songs from certain Internet sites, listen to streaming songs from other sites, and share their favorites with friends. Others turn to satellite radio. Let's look at each area.

### Satellite Radio

Satellite radio is a technology through which a consumer can receive streaming channels of music and/or talk through a special receiver (see Figure 11.6). Even though it is connected to the word "radio," the activity has little to do with the technology of broadcasting as it developed over the past century. In 2008, the two competing players in the satellite radio market, Sirius and XM, merged to become Sirius XM Radio. Sirius XM makes money from subscriptions (which cost about $20 a month) as well as through advertising on some of the hundreds of channels it offers that feature a wide variety of formats. Sirius XM produces the programs, sometimes in joint ventures with other firms (Oprah's Harpo Productions, for example, produces programming for the channel *Oprah and Friends*). The channels are uploaded to satellites and can be picked up in most places around the country by receivers sold at stores such as Best Buy. In addition, Sirius XM has made deals with major car companies to offer their receivers as original equipment. Some of the equipment is portable, making it possible to listen at home and while outdoors, as well as in the car.

In the years leading up to the merger of Sirius and XM, observers worried that the combination could create a behemoth that would set prices and squeeze consumers. Yet by 2012, Sirius XM had 24 million subscribers—not a small number, but not the large proportion of the population that some had predicted. Ominously for the firm, several years of high growth seem to be slowing, and most new subscribers enter because of a free year of programming that comes with a new car they bought. Radio industry analysts now believe that although satellite radio may have an enduring role to play in the U.S. media system, it is not a fundamental threat to broadcast radio.

---

## THINKING ABOUT MEDIA LITERACY

Although most of this chapter discusses radio audiences in terms of individual listeners, many stores also use radio as part of the shopping experience they offer. Some stores use satellite radio in particular. Why do you think they use satellite radio instead of terrestrial radio? What might be some advantages and disadvantages?

---

1. Sirius and XM both produce live and taped programming, ranging broadly from Alanis Morissette to sports and news.

2. The programming is beamed to satellites from dishes operated by each company.

3. The satellites broadcast the signal back to Earth, where it's picked up directly by receiver units. The signal is also received and rebroadcast by repeater stations in metropolitan areas. XM uses two geostationary satellites (right) that remain constantly above the United States. Sirius uses three satellites, two of which are always over the country.

4. A receiver buffers the broadcast for a few seconds, so if it loses the satellite signal, it can use one from a repeater station, helping ensure a continuous broadcast. Overpasses and tall buildings are particular problems.

**Figure 11.6**
How satellite radio works

## MEDIA TODAY & CULTURE DIVERSITY PROGRAMMING ON SATELLITE RADIO

In 2007, the two primary providers of satellite radio in the United States, Sirius and XM radio, moved to merge. The U.S. Justice Department approved the merger without conditions in 2008. The Federal Communications Commission offered its own approval several months later, but the commission added some conditions as part of the approval. In addition to setting a price cap and paying back fines, the new company was required to allocate 8 percent of its channels to noncommercial and minority programming.[1] The exact number came down to six channels from each service, for a total of 12.[2] Companies leasing these channels could not have had a previous relationship with Sirius or XM.[3]

After some delay, Sirius XM set the conditions for the companies who could lease the channels. The company sought programming that represented "diverse viewpoints and/or diverse entertainment content."[4] Further, the company sought "improved service to historically underserved audiences [and] original content of a type not otherwise available to Sirius XM subscribers."[5] Ultimately, Sirius XM would choose the companies that would lease the channels and provide the programming for it.

Ahead of the deadline for applications in January 2011, several companies and organizations protested the definition on grounds of vagueness and ambiguity and offered a petition of them.[6] Some of those groups included Radio One, a company that attempts to reach black audiences, and the Minority Media and Telecommunications Council. The RSS Network, which provides Spanish-language programming, protested that the petition would only delay the leasing of the stations.[7]

In the end, five organizations got licenses, including Howard University, Brigham Young University, Eventus/National Latino Broadcasting, WorldBand Media, and KTV Radio.[8] Howard University would offer programming for African Americans from historically black colleges and universities. BYU would offer programming for Mormons. Eventus and WorldBand Media would offer Spanish-language programming. And KTV would offer Korean-language programming. Programming would include music and talk from all the lease holders.

For more on the merger, see the FCC website: http://transition.fcc.gov/transaction/xm-sirius.html

## Online Radio

Online radio could more appropriately be called **audio streaming** because it involves the flow of music or other audio signals to a computer via the packet-switching technologies that are at the core of the internet. As we noted earlier, unlike a song downloaded from the web, streaming music is not designed to be saved by the computer through which it is playing, unless a special recording device captures it and translates it into a savable format (e.g., MP3). Thousands of websites offer streaming music. When they provide it, they pay royalty fees to rights organizations representing the publishers and artists. Many of these sites earn money when a listener clicks to buy a song from a digital music store linked to the site. Often the sites also make money through advertising. We can distinguish between two broad types: *streaming by category or interest* and *streaming on demand*.

**Streaming by Category or Interest** Companies that adopt this strategy offer music based around genres the listener chooses (e.g., rock, hip-hop, jazz) or around personalization, offering the specific types of music the listener seems to like. Personalization of music is a growing, if complex, activity. You may be familiar with the way the popular music streaming site Pandora carries out this activity. Pandora describes itself as "a new kind of radio—stations that play only music you like."[10] It supports itself through a "freemium" model: you can get it free, but you will receive ads. If you pay a monthly fee, the ads go away, and you will get higher-quality audio.

**audio streaming**
practice in which an audio file is delivered to a computer-like device from a website so that it can be heard while it is coming into the device but cannot be saved or stored

Pandora attempts personalization by first systematically analyzing the musical tracks of songs ("melody, harmony, instrumentation, rhythm, vocals, lyrics ... and more"). When you first use the site, it asks you to note a favorite artist, song, or genre, and Pandora's computers work to construct a flow of sounds (it actually has comedy tracks as well as music) that its formulas predict you will appreciate. People disagree on how well it works. Pandora asks listeners to give its computer program feedback (thumbs up, thumbs down) to help the computer adjust the choices. If you find the personalization doesn't work, you can still turn to Pandora's genre stations and go with the flow.

**Streaming on Demand** Many listeners don't want computers choosing their streams. They want to pick individual tracks and albums by themselves. Rhapsody and Spotify are two firms that offer this type of service. These companies have also adopted a "freemium" model, offering a limited version without charge (but with ads) and a more robust service for a monthly fee. Visitors can choose an artist and are offered the possibility of playing individual tracks or entire albums. Both services also offer a streaming-by-category option based on music genres; Spotify calls this service "playlist radio."

Another form of streaming on demand involves music videos. As noted in chapter 10, a popular site for this activity is VEVO, which is owned by Sony Music, Universal Music, and Abu Dhabi Media. VEVO describes itself as "the world's leading all-premium music video and entertainment platform." With "all-premium," VEVO is distinguishing itself from another streaming-on-demand music powerhouse, YouTube, which Google owns. Many artists have "official" YouTube channels where visitors will typically find music videos as well as fan-related paraphernalia. As it turns out, Google and VEVO have a strong relationship. Google makes deals to place VEVO videos on many websites in exchange for being able to serve ads with the videos. Google and VEVO then share the advertising revenue. You can also find VEVO videos on YouTube.

Most online radio firms—whether they stream by category or on demand—allow listeners who pay for the service to receive it on a number of platforms, including laptops, desktops, smartphones, tablets, and some car audio systems. They also trumpet the ability of subscribers to share what they are hearing with friends. Spotify, for example, is equipped to feed your listening activity directly to your Facebook friends. (Spotify requires you to register via Facebook; you may or may not like this idea.) On-demand firms also allow people to save the lists of streams they have created. Say, for example, you are interested in movie scores in Warner Bros. films. By clicking through Rhapsody, you could create a list of music that, as a group, represents your understanding of Warner Bros. movie scores. You could then "publish" this list on Rhapsody so that any subscriber, by clicking on a link, could hear all the pieces you've strung together.

## THINKING ABOUT MEDIA LITERACY

Many websites, including music-oriented ones such as VEVO and Spotify, require that users use their Facebook or Twitter accounts to register and participate. Do you agree with this practice? What advantages does this practice offer the user? How about the companies? Should companies be, required to offer an alternative for those who do not wish to use Facebook or Twitter? Why or why not?

## Traditional Radio's Responses to Digital Music

You may have noticed that the preceding examples given for online radio—streaming by category and streaming on demand—are services not owned by companies that own terrestrial radio companies. VEVO is a product of the recording industry's attempts to find ways to profit from convergence in the age of digital-music piracy. Google, Rhapsody, and Spotify are based solely in the internet world; Wall Street analysts call these businesses "pure-plays," indicating that they are not related to traditional (or "legacy") media.

But legacy media firms—in this case, terrestrial radio companies—are not asleep when it comes to digital competition. So far, they see satellite radio as only a minor annoyance to their business, but they know that online radio is a much bigger competitive force. One optimistic mantra that some radio executives repeat is that people like the "curation" function of traditional radio. That is, people rely on their favorite stations to tell them about new music. Then they go online to find those songs—to illegally download them or to legally stream or purchase them.

---

## THINKING ABOUT MEDIA LITERACY

Radio station executives put a lot of energy into narrowing down the number of representative songs they play on the air each day—a process they call "curation." Given that stations choose music to draw listeners and attract advertisers, how important do you think the radio station's curation function is in the contemporary industry environment? Many music websites allow users to perform this same curation function for their own personal preferences and share these preferences with their social networks. Do you think individual curation activities will match or supersede those of radio stations in the future? Why or why not?

---

One way terrestrial radio companies have tried to keep people listening is by using what they call HD radio to multiply the number of stations they use for this curation function. **HD**, or **hybrid digital/analog radio**, is a system in which digital signals of AM and FM stations are sent along with the traditional analog station sounds on the same frequencies allocated to the analog stations. The technology was developed by the company iBiquity Digital in 1991 and was approved for use by the FCC in 2002. HD stations simulcast programs digitally, providing listeners with better audio quality than traditional radio, as well as side channels that allow for additional programming. HD radio programming is free, but people who want to listen must have a special receiver to get the signals. So far, only a small percentage of American adults say they have ever listened to HD radio, and the technology doesn't seem to be drawing nearly the interest that internet radio is generating. Radio executives are hoping that the auto industry will help by installing HD radios in new cars.

Yet as we have just seen, this idea that terrestrial radio—AM, FM, or HD—has a special function doesn't hold up. The internet's new music distribution and exhibition platforms perform many of the same functions that contemporary AM and FM stations do and are available when people want them. Online radio offers many vehicles for curation, including ways to learn what your friends are hearing when they are hearing it. Online radio outlets help guide listeners through the thicket of songs that they feel they should know about or might want to learn about. In fact, internet radio sites often

**HD (hybrid digital/analog) radio**
a system in which digital signals of AM and FM stations are sent along with the traditional analog station sounds on the same frequencies allocated to the analog stations

present a lot of information about the music they are playing, including biographies of the artists and discographies (i.e., lists of the records they have put out).

The one advantage that broadcast radio has retained is its presence in virtually all automobiles. Americans report that fully one-quarter of their music listening takes place in the car, and much of that is still captured by traditional radio stations. The relative lack of in-car competition may represent only short-term relief, however. With the increasing ability to connect car systems to mobile devices, it will not be long before many people have the choice to stream sounds from the internet virtually anywhere, including from behind the steering wheel.

Astute radio executives realize that the changes in music-listening habits we see are only beginning. They are determined to find a way to join the online world rather than fight it. Therefore, broadcast radio executives are moving rapidly to work with internet radio. Just about every radio station's management realizes that it has to have a website. The site streams what the terrestrial radio station is playing, but it goes beyond that to engage the user with the personality that the station aims to project. Consider the website of Power99FM, one of five Clear Channel radio stations in Philadelphia. This station focuses on "bangin hip hop and R&B," to quote the site. The website is filled with songs, music videos, and in-studio performances that reflect the radio station's theme. Listeners can go to the site to find out about the station's contests and promotions. You can sign up for a VIP club membership to "enter exclusive online contests for concert tickets, hot prizes, movie passes, sporting event tickets, cash, trips, cars, you name it." Surrounding all this content is a large promotional and advertising environment, with advertising for local and national companies. In addition, the site connects to iheartradio.com, Clear Channel's platform for the websites of its 350+ stations. The site also allows you to stream albums for free, create a personal playlist of music videos, and see various kinds of ads, some of which (e.g., movie trailers) are integrated into the site as if they are merely more Clear Channel content.

All these activities demonstrate the power of Clear Channel to create deals with recording companies and artists for the right to post material across Clear Channel's many websites. Like other internet music sites, visitors can purchase albums online from the site, for which the company gets a transaction commission. In fact, with the idea of guiding consumers to purchase music, Clear Channel was among the radio groups to cheerlead a 2007 development in HD radio technology: users who "tag" a song on a special HD receiver now have the option to purchase it or find more information about it when their iPod is synced with iTunes software.

The websites of stations owned by CBS Radio, Citadel, and other firms have many of the same features as the Clear Channel sites. CBS owns Last.fm, which its website says "lets you effortlessly keep a record of what you listen to from any player. Based on your taste, Last.fm recommends you more music and concerts!" It also tries to facilitate discussions ("community") around the music. It provides streams of its radio stations' programming, with specially inserted commercials. These activities reflect a changing radio industry that senses it must define itself—to its audiences and its advertisers—as far more broad than AM and FM radio.

## Media Ethics and the Construction of Radio Audiences

Our excursion through the radio business provides an opportunity to explore an issue that relates particularly to radio but also is relevant to many parts of the media system: the issue of how the industry "constructs" its audience. Recall from

chapter 3 that media companies construct audiences in the sense that they attach demographic, lifestyle, and psychographic labels to people based on research and then
often act as if these labels reflect the truth about the people who read and hear their
materials. The problem is that all attempts to describe who people are and what they
want conflict with the reality that individuals are complex and that any descriptions
of them will inevitably not provide a "full" picture even if the facts presented are correct. From a media-literate standpoint, the best way to look at audience research is
to ask three questions:

- How do the methods used in audience research affect the kinds of facts collected
  about the people who use a medium?
- How do these facts, in turn, lead to certain ideas or pictures of those people?
- How do these ideas and pictures affect the extent to which, and the way in
  which, advertisers want to spend money to reach them?

These might not seem like questions that relate to media ethics, but they sometimes are. For example, research firms may use methods that underrepresent certain social groups. As a result, advertisers might not try to reach those groups, and
so media firms might not try to create materials with them in mind. Just this sort of
problem happened with Arbitron's Portable People Meter (the PPM), which we discussed earlier. When the company rolled out the technology to replace the diary in
a few cities during the mid-2000s, the ratings for stations programming to African
Americans and Latinos dropped drastically. A station in Philadelphia changed its
format away from certain African American sounds after the findings were released.
But soon executives at stations targeting African American and Latino audiences
began to complain that Arbitron had not included enough people with those characteristics in its PPM samples. This resulted in the ratings for their radio stations
dropping drastically. There were angry protests, and an industry group called the
Media Ratings Council threatened not to certify the PPMs in various cities if Arbitron didn't fix its samples. Arbitron executives agreed to make their panels more
representative.

The Media Ratings Council does perform an important service for the advertising
industry in making sure the sampling procedures of research firms meet statisti-
cians' standards. In this case, the council's intervention helped keep certain formats
alive for African American and Latino audiences in particular areas. But sometimes,
even though the statistical approaches are acceptable, the very method of audience
research and the very categories of questions asked of the audience may lead to
findings that make claims that either overplay or underplay the medium's importance in society.

Take radio's use of diaries as an example. Apart from major cities, radio station
ratings—and trends in radio listening—are still based on the sheets Arbitron asks
individuals to fill out at certain times during the year. The chart requires participants to note the stations they listen to by the quarter hour. Radio executives read-
ily admit that the diary is a highly flawed measurement. Because so much listening
is carried out in a car, it is unlikely that most people fill out the diary as they are
listening—that is, while driving. Arbitron considers that most people fill them out
at the end of the listening day or even a few days afterward. It's likely that people
write down only the stations that they typically like. Yet most claims about radio
station ratings, about time spent listening, and about radio's popularity in society
come from those ratings.

Compared to the diary, the introduction of the PPM created an entirely different sense about how people listened to radio. Arbitron found, for example, that individuals with PPMs listened to more stations—and for a shorter time per station—than people who wrote diaries. Were the people different, or did the methods determine the results? It's quite likely the different methods led to the different findings. In fact, the PPM has its own built-in bias toward reporting that people tune in to more stations than they actually care to hear. It works by picking up a radio station's sounds, and when a person just passes by a radio station's sound, that doesn't mean that he or she is really listening.

A final bit of radio ratings bias we'll mention has to do with the industry's definition of a quarter hour of listening. Arbitron tells diary participants that to put an entry in the diary that says they listened for a quarter hour (the minimum amount), they have to have listened for at least five minutes. So a person who listens for five minutes at the top of the hour, for five minutes 20 minutes later, and for five minutes 10 minutes after that would check off listening in three quarter-hour boxes. Arbitron would report these 15 total minutes as 45 minutes spent with radio. This may not be a listening pattern that is common, but it underscores the flaw that the quarter hour injects into the system. Interestingly, with the Portable People Meter, Arbitron has minute-by-minute data but continues to use 15 minutes as the minimum time period. When asked why, an Arbitron executive answered that the industry prefers that unit of measurement. One reason may be that it overstates radio listening in ways that help the radio stations that, after all, pay Arbitron for the service. (The Arbitron executive didn't disagree when the possibility was presented to her.)

All these activities that influence ratings affect the ideas that radio executives hold about how people use the medium, how long they spend with it, and the kinds of formats that will be successful in this environment. More broadly, they influence the "facts" about radio that industry officials present to the larger society—to policymakers, academics, and other citizens who are trying make sense of how radio as a business fits into the new media world. To release data that claim, for example, that teenagers and young people still have high "time spent listening" to radio without placing enormous warnings around the findings (for people who don't know the methods that created the data) is ethically suspect. When told that, contrary to Arbitron data, many college students say in class that they hardly listen to radio for any length of time, a radio station executive in the same city responded that young people simply won't admit listening because radio is not a cool medium.

Which listening pattern is correct—what the students report in class or the radio ratings? This review of audience construction suggests the answer is far from clear. It's an issue to consider when you think about audience research in all media industries.

# CHAPTER REVIEW

 Visit the Companion Website at www.routledge.com/cw/turow for additional study tools and resources.

## Key Terms

You can find the definitions to these key terms in the marginal glossary throughout this chapter. Test your knowledge of these terms with interactive flash cards on the *Media Today* companion website.

| | | |
|---|---|---|
| amplitude modulation (AM) | format consultants | national spot advertising |
| audio streaming | format networks | network |
| barter | frequency modulation (FM) | network advertising |
| billboards | fringe listeners | noncommercial stations |
| burn music test | HD (hybrid digital/analog) radio | on-air talent |
| commercial stations | listening patterns | patent trust |
| core audience | local advertising | playlist |
| dead air | music activity level | portable people meter (PPM) |
| drive time | music sophistication | radio promotion |
| focus groups | music style | rating point |
| format | music time period | streaming audio |
| format clock (format wheel) | narrowcasting | syndicator |

## Questions for Discussion and Critical Thinking

1. With websites such as Pandora now becoming available in cars, how do you think terrestrial radio might be affected? How might terrestrial radio respond to these new developments?

2. Say you have the chance to develop a radio station's format in your area. Who would be your target audience and why? What music would you use to attract them and why?

3. Unlike television or film, radio is still often considered a "local" medium that emphasizes reaching "local" audiences. How do the stations in your area establish themselves as part of the local community? Are their methods effective? Why or why not?

4. Let's say more and more Americans started taking mass transit to and from work. How would that affect terrestrial radio, and what (if anything) could radio stations do about it?

## Case Study
### RADIO'S PEOPLE METER RATINGS

**The Idea** When Arbitron instituted portable people meter (PPM) ratings in Philadelphia and Houston in 2007, it changed the way advertisers and radio station owners thought of their audience. In Philadelphia, the first sets of ratings showed dramatic differences from the old diary method of keeping track of people's listening habits. Some stations even changed their formats because of the findings. The PPM is an example of how an audience measurement technology can change the nature of reality for a media industry with regard to its audience. These events caused a lot of controversy and deserve to be examined in more detail.

**The Method** Using a periodical database, follow the discussions that radio and advertising executives have had over the past several years about problems with Arbitron's diary method and about the benefits and problems associated with the PPM technology. If everyone understood the problems with the diary method, why were station owners loath to move over to the portable people meter? What problems did Arbitron find when it tried to implement the new technology? How hard was it to roll out the technology in Philadelphia, in Houston, and beyond? Is it right to assume that the PPM gives the radio stations and their advertisers the correct read on what stations are most popular and when? Do you think it represents the last word on radio ratings?

Write a report of your findings that addresses these questions and this more sociological one: in what ways does the PPM experience show how an audience measurement technology can change the nature of reality for a media industry with regard to its audience?

# The Movie Industry 12

> "The words 'Kiss Kiss Bang Bang'—which I saw on an Italian movie poster—are perhaps the briefest statement imaginable of the basic appeal of the movies."

**PAULINE KAEL, MOVIE CRITIC**

## CHAPTER OBJECTIVES

1  Explain the history of movies in the United States and how it affects the industry today

2  Analyze the production, distribution, and exhibition processes for theatrical motion pictures in the United States and recognize the major players in each realm

3  Describe how movies are financed and how they make money through various exhibition arrangements

4  Analyze the relationship between movie distributors and theaters

5  Explain the impact of new technologies and globalization on the movie industry

6  Consider the impact of American movie culture on world culture

You may not see the movies as a place to go for a "date." (A lot of people say they don't really date anymore, anyway.) Still, the website wikiHow (to do anything) actually has an article called "How to Act on a Movie Date." In September 2012 it was edited by someone called Flickety "and 26 others." "Movie dates," it begins, "are a great way to spend time together without the added pressure of making deep conversation. To make your date even more of a breeze, here are a few guidelines on how you should act as well as strategies for initiating kissing." The list that follows includes such helpful hints as "don't forget to brush your teeth" and "if you plan to kiss, you and your date might want to head to the back."

For dates or not, movie theaters still do attract teens and young adults in larger numbers than any other age group. But theatergoing is by no means limited to teens and young adults. Check out the Saturday and Sunday afternoon theater hordes around malls, and you'll see a lot of children and their parents. Married adults with older kids attend movie theaters fairly often, and senior citizens frequent early evening shows.

But movie theaters are just the beginning—or a stop along the way—of a march across media platforms that many movies take in the digital age. As we will see in the pages that follow, convergence has become a critical part of the movie industry. If you missed the theatrical showing of a film, you will probably be able to watch it on a multitude of digital windows, from pay-per-view on your big-screen TV to your smartphone.

It may seem odd that in the 21st century we talk about "movies" as a separate category of audiovisual experience—different, for example, from "television shows" and "videos"—even when we often don't see them in movie theaters. The industry works hard to maintain this distinction even as it pushes convergence to the point where the theater is only the start of a movie's movement through the media system. To many in the audience, "the movies" means "Hollywood." Hollywood, in turn, represents a place and level of excitement and star power not to be matched by other audiovisual industries.

This chapter goes beyond the glitz and glamour of movies to sketch what popular media presentations of the industry rarely explain: how the motion picture industry actually works. What companies are involved in production, distribution, and exhibition? Where does the money come from to support these activities? To what extent is convergence changing the way motion picture executives do their jobs? To what extent is convergence changing the nature of "movies"? And how do executives try to keep the distinctiveness of movies in the age of audiovisual convergence?

To begin answering these questions, we have to first understand how the notion of "the movies" and Hollywood took hold in American society and in the American imagination. Our timeline and our themes begin with magicians in the late 18th century.

## The Rise of Motion Pictures

Magicians were the master showmen of Europe and the United States in the 1800s. What most people in their audiences didn't know was how important projected images were in their acts. As early as the 1790s, magicians used slides to project mystical pictures onto smoke rising from canisters in their darkened theaters. This "magic lantern" presentation grew more sophisticated through the 1800s. It makes sense, then, that magicians were particularly interested in the experiments that inventors in the latter part of the century were conducting in creating and projecting moving pictures. All of these inventors' devices involved preparing a series of drawings of objects in which each drawing was slightly different from the one before it. When the drawings were made to move quickly (say, if they were pasted next to one another on the side of a revolving drum), it appeared to the viewer that the objects were moving.

While some inventors were trying to make still drawings appear to move, others were developing the same idea using photographic images. One particularly important figure was Eadweard Muybridge, who immigrated to the United States from England. In 1878, Leland Stanford, an entrepreneur, politician, and horse breeder, recruited Muybridge to settle a $25,000 bet that he had made; he had bet that all four feet of a galloping horse were sometimes off the ground at the same time. Muybridge set up 24 cameras close to one another at a racetrack to take photos as a horse ran by. Stanford got his money; the photographs showed all four feet off the ground.

If none of this sounds like the modern movie to you, welcome to historical theme 1. You might well have anticipated it from previous chapters:

1. *The movies, as we know them, did not arrive in a flash as a result of one inventor's grand change.*

"OK, but what does Muybridge have to do with movies?" you may ask. The answer is that Muybridge's work got inventors to think that motion picture photography might be possible. The next trick was to be able to take 24 photographs with one camera rather than with 24 different cameras. Explore the timeline (Figure 12.1), and you'll notice a succession of innovations by several people that led to what we today call the motion picture. It would be wrong to say that one person invented the movies. Thomas Edison played a large part in developing the motion-picture camera and projector, as the timeline shows, but so did his assistant William Dickson, as well as inventors Thomas Armat and C. Francis Jenkins, Louis and Auguste Lumière of France, and Robert Paul, a competitor in England.

These people and more struggled over the technology that pointed movies in a particular direction: reels of developed photographic film projected on a screen in front of large audiences. It didn't have to be that way. Edison initially conceived of making money from the motion picture by showing it in a small box that one person could peer inside for a nickel. The Lumière brothers explored a more lucrative path in 1894, demonstrating that popular interest could be whipped up, and lots of money could be made by projecting movies to many people simultaneously. Edison came to accept this approach as well.

## THINKING ABOUT MEDIA LITERACY

Edison's nickelodeon allowed one person at a time to view the playing movie through a peephole. Eventually, projection onto large screens became the industry norm for showing movies to audiences. Why do you think projecting onto a screen became more popular? Do you think today's web-enabled devices bring us back to a time similar to the nickelodeon? Why or why not?

Both Thomas Edison and the Lumières saw the motion picture as a storytelling medium. Noteworthy early Lumière titles were *Workers Leaving the Lumière Factory*, *The Arrival of a Train at La Ciotat Station*, and *The Sprinkler Sprinkled*. Early Edison films included *The Kiss*, *Aunt Sallie's Wonderful Bustle*, *Automobile Parade*, and *An Artist's Dream*. But neither Edison nor the Lumières created their products by themselves from start to finish. They, and those who came after them, saw moviemaking as a collective activity. Individual innovators did emerge who had the creativity to guide collective storytelling in the new medium. Frenchman George Méliès, Americans Edwin S. Porter and D. W. Griffith, and Russians Sergei Eisenstein, Lev Kuleshov, and Dziga Vertov are among those who developed the styles of plotting, acting, and especially editing that defined what movies became for generations to come. As talented as these people were, they had to work with many others to complete their "photoplays."

If you go online to view movies associated with any of these artists or with the early movie companies such as Edison, Biograph, or Vitagraph, you will probably conclude that what you see has little to do with what you think of as movies today. The reason has to do with theme 2:

2. *The movie as a medium of communication developed as a result of social, legal, and organizational responses to the technology during different periods.*

Let's start with the social and organizational responses to the movie technology that the film pioneers developed. The technology allowed the creation of what were called "silent movies." It may seem obvious to say that films were called "silent" because they carried no sound. Actually, though, the film producers and exhibitors ensured that the viewing experience wasn't at all silent. Movie theaters hired musicians (individual

# Figure 12.1 Timeline of the Movie Industry

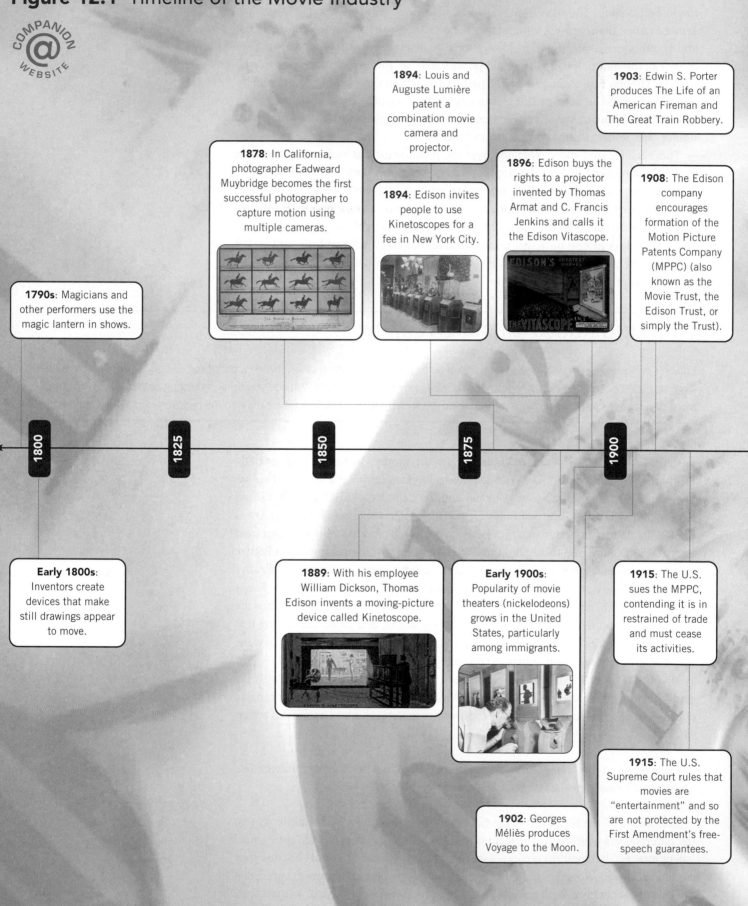

**1790s**: Magicians and other performers use the magic lantern in shows.

**1878**: In California, photographer Eadweard Muybridge becomes the first successful photographer to capture motion using multiple cameras.

**1894**: Louis and Auguste Lumière patent a combination movie camera and projector.

**1894**: Edison invites people to use Kinetoscopes for a fee in New York City.

**1896**: Edison buys the rights to a projector invented by Thomas Armat and C. Francis Jenkins and calls it the Edison Vitascope.

**1903**: Edwin S. Porter produces The Life of an American Fireman and The Great Train Robbery.

**1908**: The Edison company encourages formation of the Motion Picture Patents Company (MPPC) (also known as the Movie Trust, the Edison Trust, or simply the Trust).

**Early 1800s**: Inventors create devices that make still drawings appear to move.

**1889**: With his employee William Dickson, Thomas Edison invents a moving-picture device called Kinetoscope.

**Early 1900s**: Popularity of movie theaters (nickelodeons) grows in the United States, particularly among immigrants.

**1915**: The U.S. sues the MPPC, contending it is in restrained of trade and must cease its activities.

**1902**: Georges Méliès produces Voyage to the Moon.

**1915**: The U.S. Supreme Court rules that movies are "entertainment" and so are not protected by the First Amendment's free-speech guarantees.

1800  1825  1850  1875  1900

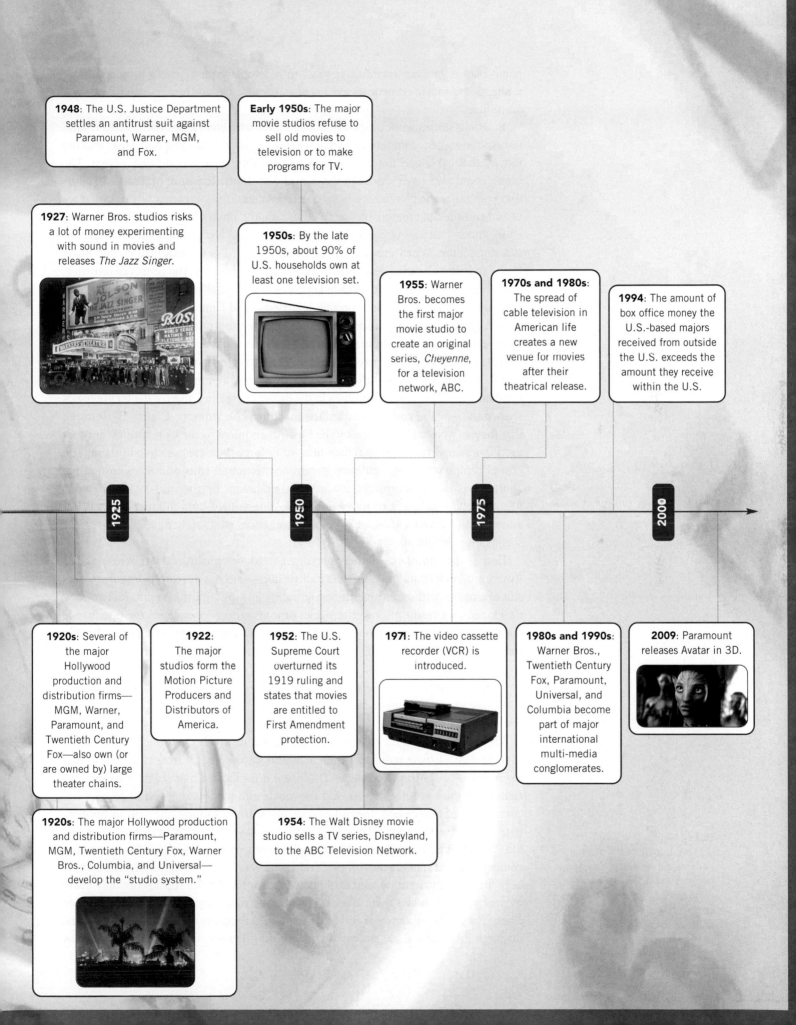

**1948**: The U.S. Justice Department settles an antitrust suit against Paramount, Warner, MGM, and Fox.

**Early 1950s**: The major movie studios refuse to sell old movies to television or to make programs for TV.

**1927**: Warner Bros. studios risks a lot of money experimenting with sound in movies and releases *The Jazz Singer*.

**1950s**: By the late 1950s, about 90% of U.S. households own at least one television set.

**1955**: Warner Bros. becomes the first major movie studio to create an original series, *Cheyenne*, for a television network, ABC.

**1970s and 1980s**: The spread of cable television in American life creates a new venue for movies after their theatrical release.

**1994**: The amount of box office money the U.S.-based majors received from outside the U.S. exceeds the amount they receive within the U.S.

1925    1950    1975    2000

**1920s**: Several of the major Hollywood production and distribution firms—MGM, Warner, Paramount, and Twentieth Century Fox—also own (or are owned by) large theater chains.

**1922**: The major studios form the Motion Picture Producers and Distributors of America.

**1952**: The U.S. Supreme Court overturned its 1919 ruling and states that movies are entitled to First Amendment protection.

**1971**: The video cassette recorder (VCR) is introduced.

**1980s and 1990s**: Warner Bros., Twentieth Century Fox, Paramount, Universal, and Columbia become part of major international multi-media conglomerates.

**2009**: Paramount releases Avatar in 3D.

**1920s**: The major Hollywood production and distribution firms—Paramount, MGM, Twentieth Century Fox, Warner Bros., Columbia, and Universal—develop the "studio system."

**1954**: The Walt Disney movie studio sells a TV series, Disneyland, to the ABC Television Network.

piano players or even entire orchestras) to accompany the theater's presentation of a film. Some movie companies even sent musical scores to theaters exhibiting their silent films.

In telling stories without spoken dialogue, the film companies had to create ways to help the audience understand what was taking place. They inserted cards into the movies that explained the context and told viewers what people were saying. The music could also give clues as to the comedic or dramatic nature of a scene. To further emphasize the plot, actors exaggerated their emotions to points beyond what we would considerable reasonable today. Above all, the photoplay creators helped audiences know what was going on by drawing on historically popular genres of American storytelling. When movies told tales of the Wizard of Oz and Joan of Arc, many in the audience already knew what to expect. More generally, the genres of romance, adventure, and comedy had already been popular in prior media such as books and magazines. Silent movies built on that knowledge and familiarity.

Still, there were some in society who didn't like the stories that movie companies were telling in order to draw audiences. As the timeline testifies, public fears arose that the vivid nature of the new medium might lead some in the audience to copy immoral or illegal activities—how to rob a bank or how to immodestly consort with the opposite sex. These social responses to the movie companies' uses of the technologies shaped the way the companies used the medium. The Supreme Court's 1919 ruling that movies were not protected by the First Amendment to the Constitution encouraged states and even cities to censor films or to force their creators to edit them. The cost of coping with many different government-required edits of movies around the country led movie companies toward self-regulation. By the mid-1930s, creators' ideas of what an American movie could be were guided by a mixture of considerations that involved a sense of what large audiences would pay to see and what the social norms would allow.

Despite the importance of these pressures, the development of the movies—and of Americans' understanding of movies in their lives—did not develop primarily as a result of tensions with governments and advocacy groups around content. Rather, they developed as a result of power struggles among various companies for dominance over changing movie technologies and paths to the audience. This point ties directly to the third historical theme:

3.  *The movie industry developed and changed as a result of struggles to control its distribution channels to audiences.*

The timeline charts the movement from the era in which the founding companies tried to control their industry through patents to the rise of firms that challenged them and, by 1920, replaced them. These new firms located most of their production facilities in the Los Angeles area, and the movie industry became identified with the community of Hollywood. Instead of controlling their business through technology patents, the five Hollywood "majors" (Metro-Goldwyn-Mayer, Warner Bros., Columbia, Twentieth Century Fox, and Universal) chose two broad methods for controlling competition and creating movies efficiently. One was vertical integration—the control of production, distribution, and exhibition. The most powerful studios not only made movies and distributed them but also owned the most important theaters in major cities. The studio system was the other method the majors used to control their industry. It involved the star system as well as A and B movie units. The **star system** was

**star system**
an operation designed to find and cultivate actors under long-term contracts, with the intention of developing those actors into famous "stars" who would enhance the profitability of the studio's films

designed to find and cultivate actors under long-term contracts, with the intention of developing those actors into famous "stars" who would enhance the profitability of the studio's films. **A films** were expensively made productions featuring glamorous, highly paid stars; think of *Gone with the Wind*. **B films** were made more quickly, with much smaller budgets. The Ma and Pa Kettle series of comedy movies from that era is an example.

**A films**
expensively made productions featuring glamorous, highly paid stars

**B films**
lower-budget films that were made quickly

The ability of the five major movie companies to create the audiovisual stories that most audiences watched at least weekly from the 1920s through the early 1950s gave them enormous cultural power. The studio system heralded the glitz, romance, drama, and adventures of the movies—and of the stars in the movies—so that "Hollywood" and "the movies" became synonymous with these qualities.

The movie industry has changed quite often. One critical pivot point was when the financially precarious Warner Bros. took the financial risk of experimenting with sound in movies. The hallmark film of this effort, 1927's *The Jazz Singer*, started a revolution in moviemaking. From that point onward, movies would be defined by the way sound—speech, audio effects, and music—worked together with action to make the moving pictures move audiences.

Keep going down the timeline, and you'll see more changes in the shape of the movie industry. With the Paramount Consent Decree of the late 1940s, the government forced the breakup of the vertical integration that gave just a few companies a grip over their industry. A few years later, the growing popularity of television drew audiences away from movie theaters and further eroded the power of the major studios. Movies changed from products that people saw regularly on a weekly or even twice-weekly basis to special events that the studios promoted as reasons to get out of the house. The "B" series pictures that had sustained Hollywood essentially left the theaters. But the movie companies did find a new home for the form: television.

Follow the timeline further, and you'll see how a stream of new technologies—cable television, the videocassette recorder, the DVD player, and the internet—posed new challenges for the industry. The movie industry today is far different from the industry of *The Jazz Singer* days or of the days that made the great films you can see on the TCM cable channel. Yet the industry has managed to keep its association with glitz, stars, and high-profile entertainment.

How does "Hollywood" work today? Let's find out.

## An Overview of the Modern Motion Picture Industry

The most appropriate name for the enterprise that we're dealing with in this chapter is the theatrical motion picture industry, so called because the business is set up in such a way that much of its output (movies) initially goes to theaters. Virtually all **theatrical films** now made commercially in the United States appear in nontheatrical locations *after* they have completed their runs in movie theaters in the United States and abroad. These movies are typically made available for rental or sale; shown in hotels, airplanes, and homes on pay-per-view systems; shown on cable, satellite, and broadcast TV; downloaded or streamed from the internet to computers, TV sets, and mobile phones; and more. Still, "the movie industry" continues to refer to the industry that produces films that will first be exhibited ("featured") in theaters.

**theatrical films**
films created to be shown first in traditional movie theaters

**box office receipts**

the sum of money taken in for admission at movie theaters around the country

According to the Motion Picture Association of America (MPAA), in 2011 North Americans (in the United States and Canada) purchased about 3.9 billion tickets to see theatrical films. The number of tickets sold has been going down, from 5.2 billion in 2002, despite an increasing population. Spending, though, has gone up from the 2002 figure of $9.1 billion in **box office receipts**—the sum of money taken in for admission. In 2011, North Americans spent $10.2 billion on movie tickets, at an average price of $7.93 per ticket. The average ticket price has gone up sharply over the past few years, from $6.88 in 2007. That is because more and more people are paying more than the regular ticket price to see movies in 3D and wide-screen IMAX. You might still feel that the $7.93 is low in comparison to what you pay to see a film, but keep in mind that this price includes discounts for senior citizens and children. Moreover, prices in some parts of the country are a good deal lower than those in other areas. In Times Square, New York City, for example, adult moviegoers typically pay $13.00 per person or more to see a non-3D, non-IMAX presentation of a new movie. Across the river in some parts of Brooklyn, the price might be a couple of dollars lower.

Going to the movies continues to be most common among young people. People 12 to 24 years old make up 35 percent of frequent moviegoers (those who go to the movies once a month or more), even though these people make up only 18 percent of the nation's population. People aged 25–39 represent 28 percent of the ticket holders, which is seven percentage points higher than their percentage in the population. In contrast, Americans aged 60 and older, who make up about 19 percent of the population, account for only 12 percent of the admissions (see Table 12.1).

**Table 12.1** Age Groups of North American Frequent Moviegoers

|  | 2–11 | 12–17 | 18–24 | 25–39 | 40–49 | 50–59 | 60+ |
|---|---|---|---|---|---|---|---|
| % of population 2011 | 14% | 8% | 10% | 21% | 14% | 14% | 19% |
| % of frequent moviegoers 2011 | 7% | 16% | 19% | 28% | 9% | 9% | 12% |

Frequent moviegoers are people who see movies in theaters at least once a month. Source: Motion Picture Association of America, "Theatrical Market Statistics," 2011, accessed November 29, 2012.

## THINKING ABOUT MEDIA LITERACY

Why do you think the most frequent moviegoers are aged 12–24? What are features unique to them that do not appear in the other age ranges (25–39 and 60+)? From your own viewing experiences, in what ways do you see the industry trying to address those aged 12–24? How about those aged 25–39 or 60+?

**blockbusters**

films that bring in more than $200 million at the U.S. box office

From 2005 through 2011, between 500 and 600 movies a year made it to the approximately 40,000 movie screens in U.S. theaters. Industry executives tend to pay most attention to the movies that bring in more than $200 million at the U.S. box office; they call such films **blockbusters** (see Table 12.2). There aren't very many blockbusters each year, but they tend to bring in a high percentage of the money that theatrical films as a whole make at the box office. In 2011, 2 movies made more than $300 million, 4 films made between $200 and $300 million, and 19 films brought in between $110 and $200 million. Together, the top 10 movies of 2011 brought in $2.4 billion, which constituted about 27 percent of total domestic box office revenue.

**Table 12.2** Top 10 Grossing Films, Worldwide Box Office, Not Adjusted and Adjusted for Inflation

| Rank | Title | U.S. distributor, initial release date | Gross (US$ billions) |
|---|---|---|---|
| **Not Adjusted for Inflation** | | | |
| 1 | *Avatar* | Twentieth Century Fox, 2009 | 2.78 |
| 2 | *Titanic* | Paramount Pictures, 1997 | 2.18 |
| 3 | *The Avengers* | Paramount Pictures, 2012 | 1.51 |
| 4 | *Harry Potter and the Deathly Hallows: Part 2* | Warner Bros., 2011 | 1.33 |
| 5 | *Transformers: Dark of the Moon* | Paramount Pictures, 2011 | 1.12 |
| 6 | *The Lord of the Rings: The Return of the King* | New Line Cinema, 2003 | 1.12 |
| 7 | *The Dark Knight Rises* | Warner Bros., 2012 | 1.08 |
| 8 | *Pirates of the Caribbean: Dead Man's Chest* | Buena Vista, 2006 | 1.07 |
| 9 | *Toy Story 3* | Buena Vista, 2010 | 1.06 |
| 10 | *Star Wars: Episode I—The Phantom Menace* | Twentieth Century Fox, 1977 | 1.03 |
| **Adjusted for Inflation** | | | |
| 1 | *Gone with the Wind* | Metro-Goldwyn Mayor, 1939 | 3.30 |
| 2 | *Avatar* | Twentieth Century Fox, 2009 | 2.78 |
| 3 | *Star Wars* | Twentieth Century Fox, 1977 | 2.71 |
| 4 | *Titanic* | Paramount, 1997 | 2.41 |
| 5 | *The Sound of Music* | Twentieth Century Fox, 1965 | 2.27 |
| 6 | *E.T. the Extra-Terrestrial* | Universal Pictures, 1982 | 2.21 |
| 7 | *The Ten Commandments* | Paramount Pictures, 1956 | 2.10 |
| 8 | *Doctor Zhivago* | Metro-Goldwyn-Mayer, 1965 | 1.99 |
| 9 | *Jaws* | Universal, 1975 | 1.95 |
| 10 | *Snow White and the Seven Dwarfs* | RKO Radio Pictures/Buena Vista, 1937 | 1.75 |

Source: http://en.wikipedia.org/wiki/List_of_highest-grossing_films, accessed November 29, 2012. If the dollar amounts are not adjusted for inflation, movies that were very popular when ticket prices were substantially lower than today do not make it to the list. Note that some movies are on both lists.

Movie executives pay attention to more than just U.S. theaters, however. What movie executives call the "international" (that is, non-U.S.) marketplace has been expanding rapidly. Around the world, moviegoing has been encouraged by the building of modern, air-conditioned **multiplexes**, or theaters with 8 to 15 screens, and **megaplexes**, or theaters with more than 16 screens. As a result, box office receipts in the international sector have grown substantially faster than U.S. box office revenues in recent years. Today, the dominant Hollywood movie firms are Warner Bros., Twentieth Century

**multiplex**
a modern, air-conditioned building that houses between 8 and 15 screens and has the capacity to exhibit a number of different films at the same time

**megaplex**
a modern, air-conditioned building that houses 16 or more screens and has the capacity to exhibit a number of different films at the same time

Fox, Disney, Sony Pictures (Columbia), Paramount, and Universal. During 2011, these Hollywood studios took in $13.52 billion from international box office sales. That amounted to 60 percent of their global (U.S. plus international) box office take.[1]

The decisions made in Hollywood radiate outward, influencing the films that people around the world see in their neighborhood theaters and on DVDs and TV sets. Consequently, a large part of the movie business focuses on getting films and people together in theaters. What does the "Hollywood" way of doing business look like? Let's start with production.

# Production in the Motion Picture Industry

People tend to think that when they see the symbols for Twentieth Century Fox, Universal Pictures, Warner Bros., Columbia, Paramount, and Disney at the start of films, this means that those companies produced the movies. In many cases, however, they didn't.

### The Role of the Majors

**the majors**
the six most powerful companies in Hollywood because of their distribution power

The six companies that people most associate with Hollywood are called **the majors**, and they are the most powerful companies in the movie business. Despite their prominence and power, however, these firms create only a small fraction (often one-third or less) of the movies to which their names are attached. Their names appear on screen because of their role as distributors, but more often than not, the films have been produced by other companies.

### Distinguishing between Production and Distribution

**film production firms**
companies involved in coming up with story ideas, finding scriptwriters, hiring the personnel needed to make the movie, and making sure the work is carried out on time and on budget

**film distribution firms**
companies responsible for finding theaters in which to show the movies around the world and for promoting the films to the public

The distinction between production and distribution in the movie industry is critical to understanding the film business. **Film production firms** are involved in coming up with story ideas, finding scriptwriters, hiring the personnel needed to make the movie, and making sure the work is carried out on time and on budget. **Film distribution firms**, in contrast, are responsible for finding theaters in which to show the movies around the world and for promoting the films to the public. Distribution firms often contribute money toward the production firms' costs of making the film.

When you see the phrase "a Paramount release," for example, you should be aware that this does not necessarily mean that the company's studio arm has fully financed and produced the movie. Although the Paramount studio does fully produce movies that its distribution division circulates to theaters, most of the films that it deals with as a distributor come from separate production firms. For example, the Graham King–founded GK Films and Johnny Depp's production company Infinitum Nihil were behind the well-regarded 2011 film *Hugo* that Paramount released. Paramount may have kicked in a portion of the production money, but the production firms took on a lot of the risk themselves.

### The Role of Independent Producers

Why don't the majors produce all the movies they distribute? The reason is straightforward: for a distribution firm to maintain a strong relationship with theaters, it has to provide a strong roster of films to help fill theater seats. If a distributor offers theaters fewer than 15 or 20 movies a year, theaters will not take the distributor seriously, and the distributor will not be an influential force in the movie industry. Yet movies are both very expensive and very risky to make. They typically cost tens of millions of dollars each, and many of them lose money. A firm such as Universal cannot afford to risk the amount of cash that would be required to fully fund many films. Consequently, Universal's own studio generates only 5 to 10 films itself per year, and the company picks up the rest of its distribution roster from **independent producers**—that is, from production firms not owned by distributors.

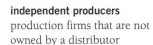

**independent producers**
production firms that are not owned by a distributor

Consider the 2007 movie *3:10 to Yuma*, which was released by the independent distributor Lionsgate. According to *Variety* it was mostly financed by its executive producer Ryan Kavanaugh and his company Relativity Media, with Lionsgate acting as an investor of $42.5 million on the $87.5 million-plus project.[2]

## The Process of Making a Movie

The process by which a movie goes from an idea in someone's head to a film that the distributor can ship to theaters is time-consuming and expensive (see Figure 12.2). Production company executives will also say that overseeing the filming and editing of their movies is only a small part of what their company does. Other important steps involve getting the idea, getting the talent, and raising the money. Only after these steps have been performed can the activities involved in the actual making of the movie take place. Let's look briefly at each stage in this process.

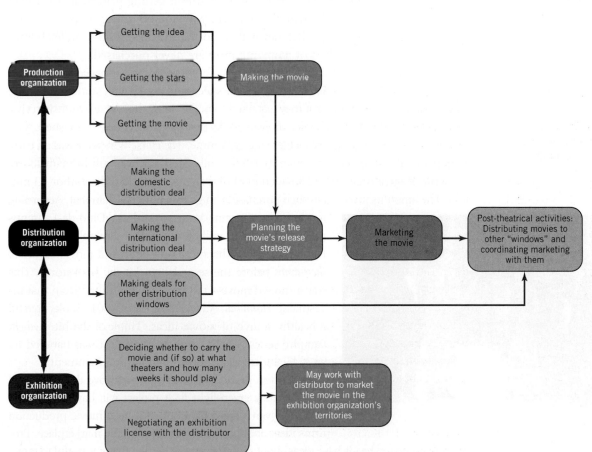

**Figure 12.2**
Producing a movie and releasing it to theaters

**scriptwriters**
individuals who create plays for the movies, with scenes and dialogue

**talent agents**
individuals who represent various creative personnel (e.g., actors, directors, authors, and screenwriters) and aim to link them with production firms in exchange for a percentage of the creators' revenues from the finished product

**pitch**
the initial presentation of a movie idea to a producer

**treatment**
detailed outline of an initial pitch to executives of a production or distribution firm; if the executives approve of the treatment, they will probably order a script to be written

**on spec**
writing a script for a film without a contract to do so, with the hope that when the script is passed along to various production firms by the scriptwriter's agent, it will be bid for and purchased

**green light**
a term used to describe production and distribution executives' approval of the making of a particular film

**Getting the Idea** An idea for a movie can come from virtually anywhere. Producers have gotten ideas for movies from television shows, comic books, toys, short stories, and newspaper articles. Scriptwriters and books (including history books) have traditionally been the most common sources, however.

**Scriptwriters** are individuals who create plays for the movies, with scenes and dialogue. Their plot ideas often come to production firms via writers' **talent agents**—individuals who represent various creative personnel (e.g., actors, directors, authors, and screenwriters) and aim to link them with production firms in exchange for a percentage of the creators' revenues from the finished product. An agent's job is to gain a reputation around Hollywood for having good creative and business ideas so that when he or she knocks on a producer's door with a suggestion, the producer will listen. Agents know what has been popular. They also know what kinds of films certain producers like to make.

An established writer's idea for a film will sometimes be only a few lines that go to the heart of the plot—for example, "A small wooden box arrives on the doorstep of a troubled married couple, who open it and become instantly wealthy. Little do they realize that opening the box also kills someone they do not know." The presentation of the idea to the producer is called a **pitch**. If the producer likes the idea (the preceding example actually came from an episode of the classic TV series *The Twilight Zone*), the writer might be paid to write a detailed outline, which is called a **treatment**. If the producer likes the treatment, the next step might be payment for a full script. Less-established writers may write an entire script without getting paid, which is called writing a script **on spec**. The writer's agent will pass around a spec script to various production firms in the hope that they will bid for it. Attractive scripts can fetch hundreds of thousands of dollars or more, but most are never purchased.

The second traditional source for film ideas—books—became especially popular in the late 1990s. Producers had long looked for successful books with stories that fit the types and budgets of films that they expected to make. Now they were furiously trying to beat one another to new books, or even books that had not yet been published, with stories that seemed to suggest a cinematic gold mine. *The Horse Whisperer* was an early example of the stampede to come. In 1994, while the book was still in manuscript, the writer's agent orchestrated an auction of film rights that netted the author $3 million. The amounts involved in such purchases can go much higher than that. According to the trade magazine *Variety*, producer Dino de Laurentis plunked down $10 million in 1999 for film rights to Thomas Harris's sequel to the successful book and movie *Silence of the Lambs* before the sequel even hit the bookstores. This was a shrewd move—the movie that resulted from that investment, *Hannibal*, was a major hit of 2001. Books are still a healthy source of movie ideas. Think of the hit *Twilight* vampire series, which started as books; it was handled by an independent distributor, Summit Entertainment.

When top production executives approve the making of a movie, they green-light it. A project will have the chance of being given a **green light** only if it fits a movie production firm's ideas about what will succeed in the marketplace. Production company heads have ideas about segments of the market that it is useful to target with particular types of films. Teens and young adults, for example, are thought to like horror films (e.g., *Halloween*). Women are thought to like romantic comedies (e.g., *He's*

Stephenie Meyer's *Twilight* vampire saga has been hugely successful as a series of books and as a movie series.

*Just Not That into You*), whereas men are typed as preferring adventure movies (e.g., *Fast Five*) or gross-out comedies (e.g., *The Hangover 2*). People over age 45 are often the targets for small-budget films (sometimes British-made) that have a subtle comedic or deeply dramatic sensibility. Think of *Sleepwalk with Me* or *Silver Linings Playbook*. Of course, many women and men attend the movies together, so executives often try to leaven movies targeted to one type of audience with some material that another type would like. An adventure film will often have a strong romantic component, for example.

## THINKING ABOUT MEDIA LITERACY

Many times we go to the movies with a variety of different people with a variety of different tastes, so movies try to appeal to a range of tastes. What is a movie that you have seen that attempts to appeal to people your own age? How did it do this? How did that same movie attempt to appeal to your parents' generation or even your grandparents' generation? Overall, how did this mix of appeals work?

The rising importance of the non-U.S. market to Hollywood has meant that, when executives green-light a film, they think about its potential around the world. Historically, most U.S.-made comedies have not "traveled" well, so a budget for a comedy typically has to be low enough to be profitable from U.S. revenues alone. Adventure films do tend to travel well, but they can be very expensive. As a result, action movies tend to emphasize violence and hair-raising stunts that usually require little knowledge of English to understand. Some of these films have been made in the United States, and others have been coproductions that blend the investment and production talents of a U.S.-based firm with those of a firm of another country such as France or India.

Increasingly, U.S. firms are making movies for other parts of the world, with the notion that they may make money even if they don't do well in the United States. For example, Universal Pictures was deeply involved in funding and distributing the 2007 installment of the British Mr. Bean comedy (*Mr. Bean's Holiday*). The Bean films traditionally do terrifically in the United Kingdom and very well in parts of Europe but are weak in the United States.

**Getting the Talent** When a production firm purchases a script or the right to use a book, its executives typically have certain actors and directors in mind. Sometimes, a major actor may get control of a property with the idea of starring in a film based on it. The actor's agent may go even further in dealing with production firms interested in the project: the agent may take a number of people from his or her roster of clients—actors, a well-known director, a highly regarded cinematographer—and tell production firms that the deal comes in a package. To many observers of the film industry, the fact that a number of talent agencies have the power to organize such major film deals with production firms is evidence that talent agencies are among Hollywood's most powerful players.

The money to pay actors and other creative personnel must, of course, come from the overall budget. The salary requirements of the most popular stars (some make more than $20 million a picture) mean that only the major studios and a few other production companies can afford to hire these stars. Sometimes a production firm will make a deal with a famous actor or director in which the actor or director takes a lower base salary but gets a percentage of the money that the production firm receives from the distributor—known as a **back-end deal** or **percentage of the gross**.

**back-end deal (percentage of the gross)**
a deal in which a production firm convinces a famous actor or director to take a lower salary in exchange for getting a percentage of the money that the production firm receives from the distributor

Stars often negotiate variations on such deals to help their careers and help movies get made. For the 2008 Warner Bros. comedy *Yes Man*, for example, Jim Carrey gave up his upfront salary (usually $22 million) to become a one-third investor in the film. He also agreed to start receiving a back-end percentage only once the studio recouped the $53 million Warner said the film cost. The deal paid off handsomely. *Yes Man* grossed about $223 million worldwide. Carrey stood to earn more than his regular salary.[3]

Some industry insiders have suggested that the high salaries stars are demanding are leading producers to hold off on hiring established, experienced actors in secondary roles in favor of more affordable relative newcomers. Rules about actors' minimum pay and working conditions have been established through deals between the Screen Actors Guild and the major production firms. Similar arrangements for screenwriters have been made by the Writers Guild of America. These **guilds** are unions established by writers, directors, actors, and other crew members to protect their mutual interests and maintain standards.

The guilds provide less highly paid workers with a collective voice. Sometimes that results in a strike. This happened in 2007 and 2008, when the major studios and the Writers Guild of America could not come to terms with the Alliance of Motion Picture and Television Producers about how much pay the writers should receive from the major studios for work that appears on the internet. The strike of more than 10,000 Writers Guild members crippled Hollywood. It ended production on TV dramas and comedies, caused the Golden Globe Awards to be canceled, and delayed a number of movie productions.

**Getting the Money** Getting a well-known actor to agree to play the lead in a movie can help a production firm get the cash it needs to make the film. Getting the money is often the hardest part of making a motion picture. The amount it costs to make a movie varies, from way more than $100 million dollars (for movies such as *Avatar*, *Spider-Man*, and *The Bourne Legacy*) to between $50 and $100 million (*The Simpsons Movie* reportedly cost about $75 million) to less than $50 million (*Knocked Up* reportedly cost $40 million to produce, and *Sparkle* cost $14 million). The word in Hollywood is that it is the most expensive movies that tend to become mega-hits. Still, a moderately inexpensive film can also reap great benefits for its production firm. *Once*, a 2007 musical romance from Ireland, cost about $150,000 to make. In the United States alone, it brought in $7 million in box office returns.[4]

A film's budget isn't typically created based on the producer's calculations of what is necessary to tell the story. Instead, a story is often chosen and developed to fit the budget that executives of a production firm can manage. Consequently, a production firm's executives decide what kinds of monetary risks they want to take (or can take). They then go about choosing a story—or tailoring one—to fit the budget they have. Take, as an example, Dimension Films, the company that produced the hit movies *Halloween* (2007) and *Halloween II* (2009). Dimension Films is a division of the Weinstein Company, an independent production and distribution firm. Dimension makes **genre films**—movies that fit classic storytelling formulas (science fiction, horror, action) and are typically relatively inexpensive to make. If a genre film becomes popular with audiences beyond its target niche, as *Halloween* did (and the *Saw* series before that), its success can make up for films that bring the production firm little return.

**guilds**
unions established by writers, directors, actors, and other crew members to protect their mutual interests and maintain standards

**genre films**
movies that fit classic storytelling formulas (science fiction, horror, action) and are typically relatively inexpensive to make

## THINKING ABOUT MEDIA LITERACY

In chapter 3, you read about the concept of hybrid genres, which bring together features of different genres into one work. These hybrids work to appeal to genres' long-standing fans and to bring in new audiences. Think of a hybrid film you have seen. What genres did the filmmakers incorporate into the piece? How did those elements appeal to traditional fans of the genre or genres? How might those elements work to attract new fans to watch it?

When millions and millions of dollars are hanging in the balance, giving a film the green light is not easy. Not only must executives believe in the script, the director, and the stars, but they also must have the money to make the film and a company to distribute it. If the production firm is part of a major studio, the chief executive officer of the studio typically discusses the proposed film with the production and distribution chiefs. Once the film and its budget are approved, the studio as a whole (encompassing both the production and distribution divisions) provides the money. It is the distribution division, however, that works to make the money back—and more—through a percentage of the box office receipts.

Independent firms have a harder time than large studios getting the money to make a film. If the independent firm has had previous successes, it may be fortunate enough to have a multi-picture distribution deal with a major that includes some financing. However, the independent may still have to use its own funds or funds borrowed from banks to make up the rest of the film's budget. The banks, of course, are hoping that the movie will make back its costs for the production firm so that they can retrieve their money with interest.

The most consistently successful independent production outfits are so tightly linked to particular distributors that they are virtually extensions of the distribution firm's own output. When it was independent, the Pixar animation firm had a distribution deal with Disney. Pixar films became so important to Disney's slate that eventually Disney decided to buy the company. More recently, Morgan Creek Productions has had a steady output deal with Universal.

Production companies that don't have long-term deals with distributors have to work a lot harder to find cash and a distributor. Sometimes wealthy investors will put up the money in the hope that they will get lucky and the film will be a hit. Sometimes an independent production firm with a record of successes (a positive track record) will be able to convince a major bank to provide a revolving credit agreement for several pictures. When a production firm is seeking a loan for part of a film's budget, the loan will be easier to get if the production firm can show that an established star has been signed for the film and that an established distribution firm has agreed to take it on and to advance it money.

A popular way for independent producers to get the money for film projects is to sell **distribution rights**: the rights to circulate a particular movie in different parts of the world. For example, a production firm's executives might get $2 million from an Asian firm that wants the rights to distribute the film to theaters (and perhaps home video rights) in Southeast Asia. Another distributor may bid $2 million for distribution rights in Australia and New Zealand. A third distributor might buy North American theatrical and home video rights. By accumulating these territory deals, often before the film is fully made, the production firm can show banks that a substantial portion of the film's budget is already in hand. Through the Internet Movie Database, you can check out the many

**distribution rights**
the rights to circulate a particular movie in different parts of the world

regional distributors involved in circulating (and financing) *The Wrestler*, a 2008 release produced by Wild Bunch, Protozoa Pictures, and Saturn Films.[5] The film turned out to be a hit in many territories. That kind of financing is, however, a difficult puzzle to put together, and in the late 2000s the economic downturn and the popularity of local films in different regions of the world made it quite difficult for independent production firms to gather substantial parts of their budgets from international presales.[6]

## Understanding film and television credits

The reason film credits can be so long is that film-making draws on the efforts of numerous people over an extended period of time. The process of taking a film or television show from idea to audiences involves several key phases and a wide assortment of skills. Based on a typical live action film, following are a few examples of workers involved in a film. Many of these workers are involved on all or multiple phases of the production.

### 1. DEVELOPMENT
Coming up with an idea, writing a script and pitching it.

| | | | | |
|---|---|---|---|---|
| Agents | Business managers | Investors | Personal Assistants | Screenwriters |
| Assistants to the producers | Consultants | Lawyers | Producers | Studio executives |
| | Executive producers | Line producers | Publicists | |

### 2. PREPRODUCTION
Developing, planning and visualizing the idea. Preparing a budget, hiring crew members, and making a schedule.

| | | | | |
|---|---|---|---|---|
| Art department assistants | Choreographers | Costume supervisors | Location assistants | Props masters |
| Art department coordinators | Concept artists | Costumers | Location managers | Set designers |
| Art directors | Construction coordinators | Dialogue coaches | Paint foremen | Set decorators |
| Artists | Construction electricians | Directors | Production assistants | Set dressers |
| Assistant directors | Construction first aid | Directors' assistants | Production designers | Set staff assistants |
| Carpenters | Construction foremen | Directors of photography | Production managers | Storyboard artists |
| Casting directors | Construction grips | Financial executives | Props builders | Stunt coordinators |
| | Construction workers | Illustrators | | Tailors/seamstresses |
| | Costume designers | | | Wardrobe |

### 3. PRODUCTION
Shooting scenes, working with cast, locations and reviewing footage.

| | | | | |
|---|---|---|---|---|
| Accounting clerks | Electricians | Payroll accountants | Property workers | Stills photographers |
| Actors | Extras | Picture car coordinators | Script supervisors | Stunt performers |
| Animal handlers | Extras casting coordinators | Picture car drivers | Set strike workers | Swing gang workers |
| Assistant accountants | First aid workers | Picture editors | Sound editors | Teachers/welfare workers |
| Assistant directors | Gaffers (lighting) | Production accountants | Sound technicians | Technical advisors |
| Boom operators | Grips (set operations) | Production coordinators | Special effects coordinators | Transportation coordinators |
| Camera loaders | Hair stylists | Production sound mixers | Special effects supervisors | Transportation captains |
| Camera operators | Makeup artists | Property masters | Special effects technicians | |
| Caterers | Office coordinators | | Standby painters | |
| Cinematographers | On-set dressers | | | |
| Drivers | | | | |

### 4. POSTPRODUCTION
Editing the film, adding titles, music and special effects.

| | | | | |
|---|---|---|---|---|
| Audio recording engineers | Dubbing editors | Film and video editors | Musicians | Special effects technicians |
| Composers | Editing room assistants | Lab technicians | Projectionists | |
| | | | Sound designers | |

### 5. DISTRIBUTION
Taking the finished product and bringing it to theaters, home video, television, online and other venues for audiences to see it.

| | | | | |
|---|---|---|---|---|
| Accountants | Distribution executives | Licensing executives | Partnership developers | Sales staff |
| Advertising executives | Financial managers | Marketers | Publicists | |

**Figure 12.3**
Understanding film and TV credits

**Getting to the Actual Making of the Movie** As you can see, a lot of work has to be done on a movie project before the actual moviemaking even begins. The moviemaking process involves a large number of people with widely different talents. To get an idea of how many people are involved, first take a look at Figure 12.3. Then watch all the credits at the end of the next movie you attend. Alternately, look up any movie on a site such as the Internet Movie Database and look at the cast and crew listings. Pay particular attention to the different jobs that are involved. Experienced personnel scout locations for certain scenes in the movie and try to minimize problems that might occur while filming there. Casting directors help the director choose many of the actors. Set designers, production designers, costume designers, makeup experts, and computer graphics personnel help create the physical shape of the space in which the actors work. Stand-ins and stunt people help actors with boring or dangerous parts of the work. The cinematographer and the film crew create the look of the film as it will appear on screen. Recording engineers make sure the sounds of the movie are appropriate (much of the dialogue will have to be rerecorded in a studio for clarity). A wide variety of personnel handle the equipment, the soundstage work, the salaries, the food, and all the other duties connected with a large project. The editor decides (usually with the director) which versions ("shots") of different scenes should end up in the final version of the film.

Because of the large number of resources involved, every extra day of filming can be an enormous drain on the production firm's budget. Keeping the production on schedule is the role of the director, who controls the pace of filming, along with the **line producer**, who makes sure the equipment and personnel are there when they are needed. Some moneylenders, worried about spiraling costs, require production firms to hire **completion bond companies**. These are insurance companies that, for a large fee, will pay any costs that exceed an agreed-upon amount for a film. When a completion bond company signs on to a movie, especially one that is in danger of going over budget, it often sends its own executives to the sites where filming is taking place. By contract, those executives have the right to take control of some of the film's activities to keep it on budget.

**line producer**
the individual who makes sure the equipment and personnel are there when they are needed

**completion bond companies**
insurance companies that, for a large fee, pay any costs that exceed an agreed-upon amount for a film

## Theatrical Distribution in the Movie Industry

When you're putting tens of millions of dollars into a movie, you want it to have a chance to reach the intended audience so that your firm can make its money back and hopefully turn a profit. As we've seen, helping a movie get that chance is the job of the distribution company. The most powerful companies in the movie business have distribution arms with a reputation of being able to place films in theaters in the United States and around the world. The major distribution firms have offices around the world, and the mandate for their personnel is twofold: to get the films they distribute into theaters and to market these films effectively to target audiences.

### Finding Movies to Distribute

The first order of business for a distributor is to get movies to distribute. You might suspect that the major distributors would have it easy, given that they are linked to studios that create their own films. Certainly, they have a simpler time of it than independent distributors. Executives in independent firms have to scour the world for the rights to films that will attract the audiences they know how to reach. But even the majors cannot afford to circulate only films that their studios make. They distribute several films from their own studio each year and get the rest from other places.

## MEDIA TODAY & CULTURE   BANNING OF HOLLYWOOD FILMS AROUND THE WORLD

As part of its distribution strategies, Hollywood creates movies that potentially have a global appeal. These blockbusters, as they often are called, deal with the fantasies of traveling throughout space or surviving alternate universes, such as the storylines seen in science fiction. They also show the high adventures of chases, mysteries, or quests. To tell these tales, the films rely on visual spectacles, incorporating action sequences, special effects, and brief dialogue. As a result, these films are critiqued for their lack of plot and character development.

Although these Hollywood films sometimes do gain immense profits through global distribution, not all films are received the same way in all countries. Some countries require a re-edit before the film can be shown in the country's theaters, whereas other countries ban them altogether. Reasons for both actions vary from country to country, and they often depend on cultural values, political climates, and other factors.

China, for example, issues guidelines through the State Administration of Radio Film and Television in China. One decree discourages more fantastical elements, including time travel, myths, reincarnation, and even negative thinking[1] and thus has discouraged such films as *Looper*, which involves an assassin killing targets sent back in time, and even *A Christmas Carol*. China also banned two-dimensional versions of James Cameron's *Avatar* to reduce its competition against locally produced works, even though the film went on to earn more than $182 million there.[2]

Other films are banned for their portrayals of local cultures. A more recent installment of *Rambo* was set in Myanmar (also often called Burma), and the film portrayed the Burmese soldiers as sadistic enemies.[3] Vietnam also bans films for their representations of the Vietnamese people, such as *Platoon* and *We Were Soldiers*. Nigeria banned *District 9* for its portrayal of Nigerians as gangsters who sleep with aliens and otherwise exploit them.[4]

Graphic and violent content also can be a reason for a film ban. Vietnam banned both *The Girl with the Dragon Tattoo* and *The Hunger Games*.[5] Germany banned public screenings of *Saw 3D* for its violation of a law about violent acts.[6] New Zealand banned *Hostel: Part II*.[7] Other reasons for films being banned in various countries include representations of sexuality and religion.

In recent years, the majors have collaborated with each other to finance and distribute particularly expensive films in order to lower their risk of losing enormous amounts of money if those films fail. For example, Warner Bros. and Sony worked together to fund the 2009 movie *Terminator: Salvation*, which cost $200 million to produce, plus the cost of marketing. The deal was that Warner would distribute the movie in the United States, and Sony would have international distribution rights.[7] Because the firms expected the film would earn more outside the United States, Sony put more money into the deal than Warner did.

### Releasing Movies

Once a distributor has set its slate of motion pictures and these pictures are completed (or nearing completion), the challenge is to choose a release date and a release pattern. The **release date** is the day on which the film will open in theaters. In setting a film's release date and release pattern, executives take into consideration the kind of film it is, how popular its actors are, its target audience, and the other films on their slate. They also try to figure out when their competitors' movies will be released.

Typically, executives schedule the release of potential blockbusters in the United States during the summer or between Thanksgiving and Christmas. These are periods when students are off from school and when many adults spend extra time with their families. Because different societies may have different moviegoing habits, a film's

**release date**
date on which the film will open in theaters

release date may be different around the world. In recent years, though, movie distributors have tended to release blockbuster films at the same time in many different countries—a practice known as a **day-and-date release**. Some executives believe that this practice discourages pirates from distributing the film online illegally because every area gets the theatrical release at the same time. More important, perhaps, is the belief that new technologies allow distributors to efficiently promote a movie across the world at the same time.

**day-and-date release**
a simultaneous release date for a movie in different countries

**Release Patterns**   In addition to the release date, distribution executives must agree on the pattern in which the movie will be released in theaters around the country. Three release patterns are common in the United States:

- A **wide release**, the most common pattern, typically involves opening a film in more than 600 theaters simultaneously. **Saturation releases** involve opening the film in more than 2,000 theaters simultaneously. Putting a film in thousands of theaters beginning the same weekend is increasingly common because it creates hype for potential blockbusters around the country (and the world) at the same time. In 2012, Warner Bros.' *Wrath of the Titans*, Relativity Media's *Mirror Mirror*, and Paramount's *Mission: Impossible—Ghost Protocol* all opened in wide or even saturation release.

**wide release**
the opening of a film in more than 600 theaters simultaneously, usually accompanied by a large publicity campaign to incite people to see the film; the most common release pattern in the United States

**saturation release**
the initial release of a film in more than 2,000 theaters simultaneously

- A **platform release** involves the initial release of a movie in far fewer theaters in a relatively small number of areas. Executives are likely to choose this approach for films that they feel have potentially wide appeal but that need time for media reviews and other discussions of the film to emerge and ignite interest among the target audience. They hope to increase the number of theaters showing the film as the movie's popularity builds, thus encouraging the snowballing of attendance. Twentieth Century Fox released the successful *Black Swan* in a platform release.

**platform release**
the initial release of the movie in far fewer theaters in a relatively small number of areas with the plan to release the film in more theaters as the film garners positive publicity and discussion

- **Exclusive releases** are not set up with the intention of "going wide." These films go to only a handful of carefully selected theaters around the country. Films with this distribution pattern are typically specialty films, often foreign, that their distributors believe will do well with very specific audiences in particular places around the country. The China-made movie *Back to 1942*, distributed by China Lion Entertainment, fit this bill and was released in only 17 U.S. theaters during late 2012.

**exclusive release**
the release of a film to only a handful of carefully selected theaters around the country

Of course, the number of movie theaters available to show a film is also an important consideration in determining release dates and release patterns. Theater-chain executives have their own ideas about what pictures they want in what locations, and they negotiate with the distributors regarding what pictures they will take and for how long. By law, movie distributors are not allowed to force exhibitors to book blocks of their films—a practice known as **block booking**. Paramount, for example, is prohibited from telling the Regal Cinemas theater chain that it can have a particular film only if it takes three other motion pictures. Over the decades, though, the major distributors and the major theater chains have developed ways to accommodate each other's needs.

**block booking**
when movie distributors force exhibitors to book blocks of their films

## Marketing Movies

One reason that theater chains like dealing with the major distributors is that the majors have sophisticated marketing operations. To help reduce the risk of failure, distributors

Actor Daniel Craig appeared on Jay Leno to promote the release of the newest James Bond film, *Skyfall* (Getty Images).

often conduct two types of research before a film is released. **Title testing** involves conducting interviews with filmgoers in shopping malls and other public places to determine the most alluring name for an upcoming picture. **Previewing** is a type of concept testing that takes place after a film is completed but before it is formally released: theatergoers see a preliminary (**rough cut**) version of a movie and answer survey questions about what they like or don't like about it, and the reactions may be used to re-edit parts of the film. The original sad ending of *Fatal Attraction*, for example, was changed to make it happier after it received negative audience reactions during previews.

You are undoubtedly familiar with **publicity** and advertising for movies—this can take the form of lavish parties for a film's cast on the day of the movie's premiere, with the press in attendance; interviews with the film's actors on TV programs such as *The Late Show with David Letterman* and *Entertainment Tonight*; previews of the film on YouTube and Facebook; comments posted about the film on Twitter; and free preview tickets given to college students before a film formally opens. The aim of publicity is to get favorable "buzz" going about the movie among its target audiences. The aim of advertising is to turn that buzz into actual moviegoing by telling people that the movie is playing near them and urging them to see it.

The flurry of publicity and advertising for a film is usually intense and short, taking place before and around the time the movie is released to the theaters. Although marketing can build anticipation among moviegoers, after the first weekend of its release, **word of mouth**—the discussions that people who see the movie have with their friends in person and on social media sites such as Facebook—determines whether more people will go to see it. The life of a film in theaters is no more than a few months. The greatest proportion of the money received from a film comes in during the first few weeks; in fact, executives believe that they can predict the total amount of money a movie will make by looking at how it does during that short period of time.

Distribution executives often order **tracking studies**—research on the public's awareness of and interest in a film—beginning two weeks before the film's release and continuing through the film's first month of release. Three times during each of those weeks, a company called National Research Group surveys a random sample of Americans by phone. National's operators read a list of current or soon-to-be-released films to people who say they have recently seen theatrical movies. For every film on the list, the people are asked if they are aware of it and if they want to see it. The film's marketers may use the results, which are broken down by age and gender categories, to determine whether revisions in their publicity, advertising, or even release plans are needed.

All this activity requires a lot of money. For major domestic releases in the early 21st century, marketing costs amounted to around half of the film's **negative cost**—the total cost of making and editing the movie. According to *Variety*, the negative cost of *3:10 to Yuma* came to roughly $60 million, to which distributor Lionsgate added $27.5 million for prints and advertising.[8] In rare instances, marketing a film costs even more than putting it together. *Scream*, a 1996 Miramax release that became a box office phenomenon, reportedly had a negative cost of about $15 million and more than $20 million of marketing expenses to send it into wide release. In this case, the expenses paid off. According to the movie website Box Office Mojo, the movie brought in $103 million in theatrical receipts.[9]

But not all the money made at the box office comes back to the distributor. Let's look at the exhibitor's side of the story.

shipped to a theater and then shipped back to the distributor. Many of the prints could be used again overseas, but the distributor still had to pay shipping costs. Moreover, international releases of many films have increasingly been taking place at around the same time as North American releases, in part to take advantage of global marketing activities. That practice means even greater expense for creating prints, given that the same prints cannot be reused.

Much of this print-handling process still takes place. Increasingly, though, distributors deliver movies to theaters via satellite and then project them onto a screen, thus creating digital theaters. Much of the production of movies is already carried out using digital cameras, and then the final product is later transferred to film. Even if film is used during shooting of the movie, the pictures are often transferred to computers for special effects and editing. Companies already make projectors that they claim have both the clarity and the resolution to match traditional motion picture technology. As a result, 48 percent of the 28,695 non-3D theatrical "screens" in the United States and Canada during 2011 used digital projection. Moreover, all of the 13,695 3D screens used digital projection. The number of theaters using digital projection is still growing inside and outside North America. Distribution executives see a time in the not-too-distant future when much of the toil involved in circulating films will be eliminated. Instead of making prints and paying delivery services, distributors may connect to a satellite delivery service that allows them to circulate one master copy of their product to theaters around the world at virtually the same time. To foil piracy attempts, they envision sending the digital copy in a code that could be deciphered only by particular theaters.

Distributors and theaters have collaborated on the tens of millions of dollars required to install state-of-the-art digital projectors on which to play 3D films.

## Convergence and Nontheatrical Distribution and Exhibition in the Motion Picture Industry

Theatrical distribution is the pad that launches a film into many other exhibition locations. The importance of theaters as a movie's first platform explains why distributors pay a lot of attention to marketing movies when they are first released to theaters and why distribution executives must maintain good relationships with their counterparts in the theater business. When it comes to deriving profits from motion pictures, though, nontheatrical platforms—also known as nontheatrical windows—are often crucial. Recall that distributors keep only about half the theatrical box-office receipts. If a movie reaps $30 million, then, the distributor takes back about $15 million, and the production firm receives only a portion of that. When movie companies distribute their products through other windows, they often can keep far more than half of consumers' payments. That business fact is a powerful incentive for Hollywood to develop many "post-theatrical" windows for its products.

For more than half a century, the movie industry has made extra money by circulating its movies through television outlets—broadcast networks, local stations, and beginning in the mid-1970s, cable television. As the movie timeline notes, the introduction of videocassette recorders, or VCRs, in the 1970s started an entirely new way for the movie industry to profit from its products. For the first time, Hollywood could create a major market for films sold directly to the consumer. Children's films were particularly popular, as parents bought or rented films that had been hits in the theaters (and even some that hadn't been) to show to youngsters at home. The digital video disc (DVD) replaced the videocassette in the mid-1990s. The popularity of these home-video technologies led moviemakers to lean

**sell-through outlets**
stores in which consumers buy the videos rather than just renting them

**rental outlets**
companies that purchase releases from movie distributors and then rent them to individual customers on a pay-per-day basis

Already facing tough competition from Netflix's mail-order service, Blockbuster has shuttered many of its brick-and-mortar stores. Having lost direct competition with Redbox machines that rent movie DVDs for $1 per night, the company is struggling to reposition itself as an option for streaming and rent-by-mail (to directly compete with Netflix). Redbox has also joined that streaming competition in a partnership with Verizon.

heavily on post-theatrical earnings through sell-through outlets and rental outlets. **Sell-through outlets** are stores in which consumers buy the videos rather than just renting them. Some stores, such as Target and Walmart, sell videos in physical locations, whereas others, such as Amazon, sell only online. **Rental outlets** are companies that purchase releases from movie distributors and then rent them to individual customers on a pay-per-day basis. The traditional way to carry this out has been to go to a physical ("brick-and-mortar") store such as one in the Blockbuster chain. In recent years, the rental business has seen the growth of subscription services. With Netflix, for example, a person signs up online and can receive and return DVDs by mail, with Netflix paying the postage. A newer model has been pioneered by Redbox. This company has made deals with stores such as 7-Eleven, McDonald's, and Barnes & Noble to place vending machines in or near the stores so that you can rent a DVD directly from the machine using a credit card. If you are looking for a particular film, you can go online to find out which Redbox machine in your area (if any) has it and then reserve it. After viewing, you can return the DVD to any Redbox.

With the increase in the percentage of Americans and others who have broadband connections at home, a shift has been taking place in the way the movie industry distributes its marketing as well as its finished products to consumers. Movie marketers well understand that digital convergence opens unprecedented opportunities and challenges.

## The Shift to Digital Marketing

If you've ever checked the time a movie starts on a movie exhibitor website (e.g., through Fandango or Moviefone), you are quite aware of movie companies' ability to use digital snippets from their products to vie for your attention. Ads often have movie promotional segments (trailers) embedded in them. Moreover, those exhibition sites, as well as many other places online, use short movie segments to start conversations among visitors about the film and whether (or not) someone should go. Encouraging such discussions can be a double-edged sword for a marketer because some people can trash the product. Nevertheless, as we have seen, word of mouth is critical for pushing people to see a film. Movie distributors consequently seed the web with small pieces of their movies in the goal of sparking great interest. They also hope that people will share and repost videos and that this will get target audiences engaged in and excited by the release.

Video games represent another growth area for digital segments of theatrical films. Many popular movies become the basis for video games and video-inspired toys, and those products often have elements of the movies digitally stitched into them. Take *The Lord of the Rings: The Battle for Middle Earth*. This is a game based on *The Lord of the Rings* film trilogy that uses short video clips from the movies as well as a number of voices of the film's actors. Not only can such clips help make the game feel more like the movie that spawned it, but they also may encourage people to rent or purchase the films.

## The Shift to Online and Mobile Downloads

Shifting practices in renting and buying films also point to digital convergence. In recent years, sales and rentals of movie DVDs and cassettes have diminished substantially. A key challenge for the movie industry is to keep post-theatrical sales high, even as people have the ability to interact digitally with so many other offerings on their digital devices inside and outside the home. Moreover, when so many of these offerings are free or available at low cost (including music, some books, and many handheld games), the movie industry must often convince people to pay more for its product. Hollywood executives point with hope to what they think will replace those revenues—downloads and streaming.

A movie download takes place when a person pays a company (e.g., Apple, via iTunes) to send a digital copy of a movie to his or her computer, digital TV set, or phone. The person then owns the movie, can replay it, and may (depending on the purchase terms) be able to move it to another device. A rented digital movie, by contrast, is streamed to your device but not permanently stored. If you view an "on demand" movie through your cable company, Netflix, or Hulu Plus, for example, you might be able to view the movie on your digital TV, laptop, tablet, or smartphone (depending on the technology you have), but after a certain amount of time, you will not be able to see it without paying another fee to stream it again.

## The Problem of Piracy

Profits in the motion picture industry are continually threatened in the United States and around the world because of **film piracy**, or the unauthorized duplication of copyrighted films for profit. The activity is illegal under international copyright laws, but it is rampant around the world, even in countries that have signed those laws. You can see it pretty openly in many U.S. cities, such as when street vendors are selling videos of films that are still in theaters. It is even easier to find pirated copies of movies on the internet, especially through **data locker** sites—that is, websites that rents secure password-protected areas to store files. Sometimes pirated copies are produced by someone taking a video camera into a theater to record the movie. In more sophisticated cases, pirates smuggle a movie out of the theater, copy it as a video master, and then return the original. The practice of stripping the copy-protection codes off DVDs and uploading movies to the internet means that many people can illegally download hit films for free.

Consider the ethical responsibility of the buyers of these DVDs as well as the behavior of the pirates. The U.S. movie industry estimates that such theft is costing the industry billions of dollars a year—money that it would have received if its companies had sold those DVDs or digital streams. Within the United States, federal and local law enforcement groups have been trying to combat piracy. On a global level, the U.S. government, aware of the importance of the film industry to U.S. exports, has been pressuring the governments of countries in which enforcement of copyright regulations is particularly problematic. In addition, the MPAA, the group that represents the major production and distribution companies, has hired detectives who roam the world trying to identify pirates.

As for internet piracy, which the MPAA on its website calls "a global avalanche," the organization states that it has a "multi-pronged approach," involving educating people about the consequences of piracy, taking legal action against internet thieves, working with law enforcement to detect piracy operations, and helping to advance technologies that will "allow the legal distribution of movies over the internet." Like the recording industry's RIAA (see chapter 10), the MPAA has sued Americans for

**film piracy**
the unauthorized duplication of copyrighted films for profit

**data locker**
a website that rents secure password-protected areas to store files

copyright infringement in the smallest of towns and the biggest of cities. Penalties can be severe. For example, by federal law a person caught illegally recording movies in theaters can get up to five years in prison and be fined up to $250,000.[10] Despite these possible penalties, all sorts of piracy continue.

## Media Ethics and the Motion Picture Industry

Despite its expensive and risky nature, moviemaking, in many ways, lies at the center of American popular culture. Not only are movies shown, but they are also discussed. Especially when movie companies first release films, huge waves of publicity blanket the mass media. It often becomes impossible to avoid hearing about certain movies. Moreover, movie stars and songs that come from movies are themselves major topics on television, in magazines, in newspapers, around the water cooler, in the lunchroom, and in media classes.

Some observers of popular culture look at movie companies' activities with dismay. They point out that many of these performances and discussions found across so many media in so many parts of the world are sparked by just a handful of corporations—the major movie distributors. Moreover, all the majors are tied to huge mass media conglomerates—Time Warner, Disney, Viacom (which owns Paramount), News Corporation (which owns Twentieth Century Fox), Sony (which owns Columbia), and Comcast (which owns Universal). These conglomerates use their Hollywood assets as content for their holdings in different media industries around the world. Materials get packaged, sold, and hyped many times. In this way, even extremely expensive movies have a decent chance of making their money back over time, and blockbuster hits have a chance of making stratospheric sums.

Starting from this position, critics voice two types of concern. One relates to the narrowing of cultural diversity. A second involves what they call cultural colonialism. Let's look at each of these.

### Cultural Diversity and Cultural Colonialism

**The Narrowing of Cultural Diversity** Critics of the mainstream movie industry argue that movie executives are sending a rather narrow range of stories into American theaters and homes. Many contemporary Hollywood movies, they argue, are made according to simplistic formulas that use sex and violence in ways designed to ignite the interest of the central moviegoing audience: 14- to 24-year-olds. Expensive films that can become blockbusters are the name of the game in Hollywood because they have the potential to travel across so many different media and make so much more money for the majors than small films ever will. But the major studios will not take artistic risks on such films because the stakes are so high. As a result, films that push the envelope and challenge the audience to see the world differently are few and far between.

Exhibitors also work against cultural diversity, say the critics. By cultural diversity, they mean a reflection of the broad differences that exist in and across societies. Overwhelmingly, they book movies that fit the typical Hollywood profile. Few theaters in the United States show **art films**—movies created on small budgets that often do not fit into Hollywood stereotypes and standard genres. Even fewer theaters show foreign-language films, dubbed or with subtitles. The theater chains justify their choices by saying that Americans simply won't go to see these movies in numbers that justify booking them. The critics respond that the movie industry worked for decades to

**art films**
movies created on small budgets that often do not fit into Hollywood stereotypes and standard genres

keep such films out of the mainstream in order to protect the standard Hollywood product, so it will take time, they say, for Americans to develop the habit of watching non-Hollywood-style films.

The critics add that by not encouraging Americans to see movies made in other countries, the U.S. movie industry is keeping Americans isolated from important aspects of world culture. We live in a time, they say, when business is global, and Americans—especially young people—need to be able to understand the viewpoints of other people. Watching other people's movies can help enormously in building that understanding. The U.S. movie industry's activities are counterproductive in this regard, they say.

**Cultural Colonialism** Another strong criticism lodged against the Hollywood movie industry is that it represents a leading edge of American cultural colonialism. As we noted in chapter 4, cultural colonialism is the process by which the media content of a dominating society (in this case, the United States) surrounds people of another society with values and beliefs that are not those of their own society. Rather, the values and beliefs reflected in the content tend to support the interests of the dominating society.

As you can see, this cultural colonialism is in some ways a mirror image of the narrowing of cultural diversity. The concern over the lack of cultural diversity in movies argues that American society is being harmed. The concern about cultural colonialism, in contrast, argues that American-based companies are harming other cultures. They are doing this, the argument goes, by drowning out the presentation of local cultural experiences in the media with Hollywood-based formulas.

The critics point out that this cultural colonialism helps American business by creating markets for their consumer goods. Moviemaking in the United States is big business. (In fact, filmed entertainment of all sorts, for television and home video as well as the theaters, is one of America's top exports.) At the same time, critics say, it erodes local cultures because they can't compete with U.S. marketing glitz.

One result of the U.S. movie industry's focus on the international market in recent years has been the search by the majors for smaller, more literary movies that might connect with relatively cultivated audiences around the world. The conglomerates have set up divisions such as Miramax, Fox Searchlight, and Sony Classics to handle these films. You might think that critics and producers in other countries would be happy about this development. The problem is that, so far, all but a few of the movies that these divisions and others have picked up have been English-language pictures from the United States, England, Australia, or New Zealand. Distribution executives point out in frustration that American audiences, still the largest moviegoing audiences, don't like to watch movies that have been dubbed or that have subtitles. As a result, even European film companies have been moving toward making films in English and then subtitling them for non-English-speaking lands. Americans are colonizing even the art film world, critics say.

The critics point to the majors' worldwide success as evidence that cultural colonialism is taking place. The international power of the majors, they say, has made U.S. films dominant in the box offices of many countries around the world. True, several of the conglomerates that own the studios, such as Sony, are not American. Their filmmaking activity, however, is very much based in the United States and presents the U.S. view of the world. Furthermore, critics add, the popularity of U.S. movies is merely the tip of a huge iceberg. Under the guidance of powerful multimedia conglomerates, U.S. theatrical products blanket all sorts of print and electronic media. U.S. stars, for instance,

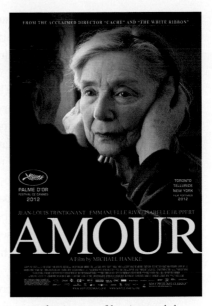

The Austrian film *Amour* did not receive much attention or promotion on U.S. television and radio stations, yet it was nominated for three Academy Awards, including best original screenplay, best foreign language film, and best director. It won the Golden Globe for best foreign language film.

are favorites the world over. And the U.S. way of life shown in the movies—with its strong commercialism, lack of environmental sensitivity, and urge toward immediate gratification—becomes an attraction for young people throughout the world.

Not surprisingly, Hollywood's supporters reject this view of their role in global culture. They point out that Hollywood employs many workers as a result of the movie industry's global reach. They add that many countries support local filmmakers and encourage them to make movies that reflect their own societies. It is not the U.S. movie industry's fault, they say, that people like Hollywood films more than those types of movies.

Hollywood's defenders also argue that people around the world like U.S. movies because they are good stories filmed in a high-quality manner. They also say that it is patronizing to believe that people in other countries see the movies in the same way that American audiences see them. Rather, these audiences accept or reject what they see in movies from the vantage point of their own cultures. They may even understand the stories differently because they are coming at them with different cultural "eyes."

This is not an argument that will go away. It may, in fact, become louder as media conglomerates increase their use of Hollywood moviemaking in their bids to create global content and take advantage of digital convergence. Where do you stand on these issues, and why?

# CHAPTER REVIEW

Visit the Companion Website at www.routledge.com/cw/turow for additional study tools and resources.

## Key Terms

You can find the definitions to these key terms in the marginal glossary throughout this chapter. Test your knowledge of these terms with interactive flash cards on the *Media Today* companion website.

| | | |
|---|---|---|
| A films | film piracy | previewing |
| art films | film production firms | publicity |
| B films | genre films | release date |
| back-end deal (percentage of the gross) | green light | rental outlets |
| | guilds | rough cut |
| block booking | independent producers | saturation release |
| blockbusters | line producer | scriptwriters |
| bookers | the majors | sell-through outlets |
| box office receipts | megaplex | star system |
| completion bond companies | multiplex | talent agents |
| data locker | negative cost | theatrical films |
| day-and-date release | on spec | title testing |
| distribution rights | percentage-above-the-nut approach | tracking studies |
| exclusive release | | treatment |
| exhibition license | pitch | wide release |
| film distribution firms | platform release | word of mouth |

# Questions for Discussion and Critical Thinking

1. Look around your home, your favorite hangouts, and your media devices. In what ways has movie industry content made its way into those spaces? Does this realization surprise you? Why or why not?

2. What do you think of the industry assertion that U.S. audiences will not attend foreign films with either dubbing or subtitling? Do you agree with their practice of avoiding these kinds of films? Why or why not?

3. A key criticism of the motion picture industry is that much of its content is derivative—stemming from comic books, books, television, and so on—and is stretched into too many sequels. Why do you think the industry relies on these sequels so much? Do you think the industry would be better off trying to make more stylistically and narratively diverse films, or would doing so be too much of a risk? Why or why not?

4. What advantages does the making of Hollywood films for a global audience offer to the industry? What advantages, if any, might these products offer global audiences? What limitations are there in assuming that global cultures are fading in light of this content?

## Case Study
### THE EXHIBITION OF INDEPENDENT AND NON-ENGLISH-LANGUAGE FILMS

**The Idea** Critics of movie exhibition in the United States argue that most Americans have no chance to become familiar with films that are off the beaten track. They specifically point to movies distributed by firms not affiliated with the major studios of Fox, Disney, Sony, Universal, Paramount, and Warner Bros. How true is this criticism in the area in which you live or attend school?

**The Method** Chart the movie theaters within 20 miles of your house. If you can find historical data, track the movies that were exhibited in them over the past three months. If you cannot find such data, track the movies that are exhibited in each theater over the next month. For each film, note the name of the production studio, the distributor, the country of origin, the language, and (if you can find it) the countries in which the film's story takes place. Write a report describing what you have found.

# 13 | The Television Industry

## CHAPTER OBJECTIVES

1   Compare and contrast broadcast, cable, and satellite television

2   Explain the role of advertisers in these three forms of television

3   Name and describe the different types of cable and satellite services

4   Identify the ways in which broadcasters, cable companies, and satellite companies produce, distribute, and exhibit programming

5   Describe the issues facing the TV industry and society in a rapidly changing TV world

> "Life doesn't imitate art. It imitates bad television."

**WOODY ALLEN, COMEDIAN/DIRECTOR**

> "I was very depressed when I was 19 … I would go back to my apartment every day and I would just sit there. It was quiet and it was lonely. It was still. It was just my piano and myself. I had a television and I would leave it on all the time just to feel like somebody was hanging out with me."

**LADY GAGA, PERFORMER/SINGER**

"Did you watch television last night?" That used to be a simple question. Either you turned on that electronic box in your home and viewed it, or you didn't. Today, though, the question can hold different meanings for different people. For some, watching TV will always be associated with viewing the box, so if they downloaded or streamed *The Voice* on their laptop computer, their phone, or their tablet, they would say they "didn't watch TV." Others might well say that they viewed television even when they saw *The Voice* or another program on their laptop or phone—or as in-flight entertainment—rather than on their traditional television set.

This ability to get programs across platforms is, of course, the very definition of convergence. Many in the audience—and many TV program creators—are happy with the activity, when it's done legally. Yet convergence is creating major tensions within the television industry. As we will see, the whole idea of what television means and how programming should be produced, sponsored, distributed, and exhibited is up for grabs as the traditional ways clash with new approaches and technologies. This chapter explores the U.S. television industry at a time of enormous change. It presents the basic building blocks for understanding how things are done now, how they are changing, why they may be changing even more in the decades ahead, and how they relate to the trends toward conglomeration and globalization—but also toward independently generated and circulated material—that that we have mentioned in previous chapters.

## The Rise of Television

To understand the television enterprise and the tensions involved in its current transformation, you have to understand how it started. It's also useful to tie TV's rise to the three historical themes we've discussed in other chapters.

### Television in Its Earliest Forms

Look at the timeline (Figure 13.1), and you'll immediately see the relevance of the first theme:

1. *Television as we know it did not arrive in a flash as a result of one inventor's grand change.*

The chronology indicates that the word "television" was used as early as 1907 in the magazine *Scientific American*. Even earlier, in 1879, the British humor magazine *Punch* published a picture of a couple watching a remote tennis match via a screen above their fireplace. Three years later, a French artist drew a family of the future watching a war on a home screen. Pretty prophetic, huh?

Although the idea of television was in the air, the reality of **television broadcasting** scanning a visual image and transmitting it, generally with accompanying sound, in the form of electromagnetic waves that when received could be reconverted into visual images—was harder to accomplish. Laboratory work started in Germany during the 1880s and continued in the United States, Scotland, Russia, and other countries throughout the next several decades. Between 1935 and 1938, the Nazi government in Germany operated the world's first regular television service, sending propaganda broadcasts to specially equipped theaters. Engineers did not consider the technology used for these performances very acceptable, however. The whirring mechanical disc that was used to scan the broadcast images had too many drawbacks. During the 1930s, a Radio Corporation of America (RCA) team brought together inventions that allowed electronic rather than mechanical scanning. RCA introduced the system at the 1939 World's Fair in New York; in introducing the new medium during formal ceremonies, President Franklin D. Roosevelt became the first U.S. president to appear on TV. Regular broadcasts began, and TV sets went on sale, but television did not take off. World War II intervened, and resources were diverted to defense production.

It was after the end of World War II—in 1946—that commercial television came into being in the United States. Even then, what was considered television continued to change. Over the decades engineers for major companies changed the television

**television broadcasting**
scanning a visual image and transmitting it, generally with accompanying sound, in the form of electromagnetic waves that when received can be reconverted into visual images

# Figure 13.1 Timeline of the Television Industry

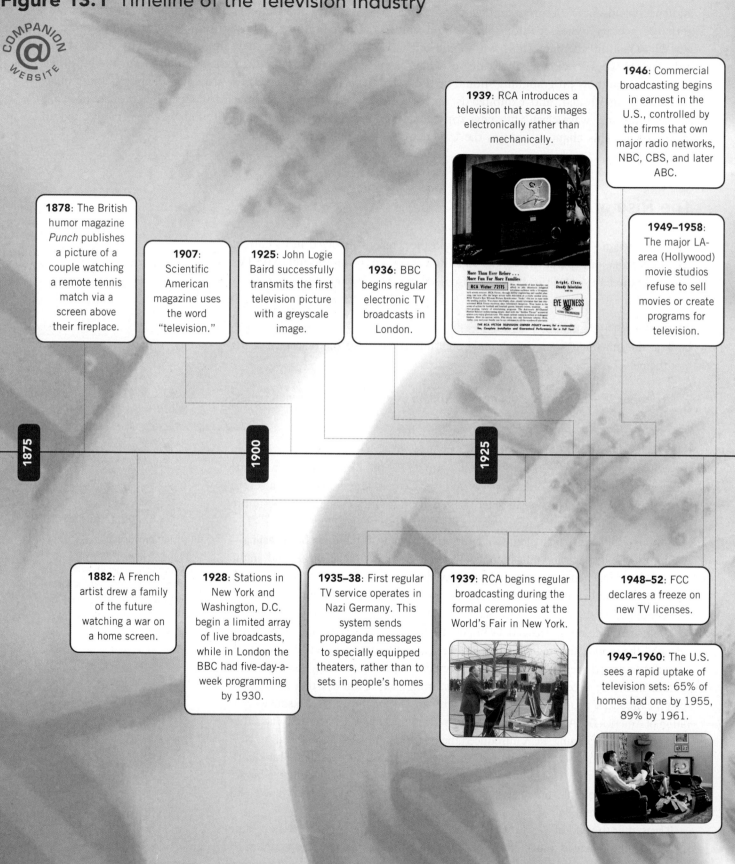

**1878**: The British humor magazine *Punch* publishes a picture of a couple watching a remote tennis match via a screen above their fireplace.

**1907**: Scientific American magazine uses the word "television."

**1925**: John Logie Baird successfully transmits the first television picture with a greyscale image.

**1936**: BBC begins regular electronic TV broadcasts in London.

**1939**: RCA introduces a television that scans images electronically rather than mechanically.

**1946**: Commercial broadcasting begins in earnest in the U.S., controlled by the firms that own major radio networks, NBC, CBS, and later ABC.

**1949–1958**: The major LA-area (Hollywood) movie studios refuse to sell movies or create programs for television.

**1882**: A French artist drew a family of the future watching a war on a home screen.

**1928**: Stations in New York and Washington, D.C. begin a limited array of live broadcasts, while in London the BBC had five-day-a-week programming by 1930.

**1935–38**: First regular TV service operates in Nazi Germany. This system sends propaganda messages to specially equipped theaters, rather than to sets in people's homes

**1939**: RCA begins regular broadcasting during the formal ceremonies at the World's Fair in New York.

**1948–52**: FCC declares a freeze on new TV licenses.

**1949–1960**: The U.S. sees a rapid uptake of television sets: 65% of homes had one by 1955, 89% by 1961.

1875    1900    1925

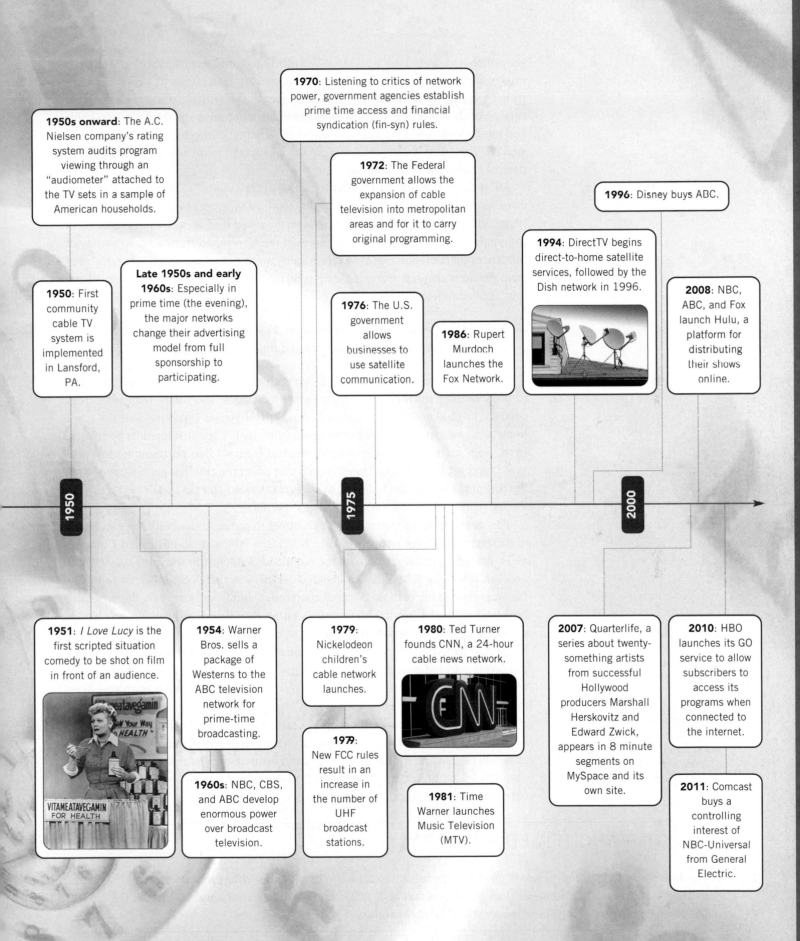

**1950s onward**: The A.C. Nielsen company's rating system audits program viewing through an "audiometer" attached to the TV sets in a sample of American households.

**1970**: Listening to critics of network power, government agencies establish prime time access and financial syndication (fin-syn) rules.

**1972**: The Federal government allows the expansion of cable television into metropolitan areas and for it to carry original programming.

**1996**: Disney buys ABC.

**1994**: DirectTV begins direct-to-home satellite services, followed by the Dish network in 1996.

**1950**: First community cable TV system is implemented in Lansford, PA.

**Late 1950s and early 1960s**: Especially in prime time (the evening), the major networks change their advertising model from full sponsorship to participating.

**1976**: The U.S. government allows businesses to use satellite communication.

**1986**: Rupert Murdoch launches the Fox Network.

**2008**: NBC, ABC, and Fox launch Hulu, a platform for distributing their shows online.

1950

1975

2000

**1951**: *I Love Lucy* is the first scripted situation comedy to be shot on film in front of an audience.

**1954**: Warner Bros. sells a package of Westerns to the ABC television network for prime-time broadcasting.

**1979**: Nickelodeon children's cable network launches.

**1980**: Ted Turner founds CNN, a 24-hour cable news network.

**2007**: Quarterlife, a series about twenty-something artists from successful Hollywood producers Marshall Herskovitz and Edward Zwick, appears in 8 minute segments on MySpace and its own site.

**2010**: HBO launches its GO service to allow subscribers to access its programs when connected to the internet.

**1960s**: NBC, CBS, and ABC develop enormous power over broadcast television.

**1979**: New FCC rules result in an increase in the number of UHF broadcast stations.

**1981**: Time Warner launches Music Television (MTV).

**2011**: Comcast buys a controlling interest of NBC-Universal from General Electric.

set, which had started out with black-and-white pictures, to include color. The technology for receiving television programs in most homes changed, as well. It went from capturing local stations' transmissions over the air with antennas to allowing reception of those stations' transmissions—and far more program channels—via cable and satellite television. And as we noted in this chapter's introduction, reception possibilities expanded (mainly beginning in the late 2000s) to include a growing array of devices connected to the internet.

All of these transformations in the nature of "television" took place not just because engineers figured out new ways to send moving and talking pictures to the home. Rather, changes in what TV "receivers" looked like, as well as in the kinds of programs that viewers could access through them, resulted from a broad variety of influences on television executives from many areas of society. You might remember from previous chapters that this idea is reflected in the second historical theme. Here it is, applied to television:

2. *Television as a medium of communication developed as a result of social, legal, and organizational responses to the technology during different periods.*

For an example, let's take the development of the television networks' approach to programming during their first and second decades. You might remember from Chapter 12 (and note in the timeline here) that Hollywood executives saw the small home screen as an obnoxious intruder onto their turf. They attributed its popularity to the huge increase in parenthood that resulted from soldiers returning from World War II and getting married. They declared that when the children got old enough for the parents to leave them at home, their parents would give up the TV and return to the movie theater for their audiovisual entertainment.

This perspective led movie studio executives to refuse to deal with the executives of the major television networks (ABC, NBC, CBS, and a small one called Dumont) as TV gained a permanent hold on the population's interest in the early 1950s. Most network television in its first commercial decade was therefore broadcast not from Los Angeles (the site of most TV production today) but from New York, the site of the broadcast networks' headquarters. In fact, rather than being made on film a la Hollywood, programs were **broadcast live**—that is, broadcast as the action was actually being performed, rather than taped, filmed, or otherwise recorded. Variety shows with vaudeville and radio stars, as well as dramas from aspiring theatrical ("Broadway") writers and actors, gave television an accessible, real-world feel that was missing from many Hollywood films. The 1950s, which historians have nicknamed the **golden age of television**, included powerful, original dramas such as *Marty*, *Judgment at Nuremberg*, and *Requiem for a Heavyweight* and such standard-setting comedy performers as Milton Berle, Sid Caesar, Imogene Coca, Carol Burnett, and Ernie Kovacs. As in radio, sponsors leased time from the television networks and owned the shows, and their advertising agencies coordinated production.

**broadcast live**
broadcast as it was actually being performed, rather than being taped, filmed, or otherwise recorded

**golden age of television**
the period of time from approximately 1949 to 1960, marked by the proliferation of original and classic dramas produced for live television

## THINKING ABOUT MEDIA LITERACY

Critics recently named the first decade of the 2000s the second "golden age" of television. What show(s) from that time do you think represent the quality of television during that time and why? What networks or channels were those shows on? Do you notice any patterns connecting the shows and their original channels?

It was an age that ended quickly. The grittiness of TV's live dramas made some major advertisers nervous. Hollywood, a world that was more upscale and populated with beautiful people, seemed to fit better with the advertisers' commercials for automobiles and other symbols of the good life. And Hollywood was finally getting interested in television. Even in the early 1950s, West Coast film producers and actors outside Hollywood's studio system had begun to sell new filmed series to television. The most important of these was created by Lucille Ball and Desi Arnaz, titled *I Love Lucy*, which became an enormous hit with audiences on CBS television. Movie and network executives were quick to recognize the advantages of having a hit on film as opposed to broadcast live. Unlike the live performances of Berle or Caesar, an *I Love Lucy* episode could be aired over and over again, or put into **syndication**. These "repeats" could even be leased to local television stations on a market-by-market basis.

By the mid-1950s, the major studios realized television wouldn't disappear from the scene, and they agreed to supply the television networks with old movies and new filmed TV series that would replace the live programming. By then television executives had accepted the idea that they were reaching as many people as the movie industry had in its heyday. And much like the movie executives of the 1930s, the TV people were worried that activist organizations angry with programming might encourage the federal government (in this case through the Federal Communications Commission, or FCC) to force changes in their programming. They therefore created a "Code of Good Practices" regarding morality in content that in many ways mirrored the self-regulatory code of the movie industry.

Despite the code, television executives of the early 1960s soon found themselves in the midst of political and social problems. Public anger over rigged quiz shows, over the large amount of violence on other shows, and over what many influential individuals in society considered idiotic entertainment ("a vast wasteland," the FCC's head called it) led to congressional hearings. Partly as a result, the networks changed their approach to selling advertising time on TV. Instead of advertisers buying the time and producing the shows themselves, network executives began to plan the schedule and order the shows, sometimes even producing them or taking part ownership in them. This planning allowed the TV networks far more control than in earlier years. Advertisers found it useful, too, because instead of putting all their television budget on one show, they could use it to buy time on various programs, thereby reaching people at different times and on different networks.

Brief though this description of the influences on the television networks' early approaches to programming is, it and the timeline should help you see the ways executives reacted to social, organizational, and potential legal reactions to their activities. The thumbnail history and the timeline also reflect the third theme:

3.  *The television industry developed and changed as a result of struggles to control its channels to audiences.*

The story of the networks' struggle to figure out the best ways to access programming and deal with sponsors is part of a larger story of the growth of the television industry. As we will see in this chapter, the TV industry today is far more than CBS,

*I Love Lucy* was first broadcast in 1951 on CBS and was soon a beloved hit. Thanks to syndication, it actually runs more frequently today than it did in the 1950s. *I Love Lucy* ran for six years of original episodes (180 total) and stopped production in 1957, despite the fact that it was still the number one show on American television. Lucille Ball and Desi Arnaz insisted on filming the shows in front of a live studio audience using three separate cameras, allowing the show to be edited into its final form. This audiovisual approach became the path many sitcoms took. More important, the filming of *I Love Lucy*—at a time when video recording was not used and most television was "live" and not well-preserved—ensured that high-quality prints of *I Love Lucy* would allow viewing long into the future.

**syndication**
the licensing of mass media material to outlets on a market-by-market basis

**television program ratings**
audits of people's viewing behaviors that gauge which shows households are viewing and how many are viewing them; they help network executives decide which shows should stay, which should be dropped from the lineup, and how much advertisers should pay to hawk their products during breaks in the program

NBC, and ABC. Even during the 1950s and 1960s, though, those three networks made up only part of the larger television industry. The timeline reflects some of the most important players: the production firms (some owned by the networks, others part of the Hollywood studios, others independent) that created the programs; the television stations that took the network program feeds and broadcast them to geographical areas; the A. C. Nielsen company, which supplied **television program ratings**, or audits of people's viewing behavior, that helped the networks decide what programs to choose; the advertisers and advertising organizations that helped pay the bills; and even the Federal Communications Commission, which decided which channels would be available in different parts of the country.

These organizations and others have been very much involved in struggles to control what television audiences see, when, and how. During the 1960s and 1970s, for example, the television networks competed fiercely with one another for the largest audience as well as for advertising money. At the same time, advertisers competed with one another for the best slots for their commercials. The advertisers also often made it clear to the networks that the programs they put on should not present views that insulted the idea of buying products and living the good life. The FCC, for its part, tried to pressure the networks to tone down violence on their programming and to inject more educational elements into children's programming. Activists started advocacy organizations such as Action for Children's Television to encourage the FCC and other government agencies to keep the pressure on the networks and their sponsors. And Nielsen created an entirely different set of pressures: the ratings released by the firm became the basic criteria against which advertisers and networks judged the success of programs. Advocacy groups tried to persuade industry executives that they should evaluate the programs by quality as decided by groups of citizens rather than as popularity contests. Other critics carped that the ratings were flawed and didn't reflect popularity accurately.

Struggles among these organizations to create and control the various TV channels to audiences certainly didn't stop in the 1970s. As the timeline indicates, the organizations with power in the industry changed over time. Cable television firms, cable networks, satellite firms, and internet service providers (with many of the biggest also selling cable service) were among the most important players over the next few decades. Bolstered by changing government regulation that they influenced through lobbyists and new television technologies that they helped to produce, they dramatically changed the amount and kinds of "television" programming Americans receive and the amount of money Americans pay to receive the programming.

The television industry continues to change as companies react to new challenges, especially those involving convergence. As we suggested in this chapter's introduction, even the definition of "television" is in flux as programs that appear on the big home screen—or that are similar to those that appear up on the big home screen—show up on the web and mobile phones. For the purposes of this chapter, we will define television programming as audiovisual material created by businesses to be part of a flow or gathering of material aimed at particular audiences and financed by advertising and/or audience payments. The definition is a mouthful. It is, however, meant to distinguish television from two other forms of audiovisual materials: amateur productions, or the sort you can find on YouTube (hence "material created by businesses"), and movies (hence the explanation that the product must be created to be "part of a flow or gathering of material" such as a channel rather than promoted as a standalone work). Admittedly, making these distinctions can get difficult, and as convergence destroys the boundaries of these categories, the need to make them may one day disappear. Still, practitioners today do recognize a television industry that they insist works differently from both amateur videomaking and moviemaking. Let's look at the most important elements of the contemporary TV industry as they define it.

## An Overview of the Contemporary Television Industry

It's useful to think of the television world as divided into three domains:

- Television broadcasting
- Subscription cable and satellite services
- Online and mobile platforms

Each area has its own technologies, its own key players, and its own special programming. Yet convergence is very much at play here: The domains are quite connected to one another. Programming from the "television broadcasting" mode shows up in the subscription cable and satellite space, and programs from there can be found on the web and other digital platforms. Let's take a brief overview of each domain and then explore how production, distribution, and exhibition work in each.

### Television Broadcasting

Television broadcasting, or the broad, over-the-air transmission of audiovisual signals, has historically been the most popular of these three domains. Its signals are transmitted from towers owned by local stations on frequencies allocated to them by the Federal Communications Commission. People with the right kind of television equipment can receive the signals without charge by simply turning on a television set.

About 1,800 television stations existed in 2012. Each station is licensed by the Federal Communications Commission to send out signals in a particular area of the country. Until recently, the FCC gave out licenses to operate on frequencies in one of two bands of the electromagnetic spectrum: the VHF band and the UHF band. Because VHF could deliver clear pictures to more people than UHF could, VHF stations were considered more valuable. By FCC ruling, however, in 2009 all stations moved to a new part of the spectrum, to broadcast using digital rather than analog technology. The part of the spectrum previously used by television stations was auctioned by the government for use by other companies and public service organizations. Newer TV sets are able to receive the digital signals. But Americans with older analog sets in their homes had to purchase special equipment so that their old TVs would be able to receive the new over-the-air digital signals. Research firm Gfk estimated in 2012 that 17.8 percent of U.S. households—about 20.7 million of them, representing 53.8 million people—receive television exclusively through broadcast signals.[1] People who pay for cable and satellite television subscriptions can also bring in most of the over-the-air channels through set-top boxes, as we will see.

The movement to digital broadcasting from analog broadcasting in 2009 was considered a monumental change in the television industry. The change was described by David Rehr (National Association of Broadcasters CEO and president) as "the most significant advancement of television technology since color TV was introduced." Because this switchover was mandated by the government, coupons for digital converter boxes (in the amount of $40 off the purchase of a converter) were subsidized through the government and made available to citizens of all income levels.

Source: "Broadcasters Prepare for DTV Transition," http://www.twice.com/video/tv/broadcasters-prepare-dtv-transition/31096, accessed February 8, 2013.

**commercial stations**
broadcast television stations that support themselves financially by selling time on their airwaves to advertisers

**noncommercial stations**
broadcast television stations that do not receive financial support from advertisers, but rather support themselves through donations from listeners and private foundations and from commercial firms in return for mentioning the firm or its products in announcements at the beginning and end of programs airing on the station

**billboards**
mentions of a sponsor's name or products at the start or end of programs airing on the station

**underwriting**
when a company pays to sponsor a program on a noncommercial station

**television network**
an organization that distributes television programs, typically by satellite and microwave relay, to all its affiliated stations, or stations that agree to carry a substantial amount of the network's material on an ongoing basis, so that the programs can be broadcast by all the stations at the same time

**Big Four commercial networks**
the four largest television networks: ABC, CBS, Fox, and NBC

**vertically integrated**
circumstance in which an organization has control over a media product from production through distribution to exhibition

**broadcast outlets**
organizations that transmit broadcasting signals

**O&Os (owned and operated stations)**
broadcast television stations that are owned and operated by a network that often provides a regular schedule of programming materials for broadcast

**Table 13.1** The Top Five and Bottom Five Broadcast Television Markets in the United States, 2012

| Rank | Designated market area (DMA) | TV households | % of U.S. |
|------|------------------------------|---------------|-----------|
| 1 | New York, NY | 7,384,340 | 6.468 |
| 2 | Los Angeles, CA | 5,613,460 | 4.917 |
| 3 | Chicago, IL | 3,484,800 | 3.052 |
| 4 | Philadelphia, PA | 2,949,310 | 2.583 |
| 5 | Dallas—Fort Worth, TX | 2,588,020 | 2.267 |
| 206 | Helena, MT | 28,260 | 0.025 |
| 207 | Juneau, AK | 26,320 | 0.023 |
| 208 | Alpena, MI | 16,910 | 0.015 |
| 209 | North Platte, NE | 14,720 | 0.013 |
| 210 | Glendive, MT | 4,050 | 0.004 |

Source: Television Bureau of Advertising, http://www.tvb.org/media/file/TVB_Market_Profiles_Nielsen_Household_DMA_Ranks2.pdf, accessed October 9, 2012.

About 1,400 stations are what people in the TV industry call commercial; 400 others are noncommercial. **Commercial stations** make their money by selling time on their airwaves to advertisers. **Noncommercial stations** receive support in other ways, such as viewer donations and donations from private foundations and commercial firms in return for billboards. **Billboards** are mentions of a sponsor's name or products at the start or end of programs airing on the station. When a company pays to sponsor a program on a noncommercial station, that is called **underwriting**.

The television industry in the United States is divided into 210 broadcast television markets. New York City is the largest, followed by Los Angeles and then Chicago. The New York City market boasts about 7.5 million homes. Glendive, Montana, the smallest market, has 4,000 (see Table 13.1).

More than 80 percent of local TV stations have linked up or affiliated with a television network for at least part of their broadcast day. A **television network** is an organization that distributes television programs, typically by satellite and microwave relay, to all its affiliated stations, or stations that agree to carry a substantial amount of the network's material on an ongoing basis, so that the programs can be broadcast by all the stations at the same time. ABC, CBS, Fox, and NBC are the broadcast networks that regularly reach the largest numbers of people. They are advertiser-supported, as are two smaller networks: the CW (owned by CBS and Time Warner) and ION. A number of commercial Spanish-speaking networks also exist. The biggest are Univision, TeleFutura (owned by Univision), and Telemundo (owned by NBC Universal). The Public Broadcasting Service (PBS) is the network for noncommercial stations. The **Big Four commercial networks**—ABC, CBS, Fox, and NBC—are the giants of the broadcast television business, primarily because of their role in coordinating the distribution of shows to hundreds of local stations, which then transmit the shows to homes.

But ABC, CBS, Fox, and NBC are more than just distributors. They are **vertically integrated** operations. Each company has divisions that produce news, sports, situation comedies, dramas, and other types of programs for use on the network. Each company also owns stations (sometimes called **broadcast outlets**) in the biggest cities; these outlets serve as exhibition anchors for their respective networks. In the TV industry, these local stations are called **O&Os**—short for **owned and operated**.

Local stations that are not owned by broadcast networks and yet transmit their signals and programs are called network affiliates. **Network affiliates** transmit the network's **program feed** (i.e., the succession of shows) on a daily basis. Each network makes money from commercials that show up during the program feed. Depending on the specific deal between network and affiliate, sometimes the network shares those revenues with a local station, and sometimes the station pays for the right to carry the network show, which attracts an audience the local station could not hope to attract on its own. Having a large audience is important to the station because each network sets aside time during programs for the local station to sell advertisements. Popular network shows bring in more viewers and therefore more money to local stations than they could hope to bring in without the distribution clout of the networks.

Many affiliates are part of **station groups**, or collections of broadcast television stations owned by a single company. In the wealthiest station groups, such as Allbritton Communications, each station is an affiliate of one of the major networks. Stations in other groups hook up mainly with CW or ION. According to the Federal Communications Commission, no group may own more than two television stations in any market. That dictum is based on the desire to limit the power of broadcast groups in any one area. The FCC has also ruled, however, that a company can own two networks as long as both are not among the Big Four networks. A station not affiliated with one of the Big Four networks is called an **independent broadcast station**. (Industry executives often consider CW and ION affiliates to be independents because they air relatively few hours of network programming per week.) Practically speaking, independents must find all (or almost all) of their programming themselves. Actually, even network affiliates and O&Os must look to sources other than ABC, CBS, Fox, and NBC for some of their programming. The reason is that the Big Four do not distribute 24 hours' worth of shows. As we will see later in this chapter, the broadcast industry has no shortage of companies trying to interest independents, affiliates, and O&Os in programming.

With the help of advertising agencies (which chapter 3 discusses in some detail), advertisers pay for time between programs and segments of programs. In return, broadcasters allow advertisers to use this time to air **commercials**—short audiovisual pieces that call attention to their products or services. In 2011, advertisers spent about $59 billion on television broadcast advertising.[2] Viewers of broadcast TV do not have to pay to receive the programming. Consequently, historically almost all the money that broadcast stations and networks receive has come from a single revenue stream—commercials. In recent years, though, stations and their networks have begun to make money from the two other domains—subscription television and online and mobile platforms—mentioned earlier. Local stations (and the networks that sometimes own them) now make about a billion dollars a year charging cable and satellite systems for the right to pick their broadcasts off the air and retransmit them to subscribers; these are called **retransmission fees**. Stations and networks are also beginning to take advantage of digital media to develop sources of revenue other than broadcast commercials; in 2008 they brought in about $3.5 billion that way.

## Subscription Cable, Telco, and Satellite Services

People in the TV industry sometimes refer to cable, telco (short for "telecommunications company"), and satellite services collectively as multichannel subscription video programming distributors. Unlike with broadcasting (which anyone with the right technology in the right location can pick off from the air), consumers must subscribe

**network affiliates**
local broadcast television stations that are not owned by broadcast networks and yet transmit network signals and programs on a daily basis; in return, the network promises to compensate the affiliate with a portion of the revenues received from advertisers that have bought time on the network

**program feed**
the succession of shows sent from a network to its network affiliates

**station groups**
collections of broadcast television stations owned by a single company

**independent broadcast station**
a station not affiliated with one of the Big Four networks

**commercials**
short audiovisual pieces that call attention to advertisers' products or services

**retransmission fees**
the money television networks and local stations charge cable and satellite firms for the right to carry their material

**Table 13.2** Top Ten Multiple Systems Owners, June 2012

| Rank | MSO | Subscribers (millions) |
|---|---|---|
| 1 | Comcast Corporation | 22.1 |
| 2 | Time Warner Cable | 12.5 |
| 3 | Cox Communications, Inc. | 4.7 |
| 4 | Charter Communications, Inc. | 4.3 |
| 5 | Cablevision Systems Corp. | 3.3 |
| 6 | Bright House Networks | 2.1 |
| 7 | Suddenlink Communications | 1.2 |
| 8 | Mediacom Communications | 1.0 |
| 9 | CableOne Inc. | 0.68 |
| 10 | WideOpenWest Networks | 0.46 |

Source: http://www.ncta.com, accessed October 10, 2012.

to get these services. As with broadcasting, advertisers pay the cable, telco, and satellite services to have their commercials shown during some of the programming. Both revenue streams are substantial, although the money received from subscriptions is far greater than advertisers' contributions. In 2010, American consumers paid around $81 billion to receive cable or satellite programming. Advertisers paid $29 billion to advertise on these services.[3]

**The Cable Television Business** "**Cable television**" refers to businesses that provide programming to subscribers via a wire (historically a coaxial cable, but increasingly a fiber optic line). The cable television business is by far the most developed in the cable and satellite area. Stripped to its basics, a cable is a type of flexible tube or pipe through which programs are exhibited in the home. The retailer that physically installs the cable and markets the program service to consumers in a particular geographic area is called a **cable television system**. A cable television firm that owns two or more cable systems is a **multiple system owner (MSO)** (see Table 13.2). Every cable system has a limit to how many channels it can carry. Each system offers consumers in its community an array of channels that includes special networks as well as independent local broadcast stations and network affiliates. Though they are called cable networks because they first appeared on cable, the nonbroadcast channels are more appropriately called **subscription networks** because people pay a monthly fee (a subscription) to receive them via cable or satellite. In 2011, Americans spent $56.9 billion on cable TV subscriptions.[4]

**The Telco Business** In recent years, traditional telephone service providers, notably AT&T and Verizon, have also begun to offer a multichannel television service in many parts of the country and now compete with the cable TV firms. Although they wouldn't be called cable companies by people in the business, Verizon and AT&T do use wire technologies (as opposed to the unwired satellite approach) to reach people's homes. Some people in the business call them the **telcos** (short for "telecommunications companies"). Verizon and AT&T have different technical philosophies, but they share the idea of using advanced communication lines called fiber optics to send cable programming to TV sets. In years to come, the telcos, especially Verizon,

---

**cable television**
television service provided to subscribers by signals sent through a wire (usually a coaxial cable, but increasingly via fiber optic lines)

**cable television system**
the cable television retailer that physically installs the cable and markets the program service to consumers in a particular geographic area

**multiple system owner (MSO)**
a cable television firm that owns two or more cable television systems

**subscription networks**
nonbroadcast program channels for which people pay a monthly subscription fee to receive them via cable or satellite

**telcos**
telephone companies that offer television and internet services

could pose a formidable threat to providers of television services. At this point in time, though, the threat posed by the telcos to traditional cable firms and to the satellite business is small because they are just beginning to roll out their services widely. In 2010, they brought in about $3.9 billion from subscribers.

**The Satellite Business** "**Satellite television**" means programming that comes directly to the home from a satellite orbiting the earth. In 2010, about 60 percent of U.S. households with a TV were hooked up to a cable service, 7 percent got TV through telco services, and 33 percent subscribed to a satellite operation. You may have seen old-style satellite dishes, the large structures that typically sat behind people's homes. The backyard satellite dish business was built in the 1980s on the proposition that a homeowner could cut out the cable system by installing a dish-shaped instrument in the backyard and getting programs directly from the satellite that sends them to the cable system. Unfortunately for the homeowners, though, most networks now encode their programs so that a person with a dish cannot view them free of charge. Most of the backyard receivers have been replaced by **direct broadcast satellite (DBS) technology**. Introduced in 1994, it allows a household to receive hundreds of channels. The signals are delivered digitally to a small dish installed on the side of a dwelling; a set-top box decodes digital signals so that they appear on the TV set. The DBS satellites operate from orbits directly above the earth's equator and just over 22,000 miles up. DirecTV and Dish Network are currently the largest DBS companies in the United States.

## Online and Mobile Platforms

By late 2010, 83.6 million (71 percent) of the 117.5 million households in the United States were connected to the internet.[5] About half of those homes were connected to the internet via cable modems, which means they typically had speeds high enough to stream videos or download them much faster than older forms of internet connections (see chapter 3 for more background). This rise in the percentage of American homes with broadband (high-speed) internet in the late 2000s saw an increase in the streaming of audiovisual materials. A similar growth took place in the mobile area. By 2010, about half the population had smartphones with Wi-Fi and cellular networks that allowed them to view videos. Tablets such as the iPad also allow for mobile viewing, and their numbers have soared; by early 2012 nearly 20 percent of Americans had a tablet.

The increasing ability of Americans to view video materials online and on mobile devices paralleled the growth of material for them to watch. Although many of these items were short and produced by amateurs (see most of the videos on YouTube, for example), broadcast networks, local stations, cable companies, satellite firms, and telcos have begun to use online and mobile technologies to distribute their programs as well. Why would broadcast and cable networks arrange for their programs to be viewed via the internet? Here we return to a central theme of this text: convergence. Executives for these firms realize that it is rather easy to make digital copies of broadcast and cable programs and make them available illegally on a variety of platforms. There is, in fact, a robust illegal circulation of television programs on the web. Television executives believe that they

**satellite television**
programming that comes directly to the home from a satellite orbiting the earth

**direct broadcast satellite (DBS) technology**
technology that allows a household to receive hundreds of channels, from signals that are delivered digitally from satellites operating in orbit to a small dish installed on the side of a dwelling; a set-top box decodes digital signals so that they appear on the TV set

With more and more people owning tablets and other mobile-technology products, watching TV online is becoming more and more prevalent. The notion of "watching TV" has fundamentally changed in recent years and will continue to evolve in response to new technologies.

must find business models that encourage people to view programs legitimately in digital spaces. Many of their activities online and in the mobile realm are aimed at trying to experiment with different business models to find the best ones.

Another related reason cable and broadcast firms are allowing their programs to be viewed online and on mobile devices is executives' belief that in a fragmented media world they have to be on technologies their potential audiences use—and audiences, especially young audiences, increasingly take digital convergence for granted. The CW, for example, is a network that aims at teens and young adults. Its leaders know that their audiences might be at least as comfortable viewing programs on laptops and phones as they are using traditional television sets. They consequently place a lot of episodes online and try to sell advertisers on the idea of sponsoring both the broadcast and online feeds.

The television industry's acceptance of convergence does not, however, mean that the activity is profitable. Cable companies *are* making lots of money providing general entry to the internet—about $20 billion in 2010. But when it comes to making money from the professionally produced programming we associate with "television," the amount is negligible compared to the revenues generated through the broadcast and subscription domains. There certainly are interesting TV-like developments in the internet and mobile spaces, as we will see in this chapter. For the foreseeable future, though, it seems clear that competition over television programming and audiences will be among broadcast, cable, and satellite providers.

To get an idea of how these providers are jockeying for viewers' eyeballs—and what the online and mobile domain adds to this mix—we have to understand the basic elements of the evolving television industry. To do that, we turn to our familiar categories of production, distribution, and exhibition. Production takes up the lion's share of this discussion, simply because there are so many different ways to look at it.

## Production in the Television Industry

"Production" is a tricky word when it comes to the television business. In the broadest sense, at least three forms of production are going on at different levels of the industry. To get a sense of what this means, think of your local cable television system. Chances are your local cable system produces very few of its own programs. (Maybe it aids in the production of an access channel, where local officials and citizens can state their problems and parade their interests.) But making shows is not the only way a cable TV system can be involved in production. Your local system is very much involved in producing the number and nature of network channels that it offers potential subscribers; this menu of channels is called a **lineup**.

Each network is also engaged in a second sort of production. For example, the MTV network creates its **format**—the flow of series, news, and videos that defines MTV's overall personality and helps it stand apart from other networks in cable system lineups. Of course, MTV personnel select the programs that are crucial building blocks of their network. However, these programs are often created by other firms that have very little input into decisions about the formats or lineups in which they appear.

Trying to understand production in the television world, then, means getting a grip on the considerations that affect the lineup of channels, the formats of individual channels, and the elements of individual programs. Let's look at each of these categories as they relate to the subscription (cable/satellite/telco), broadcast TV, and online/mobile businesses.

**lineup**
the menu of channels that a cable television system offers potential subscribers

**format**
a collection of elements that constitutes a channel's recognizable personality, created through a set of rules that guide the way the elements are stitched together with a particular audience-attracting goal in mind

## Producing Cable and Satellite Channel Lineups

Creating a channel lineup is a high-priority job for cable and satellite exhibitors. Executives from these companies believe that the number and kinds of programming networks that they offer potential customers are major features that attract people to pay for their service. For instance, take MTV, Nickelodeon, VH1, E!, CNN, C-Span, TBS, AMC, ESPN, ESPN2, the Cartoon Network, HBO, or another network. For which of these networks would you consider subscribing to another service if your cable or satellite system didn't carry it?

With so much riding on customer satisfaction, you would think that cable and satellite executives would simply poll their customers and put on everything they want to see. The firms do, in fact, conduct surveys of consumers, and executives do look at ratings reports that indicate how many people watch different networks. Nevertheless, the choice of networks is based as much on three other considerations as on consumer feedback:

- The technological limitations of the system
- The amount of money a network demands from exhibitors
- Whether or not the exhibitor owns a piece of the network

**Technological Limitations** Technological limitations restrict the number of channels that a cable or satellite service can deliver. High-definition TV (HDTV) signals use substantially more bandwidth than standard TV signals, a factor that has affected the number of HDTV channels that cable and satellite firms have offered. As a telecommunications analyst said in 2007, "HDTV takes an enormous amount of (transmission) capacity. They're going to be sticking 10 pounds of potatoes into a 5-pound bag. Something will have to give." The increasing popularity of HDTV sets and competition with Verizon's very high-capacity FIOS system have been encouraging satellite and cable firms to add more HD channels. That feat is technologically easier for satellite firms than for cable companies, which have to implement major system upgrades across neighborhoods to add capacity. All the services, though, have to weigh the often huge cost of adding channels and other services against the additional subscribers they may bring.

**Covering Costs** In addition to technological limitations and the costs of upgrades, the lineups set by cable and satellite exhibitors depend on the amounts of money that particular networks charge exhibitors for carrying their networks. These costs are called **license fees**. The notion that a subscription video network should charge exhibitors for carrying it goes back to the early 1980s, when advertising support for cable networks such as CNN and A&E was meager and cable systems agreed to chip in to help the networks survive.

Cable and satellite systems typically pay between 15 and 25 cents per month for each subscriber for many of the networks they carry. ESPN and its sister channels, an exceedingly popular set of channels, demand more than $4 per subscriber per month. With millions of subscribers out there, this can add up to money that the delivery service could use for technology upgrades. Consequently, when cable and satellite systems make decisions about their lineups, the mix of channels that they choose is influenced by the amount they will have to pay to those channels. A channel that charges more than another with the same level of audience popularity will have less chance of getting on a system than the one that demands lower license fees.

**license fees**
the costs that particular networks charge exhibitors for carrying the networks' lineups in the exhibitors' cable or satellite systems

Some sporting events, such as Ultimate Fighting Champion matches, are available to view only on PPV.

**tiering**
the strategy by which different levels of television programming are priced differently

**pay-per-view (PPV)**
a transaction in which a cable provider, satellite company, or telco charges the customer for viewing an individual program, such as a boxing event, a live broadcast of a concert, or a newly released motion picture

**video on demand (VOD)**
a television viewing technology whereby a customer uses the remote control to navigate to a menu of programs and then click on the program he or she wants to watch; unlike pay-per-view, in which the customer has to wait for the show to appear at a certain time, the program immediately appears for viewing

**head end**
a cable system's regional delivery location

Part of the way cable systems pay for many of these channels and make technological improvements is to make money from advertising on them. Advertising-supported channels such as CNN or Lifetime typically leave room for the companies that carry them to insert commercials from national or local companies interested in reaching people in particular areas served by the satellite, cable, or telco operation. Of course, another way that a cable or satellite system can bring in revenues is to charge subscribers more money. Still, the possibility of competition and a desire for consumer goodwill have led firms to keep their most basic rates relatively low and to charge more for extra packages of programs. The relatively low rate often offers the customer all the broadcast channels available in the area, channels with local government and other "access" programming, and a relatively small number of subscription channels, such as TBS and TNT. To get more clusters of channels, the subscriber must pay more. This strategy of charging different amounts for different levels of programming is called **tiering** (it's not spelled "tearing," though some people might cry when they see their bills). The number and variety of tiers have gone up dramatically in recent years, especially among cable firms. They include packages of movie channels (e.g., HBO and Cinemax), sports, Spanish-language channels, international channels, and more.

Another way to make money is through **pay-per-view (PPV)** or **video on demand (VOD)** or by renting digital video recorders. In pay-per-view programming, the cable or satellite company charges the customer for viewing an individual program, such as a boxing event, a live broadcast of a concert, or a newly released motion picture. The customer must wait for the specific time that the program airs to view it, or the customer can use the DVR he or she rents per month to capture the program at that time. With video on demand, a customer uses a remote control to navigate to a menu of programs and then click on the program he or she wants to watch. Unlike PPV, where the customer has to wait for the show to appear at a certain time, the program immediately appears for viewing. As this description suggests, VOD requires the customer to be able to communicate directly with the computer providing the programming. That is possible in most cable and telco television systems because the wire connected to the television carries a signal two ways—from the system's regional delivery location (called the **head end**) to the home set and back. Satellite companies, however, don't typically provide the ability of a home television remote to communicate instantly with the computers delivering the programming. Consequently, they cannot offer true video on demand. They try to make up for it by providing their customers with digital video recorders that download selections viewers might want to try, but the selections are more limited than the ones that cable firms provide. Seeing a competitive advantage, cable firms and telcos have been trumpeting their VOD offerings, many of which are free and some of which are high-definition.

**The Exhibitors' Ownership Role in the Network** A third important consideration that influences the lineup of a cable system is whether or not the multiple system owner (MSO) or its parent company owns the network. It stands to reason that if a company has a financial interest in the success of a channel, it will include it. For example, if you live in an area served by Comcast, you'll probably find that it carries SportsNet, E!, Style, the Golf Channel, and G4—all owned wholly or partly by Comcast. Time Warner Cable similarly carries networks that it owns. That doesn't mean that cable systems that do not own these channels will not carry them. It does mean, however, that if a major cable MSO decides to create a channel, it will put it on enough systems in favorable channel locations to give it a good chance of success. That kind of boost would not be so easily available to independent companies with interesting channel ideas.

## Producing Broadcast Channel Lineups

The practice of creating lineups is just beginning to happen in the broadcast industry. Since late 2009, broadcasters have been sending all their programs in digital form. With digital technology, broadcasters now have the ability to send high-definition signals, which they could not do under the old analog system because their bandwidth wouldn't allow it. The digital frequencies do allow it, but broadcasters have decided that they will not always use their new digital frequencies for **high-definition television (HDTV)**. They may send out HDTV signals during the evening, when the large number of viewers available justifies beaming shows in expensive, spectrum-hogging HDTV, but at other times, many broadcasters reason, they can make more advertising money by doing what is called **channel multiplexing** or **multichannel broadcasting**—that is, splitting their new digital signals into two, three, or even four separately programmed channels and sending them in the form of a complex signal that is separated at the receiving end, instead of broadcasting one channel of HDTV. So rather than just broadcasting channel 6, a network could broadcast on channels 6a, 6b, 6c, and 6d.

This is where questions related to program lineups enter the picture. Should each channel aim as broadly as possible, or should each channel focus on a particular topic (e.g., food or sports), as many cable systems do? Should the stations target people at home, in school, in hospitals, in nursing homes, or at work? Should the channels be related to one another thematically—all of them programming news but programming different types of news, for example? How different should the channels be from the offerings of other stations? How involved should the network with which the local station is affiliated be in creating programming for the channels? What will advertisers think about all this?

These are among the questions TV broadcasters have begun to ask about their new digital world. They also face the challenge of trying to persuade—or get the government to require—local cable systems to carry their digital and HDTV signals. Although federal law requires cable systems to carry local stations, the cable firms are reluctant to carry the multiplexed channels of these stations. They argue that these channels would take up so much space on their systems that they would interfere with the systems' ability to carry the popular national networks that cable outlets typically exhibit.

## Producing Online/Mobile Lineups

The same considerations that drive executives in the cable and broadcast arenas also come up among leaders of websites and mobile applications. Although you may think of a website or app as a single channel, chances are if it provides video choices, it

**high-definition television (HDTV)** a television display technology that provides picture quality similar to that of 35mm movies with sound quality similar to that of today's compact discs. Some television stations have begun transmitting HDTV broadcasts to users on a limited number of channels, generally using digital rather than analog signal transmission

**channel multiplexing (multichannel broadcasting)** sending multiple signals or streams of information on a carrier at the same time in the form of a single complex signal and then recovering the separate signals at the receiving end

actually offers its video options in arrangements by themes or types. YouTube, for example, actually does use the word "channels" for its arrangement of choices according to certain themes—for example, entertainment, sports, comedy, politics, and NHL video. Hulu's home page combines links to collections of episodes of popular programs (e.g., *Modern Family*, *Glee*) as well as collections of programs from the program networks that own Hulu: NBC Universal Television Group, Fox Broadcasting, and Disney-ABC Television Group. Ownership is also an obvious issue for MSNBC's mobile app, which divides into collections of NBC-owned shows (e.g., *Hardball*, *Rachel Maddow*, *Meet the Press*) and topics (weather, travel, health). The point is that the decision about what program categories to offer may well have as much to do with the types of programs the digital service can access as with the themes that channel creators would like to offer.

## Producing Individual Channels

Once a television service has a channel, it has to find a way to fill the time. The task of producing any channel itself is huge, whether it is carried out for a subscription TV network such as CNN or for a broadcast station. Programmers—the people in charge of operations as different as the Weather Channel and MTV on subscription video and WWOR (channel 9) in New York and KNBC (channel 4) in Los Angeles on broadcast TV—have to fill 24 hours of airtime every day of the year. Clock-based programming isn't typically a requirement for "on demand" programs on cable or satellite or online. Offerings are set out for visitors to access as they wish; some are removed after a certain period. Populating these sorts of channels still requires a good deal of thought, however, for the menu of possibilities can either invite or chase away intended audiences.

**Determining the Channel's Intended Audience**   The most basic issue that confronts a programmer online, in cable, or in broadcast relates to the intended audience: whom should the programmer try to attract as viewers? This critical question is typically thrashed out by a number of top executives in the organization. The answer generally depends on four interrelated considerations:

- The competition
- The available pool of viewers
- The interests of sponsors
- The costs of relevant programming

**competition**
the programming alternatives that already exist

"**Competition**" refers to the programming alternatives that already exist. If a channel that emphasizes history is already succeeding, starting a similar channel may not be useful unless you are sure that you have a clearly more attractive way of doing it or that there are enough people who are interested in history to accommodate two somewhat different approaches to the subject. But even if there are enough history buffs around, executives who are thinking of starting a second history channel must ask whether there are enough advertisers that want to sponsor programs on such a channel. If the channel is in the cable/satellite domain (as it probably would be), the executives have to ask whether they could successfully place a second history channel on enough systems to interest advertisers. They also have to ask whether the costs of history programs would be appropriate in view of the projected revenues that would be received from advertisers that want to reach the projected audience. If the programs would be so expensive that the channel wouldn't be able to recover the costs from advertisers and cable subscriptions, such a channel wouldn't succeed, regardless of how interesting it was.

Programmers for cable/satellite/telco channels often focus on rather specific topics to guide their choices of materials. That's also true of many websites with video. They aim to reach people with particular lifestyle habits or interests—an available pool of viewers. Think of HGTV (Home and Garden Television) or the Golf Channel. In contrast, broadcast stations, because they are well known and accessible to virtually everyone in their area, do not differentiate themselves so narrowly. When they go after new audiences, they choose broad segments of the population that advertisers want to reach. In some large cities, for example, where the FCC added several stations and increased competition for audiences, a few stations have decided to pursue Spanish-speaking viewers, or non-English-speaking viewers generally, to maximize their profits.

**Ratings** In the television industry, the audits of people's television viewing behavior that help to determine where much of the money for programming and advertising should go are called **ratings**. Nielsen Media Research dominates this business. The stations, networks, and major advertisers foot most of the bill for the firm's reports. Nielsen uses meters and diaries to determine what people are watching and when.

For a snapshot of what America is watching, Nielsen uses an instrument called a **people meter**. The company installs this small box on all of the television sets in more than 20,000 homes that it has chosen as a representative sample of the U.S. population. The meter holds a preassigned code for every individual in the home, including visitors. The research firm asks each viewer to enter his or her code at the start and end of a TV viewing session. Information from each viewing session is transmitted to Nielsen's computers through television lines and is the basis for the firm's conclusions about national viewing habits.

However, meters in 20,000 homes scattered around the country can't tell stations in the 210 individual television markets around the country how many people are watching the stations and who these people are. To get these data, Nielsen uses two approaches. For nonstop research on 56 markets, Nielsen uses people meters. The rest are monitored through household meters and diaries. In the smaller markets Nielsen finds a way to generalize about the habits of individual viewers by comparing the data collected from the household meters with entries in diaries that are distributed four times a year to another sample of households in the same markets. Nielsen asks the family members to fill in the viewing experiences for each member of the household for a month. These diaries are also used to determine viewing habits during four months of the year—February, May, August, and November—in all 210 television markets. Broadcast industry workers call these months the **sweeps** because the ratings measurements during these periods are comparable to giant sweepstakes in which winners and losers are determined.

Nielsen's results are arrayed as ratings and shares. Ratings and shares, in turn, can be discussed in household and people terms. **Household ratings** represent the number of households in which the channel was turned on, compared with the number of households in the channel's universe (the local area, or the number of people who receive the cable network). **People ratings** refer to particular demographic categories of individuals within each household—for example, those aged 18 to 49 or those who are female. For a particular channel during a particular time, a **household share** represents the number of households in which the channel was

**ratings**
audits of people's television viewing behavior that help to determine where much of the money for programming and advertising should go

**people meter**
a small box installed by Nielsen on television sets in about 20,000 homes that it has chosen as a representative sample of the U.S. population. The meter holds a preassigned code for every individual in the home, including visitors. Nielsen asks each viewer to enter his or her code at the start and end of a TV viewing session. Information from each viewing session is transmitted to Nielsen's computers through television lines and is the basis for the firm's conclusions about national viewing habits.

**sweeps**
the survey of TV viewing habits in markets across the United States, as performed by Nielsen four times per year—during the months of February, May, August, and November; competition among TV programmers is especially keen during these periods

**household ratings**
ratings that represent the number of households in which the channel was turned on, compared with the number of households in the channel's universe (the local area, or the number of people who receive the cable network)

**people ratings**
particular demographic categories of individuals within each household—for example, those aged 18 to 49 years or those who are female

**household share**

the number of households in which a particular channel was turned on compared with the number of TV-owning households in the area where the channel could be viewed

**reach**

the percentage of the entire target audience to which a media outlet will circulate

**national rating points**

a measure of the percentage of TV sets in the United States that are tuned to a specific show; in 2001, each national rating point represented just over 1 million U.S. homes with TVs

**average commercial minute**

Nielsen's reporting standard for determining ratings and household viewing during commercials; this information gives advertisers measurements not just for each program taken as a whole, but also for the commercials that run during the programs

**C3 standard**

Nielsen technique of measuring the average commercial minute of a program by including in the ratings people who recorded commercials on DVRs and viewed them within a three-day period

turned on compared with the number of TV-owning households in the area where the channel could be viewed.

Because of their wide **reach**, or the percentage of the entire target audience to which they circulate, broadcast networks often answer to advertisers in terms of their **national rating points**. In 2012, every national household rating point represented 1,175,000 households (about 1 percent of U.S. homes with a TV). National people ratings are expressed in terms of the number of individuals in the United States who fit into a particular category. Each rating point in the 18- to 49-year-old category, for example, represents 1 percent of the U.S. total for people 18 to 49.

For example, if the *Late Show with David Letterman*—which is exhibited nationally on CBS—receives a 5.4 household rating and a 16 household share, what does that mean? The rating means that of the 117.5 million households in the United States that own a TV set, 5.4 percent (6.3 million households) had at least one TV tuned to Letterman. That may look like a very small percentage, but the program airs at 11:30 p.m. (EST and PST), when many people are asleep. The 16 household share means that of the households in which people were viewing TV at that time of night, about one in six (about 16 percent) had a set tuned to Letterman. Of course, households often have people viewing different TV sets. Increasingly, then, networks and their advertisers prefer ratings and shares to be expressed not in terms of households but in terms of categories of individuals who are viewing. So, for example, you might read in the trade press that Letterman received a 19 share among the 18- to 49-year-olds in its audience.

Nielsen reports each program's rating and share for a particular night to its clients (typically advertising executives). In the 2000s, advertisers began to pressure Nielsen to report ratings and shares not just for the average viewing of programs but also in terms of the viewing of commercials within and around the shows. After all, for advertisers, the shows are there mainly to get the right people to watch the commercials. Nielsen determines ratings and household viewings during commercials and reports them in terms of the **average commercial minute**. That way, advertisers have measurements not just for each program taken as a whole but also for the commercials that run during the programs. In addition, Nielsen determines the ratings for a program and its average commercial minutes not just by counting the people who viewed it at the actual time it ran on broadcast or cable. The company includes in the ratings people who recorded it on a DVR and viewed it within a three-day period. The reason for this is that by 2011 about 42 percent of U.S. households had a DVR-connected TV set; 18- to 49-year-old women, it turns out, spend 10 percent of their viewing time with a DVR.[6] The TV networks argue that advertisers should take viewing through DVRs into account as well as so-called live viewing. This approach—measuring the average commercial minute of a program within a three-day window—is called the **C3 standard** and is used for today's ratings reports.

Preliminary evidence suggests that the commercial ratings of some shows rise substantially when time-shifting via DVRs is added to the picture. However, the ratings do not take into account viewing on the web and mobile media. For this reason, Nielsen has developed what the company calls its Cross-Platform Homes and Extended Screen Ratings system. The company audits all use of desktops and laptops in nearly half the homes in Nielsen's National People Meter sample. This audit, says the company, gives its clients "a singular view of how everyone in the house watches TV, surfs, and streams, generating vital insights into the relationships between these activities." And in a strong nod to convergence, a video on

| Time Slot | Network | | | |
|---|---|---|---|---|
| | ABC | NBC | CBS | FOX |
| 8:00 p.m. | Last Resort | The Rock | Big Bang Theory | Mobbed |
| 8:30 p.m. | | 1600 Penn | Two and a Half Men | |
| 9:00 p.m. | Grey's Anatomy | The Office | Person of Interest | Glee |
| 9:30 p.m. | | 1600 Penn | | |
| 10:00 p.m. | Scandal | Rock Center with Brian Williams | Elementary | Local Programming |
| 10:30 p.m. | | | | |

## Figure 13.2

Prime-time lineups on Thursday evenings for the four major national networks (as of January 10, 2013).

Nielsen's site says, "Imagine knowing who's viewing what wherever, whenever, on whatever, and applying it to a variety of cross-platform business models." Nielsen says it can do that—present ratings numbers for programs across conventional TV, desktop, and laptop viewing. The video acknowledges that this approach doesn't take into consideration other platforms where people view television programs, such as smartphones and tablets. That, says the video, will come soon.[7]

**Preparing a Schedule** The size of a program's audience helps determine the amount of money a station or network can charge an advertiser for time during that program. Consequently, ratings are always on the minds of the programmers who produce schedules for their stations or networks. Many broadcast and cable/satellite channel programmers break down their work into creating discrete **schedules**, or patterns in which programs are arranged, for different **day parts**, or segments of the day as defined by programmers and marketers. The most prominent of these day parts is the period from 8:00 to 11:00 p.m. (or from 7:00 to 10:00 p.m. in the central and mountain time zones), when the largest number of people are viewing. Called **prime time**, these are the hours in which the Big Four broadcast networks put on their most expensive programs (see Figure 13.2 for a sample of a prime-time schedule) and charge advertisers the most money for commercial time (30 seconds is the most common). Prime time is the most prestigious day part, although not necessarily the most profitable. CBS, for example, makes more profits from its afternoon soap opera schedule (for which it pays relatively little) than from its pricier evening fare.

**schedules**
patterns in which programs are arranged

**day parts**
segments of the day as defined by programmers and marketers

**prime time**
the hours in which the Big Four broadcast networks put on their most expensive programs and charge advertisers the most money for commercial time

## THINKING ABOUT MEDIA LITERACY

Prime time is more prestigious than other day parts, and in turn the programming for it is also more expensive. Choose a broadcast station in your area and compare the schedules for the afternoon and the evening. What kind(s) of programs do you find? What kinds of audiences are the shows trying to attract? From these observations, why do you think the costs are so different?

In prime time, as in all day parts, the different goals of different channels lead to different schedules. As noted earlier, household ratings are usually not as important to advertisers and programmers as individual ratings. Age, gender, and sometimes ethnicity are particular selling points. When adults are the targets, most programmers start with the assumption that they must attract mostly people between 18 and 49 years old because this is the market segment that most television advertisers want to reach. Although people older than 50 actually have more money than those who are younger, many advertisers believe that once people pass the age of 49, they are not as susceptible as younger adults to new product ideas. Advertisers are also aware that people who are 50 and older are less likely than younger adults to be taking care of children at home. More people in a household means more repeat purchases of goods such as soap, cereal, and frozen foods.

**series**
a set of programs that revolve around the same ideas or characters

The building block of a television schedule is the **series**—a set of programs that revolve around the same ideas or characters. Series can be as varied as *Grey's Anatomy*, a weekly dramedy about physicians in a Seattle hospital; *Nightline*, a daily late-night news and interview program; or *Are You Smarter Than a 5th Grader?*, a game show that pits an adult's knowledge against knowledge held by kids. Series are useful to programmers because they lend predictability to a schedule. Programmers can schedule a series in a particular time slot with the hope that it will solve the problem of attracting viewers to that slot on a regular basis.

**audience flow**
the movement of audience members from one program to another

**lead-in**
a program that comes before, and therefore leads into, another program

Programmers generally try to bring viewers to more than just one show on their station or network. Their goal is to attract certain types of people to an entire day part so that the ratings for that day part—and therefore its ad fees—will be high. Keeping people tuned to more than one series also means keeping them around for the commercials between the series. In TV industry lingo, the challenge is to maximize the **audience flow** across programs in the day part.

**sampling**
trying out a new program by watching it for the first time

**lead-out**
the program that follows the program after the lead-in

**hammock**
the strategic placement of a program between two other programs; positioning a new series between two well-established shows that appeal to the same target audience often gives the right viewers an opportunity to sample the new series

That's a tall order when so many viewers clutch that ultimate ratings spoiler, the remote control, securely in their hands for the duration of their viewing sessions. The idea of audience flow is particularly precarious when a substantial portion of households have digital video recorders that can capture one network's program while they watch a different channel. Still, Nielsen ratings do suggest that certain scheduling techniques can improve audience flow. One is the use of a strong lead-in to programs that follow. A **lead-in** is a program that comes before, and therefore leads into, another program. Ratings suggest that a strong lead-in tends to bring its audience to sample the program that comes after it. The chance for **sampling**, or trying a new series for the first time, is also increased if the **lead-out**—the program that follows the new series—is popular. Many people who are interested in seeing the first and third programs will stick through the second if they consider it at all good.

**time slot**
a particular position in the schedule

Say you're a programmer and have a new series that you want to give the maximum chance to succeed. By the logic of lead-ins and lead-outs, you should place the new series between two well-established shows that appeal to the same audience. This position, known as a **hammock**, gives the right viewers an opportunity to sample the show.

**counterprogramming**
scheduling a program that aims to attract a target audience different from those of other shows in the same time slot; often done to avoid competing directly with a popular series

Sometimes what seems like a good program for a particular position in the schedule, or **time slot**, may be judged unacceptable because it is aimed at the same kinds of people (in terms of age, gender, ethnicity, or interests) who are flocking to a popular program on another channel at the same time. When programmers don't want to compete directly with a popular series, they turn to **counterprogramming**—scheduling a program that aims to attract a target audience different from that of other shows in a particular time slot. For example, in 2007 some local stations began to place game shows in the late afternoon (4:00 to 6:00 p.m.) time slot as counterprogramming to talk shows that their competitors were running at that time.

## Producing Individual Programs

To program producers, being successful doesn't just mean coming up with an idea that programmers like (as difficult as that may be). It also means coming up with an idea that programmers for local stations, broadcast networks, cable/satellite networks, or websites need—at a cost they can afford. Making shows for websites is the most experimental part of television production. The past several years have seen the rise of a large number of firms creating programs of various lengths for the digital world. Their goal is to get upfront funding from entrepreneurs who will also help them secure distribution in ways that will attract advertisers and pay for the shows. High-profile Hollywood talent has been involved in web-initiated programming for several years. When the Budweiser beer company started Bud.TV in 2006, it turned for material to Kevin Spacey's Trigger Street Productions, Matt Damon's LivePlanet Productions, and Warner Bros. Television's Studio 2.0, an outfit created for less expensive web-based projects. Consider, too, the path of Emmy award–winning writer/ producer team Marshall Herskovitz and Edward Zwick (*My So-Called Life*, *Thirty-Something*, *Glory*). In 2007, they decided to take the pilot of an ad-sponsored program called *Quarterlife* that did not make it to traditional network television and recreate it in smaller bits as an internet series. They enlisted the enormously popular site MySpace (owned by News Corporation) to distribute the series' 36 episodes and did not count out showing it elsewhere on the web. The endeavor wasn't wildly popular, but their move did point to a distribution platform for new professionally created television programming outside of the traditional channels. It's a new world for video professionals, and it stretches the term "television" far beyond what people would have thought a decade ago.

Take a look at the programs available on Koldcast.tv to get an idea of the fare available nowadays on a small but ambitious distribution venue. For another example, check out the giant video distributor YouTube. In recent years it has been offering funds to promising production firms, some led by people with Hollywood track records. YouTube executives hope to attract large audiences for such "professionally" produced material on its territory. The executives believe advertisers will feel more comfortable placing ads alongside this fare rather than alongside the amateur and often raunchy videos currently typical of YouTube.

At this point, though, production of programs aimed at the web and other digital spaces is risky from a business standpoint. Broadcast and subscription television are the places where production makes by far the most money. For many production companies, the biggest prize is an order for a prime-time series from one of the broadcast networks. Landing this prize can be tough because often network-owned production companies seem to have an inside track. Even apart from the competition with the networks' production divisions, however, the chances of getting such an order are not high. Network programming executives meet with many producers to hear brief summaries of program ideas. Creators may present several of these summaries, called **pitches**, in one sitting. Most of the time, the network people say that they are not interested. Sometimes they tell the creators that they will pay for a **treatment**, a multipage elaboration of the idea. The treatment describes the proposed

**pitch**
brief summary of a program idea

**treatment**
a multipage elaboration of a television series producer's initial pitch to network programming executives; the document describes the proposed show's setup and the way in which it relates to previous popular series

show's setup and how it relates to previous popular series. It also discusses the collection of elements that will propel the series and give it a recognizable personality—the setting, the characters, typical plots, and the general layout, tone, and approach. This collection of elements, which often are created using a set of rules that guide the way elements are stitched together with a particular audience-attracting goal in mind, is called the format of a show. (We have already seen how networks such as MTV can have formats.)

If network officials like the format and believe that it fits their programming strategy, they may commission research known as **concept testing** to try out this idea and the ideas of other producers with audiences. Concept testing involves reading one-paragraph descriptions of series formats to people who fit the profile of likely viewers. Sometimes these people are contacted by phone, and sometimes they are questioned in preview theaters where they have been invited to evaluate new shows. Researchers ask these viewers if they would watch the series based on the descriptions. If a producer's concept rates well with the appropriate audience, the interested network may contract for a sample script and a test program, called a **pilot**.

When the pilot is completed, the network tests it too. Often the process involves showing the pilot to a group of target viewers, either on specially rented cable TV channels or in **preview theaters**. When cable TV is used, the individuals chosen are asked to view a movie or series pilot on the channel at a certain time. After the program, the viewers are asked questions over the telephone about what they saw. Viewers in preview theaters sometimes sit in chairs equipped with dials that they can use to indicate how much they like what they see on the screen. These responses, along with the viewers' written comments, help network executives decide whether or not to commission the series.

Let's assume that everything works out fine with a series' concept testing and pilot. The network executives then give the production company a contract for several episodes—typically 13. The contract is for permission—called a **license**—to air each episode a certain number of times. You might think that with such a deal in hand, production firm executives would be wildly ecstatic, sure that the show will enrich their firm. Not so fast. For one thing, the network may reduce the firm's potential profits by asking for co-ownership of the show as a way of paying for the risk the network is taking to fund and air it. Moreover, even with network backing, the show may not last long. Many prime-time series receive bad ratings and are yanked by the networks even before their first 13 episodes have aired.

Another factor that makes production executives nervous is that network licensing agreements typically do not cover the full costs of each episode—even for shows from companies the networks own. If an hour-long drama is slated to cost the production firm $2.5 million per episode, the network may pay $1.5 million. The producers then have to come up with $1 million per episode themselves. Over 13 episodes, that will put them $13 million in a financial hole.

Why would any company do that? The answer is that in a convergence world production firms see network broadcast as only the first of a number of TV domains in which they can make money from their series. They can make money from local stations, from cable networks, from stores, from the internet, from mobile apps, and from broadcasters outside the United States. And if a show succeeds on TV, these extra windows can become gold mines. But to learn more about how the money comes in, let's shift the discussion from production to distribution.

**concept testing**
research commissioned by network executives in order to determine whether the format of a proposed series appeals to members of the series' target audience; this often involves reading a one-paragraph description of series formats to people who fit the profile of likely viewers

**pilot**
a single episode that is used to test the viability of a series

**preview theaters**
venues to which members of a target audience are invited to engage in concept testing or to evaluate newly completed series pilots

**license**
the contract between a production company and network executives that grants the network permission to air each episode a certain number of times; usually 13 episodes of a series are ordered

# Distribution in the Television Industry

As we noted earlier, a broadcast television network is involved in both the production and the distribution of material. When a network licenses programs from its own production divisions or from outside producers, it sends them to its affiliates, which then broadcast them (usually simultaneously) to homes. A similar activity happens in the cable and satellite businesses. TV distributors on the web tend not to pay license fees. Hulu and Koldcast, for example, pay the program owners a percentage of the revenues they get from ads around the show. YouTube has taken a different approach, though. To jumpstart interest in its professionally produced channels, the Google-owned service has paid producers it has enlisted fees from a $100 million pot the company allocated to get promising programs off the ground and on its network.

Note that local broadcast stations do not always rely on the broadcast "nets" for programs. One reason is that stations not affiliated with networks need to get their programming from somewhere. Another reason is that even network-affiliated stations do not broadcast the network feed all the time. Certain hours in the morning, in the afternoon, in the early evening, and after 1:00 a.m. belong to the stations. Therefore, they can take for themselves all the ad revenue they bring in during these periods, but first they must find programs that attract an audience at a reasonable price.

Many non-network distributors are willing to help local stations find attractive shows through syndication—licensing programs to individual outlets on a market-by-market basis (see Table 13.3, which presents ratings of the top 20 syndicated programs during a week in 2012). One way to attract audiences "off network" is with programs that are newly created for syndication. Examples are the celebrity news program *Entertainment Tonight*, the talk show *The Ellen DeGeneres Show*, and the game show *Wheel of Fortune*, which are made to be shown every weekday, which is typical of new syndicated programming. This five-day-a-week placement is called **stripping** a show. Local programmers believe that, in certain day parts, putting the same show in the same time slot each weekday lends predictability to the schedule that target audiences appreciate.

**stripping**
five-day-a-week placement of a television show; programmers believe that, in certain day parts, placing the same show in the same time slot each weekday lends a predictability to the schedule that target audiences appreciate

## THINKING ABOUT MEDIA LITERACY

Take a closer look at Table 13.3, which lists the most popular shows in syndication. Do any of the listings there surprise you? Were you surprised to see some showing missing from the list? Why or why not? What do you think the list says?

Stripping is also a popular tactic in **off-network syndication**—in which a distributor takes a program that has already been shown on network television and rents episodes of that program to TV stations for local airing. Consider *Law & Order: Criminal Intent*, a police and law drama that was produced by Wolf Films and NBC Universal and shown on a first-run basis on NBC television and USA cable network. In 2007, NBC Universal Domestic Television Distribution syndicated it to local stations on a stripped basis. The distributor made deals with stations covering 95 percent of the country.

If producers fail to place their reruns on local stations, there are other avenues that they can use. Cable and satellite networks have become voracious consumers of off-network programming, in part because these programs are less expensive than new shows and in part because they reliably attract certain categories of viewers. Nick at

**off-network syndication**
a situation in which a distributor takes a program that has already been shown on network television and rents episodes of that program to TV stations for local airing

**Table 13.3** Top 25 Syndicated Shows for the Week Ending September 23, 2012

| Rank | Program | Dist | Days | HH rating | Viewers (000) |
|---|---|---|---|---|---|
| 1 | ESPN NFL REGULAR SEASON | ESP | M...... | 10.5 | 16462 |
| 2 | BIG BANG-SYN (AT) | WB | MTWTF.. | 7.0 | 10931 |
| 3 | JUDGE JUDY (AT) | CTD | MTWTF.. | 6.7 | 9239 |
| 4 | WHEEL OF FORTUNE | CTD | MTWTF.. | 6.3 | 9510 |
| 5 | JEOPARDY (AT) | CTD | MTWTF.. | 5.6 | 8386 |
| 6 | 2012 REG SEASON GAMES | NFL | ...T... | 5.2 | 7968 |
| 7 | TWO-HALF MEN-SYN (AT) | WB | MTWTF.. | 4.7 | 7004 |
| 8 | BIG BANG WKND B (AT) | WB | ......S | 4.6 | 7151 |
| 9 | FAMILY FEUD (AT) | 2/T | MTWTF.. | 4.0 | 5865 |
| 9 | BIG BANG WKND A (AT) | WB | ......S | 4.0 | 6191 |
| 11 | FAMILY GUY-MF-SYN (AT) | 2/T | MTWTF.. | 3.7 | 5655 |
| 12 | ENTERTAINMENT TONIGHT(AT) | CTD | MTWTF.. | 3.6 | 4967 |
| 13 | FAMILY GUY-WK-SYN (AT) | 2/T | ......S | 3.5 | 5301 |
| 14 | 2012 NFL REG SEA PREKICK | NFL | ...T... | 3.1 | 4519 |
| 14 | DR. PHIL SHOW (AT) | CTD | MTWTF.. | 3.1 | 3980 |
| 16 | 2012 NFL REG SEA POSTGUN | NFL | ...T... | 3.0 | 4502 |
| 17 | INSIDE EDITION (AT) | CTD | MTWTF.. | 2.9 | 4035 |
| 18 | MONK-SYN (AT) | NBU | ......S | 2.8 | 4127 |
| 19 | LAW & ORDER-SYN (AT) | NBU | ......S | 2.7 | 3723 |

These are the top nationally syndicated shows, which Nielsen defines as shows for which the distributors sell national advertising. For syndicated shows that air on multiple days, the viewership shown is the average of all telecasts. "HH rating" stands for household rating. 2/T: Twentieth Television; CTD: CBS Television Distribution; ESP: ESPN NBU: NBC Universal; NFL: National Football League; SPT: Sony Pictures Television; WB: Warner Bros. Note: Although *The Simpsons* repeats are available nationally, Nielsen does not count the show's ratings in the weekly syndicated ratings because *The Simpsons* does not sell any national advertising in syndication.

Source: http://tvbythenumbers.zap2it.com/2012/10/02/syndicated-tv-ratings-big-bang-theory-wins-again-dr-phil-retains-top-talker-spot-for-week-of-september-16th/151017/© 2010 The Nielsen Company. All Rights Reserved.

**out-of-home locations (or captive audience locations)**
places such as airline waiting areas and store checkout lines where people congregate and likely pay attention to TV clips and commercials

Night and TVLand are two subscription video networks that air television programs that people in their thirties and forties viewed when they were young. Lifetime goes after programs that in their broadcast network lives were popular with women, and the Family Channel looks for material that few moms and dads would find objectionable.

Another venue for making extra money from television programs is what marketers call **out-of-home locations**, sometimes called **captive audience locations**. These include such places as airline waiting areas and store checkout lines where people congregate and likely pay attention to TV clips and commercials. CNN distributes its news programming as the CNN Airport Network. NBC sends parts of its programs to a supermarket checkout TV network. CBS provides some of the news and entertainment programs it owns to airlines; it also owns a network that sends some of its programs (with commercials) to health care offices. ABC News provides material for a company that puts video screens on gas station pumps.

## THINKING ABOUT MEDIA LITERACY

Think for a moment about all the screens that feature programming outside your home. Where do you find them? Why do you think the screens are there? What kinds of programming do they show? What advantages do these screens offer, if any? What disadvantages do they offer, if any?

Foreign countries have also been a useful market for certain types of reruns. Broadcasters around the world purchase U.S.-made series as components of their schedules. The popularity of programs from the United States rises and falls, and in many cases homegrown programming gets better ratings than the U.S. material. Generally speaking, action dramas do better than sitcoms in this market because American humor doesn't cross borders as easily as sex appeal (*Baywatch* was popular around the world) and violence (so was *Walker, Texas Ranger*). During the late 2000s, the increase in digital television channels in some countries led both new networks looking to raise their profiles and established networks wanting to stem audience losses to scramble for highly polished programs at reasonable prices. U.S. firms have been ready to fill the gap. In Spain, for example, the Telecinco network signed a deal with NBC Universal to show the new drama series *Trauma: Life in the ER* and the older *Parenthood* movies. "U.S. dramas bring prestige and work well for Spanish channels," said a Madrid-based research company executive.

Captive-audience locations, such as checkout lines, airports, airplanes, and even the backseats of New York City cabs, provide an opportunity for networks and advertisers to reach viewers (or potential customers, for advertisers) at a time when they are likely to actually view the programming that is put in front of them.

Note that a reverse flow of programs is also taking place. The increase in channels in the United States, combined with the need for less expensive programming, has led programmers to scour the world for series ideas. They may decide to copy an international series idea for use in the United States—even using the same basic scripts, but adapting the program to suit their idea of what their American audience wants. Examples include NBC's sitcom *The Office*, CBS's reality show *Big Brother*, and HBO's drama *In Treatment*, which are based on British, Dutch, and Israeli versions, respectively.

The internet has become a competitor to the traditional TV set for viewers' time, and so have video games and the DVD player. TV ratings are slipping as a result, and advertising rates are not rising as high as license fees in many cases. Producers and network executives are trying to find ways to profit from the programs that they make and circulate.

**Encouraging Viewers to View Programs with Commercials on the Internet** An increasing number of homes have been paying for fast broadband connections to the internet. Such fast connections allow users to view audiovisual presentations with acceptable clarity, and as a result, just about every television network is posting much of its programming on the web for people to view. The shows **stream**—that is, they start playing when you click on their links—and they are not designed to be saved on the user's computer. The program streams come with commercials that are much fewer in number and shorter in time than the ones people see on traditional TV. The catch, however, is that online a viewer cannot speed through ads.

**stream**
the act of sending digital materials so they can be heard or viewed as they are sent, without having to be saved first

Different networks have different philosophies about how much programming to put online and where. The biggest networks, though, have decided that putting shows only on their own sites is not enough. CBS, for example, has been making

## MEDIA TODAY & CULTURE  LACK OF DIVERSITY IN TELEVISION PROGRAMMING

Following on the success of the *Sex and the City* franchise, HBO debuted the series *Girls* in early 2012. Created by Lena Dunham, *Girls* follows four 20-something women living in New York City. *Girls* drew criticism for its homogeneity—all of the main cast members are white.[1]

According to figures from the last major census, diversity in the United States is expanding. Both Hispanic and Asian populations have grown at faster rates recently, whereas the Caucasian population has grown at a slower rate.[2] Television programming, however, offers little reflection of the growing diversity in the United States, in either news or prime-time entertainment.

Cable news outlets still feature an overwhelming majority of white males, according to a study conducted by Media Matters for America. The study, titled "Locked Out: The Lack of Gender and Ethnic Diversity in on Cable News," shows that in the examined time frame 67 percent of guests on cable news programs were male and 84 percent of guests were white. Some groups, such as Asian Americans and Arab Americans, appeared less than five times within the month studied. No Native Americans appeared whatsoever.[3]

Prime-time entertainment programming offers similar rates of diversity in representations. In general, television shows feature almost all-white casts. Newer example comedies include *The Big Bang Theory*, *30 Rock*, and *How I Met Your Mother*. Slightly older example comedies include *Sex and the City*, *Friends*, and *Seinfeld*. Newer example dramas include *NCIS* and *Brothers and Sisters*.

If shows integrate more diverse characters into their storylines, they usually incorporate one or two minority characters. For example, *The Big Bang Theory* includes Rajesh Koothrappali and his sister Priya Koothrappali, who both are from India. The drama *Bones* features Muslim intern Arastoo Vaziri. A few shows do attempt to offer more diversity in their casts, with representatives of multiple ethnic groups, such as dramas *Hawaii Five-O* and *Lost* and the comedy *Community*. Only a small handful of shows have featured casts of primarily non-white characters, such as *My Wife and Kids*, *The George Lopez Show*, and *Everybody Hates Chris*.

A roundtable hosted by the *New York Times* noted that diversity issues extend beyond representations within shows.[4] These issues include the people working behind the scenes as writers, directors, and producers as well. Though Tina Fey is quite visible in her roles as creator, writer, producer, director, and actor, the presence of other women in television production remains about 26 percent of the total across all the roles in entertainment production, according to the Center for the Study of Women in Television and Film.[5] They are most prominent among producers at 38 percent and least prominent as directors of photography at 4 percent.

deals with many sites on the web, including TV.com (in which it has invested), to display links to its shows. Sites that bring viewers to CBS programs share in ad revenues. NBC Universal, Fox, and Disney are among the firms invested in Hulu, which streams their programs and others'.

Some observers contend that the major networks are—or soon will be—cannibalizing their audiences by placing their first-run prime-time programs for viewing on the web. That is, they say people will watch the programs online (where there are fewer and less expensive commercials) and so make it difficult for the networks to profit from prime-time showings. Network executives disagree, arguing that web versions allow fans to view shows they miss occasionally and that they create new fans who end up watching the programs in their broadcast time slots. Either way, cable and satellite executives are annoyed that the programs can be found for free online. They note that they pay money to carry those shows and other programming, and they worry that increasing numbers of households will drop their subscription TV contracts and simply view many entertainment and news programs online—and purchase some from digital retailers such as iTunes and Amazon. Comcast, Time Warner, and other cable firms have therefore support a program their executives call

"TV Everywhere"—a password system for the web that prevents viewers from watching a program on, say, Hulu unless they pay for a subscription service. HBO Go is an online service that fits this description. You can use it only if you subscribe to HBO via cable or satellite firm.

## Exhibition in the Television Industry

Local stations, cable systems, satellite delivery systems, and wired phone and wireless phone companies take on the role of exhibitor when they deliver material directly to viewers. Like theaters in the movie business and stores in the book publishing industry, the broadcast exhibitors are retailers. Their business is to attract the number and the kind of viewers who can help them make a profit for their shareholders.

The early 21st century finds the television exhibition system in the midst of a major upheaval. Local broadcasters—the bedrock of the medium since its commercial introduction in the late 1940s—are facing ever-escalating competition from the cable, satellite, internet, and even mobile phone businesses. Moreover, those other businesses have the potential for making money from both subscription fees and advertising, whereas local broadcasters make money only from advertising. To make matters even more difficult for local broadcasters, as a result of the increased number of channels that cable and satellite services bring into people's homes, ratings for the network programming and local programming that broadcast stations deliver have been declining rather steadily. Local television stations still make money, but observers wonder whether this will still be true later in this century as hundreds of channels race into American homes.

Network affiliates are particularly worried about the declining ability of ABC, CBS, Fox, and NBC to grab the lion's share of the U.S. television audience. Local TV executives are also concerned about the networks' strong and increasing participation in the subscription video world. Disney-owned ABC controls cable/satellite networks ESPN, ESPN2, the Disney Channel, and ABC Family, among others. NBC Universal controls MSNBC, CNBC, USA, Syfy, and Bravo. All the broadcast networks are placing hit programs on the web, with the consequence that viewers don't have to watch local channels (and their commercials) to see prime-time TV. Network executives reply that because their O&O properties are extremely important to them (as a group they often make more profits than the networks), they would not do anything that would fundamentally harm local service. They are also helping the local stations to beef up their websites, where they make money from advertising. Nevertheless, the tension between the two parties continues.

Tensions are also running high in the cable exhibition business. For decades cable systems were the only major exhibitors competing with local TV stations. Now cable operators worry that their power will be eroded substantially by DBS firms such as DirecTV and DISH, as well as by broadband services from Verizon and AT&T that duplicate cable services. An activity that concerns all these businesses is what the industry people call "cutting the cord," which is when subscribers who are fed up with paying high fees for so many channels they don't watch decide to stop service and just watch programs over the air and via the internet. Some of what they view, they may view on their laptops via sites that connect them to illegally copied programs. But they also may use devices such as Apple TV, Roku, Nintendo's Wii, and Microsoft's XBox game player to stream programs from Hulu Plus, Netflix, Amazon Prime, and other program-rich sites to their television sets. They may have to pay for access to the shows or for individual programs, but they may feel this is still less expensive than a cable or satellite subscription.

At this point it seems that far less than 10 percent of American households have disconnected from a multichannel subscription service with the intention of using the web for their television viewing. Industry observers suggest that the numbers will grow substantially as ways to access television shows outside subscription services grow. The cable and telco providers will still be able to make money by selling the cord-cutters high-speed internet service. Still, this sort of shift would change the industry. For one thing, satellite firms will lose because it is much more expensive to offer internet connections via satellite than via cable. For another, cord cutting will undermine the entire system of charging subscribers for a broad band of niche channels relatively few of them visit. Critics of the industry contend that people should not have to pay for so much they don't watch. Cable-industry leaders respond that this approach it what has allowed the diversity of program networks that exists on cable television systems. They clearly hope that Americans will continue to subscribe to both their programming and their internet services.

## Media Ethics: Converging Screens, Social Television, and the Issue of Personalization

You may have noticed a basic point that has flowed through our discussion of television in this chapter: Watching TV no longer only means viewing the box in your living room or bedroom. In fact, taking advantage of digital convergence, television industry executives are eager to move their programs across many platforms with the aim of eking revenue from advertisers as well as from viewers at every stop. Cable, satellite, and telco exhibitors see digital convergence as bringing a different opportunity. Because of their worry that their customers will cut the cord if they can view many of their favorite programs online, the subscription services have pressured the networks they carry that also place programs on the web to join "TV Everywhere" programs. Such programs allow cable, satellite, and telco subscribers—and only them—to enter websites, tablet apps, or smartphone apps to view many of the programs they could view on the network's "regular" channel. So, for example, if your home gets Comcast cable, you can view HBO's *Boardwalk Empire* on your computer, tablet, or phone wherever you have a high-speed connection. Although many networks have fallen in line with the exhibitors' requests, some still release their newest programs to Netflix, Hulu, or their own websites. In view of the tensions this causes with their powerful exhibitors, it remains to be seen how long this open-viewing activity will continue.

## THINKING ABOUT MEDIA LITERACY

In the era of converging technologies, cable providers worry that consumers want to "cut the cord" and just watch their favorite shows online. What advantages does this option offer consumers? What disadvantages does this option bring to cable providers? What, if anything, do you think cable providers could do to remain competitive?

The TV industry's realization that people use several screens in their daily lives has led to yet another development: social television, which refers to a person's use of one screen for viewing a program while he or she uses another screen for learning more about the program and discussing it with others. IntoNow, owned by Yahoo, is a popular app for doing that. The technology is able to detect what you're watching, live, on 130 channels. Once it knows what you're viewing, IntoNow finds relevant real-time Twitter mentions of the show and serves up stories from Yahoo's news database according to what is going on in the program. The hope is that these feeds and the viewing will encourage the app's users to discuss what is taking place on one or the other screen.

IntoNow is only one of several attempts to take advantage of the TV industry's awareness that people often have an internet-connected digital device in their hands or on their laps while they are viewing television. An example for a specific show is the tablet app that TBS began circulating in 2012 for Conan O'Brien's late-night show on the network. A variation on the broader TV app (found in MyTVBuddy and Tapcast, for example) is for the app to link its members not just to other users of the app but also to their Facebook friends, thus potentially building the membership for app. As you might have guessed, the aim of these applications is to offer the participants to advertisers, who might serve different commercial messages on the tablet or phone depending on what is taking place in the show or what people are discussing.

In fact, advertisers are fascinated by the possibility of not just reaching but even interacting with people when they are viewing television on one or another digital screen. The activity is called "addressable television." It involves the ability to learn information about the individuals who are viewing and send them particular commercial messages. You may recall from our chapter on advertising that this type of activity is taking place quite actively online as well as on tablets and smartphones. Digital advertising leaders are trying hard to make it work for cable- and satellite-delivered channels, which don't share the same technical specifications as the internet-related media. Already it is quite possible for companies such as Visible World to send different commercials to different homes based on information about the homes that the cable company provides that firm. Visible World can send variations of the same commercial—with different types of people or different music—to different homes based on information stored on the homes' set-top box. Although these activities are still expensive and experimental, many in the television industry expect that in years to come commercials will be customized based on data that cable firms, advertisers, ad agencies, and others hold about particular households and even individual viewers.

For example, your TV may get a commercial from Kay Jewelers while your neighbor gets one from Tiffany. Moreover, on the tablet you're using to send messages to friends about the program you're co-viewing, you may begin to see discount ads for Kay, whereas your neighbor finds an invitation to a special viewing of an expensive new Tiffany line at the nearby mall. When you learn about this difference during a conversation with your neighbor, you ask yourself, "Why is this happening?" Well, maybe the cable company has determined that your household income is lower than that of your neighbor, and your pattern of program viewing and the record the company has gathered of your supermarket purchases had led it to suspect that you would be a Kay Jewelers type more than a Tiffany's type.

Insulted? Perhaps you should be. The more preferred outcome, for the purpose of this book, though, is for you to think more broadly about the possible impact of bringing huge amounts of data about individuals and households to the television screen, broadly defined. What will it mean for society when people wonder whether the commercials, the discounts, and maybe even the television programs they are receiving on various screen are being personalized based on what the advertisers know about them? Will people be nervous because they believe advertisers, networks, and exhibitors are defining them in ways that conflict with their understanding of themselves? Will people try to change their mobile, online, and even cable TV viewing habits in order to get better profiles that yield them better status and marketing offers? What are the ethics of media and marketing firms personalizing the screens and social media environments you receive based on information—even anonymous information—they have attached to you without your knowing it or giving your permission?

You may remember from the advertising chapter that critical observers see this issue as a major one for a lot of online and mobile advertising today. So far, these data-collection and personalization activities have not become part of the environment of the big home TV set or the little screens around them. Yet because television reaches so many Americans with powerful news, entertainment, and sports stories, marketers are chomping at the bit to bring the data techniques they have been developing for the web to those home screens. Do you think their audiences should have a say in whether and/or how they do it?

# CHAPTER REVIEW

Visit the Companion Website at www.routledge.com/cw/turow for additional study tools and resources.

## Key Terms

You can find the definitions to these key terms in the marginal glossary throughout this chapter. Test your knowledge of these terms with interactive flash cards on the *Media Today* companion website.

| | | |
|---|---|---|
| audience flow | household ratings | program feed |
| average commercial minute | household share | ratings |
| Big Four commercial networks | independent broadcast station | reach |
| billboards | lead-in | retransmission fees |
| broadcast live | lead-out | sampling |
| broadcast outlets | license | satellite television |
| C3 standard | license fees | schedules |
| cable television | lineup | series |
| cable television system | multiple system owner (MSO) | station groups |
| channel multiplexing or multichannel broadcasting | national rating points | stream |
| | network affiliates | stripping |
| commercial stations | noncommercial stations | subscription networks |
| commercials | O&Os (owned and operated stations) | sweeps |
| competition | | syndication |
| concept testing | off-network syndication | telcos |
| counterprogramming | out-of-home locations (or captive audience locations) | television broadcasting |
| day parts | | television network |
| direct broadcast satellite (DBS) technology | pay-per-view (PPV) | television program ratings |
| | people meter | tiering |
| format | people ratings | time slot |
| golden age of television | pilot | treatment |
| hammock | pitch | underwriting |
| head end | preview theaters | vertically integrated |
| high-definition television (HDTV) | prime time | video on demand (VOD) |

## Questions for Discussion and Critical Thinking

1. Check out the evening broadcasting schedule for your local ABC, NBC, CBS, or Fox station. Do you see any of the tactics described in this chapter in use, such as lead-ins, lead-outs, and hammocks? Do you think the network's choices are effective? Why or why not?
2. Much research goes into defining audiences and determining their viewing habits, so much so that some critics claim, "Audiences are not real things. They are constructed by media firms." What do you think this statement means? Do you agree with it? Why or why not?
3. Some critics claim that too much violence, sex, and stereotyping pervade television programming, and they also claim that these representations negatively influence audiences, particularly children. What do you think of these claims? Do you agree or disagree? Why or why not?

## Case Study
### OUT-OF-HOME TELEVISION

**The Idea** As noted in the chapter, television can now be seen in many places outside the home, and the major providers of broadcast and cable programming (CBS, NBC-U, ABC) are providing some of that material. How common is out-of-home television where you live, and who is providing it?

**The Method** Use your postal zip code as the geographic territory and try to uncover the use of out-of-home television sets in stores, health care offices, travel depots, and other waiting and shopping areas. What is the programming like, and what is the format? Is the material repurposed—that is, taken from general broadcast or cable TV—or is it new material? Try to determine who the program producers and distributors are in each case. Write a report of your findings.

# 14 | The Video Game Industry

## CHAPTER OBJECTIVES

1   Sketch the development of video games

2   Describe video game genres

4   Sketch the production, distribution, and exhibition of video games

5   Chart major social controversies surrounding video games

> "I like video games, but they're really violent. I'd like to play a video game where you help the people who were shot in all the other games. It'd be called 'Really Busy Hospital.'"
>
> **DEMETRI MARTIN, COMEDIAN**

The headline of a December 5, 2012, article from *Advertising Age* announced the startling news: "New 'Call of Duty' Reaches $1 Billion Faster Than 'Avatar.'" The story went on to report that "*Call of Duty: Black Ops II*, the latest installment in Activision Blizzard's best-selling video-game franchise, topped $1 billion dollars in retail sales within the first 15 days of release." In a press release, Activision triumphantly noted a number of milestones: The new game hit a billion dollars one day faster than the 2011 edition of *Call of Duty: Black Ops*. Its faster earning rate than the movie *Avatar* meant that a video game had raked in money quicker than the record holder for theatrical films. The total worldwide revenues for all versions of the *Call of Duty* video game were, by early December 2012, greater than the worldwide box office receipts for the top 10 grossing movies of that year. And, the press release noted, "sales of the 'Call of Duty' franchise have exceeded worldwide theatrical receipts for *Harry Potter*

and *Star Wars*, the two most successful movie franchises of all time."

That's quite a bit of boasting for one press release. Activision Blizzard didn't point out that whereas a ticket to *Avatar* probably averaged around $10 (the price varied, depending on whether people saw it in the 2D or the more expensive 3D format), *Call of Duty: Black Ops II* cost far more: about $50 dollars on sale from Amazon in December and $80 or more for a collector's "hardened edition" that included a case, maps, and other items. The higher price meant the game company could reach a billion dollars with fewer purchases than the move distributor. The comparison with *Avatar* also didn't take into account DVD sales, DVD rentals, and video-on-demand payments to view the film on cable or via internet services such as Netflix. With all these revenues taken into consideration, *Avatar's* grosses in December 2012 trumped those of *Black Ops II*.

Nevertheless, the huge sales associated with the video games raise a key point: video games are a big business in the United States and around the world. In fact, the annual revenue of the industry exceeds $78 billion.[1] This chapter explores this important media industry. It looks at the kinds of games that are out there; the production, distribution, and exhibition processes that create and circulate them; and the social issues that surround them.

## The Video Game Industry and Convergence

Including a chapter about the video game industry is rather unusual for an introductory text on media and society. Yet the production, distribution, and exhibition of video games have, in the past three decades, become major industrial activities that ought to be included in mainstream discussions of media in society. As we explore this relatively new industry in the final chapter, it's important to point out that convergence is a major theme.

That shouldn't be surprising. Throughout this book we have noted that media industries in the 21st century must be understood in terms of convergence, with companies and audience members moving content across media boundaries and often reshaping the content to fit different needs. We have seen how the relatively recent desktop and mobile business worlds have become important parts of the converging system. People experience convergence when they watch television, read newspapers, listen to radio, and read books and more on their mobile devices, tablets, and desktop computers, as well as on their television sets. Digging deep into that media system, we have seen how leaders in traditional media fields—advertising and public relations as well as the book, newspaper, magazine, recording, radio, movie, and television industries—understand that they have to link their products to a variety of media, analog as well as digital, to survive and grow. Fashion magazine publishers, for example, tie their periodicals' names to fashion shows in malls, on television, and on the web in order to reach their audiences. Here we will see how video games fit into this pattern.

## The Rise of the Video Game Industry

So what are video games? Here we will define them as entertainment products powered by computer chips and displayed on monitors that require users to experience and interact with challenges in a series of tasks. The products leading to today's video games go back several decades. Read through the timeline (Figure 14.1) on the nearby page. You might notice that the development of video game technology—and the development of the video game industry—echoes the three historical themes we have explored in other chapters. Let's take a look together.

1. *The video game did not arrive in a flash as a result of one inventor's grand change.*

The birth of video games can be traced back to two separate developments that initially were unrelated to the computer.[2] The first development was the advent of the **pinball machine**, a coin-operated game in which a player scores points by causing metal balls to move in certain directions (often using flippers) inside a glass-covered case. These games were made popular by David Gottlieb beginning in the early 1930s

**pinball machine**
coin-operated game in which a player scores points by causing metal balls to move in certain directions (often using flippers) inside a glass-covered case

# Figure 14.1 Timeline of the Video Games Industry

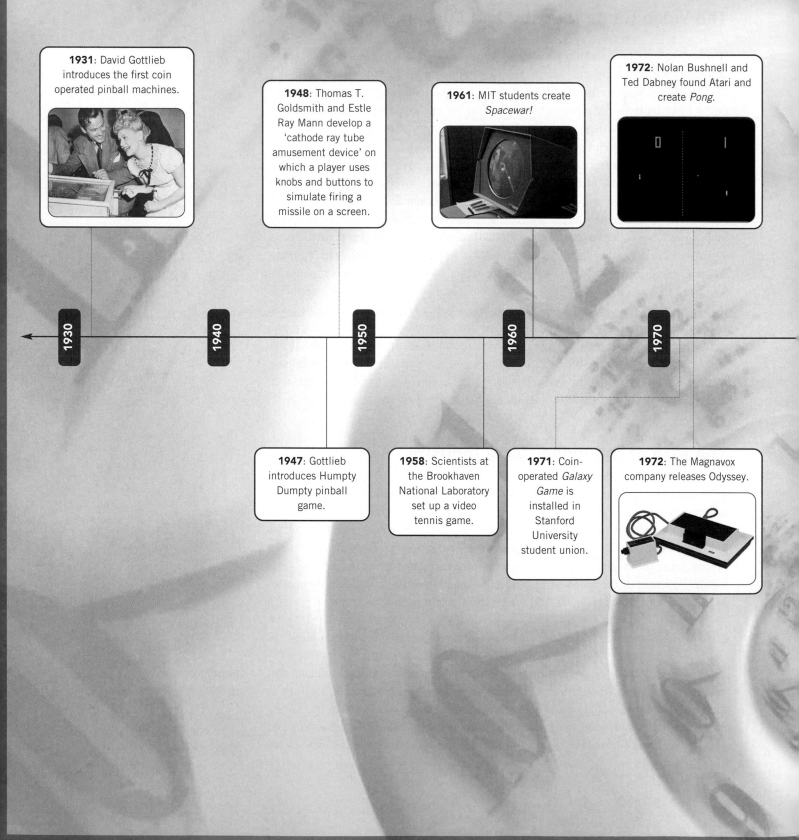

**1931**: David Gottlieb introduces the first coin operated pinball machines.

**1948**: Thomas T. Goldsmith and Estle Ray Mann develop a 'cathode ray tube amusement device' on which a player uses knobs and buttons to simulate firing a missile on a screen.

**1961**: MIT students create *Spacewar!*

**1972**: Nolan Bushnell and Ted Dabney found Atari and create *Pong*.

1930 1940 1950 1960 1970

**1947**: Gottlieb introduces Humpty Dumpty pinball game.

**1958**: Scientists at the Brookhaven National Laboratory set up a video tennis game.

**1971**: Coin-operated *Galaxy Game* is installed in Stanford University student union.

**1972**: The Magnavox company releases Odyssey.

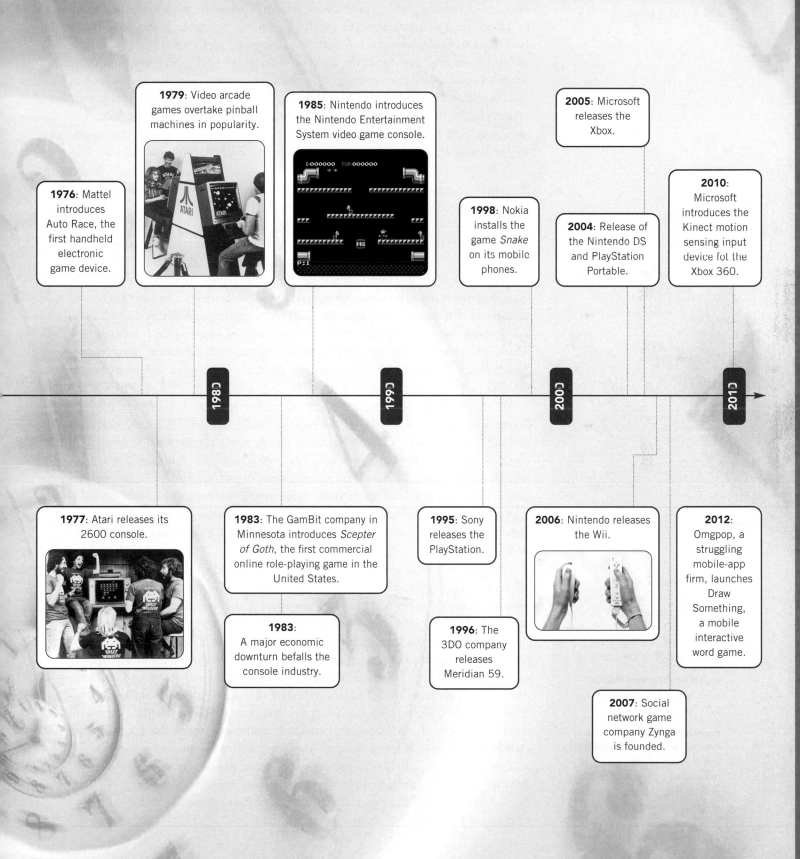

**1976**: Mattel introduces Auto Race, the first handheld electronic game device.

**1979**: Video arcade games overtake pinball machines in popularity.

**1985**: Nintendo introduces the Nintendo Entertainment System video game console.

**1998**: Nokia installs the game *Snake* on its mobile phones.

**2005**: Microsoft releases the Xbox.

**2004**: Release of the Nintendo DS and PlayStation Portable.

**2010**: Microsoft introduces the Kinect motion sensing input device for the Xbox 360.

**1977**: Atari releases its 2600 console.

**1983**: The GamBit company in Minnesota introduces *Scepter of Goth*, the first commercial online role-playing game in the United States.

**1983**: A major economic downturn befalls the console industry.

**1995**: Sony releases the PlayStation.

**1996**: The 3DO company releases Meridian 59.

**2006**: Nintendo releases the Wii.

**2012**: Omgpop, a struggling mobile-app firm, launches Draw Something, a mobile interactive word game.

**2007**: Social network game company Zynga is founded.

1980

1990

2000

2010

**entertainment arcades**
commercial locations featuring coin-operated machines such as pinball machines, fortune tellers, and shooting games

at **entertainment arcades**—commercial locations featuring coin-operated machines such as pinball machines, fortune tellers, and shooting games.

While the mechanical pinball game was a fixture of arcades, scientists working on video electronics and computers were amusing themselves with games that could be played on TV-like displays. In 1958, for example, scientists at the Brookhaven National Laboratory set up a video tennis game on an oscilloscope for play during its annual visitors' day. Similarly, computer students at MIT, Stanford, and other schools began to use their universities' computer systems to create games such as *Spacewar!* that were tied to their love of science fiction. Activities like these that were taking place at the University of Utah influenced Nolan Bushnell and Ted Dabney to start Atari in 1972—the first successful U.S. company to create and sell video arcade games. It was Atari that really got the ball rolling toward a video game industry.

2.   *The video game as a medium of communication developed as a result of social and legal responses to the technology during different periods.*

As this brief description of the beginning of the video game industry suggests, the development of the technology initially took place in the social context of what today would be called "geek" culture. It was developed by highly educated computer science students at top universities who applied their skills in order to have fun as well as meet new technical challenges. In the 1970s, enterprising businesspeople who knew about these developments took the gutsy step of adapting for broad interests what those young, highly educated niches of U.S. society were doing. Their console games struck a chord with large segments of the nation, as well as with many people in other parts of the world.

Yet social responses to the growing console industry changed in the early 1980s. A severe downturn in console-based video games during this period severely hurt Atari and other console-game makers. Instead, many gamers were attracted to games that could be used with the newly available personal-computer technology. Companies sold disks that could be played on specific computers—for example, the Commodore 64, the Apple II, and the IBM PC. Strategy video games and simulation video games—genres that had already been used for some consoles—caught on as particularly appropriate for computer play, with hits including *Dune* (strategy) and *SimCity* (simulation).

**bulletin boards**
software that allows users to exchange messages with other users, read news and public articles, and perform other activities such as play games

**multiuser dungeons (MUDs)**
early text-based online fantasy role-playing games

**massively multiplayer online role-playing games (MMORPGs)**
video games in which a large number of players—as many as hundreds of thousands—interact with one another in virtual worlds

Through the 1980s, social change connected to a different new technology again affected video games. This time it was the internet, and again the new approach to gaming related to "geeky" circles. As the internet began to be used by more and more academics in the 1980s, it too became a location for playing games. People even figured out how to use internet **bulletin boards**, in which many users could send messages to one another, as a place where many people could share a game. Multiplayer computer games that combined elements of chat rooms and fantasy role-playing games, such as *Dungeons & Dragons*, emerged as extremely popular in these environments, and the games became known as **multiuser dungeons (MUDs)**. They were the predecessors of today's popular **massively multiplayer online role-playing games (MMORPGs)**, such as *World of Warcraft*, that boast millions of players worldwide.

By the time the early 1990s came around, then, the basic types of video game vehicles had been established. Although some platforms lost popularity, the next decade would reveal that many different types of video game platforms—consoles, computers, handheld, and internet—could coexist.

3.  *The video game industry developed and changed as a result of struggles to control its channels to audiences.*

The movement of video game makers toward a number of different technologies reflects larger changes that were taking place within American society and within the industry. As Americans began using computers and mobile phones, game makers created software for those channels. They also developed different types of games for men and women. For example, the idea was (and still is) that men are more interested in action-adventure games that may take a long time to finish, whereas women are attracted to short puzzle-like games that avoid violence. Different companies tended to gravitate toward creating or distributing different types of games as well (we'll discuss more of that later). Over time, some software companies, such as Electronic Arts and Activision, became powerhouses with the ability to spend the most money on game production, advertise the most, and grab the most press attention.

A similar concentration of power eventually developed among console manufacturers, with three firms—Sony, Nintendo, and Microsoft—controlling that video game channel. Before Microsoft entered the fray in 2001, the competition was between three companies—Sony, Nintendo, and Sega. Sony's PlayStation became so popular that Sega stopped making consoles in 2001, and Nintendo lagged far behind in sales. Moreover, it took a while for Microsoft to be a serious competitor. Over time, Microsoft's Xbox and its successor, the Xbox 360 (released in 2005), cut into Sony's lead. In 2007, Nintendo came roaring back into competition with Sony and Microsoft via its new console: the Wii. The Wii represented a kind of counterprogramming to the gaming approaches of Sony and Microsoft. Hard-core gamers—mostly male 15- to 34-year-olds—prefer the Xbox 360 platform for its superior graphics, more "hard-core" adventure titles, and strong online capabilities. PlayStation has lost some market share to Xbox 360 but continues to be popular among avid gamers because of the wide variety of titles available on the platform. The Wii, by contrast, is a gaming platform that Nintendo purposely built for people who may be intimidated by PlayStation and Xbox controllers. As a result, the Wii captured a broader audience than its competitors, proving very popular with women and children.

Through these struggles among firms, and similar to the other industries we have seen in this book, the industry players have had to contend with controversies. Most of the public anger directed toward them has revolved around sex and violence in games, though there also have been strong complaints about stereotyping of various ethnic and racial groups as well as women in the video games. Evident in the timeline, however, is a reaction that we have seen in many of the industries covered in *Media Today*: self-regulation. In 1994, stung by criticism of violent content in video games such as *Night Trap*, *Mortal Kombat*, *Lethal Enforcers*, and *Doom*, the video game industry association, the Entertainment Software Association, established the Entertainment Software Rating Board (ESRB). The approach it adopted is similar to what goes on with movie and television self-regulation. As chapter 5 notes, the board assigns ratings to games based on their content, and next to the ratings are descriptions of problematic content in the games. By July 2012 the ESRB had assigned more than

XBox 360, popular with hard-core gamers, is also the platform for some other popular, less traditional video games such as *Dance Central*.

22,000 ratings to titles submitted by more than 350 publishers.[3] The ratings have not stopped controversies about game content. We will discuss this topic in more detail later in the chapter. First, let's get an overview of the industry.

## The Contemporary Shape of the Video Game Industry

Today, video games are extremely popular with a wide segment of the population. *The Atlantic* magazine reported in 2011 that 67 percent, or more than two-thirds, of U.S. households, hold individuals who play video games.[4] According to the Entertainment Software Association in 2012, the average video game player is 30 years old and has been playing games for 12 years. The average number of hours the players spend on the games per week is eight. Females make up 47 percent of the gaming population, and males constitute 53 percent. To disabuse people of the stereotype that most gamers are teenage boys, the association points out that "women 18 or older represent a significantly greater portion of the game-playing population (30%) than boys age 17 or younger (18%)." The association also states that "42 percent of game players believe that computer and video games give them the most value for their money, compared with DVDs, music, or going out to the movies."[5]

All that playing drives a lot of spending. According to data compiled by the NPD Group and released by the Entertainment Software Association, consumers spent $24.75 billion on video gaming (including purchases of hardware, content, and accessories) during 2011.[6] Of revenue gained from content sales, 69 percent was from purchases of physical games—for example, console cartridges or computer software. The proportion of money people spent on various digital downloads of games—for example, on the web or mobile apps—has been growing. In 2009 digital downloads represented only 20 percent of sales, whereas in 2011 it had increased to 31 percent.

As the preceding data suggest, today the term "video game" stands for a complex industry with several different types of products and different production, distribution, and exhibition processes. They make up a big business. In the United States alone, video game companies—ones that sell consoles and accessories and the ones that sell games—brought in between $20 billion and $25 billion in 2010. From the preceding discussion and from what you may know about video games, you can understand that any discussion of the business has to take into consideration two key features: the hardware and the software.

### Video Game Hardware

**hardware**
the device or console on which video games are played

"**Hardware**" refers to the devices on which the video games are played, and a number of types of hardware coexist. Games are sold for gaming consoles, desktop or laptop computers, interactive television connections, handheld game devices, and mobile devices. During 2011, Americans spent about $8.2 billion on hardware and physical accessories (such as carrying cases) for the hardware. Let's look briefly at each type of hardware.

**Gaming Consoles** Gaming consoles are optimized for the speed and graphics that many games require. You could get many of the same features on a desktop or laptop computer, but you'd likely have to know a lot about ordering special components, and you'd undoubtedly pay a lot more money than if you bought a standard computer. Three companies—Sony with its PlayStation, Microsoft with its Xbox, and

Nintendo, with its Wii—make the consoles that people associate with contemporary gaming. Because of the Wii console's broad appeal, 95 million had been sold by 2011. Meanwhile, 67 million Xbox consoles and 63 million PlayStation3 consoles had been purchased.[7]

Convergence has deeply impacted the design and functionality of video game consoles. Whereas early consoles were used solely for game play, today's models can serve many different functions. The Xbox 360 can be used to play DVDs, and the PlayStation3 can play both DVD and Blu-ray discs. These consoles can also be connected to the internet, so users can download games and play with other users. Various apps can also be downloaded, allowing users to stream video (via apps such as Netflix, Hulu Plus, and Amazon Prime), check sports scores (via the ESPN, NFL Sunday Ticket, or MLB.tv apps), or play music (through apps such as Last.fm and Pandora). Through convergence, consoles are quickly becoming more than just vehicles for game play, to act as multipurpose entertainment portals.

**Desktop or Laptop Computers** Computer game players seem to prefer strategy games over the adventure games that console players tend to buy. Although games purchased to play on the computer were extremely popular in the 1990s, sales declined as consoles became attractive to hard-core gamers and as broadband connections to internet gaming increased and allowed for more sophisticated graphics and animation. Whereas buying game software for stand-alone computers is becoming less common, playing games online is rapidly gaining popularity. Gambling online is illegal in the United States, but Americans do access sites elsewhere in the world to participate in these activities too.

Aside from gambling sites, however, you can go to many websites that offer games to play. Most fall under the casual gaming category; this is a popular category supposedly preferred by women aged 25 years and older. It includes puzzle, card, board, and word games, sometimes with fictional characters. The Casual Games Association, an industry trade group, estimates that more than 200 million people worldwide play such games on the internet.[8] Pogo is a website that specializes in these sorts of games, featuring titles such as *Mahjong Garden Deluxe* and *World Class Solitaire*. Pogo (along with Yahoo! Games and many other sites) also has arcade-like games and sports games. If, as a **casual gamer**, you want to play games for free, you will see a lot of ads; some even interrupt game play. Pogo allows you to get rid of the ads by paying a fee to play, and you can join Club Pogo to play a wide range of games without ad interruptions.

People interested in the more intense, complex, and often violent adventure platforms aimed at hard-core gamers can also find them online, along with chat rooms to discuss them. On Gametap.com, for example, you can find games such as *Battlestations Midway*, *Shock Troopers*, and *Tomb Raider*. Some of them are free (in exchange for viewing ads), whereas others charge users to play. Increasingly popular with hard-core gamers are sites for massively multiplayer online role-playing games. In an MMORPG, a player uses a client to connect to a server, usually run by the publisher of the game, which hosts the virtual world and stores information about the player. The user controls a character represented by an **avatar**—a character that represents the user and that can be directed to fight villains, interact with other characters, acquire items, and so on.

MMORPGs have become extremely popular since the wider debut of broadband internet connections, boasting millions of subscribers from hundreds of different

**casual gamers**
women and men who are older than the hard-core types and/or who like to play less intense (though not necessarily less difficult) games than the hard-core types; these games include puzzle, card, board, and word games

**avatar**
a character that represents the user within a virtual world

Visitors to a video game convention in Lucca, Italy, try out the newest *World of Warcraft*—by far the most popular MMORPG to date.

**handheld game devices**
portable machines used primarily for game playing

**mobile device**
multipurpose handheld computing device that can be used as a portable gaming platform

**social games**
games played through social networks

**video game publishers**
companies that coordinate the production of video games

countries. *World of Warcraft*, with its three expansions, is the world's most-subscribed-to MMORPG, with 11.5 million subscribers in 2009.[9]

**Handheld Devices, Interactive Television, and Mobile Devices** **Handheld game devices** are portable machines that are primarily designed for game play. During the late 2000s and early 2010s, the Nintendo DS (and its successor, the Nintendo 3DS) dominated the market, outselling the PlayStation Portable (and its 2012 iteration as the PlayStation Vita). With the increasing popularity of multipurpose mobile devices, however, handheld game device sales have plummeted in recent years.

Interactive television (iTV) is another area in which games have been growing strongly. Cable, satellite, and telco operators are charging customers beyond basic fees to access playing areas with their remote-control devices. Much of the iTV gaming is done via the set-top box, so that even satellite companies (whose technologies do not allow for two-way interactions with customers) can get in on the action. In 2012, for example, Dish Network was one company offering a game subscription service. Its customers could get Dish Games, a collection of games including *Yahtzee* and *Scrabble Scramble*, priced at $5 per month.

An increasingly popular portable gaming platform is the **mobile device**. The devices' capability for carrying games with sophisticated graphics has grown as the mobile system and devices have gotten faster at sending, retrieving, and processing data, with better graphics and memory capability. Typically, phone and tablet owners purchase games through the app store of the device's manufacturer or the creator of its operating system. Although some games cost money, many run on the "freemium" model that has been discussed in previous chapters. Basic versions of freemium games are free to download, but users must pay to eliminate advertisements, access additional levels of the game, or purchase in-game items (such as weapons or character accessories). Game companies have learned that gamers are sometimes more willing to spend money within the game once they have tested it and like it than they are to pay a high price for the game upfront.

Many mobile games are played through social networks such as Facebook and are set up to allow many players to make their moves at different times. These **social games** are among the world's most popular, attracting tens of millions of players. By linking to their Facebook accounts, players serve as promotional agents for the game, advertising their in-game activities to their friends. Among the companies that make such games are Zynga and Playfish (which was purchased by gaming giant Electronic Arts in 2009). *FarmVille*, *Words with Friends*, *CityVille*, *Mob Wars*, and *The Sims Social* are a few of the most popular social games.

## The Production of Video Game Software
In 2011, Americans spent just about double the amount on software ($16.5 billion) that they spent on hardware ($8.2 billion). To serve this market, there is a huge number of video games to fit a wide variety of tastes. The companies that coordinate the production of video games are called **video game publishers**. Publishers in the video game industry serve a function similar to that of publishers in other media

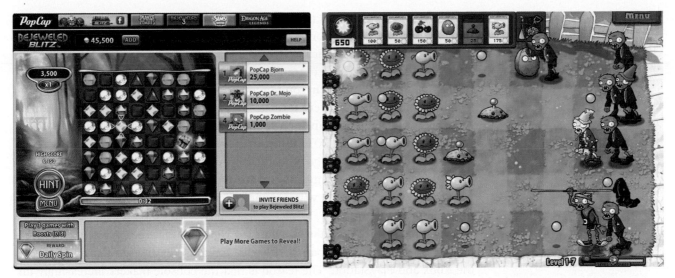

*Bejeweled* and *Plants vs. Zombies* are two popular social games that can be played from your smartphone, tablet, or any electronic device. They are often part of social media sites such as Facebook.

industries we have seen—for example, the book industry. Video game publishers search for products that they believe will succeed in the marketplace. Often the publishers finance the games' creation or have staffs of video game developers that develop the games themselves. Large video game companies arrange for the marketing and distribution of their games to their intended audiences. Smaller publishers will partner with special distribution firms (sometimes the larger video game firms) to help them get the material out to the marketplace.

The major hardware makers have publishing divisions that produce games specific to their systems; the intention is to persuade people to buy their systems because of the games exclusively associated with them. For example, Nintendo turns out the *Super Mario* and *Pokémon* titles, among others, exclusively for the Wii, Nintendo 3DS, and so on. Sony turns out the *Gran Turismo* racing game for PlayStation devices. Microsoft has an exclusive deal with Bungie Studios (which it used to own fully and in which it still has an equity stake) to produce the *Halo* series for Xbox.

The launch of *Halo 3* in 2007 illustrates the utility of this sort of exclusivity from the console-maker's standpoint. The game's global sales reached $170 million on its first day, making it the biggest launch in video game history to that point. By the end of the first week, it had reached sales of $300 million globally.[10] Not incidentally, from Microsoft's standpoint, the game's release was associated with a spike in sales of the XBox 360, the only console on which anyone could play the game. According to initial reports from retailers worldwide, XBox 360 console sales nearly tripled compared with the weekly average before the launch of the new game.[11]

Although video games made by console and handheld manufacturers exclusively for their devices get a lot of marketing and press attention, by far the largest number of games are made by what the trade calls **third-party publishers**—companies that are unaffiliated with hardware companies. Because of their unaffiliated status, third-party publishers typically create games that work on a variety of systems. Electronic Arts is probably the most powerful third-party game publisher. Some of its top sellers include *The Sims* series, the *Need for Speed* series, the *Battlefield* series, and the *Madden NFL* series, which are all available on a myriad of platforms. Other key third-party publishers are Activision Blizzard (*World of Warcraft* and *Call of Duty*), Ubisoft (*Assassin's Creed* and *Prince of Persia*), and Take-Two Interactive (*Grand Theft Auto* and *Borderlands*).

**third-party publishers**
companies that are unaffiliated with hardware companies and that typically create games that work on a variety of systems

Before digging a bit into the nature of software, it's useful to make three other points about its production. One is that the industry sometimes categorizes "video" games more specifically than the way we have here. The Entertainment Software Association, for example, distinguishes between "computer games" (games people play on their computers), "video games" (games people play on consoles), and "other delivery formats" (e.g., downloaded games, games bought by subscriptions, gaming apps on mobile devices). It turns out that the "other" category is quite large; in 2011 it made up around 43 percent of the $16.5 billion Americans spent on video game content in the broader sense in which we have defined it. In its narrower meaning, video games (i.e., console games) brought in 53 percent of the revenues, whereas computer games represented a small proportion, about 6 percent.[12]

The second point to make about video games is that they are often quite expensive to produce. That's particularly true for console games, especially those for the Xbox and PlayStation. The reason is that the console makers increasingly improve the graphics capabilities of the machines. If a game development company wants to compete on those platforms, its leadership must hire more—and more sophisticated—programmers to create the games. Their work probably also takes a lot more time to finish than was the case with earlier games. As a result, the most high-profile console games today can cost as much to produce as theatrical films. Activision Blizzard's *Spider-Man 3* game, for example, cost $35 million, not including the marketing and sales expenses.[13] (The associated movie, Sony's *Spider-Man 3*, did have a production budget of $258 million, but this large of a budget is unusual even for blockbuster films.)

These high costs lead to the third point: observers of the industry agree that it has become more and more "hit driven" through and since the 2000s. The high cost of making console games means that even the biggest firms such as Activision Blizzard and Electronic Arts concentrate their attention and their marketing on just a few games with the goal of making sure they are the top sellers. Sequels of hits become common because firms want to lower their risks when they spend huge amounts of money on games. The result, say critics, is that the biggest firms with the most expertise are pursuing formulaic blockbusters rather than exploring creative uses of technology and storytelling.

Despite the high risks associated with producing games today, companies are still producing a variety of types of games for the different devices on which people play games. Let's take a look.

**Software Genres** As we saw in chapter 2, creators in every mass media industry think of content in terms of categories, or genres. This approach helps them understand how to create in that genre; it often helps distributors and exhibitors in sending, marketing, and choosing titles for certain outlets; and it sometimes helps consumers who are thinking about what materials they want to watch, play, or hear. Most of the people who create video games for consoles, portables, and computers broadly categorize what they do as entertainment, meaning that the games are intended primarily for enjoyment. In fact, the variety of video games is so great that aficionados have developed several subgenres of entertainment to describe them and even subtypes to further differentiate content. Below, adapted from writings about video games posted on *Wikipedia*, are short explanations of the 10 most important entertainment subgenres.

## Action Games

Action games are those that present challenges that emphasize combat or involve attempts to escape being captured or killed. As a category, action games probably have the largest number of subtypes among video games. Three popular subtypes are shooter, competitive fighting, and platform games.

- Shooter games involve a character going through a dangerous environment hunting for bad guys. First-person shooter video games show the environment from the perspective of the character with the weapon; that character (whose full body you don't see) is controlled by the player. In third-person shooter games, by contrast, the player does see his or her character moving through the environment as the players uses the controls. Popular examples of shooter games include *Halo*, *Call of Duty*, and *Resident Evil*.
- Competitive fighting games emphasize one-on-one combat between two or more characters, one or more of whom may be controlled by the computer. Examples are *Mortal Kombat*, *Virtua Fighter*, and *SoulCalibur*.
- Platform games involve traveling by running and then jumping between levels and over obstacles in order to avoid being eliminated and to reach a goal. *Super Mario Bros.*, the best-selling video game of all time, first released in 1985, is a well-known example. More recent entries are *Banjo Kazooie* and *Psychonauts*.

Here journalists see the new *Halo 4* for the first time during a world video games expo in June 2012 in Los Angeles. This is a first-person shooter game that, according to Microsoft, had over 1 million players in the first 24 hours of its release on the Xbox Live platform.
Source: "Microsoft's Halo 4 Sales, Entertainment Franchise," Bloomberg Television, November 6, 2012, http://www.bloomberg.com, accessed February 8, 2013.

## Adventure Games

Adventure games are characterized by their focus on exploration and a story rather than on challenges that require the quick use of reflexes. One *Wikipedia* writer states, "Because they put little pressure on the player in the form of action-based challenges or time constraints, adventure games have had the unique ability to appeal to people who do not normally play video games. The genre peaked in popularity with the 1993 release of *Myst*."[14] Games that fuse adventure elements with action gameplay elements are sometimes referred to as adventure games. A popular example is Nintendo's *Legend of Zelda* series.

## Casual Games

As discussed previously, casual games are challenges with fairly straightforward rules that make them easy to learn and play. Social games tend to be of the casual type. The word "casual" probably comes from the idea that a person can get into the game quickly and doesn't have to devote a major commitment of time to learning rules and developing skills for the game. Such commitment is often required for people who want to play adventure games and games from other genres listed. Note that being deemed "casual" doesn't mean that a game is easy. As discussed in prior sections, these games often take the form of puzzle, card, board, and word games.

## Simulation Games

Sometimes called sim games, simulation games involve players in the creation and cultivation of certain worlds that are designed to be realistic. The idea is to see whether you can excel at accomplishing a task. The task might be sprawling—for example, building urban environments (*SimCity*) or a farm (*FarmVille*). Or it might be narrower in focus, related to particular industries (*Stock Exchange, Roller Coaster Tycoon*). It might be even narrower still, focusing, for example, on raising pets (*Neopets*) or flying jets (*MS Flight Simulator*).

## Strategy Games

Think of chess. Strategy games require a careful assessment of a situation and wise actions in order to win a competition or war. The difference between strategy and action games is that action games center almost entirely on actual combat, whereas strategy games expect the player to focus on political diplomacy, the historical context, the procurement of resources, and the larger placement of troops. Two subcategories of this genre are real-time strategy (RTS) games and turn-based strategy (TBS) games. In TBS games, each player gets turns to move the units. After a user completes his or her turn, the opponent gets a chance; examples are *Poxnora* and *Silent Storm*. In RTS games, a story unfolds, participants play ongoing roles, and events of the game's story take place in real time and keep happening even if one of the players takes a break. *Company of Heroes* and *Halo Wars* are prominent examples.

## Sports Games

One could argue that some sports games really belong to the category of action games and that others are a combination of action and strategy games. But producers, distributors, exhibitors, and consumers of video games consider sports-related games to constitute a separate category. Some games focus on playing the sport (the *Madden NFL* series is an example). Others focus on the strategy behind the sport, such as *Football Manager*.

Of course, not all video games fall under the entertainment genre. A much smaller, though socially important segment falls under the education genre. To quote a *Wikipedia* article on the topic, educational video games "are specifically designed to teach people about a certain subject, expand concepts, reinforce development, understand an historical event or culture, or assist them in learning a skill as they play."[15] You may be familiar with *Reader Rabbit, Zoombinis, Mavis Beacon Teaches Typing*, or *The Big Brain Academy: Wii Degree*. Instead of education, some in the video game industry use the term "**edutainment**" to describe such teaching-oriented games. The reason is that they are designed to be a lot of fun as well as provide educational outcomes for specific groups of learners.

**edutainment**
teaching-oriented video games that are designed to have educational outcomes for specific groups of learners

### Advertising Content and Video Games

It stands to reason that advertisers would be interested in a rapidly growing medium such as video games. Prior to 2009, their interest in video games centered on a desire to reach young men, who were assumed to be the dominant players. Beginning around 2009, though, the rise of casual social games (especially *FarmVille*) online as well as in the form of mobile apps marked the entry of a wider representation of the American public to the gaming world. Older players and females began participating at rates that, in some cases, matched or exceeded the proportion of young males.[16] This influx of a large, diverse audience of players led advertisers to believe they could target different types of people by gender, race, marital status, and more, based on the games they play. As a result, advertisers began to apply techniques to target game audiences and lead them to feel favorably toward products and hopefully buy them. The two most prominent ways in which they go about this are by creating custom games and by embedding ads in games.

**Creating Custom Games** To create a custom game (sometimes called an "adver-game"), an advertiser partners with a game company or hires developers to create a game that is exclusive to that marketer. Once the game is created, it is usually linked to the advertiser's website or Facebook fan page. For example, cereal brands such as Kellogg's Froot Loops and General Mills' Lucky Charms launched games aimed at children during 2011. The firms promoted the games and their web location on the cereal boxes. Although they could not ask children's names because of the Children's Online Privacy Protection Act (see chapter 5), they could place cookies on visitors' browsers and learn about their online habits. Similarly, automaker Ford placed a game on its website that extended Ford's relationship with the television detective series *White Collar* on the USA Network. At the time, the carmaker's Fusion model was the official vehicle for *White Collar*. The online game *36 Hours*, based on the USA series, aimed to draw viewers by encouraging them to solve weekly mysteries and earn points toward *White Collar* merchandise as well as a chance to win a 2011 Fusion Hybrid. The contest portion of the game provided Ford with an opportunity to get the names of the players and to link that information with data gathered about them online and perhaps offline—perhaps during visits to Ford stores.

Not all games promote specific commercial products and services. Some organizations create and distribute games to encourage players to adopt commercial or political beliefs through the playing of games. The U.S. Army, for example, has released multiple versions of its game *America's Army* free in CD/DVD form and for online play. In addition, the Army collaborated with the video game company Red Storm Entertainment to develop and distribute *America's Army: True Soldiers*. Released in 2007, it was created specifically for the Xbox 360 and given an industry rating as acceptable for teens—the target audience for military recruitment. Clearly, the Army meant for its ideology to be built into the game and internalized by potential recruits. Before its appearance, the game's website noted,

> Red Storm and the Army are working together to make sure that *America's Army: True Soldiers* game play experience is an authentic Army experience. [The game] accurately portrays the values that guide Soldiers in the U.S. Army, by specifically incorporating gameplay based on mission accomplishment, teamwork, leadership, rules of engagement, and respect for life and property. Just like in real combat, honor and respect must be earned, and in the game the Play-Lead-Recruit feature allows players to earn respect as they move up through the ranks and become a true leader.

**Embedded Ads** Some companies or organizations don't want to go through the trouble of paying for and distributing games, but they do want to reach certain target audiences. To accommodate them, game publishers increasingly place ads or products

During the 2008 election, the Obama campaign partnered with Electronic Arts games and placed "early voting" ads in 18 video games, including *NBA Live*, *Madden NFL*, *Battleship*, *Tetris*, *Burnout* and *Need for Speed*. An image of the presidential candidate with a message encouraging people to get out for early voting showed up in billboards and arenas within the video games. Studies found that video gamers who saw the ads embedded in their video games were 120 percent more likely to have a positive attitude toward the presidential hopeful and 50 percent more likely to vote for him. Needless to say, Obama's campaign repeated this strategy for the 2012 elections. Source: "Obama Taps Video Games for Early Voting," *AdWeek*, September 14, 2012, http://www.adweek.com/news /technology/obama-taps-video -games-early-voting-143717, accessed February 8, 2013.

**dynamic in-game advertising**
the process of sending ads into video games while individuals are playing and of changing the ads and offering different sponsored downloads depending on the players' game setting and level

in the action so that players will see the commercial messages or use the products in the course of their play. The game publishers realize that ad insertion increases their revenues without adding much to development costs. To draw advertisers, they have learned to make embedded ads look realistic and "natural." In racing games, for example, cars often pass billboards with the names of products whose companies have paid for their presence. In fact, even the model of the car that the player is driving may be offered because its manufacturer paid the gaming company. As this activity becomes routine, some companies are going one step further by giving people free add-ons that provide more characters or levels to the games.

The Century 21 real estate company used this technique in a mobile game called *We City* in 2011. According to an eMarketer report, *We City* appealed to Century 21 because at that time it had a large player base of 15 million people. Moreover, most of the players of the game were between 25 and 44 years old, and that fit Century 21's target audience. The real estate agency's goal was to encourage *We City* players to view a 30-second video ad. The firm rewarded people who viewed the entire clip with virtual currency to use in the game. The approach pleased the company: players viewed the video 300,000 times, and a post-campaign survey suggested a 40 percent rise in awareness of the Century 21 brand among those who played *We City* during the time of the ad campaign.[17]

But marketers and game publishers see these activities as only the beginning of a highly sophisticated process of targeting players with ads and add-ons that are specific to what the companies know about them. They realize that with increasing numbers of gamers playing online, it will be possible to send them these features on the fly, while they are playing, and to change the ads and offer different sponsored downloads depending on their game setting and level. This activity is called **dynamic in-game advertising**, and it is drawing a lot of attention from marketers, game firms, and technology companies.

## Distribution and Exhibition of Video Games

There are many ways to get games to the player. As noted, some cable systems and telcos stream games to computers; the games do not remain on the computer. In the case of mobile games, the software is downloaded, and it must come directly to the mobile device; some of the payment is shared by the creator with the mobile service provider. Video games for consoles and handhelds and sometimes for PCs are downloaded from the internet or distributed on disks or cartridges to wholesalers and a variety of stores. In the brick-and-mortar world, you can find collections of the top games (and consoles) in huge retailers such as Walmart and in toy outlets such as Toys "R" Us, as well as in consumer electronics stores such as Best Buy. There are also specialized video game retailers, such as GameStop, that sell a wider variety of titles. In addition, you can purchase video games online at Amazon.com or through many other online retailers. Used games show up in GameStop as well as on many websites, including eBay. Video games can also be rented through mail services such as GameFly and at physical locations such as at Redbox kiosks.

Part of the process of distribution and exhibition involves signaling to prospective players whether a particular game will fit their technology. As we have seen with Microsoft and *Halo*, sometimes a company with a financial interest in a particular operating system or console will want to have exclusive rights to certain game software, at least for a while. Sometimes, a distributor may license a game from a producer with an agreement not to distribute it. Square Enix, formerly known as Eidos Interactive, the publisher of the Lara Croft game *Tomb Raider: Legend*, had Nixxes Software work on the Windows-PC and Xbox versions of the game while Buzz Money Software developed the PlayStation 2 version, and Humansoft worked out the Nintendo DS and Game Boy Advance versions. Starting with Windows and Xbox in April 2006, the platform-specific incarnations rolled out across months, with the handheld version debuting in December of that year. The game has been so popular that an updated version for the PlayStation 3 (in HD) came out in 2011.[18]

## Video Games and Convergence

The cross-platform nature of the games we've just discussed is evidence of digital convergence at work. In fact, much of video game publishing involves deciding whether, when, and how to roll out digital versions of software across boundaries created by different systems for play. When it comes to multiplayer games, publishers will enable users to play the games online as well as on their individual consoles. For example, some Microsoft multiplayer games allow people who have an Xbox 360 to interact with people who are playing on their Windows PC or on their Windows Phone.

As you might expect from the other media we have explored throughout this book, convergence doesn't stop with the movement of entire copies of games across different platforms. Game publishers have a strong interest in leading as many people as possible in their target audiences to learn about and buy their products. So when Activision Publishing released *Call of Duty: Black Ops II* (developed by Treyarch) in 2012, for example, the company also released the soundtrack of the game. It hyped the soundtrack by publicizing that its main theme was written by Trent Reznor, leader of the band Nine Inch Nails and Academy Award–winning composer of the score for the English-language version of the movie *The Girl with the Dragon Tattoo*. The aim was clearly to give fans of the *Call of Duty* game series and fans of Reznor (perhaps an overlapping population) an additional reason to pay attention to the *Black Ops II* release.

Publishers of especially popular games encourage convergence—not all of it digital—because they make money from licensing characters, music, plots, or other aspects of their games to companies in other media industries. For a familiar example, just type Super Mario Brothers into Amazon's search engine. Results will include a variety of the kid-friendly Brooklyn plumbers' adventures on various Nintendo platforms. But you will also be able to buy Super Mario Brothers toys (several types of figurines and plush dolls), TV episodes, peel-and-stick wall decals, bedsheet sets, pillowcases, party napkins, hats, and cherry-cola lip balm, as well as the game's music track and more.

Lara Croft, of the *Tomb Raider* series, is an especially noteworthy example of a video game character who crossed media boundaries to become a major cultural figure. She first appeared in the 1996 *Tomb Raider* video game, where she competed with a rival archaeologist to find an ancient artifact. Even as she enjoyed other adventures in *Tomb Raider* games, she moved into other digital and non-digital media. These included dozens of comic book issues, two novels, two motion pictures, a CD and MP3s of the movie soundtrack, and short animated films on the web. You can also buy Lara Croft paraphernalia such as character outfits, wigs, figurines, mouse pads, toy pistols, and shoulder holsters. Although the Super Mario Brothers and Lara Croft represent characters originating within the video game landscape and migrating to other platforms, video games also provide a vehicle for extending storylines originating in other media forms. For instance, the book series *Lord of the Rings* has spawned a very successful movie franchise as well as a popular video game series.

## Media Ethics: Confronting Key Issues

By this point in the book, you have probably noticed that all the media industries we discuss are embroiled in controversies that touch on ethical issues. The video game industry is no different. Three enduring concerns center on content, privacy, and self-regulation. Let's take a look at some examples. As we sketch them, consider how they make two broad points. First, think about how the controversies reflect the unique nature of the videogame industry. But second, think about how quite similar issues can and do arise in virtually all of the other industries we've explored.

*Tomb Raider*, which has been a success in both the film and video game worlds, has also been the subject of controversy with respect to the way Lara Croft's character is typically portrayed as a very sexualized, scantily clad woman.

### Concerns about Content

Lara Croft is a good place to start. The *Guinness Book of World Records* calls her "the most recognized female video game character." She has many admirers who point out that she is athletic, strong, and proactive—which they claim is a great image for women in a video game. But the Croft character also has touched off strong negative reactions. Critics say that her sexy frame reinforces unrealistic ideals about the female body, that she is there to embody male fantasies, and that she is a negative role model for young girls. They also claim that the game's publisher and developer downplay the character's sex appeal when they are speaking to groups but emphasize it in their advertisements.

Images of women, as embodied by Lara Croft and other characters, are by no means the only controversial aspect of video games. Consider the *Grand Theft Auto* series. Published by Rockstar Games (which is owned by Take-Two Interactive), it had created 15 editions of the popular game by 2013. It has sold tens of millions of copies worldwide, mainly for Windows computers and the Xbox 360, though some versions are available in mobile versions. From its first incarnation in 1997, the game raised consternation because of its violence and sexual content. In 2005, *Grand Theft Auto: San Andreas* was skewered by angry parents and advocacy groups as morally bankrupt. They argued that it teaches people how to engage in a crime spree with gusto. Other games within the *Grand Theft Auto* series were castigated for their stereotypes of groups such as Haitians and Cubans as belonging to criminal gangs. In 2009, the *Guinness Book of World Records* called it the most controversial video game series in history. It calculated that over 4,000 articles had been published about it. Such articles have included laudatory comments about its innovativeness, but also many accusations of glamorizing violence, corrupting gamers, and even encouraging real-life crimes.[19] Video games such as *Grand Theft Auto* often enter the public debate about violence—especially teen violence. For instance, in the aftermath of the Columbine High School shooting in 1999, the games *Doom* and *Quake* moved to the center of a renewed nationwide debate about the possible harmful effects of violent video games. Although research on the subject offers mixed conclusions, the subject remains central in public discourse.

What factors encourage the creation of video game content that substantial numbers of people consider offensive? There is no easy answer. One view is that when creators of the games present sexist, violent, and/or ethnically derogatory portrayals, they are reflecting the attitudes of the people who play the games. The players may not shout those views in public, but they have no problem connecting with stories that build conflict or excitement by giving characters various negative sexually, ethnically, or racially stereotyped characteristics and pitting them against one another.

Many people who work on video games, though, believe that such images are socially harmful because they reinforce the idea that violence is the solution to problems and that particular groups in society have undesirable characteristics. These workers believe they have a responsibility to convince their coworkers and industry leaders to be sensitive to problematic depictions. One way some industry players have attempted to improve these presentations is by increasing the number and prominence of game creators with diverse backgrounds so that they can quash negative portrayals and be at the forefront of thinking up creative ways to use people of various backgrounds in less violent but compelling ways that will attract large audiences.

One of the major issues raised among people who observe the gaming industry is why there are so few women involved. According to a 2013 article in the *Boston Globe*, women account for only 11 percent of game designers and 3 percent of programmers. The article goes on to describe how "female workers are frequently subjected to unequal treatment, harassment, and hostile atmospheres. At last year's industry convention in San Francisco, for example, one company hired topless models for a professional networking event." Additionally, it notes that female video game programmers earn an average of $10,000 less per year than their male counterparts, and female designers make an average of $12,000 less.[20]

John Vanderhoef, a doctoral student at the University of California, Santa Barbara, tracked a Twitter discussion on just this topic among people who work in the video game industry. The tweets brought to light many charges of discrimination against women in the games industry.[21] These issues also came up in a frank essay on a site for gaming practitioners. One of the site's editors, Leigh Alexander, who also works in the video game industry, argued, "Every single one of us [women] can tell you at least one horror story. Most of us have more than one. Booth babes, incidences of sexism, [and] using attempted rape as a *Tomb Raider* 'character builder.'" She then added, "None of these are things we should shut up about." It's important, she noted, to ask game developers "harder questions" with the aim of creating "a healthy industry with diverse products by and for anyone that wants to participate."[22] It's a worthy goal that many say is still far from being realized.

Among Zynga's popular games that the firm distributes online (at zynga.com) and via Facebook are Farmville and Words with Friends. Zynga explicitly states in its privacy policy that it is collecting information about its users, based on their physical location (if playing on mobile devices such as smartphones or tablets) and any information you may have posted on Facebook. Many of the gamers may not realize that.

## Concerns about Privacy

Many people probably think of the issues we've just discussed when they think about concerns with video games—sex, violence, and possibly social stereotypes. It is probably less likely that they think they are being followed and profiled when they play a game. Increasingly, though, that ought to be a consideration.

Consider *FarmVille*, *CityVille*, and the many other games published by Zynga. Perhaps you've played them on your web browser or while on a social networking site (SNS) such as Facebook or Google+. Well, if you read Zynga's privacy policy, you'll learn that Zynga is collecting loads of information about you as you play. Depending on what the SNS considers public information by default as well as your privacy settings, Zynga

> may access and store your first and last name, your profile picture or its URL, your user ID number, which is linked to publicly available information such as name and profile photo; the user ID numbers and other public data for your friends; the login e-mail you provided to that SNS when you registered; your physical location and that of your access devices; your gender; your birthday.[23]

Not sure what Facebook or Google+ give up about you by default? Not sure about your privacy settings? Research shows that many people don't know these things, and it's likely Zynga gathers a lot of information people might not have wanted the company to know. Zynga also uses cookies and other tracking devices to follow what you do if you visit its website or play one of its games in an app. Moreover, the privacy policy states,

> If you play Zynga games on your mobile telephone or other mobile device, including iPads and tablets, We collect mobile device identifiers, including MAC Address, and IP Address. In certain games we will create and assign to your device an identifier that is similar to an account number. We may collect the name you have associated with your device, device type, telephone number, country, and any other information you choose to provide, such as user name, character name, geo-location or e-mail address. We may also access your contacts to enable you to invite friends to join you in the Service.[24]

Even when Zynga or other game companies are not linking your actions to personally identifiable information, they are often carefully tracking your in-game activity. By embedding triggers in the game, publishers can observe user patterns that can provide useful marketing data and guide future game design.

Zynga's tracking of the visitors to its website and apps is by no means unusual. As we noted in chapter 6, most publishers and marketers follow people's activities online and use—and trade—that information for marketing purposes. In addition to these funds of knowledge, marketers themselves have been taking advantage of the constantly decreasing costs of computer power to create their own databases from information they learn about their customers, by asking them and by keeping records of their purchases. These storehouses of information are called **transactional databases**. A marketer that wants to learn more about the customers in its transactional database can turn to a data-gathering firm such as Acxiom. The company will match the names and addresses of the marketer's customers against its data on more than 124 million households. The resulting merged file could supply the marketer with a wealth of new information about each customer's purchasing behavior, estimated income, credit extended by mail-order firms, investments, credit cards, and more.

**transactional databases**
databases that store and sort large quantities of data that reflect transactions—such as logs of phone calls, e-mails, mailings, or purchases

## Concerns about Self-Regulation

As you might imagine, this controversy about privacy has reached the halls of government. Critics of data collection by media firms have tried to persuade regulators and lawmakers to enact laws to stop those activities. Critics of the content of certain video games have also complained to lawmakers for action on the grounds that young people have been harmed. In both these cases, government response has tended to center on pressuring the companies that make up the industry to clean up their act. Industry critics and industry leaders disagree about how much this self-regulation has succeeded in erasing problems in the video game industry, on the web, or in the mobile space. Let's take a look at the arguments as they relate to privacy and content.

**Privacy and Self-Regulation** When it comes to privacy, the U.S. government has mixed laws about collecting data. The existing laws relate to personal data about children, people's health records, and aspects of their bank and credit card records. Chapter 5 discusses the Children's Online Privacy Protection Act (COPPA), a law that requires websites (including game sites) to get parents' permission to ask children for information about themselves. By federal law, some aspects of medical privacy and credit data (e.g., your prescription drugs and specific purchases on your credit card) also require permission from the individual. These exceptions aside, the federal government in the early 21st century stayed away from imposing particular rules on the use of personal information by websites. The reason: to encourage web commerce.

Instead, lawmakers at the federal level have agreed with digital marketers and publishers that the best way forward is through self-regulation. Consistent with this approach, the Federal Trade Commission (FTC) has suggested four broad principles that it expects those engaged in the web and mobile industries to follow when it comes to handling information about people that identifies them personally through items such as their names, postal address, and e-mail address. These "fair information practice principles" (FIPPs) include the following:

- Notice (or Awareness): Visitors to a site or app should be made aware of the company's information practices—and the information practices of other firms who take people's information at those locations—before any personal information is collected from the visitors.
- Choice (or Consent): The visitors should have the option of making decisions about how their data will be used during the current session on the site or app, as well as in the future. That is, the visitor should have the option of opting into the company's collection of data (the firm should not collect data unless the person gives the OK) or opting out (the firm will collect the data unless the visitor says no).
- Access: The visitor should be able to view the data collected and challenge it if the visitor considers it inaccurate.
- Security: The data collection and storage should take place in ways that stop people and firms from getting the data if they have no right to the data.

These principles are quite broad, they are not backed up by law, and they relate only to data that the FTC suggests will lead to the specific knowledge of the name and address of the person. Nowadays, most web marketers and game publishers contend that self-regulation will work to safeguard the public's privacy. They say that they understand people's desire to keep certain information confidential and secure. They also insist, however, that many individuals are willing to give up information about themselves if, in return, they get something that they consider valuable. Many privacy advocates agree that people should have the right to decide whether they want to give up private information as part of a transaction. But they insist that the FIPPs should cover all data, not only obviously personal data. They also disagree with the web marketers and publishers on the way in which consumers should be informed about the data that will be collected about them, often without their knowledge.

Industry representatives continue to insist that interactive sites and marketers could regulate themselves through an opt-out approach, although some sites still tell their visitors nothing about the information they collect about them. Compounding all these arguments is the international nature of the issue. The European Union requires an opt-in approach, for example, and U.S. companies have to promise to accept the stricter EU rules when they deal with European consumers.

Note, too, that these privacy issues are related not only to the web but also to mobile apps and video games on several platforms that are connected to the internet. Moreover, as home-based television viewing becomes a two-way activity, getting data about what individuals do with the medium will also interest marketers and, possibly, certain branches of government. As these types of surveillance take place, various advocacy groups will argue against them and ask for legal safeguards against the misuse and abuse of people's data. Clearly, the fight over U.S. consumer privacy and the merits of self-regulation in the digital age will continue.

**Video Game Content and Self-Regulation** The success of self-regulation is also in dispute when it comes to the content of video games. As discussed previously, the video game industry has set up a rating system much as the movie and television industries have done. Government regulators don't want to censor games out of concern that they would be overriding the firms' freedom of speech, but they also try to pressure the industry to act responsibly, to calm anger around the sex and violence of certain games on the part of consumers, especially parents. Like the movie and TV businesses, the video game industry argues that its ratings system effectively categorizes games so that buyers can make informed purchase decisions. The six ratings (apart from "rating pending") are EC (early childhood), E (everyone), E 101 (everyone 10+), T (teen), M (mature—17 and older), and AO (adults only). Content descriptors run a wide gamut from "alcohol reference" to "intense violence" to "use of tobacco." Table 14.1 presents a look at top video games and their ratings.

Despite this ratings system, some games have raised consternation among critics. Regardless of the public outcry surrounding *Grand Theft Auto: San Andreas* (discussed previously), the game was given an M by the ratings agency. Critics claimed that the rating and the accompanying descriptors were problematic because they didn't inform parents regarding the true level of violence and sex in the game. The controversy got hotter when players discovered that use of a certain code would unlock an explicit sex scene in the game. Even though Rockstar insisted that the sex scene and code were the work of a hacker, advocacy groups and politicians such as Hillary Clinton attacked the company for misleading the ESRB, retailers, and parents. Rockstar pulled the game from the shelves at great cost, deleted the scene, and put it back on the market. Nevertheless, the incident served as an opportunity for groups to rail against retailers for allegedly selling games to kids as young as nine years old.

Take-Two Interactive's Rockstar Games sparked a game-selling controversy again in 2007, with a game called *Manhunt 2*. Its central character is an inmate who escapes a mental asylum, murdering guards and prisoners. The game was banned in

**Table 14.1**  ESRB Ratings of Top-Rated Video Games

| Title | ESRB Rating |
| --- | --- |
| Assassin's Creed: Revelations | Mature |
| Batman: Arkham City | Teen |
| Battlefield 3 | Mature |
| Call of Duty: Black Ops | Mature |
| Call of Duty: Modern Warfare 3 | Mature |
| Civilization V | Everyone 10+ |
| Dragon Age II | Mature |
| Elder Scrolls V: Skyrim | Mature |
| Gears of War 3 | Mature |
| Just Dance 2 | Everyone |
| Just Dance 3 | Everyone 10+ |
| Madden NFL 12 | Everyone |
| Portal 2 | Everyone 10+ |
| Rift | Teen |
| Star Wars: The Old Republic | Teen |
| Starcraft II: Wings of Liberty | Teen |
| The Sims 3 | Teen |
| The Sims 3: Generations | Teen |
| The Sims 3: Medieval | Teen |
| World of Warcraft: Cataclysm | Teen |

Source: Adapted from http://www.theesa.com/facts/pdfs/ESA_EF_2012.pdf, 8–9, accessed November 23, 2012.

the United Kingdom, Ireland, and Italy, and it was given an AO rating by the ESRB. Take-Two's chairman Strauss Zelnick defended the game on artistic grounds, stating that "the Rockstar team has come up with a game that fits squarely within the horror genre and was intended to do so." He added, "It brings a unique, formerly unheard of cinematic quality to interactive entertainment, and is also a fine piece of art." Take-Two's financial situation was precarious, however, and Zelnick knew that major retailers such as Walmart would not carry a title with an AO rating. Moreover, Sony and Nintendo do not allow AO-rated games on their systems. So Rockstar toned down the sadism, and the ESRB gave it an M.

To some critics, the change was beside the point. They argued that even M-rated games in stores were getting into the wrong hands because game retailers too often sold M-rated video games to kids as young as nine years of age. They cited research at the Harvard School of Public Health that 81 percent of M-rated games were mislabeled and had missing content descriptors, thus potentially misleading parents. The ESRB replied that the researchers had exaggerated problems they found and that a long list of content descriptors on packages would be impractical. Clearly, though, the arguments surrounding video game producers, retailing, and ratings are not over.

In fact, it's pretty safe to say that this is true about all the media industries we've covered in this book, as well as those we haven't looked at in detail. As we have noted more than once, media practices often affect the ways members of a society—you and I—see our world and carry out our daily lives. It should not be surprising that we all argue about them as well as enjoy them and try to influence them.

## MEDIA TODAY & CULTURE  WOMEN AND VIDEO GAMES

The typical video game player is stereotyped as a teenage boy playing his games home alone, but industry statistics paint a different picture. According to the Entertainment Software Association, females make up 47 percent of all players, and adult women make up the fastest-growing audience segment. What's more, adult women make up a greater percentage of overall players than boys ages 17 and younger.[1]

Despite their growing presence among the video game audience, female characters remain conspicuously absent as heroes in the games themselves. One study found that out of 669 games, just 24 offered only female lead characters, while less than 300 offered the option of a female character. This study connected these findings with video game sales, which concludes that games with male-only leads far outsell games with female-only leads.[2] As a result, the industry remains reluctant to create games with just female leads and to commit the funds for marketing them.

Even within the video games, representations of women remain hypersexualized and objectified. Female lead characters often wear skimpy clothing and get drawn with enhanced breasts, small waists, flat stomachs, and long legs. The Lara Croft character in the *Tomb Raider* series is the most popular example of this. When the video game first was adapted for film with Angelina Jolie in the role of Lara Croft, debates flew about the character's bust size decreasing. Later iterations of the video game character showed designers reducing her bust size.[3]

In some video games, women serve as objects of violence. In the *Grand Theft Auto* series, for example, beating up, raping, and killing female prostitutes becomes a way to earn points and advance in the game narrative. *Duke Nukem Forever* is premised on the idea that aliens are kidnapping the women of Earth, and the goal is to get them back. The game encourages slapping around women to calm them down, procuring them for sex, and even killing them.[4]

For women and girls seeking fun video games that demonstrate positive role models for them, the current industry options prove lacking. One father got so frustrated he hacked into *The Legend of Zelda* and recast the male character Link as a female. The father, Mike Hoye, previously had been reading the dialogue and other onscreen information to his 3-year-old daughter and switching the pronouns. Hoye wrote in his blog, "I'm not having my daughter growing up thinking girls don't get to be the hero and rescue their little brothers."[5] The story garnered much press and a lot of positive support.[6]

# CHAPTER REVIEW

Visit the Companion Website at www.routledge.com/cw/turow for additional study tools and resources.

# Key Terms

You can find the definitions to these key terms in the marginal glossary throughout this chapter. Test your knowledge of these terms with interactive flash cards on the *Media Today* companion website.

avatar

bulletin boards

casual gamers

dynamic in-game advertising

edutainment

entertainment arcades

handheld game devices

massively multiplayer online

   role-playing games

   (MMORPGs)

mobile device

multiuser dungeons (MUDs)

pinball machine

social games

third-party publishers

transactional databases

video game publishers

# Questions for Discussion and Critical Thinking

1. To what extent is media convergence already part of your everyday life?

2. Some observers have commented that parents in some families feel like immigrants to the United States when the family brings computers and gaming platforms into the home for the first time. That is because, as in immigrant families, the children often "speak the language" better than the parents do. Did your family's experience with technology fit this description? Do you have any friends whose experiences fit this description?

3. Where do you stand on the issue of video game violence? Why?

4. Are you concerned about being tracked by marketers while you use digital devices? Why or why not?

5. Video game addiction is considered a diagnosable and serious psychological condition in several countries. Do you agree that this is a serious problem? Why or why not?

## Case Study
### GOOD GUYS AND BAD CHARACTERS IN VIDEO GAMES

**The Idea** In real life, it may well be that it's hard to distinguish bad characters from good ones. In some video games, though, the creators may systematically create differences between the good and bad guys to make it clearer whom to shoot, capture, and/or dislike. That may be especially true with action games. Is it?

**The Method** Each class member should choose two popular action games and conduct a systematic analysis of characters in the game who are clearly bad, characters who are clearly good, characters who are a mixture of good and bad, and characters about whom you can't tell. After familiarizing yourselves with the games you will examine, you and your fellow class members should cooperate on creating a coding sheet that you will use to analyze each game character. On the sheet, list features of that character—physical characteristics (e.g., human, animal, amount of hair, location of hair, hair color, tall/short, female/male, and more), clothing characteristics, tone of speaking, gender, perceived age—and more.

After making sure you all are defining the features in the same way, each person should code each character that shows up in the game during a particular period of time. Bring all your data together and note whether the good and bad characters are similar or different. Discuss various ways to think about what you have found.

# Epilogue

## The Need For Transparency

Let us not look back in anger, nor forward in fear,
but around in awareness.

*James Thurber*

It is easy to sit up and take notice.
What is difficult is getting up and taking action.

*Al Battista*

As the examples we've explored throughout this text suggest, a central concern in the converging world of media today relates to people's lack of knowledge about what powers and what agendas lie behind the news, information, and entertainment that confront them across so many channels. People find it difficult to keep straight the maze of ownerships, alliances, and entanglements that affect so much of what we see and hear today. Corporate relationships within Sony affect the circulation of music and characters from video games to recordings to movies and back. Internal organizational rearrangements within Time Warner affect everything from the lineup of your local cable system to the kinds of news you get from *Time, Sports Illustrated, Entertainment Weekly,* and CNN—and how the news travels across these sources.

The easy (and understandable) reaction is to simply throw up your hands and say "It's impossible to follow these issues. All of the media world is manipulated in ways we can't understand, so I'll just distrust it all." This is the path of cynicism. It's an approach that will make you suspect everything you come across in almost every medium, even when that response isn't warranted. You'll shut yourself off from good stuff, and you won't learn to be an educated critic of what is going on in the media or the world at large.

The other, better reaction is to apply the media literacy skills that you've learned through this book in two ways. The first way is to try to keep track of the connections among the media that produce, distribute, and exhibit the materials that you use on a regular basis. What companies create these materials? Are they part of conglomerates, joint ventures, or alliances of other types? Do any of these relationships explain the kinds of content you are getting in the ways you are getting them? If so, can you figure out whether any corporate strategies might explain why these materials and not others are being released—and why one perspective and not another is being used?

The second way to apply your media literacy skills is to take action. Work with individuals or groups to convince mass media organizations to be more open about the corporate connections that go into creating their content. Demand that entertainment and news organizations routinely disclose when press releases or public relations organizations are involved in instigating or contributing to a story. Insist that media firms prominently divulge all product placements. Write to executives of public relations and "communication services" firms to demand that they work with media companies to inform the public when the products of their activities make it into print, on the air, on film, or on the Web.

It's unlikely that media executives will take kindly to such requests. It's also unlikely that the government can force these sorts of corporate disclosures, because that is probably unconstitutional. Yet consistent, insistent pressure by various public groups for openness about the ways in which marketers and PR practitioners influence twenty-first century mass media might, over time, lead corporations to provide substantially more background about the commercial and political influences behind the mass media than the public now receives. Working toward more transparency in media today might well pay off big time in terms of what we will know about media tomorrow.

# Notes

## Main Text

### Chapter 4

1. Abby Klaasen, "MTV Lures to Its Website Those Who Don't Buy TV," Advertising Age, October 9, 2006, 8.
2. Quoted in Joseph Turow, Niche Envy: Marketing and Discrimination in the Digital Age (Cambridge, MA, MIT Press, 2006), 43.
3. http://www.hkstrategies.com/company/sustainability/about-us, accessed January 21, 2013.
4. http://www.linkedin.com/company/pbn-hill-knowlton-strategies/media-relations-1186338/product?trk=biz_product, accessed January 21, 2013.
5. David Goetzl, "Ram Drives A&E 'Longmire' Sponsorship, Integration," MediaDailyNews, April 19, 2012, http://www.mediapost.com/publications/article/172812/ram-drives-ae-longmire-sponsorship-integration.html#axzz2IeZ8FzOY, accessed January 21, 2013.
6. Ross Fadner, "Ford Web Series Focuses on Eco Education," Marketing Daily, April 19, 2012, http://www.mediapost.com/publications/article/172794/ford-web-series-focuses-on-eco-education.html?print#axzz2IeZ8FzOY, accessed January 21, 2013.
7. Scott Cutlip, The Unseen Power (New York: Lawrence Erlbaum, 1994), 768.
8. http://www.columbia.edu/itc/journalism/j6075/edit/ethiccodes/PRSA.html, accessed January 21, 2013.
9. Sut Jhally, "Advertising at the Edge of the Apocalypse," http://www.sutjhally.com/articles/advertisingattheed/, accessed January 21, 2013.

### Chapter 5

1. Roger Yu and Jon Swartz, "Internet Community Cheers Power of Protest," USA Today, January 18, 1012, http://www.usatoday.com/tech/news/story/2012-01-19/sopa-protest-shows-internet-power/52654106/1, accessed May 18, 2012.
2. The quote is from the U.S. Supreme Court case New York Times Co. v. Sullivan (1964), 271–272. The case quoting it is Time Inc. v. Hill, 385 U.S. 374 (1967).
3. Roth v. United States, 354 U.S. 476 (1957).
4. Bill Katovsky and Timothy Carlson, Embedded: The Media at War in Iraq (Guilford, CT: Lyons Press, 2004).
5. Paul Weidman, "Rules of Embeddedness," Sante Fe New Mexican, September 10, 2004, 32. See also Kevin Smith, "The Media at the Tip of the Spear," Michigan Law Review 102, no. 6 (May 2004): 1329.
6. Julie Bisceglia, "Parody and Fair Use," Entertainment Law Reporter, May 1994.
7. "Weird Al Yankovic Still Weird and White and Nerdy," New Zealand Herald, March 3, 2007, via Nexis.

8. Federal Communications Commission, "Best Practices for National Spectrum Management," http://transition.fcc.gov/ib/sand/irb/bestpractices.html, accessed January 21, 2013.
9. Tricia Duryee, "Two Consumer Groups Try to Black Google's Acquisition of AdMob," PaidContent.org, December 28, 2009.
10. Jim Puzazzanhara, "FCC to Fine Univision $24 Million," Los Angeles Times, February 25, 2007, A20.
11. "Skechers Pays $40 Million to Settle Toning Claims," Advertising Age, May 16, 2012.
12. Stuart Elliot, "A Coalition of Marketers Is Accelerating Efforts to Sponsor 'Family Friendly' Prime-Time Television," New York Times, March 31, 2000, http://www.nytimes.com/2000/03/31/business/media-business-advertising-coalition-marketers-accelerating-efforts-sponsor.html, accessed January 21, 2013.
13. Elliot, "Coalition of Marketers."
14. Association of National Advertisers, "Alliance for Family Entertainment," PaidContent.org
15. Bob Steele, "Ask These 10 Questions to Make Good Ethical Decisions," http://www.poynter.org/latest-news/everyday-ethics/talk-about-ethics/1750/ask-these-10-questions-to-make-good-ethical-decisions/, accessed January 21, 2013.
16. Clifford Christians, Kim Rotzoll, and Mark Fackler, Media Ethics, 4th ed. (White Plains, NY: Longman, 1995).

### Chapter 6

1. Ross Fadner, "As Millennials Grow Up, Big TV Faces a Race against Time," Mediapost, May 23, 2012.
2. Steve Smith, "'What Did I Miss?' TV Attention Suffers a Big Hit from Second Screens," Mediapost, May 24, 2012,
3. http://pewinternet.org/Trend-Data-(Adults)/Device-Ownership.aspx, accessed November 18, 2012.
4. http://pewinternet.org/~/media//Files/Reports/2012/PIP_Digital_differences_041312.pdf
5. "Advertising Spending Online Expected to Surpass Print This Year," Los Angeles Times, January 20, 2012, http://latimesblogs.latimes.com/technology/2012/01/advertising-spending-online-expected-to-surpass-print-this-year.html, accessed February 11, 2013.
6. Stewart Miles, "Android Users Finally Buying Paid Apps, Download Numbers Catching iPhone," Pocket-lint, August 29, 2012, http://www.pocket-lint.com/news/47102/android-users-finally-buying-paid-apps, accessed October 27, 2012.
7. Pew Research Center's Project for Excellence in Journalism, "Future of Mobile News," October 1, 2012, http://www.journalism.org/analysis_report/device_ownership, accessed October 27, 2012.
8. Pew Research Center's Project for Excellence in Journalism, "Future of Mobile News."
9. Pew Research Center's Project for Excellence in Journalism, "Future of Mobile News."

**10.** Paul Sloan, "Apple by the Numbers," CNET, October 23, 2012, http://news.cnet.com/8301-13579_3-57537667-37/apple-by-the-numbers-35b-apps-downloaded-100m-ipads-sold/, accessed January 22, 2013.

## Chapter 7

**1.** Thomas Catan and Jeffrey A. Trachtenberg, "U.S. Warns Apple, Publishers," *Wall Street Journal*, March 9, 2012, http://online.wsj.com/article/SB1000142405297020396120457726783176748921 6.html, accessed June 10, 2012.

**2.** Association of American Publishers, "Bookstats Publishing Formats Highlights," http://www.publishers.org/bookstats/formats, accessed June 11, 2012.

**3.** *Communications Industry Forecast, 2011–15* (New York: Veronis Suhler Stevenson, 2012), section 14, p. 10.

**4.** "Zondervan Released Enhanced eBook of Rick Warren's Best-Selling 'The Purpose Driven Life,'" PR Newswire, January 26, 2011, via LexisNexis.

**5.** "Fifty Shades of Grey," *Wikipedia*, http://en.wikipedia.org/wiki/50_Shades_of_Grey, accessed July 30, 2012.

**6.** *Communications Industry Forecast, 2011–15*, section 14, p. 3.

**7.** Michael Meyer, "My Advance," *New York Times*, April 10, 2010, http://www.nytimes.com/2009/04/12/books/review/Meyer-t.html?_r=1, accessed June 21, 2012.

**8.** *Communications Industry Forecast, 2011–15*, section 14, p. 4.

**9.** *Communications Industry Forecast, 2011–15*, section 14, p. 4.

**10.** Julie Bosman, "Jonah Lehrer Resigns from the *New Yorker* after Making Up Dylan Quotes for His Book," *New York Times*, July 30, 2012, http://mediadecoder.blogs.nytimes.com/2012/07/30/jonah-lehrer-resigns-from-new-yorker-after-making-up-dylan-quotes-for-his-book/, accessed July 30, 2012.

## Chapter 8

**1.** *Communications Industry Forecast, 2011–15* (Veronis Suhler Stevenson, 2011), part 16, p. 14.

**2.** Richard Karpel and Ken Fleming, "Total and Minority Newsroom Employment Declines in 2011 but Loss Continues to Stabilize," American Society of Newspaper Editors, April 4, 2012, http://asne.org/Article_View/ArticleId/2499/Total-and-minority-newsroom-employment-declines-in-2011-but-loss-continues-to-stabilize.aspx, accessed on June 26, 2012.

**3.** Rick Edmonds, "Building Digital Revenues Proves Painfully Slow," State of the News Media 2012, Pew Research Center's Project for Excellence in Journalism, April 11, 2012, http://stateofthemedia.org/2012/newspapers-building-digital-revenues-proves-painfully-slow/, accessed June 28, 2012.

**4.** Rick Edmonds, "Building Digital Revenues Proves Painfully Slow," State of the News Media 2012, Pew Research Center's Project for Excellence in Journalism, April 11, 2012, http://stateofthemedia.org/2012/newspapers-building-digital-revenues-proves-painfully-slow/, accessed June 28, 2012.

**5.** *Communications Industry Forecast, 2011–15* (Veronis Suhler Stevenson, 2011), part 16, p. 9.

## Chapter 9

**1.** Brooks Barnes, "In the Footsteps of Marvel," *New York Times*, July 9, 2012, B1.

**2.** *Magazine Media Factbook* 2012/13 (New York: MPA, 2012), 95, http://www.magazine.org/advertising/factbook2012.aspx

**3.** See http://www.totembrandstories.com/en/clients/kraft-foods.aspx, accessed July 10, 2012.

**4.** http://www.seventeenmediakit.com/r5/home.asp, accessed July 11, 2012.

**5.** "Forbes Events," http://www.forbesmedia.com/events-overview, accessed July 12, 2012.

**6.** "Forbes Properties," http://www.forbesmedia.com/properties-overview, accessed July 12, 2012.

**7.** J. W. Click and R. N. Baird, *Magazine Editing and Production* (William C. Brown, 1990), 2661.

**8.** "Men's Health Media Kit 2012," http://www.menshealth.com/mediakit/pdfs/1-General/4-MH12_Full_Media_Kit.pdf, Accessed July 16, 2012.

## Chapter 10

**1.** http://www.techspot.com/news/45182-riaa-appeals-jammie-thomas-rassets-damage-reduction.html

**2.** See "Sony BMG v. Tenenbaum," *Wikipedia*, http://en.wikipedia.org/wiki/Sony_BMG_v._Tenenbaum, accessed August 6, 2012; Milton Vilencia, "Student Fights Music-Sharing Fine," *Boston.com*, April 5, 2011, http://www.boston.com/news/local/massachusetts/articles/2011/04/05/student_fights_music_sharing_fine/, accessed August 6, 2011.

**3.** Cited in RIAA, "Piracy Online: Scope of the Problem," http://www.riaa.com/physicalpiracy.php?content_selector=piracy-online-scope-of-the-problem, accessed August 3, 2012.

**4.** Cited in RIAA, "Piracy Online: Scope of the Problem."

**5.** "*Smash* (The Offspring Album)," *Wikipedia*, http://en.wikipedia.org/wiki/Smash_(The_Offspring_album), accessed August 6, 2012.

**6.** NDP, "Demographics: NDP Annual Music Study, 2011," courtesy NDP; http://www.census.gov/compendia/statab/cats/population.html

**7.** "The Nielsen Company & Billboard's Music Industry Report," Business Wire, January 5, 2012.

**8.** Joshua Friedlander, "News and Notes on 2011 RIAA Music Shipment Data," RIAA, accessed July 30, 2012.

**9.** You can see this spreadsheet here: http://www.informationisbeautiful.net/2010/how-much-do-music-artists-earn-online/.

**10.** http://en.wikipedia.org/wiki/Live_Nation_(events_promoter), accessed December 11, 2012.

**11.** http://www.universalmusic.com/company

**12.** http://www.wmg.com/

**13.** "The Nielsen Company & Billboard's 2011 Music Industry Report," Business Wire, January 5, 2012, 2http://www.businesswire.com/news/home/20120105005547/en/Nielsen-Company-Billboard%E2%80%99s-2011-Music-Industry-Report, accessed December 11, 2012.

**14.** Joseph Menn, "Digital Lockers a Growing Concern," Reuters, January 20, 2012, http://www.reuters.com/article/2012/01/21/us-digital-piracy-idUSTRE80K05120120121, accessed August 10, 2012.

**15.** Joseph Menn, "Digital Lockers a Growing Concern."

## Chapter 11

**1.** "Radio," *Wikipedia*, http://en.wikipedia.org/wiki/Radio, accessed August 21, 2012; "Edouard Branly," *Wikipedia*, http://en.wikipedia.org/wiki/%C3%89douard_Branly, accessed August 21, 2012.

2. Jennifer Watts, "FCC's Quarterly Station Count Indicates That Radio Is Still Growing in U.S.," Radio Survivor, http://www.radiosurvivor.com/2012/07/19/fccs-quarterly-station-count-indicates-that-radio-is-still-growing-in-u-s/, accessed August 23, 2012.

3. "Radio Locator," http://radio-locator.com/cgi-bin/locate?select=city&city=Philadelphia&state=PA&band=Both&is_lic=Y&format=&dx=0&radius=&freq=&sort=freq&sid=, accessed August 23, 2012; http://www.greatermediaphiladelphia.com/, accessed December 11, 2012.

4. Arbitron, "Radio Today 2011," http://www.arbitron.com/downloads/Radio_Today_2011.pdf, accessed August 23, 2011; Arbitron and Edison Research, "The Infinite Dial, 2012," http://www.edisonresearch.com/home/archives/2012/04/the-infinite-dial-2012-navigating-digital-platforms.php, accessed August 23, 2012.

5. Arbitron, "Radio Today 2011," 12, http://www.arbitron.com/downloads/Radio_Today_2011.pdf, accessed August 23, 2011.

6. Communications Industry Forecast, 2011–15 (New York: Veronis Suhler Stevenson), section 18, p. 10. This volume presents only the 2011 data. The 1981 data comes from an earlier VSS forecast.

7. Arbitron, "Radio Today 2011," 15–30, http://www.arbitron.com/downloads/Radio_Today_2011.pdf, accessed August 23, 2011.

8. http://www.dialglobal.com/index.php/delivery-choices, accessed January 29, 2013.

9. http://www.hollywoodreporter.com/news/radio-industry-grows-annual-advertising-revenue-292439

10. "About Pandora," http://www.pandora.com/about, accessed August 27, 2012

## Chapter 12

1. Andrew Stewart, "Hollywood B.O. Rides O'seas Boom," Variety, January 14, 2012, accessed online (by subscription) on September 9, 2012.

2. http://www.boxofficemojo.com/movies/?id=scream.htm, accessed January 29, 2013.

3. Dade Hayes, "Powering Up the Last Indie," Variety, January 21, 2009, 1.

4. Dade Hayes, "Powering Up the Last Indie," Variety, January 21, 2009, 1.

5. http://www.imdb.com/title/tt1125849/companycredits

6. http://www.boxofficemojo.com/movies/?id=yesman.htm, accessed January 30, 2013.

7. Pamela McClintock, "Summer's Bottom Line," Variety, August 20–26, 2007, 42.

8. Lauren A. E. Schuker, "Indie Firms Suffer Drop-off in Rights Sales," Wall Street Journal, April 20, 2009, B-1.

9. Pamela McClintock, "B.O. History Lesson," Daily Variety, May 26, 2009, 1.

10. MPAA, "Content Protection FAQ," http://www.mpaa.org/content-protection/faq, accessed January 29, 2013.

## Chapter 13

1. National Association of Broadcasters, "Over-the-Air TV Viewership Soars to 54 Million Americans," June 18, 2012, http://www.nab.org/documents/newsroom/pressRelease.asp?id=2761, accessed October 10, 2012.

2. Advertising Age Data Center, "US Spending by Media Sector," http://adage.com/datacenter/datapopup.php?article_id=231559, accessed September 28, 2012.

3. Communications Industry Forecast, 2011–15 (New York: Veronis Suhler Stevenson, 2011), section 12, p. 9.

4. http://www.ncta.com/Stats/CustomerRevenue.aspx

5. Communications Industry Forecast, 2011–15 (New York: Veronis Suhler Stevenson, 2011), section 6, p. 14.

6. http://tvbythenumbers.zap2it.com/2011/03/23/dvr-penetration-grows-to-39-7-of-households-42-2-of-viewers/86819/; http://blog.nielsen.com/nielsenwire/media_entertainment/as-tv-screens-grow-so-does-u-s-dvr-usage/, accessed October 10, 2012.

7. "Nielsen Cross-Platform Homes—Extended Screen Ratings," http://www.nielsen.com/us/en/measurement/television-measurement.html, accessed September 29, 2012.

## Chapter 14

1. http://www.reuters.com/article/2012/06/01/us-videogameshow-e3-show-factbox-idUSBRE8501IN20120601

2. Much of this brief historical sketch is based on a wide variety of articles on Wikipedia as well as on Steven Kent, The Ultimate History of Video Games (New York: Three Rivers Press, 2001).

3. http://en.wikipedia.org/wiki/Entertainment_Software_Rating_Board, accessed December 7, 2012.

4. Nicholas Jackson, "Infographic: Video Game Industry Statistics," The Atlantic, http://www.theatlantic.com/technology/archive/2011/06/infographic-video-game-industry-statistics/239665/, accessed November 4, 2012.

5. "Essential Facts about the Computer and Video Game Industry," Entertainment Software Association, http://www.theesa.com/facts/pdfs/ESA_EF_2012.pdf, accessed November 5, 2012.

6. "Essential Facts about the Computer and Video Game Industry," Entertainment Software Association, http://www.theesa.com/facts/pdfs/ESA_EF_2012.pdf, 10, accessed November 5, 2012.

7. http://www.reuters.com/article/2012/06/01/us-videogameshow-e3-show-factbox-idUSBRE8501IN20120601, accessed January 29, 2013.

8. http://www.casualgamesassociation.org/about.php, accessed November 5, 2012.

9. Mike Wilcox, "A Challenge That Lets You Grow Wings," The Age (Melbourne), September 17, 2009, 24.

10. Michael Sansbury, "X-Box Outplays Rivals and Movies," The Australian, October 11, 2007, 36.

11. Langston Werz Jr., "Video Games," Charlotte Observer, October 11, 2007, 36.

12. "Essential Facts about the Computer and Video Game Industry," Entertainment Software Association, http://www.theesa.com/facts/pdfs/ESA_EF_2012.pdf, 10, accessed November 5, 2012.

13. "Video Game Publisher," Wikipedia, http://en.wikipedia.org/wiki/Video_game_publisher, accessed November 5, 2012.

14. "Video Game Genres," Wikipedia, http://en.wikipedia.org/wiki/Video_game_genres, accessed January 30, 2013.

15. "Outline of Video Games," Wikipedia, http://en.wikipedia.org/wiki/Outline_of_video_games, accessed January 31, 2013.

16. See Paul Verna, "Gaming for Marketers," eMarketer, October 2011, 3.

17. See Paul Verna, "Gaming for Marketers," eMarketer, October 2011, 11.

18. http://en.wikipedia.org/wiki/Tomb_Raider:_Legend, accessed November 11, 2012.

19. http://en.wikipedia.org/wiki/Grand_Theft_Auto_(series), accessed November 15, 2012.

20. http://www.bostonglobe.com/business/2013/01/27/women-remain-outsiders-video-game-industry/275JKqy3rFylT7TxgPmO3K/story.html, accessed January 30, 2013.

21. John Vanderhoef, "Women Game Makers Speak Out," CWC Media Industries Project, December 4, 2012, http://www.carseywolf.ucsb.edu/mip/women-game-makers-speak-out, accessed December 7, 2012.

22. Leigh Alexander, "Opinion: In the Sexism Discussion, Let's Look at Game Culture," Gamasutra, July 16, 2012, http://www.gamasutra.com/view/news/174145/Opinion_In_the_sexism_discussion_lets_look_at_game_culture.php#.ULkmW-Oe85R, accessed December 7, 2012.

23. http://company.zynga.com/privacy/policy, accessed November 15, 2012.

24. http://company.zynga.com/privacy/policy, accessed November 15, 2012.

# Boxed Text

## Chapter 3

1. http://popwatch.ew.com/2012/05/04/mark-harris-tvs-diversity-dilemma/

2. http://www.imdb.com/title/tt1772752/

3. http://jezebel.com/5912440/an-oasis-of-racially-diverse-television-is-right-under-our-noses

## Chapter 4

1. http://www.pewsocialtrends.org/2012/06/19/the-rise-of-asian-americans/

2. http://www.washingtonpost.com/lifestyle/style/asian-americans-face-new-stereotype-in-ads/2011/08/11/gIQAiMzvZJ_story.html

3. http://www.adweek.com/adfreak/are-ranjit-and-chad-endearing-or-offensive-12957,

4. http://www.cbsnews.com/8301-505123_162-42744269/is-metropcss-new-commercial-racist-many-say-ranjit-and-chad-are-indian-tech-help-stereotypes/

5. http://www.cbsnews.com/8301-505123_162-42744943/its-racist-but-it-works-metropcss-ranjit-and-chad-commercials-boost-sales/?tag=bnetdomain

## Chapter 5

1. Bruce Einhorn, "Facebook, Twitter Growth in China Has Lots of Caveats," Bloomberg Businessweek, September 28, 2012, http://www.businessweek.com/articles/2012-09-28/facebook-twitter-growth-in-china-has-lots-of-caveats, accessed January 21, 2013.

2. http://www.weibo.com/

3. http://renren.com/, http://www.kaixin001.com/, http://www.qq.com, http://www.51.com

4. http://www.sec.gov/Archives/edgar/data/1326801/000119312512034517/d287954ds1.htm

## Chapter 7

1. http://ebooks.nypl.org/F1EFD9A2-64AE-4E2F-82C0-7284E74077E0/10/257/en/Default.htm

2. http://www.cnn.com/2011/10/26/living/digital-libraries/index.html

3. http://www.overdrive.com/resources/drc/Default.aspx?type=ebook

4. http://www.nytimes.com/2012/04/12/technology/personaltech/e-books-are-easier-to-borrow-just-be-prepared-to-wait.html?pagewanted=all

5. http://www.nytimes.com/2012/04/12/technology/personaltech/e-books-are-easier-to-borrow-just-be-prepared-to-wait.html?pagewanted=all

6. http://www.nytimes.com/2011/12/25/business/for-libraries-and-publishers-an-e-book-tug-of-war.html

7. http://mediadecoder.blogs.nytimes.com/2011/02/27/a-limit-on-lending-e-books/

8. http://www.nytimes.com/2011/12/25/business/for-libraries-and-publishers-an-e-book-tug-of-war.html

9. http://www.nytimes.com/2011/12/25/business/for-libraries-and-publishers-an-e-book-tug-of-war.html

## Chapter 8

1. http://www.nielsen.com/us/en/insights/reports-downloads/2012/state-of-the-hispanic-consumer-the-hispanic-market-imperative.html

2. http://msnlatino.telemundo.com/mujer_de_hoy

3. http://www.adweek.com/news/technology/telemundo-ivillage-partner-target-hispanics-141925

4. http://stateofthemedia.org/2011/hispanic-media-fairing-better-than-the-mainstream-media/

## Chapter 9

1. http://www.imdb.com/title/tt1608180/

2. http://www.marieclaire.com/sex-love/dating-blog/overweight-couples-on-television

3. http://www.jennsylvania.com/jennsylvania/2010/10/ive-got-your-counterpoint-right-here-marie-claire.html

## Chapter 10

1. Rana A. Emerson, "'Where My Girls At?': Negotiating Black Womanhood in Music Videos," Gender and Society 16, no. 1 (Feb. 2002): 115–135.

## Chapter 11

1. http://news.cnet.com/8301-1035_3-10000241-94.html

2. http://siriusbuzz.com/are-minority-channels-coming-soon.php

3. http://thehill.com/blogs/hillicon-valley/technology/156633-sirius-xm-leases-channels-to-minority-communities

4. http://www.siriusxm.com/qualifiedentity

5. http://www.siriusxm.com/qualifiedentity

6. http://radioworld.com/article/who-could-lease-sirius-xm-channels-is-in-dispute/4282

7. http://www.fmqb.com/article.asp?id=2163976

## Chapter 12

1. http://business.blogs.cnn.com/2011/04/14/china-bans-time-travel-for-television/
2. http://boxofficemojo.com/movies/?page=intl&country=CH&id=avatar.htm
3. http://www.telegraph.co.uk/news/uknews/1579082/Banned-Rambo-film-hot-property-in-Burma.html
4. http://edition.cnn.com/2009/SHOWBIZ/Movies/09/21/nigeria.film.outcry/
5. http://www.tuoitrenews.vn/cmlink/tuoitrenews/lifestyle/teenage-horror-movie-banned-for-vulgar-scenes-1.71686
6. http://www.schnittberichte.com/news.php?ID=3600
7. http://www.censorship.govt.nz/oflcdd/DocProps.asp?PubNum=701222

## Chapter 13

1. http://www.hollywoodreporter.com/live-feed/lena-dunham-hbo-girls-racism-backlash-321548

2. http://2010.census.gov/news/releases/operations/cb11-cn125.html
3. http://mediamatters.org/research/diversity_report/
4. http://www.nytimes.com/roomfordebate/2012/04/25/minorities-in-movies-and-television
5. http://womenintvfilm.sdsu.edu/research.html

## Chapter 14

1. http://www.theesa.com/facts/gameplayer.asp
2. http://penny-arcade.com/report/editorial-article/games-with-female-heroes-dont-sell-because-publishers-dont-support-them
3. http://www.smh.com.au/news/World/Real-appeal/2005/05/21/1116533572111.html
4. http://webcache.googleusercontent.com/search?q=cache:Re-jh4eZClwJ:msmagazine.com/blog/blog/2011/06/28/no-comment-duke-nukem-forever/+&cd=3&hl=en&ct=clnk&gl=us&client=firefox-a
5. http://exple.tive.org/blarg/2012/11/07/flip-all-the-pronouns/
6. http://exple.tive.org/blarg/2012/11/21/fifteen-minutes-of-forever/

# Photo Credits

## Part 1

### Chapter 1
Opener: © Anton Gvozdikov/Shutterstock

Page 7: © Creatas/Thinkstock; page 12: © Digital vision/Thinkstock; © iStockphoto/Thinkstock; page 14: © iofoto/Shutterstock; page 18: © NBCU Photo Bank via Getty Images; page 23: © Hans Laubel/iStockphoto.com

### Chapter 2
Opener: © Bravo/Photofest

Page 30: © Library of Congress; page 32: © Sony Pictures Classic/Photofest; page 39: © PBS/Photofest; page 44: © Alinari via Getty Images; page 48: © FX Network/Photofest

### Chapter 3
Opener: © Songquan Deng/Shutterstock

Page 67: © FOX/Photofest; page 74: © WireImage; page 80: © Terekhov Igor/Shutterstock; page 84: © Hancu Adrian/iStockphoto.com

### Chapter 4
Opener: © Gioadventures/iStockphoto.com;

Page 93: © AMC/Photofest; page 112: © KPegg/Shutterstock; page 114: © WireImage; page 119: © Showtime

### Chapter 5
Opener: © Google and the Google logo are registered trademarks of Google Inc., used with permission

Page 128: © New York Public Library/Oscar Lion Collection; page 134: © Fox Network/Photofest; page 145: NBC/Photofest © NBC; page 149: The Weinstein Company/Photofest © The Weinstein Company

### Preface
Opener: © pictafolio

Page 159: © Stockbyte/Thinkstock; page 160: © Columbia Pictures/Photofest © Columbia Pictures; page 162: © LoudDoor; page 163: © Buena Vista Images

## Part 2

### Chapter 6
Opener: © Bloomberg via Getty Images

Page 169: © Computer History Museum (www.computerhistory.org); © Computer History Museum (www.computerhistory.org); Timeline pages 172/173; US Army Photo/Wikimedia Commons/Public Domain; Wikimedia Commons; User: Boffy b/Wikimedia Commons/CC-BY-SA-3.0/GFDL; Silvio Tanaka/Wikimedia Commons/CC-BY-2.0; 1000 Words/Shutterstock.com; bloomua/Shutterstock.com; D. Hammonds/Shutterstock.com; page 179: © Google and the Google logo are registered trademarks of Google Inc., used with permission; page 184: © iStockphoto/Thinkstock; page 187: © AFP/Getty Images

### Chapter 7
Opener: © Olaf Speier/Shutterstock

Timeline pages 194/195: iStockphoto/Thinkstock; iStockphoto/Thinkstock; Photos.com/Thinkstock; iStockphoto/Thinkstock; N. Orr/Wikimedia Commons/Public Domain; Brand X Pictures/Thinkstock; Hammatt Billings/Wikimedia Commons/Public Domain; iStockphoto/Thinkstock; User:NotFromUtrecht/Wikimedia Commons/CC-BY-SA-3.0/GFDL; Susan Montgomery/Shutterstock.com; page 201: © Getty Images; page 205: © Annette Shaff/Shutterstock.com; Annette Shaff/Shutterstock.com; page 211: © FilmMagic; page 214: © Karel Noppe/Shutterstock

### Chapter 8
Opener: Courtesy of Ryan Frank

Timeline pages 222/223: J. L. G. Ferris/Victorian Traditions/Shutterstock.com; MidoSemsem/Shutterstock.com; Baath-Holmbert, Cecelia/NYPL/Public Domain; George K. Warren/Wikimedia Commons/Public Domain; NYPL, NYPL, villorejo/Shutterstock.com, NYPL, NYPL, Comstock/Thinkstock; Norman Chan/Shutterstock.com; page 230: © Google and the Google logo are registered trademarks of Google Inc., used with permission; page 234: © Fazon1/iStockphoto.com; page 236: © iStockphoto/Thinkstock; page 238: © Getty Images

### Chapter 9
Timeline pages 248/249: Wikimedia Commons/Public Domain; NYPL; NYPL; NYPL; NYPL; Library of Congress/Public Domain; Photofest; Ingram Publishing/Thinkstock; Bloomberg/Getty Images; page 252: © SKOdonnell/iStockphoto.com; page 258: © Bloomberg/Contributor; page 262: © AFP/Getty Images; page 266: © Ingram Publishing/Thinkstock

### Chapter 10
Opener: © Alex Skopje/Shutterstock

Timeline pages 274/275: Library of Congress/Public Domain; lynea/Shutterstock.com; nito/Shutterstock.com; tele52/Shutterstock.com; MadTatyana/Shutterstock.com; Northfoto/Shutterstock.com; Dmitry Melnikov/Shutterstock.com; page 286: © Featureflash/Shutterstock.com; page 288: © Brad Camembert/Shutterstock.com; page 290: © Time & Life Pictures/Getty Images; page 291: © Blend Images/Shutterstock; page 296: © Washington Post/Getty Images

## Chapter 11

Opener: © iStockphoto/Thinkstock

Timeline pages 304/305: Nicku/Shutterstock.com; SpbPhoto/Shutterstock.com; iStockphoto/Shutterstock.com; Photofest; Everett Collection/Shutterstock.com; Hadi Djunaedi/Shutterstock.com; Hadrian/Shutterstock.com; Wasan Srisawat/Shutterstock.com; Hemera/Thinkstock; page 307: © nelis/iStockphoto; page 317: © Getty Images; page 324: © FilmMagic

## Chapter 12

Opener: © Deklofenak/Shutterstock

Timeline pages 338/339: Eadward Muybridge/Library of Congress/Public Domain; NYPL; Photofest; Library of Congress/Public Domain; Everett Collection/Shutterstock.com; Everett Collection/Shutterstock.com; Warner Bros. Pictures/Photofest; R. Gino Santa Maria/Shutterstock.com; Zoltan Pataki/Shutterstock.com; 20th Century Fox/Photofest; page 346: © Joe Seer/Shutterstock.com; page 354: © NBCU Photo Bank via Getty Images; page 357: © Gemenacom/Shutterstock; page 358: © Rob Wilson/Shutterstock.com; page 361: Sony Pictures Classics/Photofest © Sony Pictures Classics

## Chapter 13

Opener: © Colorvsbw/Shutterstock

Timeline pages 366/367: Photofest; Photofest; Photofest; CBS Television/Photofest; Katherine Welles/Shutterstock.com; Christian Delbert/Shutterstock.com; page 369: © CBS Television; page 371: © Getty Images; page 375: © 1000 Words/Shutterstock.com; page 378: © Zuffa LLC via Getty Images; page 389: © Oksana Perkins/Shutterstock

## Chapter 14

Opener: © Barone Firenze/Shutterstock.com

Timeline pages 398/399: Everett Collection/Shutterstock.com; Joi Ito/Wikimedia Commons/CC-BY-2.0; User: Bumm13/Wikimedia Commons/Public Domain; User: Evan-Amos/Wikimedia Commons/Public Domain; Photofest; Photofest; Courtesy Taylor & Francis; User: Evan-Amos/Wikimedia Commons/Public Domain; page 401: © Barone Firenze/Shutterstock.com; page 404: © marcello farina/Shutterstock.com; page 405: © PopCap Games/Electronic Arts, Inc.; © PopCap Games/Electronic Arts, Inc.; page 407: © Barone Firenze/Shutterstock.com; page 410: Electronic Arts, Inc./Corbis News; page 412: © Photofest; page 413: © Bloomberg via Getty Images

# Index